THE BRICS-LAW\
GLOBAL CO(

In the international trade and development arena, new economies have created a regional bloc that is known as BRICS – Brazil, Russia, India, China and South Africa. Initially conceived to drive global change through economic growth, the financial crisis and reversal of fortunes of the BRICS nations have raised questions about their ability to have an impact on the governance of global affairs. This book explores the role of law in various areas of BRICS cooperation including: trade, investment, competition, intellectual property, energy, consumer protection, financial services, space exploration and legal education. It not only covers the specifics of each of the BRICS nations in the selected areas, but also offers innovative and forward-looking perspectives on the BRICS cooperation and their contribution to the reform of the global governance networks. This is a unique reference book suitable for academics, government officials, legal practitioners, business executives, researchers and students.

ROSTAM J. NEUWIRTH is Professor of Law and Programme Coordinator of Master of International Business Law (IBL) at the Faculty of Law of University of Macau (China). He holds law degrees from the European University Institute in Florence (PhD), McGill University in Montreal (LL.M) and the Karl-Franzens University of Graz (Mag. iur.). Before joining Macau University, he taught at two Universities in India and worked in the *Völkerrechtsbüro* (International Law Bureau) of the Austrian Federal Ministry for Foreign Affairs.

ALEXANDR SVETLICINII is Assistant Professor of Law at the University of Macau. Dr. Svetlicinii received his law degree at the Free International University of Moldova, his LL.M in International Business Law at the Central European University, and Master of Research in Law and his PhD in Law at the European University Institute. His primary fields of expertise are competition law, international trade and investment law, and alternative dispute resolution. Dr. Svetlicinii served as a nongovernmental advisor to the International Competition Network and as a legal expert in a number of research projects conducted by the EU Commission.

DENIS DE CASTRO HALIS is a Brazilian scholar who has been working in China since 2005. Since 2007, he has been at the Faculty of Law of the University of Macau, having served as a coordinator and as a Senate member. He has a strong interdisciplinary background, holding degrees in law, social sciences, and philosophy. His investigations vary from business and company law to legal and social theories. He is also a radio commentator.

THE BRICS-LAWYERS'
GUIDE TO GLOBAL
COOPERATION

Edited by

ROSTAM J. NEUWIRTH
University of Macau

ALEXANDR SVETLICINII
University of Macau

DENIS DE CASTRO HALIS
University of Macau

CAMBRIDGE
UNIVERSITY PRESS

University Printing House, Cambridge CB2 8BS, United Kingdom

One Liberty Plaza, 20th Floor, New York, NY 10006, USA

477 Williamstown Road, Port Melbourne, VIC 3207, Australia

314-321, 3rd Floor, Plot 3, Splendor Forum, Jasola District Centre, New Delhi - 110025, India

79 Anson Road, #06-04/06, Singapore 079906

Cambridge University Press is part of the University of Cambridge.

It furthers the University's mission by disseminating knowledge in the pursuit of education, learning and research at the highest international levels of excellence.

www.cambridge.org
Information on this title: www.cambridge.org/9781108402743
DOI: 10.1017/9781108236102

© Cambridge University Press 2017

First published 2017
First paperback edition 2018

A catalogue record for this publication is available from the British Library

Library of Congress Cataloging in Publication data
Names: Neuwirth, Rostam J. | Svetlicinii, Alexandr. | De Castro Halis, Denis.
Title: The BRICS-lawyers' guide to global cooperation / edited by Rostam J. Neuwirth, Alexandr Svetlicinii, Denis De Castro Halis.
Description: New York : Cambridge University Press, 2017. | Includes bibliographical references and index.
Identifiers: LCCN 2017020968 | ISBN 9781108416238 (hardback)
Subjects: LCSH: International economic relations. | Foreign trade regulation. | Corporation law – BRIC countries. | BRIC countries – Foreign economic relations. | International economic integration. | BISAC: LAW / International.
Classification: LCC K3823 .B75 2017 | DDC 337 – dc23 LC record available at https://lccn.loc.gov/2017020968

ISBN 978-1-108-41623-8 Hardback
ISBN 978-1-108-40274-3 Paperback

To my wife Pui Mang and our children Elam and Lea for their support and understanding when at home and when abroad.

ROSTAM

To my beloved parents, Igor and Valentina, for their unconditional support.

ALEXANDR

To my parents, Livio and Sarah, for their good parenting and the sacrifices they made for me.

To my wife Inês Hong (Hong Weng Ian) for her companionship and our amazing years together.

DENIS

CONTENTS

FIGURES

xii

TABLES

CONTRIBUTORS

DENIS DE CASTRO HALIS is a scholar who has been working in China since 2005, after having taught and coordinated research activities in Rio de Janeiro, Brazil. Since 2007, he has been located at the Faculty of Law of the University of Macau, where he has served as the coordinator of the Service Teaching Program and is a Senate member. He is a PhD candidate in law (in the Netherlands) and in sociology (in Macau), and he holds a master's degree in legal and social sciences (Fluminense Federal University, Brazil); he has two postgraduate degrees, one in contemporary philosophy and the other in education of social sciences (State of Rio de Janeiro University). He earned bachelor's degrees in social sciences (State of Rio de Janeiro University, Brazil) and in law – cum laude (Federal University of Rio de Janeiro, Brazil). He is also a member of the Brazilian Lawyers Association and several academic associations. He regularly participates and organizes sessions in international conferences, such as the International Association of Legal and Social Philosophy (IVR) and the Law and Society Association. In addition to several papers and book contributions in the areas of business law (including company law), Asian studies, sociolegal studies, fundamental rights and theory of law, he has published a book in Portuguese on the legal pragmatism of Oliver Wendell Holmes Jr.

FABIO DE SÁ E SILVA is assistant professor of international studies and Wick Cary professor of Brazilian studies at the University of Oklahoma. Before he was a research fellow at Harvard Law School's Center on the Legal Profession and a senior researcher at the Institute for Applied Economic Research (IPEA) in Brazil, where he has also served as the chair for Studies on State and Democracy and was the president's chief of staff. Before joining IPEA, Fabio was involved in several projects on justice and security reform in Brazil, with an emphasis on promoting access to justice and improving the criminal justice system. Fabio holds a law degree from the University of São Paulo School of Law, a master's of law from the University of Brasília, School of Law and a PhD in law and public policy from

Northeastern University. He has received several fellowships and grants from institutions such as the CAPES Foundation, Northeastern University and the Oñati International Institute for the Sociology of Law. Fabio studies the social organization of law and lawyering in a variety of institutional settings relevant to policy making and development in contemporary Brazil and Latin America, such as public interest organizations, legal reforms and rule of law campaigns, corporate law firms and government lawyers' offices. He has extensively taught and published on these topics.

FERNANDO DIAS SIMÕES is an assistant professor in the Faculty of Law of the University of Macau (China). He holds a PhD from the University of Santiago de Compostela (Spain) and a bachelor's degree from the University of Coimbra (Portugal). He is a senior research fellow at the University Institute of European Studies (IUSE) (Italy) and a senior research associate at Global Law Initiatives for Sustainable Development (gLAWcal) (United Kingdom). He has been EU Commission Marie Curie Fellow at Beijing Normal University (China) and was a visiting scholar at the Faculty of Law of McGill University (Canada) and Emory University School of Law (United States). He is currently the principal investigator in a research project at the University of Macau and research unit coordinator of two research projects funded by the European Commission. He also serves as Rapporteur for the Oxford International Organizations (Oxford University Press and Manchester International Law Centre). His main research interests include international arbitration, contract law and consumer law.

JENYA GRIGOROVA holds a PhD in international law from the Sorbonne Law School (University of Paris 1, Panthéon-Sorbonne). She was a teaching assistant at the Sorbonne University and junior lecturer (ATER) at the University of Evry Val d'Essonne. Her PhD thesis, defended in 2016 under the supervision of Professor Helene Ruiz Fabri, focuses on the international regulation of trade in energy resources. Jenya holds master's degrees from the University of Paris 1 (international economic law) and Sofia University (international law). An LLM scholar (dean's award) at NYU School of Law, she has previously been a Bluebook trainee at the Legal Service of the European Commission, a research fellow at the Energy Charter Secretariat and an intern at the European Court of Justice. Jenya's research interests include international trade law, particularly WTO law; issues related to energy regulation on both international and regional levels; international investment law; and environmental law. Jenya has published extensively in French, English and Bulgarian on various pressing issues in international trade relations, in particular trade in the energy sector and specific aspects of European law relating to EU restrictive measures and EU environmental policy measures. Jenya also regularly serves as a judge for moot court competitions, such as the ELSA Moot Court Competition in WTO law and the Philip C. Jessup International Law Moot Court Competition.

UMAKRISHNAN KOLLAMPARAMBIL is an associate professor in economics at the University of Witwatersrand, Johannesburg, South Africa, where she teaches graduate courses in advanced econometrics and development. She holds an MPhil in applied economics and a PhD in economics from Jawaharlal Nehru University, New Delhi. Her research interests include topics in the broad area of development economics and the economic analysis of international economic law. She has published research articles in the *Journal of Development Studies, African Development Review, Development Southern Africa, Indian Journal of Economics, Asian Economic Review, Foreign Trade Review*, among others. She has received a U.S. Government Scholarship for the International Leadership Exchange Program (theme: U.S. financial systems), a PhD internship fellowship at the United Nations University-Institute for New Technologies Maastricht and the University Grants Commission-Junior Research Fellowship, New Delhi.

SALVATORE MANCUSO earned his bachelor of law degree at the University of Palermo (Italy) and obtained his PhD in comparative law at the University of Trieste (Italy) with a specialization in African law. He holds a chair at the Centre for Comparative Law in Africa and is an honorary professor of African law at the Centre for African Laws and Society of Xiangtan University (China). He is also a visiting professor at the University of Paris I, Panthéon-Sorbonne. He has been a professor of comparative law and legal anthropology at the University of Macau; an adjunct professor at the University of Trieste; and a visiting professor at the Universities of Limoges, Réunion and Lisbon; he has given lectures at the Universities of Trento, Salerno and Palermo (Italy); Asmara (Eritrea); Bissau and Ghana–Legon in Accra (Ghana); Mauritius; Eduardo Mondlane in Maputo (Mozambique); Instituto Superior de Ciências Jurídicas e Sociais (Cape Verde); and National Taipei University, University of Political Sciences and Law in Beijing, and East China University of Political Sciences and Law in Shanghai (China). He has published and edited many books and several articles on comparative and African law. He is a member of the International Academy of Comparative Law and is secretary-general of the Juris Diversitas group. He is the editor-in -chief of the *Journal of Comparative Law in Africa* and is a member of the editorial board of several law journals that are focused on African law.

JULIA MOTTE-BAUMVOL is an associate professor with tenure at the University of Paris Descartes Law School (Paris V). She holds a master's degree from the University of Paris 2, Panthéon Assas (public international law) and a PhD degree on WTO law (University of Paris 1 Panthéon-Sorbonne). She was a postdoctoral researcher at the University of Geneva and research fellow at the Graduate Institute (Geneva). Julia has published several papers on the interaction between public international law and international economic law. Her current research explores new mechanisms emerging from international economic law that enhance the effectiveness of soft law instruments on the regional and global levels. Julia has initiated and led international research collaborations involving professors from France, Denmark, Italy and Brazil. She has been awarded research grants from France (French Ministry of Justice, CSI/UNS) and Brazil (Fapergs). Julia is the head of the Law Clinic, Business and Human Rights, at the University of Evry Val d'Essonne. She is fluent in French, English and Portuguese and has attained an intermediate level in Mandarin.

DEBANSHU MUKHERJEE leads the corporate law and financial regulation vertical team at Vidhi Centre for Legal Policy, which is a New Delhi-based think tank. He advises the government of India on several law reform projects in the area of corporate law and financial regulation. He has recently advised the Ministry of Finance in designing and drafting a Bankruptcy Code for India. He has also advised the Ministry of Corporate Affairs on reforming India's company law, known as the Companies Act. He served as a member of a government-appointed committee for drafting rules for the National Company Law Tribunal. He has advised India's central bank, the Reserve Bank of India, on several areas of financial regulation. Before joining Vidhi as a member of its founding team, Debanshu was a lawyer with AZB & Partners, a full-service law firm in India. Debanshu is a graduate of Oxford University and the Hidayatullah National Law University.

ROSTAM J. NEUWIRTH is Professor of Law at the Faculty of Law of the University of Macau, where he also is the coordinator of the

International Business Law Program in the English language. He received his PhD degree from the European University Institute (EUI) in Florence (Italy), and he also holds a master's degree in Law (LLM) from the Faculty of Law of McGill University in Montreal (Canada). His undergraduate studies were spent at the University of Graz (Austria) and the Université d'Auvergne (France). Before his appointment as an assistant professor at the University of Macau in 2007, he was a visiting professor at the West Bengal University of Juridical Sciences in Kolkata (India) and held a POROS Chair in European Union Law at the Hidayatullah National Law University in Raipur (India). Prior to his teaching assignments in India, he worked for two years as a legal advisor in the Department of European Law in Department I.4 (European Law) of the Völkerrechtsbüro (International Law Bureau) of the Austrian Federal Ministry for Foreign Affairs.

LIER PIRES FERREIRA is a postdoctoral fellow in political science at Fluminense Federal University. He has a PhD in international law from the State University of Rio de Janeiro, a master's in international relations from Pontifical Catholic University of Rio de Janeiro, and a bachelor's degree in law and social sciences from Fluminense Federal University. He has a postgraduate degree in politics and strategy at the War College and is a professor at PPGCPRI/UCAM, IBMEC-RJ and CP2. He is the author and editor of many academic books, including *Course of Political Science* (2013); *Course on Private International Law* (2012); *International Law, Oil and Development* (2011); *Course of Legal Sociology* (2011); *Course of General Theory of the State* (2009); *International Environmental Law and Oil Law* (2009); *Human Rights and International Law* (2009); and *State, Globalization and Regional Integration* (2003). He has been a coordinator of graduate and postgraduate programs and teaches in the following areas: international law, international relations and social sciences.

LILIAN RICHIERI HANANIA is an attorney (admitted to the bar in Brazil and France), a collaborator at the Centro de Estudos Sociedade e Tecnologia (CEST – University of São Paulo – USP, Brazil), and an associate researcher at the IREDIES (University of Paris 1, Panthéon-Sorbonne) and the CUREJ (University of Rouen). She graduated from the Law School of the University of São Paulo (USP, Brazil) in 2001 and obtained a master's degree in international economic law in 2003 and a PhD in international law in 2007 from the University Paris 1. Her PhD thesis, as well as her recent publications and lectures, addresses international economic law, international cultural law and sustainable development, with an emphasis on the 2005 UNESCO Convention on the Protection and Promotion of the Diversity of Cultural Expressions. In addition to her work as a consultant since 2003, she has worked in law firms in São Paulo, Paris and Houston and has served as legal counsel in a global technology firm. She taught international law and international relations at the University of Paris 1 for four years and worked at the International Economic Affairs Division of the French Ministry of Foreign and European Affairs for almost three years. She is also among the first members of the RIJDEC (Réseau international de juristes pour la diversité des expressions culturelles), an international network of lawyers founded at the Law School of Laval University in Québec, and has been actively contributing to its work on the 2005 Convention on the Diversity of Cultural Expressions.

CHRISTIANE ITABAIANA MARTINS ROMÊO is a postdoctoral fellow in political science at Fluminense Federal University. She obtained a PhD and a master's degree in political science from the University of Rio de Janeiro Research Institute, after earning bachelor degrees in social sciences from Federal Fluminense University and in law from the Pontifical Catholic University of Rio de Janeiro. She is a professor of political science and international relations in the International Relations Department at IBMEC-RJ. Her research interests are on political theory, Brazilian political thought, BRICS, bilateral relations between Brazil and China, international political economy, and international organizations.

ALEXANDR SVETLICINII is an assistant professor at the Faculty of Law of University of Macau where he also serves as associate program coordinator for the Master of International Business Law. Before joining the University of Macau, Dr. Svetlicinii was a senior researcher at the Jean Monnet Chair of European Law of the Tallinn Law School, Tallinn University of Technology. Dr. Svetlicinii received his law degree from the Free International University of Moldova (Chisinau), an LLM in international business law (cum laude) with a specialization in EU law from Central European University (Budapest), and a master's degree in research (law) and a PhD in law from the European University Institute (Florence). In addition to his academic work, Dr. Svetlicinii has acted as a nongovernmental advisor to the International Competition Network and has worked as a freelance expert in a number of international projects related to competition law enforcement.

ALIOUNE BADARA THIAM is a lecturer in law at Gaston Berger University of St. Louis. He studied law at the University of Dakar before moving to China, where he earned an LLM degree in international law and Chinese law at Wuhan University. He obtained his PhD degree from the University of Macau. His dissertation examined avenues to foster legal integration in Africa, with particular emphasis on the Organization for the Harmonization of Business Law in Africa (OHADA), the African Intellectual Property Organization (OAPI) and the inter-African Conference on Insurance Market (CIMA). While doing his PhD, Alioune won the doctoral scholarship award of The Hague Academy of International Law in 2012, and he completed several internships, including one at the CIMA headquarters in Libreville and another at the OAPI in Yaoundé. Back in Senegal he teaches courses on business law, African institutions of trade and doing business in emerging countries in several institutions, including the Ecole Supérieure de Commerce (SUPDECO), the British Business College (BBC) and the Bordeau Management School (BEM). Dr. Thiam is committed to exploring issues in the area of business law and comparative law from a multidisciplinary point of view, as well as from national, regional and international angles. His research interests lie in international trade and investment law, corporate law, intellectual property, regional integration in Africa and China–Africa relations. He has published widely in these areas in international law journals.

GUILHERME VARGAS CASTILHOS is a lawyer in Brazil specializing in the area of international economic law. He holds a master's degree in international business law from the University of Macau and a bachelor's degree in law from the Federal University of Pelotas (UFPel), Brazil. He has gained research experience during his period in Macau and in Mainland China and has translated academic legal papers (Portuguese and English). His dissertation presented a comparative law perspective of the foreign investment legal framework of Brazil and Mainland China. His areas of interest are international business and trade law, international contracts, arbitration and commercial dispute resolution, tax law and BRICS countries' economic legal systems.

ANTONIOS VLASSIS is a lecturer and FNRS (Scientific Research Fund-Belgium) researcher at the Center for International Relations Studies (CEFIR-University of Liege). Previously, he was a visiting professor at the Université libre de Bruxelles (ULB-Belgium) and was a postdoctoral research fellow and lecturer at the Center for Integration and Globalization Studies (CEIM-Quebec University of Montreal). From 2009 to 2014, he also edited the newsletter, "Culture, Trade and Digital Technologies," which was published by the CEIM for the International Organization of Francophonie. He was also a contributor to the CEIM's report, *For a Diversified Networked Culture: Bringing the Convention on the Protection and Promotion of the Diversity of Cultural Expressions in the Digital Age*, which was produced on behalf of the Ministry of Foreign Affairs of France. He received his PhD in international relations and political science from SciencesPo Bordeaux-Montesquieu University of Bordeaux IV. His research and teaching fields focus on the global governance of cultural industries, cultural diplomacy and cultural globalization. His scientific contributions have appeared in the *European Journal of Communication, International Journal of Cultural Policy, Third World Quarterly, Études International*es, *Politique et sociétés*, as well as in edited books published by several presses. His PhD thesis was published in 2015 under the title, *Global Governance and Culture: From Exception to Diversity*.

RICARDO BASÍLIO WEBER is a postdoctoral fellow in political science at Fluminense Federal University. He holds a PhD in international politics from Pontifical Catholic University of Rio de Janeiro, a master's in political science from Fluminense Federal University, and a bachelor's degree in social sciences from the State University of Rio de Janeiro. He is currently a professor of international politics and academic dean of the International Relations Department at IBMEC-RJ.

JIA YAO works as an associate professor in the Institute of Law of the Chinese Academy of Social Sciences. She is also the editor of *Global Law Review*, one of the leading legal journals in China. She obtained her PhD from the Law School of Renmin University of China in 2009, majoring in economic law. Her main research areas are civil law, consumer law and financial law. In 2012, she published a monograph titled *Regulation of Individual Financial Credit Investigation*, and she has also published several academic papers in reputed Chinese journals.

PETER K. YU is professor of law and co-director of the Center for Law and Intellectual Property at Texas A&M University School of Law. Before joining Texas A&M University, he held the Kern Family Chair in Intellectual Property Law and was the founding director of the Intellectual

Property Law Center at Drake University Law School. He served as Wenlan Scholar Chair Professor at Zhongnan University of Economics and Law in Wuhan, China, and was a visiting professor of law at Hanken School of Economics, the University of Haifa, the University of Helsinki, the University of Hong Kong, the University of Strasbourg, and Washington and Lee University. He also founded the nationally renowned Intellectual Property & Communications Law Program at Michigan State University, at which he held faculty appointments in law, communication arts and sciences, and Asian studies. Born and raised in Hong Kong, Professor Yu is a leading expert in international intellectual property and communications law. He also writes and lectures extensively on international trade, international and comparative law, and the transition of the legal systems in China and Hong Kong. A prolific scholar and an award-winning teacher, he is the author or editor of six books and more than one hundred law review articles and book chapters. He serves as the general editor of the *WIPO Journal* published by the World Intellectual Property Organization (WIPO) and chairs the Committee on International Intellectual Property of the American Branch of the International Law Association.

JUAN-JUAN ZHANG received her bachelor's degree in English and BL degree in economic law from Tianjin University, China, and was awarded a JM degree from Southwest University of Political Science and Law, China. She is currently a PhD candidate at the University of Macau, Faculty of Law. Ms. Zhang is also a lecturer at the Faculty of Law and researcher at the Centre of Latin American Studies at the Southwest University of Science and Technology, China. From January to December 2014, she was a visiting scholar at the Institute of CUENCA of Pacific of Colima University, Mexico. Ms Zhang has published more than ten academic papers and has been involved in six research projects at different levels of funding. She is currently working in the areas of WTO law, competition law and comparative law.

YUN ZHAO is a professor of law at the University of Hong Kong and is currently the director of the Center for Chinese Law at Hong Kong University. He teaches introduction to Chinese law, China trade law, PRC information technology law, and online dispute resolution. He is an arbitrator of the Hong Kong International Arbitration Center, South China International Economic and Trade Arbitration Commission, and Guangzhou Arbitration Commission; an arbitrator of Lehman-Brothers-Related Investment Products Dispute Mediation and Arbitration Scheme; and a panelist of the

Asian Domain Name Dispute Resolution Center and of the Online Dispute Resolution Center of the CIETAC in Beijing. He is also a founding council member of the Hong Kong Internet Forum (HKIF), an honorary member of the Hong Kong Construction Arbitration Center, and a member of the International Institute of Space Law at Paris.

ACKNOWLEDGMENTS

We the editors wish to express our sincere appreciation to the people, institutions and organizations without which this book would have never been possible.

Most importantly, we are extremely grateful to each and all of the book contributors who, from their different disciplines and regions of the world, have come together to discuss and debate various legal issues in the BRICS cooperation and their future contribution to the global governance.

We acknowledge the continuous support for our collaborative research granted by the University of Macau and its Faculty of Law headed by Dean Professor Tong Io Cheng, as well as its associate deans, Professor Augusto Teixeira Garcia and Professor Wei Dan. We benefited from the support accorded by the Research and Development Administration Office under the leadership of Vice-Rector Professor Rui Martins and by the Centre for Teaching and Learning Enhancement under the leadership of Professor Spencer A. Benson. At various stages of this project we also received research and technical assistance from our postgraduate students: Daisy Nogueira, Chirindza Nacita Cirlene Lourenço, Liao Jieke, Zhang Dongqiao, Guo Bochuan and Yan Jieqiong.

This project started out of our friendship and collegiality, but was strengthened by discussions and feedback during several academic conferences where we had an opportunity to present our BRICS-related research. Among these, the following deserve special mention: the University of Macau, Faculty of Law, which hosted the Asian Regional Conference on Recent Trends in Dispute Resolution: Mechanisms and Processes (September 8–9, 2016) with special thanks to Muruga Perumal Ramaswamy and Anton Cooray; the University of Hong Kong, Faculty of Law, which hosted the annual conference of the Law, Literature and the Humanities Association of Australasia (December 8–10, 2016); Fudan University, School of International Relations and Public Affairs, which hosted the International Symposium on Development and Governance in the BRICS (September 24–25, 2016) with special thanks to Yijia Jing and

Jose A. Puppim de Oliveira; Fudan University, Center for BRICS Studies, which hosted the international seminar, BRICS Cooperation and the New Order of Global Governance in the Framework of G20 (August 7, 2016) with special thanks to Shen Yi, Jiang Shixue, Tian Huifang and Aravind Yelery; the Federal University of Juiz de Fora, Faculty of Law, which hosted the Law and Innovation colloquium, Fundamental Rights: New Approach and Globalization Challenges (June 27–July 2, 2016) with special thanks to Cláudia Toledo and Marcos Chein Feres; the University of Oslo, Centre for Development and the Environment, which hosted the Norwegian Association for Development Research conference, Beyond North and South: Constructing Global Governance for the 21st Century' (November 24–25, 2016); the National University of Singapore, Faculty of Law, which hosted the Inaugural Asian Law and Society Association conference, Law and Society in Asia: Defining and Advancing the Field (September 22–23, 2016) with special thanks to Lynette Chua, Andrew Harding and George Radics; the Louisiana State University, which hosted the fourth annual conference of the Juris Diversitas, Unity and/or Diversity: An International, Interdisciplinary Conference on Comparative Law (May 30–June 1, 2016) with special thanks to Olivier Moréteau; the Law and Society Association, which hosted its 2016 conference, At the Delta: Belonging, Place and Visions of Law and Social Change, in New Orleans (June 1–5, 2016) with special thanks to Hiroshi Fukurai; the Society of International Economic Law, which hosted the fifth conference of the Postgraduate and Early Professionals/Academics Network at the University of Luxembourg (April 14–15, 2016) with special thanks to Matthew Happold, Freya Baetens, Geraldo Vidigal and Jose Caiado; the United Nations Commission on International Trade Law, the Regional Centre for Asia and the Pacific, which hosted the 2016 UNCITRAL Emergence Conference: Regional Perspectives on Contemporary and Future Harmonization Agenda in International Trade Law (December 13–14, 2016), with special thanks to João Ribeiro; the Federal University of the State of Rio de Janeiro, which hosted a seminar titled China in the International Context: Politics, Law and Administration (July 4, 2016) with special thanks to José Carlos Buzanello; and the Instituto Brasileiro de Mercado de Capitais, which hosted an international law seminar (July 4, 2016) with special thanks to Jose Luiz Niemeyer dos Santos Filho.

Many other individuals deserve a note of appreciation for their friendship and collaboration in this and other projects that were instrumental in promoting collaborative and interdisciplinary research that preceded the present work. They are Aleksandar Pavkovic, Thomas Mertens, Fernanda

Duarte Lopes Lucas da Silva, Alexandre Kehrig Veronese Aguiar, Otavio Luiz Rodrigues Jr., Kay-Wah Chan, Mahendra P. Singh, Colin Picker, Heng Wang, Christiaan De Beukelaer, Lauro da Gama e Souza Júnior, Jingxia Shi and Vera Lúcia Raposo.

Many thanks are given to the Cambridge University Press, especially to our editor John Berger and to Claudia Bona-Cohen, Gail Naron Chalew and Vijay Kumar Bhatia for guiding us through the entire publishing process. We are grateful to the anonymous peer reviewers for their appreciation and support, as well as to the language proofreaders who helped improve the quality of the work.

Our families and companions also deserve special mention for being patient when we were not, and for being tolerant when we were not there.

Denis, Rostam and Alexandr at the International Symposium on Development and Governance in the BRICS, Fudan University, Shanghai, September 2016.

~

Introduction

ROSTAM J. NEUWIRTH, ALEXANDR SVETLICINII AND
DENIS DE CASTRO HALIS

The term 'BRICS' is an acronym made from the initials of the five countries of Brazil, Russia, India, China and South Africa. The concept was
originally coined in 2001 as 'BRIC' in the context of an economic report.[1]
Eight years later, the first BRIC Summit, attended by the leaders of the
four countries of Brazil, Russia, India and China, was held in Yekaterinburg (Russia). Having been joined by South Africa in 2011, BRICS evolved
from an idea drawn from an economic viewpoint to its later establishment
as a "dialogue and cooperation platform" in political terms.[2] Initially, the
BRICS countries were hailed as an emerging driver of global change due
to their strong economic growth in the aftermath of the financial crisis.[3]
More recently, their relative diversity, as well as the internal political problems they face, has led to increasing doubts about their ability to have a
lasting impact on the governance of global affairs.[4]

In short, the relatively young history of the BRICS platform displays
the complex interplay between economic and political factors, which are

---

[1] See Jim O' Neill, 'Building Better Global Economic BRICs', *Goldman Sachs Global Economics Paper* No. 66 (November 30, 2001); available at www.goldmansachs.com/our-thinking/archive/archive-pdfs/build-better-brics.pdf [accessed on 22 December 2016].

[2] See Oliver Stuenkel 'The Financial Crisis, Contested Legitimacy, and the Genesis of Intra-BRICS Cooperation' (2013) 19 *Global Governance* 611–630; Oliver Stuenkel, *The BRICS and the Future of Global Order* (Lanham, MD: Lexington Books, 2015); Lucia Scaffardi, 'BRICS, a Multi-Centre "Legal Network"?' (2014) 5 *Beijing Law Review* 140–148.

[3] See e.g. Cedric de Coning, Thomas Mandrup, and Liselotte Odgaard (eds.), *The BRICS and Coexistence: An Alternative Vision of World Order* (London: Routledge, 2015); Sonia E. Rol-land, 'The BRICS' Contributions to the Architecture and Norms of International Economic Law' (2013) 107 *American Society of International Law Proceedings* 164–170.

[4] See e.g. Francesca Beausang, *Globalization and the BRICs: Why the BRICs Will Not Rule the World for Long* (London: Palgrave Macmillan, 2012); Christian Brutsch and Mihaela Papa, 'Deconstructing the BRICS: Bargaining, Coalition, Imagined Community, or Geopolitical Fad?' (2013) 6 *Chinese Journal of International Politics* 299–327; Harsh V. Pant, 'The BRICS Fallacy' (2013) 36(3) *Washington Quarterly* 91–105.

both subject to fluctuations in accordance with the tides of change. Scholarship and academic debate so far have reflected these changes from either an economic or a political perspective. But it is between politics and economics that law is called on to make an important contribution. Against the background of cyclical political and economic fluctuations, the law's contribution lies precisely in its ability to provide stability and predictability through the rule of law. Generally, and with a few notable exceptions,[5] the role of law, legal norms, institutions and processes has not yet been duly considered, both in the context of BRICS cooperation and in the relevant scholarship.

At the same time, it should be noted that the BRICS countries already recognize the importance of cooperation in the legal field. On December 11–12, 2014, the first BRICS Legal Forum was held in Brasília (Brazil) and was attended by legal professionals from the five countries. There, more than 200 representatives of the legal profession discussed various topics of common interest: legal guarantees, cooperation and development, financial legal cooperation, cross-border legal services and dispute resolution mechanisms. The second BRICS Legal Forum was held on October 13–16, 2015, in Shanghai (China) and focused on the domestic rule of law and the international rule of law from the perspective of developing countries, the financial-legal cooperation of the BRICS countries, and dispute resolution mechanisms. Most recently, the third BRICS Legal Forum was held on September 10–12, 2016, in New Delhi (India), with a special focus on dispute resolution mechanisms.

In this context, the book aims to remedy the unjustified absence of law in the bifurcated (politics and economics) debates and to stress the importance of the legal dimension in practice and scholarship for the BRICS countries' successful cooperation. First, we advocate the significance of the role of law in determining and securing a sustainable format for BRICS cooperation. Second, we emphasize the need for a conceptually coherent framework for BRICS cooperation that duly comprises the various

---

[5] See e.g. Robert B. Ahdieh, Zhu (Julie) Lee, Srividhya Ragavan, Kevin Noonan, and Clinton W. Francis, 'The Existing Legal Infrastructure of BRICs: Where Have We Been and Where Are We Going?' (2007) 5 *Northwestern Journal of Technology and Intellectual Property* 503–524; Mikhail Antonov, 'Systematization of Law: The BRICS Context and Beyond' (2015) 2 *BRICS Law Journal* 7–14; David B. Wilkins and Mihaela Papa, 'The Rise of the Corporate Legal Elite in the BRICS: Implications for Global Governance' (2013) 54 *Boston College Law Review* 1149–1184; Mihaela Papa, 'BRICS as a Global Legal Actor: From Regulatory Innovation to BRICS Law?' (2014) 20 *federalismi.it* 2–45; available at www.federalismi.it/document/29102014124345.pdf [accessed on 22 December 2016].

'layers' or different fields of cooperation. Summed up, this book emphasizes the role of law as providing the 'mortar' that binds and holds together the individual 'bricks' used to lay the foundational stones for the global governance system of the future.

To demonstrate the actual and potential contribution that law, in the form of substantive and institutional norms, can make for BRICS cooperation specifically, and for the global governance infrastructure more generally, we structure our discussion around four major questions. First, we test the concept of BRICS cooperation as such by questioning whether and why these countries should engage in cooperation at all. Second, we assess areas on which they should focus their cooperation. Once the areas for cooperation are identified, we focus our discourse on the third question, which concerns the methods and ways of cooperation, with a special focus on the actual and potential role of law. Finally, the fourth question posed by our contributors concerns the objectives and directions for BRICS cooperation in the selected fields.

To realize these broad objectives, we narrow the scope of our analysis to selected fields for BRICS cooperation. These diverse areas are presented by experts from those fields. In spite of their diversity, these fields are nonetheless connected and, therefore, are structured in the form of a model of concentric circles or layers expanding from the core of so-called economic issues to economy-related and non-economic issues. Their selection and assessment were done with the view of formulating recommendations for the establishment of a conceptual and practical legal framework for the successful implementation of the objectives and strategies developed by the BRICS at their annual summits and specialized meetings. Using this method, we aim to contribute to the understanding not only of the BRICS countries domestically and regionally but also of their constructive role in various frameworks of cooperation at the multilateral or global level. This means that the book is mainly aimed at identifying priority areas for mutual cooperation with the goal of formulating new ideas for the governance of global affairs altogether.

Following these rationales, the narrative is begun by Rostam J. Neuwirth (Chapter 1), who considers the concept of 'enantiosis' in relation to the BRICS countries' specific features – a unique combination of 'unity in diversity' – which can play a constructive role in their cooperation and in shaping the future global order. An economic excursus into the trade relations of the BRICS nations is provided by Umakrishnan Kollamparam-bil (Chapter 2), who uses trade statistics to demonstrate the China-centric pattern of intra-BRICS trade and calls for an increase in trade among the other BRICS members. This chapter also raises challenges for the future expansion of intra-BRICS trade: the lack of diversity in the structure and direction of trade, as well as the absence of world technology leaders and net capital exporters within BRICS.

The discussion of the role of BRICS in global trade is continued by Alexandr Svetlicinii and Zhang Juan-Juan (Chapter 3), who discuss the BRICS countries' participation in the World Trade Organization (WTO) and, more specifically, in its dispute settlement mechanism (DSM). The BRICS nations have continuously declared their support of the WTO as a multilateral negotiations and rule-making platform for international trade governance, and their participation record in the WTO DSM indicates a certain degree of policy coordination that could be channeled into a more proactive stance on the reform of the WTO, its processes and its institutions. Investment can still catch up with trade, which is the central theme of the chapter coauthored by Denis De Castro Halis and Guilherme Vargas Castilhos (Chapter 4). While BRICS cooperation in the global trade governance framework has been pronounced, the bloc's collective contribution to the field of investment regulation has been less visible, as each of the BRICS countries tends to follow its original approach toward the regulation of foreign investment in line with its national economic interests. The divergence in the national investment strategies of the BRICS countries is vividly demonstrated by Alioune Badara Thiam (Chapter 5), who discusses the example of BRICS development cooperation with African countries, which is currently led by China. Another example of the current divergence of the BRICS countries' national policy priorities – the energy issues raised in the WTO DSM and WTO negotiations – is addressed by Jenya Grigorova and Julia Motte-Baumvol (Chapter 8). The combination of convergences and discrepancies in the field of energy policy is another example of the 'enantiosis' of BRICS. Another field in which BRICS cooperation has been largely bilateral is space cooperation, which has been led by China and Russia. Chapter 14, written by Yun Zhao, provides a number of reasons why multilateral cooperation has not yet been realized in that important high-technology field.

Examining trade-related issues, Alexandr Svetlicinii, in Chapter 6, discusses the current state of affairs in the enforcement of competition rules and the potential role that BRICS countries can play in the international coordination of competition enforcement. This discussion is especially timely in light of the current impasse in the international competition law negotiations in the WTO Doha Round and the proliferation of national competition law regimes with extraterritorial applications of their competition rules. Intellectual property negotiations and the role of BRICS in shaping an international consensus on the levels of protection and enforcement are discussed by Peter K. Yu in Chapter 7.

Christiane Itabaiana Martins Romêo, Lier Pires Ferreira and Ricardo Basílio Weber (Chapter 9) analyze the role of the recently established New (BRICS) Development Bank in light of the current realities of international economic law and from the perspective of the international political economy. The closely related field of financial regulations is explored by the Indian policy expert, Debanshu Mukherjee (Chapter 10). Using the example of India, the author discusses regulatory capture and other factors that affect the performance of financial regulators and calls for greater coordination and knowledge sharing among the BRICS countries as a way to foster the development of robust financial markets in these economies.

The rising demand for BRICS studies in the field of law and legal cooperation has been voiced by numerous actors. Notably, the BRICS Business Council has recently urged the BRICS governments to 'begin negotiations on regulatory coherence and convergence between the BRICS countries, and promote a closer relationship amongst regulatory authorities'.[6] Along similar lines, the BRICS Think Tanks Council has called on the BRICS governments to enhance their efforts in international rulemaking and reform of the multilateral governance institutions.[7] On October 14, 2015, the second BRICS Legal Forum in Shanghai set up the BRICS Dispute Resolution Center,[8] which acts as an alternative dispute resolution (ADR) platform for BRICS enterprises and is expected to attract significant attention from businesses and legal practitioners in BRICS countries and beyond. The present volume answers these emerging needs by supplying several contributions concerning law cooperation in particular fields. Salvatore Mancuso (Chapter 11) explores the possibility of developing a methodological approach based on a comparative law methodology that would provide for the development of common

---

[6] BRICS Business Council, *Facing Challenges, Building Confidence* (Second Annual Report 2014–2015), available at en.brics2015.ru/load/381263 [accessed on 22 December 2016], p. 4.

[7] BRICS Think Tanks Council, *Towards a Long Term Strategy for BRICS* (2015); available at http://www.nkibrics.ru/system/asset_docs/data/54cb/6585/6272/6974/2913/0000/original/Towards_a_long-term_strategy_for_BRICS_-_Recommendations_by_the_BRICS_Think_Tanks_Council.pdf?1422615941 [accessed on 22 December 2016].

[8] BRICS Dispute Resolution Center Shanghai; available at www.shiac.org/BRICS/index_E.aspx [accessed on 22 December 2016].

principles on contract law in the BRICS countries. Fernando Dias Simões (Chapter 13) analyzes the suitability of the newly established BRICS Dispute Resolution Center for the needs of the end users in the fields of commercial and investment arbitration.

In 2015, the leading universities from the BRICS countries adopted the Beijing Consensus, which resulted in a decision to establish a BRICS Universities League. In 2016, they took the next step in that direction – the establishment of the BRICS Network University. The first Forum of the BRICS Network University was held in Yekaterinburg on April 6–9, 2016.[9] It should be expected that this development will be followed by a significant impetus for further research cooperation among BRICS universities in various fields, including law and public administration.[10] The Brazilian scholar Fabio de Sa e Silva (Chapter 16) addresses this emerging field of intra-BRICS cooperation by analyzing the historical features, challenges and strategies of legal education reform in Brazil, India, China, Russia and South Africa, with the aim of discovering new opportunities for cooperation and mutual learning. Law schools in the BRICS countries are increasingly being asked by government authorities and practitioners to step up their BRICS-related legal research and education. To face that challenge, the universities must build synergies among BRICS legal scholars, just as was achieved among the group of contributors assembled for the production of this book.

In addition to analyzing the emerging fields of BRICS cooperation, this book explores themes that have not yet been sufficiently addressed by the BRICS platform. The following contributions represent just a few examples of such fields where law and legal norms could play an important role in intra-BRICS cooperation and its impact on the global level. The Chinese scholar Jia Yao (Chapter 12) addresses the emerging global trend of 'consumer sovereignty' and argues for more intensive intra-BRICS cooperation in the field of consumer protection (consumer protection policy, food safety, consumer contracts, product liability, e-commerce and consumer public interest litigation), which would match the growing communication between consumer associations and other stakeholders. Lilian Richieri Hanania and Antonios Vlassis (Chapter 15) examine the existing

---

[9] See Iana Smagina, 'The First Forum of the BRICS Network University', (2016) 3(1) *BRICS Law Journal* 144–151.

[10] See Lucia Scaffardi and Veronica Federico, 'The BRICS in the Spotlight: A Research Agenda' (2014) 1(1) *BRICS Law Journal* 112–119.

potential for BRICS cooperation in the field of cultural industries and the creative economy and propose a BRICS agenda in the realm of culture, cultural diversity and the creative economy, founded on the 2005 UNESCO Convention on the Protection and Promotion of the Diversity of Cultural Expressions.

1

The Enantiosis of BRICS

BRICS La[w]yers and the Difference that They Can Make

ROSTAM J. NEUWIRTH

Enantiosis is a Figure, by which things very different or contrary are compared or placed together, and by which they mutually, set off and enhance each other.[1]

I. Introduction

Diversity is a defining feature of the world. Indeed, the world displays enormous diversity biologically, culturally, politically, economically and even legally. In these contexts and when contrasted with uniformity, diversity causes severe conceptual, cognitive and, eventually, practical problems, especially in the area of law. Paradoxically, while diversity also bears relevance to law itself, it is law that is supposed to give sense and practical recognition to diversity in all aspects of life. For instance, in biology diversity is the guarantee for 'evolution and for maintaining life sustaining systems of the biosphere'.[2] In culture diversity is a 'defining characteristic of humanity' and 'creates a rich and varied world'.[3] In politics diversity is said to be an 'engine, generating possibility'.[4] Moreover, in economics diversity is not a 'void theoretical construct',[5] but has, for instance, been

---

[1] Thomas Gibbons, *Rhetoric; or, a View of Its Principal Tropes and Figures* (London: J. and W. Oliver, 1767), p. 248.

[2] Recital 2 of the Preamble of the Convention on Biological Diversity (CBD), Rio de Janeiro, 5 June 1992, in force 29 December 1993, 1760 UNTS 79.

[3] Recitals 1 and 3 of the Preamble of the UNESCO Convention on the Protection and Promotion of the Diversity of Cultural Expressions (CDCE), Paris, 20 October 2005, in force 18 March 2007, 2440 UNTS 31.

[4] See Nancy S. Struever, *Rhetoric, Modality, Modernity* (Chicago: University of Chicago Press, 2009), p. 78.

[5] See Carlo D'Ippoliti, 'Economics and Diversity' (2011) 33(4) *Journal of the History of Economic Thought* 562–4 at 563.

argued to 'be a major factor in the fostering of innovation and growth'.[6] In international trade the diversity of the world and its wants is – as captured by the economic theory of comparative advantage – the prime incentive to engage in the cross-border exchange of goods and services.[7] Last but not least, in international law diversity has been linked to the problem of the fragmentation of international law.[8] However, as a different account, diversity in law on a large scale has been found not only to be 'compatible with all major legal traditions'[9] but also to be a means to guarantee the efficiency, legitimacy and sustainability of law itself.

The problems related to diversity therefore appear to lie deeper, as they can be outlined by the term *discordia concors*, which literally means 'discord in harmony', otherwise known by the maxim 'united in diversity'. In linguistic terms *discordia concors* is an oxymoron, meaning a word combining two antagonistic and apparently contradictory terms. Oxymora and related figures, like paradoxes, are becoming a defining feature of the present era, especially in the context of the 'global village'.[10] This era has already been named the *Age of Paradox*[11] and the challenges related to the governance of global affairs identified as lying in 'powerful tensions, profound contradictions and perplexing paradoxes'.[12] For law the conceptual problems of this kind have been discussed in terms of 'essentially oxymoronic concepts' as they challenge the traditional modes of legal reasoning.[13]

Another rhetorical device related to essentially oxymoronic concepts that is suitable for describing the cognitive and conceptual conflicts ensuing from two or more antonyms is 'enantiosis'; that is, a figure by which different terms or 'heterogeneous ideas are yoked by violence

---

[6] See Fabio Dercole and Sergio Rinaldi, *Analysis of Evolutionary Processes: The Adaptive Dynamics Approach and Its Applications* (Princeton: Princeton University Press, 2008), p. 120.

[7] See Thomas G. Williams, *The History of Commerce* (London: Sir Isaac Pitman, 1926), p. 1.

[8] See International Law Commission (ILC), *Fragmentation of International Law*, A/CN.4/L.682 (13 April 2006), p. 15.

[9] See H. Patrick Glenn, *Legal Traditions of the World: Sustainable Diversity in Law*, 3rd edn (Oxford: Oxford University Press, 2007), p. 359.

[10] See Marshall McLuhan, *The Gutenberg Galaxy: The Making of Typographic Man* (Toronto: University of Toronto Press, 1962), p. 31.

[11] See Charles Handy, *The Age of Paradox* (Boston: Harvard Business School Press, 1995).

[12] See James N. Rosenau, 'Governance in the 21st Century' (1995) 1(1) *Global Governance* 13–43 at 13.

[13] See Rostam J. Neuwirth, 'Essentially Oxymoronic Concepts' (2013) 2(2) *Global Journal of Comparative Law* 147–166.

together'.[14] In this sense enantiosis provides a suitable methodological framework for describing and analyzing the BRICS as a kind of multiple enantiosis of the five countries: Brazil, Russia, India, China and South Africa. The reason is that globally the BRICS display similar degrees of diversity both individually, in their internal structure, and collectively, in their mutual comparison. Ultimately, their heterogeneous features and distinct background are the main reasons for their appeal to scholars and decision makers who are interested in global governance. As will be shown, many commentators and the BRICS countries themselves have identified their main *raison d'être* as the reform of the central international instruments and institutions of global governance. Even if their rise, in the so-called Global South,[15] to use another oxymoron, seems to be based on elements of diversity, it is not the real cause of the many hopes expressed and associated with them. Consequently, it is not their diversity but the difference that the BRICS, or anyone else for that matter, can make in the process of establishing the foundations for the future global governance that gives rise to hope. In brief, it is not the difference on display but the difference that can be made and how, which are the central issues to be investigated.

Using enantiosis as the basic conceptual framework, this book therefore enquires into the dynamic nature inherent in the group of countries united by the acronym 'BRICS' with a view of assessing whether they are capable of making a difference and, if so, where and how. In this regard, the BRICS are understood as a multiple enantiosis – a rhetorical figure that refers to these countries and to their people, as well as to their respective political, economic and legal systems. Prima facie, these countries and their elements appear to be very different from or possibly even incompatible with each other. Against this backdrop, future work on the BRICS must be concerned primarily with the role of law in assisting the countries in achieving their cooperation's potential for mutually enhancing each other's governance and the governance of the world at large. To this end, the cooperation of the BRICS may be enhanced by identifying the current trends, future trajectories and new areas of cooperation or, put differently, by elaborating novel means and creative methods for the realization of their objectives through law.

---

[14] See Samuel Johnson, *Lives of the Most Eminent English Poets, with Critical Observations on their Works*, (London: John Murray, 1854), vol. 1, p. 20.

[15] See Justin Dargin (ed.), *The Rise of the Global South: Philosophical, Geopolitical and Economic Trends of the 21st Century* (Singapore: World Scientific Publishing, 2013).

II. A Short History

The origin of the BRICS already highlights the conceptual and symbolic power of ideas expressed through language.[16] This power is also strongly inherent in law, which predominantly but not exclusively functions through language.[17] To recall, the term "BRIC" was coined to ponder ways of better integrating Brazil, Russia, India and China into the arena of global economic policy making.[18] After being joined by South Africa in 2010, the BRICS countries continued to attract great international attention in mostly economic and political but also other contexts. Since then, akin to a self-fulfilling prophecy, the BRICS countries' governments have also loosely institutionalized their framework for cooperation, with regular meetings held among different levels of governments. At the highest level, since 2009 eight BRICS summits of the heads of the BRICS states or governments have been held (Yekaterinburg 2009; Brasília 2010; Sanya 2011; New Delhi 2012; Durban 2013; Fortaleza 2014; Ufa 2015; Goa 2016). The BRICS countries have qualified the nature of BRICS as a 'dialogue and cooperation platform'.[19]

An already existing vast repertory of academic literature and media coverage, which is growing daily, has supported the various hopes related to the rising significance of BRICS for global affairs and, especially, the emergence of a new global legal order.[20] Furthermore, the global attention seems to be justified in statistical terms: in 2015 the BRICS accounted for approximately 42 per cent of the world population and 30 per cent of the total landmass spread over different regions on three

[16] See also Marion Fourcade, 'The Material and Symbolic Construction of the BRICs: Reflections Inspired by the RIPE Special Issue' (2013) 20(2) *Review of International Political Economy* 256–267.

[17] See also Brian Bix, *Law, Language, and Legal Determinacy* (Oxford: Clarendon Press, 2003), p. 1.

[18] See O'Neill, 'Building Better Global Economic BRICs' (2001). *Goldman Sachs Global Economics Paper No 66* (30 November 2001); available at www.goldmansachs.com/our-thinking/archive/archive-pdfs/build-better-brics.pdf [accessed on 25 October 2016].

[19] See the Strategy for BRICS Economic Partnership (Ufa, Russia, 2015); available at http://infobrics.org/wp-content/uploads/2015/07/partnershipstrategy_eng.pdf [accessed on 25 October 2016].

[20] See e.g. Francis A. Kornegay and Narnia Bohler-Muller (eds.), *Laying the BRICS of a New Global Order: From Yekaterinburg 2009 to Ethekwini 2013* (Pretoria: Africa Institute of South Africa, 2013); Cedric de Coning, Thomas Mandrup and Liselotte Odgaard (eds.), *The BRICS and Coexistence: An Alternative Vision of World Order* (London: Routledge, 2015); and Oliver Stuenkel, *The BRICS and the Future of Global Order* (Lanham, MD: Lexington Books, 2015).

continents.[21] Equally, the BRICS reportedly make an important and growing contribution to the world gross domestic product (GDP) in terms of purchasing power parity (PPP), their share having increased from 16 per cent in 2000 to nearly 25 per cent in 2010.[22] Similar growth levels apply to their role in global trade and investment, with, for instance, their share in trade having increased from 3.6 per cent in 1990 to 15 per cent in 2010.[23] With all the BRICS countries now being members of the WTO – Brazil, India and South Africa (1995), China (2001), Russia (2012) – their impact on the regulation of multilateral trade relations can be expected to grow further.[24]

More recently, though, the hopes and optimism linked to the rise of the BRICS have been facing headwinds. Perhaps also as a reaction to their rise, commentators have questioned their ability to foster their influence on global affairs and predicted an end to their advance.[25] As one reason for their decline, their 'excessive inequality and their insufficient innovation capability' have been mentioned.[26] Others have predicted problems related to their loose connection and lack of coordination.[27] It has also been suggested that other 'newly' emerging economies will join the BRICS (e.g. Mexico, Indonesia, Turkey)[28] or replace them altogether, such as the

---

[21] See United Nations, Department of Economic and Social Affairs, Population Division, *World Population Prospects 2015 – Data Booklet* (ST/ESA/SER.A/377) (2015), pp. 12–8.

[22] See *The BRICS Report: A Study of Brazil, Russia, India, China, and South Africa with Special Focus on Synergies and Complementarities* (Oxford: Oxford University Press, 2012), pp. 1 and 33.

[23] Ibid., p. 33; see also Centre for WTO Studies, *BRICS: Trade Policies, Institutions and Areas for Deepening Cooperation* (New Delhi: 2013), pp. 214–218.

[24] See also Brendan Vickers, 'The Role of the BRICS in the WTO: System-Supporters of Change Agenda in Multilateral Trade?' in Amrita Narlikar, Martin Daunton and Robert M. Stern (eds.), *The Oxford Handbook on the World Trade Organization* (Oxford: Oxford University Press, 2012); and Sonia E. Rolland, 'The BRICS' Contributions to the Architecture and Norms of International Economic Law' (2013) 107 *American Society of International Law Proceedings* 164–170.

[25] See e.g. Ruchir Sharma, 'Broken BRICs: Why the Rest Stopped Rising' (2012) 91(6) *Foreign Affairs* 2–7; and Bruce Jones, *Still Ours to Lead: America, Rising Powers, and the Tension between Rivalry and Restraint* (Washington: Brookings Institution Press, 2014), pp. 57–80.

[26] See e.g. Francesca Beausang, *Globalization and the BRICs: Why the BRICs Will Not Rule the World for Long* (Basingstoke: Palgrave Macmillan, 2012), p. 1.

[27] See Christian Brütsch and Mihaela Papay, 'Deconstructing the BRICS: Bargaining Coalition, Imagined Community, or Geopolitical Fad?' (2013) 6(3) *Chinese Journal of International Politics* 299–327.

[28] See John Hawksworth and Gordon Cookson, *The World in 2050: Beyond the BRICs: A Broader Look at Emerging Market Growth Prospects* (PriceWaterHouseCoopers, 2006); available at www.pwc.com/la/en/publications/assets/world_2050_brics.pdf [accessed on 25 October 2016].

PINEs (Philippines, Indonesia, Nigeria and Ethiopia) taking over from the BRICS.[29] The pessimistic views have been summarized in the statement that the BRICS have lost their sheen and that their 'contribution to global order remains tentative at best and problematic at worst'.[30]

As a glass is half empty and half full at the same time, realistically it seems that, in line with economic cycles, pessimism and optimism about the future of the BRICS seem to alternate, like times of growth and times of recession. Nevertheless, the BRICS countries will survive.[31] The central questions remain, therefore, what and how their cooperation can make a difference and render everyone better off. To try to answer these questions, it is necessary to assess what has been achieved in the past and what is being undertaken presently.

III.   BRICS Cooperation: Past, Present and Future

To date, the BRICS countries have held eight summits of heads of states or governments since the first one in Yekaterinburg in 2009. These summits regularly produce numerous declarations and action plans. While the first summit was still dominated by the reform efforts of the international financial institutions in the aftermath of the global financial crisis, the subsequent summits have reflected the diversification and proliferation of areas of cooperation by a shift from the core interest in international trade and economic policy making to more peripheral fields, such as sustainable development, climate change, agriculture, poverty, energy, terrorism and sports, to mention but a few. In brief, the BRICS countries, in a relatively short time period, have managed to streamline their cooperation along two main lines of action: first, the coordination of their activities in international organizations has been improved, and, second, there has been an expansion of areas for intra-BRICS cooperation.

Evidently, the two lines of action are interrelated and can be summarized as encompassing the following focus areas:

  i. Intra-BRICS Trade and Investment Cooperation;
 ii. Cooperation in Infrastructure Financing;
iii. Industrial Development and Cooperation;

---

[29] See Michael Schuman, 'Forget the BRICs; Meet the PINEs', *Time* (13 March 2014); available at http://time.com/22779/forget-the-brics-meet-the-pines/ [accessed on 25 October 2016].
[30] See Harsh V. Pant, 'The BRICS Fallacy' (2013) 36(3), *Washington Quarterly* 91–105 at 105.
[31] See also Antoine Van Agtmael, 'Think Again: The BRICS' (2012) 196 *Foreign Policy* 76–79.

   iv. Cooperation in Transportation;
    v. Cooperation in Food Security;
   vi. Cooperation in Technical Education;
  vii. Cooperation in Financial Market Development;
 viii. Cooperation in Research and Development;
   ix. Cooperation in the Area of Culture and Tourism;
    x. Cooperation in International Issues;
   xi. Cooperation in Energy Security;
  xii. Cooperation to Build Effective Institutions;
 xiii. International Development Bank for Fostering South–South Investment.[32]

In many ways these vast areas resemble or overlap with the global challenges addressed by the 2015 Sustainable Development Goals (SDGs), which identified seventeen areas for which specific targets need to be realized by 2030.[33]

As for the long-term perspectives of BRICS cooperation, a report published in 2015 suggested the following classification of broader areas:

1. Economic Growth and Development;
2. Political and Economic Governance;
3. Social Justice, Sustainable Development and Quality of Life;
4. Peace and Security; and
5. Progress through Sharing Knowledge and Innovation.[34]

Ultimately, the problem with a possible classification, organization and realization of the principal areas of cooperation is of a conceptual nature, constrained by ideas, thoughts and language. These constraints eventually also permeate and constrain the area of law, which is needed to implement effectively the objectives formulated and laid down in various policy documents. These constraints can be exemplified by a closer look at BRICS-related research, which largely reflects the listed core areas. Some selected samples of recent publications reflect an interest first and foremost in international economic policies, including notably the subcategories

---

[32] See *The BRICS Report*, pp. xxi and 169–170.

[33] See United Nations, *Transforming Our World: The 2030 Agenda for Sustainable Development*, General Assembly A/RES/70/1 (21 October 2015).

[34] See Institute for Applied Economic Research (Instituto de Pesquisa Econômica Aplicada – IPEA), *Towards a Long-Term Strategy for BRICS: A Proposal by the BRICS Think Tanks Council* (Brasília: Institute for Applied Economic Research, 2015); available at www.ipea.gov.br/portal/images/stories/PDFs/livros/livros/151104_brics_long_term_strategy.pdf [accessed on 25 October 2016].

of international trade, finance,[35] investment,[36] taxes,[37] competition,[38] innovation[39] and the business environment.[40] Other notable nontrade, or better 'trade-related', areas are security policy, energy,[41] education,[42] food,[43] health and medicines.[44]

[35] See e.g. Luiz Fernando de Paula, 'Financial Liberalization, Exchange Rate Regime and Economic Performance in BRICs Countries', in Philip Arestis and Luiz Fernando de Paula (eds.), *Financial Liberalization and Economic Performance in Emerging Countries* (Basingstoke: Palgrave MacMillan, 2008), pp. 52–94.

[36] See e.g. David Collins, *The BRIC States and Outward Foreign Direct Investment* (Oxford: Oxford University Press, 2013); Yunyun Duan, 'FDI in BRICs: A Sector Level Analysis' (2010) 5(1) *International Journal of Business and Management* 46–52; and Karl P. Sauvant, 'New Sources of FDI: The BRICS Outward FDI from Brazil, Russia, India and China' (2005) 6(5) *Journal of World Investment & Trade* 639–709.

[37] See e.g. Salman Shaheen, 'The Future for BRICS Tax Policy Coordination' (2012) 23(7) *International Tax Review* 25–6.

[38] See e.g. Frederic Jenny and Yannis Katsoulacos (eds.) *Competition Law Enforcement in the BRICS and in Developing Countries: Legal and Economic Aspects* (Cheltenham: Springer, 2016); Adrian Emch, Jose Regazzini and Vassily Rudomino (eds.), *Competition Law in the BRICS Countries* (Alphen aan Den Rijn: Wolters Kluwer Law & Business, 2012); and Sasha-Lee Afika and Sascha-Dominik Bachmann, 'Cartel Regulation in Three Emerging BRICS Economies: Cartel and Competition Policies in South Africa, Brazil, and India – A Comparative Overview' (2011) 45(4) *International Lawyer* 975–1003.

[39] See e.g. José E. Cassiolato and Helena M. M. Lastres, 'Science, Technology and Innovation Policies in the BRICS Countries: An Introduction', in José Eduardo Cassiolato and Virginia Vitorino (eds.) *BRICS and Development Alternatives: Innovation Systems and Policies* (London: Anthem Press, 2009), pp. 1–34.

[40] See e.g. Paul Hong and YoungWon Park, *Building Network Capabilities in Turbulent Competitive Environments: Business Success Stories from the BRICs* (Boca Raton: CRC Press, 2015); Renata Lèbre La Rovere, Luiz de Magalhães Ozorio and Leonardo de Jesus Melo (eds.), *Entrepreneurship in BRICS: Policy and Research to Support Entrepreneurs* (New York: Springer, 2015); Sergio Biggemann and Kim-Shyan Fam, 'Business Marketing in BRIC Countries' (2011) 40 *Industrial Marketing Management* 5–7; Andreas Berlin, *Internationalisierung und Geschäftserfolg: Analyse des Zusammenhangs für Unternehmen der BRIC Staaten* (Wiesbaden: Springer, 2014); and Kwang Ho Chun, *The BRICs Superpower Challenge: Foreign and Security Policy Analysis* (Farnham: Ashgate, 2013).

[41] See e.g. David M. Arseneau, 'Explaining the Energy Consumption Portfolio in a Cross-Section of Countries: Are the BRICs Different?' (2012) 18(4) *Law and Business Review of the Americas* 553–584; and Huiming Zhang et al., 'Comparison of Renewable Energy Policy Evolution among the BRICs' (2011) 15 *Renewable and Sustainable Energy Reviews* 4904–4909.

[42] See e.g. Simon Schwartzman, Rómulo Pinheiro and Pundy Pillay, *Higher Education in the BRICS Countries: Investigating the Pact between Higher Education and Society* (Dordrecht: Springer, 2015) and Latika Chaudhary et al., 'Big BRICs, Weak Foundations: The Beginning of Public Elementary Education in Brazil, Russia, India, and China' (2012) 49 *Explorations in Economic History* 221–240.

[43] See e.g. International Food Policy Research Institute, *2012 Global Food Policy Report* (Washington, DC: International Food Policy Research Institute, 2013).

[44] See e.g. Robert Marten et al., 'An Assessment of Progress towards Universal Health Coverage in Brazil, Russia, India, China, and South Africa (BRICS)' (2014) 384 *Lancet*

These few examples of publications highlight the fundamental problem and major constraint met by language in classifying areas of law and policy making, especially when they are supposed to be implemented coherently. This problem is rooted in the manifold mutual connections between each of these fields. For instance, regarding economic policies alone, there are important links between trade and investment,[45] trade and taxes,[46] trade and finance, or exchange rates and stock prices.[47] Even between trade and 'trade-related' issues, such as 'trade and food'[48] or trade and education,[49] there are important and inseparable links. The same can be said about technology and energy[50] or the multiple links related to sustainable development in the context of food, energy and water policies.[51]

In short there are most likely multiple connections between all individual objectives, which raise the question of the need for more detailed or more general policy fields to be identified and objectives to be formulated. These problems are well known on the global level, on which they are discussed using different terms, such as the fragmentation of international law or the trade linkage debate made of numerous pairs of 'trade and . . . problems'.[52] Generally, these problems can be reduced to a lack

2164–2171' M. Larionova et al., 'BRICS: Emergence of Health Agenda' (2014) 9(4) *International Organisations Research Journal* 73–88; Andrew Harmer et al., 'BRICS without Straw'? A Systematic Literature Review of Newly Emerging Economies' Influence in Global Health' (2013) 9 *Globalization and Health* 15; and Peter K. Yu, 'Access to Medicines, BRICS Alliances, and Collective Action' (2008) 34(2) *American Journal of Law & Medicine* 345–94.

[45] See Matthew Gilleard, 'BRICs Attracting Investment despite their Tax Systems' (2013) 24(7) *International Tax Review* 19–21.

[46] See e.g. Charles Goulding, 'Hitting the BRICs – Brazil, Russia, India and China Tax Changes Facilitate Trade' (2005) 5(2) *Journal of Taxation of Global Transactions* 65–68.

[47] See e.g. Walid Chkili and Duc Khuong Nguyen, 'Exchange Rate Movements and Stock Market Returns in a Regime-Switching Environment: Evidence for BRICS Countries' (2014) 31 *Research in International Business and Finance* 46–56.

[48] See e.g. Zahoor Haq and Karl Meilke, 'Do the BRICs and Emerging Markets Differ in their Agrifood Imports?' (2010) 61(1) *Journal of Agricultural Economics* 1–14.

[49] See e.g. Yuan Sheng-jun, 'Educational Policies and Economic Growth in BRICs: Comparative Perspectives' (2011) 8(2) *Journal of US–China Public Administration* 188–197.

[50] See e.g. Isabel Maria Bodas Freitas, Eva Dantas and Michiko Iizuka, 'The Kyoto Mechanisms and the Diffusion of Renewable Energy Technologies in the BRICS' (2012) 42 *Energy Policy* 118–128.

[51] See e.g. Ilhan Ozturk, 'Sustainability in the Food–Energy–Eater Nexus: Evidence from BRICS (Brazil, the Russian Federation, India, China, and South Africa) Countries' (2015) 93 *Energy* 999–1010.

[52] See generally Frank J. Garcia, 'The Trade Linkage Phenomenon: Pointing the Way to the Trade Law and Global Social Policy of the 21st Century' (1998) 19(2) *University of Pennsylvania Journal of International Economic Law* 201–208; and Joel P. Trachtman, 'Trade

of coherence (or unnecessary duplication or even conflicts in policies or international laws), as well as insufficient levels of consistency between international laws, international organizations or international regimes.

These problems in global law and policy making may help explain the hopes associated with the emergence of the BRICS countries. The reason is that they point to the same source of dissatisfaction as the one expressed in the wake of the 2008 global financial crisis, namely a legitimacy crisis of the international financial order.[53] As for many 'trade and . . . problems', including the one of 'trade and finance', the legitimacy crisis seems to be rooted in the obsolete conception and inadequate architecture of the present international legal order as established in the aftermath of World War II. Again, the past, present and even future areas of cooperation between the BRICS countries seem to confirm their universality at the global level. This means that the main task and strongest arguments for the BRICS are whether or to what extent they can make a difference and how. For instance, time will tell whether the New Development Bank (NDB) (the former BRICS Development Bank), established in 2015 in Shanghai, will differ from its global counterparts, the World Bank and the International Monetary Fund (IMF).[54]

IV. The Main Incentives for BRICS Countries' Cooperation

Frequently, the reasons underlying the creation of the BRICS are said to lie in the discontent with the present global governance structures and in particular a legitimacy crisis related to the international financial order. If the BRICS are to fulfil the hopes related to an alternative global vision, they will thus have to make a difference. Evidently, this means that they cannot merely duplicate the existing governance structures. Moreover, it also means that it will not be for the BRICS countries alone to bring about the desired changes. However, if closer and well-coordinated cooperation between the BRICS countries is the foundation stone for a successful

---

and . . . Problems, Cost-Benefit Analysis and Subsidiarity' (1998) 9(1) *European Journal of International Law* 32–85.

[53] See Oliver Stuenkel, 'The Financial Crisis, Contested Legitimacy, and the Genesis of Intra-BRICS Cooperation' (2013) 19(4) *Global Governance* 611–630.

[54] See generally Stephany Griffith-Jones, *A BRICS Development Bank: A Dream Coming True?* UNCTAD Discussion Paper No. 215 (March 2014); available at http://unctad.org/en/PublicationsLibrary/osgdp20141_en.pdf [accessed on 25 October 2016]; Gregory T. Chin, 'The BRICS-led Development Bank: Purpose and Politics beyond the G20' (2014) 5(3) *Global Policy* 366–373; and Parag Khanna, 'New BRICS Bank a Building Block of Alternative World Order' (2014) 31(4) *New Perspectives Quarterly* 46–48.

reform of the international legal order, it means first formulating novel policies and subsequently implementing them based on creative laws. In this respect, the BRICS countries' diversity in political, economic, social, cultural and legal terms may prove to be crucial, and the main changes will have to come from a new mindset. This is to say that new ideas need to be molded into concepts used to define policy objectives, which then will be implemented by adequate regulatory methods and legal instruments.

As a research agenda for dealing with the complexity of governance challenges internally in the BRICS and globally, it will be necessary to develop a coherent strategy for future cooperation. Such a coherent strategy must comprise all the existing individual policy goals, from sustainability to international peace and security, as they have been laid down in the numerous BRICS declarations and action plans. For these various goals, a sound theoretical foundation for cooperation, similar to Bela Balassa's theory of economic integration, needs to be developed. To recall, Balassa identified as logical steps in the process of integration deriving from cooperation the following principal stages: free trade areas, customs unions, economic or monetary unions and complete economic integration.[55] While these stages may vary in different contexts, they still reflect some deeper driving forces behind cooperation and integration. The same driving forces can be found reflected in the process of European integration, in which the four freedoms (goods, services, persons and capital) were complemented by respective chapters on competition policy, commercial policy and the approximation of laws, to mention but a few. The same dynamic, albeit on a different scale, can be observed in the evolution of the international trading regime from the General Agreement on Tariffs and Trade (GATT 1947) to the establishment of the World Trade Organization (WTO) in 1994.[56] On a microeconomic scale, similar dynamics based on industry convergence have been apparent in economics (i.e. convergenomics) in general.[57] The same has been found to govern the creative economy, in which special tenets of products, technologies and industries are expanding concentrically from the cultural core via the creative industries to the economy as a whole.[58]

---

[55] Bela Balassa, *The Theory of Economic Integration* (London: George Allen & Unwin, 1962), p. 2.

[56] See also Paul Demaret, 'The Metamorphoses of the GATT: From the Havana Charter to the World Trade Organization' (1995) 34(1) *Columbia Journal of Transnational Law* 123–171.

[57] See Sang M. Lee and David L. Olson, *Convergenomics: Strategic Innovation in the Convergence Era* (Farnham: Gower, 2010).

[58] See e.g. Rostam J. Neuwirth, 'Global Market Integration and the Creative Economy: The Paradox of Industry Convergence and Regulatory Divergence' (2015) 18(1) *Journal of International Economic Law* 21–50.

Understanding these dynamics is highly warranted from a legal perspective, in particular in the context of convergence and an age of an acceleration of change.[59] The reason is that more frequent and rapid changes in the regulatory environment have been said to pose 'a fundamental problem for law; namely, how can law preserve its integrity over time, while managing to address the newly emerging circumstances that continually arise throughout our history?'[60] The main problem lies in the causal connection between the proliferation of regulators and the fragmentation of regulations at all levels, from local and regional to global. The causal connection lies in the fact that they mutually reinforce each other and result in overregulation, also known as a 'plethora of law',[61] a 'legal explosion',[62] 'a gigantic legislative and regulatory magma',[63] or a 'deluge of norms',[64] on the one hand and an increase in legal uncertainty and potential conflicts of norms on the other. The second important problem is that the frequent changes challenge a strongly dichotomy-based or dualist reasoning, which merely divides the world into two opposites, such as a thesis versus an antithesis or the Southern (developing) versus Northern (developed) countries.[65] In short these dichotomies are proving to be too limited and simplistic to deal with the existing diversity and complexity of the world.

This is why future law and policy making must take a more inclusive and holistic approach, based also on a new mindset or new cognitive modes. It is in this regard that cultural diversity and cultural learning through comparative cultural cognition[66] can help establish such novel and creative solutions to existing problems. This means that the existing scientific paradigm, which is largely founded on Western rationalism, is

---

[59] See e.g. James Gleick, *Faster: The Acceleration of Just about Everything* (New York: Vintage Books, 2000).

[60] See Mark L. Johnson, 'Mind, Metaphor, Law' (2007) 58(3) *Mercer Law Review* 845–868 at 845.

[61] See e.g. H. Patrick Glenn, 'Persuasive Authority' (1987) 32(2) *McGill Law Journal* 261–298 at 286.

[62] See e.g. John H. Barton, 'Behind the Legal Explosion' (1975) 27(3) *Stanford Law Review* 567–584.

[63] See Bruno Oppetit, 'Les tendances régressives dans l'évolution du droit contemporain', in Jean-François Pillebout (ed.), *Mélanges dédiés à Dominique Holleaux* (Paris: Litec, 1990), p. 317.

[64] See e.g. Andreas Heldrich, 'The Deluge of Norms' (1983) 6(2) *Boston College International and Comparative Law Review* 377–389.

[65] See also Rostam J. Neuwirth, 'Global Law and Sustainable Development: Change and the "Developing-Developed Country" Terminology' (2016) *European Journal of Development Research* 1–15; doi:10.1057/s41287-016-0067-y.

[66] See Elizabeth E. Price, Christine A. Caldwell, and Andrew Whiten, 'Comparative Cultural Cognition' (2010) 1(1) *Cognitive Science* 23–31 at 21.

meeting its inherent limitations based, especially, on dualist reasoning and binary logic.[67] It is here where the BRICS countries, with their respective diversity, can bring about change and then be able to make a difference. Still, the question remains of how they can make these differences happen. Some of the initial steps to be taken are briefly outlined next.

V.   Law and Aspects of the Future BRICS Agenda

BRICS are facing serious multilevel challenges to governance in the future. To meet them successfully, they will have to develop novel modes of cooperation. As the first step, the BRICS will have to render due attention to the role of law in the context of their cooperation and finding a way to bring about the desired changes locally and globally. The reason is that law is often neglected in the global governance debate, which is frequently dominated by either political or economic concerns. This neglect of the law has also been found to apply to the BRICS so far.[68] The law, by its nature, when applied carefully and comparatively as a 'social medicine',[69] can function as a reconciliatory force between dual opposites or even multiple divergent interests and stakeholders. Its role assumes greater importance for the BRICS countries, as their dominant method of cooperation has been described as a 'new pattern of inter-state relations, based on peer-to-peer cooperation, experiences sharing and "soft" policy transfer'.[70] In other words, as a mere dialogue and cooperation platform lacking a centralized supranational body, such a semi-institutional framework needs to rely on and be complemented by an efficient 'multicentre legal network'.[71] In contrast to the global legal system, the role, remedies and *locus standi* of private persons, both natural and legal, have to be enhanced.[72] The reason is that the law can provide the 'mortar' for an entire edifice to be built

---

[67] See Stanley J. Tambiah, *Magic, Science and the Scope of Rationality* (Cambridge: Cambridge University Press, 1990), p. 3.

[68] See Lucia Scaffardi, 'BRICS, a Multi-Centre "Legal Network"?' (2014) 5 *Beijing Law Review* 140–148 at 140.

[69] See Pierre Lepaulle, 'The Function of Comparative Law with a Critique of Sociological Jurisprudence' (1922) 35(7) *Harvard Law Review* 838–858 at 838.

[70] See also Scaffardi, 'BRICS, a Multi-Centre "Legal Network"?' pp. 140 and 145.

[71] Ibid., p. 140.

[72] See e.g. Virginia Haufler, *A Public Role for the Private Sector: Industry Self-Regulation in a Global Economy* (Washington, DC: Carnegie Endowment for International Peace, 2001); A. Claire Cutler, *Private Power and Global Authority: Transnational Merchant Law in the Global Political Economy* (Cambridge: Cambridge University Press, 2003); and Aaron Catbagan, 'Rights of Action for Private Non-State Actors in the WTO Disputes Settlement System' (2009) 37(2) *Denver Journal of International Law and Policy* 279–302.

by individual bric(k)s, to use a metaphor for the challenge of creating a new global legal order for the twenty-first century. In allusion to another recent policy debate, enantiosis can also be understood as a reminder that bric(k)s are for building bridges, not walls! This is why the notion of 'BRICS la[w]yers' aptly describes the double functional role of law.

Second, it means that the law must rely on both a comparative and a systematic method. Both elements are needed to find unity in their diversity.[73] This is supported by the BRICS countries' internal diversity, also expressed through their legal system's nature as mixed jurisdictions.[74] Additionally, the existing comparative studies on the rule of law in BRICS countries and their link to economic development[75] are promising and need to be expanded in scope and depth. An expansion in depth, for instance, should also take into account cognitive cultural aspects.[76] It should also include the search for and use of novel legal concepts and instruments, particularly in an age of paradox. Various oxymoronic policy concepts, such as 'sustainable development',[77] 'glocalisation',[78] or 'gender equality',[79] testify to the inadequacy of dichotomies or binary thinking. In this regard, future laws should aim to transcend dichotomies better and seek improved ways to implement a more holistic method of legal reasoning and decision making.

There are already concepts formulated to this end. For instance, the term 'regulatory coopetition' uses the oxymoron made of cooperation and competition to address and mitigate the negative effects of the fragmentation of international law. The defining features of regulatory coopetition have been outlined as follows:

---

[73] See also Mikhail Antonov, 'Systematization of Law: The BRICS Context and Beyond' (2015) 2(1) *BRICS Law Journal* 7–14.

[74] See generally Esin Örücü, 'What Is a Mixed Legal System: Exclusion or Expansion?' (2008) 12(1) *Electronic Journal of Comparative Law* 1–18; available at www.ejcl.org/121/art121–15 .pdf [accessed on 25 October 2016].

[75] See Nandini Ramanujam et al., *Rule of Law and Economic Development: A Comparative Analysis of Approaches to Economic Development across the BRIC Countries* (Montreal: McGill, 2012); available at www.mcgill.ca/roled/files/roled/mcgill_roled_report_2012.pdf [accessed on 25 October 2016].

[76] See e.g. Rostam J. Neuwirth, 'Law and the Mind: A New Role for Comparative Law?' in Tong Io Cheng and Salvatore Mancuso (eds.), *New Frontiers of Comparative Law* (Hong Kong: LexisNexis, 2013), pp. 11–17.

[77] See Michael Redclift, 'Sustainable Development (1987–2005): An Oxymoron Comes of Age' (2005) 13 *Sustainable Development* 212–227.

[78] See Habibul H. Khondker, 'Globalisation to Glocalisation: A Conceptual Exploration' (2005) 13(2) *Intellectual Discourse* 181–199.

[79] See Keally DeAnne McBride, *Postliberal Politics: Feminism, Communitarianism, and the Search for Community* (Berkeley: University of California, 1999), p. 68.

Regulatory theory must reflect the diversity and complexity of the world. Optimal governance thus requires a flexible mix of competition and cooperation between government actors as well as between governmental and non-governmental actors, along both horizontal and vertical dimensions. This enriched model of 'regulatory coopetition' recognized that sometimes regulatory competition will prove to be advantageous but in other cases some form of collaboration will produce superior results. In a world that is pluralistic, not simplistic, a combination of regulatory competition and cooperation will almost always be optimal.[80]

The same reasoning can be applied to the international level by virtue of the term 'international regime coopeation', which was coined to critically highlight the gaps that have opened between the different and highly fragmented international legal regimes.[81] Similarly, notions of 'multilateralizing regionalism'[82] fall into the same kind of oxymoronic categories and are of equal relevance to BRICS cooperation.[83] Related to such oxymoronic concepts are legal tools of a more holistic and dynamic nature, such as integration clauses as opposed to exceptions or so-called sunset or sunrise clauses.[84]

As the third and final aspect, the development and use of novel regulatory approaches must be conducted in synchronicity with the classification of the core areas of cooperation and then be constantly adjusted. This challenge is closely related to the research agenda for the BRICS.[85] If possible, these areas of cooperation and shared policy goals should not be listed in a hierarchical and static way but instead in a concentric and dynamic one. In this regard, the evolving concept of the creative economy can serve as a useful model for the study of these dynamics.[86] This means that the

---

[80] Daniel C. Esty and Damien Geradin, 'Regulatory Co-Opetition' (2000) 3(2) *Journal of International Economic Law* 235–255 at 235.

[81] See e.g. Rostam J. Neuwirth and Alexandr Svetlicinii, 'Law as a Social Medicine: Enhancing International Inter-Regime Regulatory Coopetition as a Means for the Establishment of a Global Health Governance Framework' (2015) 36 (3–4) *Journal of Legal Medicine* 330–366.

[82] See Richard Baldwin and Patrick Low (eds.), *Multilateralizing Regionalism* (Cambridge: Cambridge University Press, 2008).

[83] See e.g. Christophe Jaffrelot and Waheguru Pal Singh Sidhu, 'From Plurilateralism to Multilateralism? G-20, IBSA, BRICS, and BASIC', in Waheguru Pal Singh Sidhu, Pratap Bhanu Mehta, and Bruce Jones (eds.), *Shaping the Emerging World: India and the Multilateral Order* (Washington, DC: Brookings Institution Press, 2013), pp. 319–339.

[84] See e.g. Sofia Ranchordás, 'Sunset Clauses and Experimental Regulations: Blessing or Curse for Legal Certainty?' (2015) 36(1) *Statute Law Review* 28–45.

[85] See generally Scaffardi and Federico, 'The BRICS in the Spotlight', 112–119.

[86] See also Julian Cooper, 'Of BRICs and Brains: Comparing Russia with China, India, and Other Populous Emerging Economies' (2006) 47(3) *Eurasian Geography and Economics* 255–284.

emphasis should be put on the mutual relations between different goals and how they influence each other, such as the protection of the environment and economic development. Another example is the area of health governance, in which the laws governing trade, competition, technology, innovation and intellectual property, as well as intangible cultural heritage, play an equal role but are insufficiently coordinated even at the national level. To this end, the creation of an electronic BRICS-LAW database, so that BRICS countries' public authorities and other stakeholders can have instant electronic access to the relevant laws and regulations, would be an effective tool to enhance and reinforce the loose multicenter legal network. Another related proposal would be to create a permanent BRICS steering committee to oversee the coherence of all the areas of cooperation from a legal perspective. In brief, these are some initial considerations for steps already taken or to be taken in the future. Many more are necessary and need to be formulated in creative ways.

VI. Conclusion

The BRICS countries are the result of a conceptual creation. Their acronym can be seen as an enantiosis, which may or may not set free some interesting dynamics in global governance. Currently they are both hailed as the bearers of an alternate world vision or geopolitical fads. As for the future of the BRICS countries, the best way of predicting it is to create it. In this regard, the main reason for their existence is rooted in the general discontent with the present international order in place or a legitimacy crisis related to the constituent international organizations. However, to justify themselves and their existence, the BRICS countries will have to demonstrate that they can make a difference and not merely establish more institutions or additional policies duplicating the existing ones. The best way for them to do so is to draw on their own human capital and to try to set free the synergies derived from the enantiosis of their unity in diversity. That is, each BRICS country must first use its own rich internal unity in diversity as a source for the formulation of new ideas. The new ideas then need to be transformed into novel concepts used for joint coopetition with the other BRICS countries to carry the momentum for change and reform to the level of the global governance debate. This will happen automatically due to the persuasive authority vested in their successful implementation in the BRICS countries, which will simply spill over to other countries. To set such a process free, however, it is necessary to implement these new concepts – an important task primarily attributed to the role of law as the mortar and the hands of BRICS la[w]yers acting as the masons laying the bricks for the foundation of a future global legal order.

VII.   References

Afika, Sasha-Lee and Bachmann, Sascha-Dominik, 'Cartel Regulation in Three Emerging BRICS Economies: Cartel and Competition Policies in South Africa, Brazil, and India – A Comparative Overview' (2011) 45(4) *International Lawyer* 975–1003.

Antonov, Mikhail, 'Systematization of Law: The BRICS Context and Beyond' (2015) 2(1) *BRICS Law Journal* 7–14.

Arseneau, David M., 'Explaining the Energy Consumption Portfolio in a Cross-Section of Countries: Are the BRICs Different?' (2012) 18(4) *Law and Business Review of the Americas* 553–584.

Balassa, Bela, *The Theory of Economic Integration* (London: George Allen & Unwin, 1962).

Baldwin, Richard and Low, Patrick (eds.), *Multilateralizing Regionalism* (Cambridge: Cambridge University Press, 2008).

Barton, John H., 'Behind the Legal Explosion' (1975) 27(3) *Stanford Law Review* 567–584.

Beausang, Francesca, *Globalization and the BRICs: Why the BRICs Will Not Rule the World for Long* (Basingstoke: Palgrave Macmillan, 2012).

Berlin, Andreas, *Internationalisierung und Geschäftserfolg: Analyse des Zusammenhangs für Unternehmen der BRIC Staaten* (Wiesbaden: Springer, 2014).

Biggemann, Sergio and Fam, Kim-Shyan, 'Business Marketing in BRIC Countries' (2011) 40 *Industrial Marketing Management* 5–7.

Bix, Brian, *Law, Language, and Legal Determinacy* (Oxford: Clarendon Press, 2003).

Bodas Freitas, Isabel Maria, Dantas, Eva and Iizuka, Michiko, 'The Kyoto Mechanisms and the Diffusion of Renewable Energy Technologies in the BRICS' (2012) *Energy Policy* 118–128.

The BRICS Report: A Study of Brazil, Russia, India, China, and South Africa with Special Focus on Synergies and Complementarities (Oxford: Oxford University Press, 2012).

Brütsch, Christian and Papay, Mihaela, 'Deconstructing the BRICS: Bargaining Coalition, Imagined Community, or Geopolitical Fad?' (2013) 6(3) *Chinese Journal of International Politics* 299–327.

Cassiolato, José E. and Lastres, Helena M. M., 'Science, Technology and Innovation Policies in the BRICS Countries: An Introduction', in José E. Cassiolato and Virginia Vitorino (eds.), *BRICS and Development Alternatives: Innovation Systems and Policies* (London: Anthem Press, 2009), pp. 1–34.

Catbagan, Aaron, 'Rights of Action for Private Non-State Actors in the WTO Disputes Settlement System' (2009) 37(2) *Denver Journal of International Law and Policy* 279–302.

Centre for WTO Studies, *BRICS: Trade Policies, Institutions and Areas for Deepening Cooperation* (New Delhi: WTO, 2013).

Chaudhary, Latika et al., 'Big BRICs, Weak Foundations: The Beginning of Public Elementary Education in Brazil, Russia, India, and China' (2012) 49 *Explorations in Economic History* 221–240.

Chin, Gregory T., 'The BRICS-Led Development Bank: Purpose and Politics beyond the G20' (2014) 5(3) *Global Policy* 366–373.

Chkili, Walid and Nguyen, Duc Khuong, 'Exchange Rate Movements and Stock Market Returns in a Regime-Switching Environment: Evidence for BRICS Countries' (2014) 31 *Research in International Business and Finance* 46–56.

Chun, Kwang Ho, *The BRICs Superpower Challenge: Foreign and Security Policy Analysis* (Farnham: Ashgate, 2013).

Collins, David, *The BRIC States and Outward Foreign Direct Investment* (Oxford: Oxford University Press, 2013).

Cooper, Julian, 'Of BRICs and Brains: Comparing Russia with China, India, and Other Populous Emerging Economies' (2006) 47(3) *Eurasian Geography and Economics* 255–284.

Cutler, A. Claire, *Private Power and Global Authority: Transnational Merchant Law in the Global Political Economy* (Cambridge: Cambridge University Press, 2003).

Dargin, Justin (ed.), *The Rise of the Global South: Philosophical, Geopolitical and Economic Trends of the 21st Century* (Singapore: World Scientific Publishing, 2013).

De Coning, Cedric, Mandrup, Thomas and Odgaard, Liselotte (eds.), *The BRICS and Coexistence: An Alternative Vision of World Order* (London: Routledge, 2015).

Demaret, Paul, 'The Metamorphoses of the GATT: From the Havana Charter to the World Trade Organization' (1995) 34(1) *Columbia Journal of Transnational Law* 123–171.

De Paula, Luiz Fernando, 'Financial Liberalization, Exchange Rate Regime and Economic Performance in BRICs Countries', in Philip Arestis and Luiz Fernando de Paula (eds.), *Financial Liberalization and Economic Performance in Emerging Countries* (Basingstoke: Palgrave MacMillan, 2008), pp. 52–94.

Dercole, Fabio and Rinaldi, Sergio, *Analysis of Evolutionary Processes: The Adaptive Dynamics Approach and Its Applications* (Princeton: Princeton University Press, 2008).

D'Ippoliti, Carlo, 'Economics and Diversity' (2011) 33(4) *Journal of the History of Economic Thought* 562.

Duan, Yunyun, 'FDI in BRICs: A Sector Level Analysis' (2010) 5(1) *International Journal of Business and Management* 46–52.

Emch, Adrian, Regazzini, Jose and Rudomino, Vassily (eds.), *Competition Law in the BRICS Countries* (Alphen Aan Den Rijn: Wolters Kluwer Law & Business, 2012).

Esty, Daniel C. and Geradin, Damien, 'Regulatory Co-Opetition' (2000) 3(2) *Journal of International Economic Law* 235–255.

Fourcade, Marion, 'The Material and Symbolic Construction of the BRICs: Reflections Inspired by the RIPE Special Issue' (2013) 20(2) *Review of International Political Economy* 256–267.

Garcia, Frank J., 'The Trade Linkage Phenomenon: Pointing the Way to the Trade Law and Global Social Policy of the 21st Century' (1998) 19(2) *University of Pennsylvania Journal of International Economic Law* 201–208.

Gibbons, Thomas, *Rhetoric; or, a View of Its Principal Tropes and Figures* (London: J. and W. Oliver, 1767).

Gilleard, Matthew, 'BRICs Attracting Investment despite their Tax Systems' (2013) 24(7) *International Tax Review* 19–21.

Gleick, James, *Faster: The Acceleration of Just about Everything* (New York: Vintage Books, 2000).

Glenn, H. Patrick, *Legal Traditions of the World: Sustainable Diversity in Law*, 3rd edn (Oxford: Oxford University Press, 2007).

'Persuasive Authority' (1987) 32(2) *McGill Law Journal* 261–298.

Goulding, Charles, 'Hitting the BRICs – Brazil, Russia, India and China Tax Changes Facilitate Trade' (2005) 5(2) *Journal of Taxation of Global Transactions* 65–68.

Griffith-Jones, Stephany, A BRICS Development Bank: A Dream Coming True? UNCTAD Discussion Paper No. 215 (March 2014); available at http://unctad.org/en/PublicationsLibrary/osgdp20141_en.pdf [accessed on 25 October 2016].

Handy, Charles, *The Age of Paradox* (Boston: Harvard Business School Press, 1995).

Haq, Zahoor and Meilke, Karl, 'Do the BRICs and Emerging Markets Differ in their Agrifood Imports?' (2010) 61(1) *Journal of Agricultural Economics* 1–14.

Harmer, Andrew et al., "'BRICS without Straw'? A Systematic Literature Review of Newly Emerging Economies' Influence in Global Health' (2013) 9 *Globalization and Health* 15.

Haufler, Virginia, *A Public Role for the Private Sector: Industry Self-Regulation in a Global Economy* (Washington, DC: Carnegie Endowment for International Peace, 2001).

Hawksworth, John and Cookson, Gordon, *The World in 2050: Beyond the BRICs: A Broader Look at Emerging Market Growth Prospects* (PriceWaterHouseCoopers, 2006); available at www.pwc.com/la/en/publications/assets/world_2050_brics.pdf [accessed on 25 October 2016].

Heldrich, Andreas, 'The Deluge of Norms' (1983) 6(2) *Boston College International and Comparative Law Review* 377–389.

Hong, Paul and Park, YoungWon, *Building Network Capabilities in Turbulent Competitive Environments: Business Success Stories from the BRICs* (Boca Raton: CRC Press, 2015).

Institute for Applied Economic Research (Instituto de Pesquisa Econômica Aplicada – IPEA), *Towards a Long-Term Strategy for BRICS: A proposal by the BRICS Think Tanks Council* (Brasília: Institute for Applied Economic Research, 2015); available at www.ipea.gov.br/portal/images/stories/PDFs/livros/livros/151104_brics_long_term_strategy.pdf [accessed on 25 October 2016].

International Food Policy Research Institute, *2012 Global Food Policy Report* (Washington, DC: International Food Policy Research Institute, 2013).

International Law Commission (ILC), *Fragmentation of International Law: Difficulties Arising from the Diversification and Expansion of International Law*, A/CN.4/L.682 (13 April 2006).

Jaffrelot, Christophe and Singh Sidhu, Waheguru Pal, 'From Plurilateralism to Multilateralism? G-20, IBSA, BRICS, and BASIC', in Waheguru Pal Singh Sidhu, Pratap Bhanu Mehta and Bruce Jones (eds.), *Shaping the Emerging World: India and the Multilateral Order* (Washington, DC: Brookings Institution Press, 2013), pp. 319–339.

Jenny, Frederic and Katsoulacos, Yannis (eds.) *Competition Law Enforcement in the BRICS and in Developing Countries: Legal and Economic Aspects* (New York: Springer, 2016).

Johnson, Mark L., 'Mind, Metaphor, Law' (2007) 58(3) *Mercer Law Review* 845–868.

Johnson, Samuel, *Lives of the Most Eminent English Poets, with Critical Observations on their Works* (London: John Murray, 1854), vol. 1.

Jones, Bruce, *Still Ours to Lead: America, Rising Powers, and the Tension between Rivalry and Restraint* (Washington, DC: Brookings Institution Press, 2014).

Khanna, Parag, 'New BRICS Bank a Building Block of Alternative World Order' (2014) 31(4) *New Perspectives Quarterly* 46–48.

Khondker, Habibul H., 'Globalisation to Glocalisation: A Conceptual Exploration' (2005) 13(2) *Intellectual Discourse* 181–199.

Kornegay, Francis A. and Bohler-Muller, Narnia (eds.), *Laying the BRICS of a New Global Order: From Yekaterinburg 2009 to Ethekwini 2013* (Pretoria: Africa Institute of South Africa, 2013).

Larionova, M., et al., 'BRICS: Emergence of Health Agenda' (2014) 9(4) *International Organisations Research Journal* 73–88.

Lèbre La Rovere, Renata, de Magalhães Ozorio, Luiz and de Jesus Melo, Leonardo (eds.), *Entrepreneurship in BRICS: Policy and Research to Support Entrepreneurs* (New York: Springer, 2015).

Lee, Sang M. and Olson, David L., *Convergenomics: Strategic Innovation in the Convergence Era* (Farnham: Gower, 2010).

Lepaulle, Pierre, 'The Function of Comparative Law with a Critique of Sociological Jurisprudence' (1922) 35(7) *Harvard Law Review* 838–858.

Marten, Robert et al., 'An Assessment of Progress towards Universal Health Coverage in Brazil, Russia, India, China, and South Africa (BRICS)' (2014) 384 *Lancet* 2164–2171.

McBride, Keally DeAnne, *Postliberal Politics: Feminism, Communitarianism, and the Search for Community* (Berkeley: University of California, 1999).

McLuhan, Marshall, *The Gutenberg Galaxy: The Making of Typographic Man* (Toronto: University of Toronto Press, 1962).

Neuwirth, Rostam J., 'Essentially Oxymoronic Concepts' (2013) 2(2) *Global Journal of Comparative Law* 147–166.

'Global Law and Sustainable Development: Change and the "Developing–Developed Country" Terminology' (2016) *European Journal of Development Research*; doi:10.1057/s41287-016-0067-y.

'Global Market Integration and the Creative Economy: The Paradox of Industry Convergence and Regulatory Divergence' (2015) 18(1) *Journal of International Economic Law* 21–50.

'Law and the Mind: A New Role for Comparative Law?' in Tong Io Cheng and Salvatore Mancuso (eds.), *New Frontiers of Comparative Law* (Hong Kong: LexisNexis, 2013), pp. 11–17.

Neuwirth, Rostam J. and Svetlicinii, Alexandr, 'Law as a Social Medicine: Enhancing International Inter-Regime Regulatory Coopetition as a Means for the Establishment of a Global Health Governance Framework' (2015) 36 (3–4) *Journal of Legal Medicine* 330–366.

O' Neill, Jim, 'Building Better Global Economic BRICs' (2001) *Goldman Sachs Global Economics Paper No 66* (30 November 2001); available at www .goldmansachs.com/our-thinking/archive/archive-pdfs/build-better-brics .pdf [accessed on 25 October 2016].

Oppetit, Bruno., 'Les tendances régressives dans l'évolution du droit contemporain', in Jean-François Pillebout (ed.), *Mélanges dédiés à Dominique Holleaux* (Paris: Litec, 1990), pp. 317–330.

Örücü, Esin, 'What Is a Mixed Legal System: Exclusion or Expansion?' (2008) 12(1) *Electronic Journal of Comparative Law* 1–18; available at www.ejcl.org/121/art121-15.pdf [accessed on 25 October 2016].

Ozturk, Ilhan, 'Sustainability in the Food–Energy–Water Nexus: Evidence from BRICS (Brazil, the Russian Federation, India, China, and South Africa) Countries' (2015) 93 *Energy* 999–1010.

Pant, Harsh V., 'The BRICS Fallacy' (2013) 36(3) *Washington Quarterly* 91–105.

Price, Elizabeth E., Caldwell, Christine A. and Whiten, Andrew, 'Comparative Cultural Cognition' (2010) 1(1) *Cognitive Science* 23–31.

Ramanujam, Nandini, et al., *Rule of Law and Economic Development: A Comparative Analysis of Approaches to Economic Development across the BRIC Countries* (Montreal: McGill, 2012); available at www.mcgill.ca/roled/files/roled/mcgill_roled_report_2012.pdf [accessed on 25 October 2016].

Ranchordás, Sofia, 'Sunset Clauses and Experimental Regulations: Blessing or Curse for Legal Certainty?' (2015) 36(1) *Statute Law Review* 28–45.

Redclift, Michael, 'Sustainable Development (1987–2005): An Oxymoron Comes of Age' (2005) 13 *Sustainable Development* 212–227.

Rolland, Sonia E., 'The BRICS' Contributions to the Architecture and Norms of International Economic Law' (2013) 107 *American Society of International Law Proceedings* 164–170.

Rosenau, James N., 'Governance in the 21st Century' (1995) 1(1) *Global Governance* 13–43.

Sauvant, Karl P., 'New Sources of FDI: The BRICS Outward FDI from Brazil, Russia, India and China' (2005) 6(5) *Journal of World Investment & Trade* 639–709.

Scaffardi, Lucia, 'BRICS, a Multi-Centre "Legal Network"?' (2014) 5 *Beijing Law Review* 140–148.

Scaffardi, Lucia and Federico, Veronica, 'The BRICS in the Spotlight: A Research Agenda' (2014) 1(1) *BRICS Law Journal* 112–119.

Schuman, Michael, 'Forget the BRICs; Meet the PINEs', *Time* (13 March 2014); available at http://time.com/22779/forget-the-brics-meet-the-pines/ [accessed on 25 October 2016].

Schwartzman, Simon, Pinheiro, Rómulo and Pillay, Pundy, *Higher Education in the BRICS Countries: Investigating the Pact between Higher Education and Society* (Dordrecht: Springer, 2015).

Shaheen, Salman, 'The Future for BRICS Tax Policy Coordination' (2012) 23(7) *International Tax Review* 25–26.

Sharma, Ruchir, 'Broken BRICs: Why the Rest Stopped Rising' (2012) 91(6) *Foreign Affairs* 2–7.

Sheng-jun, Yuan, 'Educational Policies and Economic Growth in BRICs: Comparative Perspectives' (2011) 8(2) *Journal of US–China Public Administration* 188–196.

Strategy for BRICS Economic Partnership (Ufa, Russia, 2015); available at http://infobrics.org/wp-content/uploads/2015/07/partnershipstrategy_eng.pdf [accessed on 25 October 2016].

Struever, Nancy S., *Rhetoric, Modality, Modernity* (Chicago: University of Chicago Press, 2009).

Stuenkel, Oliver, *The BRICS and the Future of Global Order* (Lanham: Lexington Books, 2015).

'The Financial Crisis, Contested Legitimacy, and the Genesis of Intra-BRICS Cooperation' (2013) 19(4) *Global Governance* 611–630.

Tambiah, Stanley J., *Magic, Science and the Scope of Rationality* (Cambridge: Cambridge University Press, 1990).

Trachtman, Joel P., 'Trade and . . . Problems, Cost–Benefit Analysis and Subsidiarity' (1998) 9(1) *European Journal of International Law* 32–85.

United Nations, Transforming Our World: The 2030 Agenda for Sustainable Development, General Assembly A/RES/70/1 (21 October 2015).

United Nations, Department of Economic and Social Affairs, Population Division, *World Population Prospects 2015 – Data Booklet* (ST/ESA/SER.A/377) (2015).

Van Agtmael, Antoine, 'Think Again: The BRICS' (2012) 196 *Foreign Policy* 76–79.

Vickers, Brendan, 'The Role of the BRICS in the WTO: System-Supporters of Change Agenda in Multilateral Trade?' in Amrita Narlikar, Martin Daunton and Robert M. Stern (eds.), *The Oxford Handbook on the World Trade Organization* (Oxford: Oxford University Press, 2012), pp. 254–273.

Williams, Thomas G., *The History of Commerce* (London: Sir Isaac Pitman, 1926).

Yu, Peter K., 'Access to Medicines, BRICS Alliances, and Collective Action' (2008) 34(2) *American Journal of Law & Medicine* 345–394.

Zhang, Huiming et al., 'Comparison of Renewable Energy Policy Evolution among the BRICs' (2011) 15 *Renewable and Sustainable Energy Reviews* 4904–4909.

2

Diversity and Intra-BRICS Trade

Patterns, Risks and Potential

UMAKRISHNAN KOLLAMPARAMBIL

I. Introduction

The BRICS member countries are diverse not merely in their language, culture, institutions and political systems but also in their economic composition. While the dissimilarities in their political institutions, physical and financial infrastructure, levels of development, governance and cultures are expected to have a negative impact on trade relationships,[1] the diversity in their resources, factor endowment and technological capabilities is hailed in the trade literature as the fundamental rationale behind international trade.[2]

Economic diversity between countries provides a natural synergy in international trade. Russia and Brazil, as energy-surplus economies, are attractive trade partners for fast-growing members such as China and India, with their high demand for energy sources. The same is true of South Africa, a major producer of not only coal but also other mineral resources that are in high demand in India and China. On the other hand, with low levels of domestic savings, both South Africa and Brazil look to China and India as sources of foreign investment to fill their savings investment gaps. Therefore, although BRICS is not a trade agreement per se, but rather a loose political and economic association with a mandate of increased political, economic and social cooperation between the member countries based on specific bilateral agreements, there is the potential for trade and investment interdependence.

It is to this end that BRICS set up the BRICS Business Council in 2013 to promote trade, investment and economic ties between the business

---

[1] Jan Tinbergen, *Shaping the World Economy* (New York: Twentieth Century Fund, 1962).

[2] For more on the Heckscher–Ohlin model, see Robert C. Feenstra, *Advanced International Trade: Theory and Evidence* (Princeton: Princeton University Press, 2004), pp. 31–63.

communities of the member states.[3] The recent BRICS initiative establishing the New Development Bank (NDB), headquartered in Shanghai with a regional office in Johannesburg, is evidence of the close ties emerging between the BRICS countries.[4] Internationally, this is perceived as a challenge by BRICS to the existing international financial architecture, which is dominated by the developed countries, in order to highlight its dissatisfaction with the reform of the governance structures of the international financial institutions (IFIs).[5] While BRICS, as a tool for collective bargaining power to promote developing country interests, has gained attention in this context, the impact of the NDB on trade and investment promotion has received less notice. Its establishment is expected to accelerate economic cooperation between the member states, and a number of projects for cooperation have already been identified under the BRICS Roadmap for Trade, Economic and Investment Cooperation until 2020.[6]

There are many challenges in this quest for tighter trade relationships. The geographical distance between the member countries and the tight restrictions on mobility between them are fundamental obstacles. Nevertheless, their shared history has played a positive role in fostering trade relationships. Historically, India and South Africa have had close ties, as both are former British colonies. More recently, the Indian government's advocacy to end apartheid rule has continued to strengthen this relationship.[7] Similarly, the former USSR and India shared common ground during the Cold War era, despite dissimilar political regimes, with India even adopting a Soviet-style planned model of economic growth.[8] Notwithstanding the disintegration of the USSR, the close ties between India and Russia have continued. China's relationship with Russia also dramatically improved after the 1991 dissolution of the USSR.[9]

---

[3] Details on the BRICS Business Council are available at www.brics-info.org/about-the-brics-business-council/ [accessed on 31 October 2016].

[4] Details on the New Development Bank are available at http://ndbbrics.org/agreement.html [accessed on 31 October 2016].

[5] Oliver Stuenkel, *The BRICS and the Future of Global Order* (London: Lexington Books, 2015).

[6] The roadmap can be downloaded from www.unido.ru/upload/files/b/brics_roadmap.pdf [accessed on 31 October 2016].

[7] Audie Jeanne Klotz, *Norms in International Relations: The Struggle against Apartheid* (Ithaca: Cornell Studies in Political Economy, 1999).

[8] R. V. R. Chandrasekhara Rao, 'Indo-Soviet economic relations' (1973) 13(8) *Asian Survey* 793–801.

[9] Alexander Korolev, 'The strategic alignment between Russia and China: myths and reality, Singapore: Lee Kuan Yew School of Public Policy Research Paper #15–19, 2015.

There is, however, political and military strain between India and China, which is often played out through border skirmishes and through Chinese support of India's regional foe, Pakistan, which has been evident both in its military assistance and its UN Security Council votes.[10] Differences in the approaches of Russia, on the one hand, and India and China, on the other, with regards to talks on climate change are also evident.[11]

Given this complicated backdrop, it is important to take a deeper look at the trade patterns between the BRICS states, given their similarities and dissimilarities. The objective of this chapter is to analyze the trade patterns that are emerging between the BRICS states against the backdrop of their diversity, not only to identify the resulting challenges and new risks to which the members might be exposed but also to investigate the potential for enhanced trade cooperation.

The chapter is divided into several sections. The next section compares the profiles of the BRICS countries with a view to highlighting not just inter-country but also intra-country diversities that make the inter-relationships between them highly complex and are expected to have a differential impact on trade for each of them. Section III takes a closer look at the nature of and trends in their bilateral trade patterns with a view to deciphering the patterns in trade. The fourth section assesses the risks and challenges emerging from these trade patterns, specifically in the context of the ongoing Chinese economic slowdown. Section V is dedicated to assessing the trade potential for the future expansion of intra-BRICS trade. The sixth and final section concludes with some observations.

II.   Inter- and Intra-BRICS Diversity

Comprehending the diversity between and among the BRICS states is an essential first step in analyzing the trade patterns and deriving the trade potential of BRICS. BRICS cannot claim to be an association of equal or even similar countries (Table 2.1), given that the BRICS states have divergent political and legal systems. The differences in the political regimes of the members are expected to be relevant, as studies have argued that democratic countries are more likely than nondemocratic ones to

---

[10] David M. Malone and R. Mukherjee, 'India and China: conflict and cooperation' (2010) 52(1) *Survival: Global Politics and Strategy* 137–158.

[11] Marcos Degaut, *Do the BRICS Still Matter? A Report of the CSIS Americas Program*, Centre for Strategic and International Studies, October 2015, Washington, DC.

Table 2.1 *Country Profiles, 2014*

	Country area (sq. km)	Population (millions)	GDP (PPP billions USD)	Per capita income (PPP USD)	Human Development Index*
Brazil	8,514,877	203	3,364	16,592	0.755
Russia	17,098,242	144	3,576	24,930	0.798
India	32,87,263	1,295	7,389	5,704	0.609
China	95,96,961	1,361	19,794	14,543	0.727
S. Africa	1.221.037	55	725	13,300	0.666

Source: World Bank http://data.worldbank.org/data-catalog/country-profiles.
* United Nation Development Program http://hdr.undp.org/en/composite/HDI.

conclude trade agreements.[12] Sharing common legal origins is also expected to facilitate international trade.[13] While Brazil and Russia have French legal origins, China's legal origins are German, and India's and South Africa's are British.[14] There are also wide variations in the languages, religions and cultures of the BRICS countries that are expected to negatively affect the trade flows between those countries.[15] In addition to these factors, the geographical distance between the BRICS economies is also considered a potential trade dampener due to the excessive transportation costs involved.[16]

While BRICS includes China and India, both giants in terms of population and economic size, it also accommodates its newest member, South Africa, which is relatively tiny in comparison, with a GDP of under 1 trillion USD and a population of 55 million (Table 2.1). The per capita income levels also vary widely between the members, ranging from

---

[12] Edward D. Mansfield, Helen V. Milner and B. Peter Rosendorff, 'Why democracies cooperate more: electoral control and international trade agreements' (2002) 56(3) *International Organization* 477–513.

[13] Gabriel J. Felbermayr and Farid Toubal, 'Cultural proximity and trade' (2010) 54 *European Economic Review* 279–293.

[14] Rafael La Porta, Florencio Lopez-de-Silanes and Andrei Shleifer 'The economic consequences of legal origins' (2008) 46(2) *Journal of Economic Literature* 285–332; available at http://scholar.harvard.edu/files/shleifer/files/consequences_jel_final.pdf?m=1360042991 [accessed on 31 October 2016].

[15] Dale Boisso and Michael Ferrantino, 'Economic distance, cultural distance, and openness in international trade: empirical puzzles' (1997) 12(4) *Journal of Economic Integration* 456–484. See also Jacques Melitz, 'Language and foreign trade' (2008) 52(4) *European Economic Review* 667–699.

[16] Paul Krugman, *Geography and Trade* (Cambridge, MA: MIT Press, 1991).

Table 2.2 *Intra-BRICS Diversity, 2010*

	Poverty %	Gini inequality index %	Unemployment rate %	Gender inequality index	Ethnic diversity
Brazil	7.4	52.9	6.8	0.457	0.54
Russia	10.8	41.6	5.1	0.276	0.24
India	21.9	33.9	3.6	0.563	0.81
China	4.6	42.1	4.7	0.191	0.154
S. Africa	53.8	63.4	25.1	0.407	0.88

Source: World Bank, World Development Indicators; James Fearon, 'Ethnic and cultural diversity by country' (2003) 8 *Journal of Economic Growth* 195–222.

high-income countries such as Russia to upper-middle-income countries such as Brazil and South Africa to lower-middle-income countries such as China and India. The Indian income level is less than one-fourth the income level of Russia, highlighting the level of income inequality between the countries. This income gap is also reflected in the Human Development Index (HDI), which considers additional indicators such as the literacy and life expectancy levels. Both India and South Africa are faced with huge development challenges relating to the quality of life of the vast majority of their populations, as is evident from their low HDI. South Africa, which has an income level similar to that of China, has low HDI levels in comparison. This points to issues relating to higher economic inequalities within South Africa as compared to China.

There is also a wide variation in poverty rates among the BRICS members. The poverty rate, measured as the percentage of people living below the national poverty line, is higher than 50 percent for South Africa, as compared to less than 5 percent and 8 percent for China and Brazil, respectively (Table 2.2). The alarmingly high level of unemployment in South Africa is reflected in its high poverty rate, as well as in its high Gini inequality index, which is one of the highest in the world. Economic inequality aside, ethnic diversity is also the highest in South Africa, which is hailed as the 'rainbow nation' because of its racial composition. Although India has a relatively high level of poverty, its level of income inequality, as measured by the Gini inequality index, is the lowest among the BRICS countries. However, this picture is disfigured by the extremely high gender inequality index in India, which is indicative of a conservative patriarchal society. China is the most homogeneous in aspects relating to income, gender and ethnicity.

Table 2.3 *Economic Profile, 2014*

	GDP growth % (average 2011–2014)	Savings rate %	Investment rate %	Net FDI/ GDP %	Trade balance/ GDP %	Currency	Currency per USD (average 2011–2014)
Brazil	2.125	16	20	4.0	Deficit (−2.7)	Real	2.35
Russia	2.4	23	21	1.2	Surplus (7.2)	Ruble	60.9
India	6.475	31	29	1.7	Deficit (−2.3)	Rupee	61
China	8.075	50	44	2.8	Surplus (3.7)	Renminbi	6.23
S.Africa	2.275	15	20	1.6	Deficit (−1.9)	Rand	12.8

Source: World Bank, World Development Indicators.

The diversity between the BRICS countries in the sociopolitical realm is also reflected in their economic profiles. The two largest economies, China and India, have also been the two fastest-growing economies in recent times (Table 2.3). Because of this fast pace of growth, their per capita income levels have increased from the lower income category to the lower-middle income category, despite the huge size of their populations. Russia, Brazil and South Africa, in contrast, have experienced more modest levels of economic growth, which have translated into more or less stagnant per capita income levels in the recent past. The fast pace of growth in China and India has been made possible by the higher investment rates in these countries. This, in turn, has been made possible by their higher savings rates. Brazil and South Africa have savings rates that are less than one-third that of China and half that of India, and their modest savings rates are not sufficient to meet their investment requirements. Their dependence on the surplus-savings countries such as China and India to fund their savings-investment gaps is evident in Table 2.3.

The exchange rate determination mechanism of the trading partners also has an impact on their trade relationships.[17] Each BRICS country

---

[17] Christian Broda, 'Terms of trade and exchange rate regimes in developing countries' (2004) 63(1) *Journal of International Economics* 31–58.

has its own currency, and methods of determining the exchange rate also vary. Brazil and South Africa follow a freely floating exchange rate system whereby the value of their currency is not fixed, and there are no targets set by the central bank. India has a managed float system, with its central bank intervening only to curb excessive volatility. China, in contrast, has a managed float regime in which the Renminbi rate is based on supply and demand, but is also adjusted with reference to a basket of currencies. Until 2015, Russia followed the dual currency soft peg, together with automatic interventions whereby the central bank propped up the ruble when the exchange rate against the euro and the dollar exceeded its boundaries. Currently, however, Russia employs a floating exchange rate system. The diversity in the exchange rate systems within BRICS has implications for the trade balance and the sustainability of trade between its members.

The trade profiles indicate that South Africa is the most open economy, with trade accounting for 64 percent of its GDP, and that Brazil is the least open, with trade accounting for a mere 26 percent of its GDP (Table 2.4). China is among the top export markets for Brazil, South Africa and Russia. These countries meet the Chinese demand for petroleum, natural gas, iron ore and other metals and minerals.[18] China is the major source of imports for all the other BRICS countries. Trade with China is clearly the common thread that binds together the trade of the BRICS countries.

The takeaway point that emerges from this section is that while the institutional and sociopolitical diversity between the countries creates challenges for seamless trade integration, their economic diversity provides the grounds for trade and investment interdependence between the member countries. Moreover, the shared histories of some of the members have enabled them to overcome their diversity in the political sphere and bridge the geographical distance, which otherwise would have made trade cooperation more difficult.

III. Intra-BRICS Trade: Trends and Patterns

Exports from BRICS economies have shown impressive growth in recent times, with their share in world exports increasing from 8 percent in 2000

---

[18] Chukwuka Onyekwena, Olumide Taiwo and Eberechukwu Uneze, 'South Africa in BRICS: a bilateral trade analysis', South African Institute of International Affairs, Occasional Paper no. 181, April 2014.

Table 2.4 *Trade Profile 2014*

	Trade/GDP (%) #	Exports		Imports	
		Major trading partners (% share)	Goods exported	Major trading partners (% share)	Goods imported
Brazil	25	China (17), US (11), Argentina (7)	Transport equipment, iron ores, soybeans	US (17), China (12), Argentina (9)	Machinery, electrical & transport equipment, chemical products
Russia	53	Netherlands (11), Germany (8), China (7)	Petroleum, natural gas, metals	China (16), Germany (12), Ukraine (5)	Consumer goods, machinery, vehicles
India	49	EU (16), US (13), UAE (10)	Software, petrochemicals, agriculture, leather	China (13), EU (10), Saudi Arabia (7)	Crude oil, gold & gems, electronics, engineering goods
China	42	US (17), Hong Kong (15), Japan (6)	Electrical machinery, data processing equipment, apparel & textiles	South Korea (10), Japan (8.3), US (8.1)	Electrical and other machinery, oil and mineral fuels, optical and medical equipment, metal ores,
S. Africa	64	China (15), US (8), Japan (6)	Gold, diamond, platinum, other metal & minerals	China (15), Germany (10), USA (7)	Machinery, chemicals, petroleum

Data: World Bank, World Integrated Trade Systems.

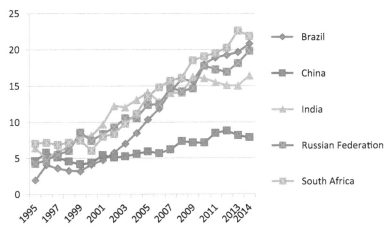

Figure 2.1 BRICS share in total imports as %, 1995–2014.
Source: Compiled from UNCTAD Statistics

to 19 percent in 2014.[19] A substantial part of this increase is due to growth in intra-BRICS exports during that period. This section will take a deeper look at the emerging trade patterns between the BRICS countries to comprehend the relative relevance of each member vis-à-vis intra-BRICS and global trade.

The increased share of intra-BRICS trade in their total imports is markedly evident in Figure 2.1. Intra-BRICS imports account for more than 20 percent of total imports for South Africa and Brazil. China's intra-BRICS imports are the lowest, and they also show the least growth.

Intra-BRICS exports, as a percentage of total exports, have also increased since the early 2000s (Figure 2.2). However, a decline in exports is very clear since 2013, which is indicative of the impact of the Chinese economic slowdown. This decrease is not surprising, because China is a major export market for South Africa, Brazil and Russia. Brazil has the highest intra-BRICS concentration, with more than 20 percent of its total exports being accounted for by intra-BRICS exports. Brazil is followed by South Africa, which has a 15 percent share. India, Russia and China are much less dependent on BRICS exports.

The largest source of intra-BRICS imports is China (Figure 2.3). The concentration of Chinese imports is the highest for Russia;

---

[19] World Trade Organization, *International Trade Statistics 2015*, p. 28; available at www.wto.org/english/res_e/statis_e/its2015_e/its2015_e.pdf [accessed on 31 October 2016].

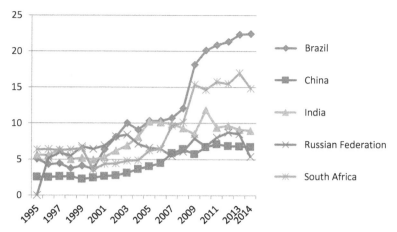

Figure 2.2 Intra-BRICS exports as a share of total exports, 1995–2014.
Source: Compiled from UNCTAD Statistics

Chinese exports account for more than 88 percent of its total intra-BRICS imports. The lowest concentration is for South Africa, whose imports from India also account for a substantial proportion of its intra-BRICS imports. China's intra-BRICS imports are predominantly from Brazil, South Africa and Russia, which is not surprising given that they are sources of petroleum, iron ore and other metals and minerals. Russian imports from South Africa and India are negligible.

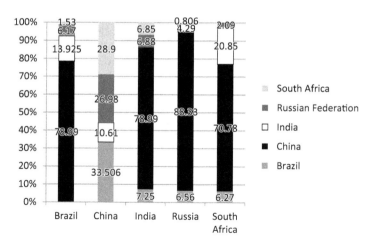

Figure 2.3 Sources of intra-BRICS imports, 2014.
Source: Computed from UNCTAD Statistics.

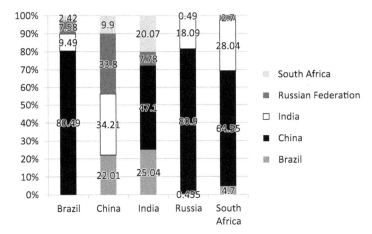

Figure 2.4 Destinations for intra-BRICS exports, 2014.
Source: Computed from UNCTAD Statistics.

China dominates as the destination of Russia's and Brazil's intra-BRICS exports, accounting for more than 80 percent of their totals (Figure 2.4). China's market domination as an export destination is lower for India and South Africa. Indian exports substantially target the Brazilian and South African markets, while South African exports target Indian, as well as Chinese markets.

A product sophistication analysis of intra-BRICS exports indicates that exports from Brazil, Russia and South Africa are overwhelmingly resource-based (Table 2.5). China seems to be the sole source of high-technology exports in intra-BRICS trade. These patterns are a cause for concern on two fronts: (1) despite increased BRICS trade, the BRICS countries continue to be dependent on developed countries for technology, indicating the limit of BRICS's power vis-à-vis the rest of the world, and (2) overdependence on resource-based trade points to the unsustainability of intra-BRICS trade, unless trade patterns change dramatically over the long run.

Given the close relationship between foreign direct investment (FDI) and international trade,[20] we briefly examine the patterns of intra-BRICS FDI stock (Table 2.6). It is clear that FDI stock from developed countries continues to dominate as the major source for all the BRICS countries

---

[20] Joshua Aizenman and Ilan Noy, 'FDI and trade – two-way linkages?' (2006) 46(3) *Quarterly Review of Economics and Finance* 317–337.

Table 2.5 *Product Sophistication in Intra-BRICS Exports (%)*

	Resource-based exports		Low-tech exports		Medium-tech exports		High-tech exports	
	2000	2007	2000	2007	2000	2007	2000	2007
Brazil	64.8	72.7	1.9	3.3	5.4	5.2	1.8	0
Russia	21	48.9	0	0	26.6	19.5	6.8	1.1
India	29.5	42.7	17.3	0	0	5.2	5.5	2.2
China	4	0	21.4	11.4	5	5.6	5.4	10.5
South Africa	44.8	58.8	2.4	5.4	13.7	10.4	0	0

Source: Compiled from Sajal Mathur and Meghna Dasgupta, *BRICS Trade Policies, Institutions and Areas for Deepening Cooperation* (IIFT New Delhi: Centre for WTO Studies, 2013), pp. 199–202.

except China, where FDI from developing countries is predominant. The intra-BRICS share in the FDI stock of the host economy is negligible for all the BRICS countries, with South Africa recording the highest at under 4 percent. The intra-BRICS share of FDI stock abroad is also not substantial, except for that of South Africa, with more than one-fifth of South African overseas assets invested within the BRICS bloc. Moreover, all the BRICS countries are net importers of investment, which underscores their continued dependence on countries outside the bloc for investments.

The point emerging from this section is that intra-BRICS trade dependence is higher for the smaller economies, such as South Africa and Brazil. Therefore, any slowdown in the large fast-growing BRICS economies such

Table 2.6 *FDI Stock Distribution, 2012 (%)*

	FDI stock source		FDI stock destination		Net stock (USD billions)
	Developed	BRICS	Developed	BRICS	WORLD
Brazil	88.96	0.42	59.09	0.14	480
Russia	79.68	0.47	77.07	0.38	90
India	61.08	0.54	39.94	2.98	138
China	18.41	1.56	13.75	2.31	811
South Africa	90.42	3.35	52.78	22.04	51

Source: Computed from UNCTAD Bilateral Investment Statistics.

as China and India is likely to hit these smaller economies because of their trade concentration. It is vital for the member economies to expand trade between all the members, rather than to concentrate on the large Chinese market. The intra-BRICS investment levels are still relatively low, and the BRICS members continue to depend on external sources of investment. We analyze the risks and challenges relating to the current trade patterns in detail in the next section.

IV. Risks and Challenges

Risks in international trade fundamentally arise from two forms of concentration: (1) product concentration in exports, especially an overdependence on commodities with high price volatility, and (b) overdependence on export markets without geographical diversity. Section II illustrated the overdependence of the BRICS countries on exports to China, which makes them susceptible to Chinese economic slowdowns. The smaller economies of South Africa, Brazil and Russia are additionally vulnerable given their overdependence on exports of commodities. The prices of commodities are known to be far more volatile than those of manufactured goods.[21] Russia has suffered the repercussions of its overdependence on petroleum and natural gas in recent years.

The economic slowdown in China has not only reduced the exports of the BRICS countries but also has had a wider impact on lowering global prices for commodities, such as oil, natural gas, precious metals, iron ore and other metals and minerals.[22] This has led to the economic slowdown of Russia, Brazil and South Africa (Table 2.7). India is the only country that seems to have overcome the Chinese slowdown, which can largely be explained by two facts: (1) as indicated in Figure 2.2, the share of intra-BRICS exports, as a proportion of India's total exports, is low, and (2) China's share as an export destination is the lowest for India among all the BRICS economies, as shown in Figure 2.4.

---

[21] UNCTAD Secretariat to the G20 Commodity Markets Working Group, *Excessive commodity price volatility: Macroeconomic effects on growth and policy options*, United Nations Conference on Trade And Development, 2012; available at http://unctad.org/en/Docs/gds_mdpb_G20_001_en.pdf [accessed on 31 October 2016].

[22] Paul Cashin, Kamiar Mohaddes and Mehdi Raissi, 'China's slowdown and global financial market volatility: is world growth losing out?' IMF Working Paper, 2016; available at https://www.imf.org/external/pubs/ft/wp/2016/wp1663.pdf [accessed on 31 October 2016].

Table 2.7 *GDP Growth Rate (%)*

Country name	Average 1990s	Average 2000s	2010	2011	2012	2014	2015
Brazil	1.88	3.39	7.53	3.91	1.92	0.10	−3.85
Russia	−4.91	5.48	4.50	4.26	3.41	0.64	−3.7
India	5.77	6.90	10.26	6.64	5.08	7.29	7.5
China	10.01	10.30	10.63	9.48	7.75	7.27	6.9
South Africa	1.39	3.60	3.04	3.21	2.22	1.55	1.25

Source: World Bank; available at www.tradingeconomics.com.

The economic slowdown in China has reduced the demand from Chinese markets, as reflected in the slowdown in the exports of the BRICS members to China (Table 2.8). The latest figures are grim, with negative growth rates for Russia, Brazil and Chinese exports.

The falling exports have, in turn, affected the trade balance of the BRICS countries. The trade balance of the BRICS states (with the exception of Brazil) has always been skewed, with imports from China overwhelmingly overshadowing exports to China (Table 2.9). This has been exacerbated by the Chinese economic slowdown, which has reduced demand from China. The trade deficit, as a percentage of total trade vis-à-vis China, was the highest for India at 54.9 percent, followed by South Africa at 46.8 percent and Russia at 15.2 percent. Brazil enjoyed a surplus of 4.2 percent, with all the members except Brazil recording a deficit vis-à-vis their trade with China. Therefore, while China is an engine of growth for the others by providing an export market, the Chinese have had more than their fair share of the markets of the rest of the BRICS countries. These deficits have grown in recent years because of the fall in Chinese imports resulting

Table 2.8 *Growth Rate of Exports to China (%)*

	2010	2011	2012	2013	2014
Brazil	73.3	30.2	5.0	7.4	−2.8
Russia	44.5	35.9	13.2	12.8	−8.3
India	37.9	23.5	−5.7	1.6	12.0
S Africa	46.6	23.7	14.7	9.8	−6.7

Source: United Nations Council for Trade and Development, UNCTAD statistics.

Table 2.9 *Bilateral Balance of Trade*

Exports	Brazil (B)	Russia (R)	India (I)	China
Russia (R)	B<R			
India (I)	B>I	R<I		
China (C)	B>C	R<C	I<C	
S. Africa (SA)	B<S	R<SA	I<SA	C>SA

Source: Computed from UNCTAD statistics.

from its economic slowdown. In the case of Brazil, the surplus it enjoyed with China has decreased following the Chinese economic slowdown. The reduced export earnings have had an impact on the exchange rates and the growth rates of the smaller BRICS states that have been unduly dependent on China for their exports.

The currencies of the commodity-exporting countries depreciated drastically following the slowdown of the Chinese economy (Table 2.10). Currency depreciation, which follows the balance of the trade deficit, is an automatic mechanism that corrects the trade balance over the long run by making exports more competitive and imports more expensive. However, this mechanism can work only if all the trading partners follow a floating exchange rate. The fact that Chinese currency has not been allowed to appreciate sufficiently over the years, despite its huge trade surplus, has been the source of major trade friction between China and its major trading partners, such as the United States and other Western

Table 2.10 *Currency Depreciation*

	Jan 2013	Dec 2015	% Depreciation
Rand	8.79	15.05	71.18
Real	2.03	3.89	91.40
RMB	6.25	6.46	3.29
Rupee	54.26	66.67	22.87
Ruble	30.30	70.42	132.39

Source: Computed from data at www.x-rates.com/average/?from= RUB&to=USD&amount=1&year=2015.

economies.[23] China devalued its currency by 2 percent in 2015 against the US dollar in an attempt to boost its exports and accelerate economic growth.[24] Therefore, the trade balance with China is not expected to improve for the other BRICS economies, despite the drastic depreciation of the ruble, the rand and the real vis-a-vis the US dollar. Addressing the issue of currency is critical for the BRICS members to ensure fair trade and competition over the long run.

This section highlighted the dangers of overconcentration, has resulted in the economic slowdown of Russia, Brazil and South Africa: It is imperative for the BRICS countries look to each other and not to concentrate solely on China as their export market. Fair trade is also needed so that the BRICS members can participate on a level playing field. This requires the value of Chinese currency to be determined by market forces. In the absence of this, the other BRICS members will continue to suffer from trade deficits with China, with no prospect of reversal.

V.   Trade Potential among the BRICS Countries

In this section, we assess the potential for trade expansion and cooperation based on three indices: (1) the trade complementary index, (2) the export similarity index and (3) the import similarity index.

A.   Trade Complementarity Index

An ideal way to assess trade potential between countries is to use the trade complementarity index.[25] The bilateral trade complementarity index measures regional export-expansion potential between trading partner countries. The index can be thought of as a correlation between Country A's exports to the world and Country B's imports from the world.[26] If Country A's export products to the world match Country B's import products from the world, this indicates that Country A and Country B are

---

[23] John A. Tatom, 'The US-China currency dispute: is a rise in the yuan necessary, inevitable or desirable?' (2007) 7(3) *Global Economy Journal*, ISSN (Online) 1524–5861.

[24] 'China rattles markets with yuan devaluation', *Bloomberg News*, 11 August 2015; available at www.bloomberg.com/news/articles/2015–08–11/china-weakens-yuan-reference-rate-by-record-1-9-amid-slowdown [accessed on 31 October 2016].

[25] Michael Michaely, 'Trade preferential agreements in Latin America: an ex ante assessment', in *Policy Research Working Paper* (Washington DC: World Bank, 1996), p. 1583.

[26] World Trade Organization & United Nations, *A Practical Guide to Trade Policy Analysis*, p. 30; available at www.wto.org/english/res_e/publications_e/wto_unctad12_e.pdf [accessed on 31 October 2016].

Table 2.11 *Trade Complementarity Index*

Exporter	Brazil		Russia		India		China		South Africa	
	pre-2010*	post-2010*	pre-2010	post-2010	pre-2010	post-2010	pre-2010	post-2010	pre-2010	post-2010
Brazil			0.44	0.37	0.39	0.35	0.44	0.45	0.5	0.45
Russia	0.35	0.33			0.46	0.5	0.27	0.31	0.37	0.37
India	0.39	0.43	0.44	0.45			0.35	0.34	0.42	0.46
China	0.44	0.47	0.52	0.53	0.36	0.33			0.45	0.46
S. Africa	0.34	0.34	0.37	0.35	0.43	0.41	0.34	0.38		

Source: UNCTAD Statistics.
* Pre-2010: average for the period 2005–2009; post-2010: average for the period 2010–2014.

complementary and that there is high potential from engaging in a preferential trade relationship between Countries A and B. The index, which takes a value between 0 and 1, indicates a higher scope for efficient trade expansion between Countries A and B when the index is higher. There are two indices for each country pair, one taking Country A as an exporter and one taking it as an importer. The two indices can be quite different. While the country whose import pattern fits with its partners' exports will create demand and act as a trade engine for the trading bloc, the one whose export pattern fits with its partners' imports will benefit from the trade cooperation by being able to increase its exports.

Brazil's highest trade complementarity within the BRICS in the pre-2010 period was with South Africa (Table 2.11). However, the trade complementarity index with South Africa has declined drastically since 2010, equalling that of China at a level of 0.45. Juxtaposing the trade complementarity figures with the shares of each country in the exports of the BRICS bloc, indications are that Brazil has the potential to explore exports to South Africa, which currently accounts for a meagre 2.8 percent of its exports.

Chinese exports complemented Russian imports the highest at 0.53, indicating a great potential to increase its exports to Russia from its share of 33.8 percent. It also had a high level of complementarity with Brazil and South Africa.

Indian exports had the highest complementarity with South African and Russian imports at 0.46 and 0.45, respectively. Ironically, these two countries account for only 20 percent and 7.8 percent of India's intra-BRICS export shares, respectively, indicating the high potential for trade between India and these two countries. Russian exports had the highest complementarity with Indian imports, driven fundamentally by its oil exports. Both India and Russia can benefit by further exploring each other's markets for exports. Although South Africa's export complementarity was the highest with India, driven by its exports of gold and precious metal, it declined in the post-2010 period. In contrast, its export complementarity with China increased from 0.34 to 0.38.

B.   Export Similarity Index

The export similarity index provides useful information on the level of the export competition between countries by highlighting distinctive export patterns from country to country.[27] The index varies between 0 and 1, with 0 indicating complete dissimilarity, and 1 representing identical export composition. Therefore, two countries with an export similarity index close to 1 are likely to be competitors in the international arena, assuming both countries target the same markets. A limitation of this index is that it is subject to aggregation bias (this is because the level of similarity decreases the more disaggregated the data are, resulting in a decline in the level of the index).[28] The UNCTAD estimates of the export similarity index presented in Table 2.12 are calculated at the three-digit level of the SITC Revision 3. While a highly similar export pattern of two countries signifies them as competitors in the world trade arena, it also indicates the potential for cooperation along the lines of the Oil and Petroleum Exporting Countries (OPEC) formed by oil-exporting countries.

A common observation is that the export similarity index has fallen across the board for all the BRICS members in the post-2010 period compared to the pre-2010 period (Table 2.12). This indicates that the economic structures of the BRICS countries are becoming more divergent with time and the level of competition between the BRICS countries has declined. The tightest competition in the post-2010 period appears to be between

---

[27] J. M. Finger and M. E. Kreinin, 'A measure of 'export similarity' and its possible uses' (1979) 89(356) *Economic Journal* 905–912.

[28] Marcus Noland, 'Has Asian export performance been unique?' (1997) 43 *Journal of International Economics* 79–101.

Table 2.12 *Export Similarity Index*

	Brazil		Russia		India		China		South Africa	
	pre-2010	post-2010	pre-2010	post-2010	pre-2010	post-2010	pre-2010	post-2010	pre-2010	post-2010
Brazil	1.00	1.00	0.34	0.29	0.39	0.35	0.29	0.24	0.42	0.38
Russia	0.34	0.29	1.00	1.00	0.31	0.40	0.15	0.13	0.32	0.30
India	0.39	0.35	0.31	0.35	1.00	1.00	0.41	0.40	0.37	0.33
China	0.29	0.24	0.15	0.13	0.41	0.35	1.00	1.00	0.24	0.23
S. Africa	0.42	0.38	0.32	0.30	0.37	0.33	0.24	0.23	1.00	1.00

Source: Computed from UNCTAD statistics.
Notes: Pre-2010: average for the period 2005–2009; post-2010: average for the period 2010–2014.

China and India at a level of 0.40, followed by Brazil and South Africa at 0.38. The limitation of the index is that, although two countries such as Brazil and South Africa are seen to be exporting similar products, their target markets could be very different; as such, the two countries would not be in direct competition. For example, South African exports of manufactured goods target the regional African market, while Brazil targets its neighboring Latin American markets. Exports are the most dissimilar between Russia and China, with the similarity index being a mere 0.13.

C. Import Similarity Index

The import similarity index provides useful information regarding distinctive import patterns from country to country. The import index of similarity signals whether the structure of the imports by product of a given country differs from that of its counterpart country. The index presented in Table 2.13 is calculated at the three-digit level of the SITC Revision 3. It varies between 0 and 1, with 0 indicating complete dissimilarity and 1 representing identical import composition. The import similarity index estimated among the BRICS countries is higher than their export similarity index. While the high level of import similarity is indicative of members competing for the same resources through trade, it is also signals the potential for cooperation and increases in their bargaining power as buyers.

The analysis in this section clearly indicates the immense potential to expand trade between the BRICS partners beyond merely trade with

Table 2.13 *Import Similarity Index*

	Brazil		Russia		India		China		South Africa	
	pre-2010	post-2010	pre-2010	post-2010	pre-2010	post-2010	pre-2010	post-2010	pre-2010	post-2010
Brazil	1.00	1.00	0.52	0.60	0.59	0.50	0.60	0.56	0.69	0.69
Russia	0.52	0.60	1.00	1.00	0.40	0.37	0.41	0.42	0.64	0.65
India	0.59	0.50	0.40	0.37	1.00	1.00	0.56	0.56	0.60	0.56
China	0.60	0.56	0.41	0.42	0.56	0.56	1.00	1.00	0.55	0.57
S. Africa	0.69	0.69	0.64	0.65	0.60	0.56	0.55	0.57	1.00	1.00

Source: Computed from UNCTAD statistics.
Notes: Pre-2010: average for the period 2005–2009; post-2010: average for the period 2010–2014.

China, as indicated by the high levels on the trade complementarity index. The falling export similarity index indicates that competition between the BRICS countries for third markets is decreasing, and the high levels on the import similarity index point to opportunities to cooperate as joint buyers.

VI. Conclusion

The objective of this chapter was to analyze the emerging trends in trade between the BRICS countries against the backdrop of their diversity, with a view to assessing the potential and the impact of increased bilateral trade. The analysis has shown that despite the diversity in their sociopolitical, economic and legal systems, as well as the geographic distance between the BRICS states, intra-BRICS trade has increased in recent years. The enhanced cooperation between the countries is evident through the establishment of the New Development Bank, which is expected to further accelerate trade and investment between the members. However, increasing intra-BRICS trade is fundamentally driven by China-centric trade. This has created risks and challenges in that the Chinese economic slowdown has negatively affected the growth of countries that have concentrated excessively on Chinese markets. The study highlights the potential for increased trade between the other members to mitigate the risks of concentrating on China.

Moreover, the relationship between the smaller BRICS members and China is often seen as reflecting the patterns of North-South trade, where the smaller countries export unprocessed resource-based commodities and import manufacturing goods from China, rather than as trade between equals. These countries therefore have become vulnerable to the excessive price volatility of commodities. A concerted effort to add value to the exports of these members, possibly assisted by Chinese and Indian foreign direct investment in the smaller countries, is required to shift this trade pattern. Intra-BRICS foreign direct investment is not substantial, either as a source or destination for the BRICS members. Increased investment between BRICS countries will likely further promote trade. Lastly, the issue of Chinese currency is also something that must be addressed in order to establish sustainable trade relationships between the BRICS countries.

This analysis has highlighted the diversity between the BRICS members, which makes a free trade agreement difficult in the immediate future. Although BRICS is not a trade agreement, the rapid growth in intra-BRICS trade in recent times indicates that increased trade cooperation is already in place between the members. In conclusion, as far as intra-BRICS trade is concerned, the limited diversity in the trade structure and direction, together with the fact that none of the members are net capital exporters, creates major challenges. The BRICS states' concentration on resource-based exports and the absence of world technology leaders within BRICS, rather than their diversity, create limits on intra-BRICS trade.

VII. References

Aizenman, Joshua and Noy, Ilan, 'FDI and trade – two-way linkages?' (2006) 46(3) *Quarterly Review of Economics and Finance* 317–337.

Boisso, Dale and Ferrantino, Michael, 'Economic distance, cultural distance, and openness in international trade: empirical puzzles' (1997) 12(4) *Journal of Economic Integration* 456–484.

Broda, Christian, 'Terms of trade and exchange rate regimes in developing countries' (2004) 63(1) *Journal of International Economics* 31–58.

Cashin, Paul, Mohaddes, Kamir and Raissi, Mehdi, 'China's slowdown and global financial market volatility: is world growth losing out?' IMF Working Paper, 2016; available at www.imf.org/external/pubs/ft/wp/2016/wp1663 .pdf [accessed on 31 October 2016].

Degaut, Marcos, *Do the BRICS still matter? A report of the CSIS Americas Program*, Centre for Strategic and International Studies, October 2015, Washington, DC.

Fearon, James, 'Ethnic and cultural diversity by country' (2003) 8 *Journal of Economic Growth* 195–222.

Feenstra, Robert C., *Advanced International Trade: Theory and Evidence*. Princeton: Princeton University Press, 2004, pp. 31–63.

Felbermayr, Gabriel J. and Toubal, Farid, 'Cultural proximity and trade' (2010) 54 *European Economic Review* 279–293.

Finger, J. M. and Kreinin, M. E., 'A measure of 'export similarity' and its possible uses' (1979) 89(356) *Economic Journal* 905–912.

Klotz, Audie Jeanne, *Norms in International Relations: The Struggle against Apartheid*. Ithaca, NY: Cornell Studies in Political Economy, 1999.

Korolev, Alexander, 'The strategic alignment between Russia and China: myths and reality', Singapore: Lee Kuan Yew School of Public Policy Research Paper #15–19, 2015.

Krugman, Paul, *Geography and Trade*. Cambridge, MA: MIT Press, 1991.

Malone, David M. and Mukherjee, R., 'India and China: conflict and cooperation' (2010) 52(1) *Survival: Global Politics and Strategy* 137–158.

Mansfield, Edward D., Milner, Helen V. and Rosendorff, B. Peter, 'Why democracies cooperate more: electoral control and international trade agreements' (2002) 56(3) *International Organization* 477–513.

Mathur, Sajal and Dasgupta, Meghna, *BRICS Trade Policies, Institutions and Areas for Deepening Cooperation*. New Delhi: Centre for WTO Studies, 2013, pp. 199–202.

Melitz, Jacques, 'Language and foreign trade' (2008) 52(4) *European Economic Review* 667–699.

Michaely, Michael, 'Trade preferential agreements in Latin America: an ex ante assessment', *Policy Research Working Paper*. Washington, DC: World Bank, 1996.

Noland, Marcus. 'Has Asian export performance been unique?' (1997) 43 *Journal of International Economics* 79–101.

Onyekwena, Chukwuka, Taiwo, Olumide and Uneze, Eberechukwu, 'South Africa in BRICS: a bilateral trade analysis', South African Institute of International Affairs, Occasional Paper no. 181, April 2014.

La Porta, Rafael, Lopez-de-Silanes, Florencio, and Shleifer, Andrei, 'The economic consequences of legal origins' (2008) 46(2) *Journal of Economic Literature* 285–332; available at http://scholar.harvard.edu/files/shleifer/files/consequences_jel_final.pdf?m=1360042991 [accessed on 31 October 2016].

Rao, R. V. R. Chandrasekhara, 'Indo-Soviet economic relations' (1973) 13(8) *Asian Survey* 793–801.

Stuenkel, Oliver, *The BRICS and the Future of Global Order*. London: Lexington Books, 2015.

Tatom, John A., 'The US-China currency dispute: is a rise in the yuan necessary, inevitable or desirable?' (2007) 7(3) *Global Economy Journal* 1524–5861.

Tinbergen, Jan, *Shaping the World Economy*. New York: The Twentieth Century Fund, 1962.

UNCTAD secretariat to the G20 Commodity Markets Working Group, 'Excessive commodity price volatility: Macroeconomic effects on growth and policy options', United Nations Conference On Trade And Development, 2012; available at http://unctad.org/en/Docs/gds_mdpb_G20_001_en.pdf [accessed on 31 October 2016].

World Trade Organization, *International Trade Statistics 2015*; available at www.wto .org/english/res_e/statis_e/its2015_e/its2015_e.pdf [accessed on 31 October 2016].

World Trade Organization and United Nations, *A Practical Guide to Trade Policy Analysis*; available at www.wto.org/english/res_e/publications_e/wto_ unctad12_e.pdf [accessed on 31 October 2016].

3

Defending Trade Multilateralism

The BRICS Countries in the World Trade Organization's Dispute Settlement Mechanism

ALEXANDR SVETLICINII AND ZHANG JUAN JUAN

I. Introduction

As early as 2003 the Goldman Sachs paper, 'Dreaming with BRICs: the path to 2050', startled the world by predicting that the BRIC (Brazil, Russia, India, China) nations would become a major force in the global economy.[1] These predictions, however, were far from suggesting that the BRIC nations would formalize their cooperation on the path to global economic leadership, which was announced at the first BRIC Summit on 16 June 2009 in Yekaterinburg (Russia).[2] In 2011 the BRIC turned into the BRICS when the South African leader Jacob Zuma joined the BRICS Summit in Sanya.[3] In 2013 China, the largest intra-BRICS trading partner,[4] surpassed the United States as the world's biggest merchandise trader,

---

[1] See Dominic Wilson and Roopa Purushothaman, 'Dreaming with BRICs: the path to 2050' (2003) *Global Economics Paper No. 99*; available at www.goldmansachs.com/our-thinking/archive/archive-pdfs/brics-dream.pdf [accessed on 26 October 2016].

[2] See Oliver Stuenkel, 'Emerging powers and status: the case of the first BRICs summit' (2014) 38(1) *Asian Perspective* 89–109.

[3] See Eiichi Sekine, 'The impact of the third BRICS Summit' (2011) 3(1) *Nomura Journal of Capital Markets* 1–6; available at www.nicmr.com/nicmr/english/report/repo/2011/2011sum04.pdf [accessed on 26 October 2016]; Laurence Boulle and Jessie Chella, 'Joining the BRICs: the case of South Africa', in Vai Io Lo and Mary Hiscock (eds.), *The Rise of the BRICS in Global Political Economy: Changing Paradigms?* (Cheltenham: Edward Elgar, 2014), pp. 99–122.

[4] China is the largest trade partner for each of the other BRICS countries with a trade share ranging from 72 percent to 85 percent in intra-BRICS trade. See Sajal Mathur and Meghna Dasgupta, 'From BRIC to BRICS: an overview', in Sajal Mathur and Meghna Dasgupta (eds.), *BRICS: Trade Policies, Institutions and Deepening Cooperation* (New Dehli: Centre for WTO Studies, 2013), p. 9; available at wtocentre.iift.ac.in/FA/Brics.pdf [accessed on 26 October 2016].

with imports and exports totaling USD 4,159 billion.[5] Russia and India have also made it into the top twenty world exporters and importers of merchandise.

As an emerging global trade leader, the BRICS alliance has firmly secured its place in the major multilateral trade forum – the World Trade Organization (WTO). Brazil, India and South Africa have been WTO members since its establishment in 1995. China joined the ranks of WTO membership on 11 December 2001.[6] Finally, Russia's accession to the WTO on 22 August 2012 completed the WTO's admission of the BRICS members.[7] At their 2013 Summit in Durban, the BRICS leaders welcomed the change in leadership brought by the election of the new WTO director general:

> We concur that the WTO requires a new leader who demonstrates a commitment to multilateralism and to enhancing the effectiveness of the WTO including through a commitment to support efforts that will lead to an expeditious conclusion of the Doha Development Agenda (DDA). We consider that the next Director General of the WTO should be a representative of a developing country.[8]

Subsequently, the Brazilian Roberto Azevêdo was elected as the new WTO director general and embarked on the uneasy task of moving the DDA forward:

> People only see us as good as our progress on Doha. That is the reality. And the perception in the world is that we have forgotten how to negotiate ... It is essential that we breathe new life into negotiations. We must send a clear

---

[5] WTO, *International Trade Statistics 2014*; available at www.wto.org/english/res_e/statis_e/its2014_e/its14_highlights1_e.pdf [accessed on 26 October 2016].

[6] For the milestones of China's WTO accession, see www.wto.org/english/thewto_e/countries_e/china_e.htm [accessed on 26 October 2016]. See also Thomas Rumbaugh and Nicolas Blancher, 'China: international trade and WTO accession', *IMF Working Paper No. 04/36*, March 2004; available at www.imf.org/external/pubs/ft/wp/2004/wp0436.pdf [accessed on 26 October 2016]; Karen Halverson, 'China's WTO accession: economic, legal, and political implications' (2004) 27(2) *Boston College International and Comparative Law Review* 319–70.

[7] For the milestones of Russia's WTO accession, see www.wto.org/english/thewto_e/countries_e/russia_e.htm [accessed on 26 October 2016]. See also Lisa Toohey, 'Barriers to universal membership of the World Trade Organization' (2012) 19 *Australian International Law Journal* 97–115; Snejina Michailova, Daniel J. McCarthy and Sheila M. Puffer, 'Russia: as solid as a BRIC?' (2013) 9(1–2) *Critical Perspectives on International Business* 5–18; Kim Van der Borght, 'Russian accession to the World Trade Organization: the slow road to trade & reform opportunities' (2013) 2 *Russian Law: Theory & Practice* 71–83.

[8] BRICS Summit eThekwini Declaration (27 March 2013), para. 16.

and unequivocal message to the world that the WTO can deliver multilateral trade deals.[9]

The BRICS countries have continuously declared their support for the WTO as a multilateral negotiations and rule-making platform for international trade. At their 2010 summit in Brasília, the BRIC countries had already stressed 'the importance of the multilateral trading system, embodied in the World Trade Organization, for providing an open, stable, equitable and non-discriminatory environment for international trade'.[10] At the same time, despite their commitment to resisting all forms of trade protectionism, all of the BRIC countries imposed new protectionist measures.[11] In the aftermath of the 2013 summit in Durban, all the BRICS countries demonstrated their support for the open, transparent and rule-based multilateral trading system by participating in various WTO engagement mechanisms, such as notification of trade-related measures, participation in the WTO dispute settlement mechanism (DSM), confirmation of the information included in the Trade Monitoring Database[12] and participation in trade policy reviews.[13] The Fortaleza Declaration adopted at the 2014 BRICS Summit contains unequivocal support for the WTO DSM as follows:

> We strongly support the WTO dispute settlement system as a cornerstone of the security and predictability of the multilateral trading system and we will enhance our ongoing dialogue on substantive and practical matters relating to it, including in the ongoing negotiations on WTO Dispute Settlement Understanding reform.[14]

The Ufa Declaration adopted at the 2015 BRICS Summit promotes 'support for working together to strengthen an open, transparent,

---

[9] WTO, 'Azevêdo launches "rolling set of meetings" aimed at delivering success in Bali' (9 September 2013); available at www.wto.org/english/news_e/news13_e/gc_09sep13_e.htm [accessed on 26 October 2016].

[10] BRIC Summit Brasília Joint Statement (15 April 2010), para. 14.

[11] See BRICS Research Group, '2010 BRIC Brasília Summit compliance assessment on world trade: fighting protectionism and disguised restrictions', 29 September 2013; available at www.brics.utoronto.ca/compliance/2010-compliance-trade.pdf [accessed on 26 October 2016].

[12] WTO, Trade Monitoring Database; available at tmdb.wto.org/ [accessed on 26 October 2016].

[13] See BRICS Research Group, *2013 BRICS Durban Summit Compliance Report*, 27 March 2013 to 1 July 2014; available at www.brics.utoronto.ca/compliance/2013-durban.html [accessed on 26 October 2016].

[14] BRICS Summit Fortaleza Declaration (15 July 2014), para. 21.

non-discriminatory and rules-based multilateral trading system as embodied in the WTO' and notes 'the importance of bilateral, regional and plurilateral trade agreements and encourage the parties to negotiations thereon to comply with the principles of transparency, inclusiveness and compatibility with WTO rules to ensure that they contribute to strengthening the multilateral trading system'.[15] The BRICS leaders' position was echoed at the meeting of their trade ministers: 'The WTO must maintain its central role in monitoring the implementation of the multilateral trade disciplines and commitments, including in the key area of dispute settlement'.[16]

The BRICS countries' role in shaping world trade can be assessed on the basis of their activity in at least three major arenas: the WTO, bilateral and regional free trade and investment negotiations, and BRICS summits and trade meetings.[17] This chapter evaluates the BRICS nations' performance in the WTO or, to be more specific, in the WTO DSM. The WTO DSM is one of the pillars of the modern multilateral trading system, labeled as 'the jewel in the crown' of the Uruguay Round.[18] As underscored by the first WTO director general, Renato Ruggiero, 'no review of the achievements of the WTO would be complete without mentioning the Dispute Settlement system, in many ways the central pillar of the multilateral trading system and the WTO's most individual contribution to the stability of the global economy'.[19] Thus, given the importance of the WTO DSM in the enforcement and interpretation of the international trade rules, the assessment of the BRICS countries' participation in and contribution to the effectiveness and legitimacy of this pillar of the multilateral trading system is a timely contribution to the discussion on the BRICS countries' role as emerging leaders in world trade.

---

[15] BRICS Summit Ufa Declaration (9 July 2015), para. 21.

[16] Ministerial Declaration of the BRICS Trade Ministers, Geneva, (14 December 2011).

[17] See Joseph Purugganan, Afsar Jafri and Pablo Solon, 'BRICS: a global trade power in a multi-polar world' (September 2014) *Focus on the Global South*, 5; available at www.tni .org/files/download/shifting_power-trade.pdf [accessed on 26 October 2016].

[18] See Peter Sutherland, 'Concluding the Uruguay Round – creating the new architecture of trade for the global economy' (2000) 24(15) *Fordham International Law Journal* 15–29 at 26.

[19] See Renato Ruggiero, 'The future path of the multilateral trading system', 17 April 1997; available at www.wto.org/english/news_e/sprr_e/seoul_e.htm [accessed on 26 October 2016]. See also Renato Ruggiero, 'Reflections after Seattle' (2000) 24(15) *Fordham International Law Journal* 30–61.

Table 3.1 *Participation in the WTO DSM: US, EU and BRICS, 1995–2015*

| | US | EU | BRICS | | | | | Total |
			Brazil	Russia	India	China	South Africa	
Complainant	109	96	27	4	21	13	0	**66***
Respondent	124	82	16	6	23	34	5	**84**
Third party	130	155	99	28	116	129	7	**204****
Total	**363**	**333**	**142**	**38**	**160**	**176**	**12**	**304*****

Source: www.wto.org/english/tratop_e/dispu_e/dispu_e.htm

* In the case DS217 *US – Offset Act (Byrd Amendment)* Brazil and India were co-complainants, www.wto.org/english/tratop_e/dispu_e/cases_e/ds217_e.htm.

** This number does not include the overlapping cases (i.e. cases where two or more BRICS countries were the third party in the same case).

*** This number does not include the overlapping cases (i.e. cases where one BRICS country was the complainant or respondent and another BRICS country was the third party).

II. Setting the Record Straight: The BRICS Countries' Participation in the WTO DSM

During the two decades of the WTO DSM (1995–2015), its members have filed a total of 501 disputes,[20] and the BRICS countries (at least one of them) have been involved in 304 cases (Table 3.1), which account for 60.68 percent of the total caseload. These numbers demonstrate a high degree of participation of the BRICS countries in this multilateral dispute settlement platform.

As original members of the WTO, Brazil and India have been the most active participants in the WTO DSM among the BRICS countries. As shown in Table 3.1, Brazil and India initiated twenty-seven and twenty-one cases, respectively. Russia, which joined the WTO in 2012, acted as a complainant in four cases, which were all submitted in the last two years.[21] China appears to be the most active BRICS respondent in the WTO DSM, with a total of thirty-four disputes filed against it since it

---

[20] This number includes both completed and pending cases. All the data in this chapter are up to date as of 31 December 2015.

[21] For an overview of Russia's WTO disputes, see Rostam J. Neuwirth and Alexandr Svetlicinii, 'The current EU/US–Russia conflict over Ukraine and the WTO: a preliminary note on (trade) restrictive measures' (2016) 32(3) *Post-Soviet Affairs* 237–71.

joined the WTO in December 2001.[22] China has also been the most active BRICS country, acting as a third party in 129 cases.[23] South Africa, despite being an original member of the WTO, has taken part in only twelve disputes as a respondent or as a third party, which generally corresponds to other African countries' participation in the WTO DSM due to their low level of development and insignificant share of international trade, limited possibilities for retaliation, low demand for action from domestic actors, lack of internal coherence and incapacity to cooperate with other countries.[24]

Compared with the major capitalist economies – the United States and the European Union – the BRICS countries have not been active complainants. During the two decades of the WTO DSM, the BRICS initiated a total of 66 disputes (13.17 percent of the total number of WTO DSM cases), while the US and the EU commenced 109 and 96 cases, respectively (Table 3.1). These numbers indicate the existence of a substantial gap between the US/EU and the BRICS in resorting to the WTO DSM. This variance could be due partly to the classical difficulties encountered by developing countries when accessing the WTO DSM: their relative lack of legal expertise in WTO law, constrained financial resources and fear of political and economic pressure (especially from the United States and the EU).[25] Nevertheless, the participation record of Brazil and India, as well as their prevalence in several important cases[26] against the United States, provides an example of the skillful navigation of the WTO DSM by developing countries. China's recent confidence in trade litigation also

---

[22] See e.g. Marcia Don Harpaz, 'Sense and sensibilities of China and WTO dispute settlement' (2010) 44(6) *Journal of World Trade* 1155–86; Kristie Thomas, 'China and the WTO dispute settlement system: from passive observer to active participant?' (2011) 6(10) *Global Trade and Customs Journal* 481–90; Liao Li and Minyou Yu, 'Impact of the WTO on China's rule of law in trade: twentieth anniversary of the WTO' (2015) 49(5) *Journal of World Trade* 837–72.

[23] See generally Yenkong Ngangjoh Hodu and Qi Zhang, *The Political Economy of WTO Implementation and China's Approach to Litigation in the WTO* (Cheltenham: Edward Elgar, 2016).

[24] See Amin Alavi, 'African countries and the WTO's dispute settlement mechanism' (2007) 25(1) *Development Policy Review* 25–42 at 38–39; Victor Mosoti, 'Africa in the first decade of WTO dispute settlement' (2006) 9(2) *Journal of International Economic Law* 427–453; Michelle Sanson, 'Facilitating access to dispute settlement for African members of the World Trade Organization' (2009) 2 *Indian Journal of International Economic Law* 1–51.

[25] See Gregory Shaffer, 'The challenges of WTO law: strategies for developing country adaptation' (2006) 5(2) *World Trade Review* 177–98 at 177.

[26] See case DS267 *US – Upland Cotton* (Brazil prevailed over the USA); case DS243 *US – Textiles Rules of Origin* (India prevailed over the USA).

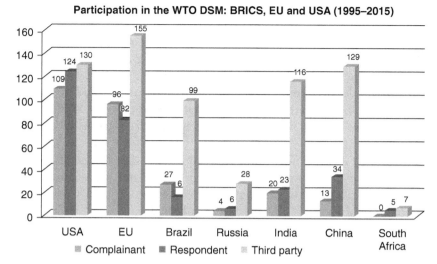

Figure 3.1 Participation in the WTO DSM: BRICS, EU and USA, 1995–2015.
Source of data: www.wto.org/english/tratop_e/dispu_e/dispu_e.htm

suggests that it is steadily learning the rules of the WTO DSM game.[27]

One of the characteristic features of the BRICS countries' involvement in the WTO DSM is the role of a third party that they have assumed in the majority of cases: there have been 204 cases in which at least one BRICS country acted as a third party (Table 3.1). For instance, China, in the fourteen years of its WTO membership, has already become the third most active third-party participant in the WTO DSM, with 129 cases, which is one case short of overcoming the United States, which now occupies the second place, the EU being the leader in this race (Figure 3.1). It has been argued that the the BRICS favoured the role of the third party because it was the least risky way to learn the rules of the WTO DSM game and to draw important tactical and strategic lessons for future disputes.[28] In addition, the procedural rules for third-party involvement are less stringent and the costs of such participation are reduced in comparison with the role of the complainant or the respondent.[29]

---

[27] See Amrita Narlikar, Martin Daunton and Robert M. Stern (eds.), *The Oxford Handbook on The World Trade Organization* (Oxford: Oxford University Press, 2012), p. 265.

[28] Ibid., p. 267.

[29] See Archana Jatkar and Laura McFarlene, 'Brazil in the WTO dispute settlement understanding: a perspective' (2013) 1 *CUTS International Briefing Paper* 1–6 at 4; available at www.cuts-citee.org/pdf/Briefing_Paper13-Brazil_in_the_WTO_Dispute_Settlement_Understanding-A_Perspective.pdf [accessed on 26 October 2016].

Table 3.2 *Basic Information on the Interaction of BRICS in the WTO DSM, 1995–2015*

	All BRICS DSM cases	Interaction case	Percentage
One BRICS country was the complainant	66	22	33.33
One BRICS country was the respondent	84	28	33.33
At least two BRICS countries were the third party	154	83	53.90
Total	**304**	**133**	**43.75**

Source: www.wto.org/english/tratop_e/dispu_e/dispu_e.htm.

III. BRICS Countries' Interaction in the WTO DSM

During the two decades of the WTO DSM, the BRICS countries have participated in 304 disputes, among which there were 133 cases in which at least two BRICS countries 'interacted' with each other in the capacity of the complainant, respondent or third party. Table 3.2 indicates that the 'interaction' rate of the BRICS in the WTO is quite high – 43.75 percent – considering that (1) Brazil, India and South Africa are original members of the WTO while the BRICS alliance was formalized only in 2009; and (2) China and Russia are latecomers to the WTO (joining in 2001 and 2012, respectively). To take into account these two factors, Table 3.3 displays the total number of cases in which at least two BRICS countries 'interacted' in

Table 3.3 *Interaction of BRICS in the WTO DSM as Third Parties, 1995–2015*

The BRICS country as the third party	Total number of BRICS interaction cases	Number of interaction cases with the country as the third party	Interaction rate (%)
Brazil	133	92	69.17
Russia (since 2012)	48	28	58.33
India	133	92	69.17
China (since 2001)	123	94	76.42
South Africa	133	7	5.26

Source: www.wto.org/english/tratop_e/dispu_e/dispu_e.htm.

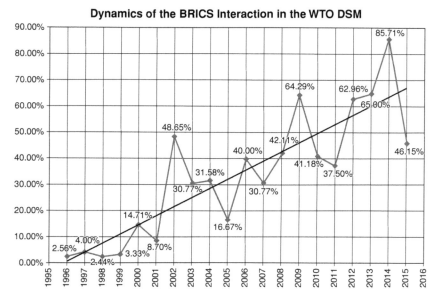

Figure 3.2 Dynamics of the BRICS interaction in the WTO DSM.
Source: www.wto.org/english/tratop_e/dispu_e/dispu_e.htm.

various capacities, as well as the 'interaction' ratio for each BRICS country based on the number of cases taking place after its accession to the WTO. The statistics show that, except for South Africa, which has generally been inactive in the WTO DSM,[30] the 'interaction' rate for all the BRICS countries exceeds 50 percent, reaching 76.42 percent in the case of China.

Since the establishment of the WTO DSM, the interaction of the BRICS countries in this dispute settlement platform has been constantly rising, reaching the participation ratio of 85.71 percent of all cases in 2014 (Figure 3.2). Table 3.4 indicates that the 'interaction' rate among the BRICS countries in the WTO DSM increased dramatically after the establishment of the BRICS in 2009: the average 'interaction' rate before 2009 was 33.87 percent, whereas after 2009 this ratio reached an average of 57.54 percent. Figures 3.2 and 3.3 also indicate that this increased interaction should be viewed against the background of the general reduction in the number of disputes filed in the WTO DSM every year. Nevertheless, the increase

---

[30] South Africa has never brought a claim in the WTO DSM as a complainant. For a discussion of South Africa's WTO DSM record, see Hilton E. Zunckel and Lambert Botha, 'The BRICS, South Africa and dispute settlement in the WTO', *SAFPI Policy Brief No. 9*, September 2012.

Table 3.4 *Intra-BRICS Interaction in the WTO DSM*

Year	Total cases filed under DSU	BRICS "interaction" cases	Percentage	Average percentage (before and after 2009)
2002	38	18	47.37	**33.87**
2003	26	8	30.77	
2004	19	6	31.58	
2005	12	2	16.67	
2006	20	8	40.00	
2007	14	4	28.57	
2008	19	8	42.11	
2009	14	9	64.29	**57.54**
2010	17	7	41.18	
2011	8	3	37.50	
2012	27	17	62.96	
2013	20	13	65.00	
2014	14	12	85.71	
2015	13	6	46.15	

Source: www.wto.org/english/tratop_e/dispu_e/dispu_e.htm.

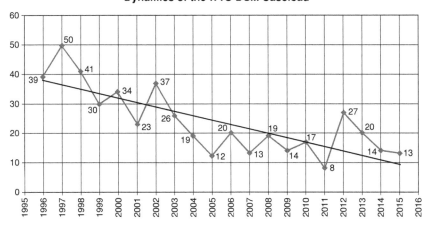

Figure 3.3 Dynamics of the WTO DSM caseload.
Source: www.wto.org/english/tratop_e/dispu_e/dispu_e.htm.

Table 3.5 *BRICS Interaction and WTO Agreements*

Agreement	Number of "interaction" cases	Percentage
General Agreement on Tariffs and Trade (GATT)	121	90.98
Protocol of Accession	16	12.03
Anti-Dumping Agreement (ADA)	27	20.30
Agreement on Subsidies and Countervailing Measures (SCM)	38	28.57
Agreement Establishing the World Trade Organization (WTO Agreement)	18	13.53
Agreement on Sanitary and Phytosanitary Measures (SPS)	14	10.53
General Agreement on Trade in Services (GATS)	5	3.76
Agreement Trade-Related Investment Measures (TRIMs)	13	9.77
Agreement on Trade-Related Aspects of Intellectual Property Rights (TRIPS)	10	7.52
Agreement on Technical Barriers to Trade (TBT)	15	11.28
Agreement on Preshipment Inspection (PSI)	3	2.26
Agreement on Rules of Origin (ARO)	2	1.50
Agreement on Import Licensing Procedures (AILP)	8	6.02
Agreement on Safeguards (AS)	14	10.53
Agreement on Agriculture (AAG)	23	17.29
Customs Valuation Agreement (ACV)	3	2.26

Source: www.wto.org/english/tratop_e/dispu_e/dispu_e.htm. The percentages add up to more than 100% because more than one agreement was involved in some cases.

in interaction after 2009 could be attributed to the growing influence and cooperation amongst the BRICS countries. With the increase in cooperation and communication amongst the BRICS countries in various trade-related areas, their interaction in the WTO DSM should continue to grow.

The 'interaction' of the BRICS countries in the WTO DSM cases concerns a wide range of topics and economic sectors. In Table 3.5 we show the scope of this interaction by indicating which WTO multilateral agreement was involved in each case. The following agreements have been the most common basis of the WTO DSM cases in which BRICS countries have

Table 3.6 *BRICS Countries as Third Parties in the WTO DSM*

Third party	The other BRICS country was the complainant	The other BRICS country was the respondent	The other BRICS country was also a third party	Total
Brazil	13	18	62	93
Russia	5	9	14	28
India	13	21	59	93
China	9	9	75	93
South Africa	1	2	4	7
Total	**41**	**59**	**214**	**314***
Percentage	**13.06%**	**18.79%**	**68.15%**	**100%**

Source: www.wto.org/english/tratop_e/dispu_e/dispu_e.htm.

* The numbers represent the number of "interactions" and not the number of cases because in some cases there were more than two BRICS countries taking part in various capacities.

'interacted': the GATT, the Anti-Dumping Agreement, the Agreement on Subsidies and Countervailing Measures and the Agreement on Agriculture. The GATT accounts for 90.98 percent or 121 cases in which at least two BRICS countries 'met' in the capacity of complainant, respondent or third party. All of the agreements appearing at the core of the BRICS countries' interaction were the subject of the DDA in the WTO negotiations.

The analysis of the cases in which at least two BRICS countries participated reveals a distinct feature of their 'interaction' in the WTO DSM – their tendency to appear in the capacity of a third party. In the total number of BRICS 'interaction' cases, there were forty-one cases in which one BRICS country was the complainant, which accounted for 13.06 percent of the total 'interaction' cases, and fifty-nine cases in which one BRICS country was the respondent, which accounted for 18.79 percent. However, in the overwhelming majority of cases (214 instances or 68.15 percent), the complainant and the respondent were non-BRICS countries while a BRICS country appeared in the capacity of a third party (Table 3.6). This tendency demonstrates the willingness and ability of the BRICS alliance members to participate actively in the WTO DSM as third parties with the objectives of voicing their positions on various trade-related issues and influencing the WTO DSM decision making in its interpretation of the WTO agreements.

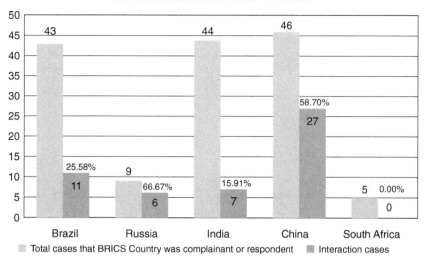

Figure 3.4   Intra-BRICS Interaction in the WTO DSM.
Source: www.wto.org/english/tratop_e/dispu_e/dispu_e.htm.

The analysis of the intra-BRICS 'interaction' in the WTO DSM indicates that, among the BRICS countries, China was the most popular 'interaction' partner for other BRICS countries. There were forty-six cases in which China acted as the complainant or respondent, in twenty-seven of which another BRICS country participated. These accounted for 58.7 percent of all the cases started by China or against it (Figure 3.4). The reason for this China-centered interaction is at least threefold: (1) being the largest BRICS economy, China has been involved in a larger number of cases, (2) China is the biggest commercial partner of the other four BRICS countries (Table 3.7), and (3) the results of China's trade disputes can have important consequences for its trade with other BRICS nations.

The number of WTO DSM cases in which BRICS countries interacted does not indicate whether this interaction was positive or negative; that is, whether the BRICS countries aligned with the same party or with each other or whether they expressed opposing views and positions on the focus issues of those cases. To ascertain the BRICS countries' position, we analyzed the completed cases in which the parties' submissions were published. As shown in Table 3.8, there were 133 interaction cases,[31] of which

---

[31] The 133 interaction cases include (1) case DS347 *EC and Certain Member States – Large Civil Aircraft (2nd Complaint)*, in which the complainant (the US) applied for the

Table 3.7 *BRICS and their Top Three Merchandise Trade Partners, 2014*

BRICS	Trade partners	Import and export trade volume (in billion USD)
Brazil	**China**	78.0
	United States	62.0
	Argentina	28.4
Russia	**China**	88.4
	The Netherlands	73.2
	Germany	70.1
India	**China**	71.6
	United States	63.3
	United Arab Emirates	60.4
China	United States	590.7
	Hong Kong, China	563.5
	Japan	307.5
South Africa	**China**	24.1
	Germany	14.6
	United States	13.0

Source: Country Report, english.mofcom.gov.cn/

98 cases were completed; only 62 cases had statements submitted by at least two BRICS countries. Of the sixty-two cases available for the present analysis, the interaction of the BRICS countries was positive in fifty-six, meaning that their positions aligned. This brings the positive interaction rate to a high 90 percent of all interaction cases in which the submissions of the parties were available for the analysis.

While the negative interaction cases are much less numerous, they deserve a more detailed explanation that highlights the opposing interests of the BRICS countries. In the 2013 case concerning the exportation of certain raw materials from China (complaints filed by the United States, the EU and Mexico),[32] Brazil and India aligned their positions against China, being large importers of the raw materials concerned. In two cases

suspension of the panel and the panel agreed to this request (no submissions published); (2) thirty-five cases that have not been completed (no submissions published); (3) four cases in which the complainant and the respondent reached mutual agreement (no submissions published): case DS287 *Australia – Quarantine Regime*; case DS391 *Korea – Bovine Meat (Canada)*; case DS469 *EU – Herring*; and case DS199 *Brazil – Patent Protection*; and (4) thirty-two interaction cases in which the BRICS country did not submit its opinion.

[32] Cases DS394/395/398 *China – Raw Materials*.

Table 3.8 *BRICS Countries' Interaction in the WTO DSM:*
Positive or Negative

Role of BRICS country	Total interaction cases (completed)	Number of positive cases	Percentage of positive cases	Number of negative cases	Percentage of negative cases
Complainant	16	13	81.25	2	12.50
Respondent	19	9	47.37	4	21.05
Third party	63	34	53.97	0	0.00
Total	**98**	**56**	**57.14**	**6**	**6.12**

Source: www.wto.org/english/tratop_e/dispu_e/dispu_e.htm.

in which China attempted to challenge the EU's anti-dumping measures concerning Chinese footwear and steel fasteners, Brazil aligned with the respondent against China, because it was applying the same 'Surrogate Country System' as the EU.[33] Despite the 2004 Memorandum of Understanding on Trade and Investment Cooperation signed between China and Brazil, in which Brazil recognized China's market economy status, the Brazilian government has not yet fully implemented that measure.[34] Finally, in a case initiated by the United States against India concerning the latter's restriction on poultry imports due to the avian influenza epidemics, Brazil, being the major exporter of poultry products, sided with the complainant against its fellow BRICS respondent.[35]

Except for the aforementioned six cases of negative interaction in the WTO DSM, the BRICS countries have always sided with each other in line with their cooperation in the Doha Development Round on issues concerning agricultural products, market access, subsidies, anti-dumping, enforcement and so on. For example, Brazil submitted proposals with the aim of reducing the burden of proof on developing countries in disputes against the subsidies of developed countries, defending the application of the concept of 'benchmarking' in cases in which there were no private investors but only state funds.[36] These issues have been addressed in

---

[33] Case DS397 *EC – Fasteners (China)* and case DS405 *EU – Footwear (China)*.
[34] See Carlos Pereira and João Augusto de Castro Neves, 'Brazil and China: South–South partnership or North–South competition?' (2011) 26 *Brookings Foreign Policy Paper* at 7.
[35] Case DS430 *India – Agricultural Products*.
[36] See Vera Thorstensen and Ivan Tiago Machado Oliveira (eds.), *BRICS in the World Trade Organization: Comparative Trade Policies* (Brasília: Institute for Applied Economic Research, 2014), p. 47.

several WTO DSM cases filed against the EU and the United States by Brazil and supported by other BRICS countries acting as third parties.[37]

At the same time, despite the stable development of the economic and trade relations among the BRICS countries, there are a number of trade-related tensions that are worth mentioning. First, there have been three cases in which one BRICS country confronted another as a complainant or a respondent.[38] Two of the cases were initiated by India against South Africa and Brazil and one by Brazil against South Africa. All of the cases concerned anti-dumping duties, and none progressed beyond the consultation stage.

According to the WTO statistics, in 1995–2014 the BRICS countries initiated 283 anti-dumping investigations against China, which accounted for 28.61 percent of the global anti-dumping investigations against that country. China's BRICS partners have adopted 202 anti-dumping measures, or 28.17 percent of the worldwide measures, while the positive outcome rate has reached 71.38 percent[39] (Table 3.9). Although these cases have not been resolved by the WTO DSM, they indicate the existing potential for tensions in the coordination of the global trade governance approach of the BRICS countries.

IV. Main Directions for BRICS Countries' Cooperation in the WTO DSM

While some developing countries have overcome the challenges of participating in the WTO DSM through various creative and innovative

---

[37] See for example case DS266 *EC – Export Subsidies on Sugar*; case DS267 *US – Upland Cotton*; case DS269 *EC – Chicken Cuts*; and case DS365 *US – Agriculture Subsidies*.

[38] Case DS168 *South Africa – Anti-Dumping Duties on Certain Pharmaceutical Products from India*; case DS229 *Brazil – Anti-Dumping Duties on Jute Bags from India*; case DS439 *South Africa – Anti-Dumping Duties on Frozen Meat of Fowls from Brazil*.

[39] At the same time, it should be noted that all the BRICS countries except India have recognized China's market economy status (MES). It has been argued that the MES had a positive impact on reducing the number of anti-dumping investigations against China. See Francisco Urdinez and Gilmar Masiero, 'China and the WTO: will the market economy status make any difference after 2016?' (2015) 48(2) *Chinese Economy* 155–72; Lara Puccio, *Granting Market Economy Status to China: An Analysis of WTO Law and of Selected WTO Members' Policy*, European Parliamentary Research Service, November 2015. However, Brazil has delayed the actual implementation of its declared intention to grant China MES in 2004. See Muruga Perumal Ramaswamy, 'Sino-Brazilian trade and anti-dumping concerns', in Vai Io Lo and Mary Hiscock (eds.), *The Rise of the BRICS in Global Political Economy: Changing Paradigms?* (Cheltenham: Edward Elgar, 2014), pp. 84–98.

Table 3.9 *Anti-Dumping Measures against China, 1995–2014*

	Worldwide	Brazil	Russia*	India	South Africa	BRICS total	BRICS percentage
Anti-dumping investigation	989	78	6	161	38	283	28.61
Anti-dumping measures	717	47	6	129	20	202	28.17
Positive outcome percentage	72.50%		60.26%	100%	80.12%	52.64%	71.38%

Source: www.wto.org/english/tratop_e/dispu_e/dispu_e.htm.
* According to WTO statistics, because Russia did not join WTO until 2012, Russia's data are not complete.

solutions,[40] others remain underrepresented in this multilateral dispute settlement platform. Even without classifying the BRICS economies as developing, this review of the BRICS countries' participation in the WTO demonstrated that, with the exception of South Africa, all the BRICS nations have managed to break existing barriers and engage in multilateral trade dispute settlement in the framework of the WTO DSM.

The enhanced positive interaction of the BRICS countries in the WTO DSM could bring economic benefits to the members of this alliance, as well as to other emerging economies and the WTO membership at large. The coordinated positions of the BRICS nations in the trade disputes under the WTO DSM could contribute to the interpretation of the WTO rules in a way that is favorable to emerging economies. The BRICS countries' shared positions in trade disputes could also contribute to their expedient resolution. For example, in 2010 both Brazil and India requested consultations with the EU concerning the seizure of generic drugs in transit from India to Brazil.[41] China joined the case as a third party.[42] As a

---

[40] See Raul A. Torres, 'Use of the WTO Trade Dispute Settlement Mechanism by the Latin American countries – dispelling myths and breaking down barriers', *WTO Staff Working Paper* ERSD-2012–03, February 2012; available at www.wto.org/english/res_e/reser_e/ersd201203_e.pdf [accessed on 26 October 2016].

[41] See *European Union and a Member State – Seizure of Generic Drugs in Transit* (Request for Consultations by India) in case DS408 (19 May 2010) and *European Union and a Member State – Seizure of Generic Drugs in Transit* (Request for Consultations by Brazil) in case DS409.

[42] See Communication by China (WT/DS408/6 and WT/DS/409/6), 30 June 2010.

result, the EU has accepted all requests for consultations, avoiding the need to establish a panel in this case.[43] It has been argued that the presence of third parties in the WTO DSM decreases the chance of a settlement and increases the odds of litigation.[44] However, if the BRICS and other key actors in global trade would coordinate their position in the WTO disputes, it would provide more of an incentive or pressure on the parties to reach a settlement through 'bargaining in the shadow of the law'[45] rather than through WTO litigation. This would also help resolve the recurrent problem of the WTO DSM – the timeliness of the dispute settlement process, including the panel process and the implementation of the results – which pushes the WTO membership to seek free trade agreements and other bilateral and regional instruments with their promises of greater expediency.[46]

In 2008, in the context of the Doha Round negotiations, China advanced the following proposals for reforming the WTO DSM: (1) developed countries should exercise proper restraint from starting cases against developing countries; (2) developed countries cannot submit more than two cases against the same developing country to the Dispute Settlement Body (DSB) in a calendar year; and (3) this restriction should not apply to the cases that developing countries start against developed countries or other developing countries.[47] At the same time, the other BRICS countries have not promoted the reform of the WTO DSM in line with their Fortaleza Declaration commitments.[48]

---

[43] For a discussion of the case, see Rostam J. Neuwirth and Alexandr Svetlicinii, 'International trade, intellectual property and competition rules: multiple cases for global "regulatory co-opetition"', in Muruga Perumal Ramaswamy and Joao Ribeiro (eds.), *Trade Development through Harmonization of Commercial Law* (Wellington: UNCITRAL Regional Centre for Asia and the Pacific, 2015), pp. 393–425 at 400–6.

[44] See Leslie Johns and Krzysztof J. Pelc, 'Fear of crowds in the World Trade Organization disputes: why don't more countries participate?' (2015) 78(1) *Journal of Politics* 88–104.

[45] See e.g. Marc L. Busch and Eric Reinhardt, 'Bargaining in the shadow of the law: early settlement in GATT/WTO disputes' (2001) 24 *Fordham International Law Journal* 158–72.

[46] See William J. Davey, 'The WTO and rules-based dispute settlement: historical evolution, operational success, and future challenges' (2014) 17(3) *Journal of International Economic Law* 679–700.

[47] Hongsong Liu, 'China's proposing behavior in global governance: the cases of the WTO Doha Round negotiation and G-20 process' (2014) 57 *Revista Brasileira de Política Internacional* 121–137 at 127; available at www.scielo.br/pdf/rbpi/v57nspe/0034-7329-rbpi-57-spe-00121.pdf [accessed on 26 October 2016].

[48] See BRICS Research Group, *2014 BRICS Fortaleza Summit Compliance Report*, 15 July 2014 to 28 June 2015; available at www.brics.utoronto.ca/compliance/2014-fortaleza.html [accessed on 26 October 2016].

When it comes to the mechanism for coordinating their participation in the WTO DSM, the BRICS countries should both build on the successful experience accumulated by the BRICS members and other emerging economies and try out innovative solutions that would be better suited to the coordination of their national trade interests and more accurately reflect their role as global trade leaders. For example, Brazil has established a well-designed institutional framework of cooperation between its government and the private sector, which allows the latter to inform the former about measures that obstruct trade and to discuss whether involvement of the WTO would be advisable.[49] This mechanism is based on the interaction of three bodies: the Chamber of Foreign Trade (CAMEX), the Private Sector Consultative Council (Conex) and the General Dispute Settlement Unit in the Ministry of Foreign Affairs (CGC-MRE), the former workplace of the current WTO director general.[50] The private sector's trade-related concerns are communicated through CAMEX and Conex to the CGC-MRE, which, in consultation with the public and private sector, decides whether the case should be submitted to the WTO DSM. After the submission of the complaint, the private sector remains involved and supplies the government with factual evidence, legal arguments and litigation funding.

The involvement of the private sector in the trade policy coordination can be achieved through the BRICS Business Council, established at the 2013 BRICS Summit in Durban.[51] At the 2014 BRICS Summit in Fortaleza, the representatives of the BRICS Business Council called for the creation of a 'dedicated BRICS business information exchange platform (BRICS Business Portal)'.[52] The BRICS business leaders noted that

---

[49] See Gregory C. Shaffer, Michelle Ratton Sanchez Badin and Barbara Rosenberg, 'Winning at the WTO: the development of a trade policy community within Brazil', in Gregory C. Shaffer and Melendez-Ortiz Ricardo (eds.), *Dispute Settlement at the WTO: The Developing Country Experience* (Cambridge: Cambridge University Press, 2014), pp. 21–104.

[50] See the biographical note on WTO Director-General Roberto Azevêdo; available at www.wto.org/english/thewto_e/dg_e/ra_e.htm [accessed on 26 October 2016]. See also Roberto Azevêdo, *Brazil and Dispute Settlement in the WTO* (*Brasil e o contencioso no OMC*) (Sao Paulo: Ed. Saraiva, 2009).

[51] See Declaration on the Establishment of the BRICS Business Council, 27 March 2013; available at www.bricsbusinesscouncil.in/htm/Decleration.pdf [accessed on 26 October 2016].

[52] Statement issued by the BRICS Business Council, 15 July 2014; available at www.bricsbusinesscouncil.in/pdf/Fortaleza1.pdf [accessed on 26 October 2016]. See also BRICS Business Council, *2013/2014 Annual Report*. At the 2013 BRICS Summit, the economic ministers approved another cooperation project – the BRICS Information Sharing and Exchange Platform. The platform was developed by the Center for BRICS Studies of

better governance of the BRICS could become an alternative to the mega-regional trade agreements, such as the Trans-Pacific Partnership (TPP) and the Transatlantic Trade and Investment Partnership (TTIP).[53] The BRICS Business Portal could also be used for the exchange of information on trade-obstructing practices (both intra-BRICS and extra-BRICS) with the aim of bringing them to the attention of the respective governments and coordinating their potential engagement in the WTO DSM.

V. Conclusion

This quantitative and qualitative review of the BRICS countries' participation in the WTO DSM indicates that this alliance of emerging economies has demonstrated both its willingness and its capacity to become an emerging leader in world trade governance. All of the BRICS countries, except for South Africa, have been active participants in the WTO DSM, regardless of the timing of their accession to the WTO. Even without being involved in the trade disputes directly as a complainant or respondent, the BRICS nations have actively been raising their concerns and expressing their positions as third parties. The qualitative analysis of the cases in which the parties' submissions have been published demonstrated that, in the overwhelming majority of cases, the positions of BRICS third parties have been aligned with each other. In this way the BRICS alliance has contributed to the promotion of the interests of emerging economies in this multilateral trading system, as well as enhanced its legitimacy.

Yet the BRICS members have not been entirely consistent in promoting their declared objectives, such as reform of the WTO DSM with the aim of increasing the expediency of trade dispute resolution and facilitating the participation of wider WTO membership in the WTO DSM. For these reasons the BRICS countries should be encouraged to enhance the coordination of their positions in the WTO DSM with the aim of creating synergies and leverage for more expedient settlement of trade disputes through 'bargaining in the shadow of the law' or contributing to the clarification of the WTO rules when disputes progress within the DSB.

Enhanced coordination of the BRICS countries' positions in the WTO DSM could be achieved by taking into account their successful experiences and by developing innovative solutions. Thus, Brazil's

Fudan University and the BRICS Business Council. See www.brics-info.org/ [accessed on 26 October 2016].

53 BRICS Business Council, 'Facing challenges, building confidence', *Second Annual Report 2014–2015*, p. 28.

experience in bringing together private sector and government represen-tatives for better coordination of the trade dispute resolution strategies could be pursued by the BRICS nations through the communication chan-nels of the BRICS Business Council. Such cooperation would allow the mitigation of intra-BRICS trade tensions and the coordination of posi-tions in extra-BRICS cases.

VI. References

Alavi, Amin, 'African countries and the WTO's Dispute Settlement Mechanism' (2007) 25(1) *Development Policy Review* 25–42.

Azevêdo, Roberto, *Brazil and Dispute Settlement in the WTO (Brasil e o contencioso no OMC*. Sao Paulo: Ed. Saraiva, 2009.

Borght, Kim Van der, 'Russian accession to the World Trade Organization: the slow road to trade & reform opportunities' (2013) 2 *Russian Law: Theory & Prac-tice* 71–83.

Boulle, Laurence and Chella, Jessie, 'Joining the BRICs: the case of South Africa', in Vai Io Lo and Mary Hiscock (eds.), *The Rise of the BRICS in Global Politi-cal Economy: Changing Paradigms?* Cheltenham: Edward Elgar, 2014, pp. 99–122.

BRICS Business Council, 'Facing challenges, building confidence', *Second Annual Report 2014–2015*.

2013/2014 Annual Report.

BRICS Research Group, '2010 BRIC Brasília Summit compliance assessment on world trade: fighting protectionism and disguised restrictions', 29 September 2013; available at www.brics.utoronto.ca/compliance/2010-compliance-trade.pdf [accessed on 26 October 2016].

'2013 BRICS Durban Summit Compliance Report', 27 March 2013 to 1 July 2014; available at www.brics.utoronto.ca/compliance/2013-durban.html [accessed on 26 October 2016].

'2014 BRICS Fortaleza Summit Compliance Report', 15 July 2014 to 28 June 2015; available at www.brics.utoronto.ca/compliance/2014-fortaleza.html [accessed on 26 October 2016].

Busch, Marc L. and Reinhardt, Eric, 'Bargaining in the shadow of the law: early settlement in GATT/WTO disputes' (2001) 24 *Fordham International Law Journal* 158–172.

Davey, William J., 'The WTO and rules-based dispute settlement: historical evolu-tion, operational success, and future challenges' (2014) 17(3) *Journal of Inter-national Economic Law* 679–700.

Halverson, Karen, 'China's WTO accession: economic, legal, and political implica-tions' (2004) 27(2) *Boston College International and Comparative Law Review* 319–370.

Harpaz, Marcia Don, 'Sense and sensibilities of China and WTO dispute settlement' (2010) 44(6) *Journal of World Trade* 1155–1186.

Hodu, Yenkong Ngangjoh and Zhang, Qi, *The Political Economy of WTO Implementation and China's Approach to Litigation in the WTO*. Cheltenham: Edward Elgar, 2016.

Jatkar, Archana and McFarlene, Laura, 'Brazil in the WTO dispute settlement understanding: a perspective', (2013) 1 *CUTS International Briefing Paper* 1–6; available at www.cuts-citee.org/pdf/Briefing_Paper13-Brazil_in_the_WTO_Dispute_Settlement_Understanding-A_Perspective.pdf [accessed on 26 October 2016].

Johns, Leslie and Pelc, Krzysztof J., 'Fear of crowds in the World Trade Organization disputes: why don't more countries participate?' (2015) 78(1) *Journal of Politics* 88–104.

Li, Liao and Yu, Minyou, 'Impact of the WTO on China's rule of law in trade: twentieth anniversary of the WTO' (2015) 49(5) *Journal of World Trade* 837–872.

Liu, Hongsong, 'China's proposing behavior in global governance: the cases of the WTO Doha Round negotiation and G-20 process' (2014) 57 *Revista Brasileira de Política Internacional* 121–137; available at www.scielo.br/pdf/rbpi/v57nspe/0034-7329-rbpi-57-spe-00121.pdf [accessed on 26 October 2016].

Mathur, Sajal and Dasgupta, Meghna, 'From BRIC to BRICS: an overview', in Sajal Mathur and Meghna Dasgupta (eds.), *BRICS: Trade Policies, Institutions and Deepening Cooperation*. New Delhi: Centre for WTO Studies, 2013; available at wtocentre.iift.ac.in/FA/Brics.pdf [accessed on 26 October 2016].

Michailova, Snejina, McCarthy, Daniel J. and Puffer, Sheila M., 'Russia: as solid as a BRIC?' (2013) 9(1–2) *Critical Perspectives on International Business* 5–18.

Mosoti, Victor, 'Africa in the first decade of WTO dispute settlement' (2006) 9(2) *Journal of International Economic Law* 427–453.

Narlikar, Amrita, Daunton, Martin and Stern, Robert M. (eds.), *The Oxford Handbook on The World Trade Organization*. Oxford: Oxford University Press, 2012.

Neuwirth, Rostam J. and Svetlicinii, Alexandr, 'International trade, intellectual property and competition rules: multiple cases for global "regulatory co-opetition"', in Muruga Perumal Ramaswamy and Joao Ribeiro (eds.), *Trade Development through Harmonization of Commercial Law*. Wellington: UNCITRAL Regional Centre for Asia and the Pacific, 2015, pp. 393–425.

'The current EU/US–Russia conflict over Ukraine and the WTO: a preliminary note on (trade) restrictive measures' (2016) 32(3) *Post-Soviet Affairs* 237–71.

Pereira, Carlos and Neves, João Augusto de Castro, 'Brazil and China: South–South partnership or North–South competition?' (2011) 26 *Brookings Foreign Policy Paper*.

Puccio, Lara, 'Granting market economy status to China: an analysis of WTO law and of selected WTO members' policy', European Parliamentary Research Service, November 2015.

Purugganan, Joseph, Jafri, Afsar and Solon, Pablo, 'BRICS: a global trade power in a multi-polar world' (September 2014) *Focus on the Global South*; available at www.tni.org/files/download/shifting_power-trade.pdf [accessed on 26 October 2016].

Ramaswamy, Muruga Perumal, 'Sino-Brazilian trade and anti-dumping concerns', in Vai Io Lo and Mary Hiscock (eds.), *The Rise of the BRICS in Global Political Economy: Changing Paradigms?* Cheltenham: Edward Elgar, 2014, pp. 84–98.

Ruggiero, Renato, 'The future path of the multilateral trading system', 17 April 1997; available at www.wto.org/english/news_e/sprr_e/seoul_e.htm [accessed on 26 October 2016].

'Reflections after Seattle' (2000) 24(15) *Fordham International Law Journal* 30–61.

Rumbaugh, Thomas and Blancher, Nicolas, 'China: international trade and WTO accession', IMF Working Paper No. 04/36, March 2004; available at www.imf.org/external/pubs/ft/wp/2004/wp0436.pdf [accessed on 26 October 2016].

Sanson, Michelle, 'Facilitating access to dispute settlement for African members of the World Trade Organization' (2009) 2 *Indian Journal of International Economic Law* 1–51.

Sekine, Eiichi, 'The impact of the third BRICS Summit' (2011) 3(1) *Nomura Journal of Capital Markets* 1–6; available at www.nicmr.com/nicmr/english/report/repo/2011/2011sum04.pdf [accessed on 26 October 2016].

Shaffer, Gregory, 'The challenges of WTO law: strategies for developing country adaptation' (2006) 5(2) *World Trade Review* 177–198.

Shaffer, Gregory C., Badin, Michelle Ratton Sanchez and Rosenberg, Barbara, 'Winning at the WTO: the development of a trade policy community within Brazil', in Gregory C. Shaffer and Ricardo Melendez-Ortiz (eds.), *Dispute Settlement at the WTO: The Developing Country Experience*. Cambridge: Cambridge University Press, 2014, pp. 21–104.

Stuenkel, Oliver, 'Emerging powers and status: the case of the first BRICs summit' (2014) 38(1) *Asian Perspective* 89–109.

Sutherland, Peter, 'Concluding the Uruguay Round – creating the new architecture of trade for the global economy' (2000) 24(15) *Fordham International Law Journal* 15–29.

Thomas, Kristie, 'China and the WTO dispute settlement system: from passive observer to active participant?' (2011) 6(10) *Global Trade and Customs Journal* 481–490.

Thorstensen, Vera and Oliveira, Ivan Tiago Machado (eds.), *BRICS in the World Trade Organization: Comparative Trade Policies*. Brasília: Institute for Applied Economic Research, 2014.

Toohey, Lisa, 'Barriers to universal membership of the World Trade Organization' (2012) 19 *Australian International Law Journal* 97–115.

Torres, Raul A., 'Use of the WTO Trade Dispute Settlement Mechanism by the Latin American countries – dispelling myths and breaking down barriers', WTO Staff Working Paper ERSD-2012-03, February 2012; available at www.wto .org/english/res_e/reser_e/ersd201203_e.pdf [accessed on 26 October 2016].

Urdinez, Francisco and Masiero, Gilmar, 'China and the WTO: will the market economy status make any difference after 2016?' (2015) 48(2) *Chinese Economy* 155–172.

Wilson, Dominic and Purushothaman, Roopa, 'Dreaming with BRICs: the path to 2050', Global Economics Paper no. 99, (2003) available at www.goldmansachs .com/our-thinking/archive/archive-pdfs/brics-dream.pdf [accessed on 26 October 2016].

World Trade Organization, 'Azevêdo launches "rolling set of meetings" aimed at delivering success in Bali' (9 September 2013); available at www.wto .org/english/news_e/news13_e/gc_09sep13_e.htm [accessed on 26 October 2016].

'International Trade Statistics 2014'; available at www.wto.org/english/res_e/ statis_e/its2014_e/its14_highlights1_e.pdf [accessed on 26 October 2016].

'Trade Monitoring Database'; available at tmdb.wto.org/ [accessed on 26 October 2016].

Zunckel, Hilton E. and Botha, Lambert, 'The BRICS, South Africa and dispute settlement in the WTO', *SAFPI Policy Brief No. 9* (September 2012).

4

The BRICS Investment Framework

Catching Up with Trade

DENIS DE CASTRO HALIS AND
GUILHERME VARGAS CASTILHOS

I. Introduction

Each and all of the five countries – Brazil, Russia, India, China and South Africa – belonging to the BRICS group have publicly recognized foreign investment (FDI) as an important driver of economic growth and development.[1] The increase of trade and investment appears to be a priority in BRICS cooperation documents.[2] This chapter raises issues and provides data that help to understand the position of each of the BRICS members in the global economy and the ways in which their companies have been investing in one another. A premise here is that mutual comprehension is necessary for trading and investment among

---

[1] They have expressly linked foreign investment to different spheres of development, as seen in the joint statement from their 2014 summit in Fortaleza, Brazil: 'Foreign direct investment (FDI) can make a positive contribution to sustainable development when integrated into national development strategies. These benefits of FDI may include, amongst others, technology transfer, skills development, enhanced research at the national level, and the establishment of stronger supply chains between domestic and foreign firms.' See: Brazil, Ministry of External Relations, 'BRICS Perspective on International Investment Agreements'; available at http://brics.itamaraty.gov.br/category-english/ 21-documents/227-brics-perspective-on-international-investment-agreements [accessed on 29 November 2016]. Their position remains the same, and significance is placed on investments related to infrastructure: 'We highlight the importance of public and private investments in infrastructure, including connectivity, to ensure sustained long term growth.' See: Ministry of Foreign Affairs, Government of India, 8th BRICS Summit Goa Declaration; available at www.mea.gov.in/bilateral-documents.htm?dtl/27491/ Goa+Declaration+at+8th+BRICS+Summit [accessed on 5 December 2016].

[2] For one such instance, see: Brazil, Ministry of External Relations, 'BRICS Trade and Investment Facilitation Plan'; available at http://brics.itamaraty.gov.br/category-english/ 21-documents/226-brics-trade-and-investment-facilitation-plan [accessed on 29 November 2016].

them to grow and that increased knowledge of their legislation concerning companies and foreign investment is an important part of that comprehension.

Indeed, regulatory frameworks are instrumental for governments wishing to stimulate or restrict the opportunities for business investments. The study of each of these countries' laws on foreign investment is thus extremely relevant for understanding current and potential economic interaction between the BRICS member companies and individuals. It serves to identify possible improvements in their domestic laws that can enhance relations and investment within the bloc.

The driving questions in this analysis concern the relevance of intra-BRICS foreign investment, the complexities involved in investing in BRICS members, and the differences and similarities in their company law frameworks related to foreign investment. The research takes into consideration the regulatory issues related to the definition of a commercial company, the distinction between a national and a foreign company, restrictions in terms of the industries that foreigners may operate in, and the legal means available to foreign investors to operate in BRICS economies.

This chapter has three core sections. The first two are important in advancing the key argument that complex regulation, lack of transparency and insufficient mutual knowledge are deterrents for business investments, particularly those that take place across international borders. They review the data from the most recent reports produced by the World Bank (WB), the World Economic Forum (WEF), and the United Nations Conference on Trade and Development (UNCTAD) and indicate the dynamic movement of BRICS in the international rankings produced by these organizations.

Section IV summarizes and analyzes relevant points concerning the regulatory frameworks of each of the BRICS countries concerning foreign investment, with a focus on their respective company laws and the legal ways that foreign enterprises can be incorporated and operate in their territories. Rather than undertaking a detailed description or comparison, it underscores existing differences and the confusion that still exists and that may restrict understanding of countries' rules needed for their cooperation to take place. Furthermore, the objective is to identify the important viewpoints of each of the countries as expressed in their laws, which can then be taken as important reference points for the other members when needing to regulate similar issues or to evaluate the likely pros and cons of a certain regulation.

II.   Investments in BRICS and Intra-BRICS

Trade and foreign investment comprise the majority of economic inter-actions between nations. It is important to note that while trade within BRICS is consistently increasing to a significant extent, foreign investment is not following this trend.[3] On this note, a 2013 report from the South African Institute of International Affairs stated,

> Trade among the BRICS countries has shown progressive growth over the past decade. Although foreign direct investment (FDI) flows in all of the countries have increased, *intra-BRICS flows do not correlate with trade figures*... Generally, *the evidence suggests that intra-BRICS countries' investment is not substantial.*[4]

UNCTAD reinforces those claims in its 2103 report:

> Overseas investment by BRICS countries is mainly in search of markets in developed countries or in the context of regional value chains. 42% of BRICS outward FDI stock is in developed countries, with 34% in the EU.[5]

Data on global foreign investment compared with that the investment between the BRICS members indicate the same. In 2015, global FDI reached an amount of USD 1.076 trillion according to UNCTAD.[6] BRICS received approximately 15 percent of that amount, which represented a total of around USD 256 billion.[7] The BRICS member receiving most of that investment was China, gaining more than half of the total amount

---

[3] As an illustration, between 2006 and 2015, intra-BRICS trade increased 163 percent, from USD 93 billion to USD 244 billion. See: Brazil, Ministry of External Relations, 'About BRICS, Economic Data and Trade Statistics'; available at http://brics.itamaraty.gov.br/about-brics/economic-data [accessed on 10 August 2016].

[4] South African Institute of International Affairs, 'Economic Diplomacy Programme Policy Briefing n. 63, March, 2013'; available at www.saiia.org.za/policy-briefings/173-brics-fdi-a-preliminary-view/file [accessed on 29 July 2016] [emphasis added]. A 2013 UNCTAD report also stated, 'Economic linkages through FDI [foreign direct investment] between BRICS countries themselves are still limited, although intra-BRICS FDI has grown faster than flows to non-BRICS over the past decade'. See: UNCTAD, Global Investment Trends Monitor, Special Edition, March 25, 2013, 'The Rise of BRICS FDI and Africa', p. 1; available at http://unctad.org/en/PublicationsLibrary/webdiaeia2013d6_en.pdf [accessed on 19 November 2016].

[5] UNCTAD, 'The Rise of BRICS FDI and Africa'.

[6] UNCTAD, World Investment Report 2016, 'Investor Nationality: Policy Challenges', Geneva, 2016, p. x, available at http://unctad.org/en/PublicationsLibrary/wir2016_en.pdf [accessed on 29 July 2016].

[7] Ibid., pp. 8 and 12.

invested in the group – around USD 135.610 billion in 2015.[8] In second place came Brazil, receiving USD 64.648 billion in 2015.[9] India followed with USD 44.208 billion received in 2015.[10] Russia and South Africa came next, receiving USD 9.825 billion[11] and USD 1.772 billion[12] respectively.[13]

Even though these numbers indicate considerable participation of BRICS in world FDI, most of these investments did not originate from the BRICS members themselves, as confirmed by the UNCTAD World Investment Report 2016:

> FDI in BRICS is highly concentrated, with China alone receiving more than 50 percent of the group's total FDI inflows in 2015. Unlike other economic groups, BRICS members are not active investors in each other's economies … : the share of intra-BRICS investment in total FDI flows to the group was less than 1 percent between 2010 and 2014, and intra-BRICS cross-border M&A sales have also been low, averaging $2 billion in 2014–2015. This reflects the minimal intra-BRICS corporate connectivity.[14]

Table 4.1 presents the share of each of the BRICS countries in global foreign investment.

From Table 4.1, it is apparent that China has been maintaining the lead, with a respectable distance from the BRICS member positioned second, be it Brazil (in 2012, 2014 and 2015) or Russia (in 2013). South Africa has remained last throughout. Finally, while Brazil's, Russia's and South Africa's inflows have been oscillating between higher and lower numbers over the years, that of India has been consistently and continuously increasing.

The data are scarce and not so recent, however, when it comes to finding the investment that each BRICS member has made in each other. In

---

8 Ibid., p. 12; Also: UNCTAD, 'Country Fact Sheet: China'; available at http://unctad.org/sections/dite_dir/docs/wir2016/wir16_fs_cn_en.pdf [accessed on 29 July 2016].

9 UNCTAD, 'Country Fact Sheet: Brazil'; available at http://unctad.org/sections/dite_dir/docs/wir2016/wir16_fs_br_en.pdf [accessed on 29 July 2016].

10 UNCTAD, 'Country Fact Sheet: India'; available at http://unctad.org/sections/dite_dir/docs/wir2016/wir16_fs_in_en.pdf [accessed on 29 July 2016].

11 UNCTAD, 'Country Fact Sheet: Russia'; available at http://unctad.org/sections/dite_dir/docs/wir2016/wir16_fs_ru_en.pdf [accessed on 29 July 2016].

12 UNCTAD, 'Country Fact Sheet: South Africa'; available at http://unctad.org/sections/dite_dir/docs/wir2016/wir16_fs_za_en.pdf [accessed on 29 July 2016].

13 Sauvant notes, 'While all four countries [South Africa was not yet a part of the group] have attracted substantial amounts of FDI, this performance has been highly uneven, whatever measure is used.' See: Karl P. Sauvant, 'New Sources of FDI: The BRICs-outward FDI from Brazil, Russia, India and China'; (2005) 6 *Journal of World Investment & Trade* 639–709 at 639.

14 UNCTAD, 'Investor Nationality: Policy Challenges', p. 12.

Table 4.1 *Annual Foreign Investment Inflow: World and BRICS (USD)*

	2012		2013		2014		2015	
	Amount	Percentage	Amount	Percentage	Amount	Percentage	Amount	Percentage
World:	1.051 trillion	100	1.042 trillion	100	1.027 trillion	100	1.076 trillion	100
Brazil	76.098 billion	5	53.060 billion	3.70	73.086 billion	5.70	64.648 billion	3.70
Russia	30.188 billion	2	53.397 billion	4	29.152 billion	2	9.825 billion	1
India	24.196 billion	1.60	28.199 billion	1.9	34.582 billion	2.7	44.208 billion	2.50
China	121.080 billion	8	123.911 billion	8.70	128.500 billion	10.1	135.610 billion	7.70
South Africa	4.559 billion	0.30	8.300 billion	0.6	5.771 billion	0.40	1.772 billion	0.09

Source: UNCTAD. Data from the respective countries "fact sheet" reports, available at http://unctad.org. [last accessed 29 July 2016].

2012, Brazil's foreign direct investment flows (outflows less inflows) from investments abroad were recorded as negative, USD 2.821 million, indicating that more funds were repatriated back to Brazil in that year than were invested in the rest of the world.[15] Historically, though, the majority of Brazil's investment is directed to neighboring countries, such as Argentina and Uruguay, which are also emerging economies with political and economic similarities. Indeed, the 'neighborhood effect' has been noted in the history of foreign investment among nations as follows:

> Historically outward investment from developing countries has been mainly within the same region. This "neighborhood effect" is associated generally with commonalities in language and culture and familiarity with location, climate and factors of production.[16]

In 2012, Russia invested a total of USD 48.822 billion in other countries. Of this amount, it invested around USD 275 million in India, USD 63 million in China, USD 2 million in South Africa and USD 3 million in Brazil.[17] India invested a total of USD 10.973 billion, of which the only notable investment in another BRICS country was in China, which received USD 50 million.[18] China is the BRICS member that invests the most in other countries. In 2012, it invested a total of USD 87.804 billion in other countries. From this amount, USD194 million went to Brazil, while India received USD 277 million. Russia, due to its proximity, was the largest recipient of Chinese investment in that year, with an amount

---

[15] See the FDI outflows in bilateral FDI statistics: UNCTAD, 'Bilateral FDI Statistics: Brazil' (2012); available at http://unctad.org/Sections/dite_fdistat/docs/webdiaeia2014d3_BRA .pdf [accessed on 6 November 2016]. As for the negative number, UNCTAD explains: 'FDI flows with a negative sign indicate that at least one of the three components of FDI (equity capital, reinvested earnings or intra-company loans) is negative and not offset by positive amounts of the remaining components. These are instances of reverse investment or disinvestment.' See: UNCTAD, 'FDI Flows'; available at http://unctad.org/en/Pages/DIAE/ Investment%20and%20Enterprise/FDI_Flows.aspx [accessed on 29 July 2016].

[16] South African Institute of International Affairs, p. 2. Moreover, according to UNCTAD, 'Some 43% of BRICS outward FDI stock is in respective neighbouring countries in Latin America and the Caribbean, East Asia, South Asia and transition economies.' See: UNCTAD, Global Investment Trends Monitor, Special Edition, 25 March 2013, 'The Rise of BRICS FDI and Africa', p. 1; available at http://unctad.org/en/PublicationsLibrary/ webdiaeia2013d6_en.pdf [accessed on 19 November 2016].

[17] UNCTAD, 'Bilateral FDI Statistics [2012]: Russian Federation'; http://unctad.org/Sections/ dite_fdistat/docs/webdiaeia2014d3_RUS.pdf [accessed on 29 July 2016].

[18] UNCTAD, 'Bilateral FDI Statistics [2012]: India'; available at http://unctad.org/Sections/ dite_fdistat/docs/webdiaeia2014d3_IND.pdf [accessed on 29 July 2016].

of USD 785 million.[19] Investment in South Africa was a negative figure of USD 815 million, meaning a reverse investment. When it comes to South Africa's investments in other BRICS countries, the UNCTAD report only offers data on India, where the African nation invested USD 9 million.[20] However, UNCTAD states, 'Among BRICS countries, South Africa shows the largest share of intra-BRICS investment. In 2011, one fifth of the outward investment stock of South Africa was concentrated in other BRICS countries, mainly China.'[21]

Hence, the UNCTAD data corroborate the argument that intra-BRICS investment is not significant in comparison with what each country invests in non-BRICS economies. This might change if their cooperation continues and gains strength.

III.   Challenges for Foreign Investment in BRICS Countries and their Economic Competitiveness

BRICS cooperation aims to complement and strengthen the bilateral and multilateral relations between its members.[22] Strategies to achieve this aim include stimulating economic growth, increasing the competitiveness of the BRICS economies, and the creation of 'a business-friendly environment for investors and entrepreneurs in all BRICS countries'.[23]

To understand some of the reasons why intra-BRICS investment remains short of its potential, it is relevant to understand the business environment in each of the countries. It is important, therefore, to investigate their regulations, level of transparency and sources of information to enhance their mutual knowledge. These are just a few of the factors that may facilitate or deter foreign investment in general and that may represent notable obstacles for the improvement of BRICS cooperation.

The 'Doing Business Report' presents the WB's assessment of a series of factors indicating the quality and efficiency of the regulatory

---

[19] UNCTAD, 'Bilateral FDI Statistics: China'; available at http://unctad.org/Sections/dite_fdistat/docs/webdiaeia2014d3_CHN.pdf [accessed on 29 July 2016].

[20] UNCTAD, 'Bilateral FDI Statistics: South Africa'; available at http://unctad.org/Sections/dite_fdistat/docs/webdiaeia2014d3_ZAF.pdf [accessed on 29 July 2016].

[21] UNCTAD, 'The Rise of BRICS FDI and Africa', p. 1; available at http://unctad.org/en/PublicationsLibrary/webdiaeia2013d6_en.pdf [accessed on 19 November 2016].

[22] Brazil, Ministry of External Relations, 'The Strategy for BRICS Economic Partnership', p. 4; available at http://brics.itamaraty.gov.br/images/partnershipstrategy_eng.pdf [accessed on 15 November 2016]. This document was adopted at the 2015 BRICS Summit in Ufa, Russia.

[23] Ibid.

Table 4.2 *Regulatory Quality and Efficiency in the BRICS Countries, 2016*

Where Is Regulation More Business Friendly? Ranking out of 189 Economies	
(1) Ease of Doing Business	(2) Ease of Starting a Business
Russia – 51	Russia – 41
South Africa – 73	South Africa – 120
China – 84	China – 136
Brazil – 116	India – 155
India – 130	Brazil – 174

Source: Doing Business 2016 World Bank Report. World Bank. Available at www.doingbusiness.org/reports/global-reports/ doing-business-2016 [accessed 16 October 2016].

frameworks of most economies. The report, first published in 2003, investigates the regulations enhancing business activity and those constraining it. The 2016 report measured ten areas involving business, including the requirements needed to start a business.[24] In brief, the report ranks countries in terms of their regulatory system, the efficiency of the established bureaucracy, and the nature of business governance. It suggests that these factors have significant consequences for an economy's strength, performance and growth.

The 2016 report ranked 189 economies along the factors above. The first ranking ('Ease of Doing Business') is more comprehensive than the second ('Ease of Starting a Business') in terms of assessing factors that facilitate business activity. Table 4.2 presents the 2016 positions of the BRICS countries in those two rankings.

Table 4.2 shows that Russia is the highest ranked of the BRICS countries in terms of 'ease of doing business', whereas India comes last. The second dimension, which is more specific, focuses on the formalities required to start a business. Here, Russia is again the highest ranked in BRICS, with

---

[24] The ten areas are starting a business, handling construction permits, obtaining electricity, registering property, obtaining credit, protecting minority investors, paying taxes, trading across borders, enforcing contracts, and resolving insolvency. World Bank, 'Doing Business 2016: Measuring Regulatory Quality and Efficiency'; available at www.doingbusiness.org/~/media/GIAWB/Doing%20Business/Documents/ Annual-Reports/English/DB16-Full-Report.pdf [accessed on 18 August 2016].

Table 4.3 *Procedures and Time to Start a Business in the BRICS Countries,
2015–2016*

Name of Country	Position in the Ranking	Number of Procedures	Time to Start a Business (Days)
Russia	41	4.4	10.5
South Africa	120	6	46
China	136	11	31.4
India	155	12.9	29
Brazil	174	11	83

Source: 'Doing Business 2016'; available at www.doingbusiness.org/reports/global-reports/doing-business-2016 [accessed 16 October 2016].

Brazil being the lowest. This second dimension also measures the number of procedures and time spent starting a business in each of these countries. Table 4.3 breaks down that data.

Table 4.3 shows that one can form a company in Russia through around four procedures and over a period of some ten days, whereas eleven procedures and eighty-three days would be required to do so in Brazil.

The relatively low positions of the BRICS countries in the two rankings[25] suggest the need for them to enhance their regulatory frameworks not only to facilitate domestic business entrepreneurship but also to receive further foreign investment. Table 4.4 presents further data concerning these countries' performance in the rankings in recent years.

These relatively low positions in these international rankings indicate problems that surely affect the competitiveness and the level of economic productivity in BRICS countries. There is evidence of these problems in the *Global Competitiveness Report 2016–2017*, produced by the WEF. This report measured the 'national competitiveness' of 138 economies by analyzing institutions, policies and factors that affect the level of productivity of an economy. Table 4.5 presents the data related to the BRICS members, from the best positioned to the worst.

Here, Brazil again occupies the last position, which reinforces the relation between the complexities of opening a business and competitiveness, while China is the BRICS country in the best position. China's position,

---

[25] Russia is the only member ranked within the first fifty positions.

Table 4.4 *Regulatory Quality and Efficiency in the BRICS Countries, 2012–2016*

Ease of Doing Business (EDB) and Ease of Starting a Business (ESB) Rankings									
2012		2013		2014		2015		2016	
EDB	ESB	EDB	ESB	EDB	ESB	EDB	ESB	EDB	ESB
Brazil 126	120	130	121	116	123	120	167	116	174
Russia 120	111	112	101	92	88	62	34	51	41
India 132	166	132	173	134	179	142	158	130	155
China 91	151	91	151	96	158	90	128	84	136
South Africa 35	44	39	53	85	54	43	61	73	120

Note: The 2012 report assessed ten areas of 183 economies; the 2013 one assessed ten areas and 185 economies; the 2014, ten areas and 189 economies; the 2015 and 2016 reports, ten areas and 189 economies.
Source: 'Doing Business Reports', from 2012 to 2016'; available at www .doingbusiness.org [accessed 15 October 2016].

however, still falls short of what is perhaps desirable for the world's second largest economy. India's current position at 39 represents a significant improvement on the previous report (2015–2016), in which it was at 55. Table 4.6 provides a view of the development of BRICS positions in this ranking over a longer period.

Table 4.5 *Economic Competitiveness of the BRICS Countries, 2016–2017*

Country	Rank
China	28
India	39
Russia	43
South Africa	47
Brazil	81

Source: 'Global Competitiveness Report 2016–2017', data on 138 countries; available at www3 .weforum.org/docs/GCR2016–2017/05FullReport/ TheGlobalCompetitivenessReport2016–2017_ FINAL.pdf [accessed 16 October 2016].

Table 4.6 *Economic Competitiveness of the BRICS Countries, 2011–2017*

	2011–2012	2012–2013	2013–2014	2014–2015	2015–2016	2016–2017
Brazil	53	48	56	57	75	81
Russia	66	67	64	53	45	43
India	56	59	60	71	55	39
China	26	29	29	28	28	28
S. Africa	50	52	53	56	49	47

Note: The 2011–12 report assessed 142 economies; the 2012–13 assessed 144 economies; the 2013–14 report, 148 economies; the 2014–15, 144 economies; the 2015–16, 140 economies; and that of 2016–17, 138 economies.
Source: 'Global Competitiveness Reports'; available at www.weforum.org/reports [accessed 16 October 2016].

From Table 4.6, it is apparent that Brazil has significantly lost ground over the years (from fifty-third to eighty-first), while Russia and India have made significant gains (from sixty-sixth to forty-third, and from fifty-sixth to thirty-ninth, respectively). China has maintained a constant ranking at around the twenty-eight mark. Finally, South Africa has improved in the period after having some worse positions and is currently in forty-seventh place.

Looking at these indicators of the business environments of the BRICS members and the data on the inflow of investment (Section II), it becomes clear that the positions in the rankings are but one of the factors that affect actual investment in the BRICS countries. While the elements that result in a country having a higher or lower position are definitely relevant in terms of facilitating or deterring foreign investment, other factors should not be dismissed. Among these are the international economic and financial situation, variances in the international price of commodities, the relation of a given country to the so-called international community, and currency values.

All these factors can justify the reasons why Brazil, for instance, occupies very low relative positions in the rankings, but has nonetheless received more foreign investment than other higher- ranked countries in some years. Conversely, Russia, despite occupying some relatively high positions in the rankings, has received fewer investments in recent years than other lower-ranked countries.

This variable reality is yet another strong reason why BRICS cooperation is necessary. It strengthens and expands the members' alternatives and choices, even when the configuration of those multiple internal and external factors changes. None of this, though, is a valid argument for not improving their regulatory frameworks and business environments, especially in terms of improving their own cooperation, as the following section points out.

IV. Legal Frameworks for the Investment of Foreign Companies in BRICS

The investigation underpinning this section identified and analyzed the main company and foreign investment laws of each of the BRICS members and found a glaring contrast between their governments' declarations on the importance of foreign investment, their expressed wishes for closer economic cooperation,[26] and their current legal realities. The bloc members continue to have different models of regulation and still have much to do to make it easier for their own investors to become familiar with each other's rules concerning investment. In the past several years, the BRICS members have constantly updated their laws, with frequent amendments, some of which must now be noted to verify the legal paths they have chosen and whether they have taken into account each other's regulations as a reference.

In addition to sector-specific laws (regulating areas such as currency exchange controls, immigration and taxation), some of the members' legal systems have clearly separate regulations for commercial and civil law issues, while others unify them. Brazil used to be an example of the first case, as until 2002 it had a Commercial Code, enacted in 1850, which regulated important business activities taking place in the country.[27]

---

[26] They made important moves particularly after the 2014 Fortaleza Summit, in which they declared, 'We are committed to raise our economic cooperation to a qualitatively new level. To achieve this, we emphasize the importance of establishing a roadmap for intra-BRICS economic cooperation. In this regard, we welcome the proposals for a 'BRICS Economic Cooperation Strategy' and a 'Framework of BRICS Closer Economic Partnership', which lay down steps to promote intra-BRICS economic, trade and investment cooperation.' 'Sixth BRICS Summit – Fortaleza Declaration'; available at http://brics2016.gov.in/upload/files/document/57566d35a13456declaration.pdf [accessed on 5 December 2016].

[27] Brazil, Commercial Code of 1850, Law 556 of 25 June 1850; available at www.planalto.gov.br/ccivil_03/leis/L0556–1850.htm [in Portuguese] [accessed on 1 August 2016].

However, as its economy and society changed, a legislative reform took place, and Brazil decided to revoke most of that Commercial Code and unify its private law under its 2002 Civil Code. Hence, the pillars of commercial and company law are now included in one code, which also regulates the traditional areas of civil law, such as obligations, contracts, civil liability, property, family and succession. In addition, a separate law on joint stock corporations (also known as the Law on Public Limited Companies or on Corporations) was passed in 1976 and subsequently modified by several amendments.[28]

After the dissolution of the Soviet Union, Russia's legal system went through significant adjustments in an attempt to be more conducive to private investment and business.[29] Government policies have been crafted to attract foreign investors through incentives such as tax exemptions and the reduction of bureaucratic procedures. As in Brazil, the Russian Civil Code is the legal instrument providing the basic principles and framework that regulate companies' activities. Not all of its four constitutive parts, however, came into effect on the same date,[30] and its content related to company law was amended in 2013 and 2014; these changes related to corporate governance and the classification of legal entities.[31] In addition to the Civil Code, two other laws concern commercial matters: the Joint Stock Companies Act and the Limited Liability Companies Act, also

---

[28] Also designated Law 6.404 of 15 December 1976. For the updated law, see: Brazil, Law 6.404 of 15 December 1976; available at www2.camara.leg.br/legin/fed/lei/1970–1979/lei-6404-15-dezembro-1976-368447-normaatualizada-pl.html [in Portuguese] [accessed on 19 November 2016].

[29] 'Despite its imperfections, the new Civil Code departs dramatically and significantly from past Soviet and Russian legislation by effectively guaranteeing both freedom of contract and protection of private property. In addition, the Code carves out major areas of economic activity to be decided by the private parties to a transaction, free from state interference. The codification of these principles, taken for granted by citizens of market democracies, denotes a legal and political revolution in a country dominated by seven decades of a command style economy, socialist ideology, and state ownership.' Lane H. Blumenfeld, 'Russia's New Civil Code: The Legal Foundation for Russia's Emerging Market Economy' (1996) 30(3) *International Lawyer* 477–519 at 479.

[30] Part I of the Civil Code entered into force in 1994, whereas Parts II, III and IV entered into force only in 1996, 2001 and 2006, respectively.

[31] Vasilisa Strizh and Brian L. Zimbler, 'Key Reforms of the Russian Civil Code for Legal Entities', *Morgan Lewis*, 7 August 2014; available at www.morganlewis.com/pubs/bf_lf_keyreformsofrussiancivilcodeforlegalentities_07aug14#sthash.I4akIOeZ.dpuf [accessed on 29 July 2016]. Also see: Deloitte, 'Doing Business in Russia 2016'; available at www2.deloitte.com/ru/en/pages/tax/articles/2016/doing-business-in-russia-2016.html [accessed on 5 December 2016].

known, respectively, as the Companies Act of 1995 and the Companies Act of 1998.[32]

Because of its historical linkage with the United Kingdom, the legal system of India is representative of the common law tradition. It is not surprising, then, that legal codification plays a less important role in the Indian context than in the legal systems of those countries belonging to the civil law tradition (such as Brazil and Russia). The main legal instrument governing companies in India is the Companies Act, which combines two different laws still in force: the Companies Act of 1956 and the Companies Act of 2013.[33]

Since the opening up of China's economic system in 1979 and its joining he World Trade Organization in 2001, China's legal system has gone through significant changes, despite remaining under a 'Chinese style of socialism'.[34] Its legal system represents a blend of a codified civil law system with Chinese-style socialism. Its main company law regulation is the Companies Law of the People's Republic of China, enacted in 1994, but already amended several times.[35]

South Africa is another country historically connected to the United Kingdom and representative of the common law tradition. Its main law regulating corporate matters is the Companies Act of 2008, which adopts a more business-friendly approach than the much-amended previous law

---

[32] Their official designations are Federal Law 208-FZ of 1995 and Federal Law 14-FZ of 1998. See: Global Investment Center, *Russia Company Laws and Regulations Handbook – Strategic Information and Basic Laws* (Washington DC: Global Investment Center, 2015), p. 25; available at https://books.google.com/books?id=y8G7CgAAQBAJ&printsec=frontcover&hl=pt-BR&source=gbs_ge_summary_r&cad=0#v=onepage&q&f=false [accessed on 29 July 2016].

[33] India, 'The Companies Act of 2013 passed by the Parliament and assented by the President of India on 29th August, 2013'; available at www.mca.gov.in/MinistryV2/companiesact .html [accessed on 19 April 2016]. Also see: India, 'The Companies Act of 1956. Act no. 1 of 1956 of 18th January, 1956'; available at https://indiankanoon.org/doc/1353758/ [accessed on 19 April 2016].

[34] This expression, together with that of 'socialism with Chinese characteristics', is commonly used to suggest that China is not a capitalist country, but neither does it follow traditional conceptions of socialism, as historically implemented or as imagined from the works of Marxist authors. The 'Chinese style of socialism' was introduced to the preamble of the Chinese Constitution in a 2004 amendment. For further information on this and the rule of law in China, see: Denis De Castro Halis, 'Rule of Law in the Mainland and in Macau ... With 'Chinese Characteristics'?' in Ming Chan et al. (ed.), *Highlights from the EACS' 14 Conference, International Institute of Macau, 2015, Macau in Coimbra*, pp. 85–101.

[35] Company Law of the People's Republic of China (Revised in 2013); available at www.fdi.gov .cn/1800000121_39_4814_0_7.html#_Toc381707457 [in English] [accessed on 9 February 2016].

of 1973 that it replaced.[36] Hence, while Brazil and Russia belong to the civil law tradition and partially regulate civil and commercial law in a more unified way, China follows a blended civil law model in which specific legislation on companies is separate from other issues. Enriching the diversity within the group are India and South Africa, both belonging to the common law tradition and having specific laws on companies.

However, perhaps what is most important for investors – and for those seeking to increase harmony among the BRICS legislative systems – to know is how the law characterizes a company and the legal differences, if any, between national and foreign companies. The legal definition of a company may be crucial to understanding its nature and purpose, the basic way in which it can be formed (the minimum number of individuals and whether existing legal entities can form companies), and the relation it holds to the ideas of separate legal personality and limited liability. It is also important to know in which economic sectors or industries foreign investment cannot operate.

In Brazil, the law provides that a company is formed by people who reciprocally bind themselves to contribute, with goods and services, to perform an economic activity and share its results.[37] Another provision states that the activity of a company is the one inherent to that of an entrepreneur subject to registration.[38] Hence, to form a company in Brazil, it is necessary to have an association of two or more people, an economic and profitable purpose and the proper registration in the designated government agency. Since 2011, however, a single person has also been able to incorporate a limited liability company.[39]

When it comes to the nationality of the company, Brazilian law uses territorial and procedural criteria to define whether it is national or foreign. The two requisites for a company to be Brazilian are to have its

---

[36] South Africa, 'Companies Act, 2008 (Act No. 71 of 2008), Chapter 1: Interpretation, Purpose and Application, Part A: Interpretation'; available at www.acts.co.za/companies-act-2008/1_definitions [accessed on 19 November 2016].

[37] Brazil, Civil Code 2002, Article 981: 'The articles of association are concluded by people who mutually undertake to contribute with goods or services for the exercise of an economic activity and the sharing of the results between them' [Authors' translation].

[38] Brazil, Civil Code 2002, Article 982: 'Save the express exceptions, a business entity is considered to be one the purpose of which is the exercise of inherent entrepreneurial activity subject to registration, and simple, all others' [Authors' translation].

[39] Brazil, Law 12.441 of 11 July 2011. This alters the Brazilian Civil Code to allow the constitution of a single person limited liability company [adds Article 980-A]; available at www.planalto.gov.br/ccivil_03/_ato2011–2014/2011/lei/l12441.htm [in Portuguese] [accessed on 1 November 2016].

headquarters in Brazil and to be incorporated under its laws.[40] When defining the nationality of a company, there is no reference to the nationality of the shareholders or the origin of the capital. Even a company in which a majority or all of its shareholders are foreign nationals and the capital invested is from abroad has Brazilian legal personality as long as its headquarters are in Brazil and it is incorporated under Brazilian law.[41] Hence, any company that does not satisfy these requisites is a foreign company. The Law of Introduction to the Brazilian Legal System reinforces this interpretation,[42] making the provision that the juristic persons bound to a collective goal, such as companies and foundations, follow the laws of the state in which they were formed.[43] Hence, a company incorporated in a foreign country shall comply with the laws of that nation and will be considered a foreign company in Brazil for all legal purposes.[44] It is important to note that although the law expressly differentiates between national and foreign companies, this distinction does not have significant implications in terms of the activities and investment of those companies. Foreign companies have the same legal guarantees and rights as national companies, with the exception of specific limitations, which are mostly specified in the Brazilian Constitution.[45]

In Russia, the Civil Code sets the framework for the operation of business,[46] providing for certain types of legal entities and defining

---

[40] Brazil, Civil Code 2002, Article 1.126: 'A national company is one that is established in accordance with Brazilian law and that has its headquarters in the country' [Authors' translation].

[41] 'If two or more foreigners, residents abroad, and bringing resources from their country, constitute a business society with its headquarters in the national territory, obeying the provisions of the current legal system, this company is, to all effects, Brazilian' [Authors' translation]. Fábio Ulhoa Coelho, *Curso de direito comercial*, 4th edn (São Paulo: Saraiva, 2008), vol. 2, p. 31.

[42] Law of Introduction to the Brazilian Legal System, Law Decree 4.657 of 4 September 1942, Article 11; available at www.planalto.gov.br/ccivil_03/decreto-lei/Del4657compilado.htm [in Portuguese] [accessed on 1 July 2016].

[43] Law of Introduction, Brazil, Article 11: 'Organizations pursuing goals of collective interest, such as companies and foundations, obey the law of the state in which they are constituted' [Authors' translation].

[44] 'A foreign company is formed according to the laws of the place in which it was established (*lex loci actus*) and where it is headquartered ' [Authors' translation]. Maria Helena Diniz, *Código Civil Anotado* (São Paulo: Saraiva, 2002), p. 587.

[45] An illustration of these limitations is found in Article 199(3) of the Brazilian Constitution of 1988, which prohibits the direct or indirect participation of foreign companies or foreign capital in the health care industry, except for the cases provided by law.

[46] Russia, 'Civil Code of the Russian Federation, Part 1, Chapter IV'; available at www.wipo.int/edocs/lexdocs/laws/en/ru/ru083en.pdf [accessed on 29 July 2016].

companies and nonprofit organizations. To understand its definition of 'company', it is necessary to consider that of 'legal entity' enshrined in Article 48 of the Russian Civil Code in the following terms:

> The legal entity shall be recognized as an organization, which has in its ownership, economic management or operative management the set-apart property and which is answerable by its obligations with this property and may on its own behalf acquire and exercise the property and the personal non-property rights, to discharge duties and to come out as a plaintiff and as a defendant in the court.[47]

Legal entities organized with the goal of acquiring profits shall be considered 'commercial organizations'; in other words, companies.[48]

As for the distinction between national and foreign companies, the legislation is not straightforward. However, the distinction can be constructed via the legal definition of 'foreign investor', expressly stated in the Law on Foreign Investments in the Russian Federation of 1999, which reads:

> 'Foreign investor' shall mean: foreign legal entities, the civil legal capacity of which shall be determined by the laws of the jurisdiction of their incorporation and which have the right to invest on the territory of the Russian Federation under the laws of the jurisdiction of incorporation; a foreign organization which is not a legal entity, the civil legal capacity of which shall be determined by the laws of the jurisdiction of its organization and which has the right to invest on the territory of the Russian Federation under the laws of the jurisdiction of its organization.[49]

Hence, it can be argued that a foreign company would be one of those foreign legal 'entities' and 'organizations' incorporated under the rules of another jurisdiction and that, according to those rules, can invest in Russia. This law also provides that foreign investors operate under approximately the same legal regime and with the same advantages as prescribed for local investors. They have legal protection for business activities carried out in Russia and can access a multitude of business sectors, with

---

[47]   Russia, Civil Code, Article 48.

[48]   Russia, Civil Code, Article 50 (1): 'The legal entities may be either the organizations, which see deriving profits as the chief goal of their activity (the commercial organizations), or those organizations, which do not see deriving profits as such a goal and which do not distribute the derived profit among their participants (the non-profit organizations).'

[49]   Article 2 of the aforementioned law, also designated Federal Law No. 160-FZ of 1999 (with several later amendments). Federal Law on Foreign Investment in the Russian Federation Passed by the State Duma on 25 June 1999; available at www.jstor.org/stable/20694022?seq=8#page_scan_tab_contents [accessed on 20 November 2016].

the exception of those that are prohibited by law or that require govern-ment approval.[50] Because of this exception, Russian companies may also be restricted from operating in certain sectors if owned or controlled to varying degrees by foreign investors that are dependent on the industry.[51]

In the context of India's law, its Companies Act of 2013 defines a com-pany as any business or enterprise incorporated following the provisions of the present act or any other past Indian company law.[52] This is a very broad definition: Rather than providing the straightforward character-istics of a company, it forces any potentially interested party to under-take unavoidable research that might still result in uncertainty, given the wide scope of the definition of company. The same law, however, expressly defines a foreign company as follows:

> Article 2
> (42) 'foreign company' means any company or body corporate incorpo-rated outside India which –
> (a) has a place of business in India whether by itself or through an agent, physically or through electronic mode; and
> (b) conducts any business activity in India in any other manner.

Another criterion for distinguishing between an Indian and a foreign company is the degree of ownership or management that the foreign investor has in the company. Companies are considered 'owned' by for-eign investors when they have more than half of a company's capital, have the capacity to appoint the majority of the company's directors, or admin-ister the company themselves.[53] Foreign investors are allowed to operate in most sectors in India, with a few exceptions, such as the lottery business,

---

[50] Foreign investors are not allowed to invest in several sectors, while some have special limi-tations imposed (such as the prohibition on owning voting rights that would give them the right to control the related Russian companies). All these restricted sectors are considered to be of strategic importance for the Russian state; examples are mining activities related to the extraction of mineral resources, the aerospace industry, the media, and military sectors. The Strategic Sectors Law (FZ-57) lists several activities for which government approval is required. See: Federal Law of the Russian Federation No. 57-FZ of 29 April 2008 on 'Proce-dures for Foreign Investments in the Business Entities of Strategic Importance for Russian National Defense and State Security'; available at www.wipo.int/wipolex/en/text.jsp?file_id=188843 [accessed on 19 November 201].

[51] Russia, 'Procedures for Foreign Investments'; available at ibid.

[52] India, *The Companies Act of 2013*, Section 2 (20): '2. In this Act, unless the context other-wise requires: . . . (20) 'company' means a company incorporated under this Act or under any previous company law.'

[53] India, Circular No. RBI /2013–14/117 A.P. Guidelines for calculation of total foreign investment in Indian companies, transfer of ownership and control of Indian compa-nies and downstream investment by Indian companies, enacted by the Reserve Bank of

gambling and betting, the manufacturing of cigars and several tobacco-related products, atomic energy and so forth.[54]

In the context of China, the main company law regulation is the Companies Law of the People's Republic of China, enacted in 1994 with further amendments.[55] As in India, the law does not offer a precise definition of a company with its features and characteristics. It simply states that any limited liability company or company limited by shares incorporated in the Chinese territory and jurisdiction is considered a company.[56] On this matter, Wang notes,

> Nonetheless, under the PRC Company Law, or at least according to the law on books, a Chinese company features the core structural characteristics of the modern business corporation, including legal personality, limited liability, centralized management, shareholder's ownership and residual claims, and free transferability of shares.[57]

Despite its 13 chapters and more than 200 articles, the Companies Law does not regulate all types of legal bodies that can be used for business activities. Indeed, the law only regulates two types of companies[58] and does not prevent other types of business entities being named as 'companies' *(gongsi)*, as long as they are endorsed under other laws of the legal system (such as those regulating foreign investment in China). Foreign investments are thus not within the primary scope of the Companies Law,

India. Section A 1(i) (b): 'Company 'Owned by non-residents' means an Indian company where more than 50% of the capital in it is beneficially owned by non-residents; Company 'Controlled by 'non-residents' means an Indian company where non-residents have the power to appoint a majority of its directors in that company'; available at https://rbi.org.in/scripts/NotificationUser.aspx?Id=8209# [accessed on 1 August 2016]. Also see: Nishith Desai Associates, 'Doing Business in India', June 2015, p. 8; available at www.nishithdesai.com/fileadmin/user_upload/pdfs/Research%20Papers/Doing_Business_in_India.pdf [accessed on 2 May 2016].

54   For a consolidated list, see: UK-India Business Council, 'Indian FDI Restrictions'; available at www.ukibc.com/india-guide/how-india/fdi-restrictions/ [accessed on 18 November 2016].

55   China, 'Companies Law of the People's Republic of China. Revised and adopted at the 18th Meeting of the Standing Committee of the Tenth National People's Congress of the People's Republic of China on October 27, 2005'; available at www.fdi.gov.cn/1800000121_39_4814_0_7.html#_Toc381707457 [in English] [accessed on 9 February 2016].

56   China, Companies Law of the People's Republic of China, Article 2: 'For the purposes of the Law, the term 'companies' refers to limited liability companies and companies limited by shares established within the territory of China pursuant to the Law.'

57   Wang Jiangyu, *Company Law in China: Regulation of Business Organizations in a Socialist Market Economy* (Cheltenham: Edward Elgar, 2014), p. 23.

58   'Limited Liability Company' ['*Youxian Zeren Gongsi*'] and the 'Company Limited by Shares' ['*Gufen Youxian Gongsi*'].

although it defines 'foreign companies' as follows: 'For the purposes of the Law, the term 'foreign companies' refers to companies incorporated outside China in accordance with a foreign country's law.'[59] Thus, the criterion is simple: An enterprise duly incorporated in accordance with the legal requisites of another country is a foreign company in China.[60]

With regard to South Africa's legal system, its Companies Act of 2008 defines a company as:

> ... a juristic person incorporated in terms of this Act, or a juristic person that, immediately before the effective date –
>
> (a) was registered in terms of the –
> (i) Companies Act, 1973 (Act No. 61 of 1973), other than as an external company as defined in that Act; or
> (ii) Close Corporations Act, 1984 (Act No. 69 of 1984), if it has subsequently been converted in terms of Schedule 2;
> (b) was in existence and recognised as an 'existing company' in terms of the Companies Act, 1973 (Act No. 61 of 1973); or
> (c) was deregistered in terms of the Companies Act, 1973 (Act No. 61 of 1973), and has subsequently been re-registered in terms of this Act.[61]

This means that to comprehend the particulars of a company, an interested party would need to review this legislation, because there is no clear-cut definition that can facilitate the actions of those who wish to become familiar with the country's company law.

In terms of distinguishing between South African and foreign companies, the same law contains three variants of foreign investor-related companies.[62] First, it states that

> foreign company means an entity incorporated outside the Republic, irrespective of whether it is a profit, or non-profit, entity; or carrying on business or non-profit activities, as the case may be, within the Republic.[63]

The second is a 'domesticated company', which is a foreign company whose registration has been transferred to South Africa while observing legal requirements, such as compliance with the laws of the original jurisdiction, having all or the greater part of its assets in the country, and having

---

[59] China, Companies Law of the People's Republic of China, Article 191.
[60] Gu endorses the statement: 'Foreign companies are those established and registered outside the territory of China and they are subject to control by foreign company laws'. Gu Minkang, *Understanding Chinese Company Law*, 2nd edn (Hong Kong: Hong Kong University Press, 2010), p. 38.
[61] South Africa, Companies Act, 2008 (Act No. 71 of 2008), Chap. 1, Part A, 1; available at www.acts.co.za/companies-act-2008/1_definitions [accessed on 19 November 2016].
[62] Ibid.   [63] Ibid.

shareholders and directors who are residents and citizens of the country.[64] Finally, an 'external company' is a foreign company carrying out either business or nonprofit activities in South Africa while subject to another section of that law.[65] Whatever their choice might be, foreign investors are able to operate in any sector, with the exception of a few for which specific laws require special government approval, such as the energy, mining, banking, insurance and defense sectors.[66]

As discussed, BRICS members have different approaches to the regulation of foreign investment. While China[67] and India have several separate regulations and some specific paths for foreigners to invest directly or to participate in business ventures, in Brazil and South Africa most such rules are combined in comprehensive laws relevant for both domestic and foreign investors. As for Russia, it occupies a sort of 'middle position' given that it has a comprehensive but separate foreign investment law.

Thus the terms 'company', 'legal entity', 'corporation', 'firm', 'partnership' and 'enterprise' are all used throughout the members' combined laws (or the available and – at times – outdated translation of those laws[68]) with more or less distinct meanings. This diversity can be particularly confusing because of the day-to-day different lay or business usage of those same terms in which technical legal concepts and distinctions do not necessarily matter. The terms 'company' and 'corporation', for instance, may

---

[64] Ibid., Section 13 (5) to (11); available at www.acts.co.za/companies-act-2008/13_right_to_incorporate_company [accessed on 19 November 2016].

[65] Ibid., Section 23(2); available at www.acts.co.za/companies-act-2008/23_registration_of_external_companies_and_registered_office [accessed on 19 November 2016].

[66] U.S. Department of State, '2012 Investment Climate Statement – South Africa, June 2012 Report'; available at www.state.gov/e/eb/rls/othr/ics/2012/191236.htm [accessed on 19 November 2016]. Also see: Norton Rose Fullbright, 'Doing business in South Africa, 2015'; available at www.nortonrosefulbright.com/files/a-guide-to-doing-business-in-south-africa-126259.pdf [accessed on 2 August 2016].

[67] In the case of China, the Standing Committee of the National People's Congress passed several amendments on specialized laws regulating foreign investment, which entered into force on 1 October 2016. They affected the Law on Foreign-Funded Enterprises, the Law on Sino-Foreign Equity Joint Venture Enterprises, the Law on Sino-Foreign Cooperative Joint Venture Enterprises, and the Law on the Protection of Investments by Taiwan Compatriots. The publicized major reason for the changes was to ease regulatory controls on foreign investment.

[68] English versions of the main domestic laws are available (even for the members with an official language other than English). In many cases, however, the English translations do not reflect the most updated versions of laws that had undergone several amendments. Moreover, these translations are not always available on the official websites of the governments' entities, but rather on the websites of private consultancy firms, which is not ideal because they are not official sources of information.

even mean the same in technical legal terms, but people rarely, if ever, refer to a small business (such as a shop or a restaurant) as a corporation. Moreover, there may be a 'non-profit company' (as in South Africa's law) that goes against both people's imagined and many countries' legal definition of 'company', which is usually linked to the profit motive. Moreover, as has been seen, the notion of 'foreign company' and its legally defined characteristics have implications for the way foreign investment can enter or not enter 'strategic sectors'. Such sectors might be absolutely forbidden, restricted, or dependent on special permission from the government, which may require a higher degree of strict scrutiny. Furthermore, members' laws contain greater or lesser distinctions between 'direct' and 'indirect' control over companies operating in those strategic sectors.[69]

A final illustration of the same legal terms referring to common ways for foreign companies to invest in their countries, but that have more or less contrasting meanings, is that of 'branches' and 'representative offices'. In some frameworks, such as those of Russia, they are formally separate entities and have distinct implications concerning, for instance, the payment of taxes. Opening a 'branch' there means having greater legal powers and capacity than opening a 'representative office'.[70] With a few distinctions, India's law[71] views a 'branch office' as taking one of three forms (the others being a 'liaison office' and a 'project office') for investors who do not want to have a legal body incorporated in the country, but want an extension of the foreign company in India to conduct certain business activities and make a profit.[72] A 'liaison office', however, also known as

---

[69] For example, a maximum number of members in the administration of a company or the maximum amount of foreign capital invested in a company.

[70] The Russian legal framework restricts the scope of action of representative offices to an auxiliary and preparatory function. Moreover, branches established in Russia can perform the functions of a representative office, albeit without being limited to that role (see Article 4 (3)). Russia, Federal Law on Foreign Investment in the Russian Federation Passed by the State Duma on June 25, 1999, Approved by the Federation Council on July 2, 1999; available at www.jstor.org/stable/20694022?seq=8#page_scan_tab_contents [accessed on 27 April 2016].

[71] In Section 6 (6) of India's Foreign Exchange Management Act of 1999 (cited earlier), there is a mention of 'branch' as well as of 'office', as if they were different entities: 'Without prejudice to the provisions of this section, the Reserve Bank may, by regulation, prohibit, restrict, or regulate establishment in India of a branch, office or other place of business by a person resident outside India, for carrying on any activity relating to such branch, office or other place of business'.

[72] Reserve Bank of India, Master Circular on Establishment of Liaison/Branch/Project Offices in India by Foreign Entities: C (1): 'a) Companies incorporated outside India and engaged in manufacturing or trading activities are allowed to set up Branch Offices in India with

a 'representative office', is meant for strict 'liaison purposes' (i.e., facilitating business promotion and exploring the possibility of a permanent presence in the country) and is thus not allowed to undertake any business activity in India for income or profit.[73] In Brazil's framework, it is arguably easier to incorporate a new company in the target investment country (and thus to have a national company) than to operate through an office (or a branch, depending on the case), which usually requires government authorization and increased scrutiny. In China, however, a positive feature of branch companies is that their establishment procedures are arguably simpler than those for other foreign investment vehicles, including for the 'wholly foreign-owned enterprise'.[74] South Africa's 'external company' is arguably a 'branch' that can represent the foreign company in the South African territory, with the freedom to start conducting business with South African counterparts in the country without preregistration.[75]

All of these differences add to the complexity of investing in BRICS because they lead to different regimes governing taxation, liability and rules on immigration,[76] which are all dependent on the legal path of

---

specific approval of the Reserve Bank. Such Branch Offices are permitted to represent the parent / group companies and undertake the following activities in India: i. Export/Import of goods. ii. Rendering professional or consultancy services. iii. Carrying out research work, in areas in which the parent company is engaged. iv. Promoting technical or financial collaborations between Indian companies and parent or overseas group company. v. Representing the parent company in India and acting as buying / selling agent in India. vi. Rendering services in information technology and development of software in India. vii. Rendering technical support to the products supplied by parent/group companies. viii. Foreign airline/shipping company; available at www.rbi.org.in/scripts/BS_ViewMasCirculardetails .aspx?id=9050 [accessed on 29 November 2016].

[73] Bank of India, Master Circular, B (1): 'A Liaison Office (also known as Representative Office) can undertake only liaison activities, i.e. it can act as a channel of communication between Head Office abroad and parties in India. It is not allowed to undertake any business activity in India and cannot earn any income in India. Expenses of such offices are to be met entirely through inward remittances of foreign exchange from the Head Office outside India'; available at www.rbi.org.in/scripts/BS_ViewMasCirculardetails.aspx?id=9050 [accessed on 29 November 2016].

[74] China, Law on Wholly Foreign-Owned Enterprises, Adopted on April 12, 1986 at the 4th Session of the 6th National People's Congress; available at http://english.mofcom.gov.cn/ aarticle/lawsdata/chineselaw/200301/20030100062858.html [in English] [accessed on 29 November 2016].

[75] Section 23 (1) of the Companies Act prescribes '1) An external company must register with the Commission within 20 business days after it first begins to conduct business, or nonprofit activities, as the case may be, within the Republic.' South Africa, Companies Act, 2008 (Act No. 71 of 2008)), Section 23, 1.

[76] Immigration laws and company laws need to be in close harmony. The members' policies need to ease the processes related to the permanence of investors and to the requirements

investment chosen. A lack of familiarity with the way that the different BRICS legislations define the same and different legal institutes does not facilitate a natural increase in the flow of direct investment among countries and populations that are becoming more aware of each other.

V. Conclusion

BRICS cooperation represents a novelty on the international scene, and it is important to understand the potential and challenges for foreign investment by investors both from outside the group and from within the group. The data, legal provisions and arguments presented here suggest that innovation must not be restricted to 'BRICS' as a new type of alliance, but that it must be fostered within each of the BRICS countries and in relation to each other. This internal and co-related innovation can facilitate the bloc's functioning and lead to further member interaction and economic growth. Moreover, greater BRICS interaction and cooperation increase the probability of generating a new model of governance in which strong diversity, rather than simply communality or neighboring territoriality, is one of the keys to success. This model enhances the mutual knowledge and dialogue of member countries, fostering synergies and the achievement of common interests and purposes.[77]

The knowledge of each other's regulatory framework does not need to have the objective of strict harmonization or the convergence of laws, which could require a long period of time, is a complex process, and may have uncertain consequences.[78] By knowing each other's laws,

---

of being a resident for those belonging to BRICS. The possibility of preferential treatment for BRICS investors and their staff has a precedent in the law of Brazil, for instance, with regard to those investors from the 'Mercosul'.

[77] As reinforced by the 2016 Goa Summit declaration: 'Recalling all our previous declarations, we emphasise the importance of further strengthening BRICS solidarity and cooperation based on our common interests and key priorities to further strengthen our strategic partnership in the spirit of openness, solidarity, equality, mutual understanding, inclusiveness and mutually beneficial cooperation.' Ministry of Foreign Affairs, Government of India, 8th BRICS Summit Goa Declaration; available at www.mea.gov.in/bilateral-documents .htm?dtl/27491/Goa+Declaration+at+8th+BRICS+Summit [accessed on 5 December 2016].

[78] Some argue, for instance, that the globalization of regulation can frequently be a story of domination in global business regulation, see e.g. John Braithwaite and Peter Drahos, *Global Business Regulation* (Cambridge: Cambridge University Press, 2000), p. 13. In the case of BRICS, it would be particularly complex to harmonize the laws of each and all of the members because they belong to different legal traditions and have different law-making and reform processes, and because such harmonization could lead to discontent among

however, the BRICS members can extract lessons from the experiences of each that have already been tested and proved and then decide on 'tested grounds' whether their own frameworks need to be reformed, adjusted, or maintained.[79] The members can facilitate each other's learning by sharing a pool of experiences and practices, and spurred by the motivation of friendly cooperation, they may decide to have common ground on issues that are not actually limited to company law and foreign investment.[80]

Hence, the issue of facilitating business and the processes for starting companies, particularly within the group, must seriously enter the BRICS academic and political agenda for discussion. Once these issues have been agreed and defined as a priority,[81] the governments and interested actors must take concrete steps to convert words into reality. In spite of the fact that the strength and novelty of BRICS come largely from the members' diversity, their reciprocal investment does not benefit from the current diversity and opacity of their regulatory frameworks. Innovation here would mean undergoing a process that could transform their current legal realities, which mirror their diversity and even roots in different legal traditions, or at least the way of knowing their legal realities. Indeed, from the point of view of foreign investors, including and particularly those from BRICS, these frameworks remain confusing both in themselves and in relation to each other. There are great contrasts in the meaning of the legal terms adopted, and internal laws are not always well

---

local players and accusations that the legal features of one member have been unduly or disproportionally imposed on the others.

[79] This could be a task for the already approved 'BRICS Business Council' and the 'Contact Group on Economic and Trade Issues' (CGETI) of the BRICS, in line with their roles as suggested in their latest Trade Ministers Communique. See: 6th Meeting of the BRICS Trade Ministers, 13 October 2016 in New Delhi, Trade Ministers Communique; available at http://brics2016.gov.in/upload/files/document/58006d2c04b26BRICSTradeMinisters Communiquefinal.pdf [accessed on 5 December 2016].

[80] An example of a tested experience whose lessons can be shared is the way that Russia has sought to enhance the mechanisms of consultation with administrators of large companies operating businesses internationally, regarding the influence of its regulatory framework over the business and investment environment. One organ created for that purpose was the Foreign Investment Advisory Council. *Russia Country Commercial Guide*; available at www.export.gov/article?id=Russia-openness-to-foreign-investment [accessed on 30 November 2016]. One might also learn from the Chinese experience of creating a negative list of industries in which foreign investors have special administrative measures they must observe, whereas foreign investment in other industries' frameworks are streamlined and simplified.

[81] Brazil, Ministry of External Relations, 'BRICS Trade and Investment Facilitation Plan'. See also Brazil, Ministry of External Relations, 'About BRICS, Economic Data and Trade Statistics'.

articulated; in some cases, they conform to a situation of 'legal pluralism', with an overlap between general and specific laws from different sources. BRICS members' cooperation is hindered by a range of factors, including a lack of translation (or no updated translation) of relevant laws into each other's languages, the lack of an accord on legal terminology, and the lack of a common investment guide that minimally co-relates terms that are similar or the same but that are in fact characterized differently.

This lack of agreement on terminology is not simply a matter of lexical rigor: The different meanings lead to different investment procedures and confusion. All this confusion represents an obstacle for legal research, translation, mutual understanding, and transparency, and it hampers the will to invest. For those who are undeterred, there is a stronger case for the hiring of third parties' assistance, which is arguably the most costly procedure in starting a business abroad.[82] Hence, it is hoped that this chapter will contribute to continuous and greater cooperation among the BRICS members and an increase in the number of specialized professionals, who will certainly be a welcome source of support in developing the alliance and the innovations that it can bring about.

VI.   References

Blumenfeld, Lane H., 'Russia's New Civil Code: The Legal Foundation for Russia's Emerging Market Economy' (1996) 30(3) *International Lawyer* 477–519.

Braithwaite John and Drahos Peter, *Global Business Regulation* (Cambridge: Cambridge University Press, 2000).

Brazil, Ministry of External Relations, 'About BRICS, Economic Data and Trade Statistics'; available at http://brics.itamaraty.gov.br/about-brics/economic-data [accessed on 10 August 2016].

'BRICS Perspective on International Investment Agreements'; available at http://brics.itamaraty.gov.br/category-english/21-documents/227-brics-perspective-on-international-investment-agreements [accessed on 29 November 2016].

---

[82] 'Most of the cost of starting a business comes from the fees of third-party professionals such as lawyers and notaries. Entrepreneurs use third-party services in business start-up mostly because the process is too complex. Economies with greater third-party involvement in business incorporation tend to have more businesses operating in the informal sector. They also tend to have less accessible laws and regulations and less efficient systems of civil justice.' World Bank, 'Doing Business 2016: Measuring Regulatory Quality and Efficiency', p. 54; available at www.doingbusiness.org/~/media/GIAWB/Doing %20Business/Documents/Annual-Reports/English/DB16-Full-Report.pdfp [accessed on 18 August 2016].

'BRICS Trade and Investment Facilitation Plan'; available at http://brics. itamaraty.gov.br/category-english/21-documents/226-brics-trade-and-investment-facilitation-plan [accessed on 29 November 2016].

'The Strategy for BRICS Economic Partnership'; available at http://brics .itamaraty.gov.br/images/partnershipstrategy_eng.pdf [accessed on 15 November 2016].

De Castro Halis, Denis, 'Rule of Law in the Mainland and in Macau... With 'Chinese Characteristics'?' in Ming Chan et al. (eds.), *Highlights from the EACS' 14 Conference, International Institute of Macau*, 2015, *Macau in Coimbra*, pp. 85–101.

Deloitte, 'Doing Business in Russia 2016'; available at www2.deloitte.com/ru/en/ pages/tax/articles/2016/doing-business-in-russia-2016.html [accessed on 5 December 2016].

Global Investment Center, *Russia Company Laws and Regulations Handbook – Strategic Information and Basic Laws* (Washington DC: Global Investment Center, 2015); available at https://books.google.com/books?id=y8G7Cg AAQBAJ&printsec=frontcover&hl=pt-BR&source=gbs_ge_summary_r &cad=0#v=onepage&q&f=false [accessed on 29 July 2016].

Gu, Minkang, *Understanding Chinese Company Law*, 2nd edn (Hong Kong: Hong Kong University Press, 2010).

Nishith Desai Associates, 'Doing Business in India', June 2015; available at www .nishithdesai.com/fileadmin/user_upload/pdfs/Research%20Papers/Doing_ Business_in_India.pdf [accessed on 2 May 2016].

Norton Rose Fullbright, 'Doing Business in South Africa, 2015'; available at www. nortonrosefulbright.com/files/a-guide-to-doing-business-in-south-africa-126259.pdf [accessed on 2 August 2016].

Sauvant, Karl P., 'New Sources of FDI: The BRICs-Outward FDI from Brazil, Russia, India and China'; (2005) 6 *Journal of World Investment & Trade* 639–709.

South African Institute of International Affairs, 'Economic Diplomacy Programme Policy Briefing No. 63, March 2013'; available at http://www.saiia.org.za/ policy-briefings/173-brics-fdi-a-preliminary-view/file [accessed on 29 July 2016].

Strizh, Vasilisa and Zimbler, Brian L., 'Key Reforms of the Russian Civil Code for Legal Entities', *Morgan Lewis*, 7 August 2014; available at www.morganlewis .com/pubs/bf_lf_keyreformsofrussiancivilcodeforlegalentities_07aug14# sthash.I4akIOeZ.dpuf [accessed on 29 July 2016].

UK-India Business Council, 'Indian FDI Restrictions'; available at www.ukibc.com/ india-guide/how-india/fdi-restrictions/ [accessed on 18 November 2016].

Ulhoa Coelho, Fábio, *Curso de direito comercial*, 4th edn (São Paulo: Saraiva, 2008), vol. 2.

UNCTAD, 'Bilateral FDI Statistics: Brazil'; available at http://unctad.org/Sections/ dite_fdistat/docs/webdiaeia2014d3_BRA.pdf [accessed on 6 November 2016].

'Bilateral FDI Statistics: China'; available at http://unctad.org/Sections/dite_fdistat/docs/webdiaeia2014d3_CHN.pdf [accessed on 29 July 2016].

'Bilateral FDI Statistics: South Africa; available at http://unctad.org/Sections/dite_fdistat/docs/webdiaeia2014d3_ZAF.pdf [accessed on 29 July 2016].

'Bilateral FDI Statistics [2012]: India'; available at http://unctad.org/Sections/dite_fdistat/docs/webdiaeia2014d3_IND.pdf [accessed on 29 July 2016].

'Bilateral FDI Statistics [2012]: Russian Federation'; http://unctad.org/Sections/dite_fdistat/docs/webdiaeia2014d3_RUS.pdf [accessed on 29 July 2016].

'Country Fact Sheet: Brazil'; available at http://unctad.org/sections/dite_dir/docs/wir2016/wir16_fs_br_en.pdf [accessed on 29 July 2016].

'Country Fact Sheet: Russia'; available at http://unctad.org/sections/dite_dir/docs/wir2016/wir16_fs_ru_en.pdf [accessed on 29 July 2016].

'Country Fact Sheet: South Africa'; available at http://unctad.org/sections/dite_dir/docs/wir2016/wir16_fs_za_en.pdf [accessed on 29 July 2016].

'FDI Flows'; available at http://unctad.org/en/Pages/DIAE/Investment%20and%20Enterprise/FDI_Flows.aspx [accessed on 29 July 2016].

Global Investment Trends Monitor, Special Edition, 25 March 2013, 'The Rise of BRICS FDI and Africa'; available at http://unctad.org/en/PublicationsLibrary/webdiaeia2013d6_en.pdf [accessed on 19 November 2016].

World Investment Report 2016, 'Investor Nationality: Policy Challenges', Geneva, 2016; available at http://unctad.org/en/PublicationsLibrary/wir2016_en.pdf [accessed on 29 July 2016].

Wang, Jiangyu, *Company Law in China: Regulation of Business Organizations in a Socialist Market Economy* (Cheltenham: Edward Elgar, 2014).

World Bank. 2016. *Doing Business 2016: Measuring Regulatory Quality and Efficiency*. Washington, DC: World Bank. DOI: 10.1596/978-1-4648-0667-4. License: Creative Commons Attribution CC BY 3.0 IGO.

5

China–Africa and the BRICS

An Insight into the Development Cooperation and Investment Policies

ALIOUNE BADARA THIAM

I. Introduction

Diverse but united, the emerging economies named the BRICS (Brazil, Russia, India, China and South Africa) are to some extent fostering hope for the revival of Africa's economy with an innovative mechanism of cooperation and a development agenda.[1] China is among a number of large new powers in the ascendant in the international system, all of which are deepening their economic relations with Africa. Hitherto China–Africa relations evolved on the foundations of political equality, support and mutual admiration. China's rise and Africa's renaissance are now progressing hand in hand. Despite the numerous controversies regarding this relationship, China is increasingly demonstrating its commitment to deepening its relations with African countries, and in turn these countries consider China as a major trade partner and investor. China also benefits from this cooperation by stabilizing its economic environment, widening its export market, satisfying its increasing need for natural resources and strengthening its identity as an emerging country.

China is coordinating its position with the BRICS in the ambit of the new economic paradigm in Africa. Putting this into a wider context, the BRICS countries have committed themselves to enhancing their

---

[1] China and India are the two demographic heavyweights of the BRICS countries with, respectively, 45 percent and 42 percent of their cumulative population. China appears to be the economic heavyweight of the group. The cumulative GDP of the four other BRICS countries together does not exceed that of China. The share of the BRICS countries in the global GDP is significant, but not proportional to their population share. The smallness of its shares in the GDP and population (3 percent and 2 percent, respectively) makes South Africa the outsider of the BRICS countries. L. Martinet, extractions. UNCTAD, 'The rise of BRICS FDI and Africa' (2013) *Global Investment Trend Monitor*, Special Edition.

cooperation and collaboration to provide Africa's own strategies with a more decisive impetus for inclusive and sustainable development. Within this new paradigm, China and South Africa may jointly support the strategy in ways that significantly promote the economic development agenda of other African countries. Africa–BRICS cooperation is a response to the major challenges facing the continent, and accession to the BRICS rank of major players would allow African countries to increase their ability to make the decisions necessary to pursue their own development goals. The trends analyzed in this chapter indicate that, overall, the BRICS countries and Africa are jointly developing a model of South–South relations that could benefit both entities. The presence of the BRICS provides real opportunities for Africa.

The question remains, however, whether BRICS's presence will generate new forms of dependence. It therefore is important to investigate the approaches underpinning these dealings and the ways in which Africa is taking advantage of them. The combined use of trade and investment requires political and legal coordination in practice. However, the different aforementioned strategies, taking shape from different perspectives, make it difficult to determine whether there is coherence in the trade and investment policies that the BRICS countries have adopted individually with regard to Africa on the one hand and their commitment to Africa on the other. This chapter aims to shed light on the BRICS countries' approaches to the trade and investment relationship with Africa. It briefly assesses the potential impact of economic relations between the BRICS countries from a bilateral standpoint before considering the BRICS–Africa relationships.

II. The Rise of a New Group of Influence in Africa

The African economies have long been dependent on Northern international financial institutions (IFIs) and donors of colonial powers. These days the young continent is taking a leap forwards, moving from neo-colonialism to a sort of neoliberalism.[2] The emerging economies that are exerting a strong influence on the international economic order are gaining market share in Africa. This new trend has given rise to the

---

[2] The European Union remains the main source of development assistance for Africa, but it is Brazil and China that African governments perceive as 'associates'. Conversely, the image of sub-Saharan Africa in developed countries continues to be that of a miserable region plunged into absolute poverty. Diplomats and Brazilian entrepreneurs perceive them as growing economies and associates.

notion that Africa's international relations are undergoing a process of change away from the North and towards the South, with connected debates over the possibility of alternative models of development.[3] Emerging economies have been cited as playing an important role in diversifying Africa's international relations and thus providing Africa new and exciting possibilities.[4] The interaction between Africa and the BRICS countries is based on trade and foreign direct investment (FDI). In this dynamic it is fair from a comparative perspective to assess the interest and commitment of the different emerging powers in Africa before examining their commitment as an organized group.

A. The Emerging Countries' Individual Interests and Strategies in Africa

The BRICS nations have been on the radar of marketers and exporters worldwide for a long time. Although China and India are the primary sources of disruptive market change, they are not alone and their growing presence is opening the space for other new economic and political actors. Each of the BRICS countries, taken individually, has its own history, interest in and strategies for conducting business in Africa. Because these relationships are difficult to assess thoroughly, the trade profile will be reported in a nutshell.

1.   History and Trade Relations between Brazil and Africa

Brazil benefited first from the geographical proximity of the South Atlantic and shares a common history with Africa.[5] Starting with the transatlantic slave trade, the links between Brazil and Africa have been based on trade in goods, economic and social interactions and exchanges of ideas and skills from the sixteenth to the early nineteenth century. In the late 1950s, the relationship between Brazil and the United States began to create favorable conditions for the revitalization of the relations between Brazil and Africa after their gradual marginalization following the independence of Brazil.

---

[3] Iyan Taylor, *The Brics in Africa: Diversifying Dependency* (Dakar: CODESRIA, 2015).

[4] Edwar Miguel, *Africa's Turn?* (Cambridge, MA: MIT Press, 2009).

[5] The Atlantic south of the equator line was the most active economic hub in the early modern world, connecting Africa, the Americas and the early colonizing European states, Portugal and Spain. Winds and ocean currents divide the Atlantic Ocean into two systems, north and south. The South Atlantic system follows the pattern of giant wheels turning counterclockwise, favouring sailing from western African ports to the Americas. The South Atlantic was dominated by merchants who traded only with Brazil.

From January 1961 to the mid-1980s, many significant changes took place in Brazilian foreign policy. This period, except for 1964, the year of Brazil's military coup, witnessed an active political and economic rapprochement with Africa. During the fifth period, extending into the twenty-first century, Africa has become one of the major interests of Brazil's international agenda. The continent is changing rapidly, and Brazil has gradually expressed more interest in supporting and participating in African development. The administration of President Luiz Inácio Lula da Silva (2003–2010) revived Brazil's interest in Africa and set it on a surer footing as part of the attempt to extend Brazil's global influence. Following this dynamic Brazil's foreign policy objectives developed opportunities for South–South cooperation. It intends to increase its diplomatic and economic influence[6] and has ambitions to head the World Trade Organization and to secure a permanent seat on the United Nations Security Council.[7] Thus, the connection with African countries can be helpful, though there are few signs of a coordinated approach towards Brazil from any individual African countries or from groups of African countries. Brazil's interest in Africa reflects its needs for energy (although in recent years Brazil has discovered significant oil deposits of its own) and commodities and to some extent a market for its technology and exports.

When Lula da Silva began to focus his diplomatic efforts on maintaining his relationship with the countries of the South, this policy was perceived as political and less pragmatic by the Brazilian business community. However, in ten years, trade between Brazil and Africa quintupled from USD 5 billion in 2002 to USD 26 billion in 2012. Almost half of its exports are manufactured products. Brazil cooperates especially with Benin, Burkina Faso, Chad and Mali on increasing the production of cotton. Regarding the World Trade Organization, these countries make a common front against the subsidies of the United States for its own cotton producers that directly affect Brazilian and African cotton producers.

---

[6] During these ten years, Brazil increased the number of its embassies in Africa from seventeen to thirty-six, and Brazil's development bank started granting credit lines, whether for airport construction in Mozambique or for the installation of electronic payment systems for the South African autobus.

[7] Brazil is among the G-4 countries, comprising Brazil, Germany, India and Japan, which support each other's bids for permanent seats on the United Nations Security Council. Each of these four countries has figured among the elected nonpermanent members of the Security Council since the UN's establishment. Their economic and political influence has grown significantly in the last decades, reaching a scope comparable to that of the permanent members.

On the import side, Africa has the capacity to benefit from Brazilian expertise in biofuels and pharmaceutical products. In mining and construction, Africa has many opportunities to gain from the expertise and market access provided by large Brazilian commodity firms, particularly in iron ore. Brazilian firms also have expertise in infrastructure, although (as in Angola) they find it hard to compete with Chinese firms.

2.   Africa–Russia Trade Relations

After the implosion of the Union of Soviet Socialist Republics (USSR) in the early 1990s, its heir, the Federal Russia, was virtually absent from the African continent for ten years: It was completely absorbed in its internal reorganization. That slightly reduced its share in the African market, which stood at 2.5 percent in 1986 and fell to 1.9 percent in 1988 and to 0.4 percent in 2001.[8] When Russia was admitted to the Paris Club in 1997, it agreed to reduce considerably most of the debts of African countries with regard to the former USSR by up to 90 percent. The countries that benefited from that reduction include Ethiopia, Somalia, Angola, Mozambique, Tanzania, Guinea and Mali.[9] It was only in 2001, the 'Year of African renaissance,'[10] that the Russian government hosted the presidents of Algeria, Egypt, Nigeria, Guinea and Gabon in Moscow. However, it was in 2006 that the most significant resumption of relations between Russia and Africa occurred, with the spectacular first African tour of President Putin to South Africa and Morocco. This tour was part of the new 'multipolar' diplomacy.

Trade between Africa and Russia has continued to increase. Since 2002, when Morocco became one of the main Russian trade partners in Africa, trade has tripled, reaching nearly USD 1.5 billion in 2005. Crude oil tops Moroccan imports from Russia, followed by iron and steel ore, while Morocco exports citrus fruits, fish meal and fresh vegetables. According to the new three-year agreement, twelve Russian ships, on the condition that they hire Moroccan seamen, have the right to fish annually 12,000 tonnes of pelagic species in Moroccan waters in the Atlantic Ocean.

The economic cooperation of Russia with Africa has reached a milestone; for example, the trade turnover with the countries of sub-Saharan Africa for the period from January to December 2015 was estimated at

---

[8] This statistic refers to the oil market in Libya and the cocoa market in Cote d'Ivoire.
[9] Gilles Troude, 'La Russie en Afrique: le grand retour?' (2009) 25 *Géostratégiques* 165–175, at 166.
[10] Mikhail Lebedev, 'La Russie qui venait du froid' (2010) *Géopolitique Africaine* 211–222.

USD 3.3 billion.[11] It was formalized in March 2016 with the launching of the Africa Business Initiative in Moscow, created with the support of business as a platform for humanitarian, economic and legal expertise. This organization aims to reconstruct and strengthen the relations between Russia and Africa by unifying efforts to promote and support the interests of Russian business in the framework of broader international cooperation on the African continent.[12] It is helping to develop and outline an approach for Russian companies to enter the African market as a whole as reliable business partners. Through this framework it will be possible to consolidate the interests of companies in different sectors, to establish joint strategic initiatives and expand Russia's presence in the investment field.

3.   India–Africa Trade Relations

India and Africa share a long history and interaction that date back to the time of ancient civilizations, including the trade ties between the Nile Valley and the Indus Valley.[13] India's shared colonial heritage with many African countries has contributed significantly to this connection, as has the migration of many Indian workers to Southern and Eastern Africa, establishing large diasporas in these areas.[14] To strengthen its global position, it was necessary for India to establish long-term and strategic partnerships with key allies. This is particularly relevant in the context of India's competitive relationship with China.

India's economic links with Africa were first developed in an ad hoc fashion by corporate bodies that championed greater investment in Africa. The government's economic diplomacy towards Africa became particularly pronounced in March 2002 when the Focus Africa program[15] was

---

[11] Kester Kenn Klomegah, 'Russia–Africa: the realities and the truths', 2016; available at http://moderndiplomacy.eu/index.php?option=com_k2&view=item&id=1484: russia-africa-the-realities-and-the-truths&Itemid=480 [accessed on 26 October 2016].

[12] Ibid.

[13] It dates back thousands of years to the days when Indian traders, using the seasonal monsoon winds, sailed to the east coast of Africa in search of mangrove poles, elephant tusks, and gold and gemstones that made their way up from what is now Zimbabwe. D. Large, 'India's African engagement', in N. Kitchen (ed.), *Emerging Powers in Africa*, LSE-IDEAS special report (2013).

[14] Ibid.

[15] The 'Focus Africa' program was launched in 2002 with a focus on seven countries of the sub-Saharan African (SSA) region – South Africa, Nigeria, Mauritius, Tanzania, Kenya, Ghana and Ethiopia, with a view to widening and deepening India's trade with Africa. The scope of this program was extended, with effect from April 2003, to include Angola,

launched alongside the five-year Foreign Trade Policy 2002–2007.[16] The New India Foreign Trade Procedure is ongoing (2015–2020), designed for regulate importing and exporting of goods in India[17] This policy is in line with India's efforts to become a permanent member of the UN Security Council, in which Africa is seen as a key support base. India aims to have increased influence on international institutions, such as the International Monetary Fund and the World Bank, by giving 'goodwill gestures' of grants to African countries that can then be counted on as allies in multilateral negotiations.[18] Underlying this political diplomacy lies India's interest in being a superpower with a growing market size and rising rate of private consumption.

Trade and investment flow from economic diplomacy, particularly in relation to commercial activities. Both India and Africa are seeking to derive economic benefits from their interactions, and this is largely reflected in the exchange of goods, services and capital between markets. Although India already had good ties with Anglophone countries in southern and eastern Africa, the country aimed to deepen its ties with Francophone and Lusophone countries in an effort to improve resource security, particularly with regard to oil and gas. India's Africa policy in general and trade policy in particular are being shaped by these multiple developments. Along with trade, Indian investment in Africa has obviously increased in recent years. Indian investors used to be most active in the areas traditionally considered to be India's comparative advantage, such as agriculture, communications infrastructure and petroleum refining. Oil constituted 84.57 percent of India's imports from West Africa in 2007–2008. Trade and investment between India and Africa are expected to grow tremendously.[19] To sustain this economic and political diplomacy,

Botswana, Cote d'Ivoire, Madagascar, Mozambique, Senegal, Seychelles, Uganda, Zambia, Namibia and Zimbabwe, along with the six countries of North Africa: Egypt, Libya, Tunisia, Sudan, Morocco and Algeria.

[16] EXIM policy 2002–2007; available at http://pib.nic.in/archieve/eximpol/eximpolicy2002/Exim%20Policy%202002–2007/contents.htm [accessed on 26 October 2016].

[17] Amanda Lucey, Mark Schoeman and Catherine Grant Makokera, 'India–Africa relations: the role of the private sector', *Institute for Security Studies Paper* (2015), p. 285.

[18] For example, the strength of African numbers in trade negotiations with the WTO and their collective bargaining power in concert with India and Brazil in the Doha Round. See, for more details, the *Indian Development Cooperation Research Report*, State of Indian Development Cooperation (Spring 2014).

[19] Trade between Africa and India more than doubled from USD 25 billion in 2007 to USD 57 billion in 2011. By 2013 trade had reached more than USD 67 billion. Projections forecast that the level of trade could increase to USD 80 billion by 2020.

in 2008 the India–Africa Forum Summit (IAFS), which is an official platform for African–Indian relations, was launched. According to the International Monetary Fund, the value of India's exports to Africa increased by more than 100 percent from 2008–2013.

4.   China–Africa Trade Relations

China's history of engagement with Africa can be traced back to the fifteenth century, when Chinese traders visited East Africa. However, the foundation for modern-day Sino-African relationships was laid in the postcolonial period, when China enlarged its cooperation framework with Africa as part of its efforts to demonstrate solidarity with emerging countries[20] China's foreign policy centers on the 'Five Principles of Peaceful Coexistence', which were first applied in a Sino-Indian cooperation agreement signed in 1954. In the year that followed, the principles were also adopted at the Asia–Africa Conference in Bandung (Indonesia), and even today they are among the effective foundations of the nonaligned movement. These five principles are as follows:

1. Mutual non-interference in internal affairs
2. Mutual respect for territorial integrity and sovereignty
3. Mutual non-aggression
4. Equality and mutual benefit
5. Peaceful coexistence

The 'Five Principles' are embedded in the concept of a 'harmonious world', which China announced in 2005 and in which Beijing comes out in favor of cooperative multilateralism.[21] In January 2006 China published a comprehensive Africa strategy for the first time, by which it intends to support the continent's development and its efforts to reach the Millennium Development Goals.[22] Two-way trade impressively rose from USD 40 billion in 2005 to USD 50 billion in 2006, making China Africa's third-largest trading partner after the European Union and the United States. Meanwhile, foreign direct investment inflows to the continent increased substantially as a result of the USD 1.9 billion new investment and business deals signed

---

[20] The classic example of Chinese support was the USD 400 million interest-free loan provided over the period 1970–1975 for the landmark 1,800-km Tanzania–Zambia railway.

[21] Thomas Fues, Sven Grimm and Denise Laufer, *China's Africa Policy: Opportunity and Challenge for European Development Cooperation* (German Development Institute, 2006); available at. www.die-gdi.de/uploads/media/4_2006_EN.pdf. [accessed on 26 October 2016].

[22] FOCAC 2006 concluded a year that was dubbed by the Chinese leadership as China's 'Year of Africa'.

at Forum on China–Africa Cooperation (FOCAC) 2006.[23] The trade and investments relations between China and Africa are still showing increases that are far ahead of those of Brazil, Russia, India and South Africa. The recent trends since the Johannesburg summit in July 2016 show that, in the next four years, trade between China and African countries should increase greatly. According to the draft Johannesburg Action Plan 2016–2018, the two sides will endeavor to increase trade to USD 400 billion by 2020, a sharp increase from the 2014 figure of USD 222 billion. The People's Republic of China and Africa have agreed to

> encourage and support the creation of logistics centres in Africa by Chinese companies, working to regulate and improve the quality of goods exported to China in Africa and to promote trade between China and Africa.

Chinese companies are also encouraged to engage in processing and manufacturing in Africa to satisfy the long-time demand for increased employment locally, technology transfer and human capacity development.

5.   Trade Profile between South Africa and the Other African Countries

The accession to power in 1994 of Nelson Mandela marked South Africa's return to the African scene. Its successful democratization and the internationalization of its economy, combined with the influence of the financial center of Johannesburg, have positioned the country among the large emerging nations. Historically South Africa's trade policy was guided by three interrelated strategies: import-substituting industrialization; the development of strategic industries such as oil, coal and arms; and the development of mineral-related exports.[24] Since 1994, South African businesses have made great strides in Africa, particularly in joint ventures, greenfield investment and mergers and acquisitions in southern Africa. The key to the success of South Africa's investment has been the state's promotional role through entities such as the Industrial Development Corporation and the Development Bank of South Africa. These entities not only provide funding but also become involved in companies by buying shares and sharing investment risks. The sectors of the South

[23] Sanusha, Naidu, 'China-African Relations in the 21st Century: A "Win-Win" Relationship' (2007) 33 *Current African Issues* 41–46.

[24] Taku Furdira, *Economic and Trade Policy Overview* (Trade Law Centre, 2011); available at www.tralac.org/files/2011/11/SA-Africa-trade-at-a-glance-20111116.pdf [accessed on 26 October 2016].

African economy that are taking a lead in investing in Africa in general and in southern Africa in particular include the mining, retail, construction/manufacturing, financial services, telecommunication and tourism sectors.

The economic power of South Africa strongly contributes to its leadership in Africa. Among the top 500 African companies, 127 are South African, which account for more than 60 percent of the turnover of these 500 companies. As mentioned South Africa's economic influence has been felt most strongly in southern Africa.[25] Many countries in the region (Namibia, Malawi, Swaziland, Botswana, Lesotho and Zimbabwe), despite their officially hostile policies in Pretoria, had historically been dependent on South Africa, participating in the Southern African Customs Union (SACU), which was created in 1910; its scope has recently been expanded to the Southern African Development Community (SADC). The quasi-public company Eskom, the leading electricity producer on the continent, illustrates this new boom. It is the dominant utility in southern Africa since 1994, and it is growing beyond the area.[26]

B. The BRICS Countries' Joint Strategies and Commitment in Africa

Many organizations are trying to solve local problems and find ways to enhance business cooperation with the African continent. The BRICS countries aim to be an alternative to the Western domination of the world economy and make the South a pillar in the international economic order. Members of the BRICS share common ideals in the pursuit of economic and social development. Reaching these common goals will be facilitated by joint initiatives of the five countries, sharing experiences and information as well as improving conditions to foster intra-group trade and investment flows. At the same time, the BRICS members are committed to making joint efforts to build a more just and fairer international order. This set of objectives requires a wide-ranging common agenda in the medium to long run.

The current economic BRICS commitments vis-à-vis Africa are becoming yet more important through three main channels: trade, foreign direct investment (FDI) and development assistance. The benefits for BRICS countries of economic cooperation with Africa are increased diplomatic support in international and regional forums, guarantees of energy

---

[25] Ibid.
[26] Philippe Gervais-Lambony, 'L'Afrique du Sud, en Afrique australe et en Afrique' (2012) *Documentation photographique no. 8088.*

security for economic growth, and increases in their exports to Africa, which will both help the BRICS countries to sustain their economic growth and boost the African economy.

The BRICS cooperation is aimed at complementing and strengthening the existing bilateral and multilateral relations between member states. The Strategy for BRICS Economic Partnership will contribute to increasing the economic growth and competitiveness of the BRICS economies in the global arena. Its purposes are to enhance market access opportunities and facilitate market inter-linkages, promote mutual trade and investment and create a business-friendly environment for investors and entrepreneurs in all the BRICS countries. The strategy also seeks to enhance and diversify trade and investment cooperation that has value-added benefits for the BRICS countries, strengthen macroeconomic policy coordination and build resilience to external economic shocks. It also strives to achieve inclusive economic growth to eradicate poverty, address unemployment and promote social inclusion. It shall also promote information exchange through the BRICS Virtual Secretariat and BRICS Economic Exchange Platform as well as agreed platforms and to consolidate efforts to ensure a better quality of growth by fostering innovative economic development based on advanced technologies and skills development with a view to building knowledge economies. Last but not least, there is a need to seek further interaction and cooperation with non-BRICS countries and international organizations and forums. To implement this strategy, BRICS members will engage with the business communities in their respective countries and encourage closer collaboration of BRICS business communities.[27]

The BRICS countries' share in the continent's FDI stock and flows is steadily increasing.[28] The rapid economic growth and industrial upgrading currently taking place in the BRICS countries provide ample scope for their firms to seek opportunities to invest in Africa, including in the manufacturing and service sectors. Indeed, the rise of FDI in manufacturing, which has positive consequences for job creation and industrial growth, is becoming an important facet of South–South economic cooperation.[29] Concentrated primarily in the natural resource sector (oil and minerals), the BRICS countries' FDI in Africa is now diversifying

---

[27] BRICS Information Centre, *The Strategy for BRICS Economic Partnership*, Ufa Summit, 9 July 2015.

[28] See UNCTAD Database (2010), 'Estimated FDI flows and stock to African countries'.

[29] UNCTAD, 'The rise of BRICS FDI and Africa'.

more and more towards sectors such as infrastructure, agriculture, manufacturing and service industries. This reinforces the potential for technology transfer and increases productivity, which is important for economic growth in resource-poor countries. For example, Chinese investments are moving towards natural resources and infrastructure to invest in agriculture and fishing.[30]

Consecutive summits have enhanced economic cooperation between the BRICS countries and Africa. The final communiqué of the Durban Summit in 2015 stated that the first BRICS–Africa dialogue, centered on the theme of 'partnership between the BRICS and Africa', has sent a positive signal of increased cooperation with African countries in the field of infrastructure to promote interconnectivity in Africa and release the development potential of the continent.

At the most recent BRICS summit held in Goa in October 2016, further commitments were made to enhance Africa's sustainable development. There has been progress in operationalizing the Africa Regional Centre (ARC) of the New Development Bank (NDB). The BRICS countries called upon the International Monetary fund (IMF) to strengthen the voice and representation of sub-Saharan Africa. They remain committed to supporting the African Union's (AU) vision, aspirations, goals and priorities for Africa's development enshrined in Agenda 2063. These declarations of intent have aroused the enthusiasm and hope of heads of state and African governments.[31]

Last but not least the BRICS is committed to working closely with all G20 members to strengthen macroeconomic cooperation, improve global economic governance, strengthen international financial architecture, support industrialization in Africa and enhance cooperation on energy access and efficiency.

III. Investing in Africa: What Makes the BRICS Unique?

International economic relations are not the best field for the expression of solidarity between states. As General Charles de Gaulle once said, states do not have friends; they have interests.[32] It would be naive to believe

---

[30] Abdoulaye Soumah, 'How China's trawlers are emptying Guinea's oceans', 2016; available at www.bbc.com/news/world-africa-36734578 [accessed on 26 October 2016].

[31] James-William Gbaguidi, 'Les BRICS en Afrique, une histoire de perception. Entre espoirs et risques de désenchantement' (2013) 248 *Afrique contemporaine* 112–113.

[32] Charles de Gaulle, 'les Etats n'ont pas d'Amis ils n'ont que des intérêts'.

that the BRICS countries, in their relations with African countries, provide the remedy for Western powers' failure to show generosity. The economic potential of the continent is in fact such that the major emerging powers, whether or not they are members of the BRICS, will not have many more scruples than Western powers in the past about maximizing their own interests at the expense of the interests of their African counterparts. The relative rise in profile of the BRICS has occurred simultaneously with internal developments within Africa, whereby, under strong pressure from IFIs and Western donors, many African states have opened up their economies through privatization. In a number of African countries, the elites have bought into the neoliberal prescriptions on how to actively attract foreign investment. These efforts have facilitated the expansion of foreign capital in Africa, mainly from emerging economies. The partnership model proposed between Africa and the BRICS countries is oriented toward three specific areas: trade, foreign direct investment and development assistance. In each of these areas, Africa already has enough experience not to repeat its past mistakes.

African exports are increasingly diversified, generating government revenue, creating added values and being reflected in income distributions. The imports of consumption products from the BRICS generally benefit African consumers, at least in the short term, and reduce their dependence on traditional partners. Consumer products from the BRICS that are sold at a low price shift imports from industrialized countries and thus offer the possibility for a growing number of less fortunate African households to gain access to property for current consumption. Lower prices of imported products also benefit firms using capital goods. In addition, the provision by the BRICS countries of less sophisticated, cheaper and better adapted equipment helps reduce the cost of investment. Cooperation with the BRICS in priority areas can enhance growth, create jobs and accelerate the development of the continent.

A recent report by the United Nations Economic Commission for Africa on the subject of cooperation with the BRICS identified several prospects that would favor the continent, particularly in the area of trade and the processing of raw materials. Other possibilities include economic development that is broad based and driven by cultural exchanges; social, scientific and technological indirect and direct trade; and foreign direct investment. Such developments could lead to the BRICS countries' more rapid dissemination of productive ideas and innovation, faster adoption of new technologies and the more efficient absorption of knowledge, which are key factors in wealth creation.

Regarding development assistance, given that most of the emerging economies are aid recipients themselves, it is understandable that the flow of financial aid from the BRICS members to African countries is relatively low compared with that from the United States, Canada, the European Union and Japan. Yet, capitalizing on their own experiences, the emerging economies are able to offer nonfinancial assistance to their African counterparts in a wide variety of sectors. Such engagement is generally characterized as South–South cooperation and seems to be the most welcome form for African countries. Assistance has been provided in various sectors, including health, agriculture, education and institution building. Given the diverse nature of the emerging economies themselves, they have been able to provide assistance to their African counterparts in different economic and social sectors. For example, Brazil and India have shared experiences in the health sector, especially in their own struggles against HIV/AIDS. Assistance in developing human resources through training has been provided generally by offering scholarships and building schools to in more focused areas such as agriculture, banking, legal issues and technical training. Brazil has built vocational training centers in postconflict areas, while India has sponsored information technology centers and training. Assistance in humanitarian causes has been provided through financial contributions as well as through personnel and materials. The Russian Federation has helped train and equip local staff to handle humanitarian and rescue issues.[33]

However, the relatively low importance of Africa in the BRICS countries' trade, compared with their increasing importance in the trade of the continent, is not without risk. All the advantages of the aforementioned dealings are still significant, but the question remains of whether Africa in the long run will fairly take advantage of development cooperation with the BRICS? Would doing so deepen Africa's dependent position? While the answers to these questions depend on the national context, as a result of their colonial legacy, the present-day economies of the African countries are characterized by lopsided dependence on the exporting of raw materials and the importing of manufactured goods.[34] This assessment was made forty years ago, and there has not been any radical departure

---

[33] United Nations, Office of the Special Adviser on Africa, *Africa's Cooperation with New and Emerging Development Partners: Options for Africa's Development* (New York, 2010).

[34] Richard Harris, 'The political economy of Africa: underdevelopment or revolution', in H. Richard (ed.), *The Political Economy of Africa* (New York: Schenkman, 1975), p. 12.

from such a strategy for most African countries; the postcolonial trajectories are still in force.[35]

African economies are integrated into the global economy in ways that are generally unfavorable to the continent and ensure structural dependence. The geo-economy of Africa depends on two production systems that determine its structures and define its place in the global system. The first production system is the exporting of tropical agricultural products: coffee, cocoa, cotton, peanuts, fruits, oil palm, fish and so on; the second production system, which is not renewable, involves the development of hydrocarbons and the extraction of minerals. This trend appears to not be able to bring sustainable growth to African countries.

IV. Conclusion

Trade, FDI and development assistance form the basis of interactions in the relations between BRICS countries and African countries. The BRICS countries have been involved in Africa as important sources of development for the continent for a long time. China is taking the lead: Its relation with Africa is more significant in terms of development cooperation. The BRICS countries taken individually provide significant opportunities to Africa, but gain more from this cooperation. Yet the fact that the participation of the BRICS countries is based on the principle of non-interference in the internal affairs of states gives African countries some freedom. Thus, African countries have increased their ability to take the necessary decisions to pursue their own development objectives and not those of their donors, ending decades of almost unilateral dependence on Western donors.

The presence of emerging economies in Africa may promote both complementary win–win and competitive win–lose outcomes. At the same time, some of the impacts of interaction may be direct and visible, reflected in bilateral relationships, while others may be indirect and less visible; for example, competition in third-country markets or for scarce global resources.

The trends analyzed in this chapter show that, overall, Africa and the BRICS countries are jointly developing a model of South–South relations that could benefit them both. For the BRICS countries, the interest in developing their relation with Africa is obvious. It gives their members access to raw materials, expands the market for their exports and allows for investments that could eventually bring them large profits and

---

[35] Taylor, *The Brics in Africa*.

strengthen their political and diplomatic prestige. Beyond these common interests, each BRICS country has specific reasons to be interested in one of the African countries. Brazil, India and South Africa aspire to gain the support of African countries to obtain a permanent seat on the UN Security Council. For Africa the prospects opened up by these new times must have a positive impact that will result in the Africa that we want.[36] It will be necessary for African countries not to be locked into the exclusive role of raw material suppliers to the BRICS countries, but instead to develop mutually beneficial common policies to accelerate the development of the continent. One has to bear in mind that individualistic strategies '*du chacun pour soi*' hide the causes of many previous failed partnerships between Africa and the world.[37] It is therefore urgent to assess which policies of African countries will help ensure that the investment in the continent is conducive to sustainable development.

V. References

BRICS Information Centre, 'The Strategy for BRICS Economic Partnership', Ufa Summit, 9 July 2015.

EXIM Policy 2002–2007; available at http://pib.nic.in/archieve/eximpol/eximpolicy2002/Exim%20Policy%202002–2007/contents.htm [accessed on 26 October 2016].

Fues, Thomas, Grimm, Sven and Laufer, Denise, *China's Africa Policy: Opportunity and Challenge for European Development Cooperation* (German Development Institute, 2006); available at www.die-gdi.de/uploads/media/4_2006_EN.pdf [accessed on 26 October 2016].

Furdira, Taku, *Economic and Trade Policy Overview* (Trade Law Centre, 2011).

Gbaguidi, James-William, 'Les BRICS en Afrique, une histoire de perception. Entre espoirs et risques de désenchantement' (2013) 248 *Afrique contemporaine* 112–113; available at www.cairn.info/revue-afrique-contemporaine-2013-4-page-112.htm [accessed on 26 October 2016].

Gervais-Lambony, Philippe, 'L'Afrique du Sud, en Afrique australe et en Afrique' (2012) *Documentation photographique no. 8088*.

Harris, Richard, 'The political economy of Africa: underdevelopment or revolution', in Richard Harris (ed.), *The Political Economy of Africa* (New York: Schenkman, 1975).

---

[36] 'The Africa We Want' is a slogan used by the UNEP. The result is Agenda 2063, a remarkable plan of action to consolidate and position Africa's priorities and concerns in the newly emerged Sustainable Development Agenda. The environment must be placed at the center of Africa's growth and transformation into a prosperous, sustainable continent.

[37] Gbaguidi, 'Les BRICS en Afrique, une histoire de perception'.

Klomegah, Kester Kenn, 'Russia–Africa: the realities and the truths', 2016; available at http://moderndiplomacy.eu/index.php?option=com_k2&view=item&id =1484:russia-africa-the-realities-and-the-truths&Itemid=480 [accessed on 26 October 2016].

Large, D., 'India's African engagement', in N. Kitchen (ed.), *Emerging Powers in Africa* (London: LSE-IDEAS Special Report, 2013).

Lebedev, Mikhail, 'La Russie qui venait du froid' (2010) *Géopolitique Africaine* 211– 222.

Lucey, Amanda, Schoeman, Mark and Makokera, Catherine Grant, 'India–Africa relations: the role of the private sector', *Institute for Security Studies Paper* (2015).

Miguel, Edwar, *Africa's Turn?* (Cambridge, MA: MIT Press, 2009).

Sanusha, Naidu, 'China-African Relations in the 21st Century: A "Win-Win" Relationship' (2007) 33 *Current African Issues* 41–46.

Soumah, Abdoulaye, 'How China's trawlers are emptying Guinea's oceans', 2016; available at www.bbc.com/news/world-africa-36734578 [accessed on 26 October 2016].

Taylor, Iyan, *The Brics in Africa: Diversifying Dependency* (Dakar: CODESRIA, 2015).

Troude, Gilles, 'La Russie en Afrique: le grand retour?' (2009) 25 *Géostratégiques* 165–175.

UNCTAD, 'Estimated FDI flows and stock to African countries', *UNCTAD Database* (2010).

'The rise of BRICS FDI and Africa', *Global Investment Trend Monitor*, Special Edition (2013).

United Nations, Office of the Special Adviser on Africa, *Africa's Cooperation with New and Emerging Development Partners: Options for Africa's Development* (New York: United Nations, 2010).

6

Global Fragmentation of Competition Law and BRICS

Adaptation or Transformation?

ALEXANDR SVETLICINII

I. Introduction

We stand ready to work with others, developed and developing countries together, on the basis of universally recognized norms of international law and multilateral decision making, to deal with the challenges and the opportunities before the world today.[1]

The economic growth of the BRICS countries[2] – Brazil, Russia, India, China and South Africa – and their increasing consolidation in the international arena as active participants in global governance have attracted significant attention from scholars in various disciplines dealing with a diverse range of global challenges, such as trade,[3] investment,[4] finance,[5] energy,[6] information technology,[7] health

---

[1] Fourth BRICS Summit, New Delhi Declaration, 29 March 2012, para. 4.

[2] See Jim O' Neill, 'Building Better Global Economic BRICs', Goldman Sachs Global Economics Paper No. 66, 30 November 2001; available at www.goldmansachs.com/our-thinking/archive/archive-pdfs/build-better-brics.pdf [accessed on 5 November 2016].

[3] See e.g. Thomas Osang, 'World Trade and Investment: Where Do the BRICs Stand?' (2012) 18 *Law and Business Review of the Americas* 515–536.

[4] See e.g. Anjali Sane, 'India and the BRICS Countries: Analysis of the Pattern of FDI (Foreign Direct Investment)' (2015) 6(4) *Journal of Commerce & Management Thought* 613–623.

[5] See e.g. Andrew F. Cooper and Asif B. Farooq, 'Testing the Club Dynamics of the BRICS: The New Development Bank from Conception to Establishment' (2015) 10(2) *International Organisations Research Journal* 1–15.

[6] See e.g. David M. Arseneau, 'Explaining the Energy Consumption in a Cross-Section of Countries: Are the BRICs Different?' (2012) 18 *Law and Business Review of the Americas* 553–584.

[7] See e.g. Christopher A. Buscaglia and Miriam F. Weismann, 'How 'Cybersafe' Are the BRICS?' (2012) 15(2) *Journal of Legal, Ethical and Regulatory Issues* 61–91.

care[8] and legal research,[9] to mention but a few. The BRICS platform itself has been seen as a 'failed alliance', a 'boom-to-bust decline', 'façade of unity', successful response to financial crisis, an increasingly influential geopolitical bloc, 'Russia's counter-hegemonic coalition', a broader developing country coalition, a stand-alone success, a competitor to G-8, a cooperation partner of G-20 and many other things.[10] Despite the divergent appreciation of BRICS achievements and approaches towards various global challenges both as a strategic alliance and as a group of influential global actors, studies of BRICS experiences in different areas continue to be made, indicating increasing interest from the scholars of various disciplines who are searching for new 'bricks' that could lay the foundation of alternative and/or innovative solutions to emerging global problems.

For various reasons, despite its global significance and widespread presence in the context of the globalization of trade flows and the liberalization of domestic and international markets, the international community has not yet managed to construct a multilateral mechanism for competition law enforcement or competition policy coordination. Unlike regional integrationist structures with a common market and supranational competition law regime, such as the European Union (EU), the BRICS countries lack a geographic connection and shared language, and their cultural, economic, political and social history reflects many more differences than common features. Despite these differences the significance of competition policy in these large global economies has prompted a certain degree of cooperation and the sharing of experience amongst them. The most visible examples of this cooperation are the biennial BRICS competition conferences, held in Kazan (Russia) in 2009,[11] in Beijing (China) in 2011,[12] in New Delhi (India) in 2013,[13] and most recently in Durban (South Africa) in 2015.[14]

---

[8] See e.g. Robert Marten, Diane McIntyre, Claudia Travassos, Sergey Shishkin, Wang Longde, Srinath Reddy and Jeanette Vega, 'An Assessment of Progress towards Universal Health Coverage in Brazil, Russia, India, China, and South Africa (BRICS)' (2014) 384 *Health Policy* 2164–2171.

[9] See e.g. Jacquelynn M. Jordan, 'The Legal Aspects of BRICS and the Contribution of Jurists' (2013) 1 *China Legal Science* 156–160.

[10] See John J. Kirton, 'Explaining the BRICS Summit's Solid, Strengthening Success' (2015) *International Organisations Research Journal* 9–31, at 10–12.

[11] First BRIC International Competition Conference, 1 September 2009, Kazan (Russia).

[12] Second BRICS International Competition Conference, 20–22 September 2011, Beijing (China); available at www.brics2011.org.cn/ [accessed on 5 November 2016].

[13] Third BRICS International Competition Conference, 21–22 November 2013, New Delhi (India).

[14] Fourth BRICS International Competition Conference, 10–13 November 2015, Durban (South Africa); available at http://brics2015.co.za/ [accessed on 5 November 2016].

The distinguished US antitrust scholar William Kovacic emphasized the significance of studying BRICS experience in competition enforcement in the following way:

> The BRICS nations supply informative contexts in which to analyze the establishment of competition policy systems at the national level and to derive further lessons about superior approaches for other jurisdictions. They provide an opportunity for both older and newer competition systems to revisit basic questions about institutional foundations for successful implementation, the life cycle of antitrust regimes, and measures of effectiveness.[15]

The emergence of the BRICS countries as pivotal actors in the sphere of competition law has been seen as a challenge to the uncontested US hegemony in this field.[16] Competition law practitioners have focused their attention on the national competition regimes of BRICS jurisdictions,[17] and academics have engaged in the comparative analysis of enforcement practices in the BRICS countries.[18] At the same time, little attention has been accorded to their potential contribution to resolving the current impasse in the development of an international competition law framework and their potential role as trendsetters for competition policy development in developing countries and for new competition law regimes in general.[19]

The present chapter attempts to fill the existing gap in the academic literature by analyzing the actual and potential contribution of the BRICS group to overcoming or shifting the international fragmentation of the competition law based on national enforcement. Analysis of current BRICS competition initiatives and cooperation mechanisms will provide a better understanding of the BRICS approach (if it exists) to

---

[15] William Kovacic, 'Competition Law in the BRICS Countries: More than an Acronym', in Adrian Emch, Jose Regazzini and Vassily Rudomino (eds.), *Competition Law in the BRICS Countries* (Alphen aan den Rijn: Kluwer Law International, 2012), pp. 324–325.

[16] See Imelda Maher, 'Competition Law Fragmentation in a Globalizing World' (2015) 40(2) *Law & Social Inquiry* 553–571.

[17] See e.g. Adrian Emch, Jose Regazzini and Vassily Rudomino (eds.), *Competition Law in the BRICS Countries* (Alphen aan den Rijn: Kluwer Law International, 2012).

[18] See e.g. Frederic Jenny and Yannis Katsoulacos (eds.), *Competition Law Enforcement in the BRICS and in Developing Countries: Legal and Economic Aspects* (Springer, 2016); Sasha-Lee Afrika and Sascha-Dominik Bachmann, 'Cartel Regulation in Three Emerging BRICS Economies: Cartel and Competition Policies in South Africa, Brazil, and India – A Comparative Overview' (2011) 45(4) *International Lawyer* 975–1003.

[19] See e.g. Ioannis Lianos, 'Global Governance of Antitrust and the Need for a BRICS Joint Research Platform in Competition Law and Policy', *CLES Research Paper Series* 5/2016, August 2016; available at www.ucl.ac.uk/cles/research-paper-series [accessed on 5 November 2016].

the role of competition enforcement, substantive and procedural competition rules, and the international cooperation in competition enforcement. Most importantly, the proposed analysis is an attempt to understand whether BRICS are capable and/or willing to move beyond a mere interest in mutual learning and the development of domestic competition laws and policies, and to work towards an international framework for competition law enforcement.

The discussion is structured as follows. Section II briefly describes the current international fragmentation of competition law, failed attempts to establish a multilateral enforcement mechanism and the emergence of the BRICS national competition regimes in that context. Section III highlights the milestones of intra-BRICS cooperation in the field of competition law and policy. In Section IV we look at the specifics of the BRICS platform and its suitability for international dialogue on cooperation in competition matters. Section V summarizes the challenges faced by the BRICS countries in formulating their own 'BRICS way' in competition enforcement cooperation. Finally, we offer concluding remarks and outline directions for future research.

II. Global Fragmentation of Competition Law and BRICS

In general, the laws that are applied to global markets are not themselves global – or even transnational! Instead, the laws of individual states govern global markets. In this legal regime, law does not perform an integrative or embedding function. It often has the opposite effect – it creates borders and concomitant tensions and conflicts.[20]

The 1948 Havana Charter foresaw the establishment of the International Trade Organization, which obliged its members to prevent 'business practices affecting international trade which restrain competition, limit access to markets, or foster monopolistic control' and set up investigation and reporting procedures for individual complaints about such practices.[21] The US Senate refused to ratify the Havana Charter,[22] thereby preventing the establishment of an international economic governance

---

[20] David J. Gerber, *Global Competition Law, Markets, and Globalization* (Oxford: Oxford University Press, 2010), p. 3.

[21] Art. 46, Havana Charter for an International Trade Organization; available at www.wto.org/english/docs_e/legal_e/havana_e.pdf [accessed on 5 November 2016].

[22] See Richard Toye, 'Developing Multilateralism: The Havana Charter and the Fight for the International Trade Organization, 1947–1948' (2003) 25(2) *International History Review* 282–305.

framework that would have simultaneously encompassed and united trade, employment and development goals under the aegis of one international organization.[23]

The importance of protecting market competition for the purpose of securing free trade has been recognized by World Trade Organization members, and in 1996 they set up the Working Group on the Interaction between Trade and Competition Policy with the mandate 'to study issues raised by Members relating to the interaction between trade and competition policy, including anti-competitive practices, in order to identify any areas that may merit further consideration in the WTO framework'.[24] WTO members recognized 'the case for a multilateral framework to enhance the contribution of competition policy to international trade and development, and the need for enhanced technical assistance and capacity-building in this area'[25] in the Doha Ministerial Declaration. However, the impasse of the Doha Round affected negotiations on competition issues, and in 2004 it was decided that competition policy 'will not form part of the Work Programme set out in that Declaration and therefore no work towards negotiations on any of these issues will take place within the WTO during the Doha Round'.[26]

Despite the suspension of the multilateral negotiations on this international framework, competition law and policy have been developing rapidly at both national and regional levels. The adoption of competition legislation became especially widespread with the end of the Cold War, when various developing countries, under the external influence of

---

[23] See Daniel Drache, 'The Short but Significant Life of the International Trade Organization: Lessons for Our Time', *Centre for the Study of Globalization and Regionalisation*, CSGR Working Paper No. 62/00, November 2000; available at http://wrap.warwick.ac.uk/2063/1/WRAP_Drache_wp6200.pdf [accessed on 5 November 2016].

[24] WTO Ministerial Declaration adopted on 13 December 1996, WT/MIN(96)/DEC, para. 20; available at www.wto.org/english/thewto_e/minist_e/min96_e/singapore_declaration96_e.pdf [accessed on 5 November 2016]. See also Bernard M. Hoekman and Petros C. Mavroidis, 'Competition, Competition Policy and the GATT' (1994) 17(2) *World Economy* 121–150; Roger Zach (ed.), *Towards WTO Competition Rules: Key Issues and Comments on the WTO Report (1998) on Trade and Competition* (Kluwer, 1999); Aaditya Mattoo and Arvind Subramanian, 'Multilateral Rules on Competition Policy: A Possible Way Forward' (1997) 31(5) *Journal of World Trade* 95–115.

[25] WTO Ministerial Declaration adopted on 20 November 2001, WT/MIN(01)DEC/1, para. 23; available at www.wto.org/english/thewto_e/minist_e/min01_e/mindecl_e.pdf [accessed on 5 November 2016].

[26] Doha Work Programme, Decision Adopted by the General Council on 1 August 2004, WT/L/579; available at www.wto.org/english/tratop_e/dda_e/ddadraft_31jul04_e.pdf [accessed on 5 November 2016].

international bodies (such as WTO, the Organization for Economic Cooperation and Development (OECD), World Bank, etc.)[27] and major trading partners[28] were incentivized to adopt competition legislation as a tool for achieving economic development.[29] By 2009 the number of national competition authorities (NCAs) joining the International Competition Network (ICN) has reached 104, from 92 jurisdictions.[30]

In the absence of a binding multilateral treaty on competition issues, international organizations are largely involved in communication, policy research, competition advocacy and the adoption of nonbinding best practices for competition enforcement. Among the supranational competition law regimes established at the regional level are the EU Internal Market, with its European Competition Network (ECN), the West African Economic and Monetary Union (WAEMU)[31] and the Caribbean Community (CARICOM)[32] where anti-competitive cross-border behavior is investigated and prosecuted under the rules of the respective regional

---

[27] See e.g. Julien Moiroux, 'The Internalization of Competition Policy: The EU and the WTO Between Boldness and Rally' (2009) 2 *Global Antitrust Review* 38–60.

[28] Competition provisions have been often included in bilateral preferential trade agreements. Although predominantly nonbinding, they have, nevertheless, fostered the development of competition legislation in the signatory countries. See Daniel Sokol, 'Order without (Enforceable) Law: Why Countries Enter into Non-Enforceable Competition Policy Chapters in Free Trade Agreements' (2008) 83 *Chicago-Kent Law Review* 231–292; Michal Gal and Inbal Wassmer-Faibish, 'Regional Agreements of Developing Jurisdictions: Unleashing the Potential', in Josef Drexl, Mor Bakhoum, Eleanor M. Fox, Michal S. Gal and David J. Gerber (eds.) *Competition Policy and Regional Integration in Developing Countries* (Cheltenham: Edward Elgar, 2012).

[29] See e.g. Dina I. Waked, 'Competition Law in the Developing World: The Why and How of Adoption and Its Implications for International Competition Law' (2008) 1 *Global Antitrust Review* 69–96.

[30] International Competition Network, 'Factsheet and Key Messages', at 1; available at www.internationalcompetitionnetwork.org/uploads/library/doc608.pdf [accessed on 5 November 2016].

[31] See Mor Bakhoum and Julia Molestina, 'Institutional Coherence and Effectiveness of a Regional Competition Policy: The Case of the West African Economic and Monetary Union (WAEMU)', in Josef Drexl et al. (eds.), *Competition Policy and Regional Integration in Developing Countries*.

[32] See Alina Kaczorowska-Ireland, *Competition Law in the CARICOM Single Market and Economy* (New York: Routledge, 2014) and 'The Objectives of the Competition Policy of the CARICOM Single Market and Economy and Their Importance to the Development of a Coherent and Comprehensive Body of Substantive CSME Competition Rules' (2012) 8(2) *Competition Law Review* 185–207; Delroy S. Beckford, 'Implementing Effective Competition Policy through Regional Trade Agreements: The Case of CARICOM', and Taimoon Stewart, 'Regional Integration in the Caribbean: The Role of Competition Policy', in Josef Drexl et al. (eds.), *Competition Policy and Regional Integration in Developing Countries*.

competition regimes. In the rest of the world, export cartels continue to be shielded from competition enforcement in their home countries (because they do not restrict competition in domestic markets),[33] and multinational corporations continue to engage in various restrictive business practices in individual jurisdictions where such practices are permitted by national competition law or where the competition authorities lack the vigor or enforcement powers to effectively combat such practices.

The BRICS countries have developed their own competition law regimes in the context of the 'universal proliferation' and 'global convergence' of competition laws.[34] The establishment of the modern competition law regime in Brazil dates back to the adoption of the 1994 Competition Act,[35] which was reformed in 2012 with the restructuring of the institutional framework for competition enforcement.[36] The Brazilian competition authority – the Council for Economic Defense – has been praised for 'leading the way to faster, more efficient and more effective enforcement and the consolidation of a competition culture in Brazil'.[37]

---

[33] See e.g. Marek Martyniszyn, 'Export Cartels: Is It Legal to Target Your Neighbour? Analysis in Light of Recent Case Law' (2012) 15(1) *Journal of International Economic Law* 181–222; Brendan Sweeney, 'Export Cartels: Is There a Need for Global Rules?' (2007) 10(1) *Journal of International Economic Law* 87–115.

[34] See e.g. Eleanor M. Fox and Michael J. Trebilcock, 'Introduction: The GAL Competition Project: The Global Convergence of Process Norms', in Eleanor M. Fox and Michael J. Trebilcock (eds.), *The Design of Competition Law Institutions* (Oxford: Oxford University Press, 2013), pp. 1–48; David J. Gerber, 'Asia and Global Competition Law Convergence', in Michael Dowdle, John Gillespie and Imelda Maher (eds.), *Asian Capitalism and the Regulation of Competition: Towards a Regulatory Geography of Global Competition Law* (Cambridge: Cambridge University Press, 2013), pp. 36–52; Leonardo T. Orlanski, 'Searching for the Basis of International Convergence in Competition Law and Policy' (2011) 4 *Global Antitrust Review* 7–47.

[35] Law No. 8,884 of 11 June 1994, published in Diário Oficial da União on 13 June 1994.

[36] See e.g. Marco Botta, 'The Brazilian Senate passes the text of the New Competition Act introducing a more efficient merger control system', 2 December 2010, *e-Competitions Bulletin* December 2010, no. 35224; Fiona A. Schaeffer, Luis Riesgo, S. Wade Angus and Michael Culhane Harper, 'Brazil's Congress approves a new competition law that significantly restructures the landscape of competition enforcement', 5 October 2011, *e-Competitions Bulletin* October 2011, no. 50116; Diego Herrera Moraes, 'The Brazilian President approves the new competition law introducing substantive reforms to the national antitrust enforcement', 30 November 2011, *e-Competitions Bulletin* November 2011, no. 42231; Fiona A. Schaeffer, Luis Riesgo, S. Wade Angus and Michael Culhane Harper, 'The Brazilian Parliament approves new competition law subject to prior significant vetoes', 1 December 2011, *e-Competitions Bulletin* December 2011, no. 50121.

[37] Vinicius Marques de Carvalho, 'Questions & Answers', in Cristianne Zarzur, Krisztian Katona and Mariana Villela (eds.), *Overview of Competition Law in Brazil* (São Paulo: IBRAC, 2015), p. 40.

The current competition law regime in Russia was set up in 2006[38] and is being enforced by the government-subordinated Federal Anti-Monopoly Service (FAS), a large administrative agency with more than 3,000 personnel, charged with the enforcement of anti-monopoly regulation, unfair competition and advertising, tariff regulation, public procurement control, foreign investment control and defense procurement.[39] In 2007 the FAS hosted the 6th Annual Conference of the ICN. In India, the 2002 Competition Act came into force in phases, starting with antitrust provisions in 2009, followed by merger control in 2011.[40] The Chinese antitrust regime is based on the 2007 Anti-Monopoly Law, which has already passed the five-year mark from the start of its effective enforcement.[41] In South Africa, the Competition Commission works under the 1998 Competition Act and enjoys significant support from the government and civil society for its transformative role in the national economy.[42]

All the BRICS NCAs have participated in the activities of the ICN, as well as the regional competition cooperation frameworks of their respective countries. The Brazilian NCA joined the 2009 MERCOSUR cooperation initiatives in the fields of antitrust and merger control.[43] The Russian FAS works with the NCAs of the Commonwealth of Independent States (CIS) on the basis of the 2000 CIS Agreement on implementation of a coordinated anti-monopoly policy.[44] The BRICS countries have also

[38] Law No. 135-FZ of 26 July 2006, as amended on 5 October 2015 (entry into force 10 January 2016).

[39] See Igor Artemyev, 'Regulator's Introduction: Recent Activities and Policy Priorities in Russia', in Adrian Emch et al. (eds.) *Competition Law in the BRICS Countries*, pp. 57–66.

[40] See e.g. Cyril Shroff and Nisha Kaur Uberoi, 'India', in Katrina Groshinski and Caitlin Davies (eds.), *Competition Law in Asia Pacific: A Practical Guide* (The Hague: Kluwer Law International, 2015), pp. 235–297.

[41] Anti-Monopoly Law of the People's Republic of China was adopted by the Standing Committee of the 10th National People's Congress on 30 August 2007 and was effective as of 1 August 2008. See e.g. Adrian Emch and David Stallibrass (eds.), *China's Anti-Monopoly Law: The First Five Years* (Alphen aan den Rijn: Kluwer Law International, 2014); Dan Wei, 'Antitrust in China: An Overview of Recent Implementation of Anti-Monopoly Law' (2013) 14(1) *European Business Organization Law Review* 119–139.

[42] See e.g. Shan Ramburuth, 'Regulator's Introduction: Recent Activities and Policy Priorities in South Africa', in Adrian Emch et al. (eds.), *Competition Law in the BRICS Countries*, pp. 207–217.

[43] See e.g. Marco Botta, 'The Cooperation between the Competition Authorities of the Developing Countries: Why It Does Not Work? Case Study on Argentina and Brazil' (2009) 5(2) *Competition Law Review* 153–178.

[44] See CIS Economic Council, Decision on directions for cooperation in the field of anti-monopoly policy of the CIS States of 12 March 2004; available at http://e-cis.info/page .php?id=23147 [accessed on 5 November 2016].

entered into a number of bilateral governmental and institutional agreements on cooperation and information exchanges: Brazil-Russia in 2001, India-Russia in 2011,[45] and Brazil-China in 2012.[46]

III.   BRICS Cooperation in the Field of Competition Law and Policy

We will continue our joint efforts aimed at improving competition policy and enforcement.[47]

This overview of competition regimes in the BRICS countries demonstrates that the establishment and development of national competition legislation, NCAs, enforcement practices and competition culture have been largely carried out outside the BRICS framework of cooperation. By the time BRICS was formalized as an international grouping in 2011[48] all its members had their competition protection frameworks in place. As a result, subsequent cooperation has been focused on the enhancement of existing competition law regimes through the processes of experience sharing, mutual learning, information exchanges and discussions of recurrent issues in competition enforcement.

The first recognition of the importance of cooperation in the field of competition law and policy was spelled out in the Brasília Declaration adopted at the 2010 BRIC Summit in Brazil, where the parties welcomed the Conference of Competition Authorities as a sectoral initiative in BRIC cooperation.[49] The Fortaleza Declaration adopted at the 2014 BRICS Summit in Brazil highlighted BRICS' understanding of the competition policy's importance for the 'open world economy with efficient allocation of resources, free flow of goods, and fair and orderly competition to the benefit of all'[50] in the following way:

---

45 A Memorandum of Understanding (MoU) between Competition Commission and Federal Antimonopoly Service was signed on 16 December 2011 in the presence of Indian prime minister Manmohan Singh and Russian president Dmitry Medvedev in Moscow.

46 See Allan Fels, Xiaoye Wang, Jessica Su and Wendy Ng, 'The Chinese State Administration for Industry and Commerce and the Brazilian Conselho Administrativo de Defesa Econômica sign a memorandum of understanding', 13 September 2012, *e-Competitions Bulletin* September 2012, no. 74336.

47 Seventh BRICS Summit Declaration (9 July 2015) Ufa, para. 25.

48 South Africa joined the BRIC countries in 2011 at the BRICS Summit in Sanya (China) on 14 April 2011. In the Sanya Declaration (para. 2), 'The Heads of State and Government of Brazil, Russia, India and China welcome South Africa joining the BRICS and look forward to strengthening dialogue and cooperation with South Africa within the forum'.

49 Second BRIC Summit Declaration (16 April 2010), Brasília, para. 27.

50 Sixth BRICS Summit Declaration (15 July 2014), Fortaleza, para. 21.

> We will continue to improve competition policy and enforcement, under-
> take actions to address challenges that BRICS Competition Authorities face
> and further enable competitive environments in order to enhance contri-
> butions to economic growth in our economies.[51]

Finally, at the 2015 BRICS Summit in Russia the BRICS countries declared their intention 'to facilitate market inter-linkages, robust growth and an inclusive and open world economy characterized by efficient resource distribution, free movement of capital, labour and goods, and fair and efficiently regulated competition'.[52] They recognized that as important emerging markets and developing countries they are faced with many similar problems related to economic development and competition. To strengthen cooperation among the BRICS competition authorities it was proposed to conclude a sectoral Memorandum of Understanding to jointly study the issues of competition in important economic sectors.[53]

The general directions for cooperation in the field of competition law and policy formulated by the political leaders of BRICS at the annual sum-mits have been followed in the sectoral cooperation developed by the BRICS NCAs. The biennial BRICS competition conferences reflect the specifics of the competition problems faced by BRICS countries as emerg-ing economies. The keynote speaker of the plenary session of the first BRIC Competition Conference noted that the specifics of the legal and economic systems of the BRIC countries have a distinct imprint on the way they enforce their competition laws, 'which may not be exactly sim-ilar to other jurisdictions, even when they might have the experience of implementing these laws for a considerable period of time'.[54] At the sec-ond BRICS Competition Conference, the chairperson of the Indian NCA emphasized the importance of BRICS cooperation in the field of compe-tition regulation, calling for 'a comprehensive international cooperation strategy'.[55] This approach was carried forward to the third BRICS Compe-tition Conference, which called for international cooperation 'on the basis

---

[51] Ibid, para. 69.

[52] Seventh BRICS Summit Declaration (9 July 2015) Ufa, para. 12.   [53] Ibid., para. 25.

[54] Dhanendra Kumar, Address at the Plenary Session 'Challenges of Competition Policy Development in the BRIC Countries', 2009 BRIC Competition Conference, 1 September 2009, para. 30; available at www.slideshare.net/compad123/international-competition-conference-bric-2009-challenges-of-competition-policy-development-in-the-bric-countries [accessed on 5 November 2016].

[55] Keynote speech by Harish Chandra Gupta, Officiating Chairperson of the Competition Commission of India, para. 30; available at www.brics2011.org.cn/english/jzlt_en/zzfy_en/201109/t20110929_119878.html [accessed on 5 November 2016].

of home-grown solutions proposed by BRICS competition authorities as well as the experience of more mature jurisdictions'.[56]

In the joint statement issued at the fourth BRICS International Competition Conference the representatives of the NCAs agreed to continue their cooperation aimed at 'improving competition law and policy enforcement in order to achieve growth in our economies and the protection of consumers'.[57] The BRICS NCAs have highlighted the importance of the 'strengthening of the cooperation and coordination between the BRICS competition authorities' and agreed 'to conclude the Memorandum of Understanding in the field of competition policy in order to strengthen the cooperation and coordination between the BRICS competition authorities'.[58] The expected forms of such cooperation include 'sharing of best practices in respect of laws, rules and policies; joint participation in capacity building initiatives such as conferences and seminars; the conduct of joint studies and coordination in enforcement proceedings'.[59]

The topics addressed at the BRICS competition conferences reflected the specific needs of these emerging and developing economies. For example, during the 2011 BRICS Competition Conference the participants discussed the issues of the control of large transnational mergers, trade barriers and anti-monopoly enforcement, anti-monopoly control over natural monopoly industries, coordination between competition policy and industrial policy, capacity building and competition advocacy, and international cooperation in anti-monopoly enforcement.[60] In addition to engaging in a discussion of emerging issues in the field of competition law and policy, the BRICS NCAs have engaged in more systematic information exchanges and communications. For example, the BRICS Working Group for Research of Competition Issues on the BRICS Markets of Social Importance, led by the Russian FAS, has declared its objectives to be the promotion of a competitive environment and the support of competitive price formation in markets of social importance. These markets

---

[56] Keynote Address by Sachin Pilot, Honorable Minister of State for Corporate Affairs; available at www.cci.gov.in/sites/default/files/event%20document/Speech_MinisterMCA_3rdBRICS_nov212013.pdf [accessed on 5 November 2016].

[57] Joint Statement of the Heads of BRICS Competition Authorities, 13 November 2015; available at www.compcom.co.za/wp-content/uploads/2015/11/JOINT-STATEMENT-OF-THE-HEADS-OF-BRICS-COMPETITION-AUTHORITIES.pdf [accessed on 5 November 2016].

[58] Ibid.   [59] Ibid.

[60] Agenda of the 2011 BRICS International Competition Conference; available at www.brics2011.org.cn//english/dhrc_en/ [accessed on 5 November 2016].

include telecommunications, pharmaceuticals and health care, construction, energy and the food industry.[61]

IV. BRICS as an Alternative Platform for International Competition Law Cooperation

The history shows that the kind of competition regimes now in place in developed countries are of recent vintage and may not be appropriate for countries at an earlier stage of development[62]

The work of the WTO Working Group on the Interaction between Trade and Competition Policy, as well as the competition policy activities of other multinational forums such as the United Nations Conference on Trade and Development (UNCTAD), OECD and the World Bank, has been criticized for the insufficient attention paid to the relationship between competition policy and developmental goals, which is of vital importance to developing countries.[63] For example, India has been very vocal in raising developmental concerns within the WTO Working Group, where it opposed the multilateral competition agreement on the following grounds:

> Until such time as developed countries are willing to consider the impact of mergers on consumers in foreign countries, to rescind the exemption of export cartels in their competition laws, to give serious consideration to enforcing the UNCTAD Set of measures to control restrictive business practices (RBPs), and to extend the benefits of "positive comity" in competition law enforcement to developing countries, the latter will have to retain the right to challenge foreign mergers and RBPs that have an effect on domestic consumers.[64]

The failure of WTO dialogue on competition policy and current efforts by the World Bank and OECD to breach the gap between competition policy

---

[61] Federal Anti-Monopoly Service, Concept of the BRICS Working Group; available at http://fas.gov.ru/international-partnership/briks/rabochaya-gruppa-briks/ [accessed on 5 November 2016].

[62] Aditya Bhattacharjea, 'The Case for a Multilateral Agreement on Competition Policy: A Developing Country Perspective' (2006) 9(2) *Journal of International Economic Law* 293–323 at 323.

[63] See e.g. Ajit Singh, 'Competition Policy, Development and Developing Countries', *Indian Council for Research on International Economic Relations*, Working Paper No. 50, November 1999.

[64] Working Group on the Interaction between Trade and Competition Policy, Communication from India, WT/WGTCP/W/216, 26 September 2002, para 3.

and development[65] indicate that international dialogue on the relationship between competition law and policy, economic development, industrial policy, and the eradication of poverty and unemployment is likely to continue until developing countries are properly 'convinced' of the need and form of a competition regime that would suit their developmental needs.

When discussing the prerequisites for the establishment of the WTO-led multilateral competition agreement, David J. Gerber pointed out that, unlike the US antitrust approach that prioritizes economic efficiency, the WTO competition law regime will have to incorporate various developmental goals, which 'will require serious and creative thought in defining the relationships among the goals themselves and relating them to the objectives of the WTO as an institution'.[66] Mindful of this diversity in objectives of competition policy, the 2007 UNCTAD Model Competition Law provided that the objective of competition law is to prevent restrictive business practices 'which limit access to markets or otherwise unduly restrain competition, adversely affecting domestic or international trade or economic development'.[67] The UNCTAD commentary is, however, concerned that the inclusion of public interest goals in competition law may outweigh the 'original objective' of competition law, which is to address the impact of certain commercial practices on competition.[68]

When they began cooperating in this field, the BRICS countries acknowledged their acceptance of the multiple goals that can be pursued in competition law and policy. The national competition legislation of BRICS countries attributes a variety of public policy objectives to competition enforcement: the social function of property (Brazil), the position of historically disadvantaged people (South Africa), freedom of

---

[65] See e.g. World Bank/OECD initiative Promoting Effective Competition Policies for Shared Prosperity and Inclusive Growth; available at www.worldbank.org/en/events/2015/06/23/promoting-effective-competition-policies-for-shared-prosperity-and-inclusive-growth#1 [accessed on 5 November 2016] or World Bank/ICN Competition Policy Advocacy Awards; available at www.wbginvestmentclimate.org/publications/the-competition-policy-advocacy-awards.cfm [accessed on 5 November 2016].

[66] David J. Gerber, 'Competition Law and the WTO: Rethinking the Relationship' (2007) 10(3) *Journal of International Economic Law* 707–724 at 722.

[67] UNCTAD, 2007 Model Law on Competition (TD/RBP/CONF.5/7/Rev.3), Chapter I; available at http://unctad.org/en/Docs/tdrbpconf5d7rev3_en.pdf [accessed on 5 November 2016].

[68] UNCTAD Model Law on Competition (2015) – Revised Chapter I (TD/RBP/CONF.5/7/Rev.3), para. 14, http://unctad.org/meetings/en/SessionalDocuments/tdrbpconf8l1_en.pdf [accessed on 5 November 2016].

economic activity (Russia), and the development of a socialist market economy (China).[69] As a result, the BRICS platform could potentially become an alternative venue for international dialogue on the goals and objectives of competition law and policy; it would likely be more receptive and accommodating to the needs of developing countries in their attempt to develop a national competition law regime that would be suitable for the developmental and other public policy objectives they might want to pursue. This platform could also facilitate discussion on the relationship between competition policy and the Sustainable Development Goals as formulated by the United Nations.[70]

Even from a merely comparative perspective, the BRICS countries offer a wide variety of substantive, procedural, and institutional frameworks for national competition law regimes, which could be studied and learned from. For instance, China has developed a three-headed institutional framework for the enforcement of its Anti-Monopoly Law, with the Ministry of Commerce[71] enforcing the merger control regime, the National Development and Reform Commission[72] investigating price-related anti-competitive conduct, and the State Administration of Industry and Commerce[73] handling other types of anti-competitive conduct.[74] This unique institutional framework provides for a certain 'checks and balances' mechanism within the competition enforcement mechanism, because all three enforcement authorities work towards the improvement of investigatory and decision-making practices. At the same time, in the absence of effective coordination between the competition authorities, this multipolar enforcement structure may create certain inconsistencies in the interpretation and application of competition rules. South Africa, where the competition law regime is almost two decades old, has developed a strong competition culture, and the work of competition authorities has received enormous popular support because the fight against economic exploitation by companies is seen as an extension of the fight against poverty and

---

[69] See Horacio Vedia Jerez, *Competition Law Enforcement and Compliance across the World: A Comparative Review* (Alphen aan den Rijn: Kluwer Law International, 2015), p. 15.

[70] See Sustainable Development Knowledge Platform, https://sustainabledevelopment.un .org/ [accessed on 5 November 2016].

[71] Available at http://english.mofcom.gov.cn/ [accessed on 5 November 2016].

[72] Available at http://en.ndrc.gov.cn/ [accessed on 5 November 2016].

[73] Available at http://www.saic.gov.cn/ [accessed on 5 November 2016].

[74] See Qian Hao, 'The Multiple Hands: Institutional Dynamics of China's Competition Regime', in Emch and Stallibrass (eds.), *China's Anti-Monopoly Law: The First Five Years*, pp. 15–34; Angela Huyue Zhang, 'The Enforcement of the Anti-Monopoly Law in China: An Institutional Design Perspective' (2011) 56(3) *Antitrust Bulletin* 631–663.

inequality.[75] As a result, this African jurisdiction can provide a model for promoting competition culture and mobilizing popular support for competition promotion and competition enforcement activities. Russia has accumulated substantial experience in regional cooperation and the coordination of competition laws and policies – first within the framework of the CIS on the basis of the 2000 agreement on implementation of the coordinated anti-monopoly policy[76] and currently within the Eurasian Economic Union where the Eurasian Economic Commission has been accorded certain competences in cross-border enforcement of competition rules.[77]

Another potential area of BRICS cooperation could be overseas mergers and acquisitions, as governed by the national merger control regimes.[78] With the diversity of policy goals pursued by merger control authorities throughout the world, such cooperation would be particularly warranted.[79] For example, Chinese merger control enforcement has attracted significant attention from both practitioners and policy makers due to the three-pillar structure of the merger review: competition, national security, and industrial policy.[80] Since China has a clear interest in the extraterritorial application of its Anti-Monopoly Law, its bilateral and multilateral cooperation with other competition authorities, including those from the BRICS countries, may be instrumental in avoiding enforcement conflicts and protecting its national economic interests.[81]

---

[75] See Dennis Davis and Lara Granville, 'South Africa: The Competition Law System and the Country's Norms', in Fox and Trebilcock (eds.), *The Design of Competition Law Institutions: Global Norms, Local Choices*, pp. 266–328.

[76] The agreement was signed by all CIS countries except Turkmenistan.

[77] See Vassily Rudomino and German Zakharov, 'Chapter 19: Eurasian Economic Area', in Aleksander Stawicki and Vassily Rudomino (eds.), *Competition Law in Central and Eastern Europe: A Practical Guide* (Alphen aan den Rijn: Kluwer Law International, 2014), pp. 503–516.

[78] See Haiyong Ma and Weiwei Zhang, 'Brief Analysis of the Issue of Cross Border Merger and Acquisition in BRICs' (2010) 1(1) *Research in World Economy* 43–46. The authors argue that the BRICS countries should improve the legal system of overseas acquisitions for their enterprises and confirm industrial and capital requirements on corporate acquisitions.

[79] See e.g. Deborah E. Healey, 'Strange Bedfellows or Soulmates: A Comparison of Merger Regulation in China and Australia' (2012) 7 *Asian Journal of Comparative Law* 281–318.

[80] See e.g. Li-Fen Wu, 'Anti-Monopoly, National Security, and Industrial Policy: Merger Control in China' (2010) 33(3) *World Competition Law and Economics Review* 477–497; Mark Furse, 'Merger Control in China: Four and a Half Years of Practice and Enforcement – A Critical Analysis' (2013) 36(2) *World Competition Law and Economics Review* 285–313.

[81] See Michael Faure and Xinzhu Zhang, 'Towards an Extraterritorial Application of the Chinese Anti-Monopoly Law that Avoids Trade Conflicts' (2013) 45 *George Washington International Law Review* 501–538.

V.   Challenges for the Development of the 'BRICS Way' in Competition Law Enforcement

It is true that the major challenge for BRICS has always been, and continues to be, the articulation of a common vision. Without the ability to find a common denominator, there is little reason to organize yearly summits to debate global issues.[82]

The viability of BRICS as an alternative platform for international dialogue and cooperation on matters of competition law and policy will depend to a large degree on the ability of this global alliance to formulate its own 'BRICS way' of dealing with competition law enforcement, which has cross-border effects on foreign markets and foreign companies. Another challenge for the formulation of the 'BRICS way' in competition law and policy is the ability of BRICS to offer a viable alternative to the current 'universal proliferation, fragmentation and convergence' framework, which currently dominates international cooperation in the field of competition law and policy.

As mentioned in Section I, BRICS countries have developed their national competition regimes largely outside the BRICS framework of cooperation and dialogue. Some BRICS countries generally regard their national competition policy as an extension or tool with which to pursue industrial policy or market regulation (China, Russia), and the others (Brazil, India, South Africa) have set up their competition authorities as independent regulators within their own field of responsibility. It seems that each BRICS country has its own understanding of the role of competition as part of its industrial or macroeconomic policy, which would pose challenges for the 'BRICS way' in competition enforcement and its relationship with other public policies (developmental, social, employment, etc.). Without such a common vision the BRICS approach to competition would mirror the 'ASEAN Way', which is characterized by decision making by consensus, non-interference in the domestic affairs of members, and recourse to informal and nonbinding agreements.[83]

In terms of international cooperation in competition enforcement, the BRICS countries tend to treat competition law and policy as a

---

[82]   Oliver Stuenkel, 'Why BRICS Matters', *E-International Relations*, 28 March 2012; available at www.e-ir.info/2012/03/28/why-brics-matters/ [accessed on 5 November 2016].

[83]   See e.g. Paul. J. Davidson, 'The ASEAN Way and the Role of Law in ASEAN Economic Cooperation' (2004) 8 *Singapore Yearbook of International Law* 165–176; Huong Ly Luu, 'Regional Harmonization of Competition Law and Policy: An ASEAN Approach' (2012) 2(2) *Asian Journal of International Law* 291–321.

primarily domestic matter, distinct from foreign trade regulation. The separate meetings of BRICS competition authorities and BRICS trade ministers[84] also indicate the separation between competition and trade issues, creating an impression that the BRICS countries are willing to cooperate primarily to share experiences, but not for building an international cooperation mechanism that could be suitable for other countries. Competition authorities and cooperation in the field of competition should be more closely linked to other areas, and joint meetings with trade ministers and other sector regulators should be encouraged.[85]

The BRICS ability to serve as a platform for international cooperation in competition matters may be also compromised by each country's vigorous defense of its national economic interests, including those affected by foreign competition enforcement. For example, in 2012 as a response to the EU Commission's antitrust investigation into the alleged pricing abuses of the Russian state-owned conglomerate Gazprom,[86] the Russian president issued a decree[87] ordering all state-owned strategic enterprises to refrain from cooperation with foreign authorities at the stage of both investigation and enforcement without prior consent from the Russian

---

[84] The trade ministers of BRICS countries have already held several joint meetings: on 7 July 2015 in Moscow, on 14 July 2013 in Fortaleza, on 26 March 2013 in Durban, on 19 April 2012 in Puerto Vallarta, on 28 March 2012 in New Delhi, and on 14 December 2011 in Geneva. The ministerial declarations primarily concerned the BRICS stance on the ongoing WTO negotiations and cooperation within other international forums, such as UNCTAD.

[85] Some inspiration from such cross-sector dialogue and cooperation can be drawn from the experience of the Energy Community, a regional governance framework for the implementation of the EU *acquis communautaire* in the non-EU countries of southeastern Europe. In 2013 the Energy Community Secretariat set up the Energy Community Competition Network; available at www.energy-community.org/portal/page/portal/ENC_HOME/AREAS_OF_WORK/Instruments/Competition/Network [accessed on 5 November 2016]; it brings together energy regulators and competition authorities from the contracting states for the exchange of information, mutual consultations and coordination of enforcement. See generally Alexandr Svetlicinii, 'Competition Law Enforcement in the Contracting Parties of the Energy Community: Current Challenges and Future Perspectives', in Dirk Buschle and Kim Talus (eds.), *The Energy Community: A New Energy Governance System* (Cambridge: Intersentia, 2015), pp. 111–137.

[86] See EU Commission, Press release IP/15/4828, 'Antitrust: Commission sends Statement of Objections to Gazprom for alleged abuse of dominance on Central and Eastern European gas supply markets', 22 April 2015; available at http://europa.eu/rapid/press-release_IP-15-4828_en.htm [accessed on 5 November 2016].

[87] Executive Order of the President of the Russian Federation No 1285 of 11 September 2012 on Measures to Protect Russian Federation Interests in Russian Legal Entities' Foreign Economic Activities.

government.[88] Earlier in 2008 the Chinese government submitted its first *amicus curiae* brief before the US court in order to shield Chinese vitamin C manufacturers from civil liability for price fixing and the limitation of exports under US antitrust law.[89] Conversely, the BRICS countries have vigorously fought foreign export cartels applying their national competition laws extraterritorially. For example, in the 1990s both Indian and South African competition authorities confronted, albeit with different results, the American soda ash export cartel, established and registered in the United States under the export cartel exemption provided by the Webb-Pomerene Act.[90]

The following factors have been identified as drivers of international cooperation in antitrust enforcement between individual jurisdictions: the level of cross-border trade, coherence of laws on the protection of confidential information, coherence of the competition law regimes, mutual trust between cooperating jurisdictions and the availability of sufficient resources.[91] It remains to be seen whether the BRICS countries will manage to accumulate the critical mass in such indicators to ensure smooth intra-BRICS cooperation in competition enforcement that could serve as a model for the rest of the world and for developing countries in particular.

VI. Conclusion

A reliable solution to the problems of the modern world can only be achieved through serious and honest cooperation between the leading states and their associations in order to address common challenges.[92]

It has been argued that the developing countries need to improve their cooperation in order to demonstrate a common stance concerning the negative effects of cross-border anti-competitive conduct on their home markets and to identify the common benefits of an eventual international

---

[88] See Marek Martyniszyn, 'Legislation Blocking Antitrust Investigations and the September 2012 Russian Executive Order' (2014) 37(1) *World Competition Law and Economics Review* 103–119.

[89] In re Vitamin C Antitrust Litigation, 584 F. Supp. 2d 546 (E.D.N.Y. 2008). See Jane Lee, 'Vitamin 'C' is for Compulsion: Delimiting the Foreign Sovereign Compulsion Defense' (2010) 50(3) *Virginia Journal of International Law* 757–791.

[90] See Martyniszyn, 'Export Cartels: Is It Legal to Target Your Neighbour?' at 199–208.

[91] See G. Deniz Both, 'Drivers of International Cooperation in Competition Law Enforcement' (2015) 38(2) *World Competition Law and Economics Review* 301–320.

[92] Sergey Lavrov, 'Russia's Foreign Policy: Historical Background' (2016) 2 *Russia in Global Affairs*; available at www.globalaffairs.ru/number/Istoricheskaya-perspektiva-vneshnei-politiki-Rossii-18019 [accessed on 5 November 2016].

cooperation mechanism in the field of competition law and policy.[93] The impasse of the Doha Round has removed the competition policy from the agenda of the WTO and passed it along for discussion in various non-governmental or regional forums. As a result, a universal proliferation of competition regimes has been developing under the general theme of fragmentation and convergence, which has not resolved the problems related to extraterritorial enforcement and international cooperation.

This analysis of the BRICS countries' experience in developing their national competition regimes and placing competition law and policy on the agenda of intra-BRICS cooperation could provide the background for an alternative international platform for dialogue and cooperation in competition matters. The viability of such a platform will depend to a large degree on the ability of BRICS countries to develop and promote a common vision or approach to competition law and policy, which would allow the accommodation of various public policy goals pursued by the emerging economies. The success of the intra-BRICS coordination of competition enforcement and their ability to balance national economic interests with considerations of international cooperation, comity and the general rejection of anti-competitive business practices will be essential for the credibility of the BRICS countries as global leaders in the competition law and policy dialogue.

In the Chinese language (Mandarin) the acronym BRICS is read as 'jin zhuan guo jia' (金砖国家), which can be literally translated as 'golden bricks organization'. It is undeniable that in the field of competition policy each of the BRICS countries has laid down important 'bricks' of experience in policy making and implementation, which can be 'built upon' by other countries developing their competition law regimes. At the same time, the current limitations to BRICS cooperation in the field of competition law and policy caution against the optimistic conclusions of whether these 'bricks' could form the foundation of an eventual multilateral cooperation mechanism for cross-border competition enforcement.

VII.   References

Afrika, Sasha-Lee and Bachmann, Sascha-Dominik, 'Cartel Regulation in Three Emerging BRICS Economies: Cartel and Competition Policies in South Africa, Brazil, and India – A Comparative Overview' (2011) 45(4) *International Lawyer* 975–1003.

---

[93] See Kim Them Do, 'Competition Law and Policy and Economic Development in Developing Countries' (2011) 8 *Manchester Journal of International Economic Law* 18–35 at 34.

Arseneau, David M., 'Explaining the Energy Consumption in a Cross-Section of Countries: Are the BRICs Different?' (2012) 18 *Law and Business Review of the Americas* 553–584.

Artemyev, Igor, 'Regulator's Introduction: Recent Activities and Policy Priorities in Russia', in Adrian Emch, Jose Regazzini and Vassily Rudomino (eds.) *Competition Law in the BRICS Countries* (Alphen aan den Rijn: Kluwer Law International, 2012), pp. 57–66.

Bakhoum, Mor and Molestina, Julia, 'Institutional Coherence and Effectiveness of a Regional Competition Policy: The Case of the West African Economic and Monetary Union (WAEMU)', in Josef Drexl, Mor Bakhoum, Eleanor M. Fox, Michal S. Gal and David J. Gerber (eds.), *Competition Policy and Regional Integration in Developing Countries* (Cheltenham: Edward Elgar, 2012), pp. 89–115.

Beckford, Delroy S., 'Implementing Effective Competition Policy through Regional Trade Agreements: The Case of CARICOM', in Josef Drexl, Mor Bakhoum, Eleanor M. Fox, Michal S. Gal and David J. Gerber (eds.), *Competition Policy and Regional Integration in Developing Countries* (Cheltenham: Edward Elgar, 2012), pp. 185–204.

Bhattacharjea, Aditya, 'The Case for a Multilateral Agreement on Competition Policy: A Developing Country Perspective' (2006) 9(2) *Journal of International Economic Law* 293–323.

Both, G. Deniz, 'Drivers of International Cooperation in Competition Law Enforcement' (2015) 38(2) *World Competition Law and Economics Review* 301–320.

Botta, Marco, 'The Brazilian Senate passes the text of the New Competition Act introducing a more efficient merger control system', 2 December 2010, *e-Competitions Bulletin*, no. 35224.

Botta, Marco, 'The Cooperation between the Competition Authorities of the Developing Countries: Why It Does Not Work? Case Study on Argentina and Brazil' (2009) 5(2) *Competition Law Review* 153–178.

Buscaglia, Christopher A. and Weismann, Miriam F., 'How 'Cybersafe' Are the BRICS?' (2012) 15(2) *Journal of Legal, Ethical and Regulatory Issues* 61–91.

Carvalho, Vinicius Marques de, 'Questions & Answers', in Cristianne Zarzur, Krisztian Katona and Mariana Villela (eds.), *Overview of Competition Law in Brazil* (São Paulo: IBRAC, 2015), pp. 25–40.

Cooper, Andrew F. and Farooq, Asif B., 'Testing the Club Dynamics of the BRICS: The New Development Bank from Conception to Establishment' (2015) 10(2) *International Organisations Research Journal* 1–15.

Davidson, Paul. J., 'The ASEAN Way and the Role of Law in ASEAN Economic Cooperation' (2004) 8 *Singapore Yearbook of International Law* 165–176.

Davis, Dennis and Granville, Lara, 'South Africa: The Competition Law System and the Country's Norms', in Eleanor M. Fox and Michael J. Trebilcock (eds.), *The Design of Competition Law Institutions: Global Norms, Local Choices* (Oxford: Oxford University Press, 2013), pp. 266–328.

Do, Kim Them, 'Competition Law and Policy and Economic Development in Developing Countries' (2011) 8 *Manchester Journal of International Economic Law* 18–35.

Drache, Daniel, 'The Short but Significant Life of the International Trade Organization: Lessons for Our Time', *Centre for the Study of Globalization and Regionalisation*, CSGR Working Paper No. 62/00, November 2000; available at http://wrap.warwick.ac.uk/2063/1/WRAP_Drache_wp6200.pdf [accessed on 5 November 2016].

Emch, Adrian, Regazzini, Jose and Rudomino, Vassily (eds.), *Competition Law in the BRICS Countries* (Alphen aan den Rijn: Kluwer Law International, 2012).

Emch, Adrian and Stallibrass, David (eds.), *China's Anti-Monopoly Law: The First Five Years* (Alphen aan den Rijn: Kluwer Law International, 2014).

Faure, Michael and Zhang, Xinzhu, 'Towards an Extraterritorial Application of the Chinese Anti-Monopoly Law that Avoids Trade Conflicts' (2013) 45 *George Washington International Law Review* 501–538.

Fels, Allan, Wang, Xiaoye, Su, Jessica and Ng, Wendy, 'The Chinese State Administration for Industry and Commerce and the Brazilian Conselho Administrativo de Defesa Econômica sign a memorandum of understanding', 13 September 2012, *e-Competitions Bulletin*, no. 74336.

Fox, Eleanor M. and Trebilcock, Michael J., 'Introduction: The GAL Competition Project: The Global Convergence of Process Norms', in Eleanor M. Fox and Michael J. Trebilcock (eds.), *The Design of Competition Law Institutions* (Oxford: Oxford University Press, 2013), pp. 1–48.

Furse, Mark, 'Merger Control in China: Four and a Half Years of Practice and Enforcement – A Critical Analysis' (2013) 36(2) *World Competition Law and Economics Review* 285–313.

Gal, Michal and Wassmer-Faibish, Inbal, 'Regional Agreements of Developing Jurisdictions: Unleashing the Potential', in Josef Drexl, Mor Bakhoum, Eleanor M. Fox, Michal S. Gal and David J. Gerber (eds.) *Competition Policy and Regional Integration in Developing Countries* (Cheltenham: Edward Elgar, 2012), pp. 291–320.

Gerber, David J., 'Asia and Global Competition Law Convergence', in Michael Dowdle, John Gillespie and Imelda Maher (eds.), *Asian Capitalism and the Regulation of Competition: Towards a Regulatory Geography of Global Competition Law* (Cambridge: Cambridge University Press, 2013), pp. 36–52.

'Competition Law and the WTO: Rethinking the Relationship' (2007) 10(3) *Journal of International Economic Law* 707–724.

Global Competition Law, Markets, and Globalization (Oxford: Oxford University Press, 2010).

Hao, Qian, 'The Multiple Hands: Institutional Dynamics of China's Competition Regime', in Adrian Emch and David Stallibrass (eds.), *China's Anti-Monopoly Law: The First Five Years* (Alphen aan den Rijn: Kluwer Law International, 2013), pp. 15–34.

Healey, Deborah E., 'Strange Bedfellows or Soulmates: A Comparison of Merger Regulation in China and Australia' (2012) 7 *Asian Journal of Comparative Law* 281–318.

Hoekman, Bernard M. and Mavroidis, Petros C., 'Competition, Competition Policy and the GATT' (1994) 17(2) *World Economy* 121–150.

Jenny, Frederic and Katsoulacos, Yannis (eds.), *Competition Law Enforcement in the BRICS and in Developing Countries: Legal and Economic Aspects* (New York: Springer, 2016).

Jerez, Horacio Vedia, *Competition Law Enforcement and Compliance across the World: A Comparative Review* (Alphen aan den Rijn: Kluwer Law International, 2015).

Jordan, Jacquelynn M., 'The Legal Aspects of BRICS and the Contribution of Jurists' (2013) 1 *China Legal Science* 156–160.

Kaczorowska-Ireland, Alina, 'The Objectives of the Competition Policy of the CARICOM Single Market and Economy and their Importance to the Development of a Coherent and Comprehensive Body of Substantive CSME Competition Rules' (2012) 8(2) *Competition Law Review* 185–207.

Competition Law in the CARICOM Single Market and Economy (New York: Routledge, 2014).

Kirton, John J., 'Explaining the BRICS Summit's Solid, Strengthening Success' (2015) *International Organisations Research Journal* 9–31.

Kovacic, William, 'Competition Law in the BRICS Countries: More than an Acronym', in Adrian Emch, Jose Regazzini and Vassily Rudomino (eds.), *Competition Law in the BRICS Countries* (Alphen aan den Rijn: Kluwer Law International, 2012), pp. 315–325.

Lavrov, Sergey, 'Russia's Foreign Policy: Historical Background' (2016) 2 *Russia in Global Affairs*; available at www.globalaffairs.ru/number/Istoricheskaya-perspektiva-vneshnei-politiki-Rossii-18019 [accessed on 5 November 2016].

Lee, Jane, 'Vitamin 'C' is for Compulsion: Delimiting the Foreign Sovereign Compulsion Defense' (2010) 50(3) *Virginia Journal of International Law* 757–791.

Lianos, Ioannis, 'Global Governance of Antitrust and the Need for a BRICS Joint Research Platform in Competition Law and Policy', *CLES Research Paper Series* 5/2016, August 2016; available at www.ucl.ac.uk/cles/research-paper-series [accessed on 5 November 2016].

Luu, Huong Ly, 'Regional Harmonization of Competition Law and Policy: An ASEAN Approach' (2012) 2(2) *Asian Journal of International Law* 291–321.

Ma, Haiyong and Zhang, Weiwei, 'Brief Analysis of the Issue of Cross Border Merger and Acquisition in BRICs' (2010) 1(1) *Research in World Economy* 43–46.

Maher, Imelda, 'Competition Law Fragmentation in a Globalizing World' (2015) 40(2) *Law & Social Inquiry* 553–571.

Marten, Robert, McIntyre, Diane, Travassos, Claudia, Shishkin, Sergey, Wang, Longde, Reddy, Srinath and Vega, Jeanette, 'An Assessment of Progress towards Universal Health Coverage in Brazil, Russia, India, China, and South Africa (BRICS)' (2014) 384 *Health Policy* 2164–2171.

Martyniszyn, Marek, 'Export Cartels: Is It Legal to Target Your Neighbour? Analysis in Light of Recent Case Law' (2012) 15(1) *Journal of International Economic Law* 181–222.

'Legislation Blocking Antitrust Investigations and the September 2012 Russian Executive Order' (2014) 37(1) *World Competition Law and Economics Review* 103–119.

Mattoo, Aaditya and Subramanian, Arvind, 'Multilateral Rules on Competition Policy: A Possible Way Forward' (1997) 31(5) *Journal of World Trade* 95–115.

Moiroux, Julien, 'The Internalization of Competition Policy: The EU and the WTO between Boldness and Rally' (2009) 2 *Global Antitrust Review* 38–60.

Moraes, Diego Herrera, 'The Brazilian President Approves the New Competition Law Introducing Substantive Reforms to the National Antitrust Enforcement', 30 November 2011, *e-Competitions Bulletin*, no. 42231.

O'Neill, Jim, 'Building Better Global Economic BRICs', Goldman Sachs Global Economics Paper no. 66, 30 November 2001; available at www.goldmansachs .com/our-thinking/archive/archive-pdfs/build-better-brics.pdf [accessed on 5 November 2016].

Orlanski, Leonardo T., 'Searching for the Basis of International Convergence in Competition Law and Policy' (2011) 4 *Global Antitrust Review* 7–47.

Osang, Thomas, 'World Trade and Investment: Where Do the BRICs Stand?' (2012) 18 *Law and Business Review of the Americas* 515–536.

Ramburuth, Shan, 'Regulator's Introduction: Recent Activities and Policy Priorities in South Africa', in Adrian Emch, Jose Regazzini and Vassily Rudomino (eds.), *Competition Law in the BRICS Countries* (Alphen aan den Rijn: Kluwer Law International, 2012), pp. 207–217.

Rudomino, Vassily and Zakharov, German, 'Chapter 19: Eurasian Economic Area', in Aleksander Stawicki and Vassily Rudomino (eds.), *Competition Law in Central and Eastern Europe: A Practical Guide* (Alphen aan den Rijn: Kluwer Law International, 2014), pp. 503–516.

Sane, Anjali, 'India and the BRICS Countries: Analysis of the Pattern of FDI (Foreign Direct Investment)' (2015) 6(4) *Journal of Commerce & Management Thought* 613–623.

Schaeffer, Fiona A., Riesgo, Luis, Wade, Angus S. and Harper, Michael Culhane, 'Brazil's Congress Approves a New Competition Law that Significantly Restructures the Landscape of Competition Enforcement', 5 October 2011, e-Competitions Bulletin, no. 50116.

'The Brazilian Parliament Approves New Competition Law Subject to Prior Significant Vetoes', 1 December 2011, e-Competitions Bulletin, no. 50121.

Shroff, Cyril and Uberoi, Nisha Kaur, 'India', in Katrina Groshinski and Caitlin Davies (eds.), Competition Law in Asia Pacific: A Practical Guide (The Hague: Kluwer Law International, 2015), pp. 235–297.

Singh, Ajit, 'Competition Policy, Development and Developing Countries', Indian Council for Research on International Economic Relations, Working Paper no. 50, November 1999.

Sokol, Daniel, 'Order without (Enforceable) Law: Why Countries Enter into Non-Enforceable Competition Policy Chapters in Free Trade Agreements' (2008) 83 Chicago-Kent Law Review 231–292.

Stewart, Taimoon, 'Regional Integration in the Caribbean: The Role of Competition Policy', in Josef Drexl, Mor Bakhoum, Eleanor M. Fox, Michal S. Gal and David J. Gerber (eds.) Competition Policy and Regional Integration in Developing Countries (Cheltenham: Edward Elgar, 2012), pp. 161–184.

Stuenkel, Oliver, 'Why BRICS Matters', E-International Relations, 28 March 2012; available at www.e-ir.info/2012/03/28/why-brics-matters/ [accessed on 5 November 2016].

Svetlicinii, Alexandr, 'Competition Law Enforcement in the Contracting Parties of the Energy Community: Current Challenges and Future Perspectives', in Dirk Buschle and Kim Talus (eds.), The Energy Community: A New Energy Governance System (Cambridge: Intersentia, 2015), pp. 111–137.

Sweeney, Brendan, 'Export Cartels: Is there a Need for Global Rules?' (2007) 10(1) Journal of International Economic Law 87–115.

Toye, Richard, 'Developing Multilateralism: The Havana Charter and the Fight for the International Trade Organization, 1947–1948' (2003) 25(2) International History Review 282–305.

Waked, Dina I., 'Competition Law in the Developing World: The Why and How of Adoption and Its Implications for International Competition Law' (2008) 1 Global Antitrust Review 69–96.

Wei, Dan, 'Antitrust in China: An Overview of Recent Implementation of Anti-Monopoly Law' (2013) 14(1) European Business Organization Law Review 119–139.

Wu, Li-Fen, 'Anti-Monopoly, National Security, and Industrial Policy: Merger Control in China' (2010) 33(3) World Competition Law and Economics Review 477–497.

Zach, Roger (ed.), *Towards WTO Competition Rules: Key Issues and Comments on the WTO Report (1998) on Trade and Competition* (Alphen aan den Rijn: Kluwer Law International, 1999).

Zhang, Angela Huyue, 'The Enforcement of the Anti-Monopoly Law in China: An Institutional Design Perspective' (2011) 56(3) *Antitrust Bulletin* 631–663.

7

Intellectual Property Negotiations, the BRICS Factor and the Changing North–South Debate

PETER K. YU

I. Introduction

Multilateral trade negotiations provide fertile grounds for studying regional and international norm setting.[1] Within these negotiations, intellectual property is one area that has shown a clear North–South divide. When intellectual property norms were first explored as part of the negotiations under the General Agreement on Tariffs and Trade (GATT), most developing countries were unfamiliar with the subject matter.[2] As a result, developed countries had an upper hand during the Uruguay Round of Multilateral Trade Negotiations (Uruguay Round), not to mention the tremendous support they received from private industries.[3]

In the past two decades, however, developing countries have quickly improved their ability to set international trade and intellectual property norms.[4] This improvement can be attributed not only to the active participation of academics and civil society organizations – from both the North and the South – but also to the developing countries' increased

---

[1] Amrita Narlikar (ed.), *Deadlocks in Multilateral Negotiations: Causes and Solutions* (Cambridge: Cambridge University Press, 2010); Amrita Narlikar, *International Trade and Developing Countries: Bargaining Coalitions in the GATT and WTO* (London: Routledge, 2003); John S. Odell, *Negotiating the World Economy* (Ithaca, NY: Cornell University Press, 2000); John S. Odell (ed.), *Negotiating Trade: Developing Countries in the WTO and NAFTA* (Cambridge: Cambridge University Press, 2006); J. P. Singh, *Negotiation and the Global Information Economy* (Cambridge: Cambridge University Press, 2008).

[2] United Nations Development Programme, *Human Development Report 1999* (New York: Oxford University Press, 1999), p. 74.

[3] Duncan Matthews, *Globalising Intellectual Property Rights: The TRIPs Agreement* (London: Routledge, 2002); Susan K. Sell, *Private Power, Public Law: The Globalization of Intellectual Property Rights* (Cambridge: Cambridge University Press, 2003), pp. 96–120.

[4] Peter K. Yu, 'Virotech Patents, Viropiracy, and Viral Sovereignty' (2014) 45 *Arizona State Law Journal* 1563–662 at 1635–54.

understanding of the intellectual property system. In the meantime, the international norm-setting environment has also slowly changed. Having acceded to the World Trade Organization (WTO) in December 2001, China has now joined Brazil and India – the two longtime leaders of the developing world – in pushing for their preferred international trade and intellectual property norms. To highlight this changing environment, Amrita Narlikar has referred to these three countries collectively as the 'new powers'.[5]

Since the early 2000s, these countries, along with Russia and South Africa, have also been lumped together under the BRICS acronym in academic and policy literature.[6] Coined by Jim O'Neill, the former chief global economist of Goldman Sachs, the term 'BRICs' initially referred to only four countries: Brazil, Russia, India and China.[7] Since its creation, however, the term has been transformed to BRICS, with a capital S, covering not only the four aforementioned countries but also South Africa. In April 2011, the five BRICS countries met for the first time in Sanya, China, to discuss issues that could benefit from greater cooperation. Since then, annual BRICS Summits have been held in New Delhi (India), Durban (South Africa), Fortaleza (Brazil), Ufa (Russia) and Goa (India).[8]

In the past few years, the popularity and collective influence of the BRICS countries have slightly declined, due in part to the economic slowdown caused by the global economic crisis and in part to the inherent challenges of lumping five drastically different economies together. Nevertheless, the BRICS countries have continued to garner academic and policy attention. As far as international norm setting is concerned, some BRICS countries, such as Brazil, China and India, have also assumed leadership in the developing world, even though the five BRICS countries have yet to utilize their collective clout as a single bloc.

To fully understand the role played by the BRICS countries in international trade and intellectual property negotiations, this chapter covers

---

[5] Amrita Narlikar, *New Powers: How to Become One and How to Manage Them* (New York: Columbia University Press, 2010).

[6] José Cassiolato and Virginia Vitorino (eds.), *BRICS and Development Alternatives: Innovation Systems and Policies* (London: Anthem Press, 2011); Andrew F. Cooper, *The BRICS: A Very Short Introduction* (Oxford: Oxford University Press, 2016).

[7] Jim O'Neill, 'Building Better Global Economic BRICs' (2001) Goldman Sachs, Global Economics Paper No. 66. For his later and much broader analysis, see Jim O'Neill, *The Growth Map: Economic Opportunity in the BRICs and Beyond* (London: Portfolio, 2011).

[8] The first BRIC Summit was launched in Yekaterinburg, Russia in June 2009. The second summit was held in Brasília, Brazil. South Africa did not join the four BRIC countries until the third summit in Sanya, China.

not only the complete BRICS coalition that consists of all five countries but also what I have referred to as 'partial BRICS alliances' – alliances that involve some but not all of the BRICS countries.[9] As noted in a previous article, a complete BRICS coalition is hard to sustain, even though it can be tremendously powerful. Instead, partial BRICS alliances are likely to be more frequently used.[10] These alliances can be formed in two ways: first, by bringing together some BRICS countries, such as Brazil, China and India, as a single negotiating bloc; or second, by teaming up some BRICS countries with other large developing countries.

This chapter focuses primarily on the presence, impact and significance of what I refer to here as the 'BRICS factor' in international trade and intellectual property negotiations. It begins by revisiting the negotiation of the Agreement on Trade-Related Aspects of Intellectual Property Rights (TRIPS Agreement). A review of the TRIPS negotiations is important because this historic agreement has made salient the inevitable compromises between developed and developing countries in international intellectual property negotiations. Such a review also highlights the important but limited roles played by a partial BRICS alliance. At the time of the TRIPS negotiations, China and Russia had yet to join the GATT/WTO.

This chapter then turns its attention to the ongoing negotiation of TRIPS-plus bilateral, regional and plurilateral trade agreements, such as the recently signed Trans-Pacific Partnership (TPP) Agreement and the yet-to-be-completed Regional Comprehensive Economic Partnership (RCEP) Agreement. The analysis of these two mega-regional agreements provides two sets of highly instructive comparisons. First, a close examination of the roles played by some BRICS countries in the TPP negotiations enables us to compare and contrast these roles with their historic roles in the TRIPS negotiations. Second, the juxtaposition of the TPP and RCEP negotiations enables us to identify and evaluate the distinctively different roles the participating BRICS countries have played in the two

---

[9] Peter K. Yu, 'Access to Medicines, BRICS Alliances, and Collective Action' (2008) 34 *American Journal of Law and Medicine* 345–94 at 362–70.

[10] *Ibid*, at 365. As I noted in comparison, 'While each partial alliance does not provide the same bargaining leverage as the BRICS coalition, it still possesses a number of attractive features. By teaming up other less developed countries with one or more of the BRICS countries, the group will have leverage that does not exist for each less developed country alone. The costs of maintaining a partial alliance [are] also significantly lower than what would be required to maintain a complete coalition. Moreover, like the BRICS coalition, partial BRICS alliances can be used strategically to help less developed countries develop their own voice. If multiple partial alliances are set up, these alliances, partial as they are, may result in the creation of a web of alliances that has immense synergistic potential'. *Ibid*.

sets of negotiations. While these countries played only indirect roles in the TPP negotiations due to their exclusion, they have taken on dominant and proactive roles in the RCEP negotiations.

Drawing on the triangular comparisons between the TRIPS, TPP and RCEP negotiations, the final section of this chapter highlights four sets of important changes that have transformed the international norm-setting environment in both the trade and intellectual property arenas. These changes involve not only the BRICS countries but also other large developing countries. Given the fact that all five BRICS countries are now WTO members, it remains to be seen what direct and indirect roles these countries will assume collectively in international trade and intellectual property negotiations. Nevertheless, if the significant roles played by partial BRICS alliances provide any useful guide, the roles that the five BRICS countries can play as a collective bloc are likely to be both far-reaching and transformative.

II.   TRIPS Negotiations

The negotiation of the TRIPS Agreement began more than two decades ago with the GATT Ministerial Conference in Punta del Este, Uruguay.[11] Held in September 1986, this conference took place at a critical point when the negotiations between developed and developing countries over the revision of the Paris Convention for the Protection of Industrial Property (Paris Convention) became deadlocked at the World Intellectual Property Organization (WIPO).[12]

During this ministerial conference, the GATT contracting parties set out their negotiating objectives for the new Uruguay Round. In a section titled 'trade-related aspects of intellectual property rights, including trade in counterfeit goods', the Ministerial Declaration stated as follows:

> In order to reduce the distortions and impediments to international trade, and taking into account the need to promote effective and adequate protection of intellectual property rights, and to ensure that measures and procedures to enforce intellectual property rights do not themselves become barriers to legitimate trade, the negotiations shall aim to clarify GATT provisions and elaborate as appropriate new rules and disciplines.

---

[11] Jayashree Watal, *Intellectual Property Rights in the WTO and Developing Countries* (The Hague: Kluwer Law International, 2001), p. 21.

[12] Peter K. Yu, 'Currents and Crosscurrents in the International Intellectual Property Regime' (2004) 38 *Loyola of Los Angeles Law Review* 323–443 at 357–8.

> Negotiations shall aim to develop a multilateral framework of principles, rules and disciplines dealing with international trade in counterfeit goods, taking into account work already undertaken in the GATT.
>
> These negotiations shall be without prejudice to other complementary initiatives that may be taken in the World Intellectual Property Organization and elsewhere to deal with these matters.[13]

In the beginning, many developing countries naively believed they could use the text of this declaration to limit the scope of the negotiations to 'primarily... trade in counterfeit goods and other such trade-related aspects'.[14] As these countries claimed, the GATT mandate did not allow for the discussion of substantive intellectual property issues. Led by Brazil and India – two future BRICS countries – developing countries insisted that only WIPO had the institutional competence to discuss those issues.[15] However, as Jayashree Watal, a former negotiator for India who now works in the WTO Intellectual Property Division, pointed out, 'This was a misreading not only of the text but also of the writing on the wall. Clearly, the negotiations were aimed not only at clarifying GATT provisions but elaborating, "as appropriate," new rules and disciplines'.[16]

To properly understand the negotiating context surrounding the TRIPS Agreement, it is instructive to recall the initial positions taken by four key negotiating parties: the United States, the European Communities (and, later, the European Union), Brazil and India. In October 1987, the United States submitted its proposal to the TRIPS Negotiating Group. As the proposal stated, 'The objective of a GATT intellectual property agreement would be to reduce distortions of and impediments to legitimate trade in goods and services caused by deficient levels of protection and enforcement of intellectual property rights'.[17]

This stated negotiating objective stood in sharp contrast to the negotiating guidelines advanced by the European Communities, which gave considerable deference to the Punta del Este Declaration and expressed preference for an instrument of a narrower scope.[18] One of its papers

---

[13] General Agreement on Tariffs and Trade, 'Ministerial Declaration on the Uruguay Round of Multilateral Trade Negotiations', 20 September 1986, (1986) 25 *International Legal Materials* 1623–7 at 1626.

[14] Jayashree Watal, *Intellectual Property Rights in the WTO and Developing Countries*, p. 21.

[15] *Ibid*, p. 24.   [16] *Ibid*, p. 21.

[17] Negotiating Group on Trade-Related Aspects of Intellectual Property Rights, Including Trade in Counterfeit Goods (TRIPS Negotiating Group), 'Suggestion by the United States for Achieving the Negotiating Objective', 20 October 1987, MTN.GNG/NG11/W/14, p. 3.

[18] TRIPS Negotiating Group, 'Guidelines Proposed by the European Community for the Negotiations on Trade-Related Aspects of Intellectual Property Rights', 20 November 1987,

explicitly stated that the negotiations 'should not attempt to elaborate rules which would substitute for existing specific conventions on intellectual property matters' or prejudice 'initiatives that may be taken in WIPO or elsewhere.'[19]

Compared with these two trading powers, Brazil and India adamantly opposed the inclusion of new substantive intellectual property norms in the GATT. At the time of the TRIPS negotiations, these two BRICS countries served as key leaders of the developing world. In July 1987, Brazil provided one of the earliest proposals from developing countries. Its proposal called on the GATT contracting parties to sign the Madrid Agreement for the Repression of False or Deceptive Indications of Source on Goods 'as a preliminary to any further discussion on the subject of trade in counterfeit goods.'[20]

Two years later, India submitted a detailed paper expressing its concerns over the objectives of the GATT negotiations. Offering a developing country's perspective on the TRIPS negotiations, this paper noted the inappropriateness of 'establish[ing] within the [GATT framework] any new rules and disciplines pertaining to standards and principles concerning the availability, scope and use of intellectual property rights.'[21] At a meeting of the TRIPS Negotiating Group, India followed up by 'making a fairly detailed intervention', discussing the objectives and principles of the new GATT instrument.[22] As the GATT Secretariat recounted,

> India was of the view that it was only the restrictive and anti-competitive practices of the owners of the [intellectual property rights] that could be considered to be trade-related because they alone distorted or impeded international trade. Although India did not regard the other aspects of [intellectual property rights] dealt with in the paper to be trade-related, it

MTN.GNG/NG11/W/16; TRIPS Negotiating Group, 'Guidelines and Objectives Proposed by the European Community for the Negotiations on Trade Related Aspects of Substantive Standards of Intellectual Property Rights', 7 July 1988, MTN.GNG/NG11/W/26.

[19] TRIPS Negotiating Group, 'Guidelines and Objectives Proposed by the European Community for the Negotiations on Trade Related Aspects of Substantive Standards of Intellectual Property Rights', p. 2.

[20] TRIPS Negotiating Group, 'The Madrid Agreement for the Repression of False or Deceptive Indications of Source on Goods: Suggestion by Brazil', 9 July 1987, MTN.GNG/NG11/W/11, p. 1.

[21] TRIPS Negotiating Group, 'Standards and Principles Concerning the Availability Scope and Use of Trade-Related Intellectual Property Rights: Communication from India', 10 July 1989, MTN.GNG/NG11/W/37, pp. 19–20.

[22] UNCTAD-ICTSD Project on IPRs and Sustainable Development, *Resource Book on TRIPS and Development* (Cambridge: Cambridge University Press, 2005), p. 121.

had examined these other aspects . . . in the wider developmental and technological context to which they properly belonged. India was of the view that by merely placing the label 'trade-related' on them, such issues could not be brought within the ambit of international trade.[23]

In view of the drastically different positions taken by the United States, the European Communities, Brazil and India, the development of new international minimum standards for the protection and enforcement of intellectual property rights in the GATT/WTO was fairly controversial from the beginning of the negotiations. As Lars Anell, chairman of the TRIPS Negotiating Group, admitted, 'When the date of the Ministerial Conference to launch the Uruguay Round was fixed it was not clear at all that it would cover intellectual property rights.'[24] Daniel Gervais also pointed out that the Punta del Este Declaration, despite its scope and potential reach, 'shows [in retrospect] how difficult it was to get [the GATT] contracting parties to accept this new subject matter.'[25]

By the early 1990s, however, it became apparent to all negotiating parties, including those in the developing world, that the inclusion of international minimum standards for intellectual property protection and enforcement was inevitable.[26] Such a resigned view was largely the result of the United States' aggressive strategies towards the hardline opposition countries,[27] its successful 'divide and conquer' tactics, the economic crises confronting many developing countries and the successful lobbying of the European Communities, Japan and the United States by global intellectual property industries.[28] By the time Canada proposed the creation of a new multilateral trade organization in October 1990, its proposal, along with the developing countries' fears of being excluded from such an organization, 'effectively ended the debate on the earlier developing country

---

[23] TRIPS Negotiating Group, 'Meeting of Negotiating Group of 12–14 July 1989: Note by the Secretariat', 12 September 1989, MTN.GNG/NG11/14, p. 4.

[24] Lars Anell, 'Foreword to the First Edition', in Daniel Gervais, *The TRIPS Agreement: Drafting History and Analysis*, 3rd edn (London: Sweet & Maxwell, 2008), p. ix.

[25] Daniel Gervais, *The TRIPS Agreement*, p. 12.

[26] Abdulqawi A. Yusuf, 'TRIPS: Background, Principles and General Provisions', in Carlos M. Correa and Abdulqawi A. Yusuf (eds.), *Intellectual Property and International Trade: The TRIPS Agreement*, 2nd edn (Alphen aan den Rijn: Kluwer Law International, 2008), p. 9.

[27] These countries included Argentina, Brazil, Cuba, Egypt, India, Nicaragua, Nigeria, Peru, Tanzania and Yugoslavia. Jayashree Watal, *Intellectual Property Rights in the WTO and Developing Countries*, p. 19, fn. 17.

[28] Susan K. Sell, *Private Power, Public Law*, pp. 96–120; Jayashree Watal, *Intellectual Property Rights in the WTO and Developing Countries*, p. 19; Peter K. Yu, 'Access to Medicines, BRICS Alliances, and Collective Action', at 365; Peter K. Yu, 'Currents and Crosscurrents in the International Intellectual Property Regime', at 412–13.

position of WIPO as the appropriate forum for lodging the results of the TRIPS negotiations.'[29]

What remained in the negotiations were the details of these new standards and specifying how these standards were to be incorporated into the new agreement without adversely affecting the protections already put in place by the extant international intellectual property conventions, such as the Berne Convention for the Protection of Literary and Artistic Works (Berne Convention) and the Paris Convention. To expedite the negotiation process and to minimize the gap between the positions of developed and developing countries, the GATT Secretariat and Chairman Anell prepared what was commonly referred to as the Anell Draft.[30]

This draft was later incorporated into the 'take it or leave it' draft of the Final Act embodying the results of the Uruguay Round. Advanced by GATT Director-General Arthur Dunkel, this draft brought together different sectors and constituted the GATT Secretariat's best judgement of what would be acceptable to all negotiating parties.[31] Although Dunkel's approach was and has remained controversial,[32] this approach and the eventual 'marriage' of intellectual property to trade proved to be effective. The negotiations quickly concluded in April 1994, and the TRIPS Agreement was adopted with minor changes as Annex 1C of the Marrakesh Agreement Establishing the World Trade Organization.[33]

The TRIPS Agreement entered into force on 1 January 1995, extending obligations to more than 130 (now over 160) WTO members. Although the developing country bloc, under the leadership of Brazil and India, strongly resisted the adoption of high intellectual property standards in the TRIPS Agreement, especially in the first few years of the negotiations, they failed to unite in their opposition towards the end and eventually

---

[29] Jayashree Watal, *Intellectual Property Rights in the WTO and Developing Countries*, p. 34.

[30] TRIPS Negotiating Group, 'Status of Work in the Negotiating Group: Chairman's Report to the GNG', 23 July 1990, MTN.GNG/NG11/W/76; UNCTAD-ICTSD Project on IPRs and Sustainable Development, *Resource Book on TRIPS and Development*, p. xiii.

[31] Jayashree Watal, *Intellectual Property Rights in the WTO and Developing Countries*, p. 37.

[32] Jagdish Bhagwati, 'Afterword: The Question of Linkage' (2002) 96 *American Journal of International Law* 126–34 at 127; Daniel J. Gervais, 'TRIPS 3.0: Policy Calibration and Innovation Displacement', in Neil Weinstock Netanel (ed.), *The Development Agenda: Global Intellectual Property and Developing Countries* (Oxford: Oxford University Press, 2008), p. 52.

[33] Jayashree Watal, *Intellectual Property Rights in the WTO and Developing Countries*, p. 40–1; Daniel J. Gervais, 'The TRIPS Agreement and the Doha Round: History and Impact on Economic Development', in Peter K. Yu (ed.), *Intellectual Property and Information Wealth: Issues and Practices in the Digital Age* (Westport, CT: Praeger, 2007), vol. 4, p. 29.

succumbed to the demands of developed countries.[34] Of all the seventy-three articles in the TRIPS Agreement, developing countries only managed to obtain 'limited concessions in the form of articles 1.1, 7, 8, 40, 41.5, 65, 66, and 67, and some minor adjustments in other provisions'.[35] While articles 7 and 8 have been considered by many policy makers and commentators, especially those in the developed world, as merely hortatory,[36] the transition periods for developing and transition countries provided in article 65 expired in five quick years after the agreement entered into effect.

At the time of the WTO's formation, two BRICS countries, China and Russia, had not yet joined the international trading body; they became members on 11 December 2001 and 22 August 2012, respectively. Together with Brazil, India and South Africa, which were among the founding WTO members, the five BRICS countries now play highly important roles in international trade and intellectual property negotiations, especially those relating to the TRIPS Agreement.

III. TPP Negotiations

Immediately after the adoption of the TRIPS Agreement, commentators were quick to extol the benefits of marrying intellectual property to trade. As Michael Ryan noted, such a marriage allowed WTO members to 'achieve treaties in diplomatically and politically difficult areas in which agreement would otherwise be elusive'.[37] In addition, policy makers and commentators were excited about the establishment of the mandatory WTO dispute settlement process, which they considered a crowning achievement of the Uruguay Round.[38] Many of them also welcomed the

---

[34] Peter K. Yu, 'Currents and Crosscurrents in the International Intellectual Property Regime', at 363.

[35] Peter K. Yu, 'Are Developing Countries Playing a Better TRIPS Game?' (2011) 16 *UCLA Journal of International Law and Foreign Affairs* 311–43 at 316.

[36] Carlos M. Correa, *Trade Related Aspects of Intellectual Property Rights: A Commentary on the TRIPS Agreement* (Oxford: Oxford University Press, 2007), p. 93; Jacques J. Gorlin, *An Analysis of the Pharmaceutical-Related Provisions of the WTO TRIPS (Intellectual Property) Agreement* (London: Intellectual Property Institute, 1999), p. 16; Margaret Chon, 'Intellectual Property and the Development Divide' (2006) 27 *Cardozo Law Review* 2821–912 at 2843.

[37] Michael P. Ryan, *Knowledge Diplomacy: Global Competition and the Politics of Intellectual Property* (Washington, DC: Brookings Institution Press, 1998), p. 12.

[38] Rachel Brewster, 'Shadow Unilateralism: Enforcing International Trade Law at the WTO' (2009) 30 *University of Pennsylvania Journal of International Law* 1133–46 at 1134; William

new TRIPS-based multilateral intellectual property enforcement norms.[39] As Jacques Gorlin proudly declared in an interview, the Intellectual Property Committee – an ad hoc coalition of major US corporations he led that successfully lobbied for the TRIPS Agreement – got 95 percent of what it wanted and was particularly pleased with the enforcement provisions.[40]

Notwithstanding this quick initial praise, developed countries began to lose patience when the enforcement of intellectual property rights remained grossly inadequate despite the adoption of the TRIPS Agreement. As Gorlin recounted candidly, 'We had assumed that most countries would accept the TRIPS obligations, and dispute settlement would fix a few... problems. What has happened, however, is that we are starting to see dispute settlement cases that cover the wholesale failure to implement TRIPS'.[41] In short, the 5 percent that developed countries failed to secure in the TRIPS negotiations came back to haunt them. With the rapid economic and technological growth in the BRICS countries, the failure of the TRIPS Agreement to induce developing countries to offer effective protection and enforcement of intellectual property rights also became costly and highly troublesome.

To address these deficiencies, the European Union and the United States began pushing aggressively for the development of bilateral and regional trade agreements in the early 2000s. Termed economic partnership agreements and free trade agreements by the European Union and free trade agreements by the United States, these international instruments seek to transplant intellectual property standards from the more powerful signatories to the less powerful ones. Because the intellectual property provisions in these agreements often mandate protections in excess of the

---

J. Davey, 'The WTO Dispute Settlement System: The First Ten Years' (2005) 8 *Journal of International Economic Law* 17–50 at 32; Rochelle Cooper Dreyfuss and Andreas F. Lowenfeld, 'Two Achievements of the Uruguay Round: Putting TRIPS and Dispute Settlement Together' (1997) 37 *Virginia Journal of International Law* 275–333 at 275; Ruth Okediji, 'Toward an International Fair Use Doctrine' (2000) 39 *Columbia Journal of Transnational Law* 75–175 at 149–50.

[39] Daniel Gervais, *The TRIPS Agreement*, p. 440; UNCTAD-ICTSD Project on IPRs and Sustainable Development, *Resource Book on TRIPS and Development*, p. 629; Carlos M. Correa, 'The Push for Stronger Enforcement Rules: Implications for Developing Countries', in *The Global Debate on the Enforcement of Intellectual Property Rights and Developing Countries* (Geneva: International Centre for Trade and Sustainable Development, 2009), p. 34; Adrian Otten and Hannu Wager, 'Compliance with TRIPS: The Emerging World View' (1996) 29 *Vanderbilt Journal of Transnational Law* 391–413 at 403.

[40] Susan K. Sell, *Private Power, Public Law*, p. 115.

[41] Peter K. Yu et al., 'Speeches: U.S. Industries, Trade Associations, and Intellectual Property Lawmaking' (2002) 10 *Cardozo Journal of International and Comparative Law* 5–35 at 10.

levels required by the TRIPS Agreement and other international intellectual property agreements, TRIPS-plus agreements threaten to ignore the local needs, national interests, technological capabilities, institutional capacities and public health conditions of many developing countries.[42]

Although the European Union and the United States initially focused on the establishment of only bilateral and regional trade agreements, the need for greater adjustment of multilateral intellectual property norms – especially those in the enforcement area – called for the development of a new form of trade agreement known as a 'plurilateral trade agreement'.[43] Using an ill-advised 'country club' approach to international trade and intellectual property norm setting,[44] these agreements enable developed and like-minded countries to team up with each other to strengthen the international minimum standards for the protection and enforcement of intellectual property rights. This approach further enhances the participating countries' bargaining positions while enabling them to avoid stalemates in international negotiations. Among the widely criticized plurilateral agreements involving new international intellectual property norms are the Anti-Counterfeiting Trade Agreement (ACTA) and the TPP Agreement. For comparative purposes, this section discusses only the latter, as the former did not involve multi-sector bargaining similar to the type of bargaining found in the Uruguay Round.

The TPP began as a quadrilateral agreement among Brunei Darussalam, Chile, New Zealand and Singapore known as the Trans-Pacific

---

[42] Peter K. Yu, 'The International Enclosure Movement' (2007) 82 *Indiana Law Journal* 827–907 at 828.

[43] Although the WTO has used this term to refer to those nonmultilateral agreements included in Annex 4 of the WTO Agreement – namely, the Agreement on Trade in Civil Aircraft, the Agreement on Government Procurement, the International Dairy Agreement and the International Bovine Meat Agreement – commentators have generally used this term to cover multi-country, multi-region agreements that are being negotiated outside the WTO, WIPO and other multilateral fora.

[44] Daniel Gervais, 'Country Clubs, Empiricism, Blogs and Innovation: The Future of International Intellectual Property Norm Making in the Wake of ACTA', in Mira Burri and Thomas Cottier (eds.), *Trade Governance in the Digital Age: World Trade Forum* (Cambridge: Cambridge University Press, 2012); Peter K. Yu, 'The ACTA/TPP Country Clubs', in Dana Beldiman (ed.), *Access to Information and Knowledge: 21st Century Challenges in Intellectual Property and Knowledge Governance* (Cheltenham: Edward Elgar, 2014). As Professor Gervais elaborated, 'This approach [is referred to] as "Country Club" because, like a country club, the membership rules are negotiated by a number of like-minded founders. Others are then invited to join, but changes to the membership rules are difficult to achieve.' Daniel Gervais, 'Country Clubs, Empiricism, Blogs and Innovation', in Mira Burri and Thomas Cottier (eds.), *Trade Governance in the Digital Age*, p. 324.

Strategic Economic Partnership Agreement or, more commonly, the 'P4' or 'Pacific 4'. As Meredith Lewis recounted,

> [The negotiations were initially] launched by Chile, New Zealand and Singapore at the APEC [Asia-Pacific Economic Cooperation Forum] leaders' summit in 2002. These original negotiations contemplated an agreement amongst the three participating countries, to be known as the Pacific Three Closer Economic Partnership...However, Brunei attended a number of rounds as an observer, and ultimately joined the Agreement as a 'founding member'. The Agreement was signed by New Zealand, Chile and Singapore on July 18, 2005 and by Brunei on August 2, 2005, following the conclusion of negotiations in June 2005.[45]

In March 2010, the TPP negotiations began with the goal of establishing an expanded agreement among Australia, Peru, Vietnam, the United States and the P4 members. Malaysia, Canada, Mexico and Japan joined the negotiations later. After nearly six years of negotiations, the agreement was finally signed in Auckland, New Zealand on 4 February 2016.

The agreement's final text contains thirty chapters, including three with significant ramifications for future international intellectual property norm setting: the investment chapter (Chapter 9), the intellectual property chapter (Chapter 18) and the dispute settlement chapter (Chapter 28). If entered into force, the original TPP Agreement would have covered '40% of global [gross domestic product] and some 30% of worldwide trade in both goods and services'.[46]

At the time of writing, the future of the TPP has become highly uncertain, due largely to President Trump's memorandum directing the United States' withdrawal from the TPP[47] as well as the reluctance on the part of other TPP partners to ratify the agreement before knowing how the new US administration would handle it. Thus far, only Japan and New Zealand have ratified the agreement. Nevertheless, regardless of the agreement's ratification status, the TPP negotiations remain important for our

---

[45] Meredith Kolsky Lewis, 'Expanding the P-4 Trade Agreement into a Broader Trans-Pacific Partnership: Implications, Risks and Opportunities' (2009) 4 *Asian Journal of the WTO and International Health Law and Policy* 401–22 at 403–4.

[46] David A. Gantz, 'The TPP and RCEP: Mega-Trade Agreements for the Pacific Rim' (2016) 33 *Arizona Journal of International and Comparative Law* 57–69 at 59.

[47] White House, 'Presidential Memorandum regarding Withdrawal of the United States from the Trans-Pacific Partnership Negotiations and Agreement'; available at www.whitehouse.gov/the-press-office/2017/01/23/presidential-memorandum-regarding-withdrawal-united-states-trans-pacific [accessed on 21 April 2017].

purposes. After all, they document not only the BRICS countries' growing influence but also their indirect impacts on international trade and
intellectual property negotiations.[48]

In general, a close analysis of the TPP negotiations and their aftermath provides four key takeaways. The first takeaway is that the negotiations show, somewhat indirectly, the BRICS countries' vocal and continued opposition to high trade and intellectual property standards set by
developed countries. Such opposition not only builds on the opposition
mounted by developing countries during the TRIPS negotiations but can
also be traced back to the 'Old Development Agenda' for intellectual property law and policy in the 1960s.[49]

The developing countries' opposition is understandable considering the
major challenges posed by high trade and intellectual property standards.
A case in point is China, the most widely discussed BRICS country in
the TPP context. The standards laid down in the agreement's government procurement and state-owned enterprises chapters would require
drastic alteration to the structure and operation of China's state-owned
enterprises.[50] The TPP electronic commerce standards chapter would also
deeply affect the Chinese censorship and information control policy.[51]
The relationship between this policy and foreign trade has been particularly sensitive, considering China's losses before both the WTO panel and
the Appellate Body in *China – Measures Affecting Trading Rights and Distribution Services for Certain Publications and Audiovisual Entertainment
Products*.[52]

The second takeaway is that the TPP negotiations remind us of the
growing threat the BRICS countries have posed to the developed world.
Although the analysis of these negotiations tend to begin with the negotiating parties, such as Australia, Canada, Japan, New Zealand, Singapore

---

[48] Peter K. Yu, 'Thinking about the Trans-Pacific Partnership (and a Mega-Regional Agreement on Life Support)' (2017) 21 *SMU Science and Technology Law Review* [forthcoming].

[49] Peter K. Yu, 'A Tale of Two Development Agendas' (2009) 35 *Ohio Northern University
Law Review* 465–93 at 468–511.

[50] Henry Gao, 'From the P4 to the TPP: Transplantation or Transformation', in C. L. Lim,
Deborah K. Elms and Patrick Low (eds.), *Trans-Pacific Partnership: A Quest for a Twenty-
First Century Trade Agreement* (Cambridge: Cambridge University Press, 2012), p. 79.

[51] *Ibid*, pp. 79–80.

[52] World Trade Organization, 'China – Measures Affecting Trading Rights and Distribution
Services for Certain Publications and Audiovisual Entertainment Products', WT/DS363/R,
12 August 2009, Panel Report; World Trade Organization, 'China – Measures Affecting
Trading Rights and Distribution Services for Certain Publications and Audiovisual Entertainment Products', WT/DS363/AB/R, 21 December 2009, Appellate Body Report.

and the United States, the outsiders are just as important as the insiders.[53] Indeed, a recent article of mine focused primarily on the TPP outsiders.[54] While commentators have analyzed ad nauseum the paradigmatic case of China's exclusion from the TPP negotiations,[55] these negotiations have also excluded the four remaining BRICS countries, as well as other key Asian economies, such as Indonesia, the Philippines, South Korea and Thailand.

To be sure, there is nothing unusual when powerful countries exclude inconsequential players from international negotiations. However, the BRICS countries are not inconsequential, and their omission deserves greater scrutiny. While China is the world's second largest or largest economy, depending on one's metrics and methodology,[56] India is the world's second most populous country and Asia's third largest economy, behind only China and Japan. Neither country was invited to the negotiations. Brazil, Russia and South Africa are equally important in their own right, yet they were also conveniently left out by virtue of the trade pact's focus on the Pacific Rim.

To a large extent, the omission of all five BRICS countries from the TPP negotiations can be analyzed by drawing on insights from the political science and international relations literature. As Shintaro Hamanaka explained,

> The formation of regional integration and cooperation frameworks can be best understood as a dominant state's attempt to create its own regional framework where it can exercise some exclusive influence … By assuming leadership, an economy can set a favorable agenda and establish convenient rules. In addition, the most powerful state can increase influence through prestige and asymmetric economic interdependence with others.[57]

The third takeaway is that the TPP negotiations reflect the increasing leverage of the BRICS countries, at least those in the Asia-Pacific region.

---

[53] Shintaro Hamanaka, 'Trans-Pacific Partnership versus Regional Comprehensive Economic Partnership: Control of Membership and Agenda Setting' (2014) Asian Development Bank, Working Paper Series on Regional Economic Integration No. 146, p. 1.

[54] Peter K. Yu, 'TPP and Trans-Pacific Perplexities' (2014) 37 *Fordham International Law Journal* 1129–81.

[55] Ibid, at 1132–51.

[56] Joseph E. Stiglitz, 'The Chinese Century', *Vanity Fair*, January 2015; available at www .vanityfair.com/news/2015/01/china-worlds-largest-economy [accessed on 23 December 2016].

[57] Shintaro Hamanaka, 'Trans-Pacific Partnership versus Regional Comprehensive Economic Partnership', pp. 1–2.

Thus far, policy makers and commentators have advanced both economic and noneconomic justifications for excluding the BRICS countries from the TPP negotiations.[58] Regardless of these justifications, however, the TPP partners' conscious and determined choice to shut these increasingly powerful emerging countries out of the negotiations has made it unclear how the former can now induce the latter to join after the regional pact's creation.

Given the BRICS countries' growing economic and geopolitical strengths, it is also difficult to see why these countries would join an agreement that is filled with rules and standards that they did not shape and cannot renegotiate.[59] Gone are the days when trade rules can be created in the developed world and then shoved down the throats of large developing countries.[60] If the BRICS countries are to eventually join this regional pact, the TPP partners will have to make significant adjustments to the pact or to provide additional incentives to entice them to join.

The final takeaway is that the TPP negotiations highlight the growing importance of the BRICS countries, especially within the Asia-Pacific region. Although China and India sat outside the TPP negotiations, the models they use and the challenges they pose are often taken into consideration when new trade and intellectual property standards are being negotiated. China, for example, was repeatedly mentioned during the negotiations as the 'elephant in the room'. Some chapters, such as those on government procurement (Chapter 15) and state-owned enterprises (Chapter 17), were clearly drafted with China in mind.

Indeed, the challenges posed by China – and, for that matter, other BRICS countries – in the regional or international trading environment have made it inevitable that the TPP negotiating parties consider the appropriateness of certain preemptory trade or trade-related norms. These parties are also likely to have evaluated the potential impact of these norms on the BRICS countries' future abilities to join the TPP. Some TPP

---

[58] Paul G. Buchanan, 'Security Implications of the TPPA', in Jane Kelsey (ed.), *No Ordinary Deal: Unmasking the Trans-Pacific Partnership Free Trade Agreement* (Wellington: Bridget Williams Books, 2010), p. 89; Meredith Kolsky Lewis, 'Achieving a Free Trade Area of the Asia-Pacific: Does the TPP Present the Most Attractive Path?' in C. L. Lim, Deborah K. Elms and Patrick Low (eds.), *Trans-Pacific Partnership*, p. 226; Peter K. Yu, 'TPP and Trans-Pacific Perplexities', at 1139–41.

[59] Peter K. Yu, 'Six Secret (and Now Open) Fears of ACTA' (2011) 64 *SMU Law Review* 975–1094 at 1090–1.

[60] Deborah Kay Elms, 'The Trans-Pacific Partnership: Looking Ahead to Next Steps', in Tang Guoqiang and Peter A. Petri (eds.), *New Directions in Asia-Pacific Economic Integration* (Honolulu: East-West Center, 2014), p. 18.

negotiating parties might also be very concerned about losing the vast and fast-growing BRICS markets. As a result, they might have paid considerable attention to the potential tension or conflict between the new TPP standards and those in preexisting trade agreements with the BRICS countries.

Moreover, some negotiating parties simply do not see the TPP solely as a trade pact. Instead, they consider it as an important strategic alliance that would help foster regional security.[61] In relation to China, for instance, some of these parties may view the regional pact as a strategic tool to ward off the threat created by a rapidly emerging China, or the so-called China threat.[62] These parties likely will have second thoughts about admitting China, and perhaps even other BRICS countries, into the TPP.

When all of these BRICS-related complications are taken into consideration, it is understandable why the BRICS countries were not invited to the TPP negotiations. It is also likely that these countries will continue to refrain from joining the agreement in the near future even if it is to enter into force.

Should the BRICS countries choose not to join the pact, however, their exclusion will raise serious questions about the benefits, significance and viability of the TPP Agreement. As Sebastian Herreros declared,

> Ultimately, the TPP will have to expand to include large, mostly Asian economies, to be a meaningful exercise. Its current commercial appeal is very modest, given the small size of most participating economies. More importantly, an agreement limited to the ... nine [and now twelve] participants would be far from a credible platform for large-scale trans-Pacific economic integration.[63]

---

[61] Paul G. Buchanan, 'Security Implications of the TPPA', p. 87; Ann Capling and John Ravenhill, 'The TPP: Multilateralizing Regionalism or the Securitization of Trade Policy', in C. L. Lim, Deborah K. Elms and Patrick Low (eds.), *Trans-Pacific Partnership*, p. 292; Olivier Cattaneo, 'The Political Economy of PTAs', in Simon Lester and Bryan Mercurio (eds.), *Bilateral and Regional Trade Agreements: Commentary and Analysis* (Cambridge: Cambridge University Press, 2009), pp. 42–50; Chad Damro, 'The Political Economy of Regional Trade Agreements', in Lorand Bartels and Federico Ortino (eds.), *Regional Trade Agreements and the WTO Legal System* (Oxford: Oxford University Press, 2007), p. 39.

[62] Paul G. Buchanan, 'Security Implications of the TPPA', p. 89; Avery Goldstein, 'U.S.–China Interactions in Asia', in David Shambaugh (ed.), *Tangled Titans: The United States and China* (Lanham, MD: Rowman & Littlefield, 2012), p. 281; Meredith Kolsky Lewis, 'Achieving a Free Trade Area of the Asia-Pacific', at 226; Jagdish Bhagwati, 'Deadlock in Durban', *Project-Syndicate*, 30 November 2011.

[63] Sebastian Herreros, 'Coping with Multiple Uncertainties: Latin America in the TPP Negotiations', in C. L. Lim, Deborah K. Elms and Patrick Low (eds.), *Trans-Pacific Partnership*, p. 274.

The continued exclusion of the BRICS countries and other large developing countries in Asia will also create complications within the existing international regulatory environment and multilateral trading system. Such complications would lead to further fragmentation, creating what commentators have referred to as the 'noodle bowl',[64] which is filled with 'a mish-mash of overlapping, supporting and possibly conflicting, obligations'.[65] In the words of former WTO Director-General Pascal Lamy, 'proliferation is breeding concern – concern about incoherence, confusion, exponential increase of costs for business, unpredictability and even unfairness in trade relations'.[66]

IV. RCEP Negotiations

A few years ago, a chapter examining the changing international trade and intellectual property norm-setting environment would have ended with the comparison between the TRIPS Agreement and the intellectual property chapter in the TPP Agreement, a key initiative launched by developed and like-minded countries. In the past few years, however, China, India and other emerging countries in the Asia-Pacific region have been actively negotiating the RCEP. This process provides an important contrast with the TPP negotiations. While China and India played rather indirect roles in the latter due to their exclusion, they have taken on dominant and proactive roles in the former.

The RCEP negotiations build on the fast-growing volumes of bilateral, regional and plurilateral negotiations that China and India have conducted in the past decade. Since the mid-2000s, China has successfully negotiated bilateral agreements with Chile, Pakistan, New Zealand, Singapore, Peru, Costa Rica, Iceland, Switzerland, South Korea, Australia and Georgia. With Brunei Darussalam, Malaysia, Vietnam and other members

---

[64] Wang Jiangyu, 'Association of Southeast Asian Nations–China Free Trade Agreement', in Simon Lester and Bryan Mercurio (eds.), *Bilateral and Regional Trade Agreements: Case Studies* (Cambridge: Cambridge University Press, 2009), p. 224; Peter K. Yu, 'Sinic Trade Agreements' (2011) 44 *U.C. Davis Law Review* 953–1028 at 978; Richard E. Baldwin, 'Managing the Noodle Bowl: The Fragility of East Asian Regionalism' (2007) Asian Development Bank, Working Paper on Regional Economic Integration No. 7; Masahiro Kawai and Ganeshan Wignaraja, 'Asian FTAs: Trends and Challenges' (2009) Asian Development Bank, Working Paper No. 144, p. 3.

[65] Simon Lester and Bryan Mercurio, 'Introduction', in Simon Lester and Bryan Mercurio (eds.), *Bilateral and Regional Trade Agreements: Case Studies*, p. 2.

[66] Pascal Lamy, 'Proliferation of Regional Trade Agreements "Breeding Concern"', 10 September 2007; available at www.wto.org/english/news_e/sppl_e/sppl67_e.htm [accessed on 23 December 2016].

of the Association of Southeast Asian Nations (ASEAN), China has also developed the ASEAN–China Free Trade Area. Taken together, China has already established bilateral or regional trading relationships with eight of the twelve TPP partners.

Similarly, India has been actively establishing bilateral and regional agreements with its trading partners, including Bhutan, Sri Lanka and ASEAN members.[67] India is also currently negotiating an economic partnership agreement with the European Union. As if these negotiations were not enough, India was instrumental in the development of the India–Brazil–South Africa (IBSA) Dialogue Forum, which features trilateral cooperation among Brazil, India and South Africa, three BRICS countries.

In November 2012, Australia, China, India, Japan, New Zealand, South Korea and the ten ASEAN members launched the negotiation of the RCEP. Building on past trade and nontrade discussions under the ASEAN+6 framework, this new regional partnership will cover not only the two most powerful BRICS countries (China and India) but also two high-income Asian economies (Japan and South Korea) as well as six other TPP partners (Australia, Brunei Darussalam, Malaysia, New Zealand, Singapore and Vietnam).[68] Once established, the RCEP will 'account for almost half of the world's population, almost 30 per cent of global [gross domestic product] and over a quarter of world exports'.[69]

Thus far, policy makers and commentators remain skeptical towards ASEAN's ability to set effective and far-reaching trade and intellectual property norms. Mark Beeson, for example, has described ASEAN as an organization 'accommodating the slowest ship in the convoy'.[70] Notwithstanding this skepticism, the RCEP may garner more interest from developing countries in the Asia-Pacific region than the TPP, given the former's potential application to China and India. The Trump administration's recent withdrawal from the TPP also raises the possibility that the RCEP will eventually overtake the TPP as the most dominant regional norm-setting exercise in the Asia-Pacific region. If so, the eventually

---

[67] Locknie Hsu, 'China, India and Dispute Settlement in the WTO and RTAs', in Muthucumaraswamy Sornarajah and Wang Jiangyu (eds.), *China, India and the International Economic Order* (Cambridge: Cambridge University Press, 2010), pp. 266–8; Wang Jiangyu, 'The Role of China and India in Asian Regionalism', in Muthucumaraswamy Sornarajah and Wang Jiangyu (eds.), *China, India and the International Economic Order*, pp. 356–8.

[68] Meredith Kolsky Lewis, 'Achieving a Free Trade Area of the Asia-Pacific', at 227–9.

[69] Department of Foreign Affairs and Trade (Australia), 'Regional Comprehensive Economic Partnership'; available at dfat.gov.au/trade/agreements/rcep/pages/regional-comprehensive-economic-partnership.aspx [accessed on 23 December 2016].

[70] Mark Beeson, *Institutions of the Asia-Pacific: ASEAN, APEC and Beyond* (London: Routledge, 2009), p. 32.

finalized RCEP Agreement will become the de facto blueprint for the development of the Free Trade Area of the Asia-Pacific (FTAAP), which APEC members pledged to create in 2009.

A greater focus on the RCEP negotiations is therefore highly important. Such a focus also highlights the increasing roles of the BRICS countries in international trade and intellectual property negotiations, in at least three ways. First, unlike the TPP negotiations, which involved only the BRICS countries' indirect participation, the RCEP negotiations feature the direct participation of China, India and other large developing countries in Asia. Notwithstanding this key difference, the TPP continues to have a direct impact on the RCEP. While the successful negotiation of the TPP Agreement led to the acceleration of the RCEP negotiations,[71] the United States' withdrawal from the TPP has also led to a slowdown of the RCEP negotiations.

Second, like the TPP negotiations, the RCEP negotiations reflect the growing leverage of the BRICS countries, at least in the Asia-Pacific region. Although commentators have distinguished the RCEP from the TPP by noting China's involvement in the former and the United States' involvement in the latter, it cannot be ignored that seven of the twelve TPP partners have participated in both the TPP and RCEP negotiations. As David Shambaugh and other commentators have aptly observed, countries in the Asia-Pacific region remain highly reluctant to pick between Beijing and Washington in developing their trade relations, despite their ongoing concern about China's growing economic and military strengths.[72] Indeed, some commentators take the position that the TPP and the RCEP will eventually merge.[73] As Meredith Lewis observed,

---

[71] Du Ming, 'Explaining China's Tripartite Strategy toward the Trans-Pacific Partnership Agreement' (2015) 18 *Journal of International Economic Law* 407–32 at 424; Shintaro Hamanaka, 'Trans-Pacific Partnership versus Regional Comprehensive Economic Partnership', p. 13; Michael Wesley, 'Who Calls the Tune? Asia Has to Dance to Duelling Trade Agendas', *The Conversation*, 19 October 2014.

[72] Ann Capling and John Ravenhill, 'The TPP', p. 293; Ellen L. Frost, 'China's Commercial Diplomacy in Asia: Promise or Threat?' in William W. Keller and Thomas G. Rawski (eds.), *China's Rise and the Balance of Influence in Asia* (Pittsburgh: University of Pittsburgh Press, 2007), p. 105; David Shambaugh, 'Introduction: The Rise of China and Asia's New Dynamics', in David Shambaugh (ed.), *Power Shift: China and Asia's New Dynamics* (Berkeley: University of California Press, 2006), p. 17; Peter K. Yu, 'TPP and Trans-Pacific Perplexities', at 1151.

[73] Kurt M. Campbell, *The Pivot: The Future of American Statecraft in Asia* (New York: Twelve, 2016), p. 193; Matthew P. Goodman, 'US Economic Strategy in the Asia-Pacific Region: Promoting Growth, Rules, and Presence', in Tang Guoqiang and Peter A. Petri (eds.), *New Directions in Asia-Pacific Economic Integration*, pp. 174–5; Meredith Kolsky Lewis,

[The merger of the TPP and the RCEP] is a definite possibility. It is hard to envision economies such as India or China agreeing in the near-term to the comprehensive liberation on trade in goods that acceding to the TPP would entail. At the same time, it also does not seem realistic that in the long-term there will be an FTAAP that does not include China. Furthermore, should Korea . . . agree to join the TPP, it would not be in China's interest to remain on the outside . . . [Thus, i]t is possible that these competing considerations will coalesce via an ultimate melding together of the TPP with ASEAN+6, such that non-TPP members of ASEAN+6 phase in their commitments over a longer and later time period.[74]

Key APEC documents such as 'Pathways to FTAAP' and 'The Beijing Roadmap for APEC's Contribution to the Realization of the FTAAP' also included both the TPP and the RCEP as possible paths to create the FTAAP.[75]

Third, the RCEP negotiations illustrate the reduced gap between developed countries on the one hand and the BRICS countries and large developing countries in Asia on the other. When the RCEP negotiations were first announced, one could not help but wonder whether the negotiations would set new regional intellectual property norms. After all, piracy and counterfeiting problems remain widespread in most RCEP negotiating parties. By the time the draft intellectual property chapter was leaked to the public, however, it became clear that the final RCEP Agreement is likely to include an intellectual property chapter that contains standards lower than those in the TPP Agreement but still much higher than those in the TRIPS Agreement.[76] Although many reasons exist to explain why the RCEP negotiating parties would accept such a chapter, it cannot be ignored that the economic and technological conditions of the BRICS

'Achieving a Free Trade Area of the Asia-Pacific', at 235; Robert Scollay, 'The TPP and RCEP: Prospects for Convergence', in Tang Guoqiang and Peter A. Petri (eds.), *New Directions in Asia-Pacific Economic Integration*, p. 235.

[74] Meredith Kolsky Lewis, 'Achieving a Free Trade Area of the Asia-Pacific', at 235.

[75] Asia-Pacific Economic Cooperation Forum, 'Pathways to FTAAP', 13 November 2010; available at www.apec.org/meeting-papers/leaders-declarations/2010/2010_aelm/pathways-to-ftaap.aspx [accessed on 23 December 2016]; Asia-Pacific Economic Cooperation Forum, 'The Beijing Roadmap for APEC's Contribution to the Realization of the FTAAP', 11 November 2014; available at www.apec.org/Meeting-Papers/Leaders-Declarations/2014/2014_aelm/2014_aelm_annexa.aspx [accessed on 23 December 2016].

[76] Peter K. Yu, 'The RCEP and Trans-Pacific Intellectual Property Norms' (2017) 50 *Vanderbilt Journal of Transnational Law* 673–740 at 720–31; Jeremy Malcolm, 'Meet RCEP, a Trade Agreement in Asia That's Even Worse than TPP or ACTA', 4 June 2015; available at www.eff.org/deeplinks/2015/06/just-when-you-thought-no-trade-agreement-could-be-worse-tpp-meet-rcep [accessed on 23 December 2016].

countries and other large developing countries have slowly caught up with those of the developed world.

In sum, the RCEP negotiations show a very different aspect and manifestation of the BRICS factor. In these negotiations, the BRICS countries are no longer outsiders trying to exert indirect influence, but are key actors that have been actively driving the negotiations. A greater scrutiny of the RCEP negotiations will therefore help us better understand what the BRICS countries could achieve in international trade and intellectual property norm setting if they chose to take on more assertive roles in international negotiations.

V. Changing International Norm-Setting Environment

The emergence of the BRICS countries in international trade and intellectual property negotiations has shown how much the norm-setting environment has changed in the past two decades. When the TRIPS Agreement was being negotiated in the late 1980s and early 1990s, intellectual property law and policy was mostly a 'new, new thing' for many countries in the South. Two decades later, however, the issue has come of age, and many developing countries that were once ignorant of intellectual property matters have now developed a good grasp of the norms needed to establish a well-functioning intellectual property system.

Thus far, the growing roles of the BRICS countries and other large developing countries have revealed four set of important changes to the international trade and intellectual property norm-setting environment. The first change concerns the types of players that have emerged in the international trade and intellectual property arenas. Although countries are usually divided between the North and the South, the arrival of the BRICS countries has raised questions about whether the newly emerging players are actually from the North or from the South.

In regard to China, for instance, it is increasingly difficult to consider as South–South agreements those free trade agreements that the country has established with other developing countries. As I noted in an article on China's free trade agreements, 'Technically, [these agreements] are not South–South agreements. They are not attempts to promote South–South or Third World solidarity. They are also not altruistic or humanitarian gestures. At best, they are East–South agreements (an intermediate category that falls between North–South and South–South agreements).'[77]

---

[77] Peter K. Yu, 'Sinic Trade Agreements', at 987.

To a large extent, the BRICS countries resemble both countries in the North and countries in the South. While they certainly have resources and capabilities to address a growing variety of issues, they still remain far behind developed countries in many areas. Because their interests align with the developed world sometimes and with the developing world at other times, their positions and policy preferences have been somewhat schizophrenic.[78] These positions and preferences are indeed so distinctive that I have referred to them as 'middle intellectual property powers'.[79] In addition to the BRICS countries, these middle powers include Argentina, Indonesia, Malaysia, Philippines and Thailand. Due to their dynamic and fast-growing nature, these emerging economies are best analyzed separately from their poorer and weaker counterparts in the developing world.[80]

The second change concerns issues that are being negotiated in the international trade and intellectual property arenas. Traditionally, these issues are negotiated along the lines of the North–South divide. Whether developing countries supported them had depended largely on whether these issues reflected the interests of the developing world. Today, however, the BRICS countries do not always make decision based on the North–South divide. Although Brazil, China and India still want to retain leadership in the developing world, they have also sided with developed countries in many negotiations – or at least in the negotiation of many items.

Because of conflicting objectives, position changes and resulting uncertainties, it is increasingly difficult for leaders from poorer and weaker developing countries to decide whether they should team up with these emerging powers.[81] Understandably, the leaders of the former will become concerned about the latter's attempt to dominate any bargaining coalition. Instead of big brothers, the larger and more powerful developing countries could easily behave like new bullies.[82] Given these complicated dynamics, the recent emergence of large developing countries may alter the alliances or bargaining coalitions that developing

---

[78] Peter K. Yu, 'The Middle Kingdom and the Intellectual Property World' (2011) 13 *Oregon Review of International Law* 209–62 at 234–5.

[79] Peter K. Yu, 'The Middle Intellectual Property Powers', in Randall Peerenboom and Tom Ginsburg (eds.), *Law and Development in Middle-Income Countries: Avoiding the Middle-Income Trap* (New York: Cambridge University Press, 2014).

[80] *Ibid*, pp. 89–91.

[81] Peter K. Yu, 'Access to Medicines, BRICS Alliances, and Collective Action', at 389–93.

[82] Peter K. Yu, 'The Middle Intellectual Property Powers', p. 104.

countries set up in the past. Such emergence may also greatly weaken the united front these countries once put up or their ability to establish what Amrita Narlikar and Pieter van Houten referred to as the 'strong South'.[83]

The third change concerns the rapid proliferation of fora for setting international trade and intellectual property norms. Although the WTO and WIPO remain the predominant fora for setting international intellectual property norms, countries have increasingly turned to other international fora, such as those governing public health, human rights, biological diversity, food and agriculture, and information and communications.[84] Countries have also explored whether negotiations should be undertaken at the nonmultilateral level instead – such as through the negotiation of bilateral, regional and plurilateral trade agreements.

In fact, both developed and developing countries have found it advantageous to negotiate international norms outside the WTO, WIPO and other multilateral fora. While developed countries initiated the negotiation of ACTA, the TPP and the Transatlantic Trade and Investment Partnership (TTIP), developing countries have participated in the RCEP negotiations, the BRICS Summit and the IBSA Dialogue Forum. At WIPO, these countries have also demanded the development of South–South collaboration projects.[85]

In the short run, nonmultilateral negotiations could allow like-minded countries to set plurilateral norms by circumventing the deadlock between developed and developing countries. In the long run, however, these negotiations will undermine the norms that developed and developing countries have worked hard to build through the WTO, WIPO and other multilateral fora.

Given these potential long-term adverse impacts, it is understandable why policy makers and commentators have widely criticized the increased fragmentation of the multilateral trading system. As WIPO Director General Francis Gurry lamented at the time of the ACTA negotiations, those developed and like-minded countries involved had 'tak[en] matters into their own hands to seek solutions outside of the multilateral system to the

---

[83] Amrita Narlikar and Pieter van Houten, 'Know the Enemy: Uncertainty and Deadlock in the WTO', in Amrita Narlikar (ed.), *Deadlocks in Multilateral Negotiations*, p. 150.

[84] Peter K. Yu, 'A Tale of Two Development Agendas', at 522–40.

[85] Catherine Saez, 'WIPO Committee on Development Agenda Suspended, Discussions Bogged Down', *Intellectual Property Watch*, 7 May 2011.

detriment of inclusiveness of the present system.[86] Eyal Benvenisti and George Downs also discussed how the growing proliferation of international regulatory institutions with overlapping jurisdictions and ambiguous boundaries would help powerful countries preserve their dominance and therefore make it more difficult for developing countries to catch up.[87]

The fourth change concerns the rhetoric used in the North-South intellectual property debate. The recent success of the BRICS countries has raised serious questions about the traditional rhetoric used in this debate. Although the TRIPS Agreement has been presented as a bargain between developed and developing countries over market access and intellectual property protection on the one hand and concessions in textiles and agriculture on the other, developing countries have repeatedly complained about the lack of a fair bargain due to power asymmetry and their limited intellectual property expertise.[88]

Nevertheless, recent developments in the BRICS countries have raised questions about whether the TRIPS bargain has been as unfair as developing countries and their supportive commentators have claimed. Consider China for example. According to the latest WIPO statistics, the country had the world's third largest volume of international applications filed through the Patent Cooperation Treaty in 2016, behind only the United States and Japan.[89] Among all corporate applicants, ZTE Corporation and Huawei Technologies had the first and second largest number of applications, respectively. In the same period, China also ranked fourth in filing international trademark applications under the Madrid system.[90]

To a large extent, the TRIPS Agreement and the market access provided by the WTO membership have helped the BRICS countries quickly develop their economies and technological capabilities. In these countries,

---

[86] Catherine Saez, 'ACTA a Sign of Weakness in Multilateral System, WIPO Head Says', *Intellectual Property Watch*, 30 June 2010.

[87] Eyal Benvenisti and George W. Downs, 'The Empire's New Clothes: Political Economy and the Fragmentation of International Law' (2007) 60 *Stanford Law Review* 595–631.

[88] Peter K. Yu, 'TRIPS and Its Discontents' (2006) 10 *Marquette Intellectual Property Law Review* 369–410 at 371–6.

[89] World Intellectual Property Organization, 'Who Filed the Most PCT Patent Applications in 2016?' 15 March 2017; available at www.wipo.int/export/sites/www/ipstats/en/docs/infographic_pct_2016.pdf [accessed on 21 April 2017].

[90] World Intellectual Property Organization, 'Who Filed the Most Madrid Trademark Applications in 2016?' 15 March 2017; available at www.wipo.int/export/sites/www/ipstats/en/docs/infographic_madrid_2016.pdf [accessed on 21 April 2017].

the fast-growing intellectual property industries have clearly benefited from greater protection and enforcement of intellectual property rights. That the TRIPS Agreement has been biased towards developed countries does not mean that it cannot also provide benefits to some key intellectual property stakeholders in developing countries.

More importantly for our purposes, if the TRIPS Agreement has considerable benefits for the BRICS countries, especially when viewed with the benefit of hindsight, one also has to think carefully about whether the TPP and the RCEP would provide similar benefits to these countries, and perhaps even other large developing countries in the Asia-Pacific region. Just because some trade and intellectual property standards are too high for these countries *now* does not mean that those standards will remain too high for them *in the near future*. Thus, as important as it is to debate whether these nonmultilateral agreements should be adopted in developing countries, it is equally important to explore what flexibilities, safeguards and correction mechanisms are needed to tailor these agreements to the needs, interests, conditions and priorities of the participating countries.

VI. Conclusion

On 1 January 1995, the TRIPS Agreement entered into effect, thereby transplanting intellectual property norms from developed countries to their less developed counterparts. Although the agreement has its strengths and contributions, many developed countries now consider it obsolete, inadequate and ineffective. As a result, they have aggressively pushed for the establishment of TRIPS-plus bilateral, regional and plurilateral trade agreements outside the WTO, WIPO and other multilateral fora.

Just as these agreements are being negotiated, developing countries are becoming more assertive in international trade and intellectual property negotiations. As a result, an inevitable clash has emerged between these two groups of countries. The ongoing negotiations of the TPP, the RCEP and other TRIPS-plus nonmultilateral agreements have revealed the important roles played by the BRICS countries, usually in the form of partial BRICS alliances. While the TPP negotiations illustrate the growing influence of these countries in international trade and intellectual property negotiations, though somewhat indirectly, the RCEP negotiations have shown their direct influence and what they could achieve by taking on more assertive roles.

In sum, the international norm-setting environment has become much more complex than it was more than two decades ago when the TRIPS Agreement was being negotiated. If new and effective international trade and intellectual property norms are to be developed, policy makers and negotiators will need to acquire a deeper understanding of this changing international norm-setting environment. Thus far, it remains unclear whether this environment will tilt the negotiations towards the developed world or the developing world. After all, the BRICS countries align their interests with the former sometimes and with the latter at other times.

Nevertheless, the dramatic changes in their negotiating positions and bargaining arrangements do suggest that these countries may not always subscribe to the positions commonly found in a traditional North–South debate. As we move forward with the negotiation of new trade and intellectual property standards between developed and developing countries, greater policy and scholarly attention will have to be devoted not only to the traditional North–South divide but also to the increasingly important BRICS factor in international trade and intellectual property negotiations.

VII. Acknowledgements

This chapter draws on research from the author's earlier articles in the *Fordham International Law Journal*, the *Houston Law Review* and the *Vanderbilt Journal of Transnational Law.*

VIII. References

Anell, Lars, 'Foreword to the First Edition', in Daniel Gervais, *The TRIPS Agreement: Drafting History and Analysis*, 3rd edn (London: Sweet & Maxwell, 2008).

Asia-Pacific Economic Cooperation Forum, 'The Beijing Roadmap for APEC's Contribution to the Realization of the FTAAP', 11 November 2014; available at www.apec.org/Meeting-Papers/Leaders-Declarations/2014/2014_aelm/ 2014_aelm_annexa.aspx [accessed on 23 December 2016].

'Pathways to FTAAP', 13 November 2010; available at www.apec.org/meeting-papers/leaders-declarations/2010/2010_aelm/pathways-to-ftaap.aspx [accessed on 23 December 2016].

Baldwin, Richard E., 'Managing the Noodle Bowl: The Fragility of East Asian Regionalism' (2007) Asian Development Bank, Working Paper on Regional Economic Integration No. 7.

Beeson, Mark, *Institutions of the Asia-Pacific: ASEAN, APEC and Beyond* (London: Routledge, 2009).

Benvenisti, Eyal and Downs, George W., 'The Empire's New Clothes: Political Economy and the Fragmentation of International Law' (2007) 60 *Stanford Law Review* 595–631.

Bhagwati, Jagdish, 'Afterword: The Question of Linkage' (2002) 96 *American Journal of International Law* 126–34.

'Deadlock in Durban', *Project-Syndicate*, 30 November 2011.

Brewster, Rachel, 'Shadow Unilateralism: Enforcing International Trade Law at the WTO' (2009) 30 *University of Pennsylvania Journal of International Law* 1133–46.

Buchanan, Paul G., 'Security Implications of the TPPA', in Jane Kelsey (ed.), *No Ordinary Deal: Unmasking the Trans-Pacific Partnership Free Trade Agreement* (Wellington: Bridget Williams Books, 2010).

Campbell, Kurt M., *The Pivot: The Future of American Statecraft in Asia* (New York: Twelve, 2016).

Capling, Ann and Ravenhill, John, 'The TPP: Multilateralizing Regionalism or the Securitization of Trade Policy', in C. L. Lim, Deborah K. Elms and Patrick Low (eds.), *Trans-Pacific Partnership: A Quest for a Twenty-First Century Trade Agreement* (Cambridge: Cambridge University Press, 2012).

Cassiolato, José and Vitorino, Virginia (eds.), *BRICS and Development Alternatives: Innovation Systems and Policies* (London: Anthem Press, 2011).

Cattaneo, Olivier, 'The Political Economy of PTAs', in Simon Lester and Bryan Mercurio (eds.), *Bilateral and Regional Trade Agreements: Commentary and Analysis* (Cambridge: Cambridge University Press, 2009).

Chon, Margaret, 'Intellectual Property and the Development Divide' (2006) 27 *Cardozo Law Review* 2821–912.

Cooper, Andrew F., *The BRICS: A Very Short Introduction* (Oxford: Oxford University Press, 2016).

Correa, Carlos M., 'The Push for Stronger Enforcement Rules: Implications for Developing Countries', in *The Global Debate on the Enforcement of Intellectual Property Rights and Developing Countries* (Geneva: International Centre for Trade and Sustainable Development, 2009).

Trade Related Aspects of Intellectual Property Rights: A Commentary on the TRIPS Agreement (Oxford: Oxford University Press, 2007).

Damro, Chad, 'The Political Economy of Regional Trade Agreements', in Lorand Bartels and Federico Ortino (eds.), *Regional Trade Agreements and the WTO Legal System* (Oxford: Oxford University Press, 2007).

Davey, William J., 'The WTO Dispute Settlement System: The First Ten Years' (2005) 8 *Journal of International Economic Law* 17–50.

Department of Foreign Affairs and Trade (Australia), 'Regional Comprehensive Economic Partnership'; available at dfat.gov.au/trade/agreements/rcep/pages/regional-comprehensive-economic-partnership.aspx [accessed on 23 December 2016].

Dreyfuss, Rochelle Cooper and Lowenfeld, Andreas F., 'Two Achievements of the Uruguay Round: Putting TRIPS and Dispute Settlement Together' (1997) 37 *Virginia Journal of International Law* 275–333.

Du, Ming, 'Explaining China's Tripartite Strategy toward the Trans-Pacific Partnership Agreement' (2015) 18 *Journal of International Economic Law* 407–32.

Elms, Deborah Kay, 'The Trans-Pacific Partnership: Looking Ahead to Next Steps', in Tang Guoqiang and Peter A. Petri (eds.), *New Directions in Asia-Pacific Economic Integration* (Honolulu: East-West Center, 2014).

Frost, Ellen L., 'China's Commercial Diplomacy in Asia: Promise or Threat?' in William W. Keller and Thomas G. Rawski (eds.), *China's Rise and the Balance of Influence in Asia* (Pittsburgh: University of Pittsburgh Press, 2007).

Gantz, David A., 'The TPP and RCEP: Mega-Trade Agreements for the Pacific Rim' (2016) 33 *Arizona Journal of International and Comparative Law* 57–69.

Gao, Henry, 'From the P4 to the TPP: Transplantation or Transformation', in C. L. Lim, Deborah K. Elms and Patrick Low (eds.), *Trans-Pacific Partnership: A Quest for a Twenty-First Century Trade Agreement* (Cambridge: Cambridge University Press, 2012).

General Agreement on Tariffs and Trade, 'Ministerial Declaration on the Uruguay Round of Multilateral Trade Negotiations', 20 September 1986, (1986) 25 *International Legal Materials* 1623–7.

Gervais, Daniel J., 'Country Clubs, Empiricism, Blogs and Innovation: The Future of International Intellectual Property Norm Making in the Wake of ACTA', in Mira Burri and Thomas Cottier (eds.), *Trade Governance in the Digital Age: World Trade Forum* (Cambridge: Cambridge University Press, 2012).

'The TRIPS Agreement and the Doha Round: History and Impact on Economic Development', in Peter K. Yu (ed.), *Intellectual Property and Information Wealth: Issues and Practices in the Digital Age* (Westport, CT: Praeger, 2007), vol. 4.

'TRIPS 3.0: Policy Calibration and Innovation Displacement', in Neil Weinstock Netanel (ed.), *The Development Agenda: Global Intellectual Property and Developing Countries* (Oxford: Oxford University Press, 2008).

Goldstein, Avery, 'U.S.–China Interactions in Asia', in David Shambaugh (ed.), *Tangled Titans: The United States and China* (Lanham, MD: Rowman & Littlefield, 2012).

Goodman, Matthew P., 'US Economic Strategy in the Asia-Pacific Region: Promoting Growth, Rules, and Presence', in Tang Guoqiang and Peter A. Petri (eds.), *New Directions in Asia-Pacific Economic Integration* (Honolulu: East-West Center, 2014).

Gorlin, Jacques J., *An Analysis of the Pharmaceutical-Related Provisions of the WTO TRIPS (Intellectual Property) Agreement* (London: Intellectual Property Institute, 1999).

Hamanaka, Shintaro, 'Trans-Pacific Partnership versus Regional Comprehensive Economic Partnership: Control of Membership and Agenda Setting' (2014) Asian Development Bank, Working Paper Series on Regional Economic Integration No. 146.

Herreros, Sebastian, 'Coping with Multiple Uncertainties: Latin America in the TPP Negotiations', in C. L. Lim, Deborah K. Elms and Patrick Low (eds.), *Trans-Pacific Partnership: A Quest for a Twenty-First Century Trade Agreement* (Cambridge: Cambridge University Press, 2012).

Hsu, Locknie, 'China, India and Dispute Settlement in the WTO and RTAs', in Muthucumaraswamy Sornarajah and Wang Jiangyu (eds.), *China, India and the International Economic Order* (Cambridge: Cambridge University Press, 2010).

Kawai, Masahiro and Wignaraja, Ganeshan, 'Asian FTAs: Trends and Challenges' (2009) Asian Development Bank, Working Paper No. 144.

Lamy, Pascal, 'Proliferation of Regional Trade Agreements "Breeding Concern"', 10 September 2007; available at www.wto.org/english/news_e/sppl_e/sppl67_e .htm [accessed on 23 December 2016].

Lester, Simon and Mercurio, Bryan, 'Introduction', in Simon Lester and Bryan Mercurio (eds.), *Bilateral and Regional Trade Agreements: Case Studies* (Cambridge: Cambridge University Press, 2009).

Lewis, Meredith Kolsky, 'Achieving a Free Trade Area of the Asia-Pacific: Does the TPP Present the Most Attractive Path?' in C. L. Lim, Deborah K. Elms and Patrick Low (eds.), *Trans-Pacific Partnership: A Quest for a Twenty-First Century Trade Agreement* (Cambridge: Cambridge University Press, 2012).

'Expanding the P-4 Trade Agreement into a Broader Trans-Pacific Partnership: Implications, Risks and Opportunities' (2009) 4 *Asian Journal of the WTO and International Health Law and Policy* 401–22.

Malcolm, Jeremy, 'Meet RCEP, a Trade Agreement in Asia That's Even Worse than TPP or ACTA', 4 June 2015; available at www.eff.org/deeplinks/2015/06/just-when-you-thought-no-trade-agreement-could-be-worse-tpp-meet-rcep [accessed on 23 December 2016].

Matthews, Duncan, *Globalising Intellectual Property Rights: The TRIPs Agreement* (London: Routledge, 2002).

Narlikar, Amrita (ed.), *Deadlocks in Multilateral Negotiations: Causes and Solutions* (Cambridge: Cambridge University Press, 2010).

International Trade and Developing Countries: Bargaining Coalitions in the GATT and WTO (London: Routledge, 2003).

New Powers: How to Become One and How to Manage Them (New York: Columbia University Press, 2010).

Narlikar, Amrita and van Houten, Pieter, 'Know the Enemy: Uncertainty and Deadlock in the WTO', in Amrita Narlikar (ed.), *Deadlocks in Multilateral Negotiations: Causes and Solutions* (Cambridge: Cambridge University Press, 2010).

Negotiating Group on Trade-Related Aspects of Intellectual Property Rights, Including Trade in Counterfeit Goods (TRIPS Negotiating Group), 'Guidelines and Objectives Proposed by the European Community for the Negotiations on Trade Related Aspects of Substantive Standards of Intellectual Property Rights', 7 July 1988, MTN.GNG/NG11/W/26.

'Guidelines Proposed by the European Community for the Negotiations on Trade-Related Aspects of Intellectual Property Rights', 20 November 1987, MTN.GNG/NG11/W/16.

'The Madrid Agreement for the Repression of False or Deceptive Indications of Source on Goods: Suggestion by Brazil', 9 July 1987, MTN.GNG/NG11/W/11.

'Meeting of Negotiating Group of 12–14 July 1989: Note by the Secretariat', 12 September 1989, MTN.GNG/NG11/14.

'Standards and Principles Concerning the Availability Scope and Use of Trade-Related Intellectual Property Rights: Communication from India', 10 July 1989, MTN.GNG/NG11/W/37.

'Status of Work in the Negotiating Group: Chairman's Report to the GNG', 23 July 1990, MTN.GNG/NG11/W/76.

'Suggestion by the United States for Achieving the Negotiating Objective', 20 October 1987, MTN.GNG/NG11/W/14.

Odell, John S. (ed.), *Negotiating the World Economy* (Ithaca, NY: Cornell University Press, 2000).

Negotiating Trade: Developing Countries in the WTO and NAFTA (Cambridge: Cambridge University Press, 2006).

Okediji, Ruth, 'Toward an International Fair Use Doctrine' (2000) 39 *Columbia Journal of Transnational Law* 75–175.

O'Neill, Jim, 'Building Better Global Economic BRICs' (2001) Goldman Sachs, Global Economics Paper No. 66.

The Growth Map: Economic Opportunity in the BRICs and Beyond (London: Portfolio, 2011).

Otten, Adrian and Wager, Hannu, 'Compliance with TRIPS: The Emerging World View' (1996) *29 Vanderbilt Journal of Transnational Law* 391–413.

Ryan, Michael P., *Knowledge Diplomacy: Global Competition and the Politics of Intellectual Property* (Washington, DC: Brookings Institution Press, 1998).

Saez, Catherine, 'ACTA a Sign of Weakness in Multilateral System, WIPO Head Says', *Intellectual Property Watch*, 30 June 2010.

'WIPO Committee on Development Agenda Suspended, Discussions Bogged Down', *Intellectual Property Watch*, 7 May 2011.

Scollay, Robert, 'The TPP and RCEP: Prospects for Convergence', in Tang Guoqiang and Peter A. Petri (eds.), *New Directions in Asia-Pacific Economic Integration* (Honolulu: East-West Center, 2014).

Sell, Susan K., *Private Power, Public Law: The Globalization of Intellectual Property Rights* (Cambridge: Cambridge University Press, 2003).

Shambaugh, David, 'Introduction: The Rise of China and Asia's New Dynamics', in David Shambaugh (ed.), *Power Shift: China and Asia's New Dynamics* (Berkeley: University of California Press, 2006).

Singh, J. P., *Negotiation and the Global Information Economy* (Cambridge: Cambridge University Press, 2008).

Stiglitz, Joseph E., 'The Chinese Century', *Vanity Fair*, January 2015; available at www.vanityfair.com/news/2015/01/china-worlds-largest-economy [accessed on 23 December 2016].

UNCTAD-ICTSD Project on IPRs and Sustainable Development, *Resource Book on TRIPS and Development* (Cambridge: Cambridge University Press, 2005).

United Nations Development Programme, *Human Development Report 1999* (New York: Oxford University Press, 1999).

Wang, Jiangyu, 'Association of Southeast Asian Nations–China Free Trade Agreement', in Simon Lester and Bryan Mercurio (eds.), *Bilateral and Regional Trade Agreements: Case Studies* (Cambridge: Cambridge University Press, 2009).

'The Role of China and India in Asian Regionalism', in Muthucumaraswamy Sornarajah and Wang Jiangyu (eds.), *China, India and the International Economic Order* (Cambridge: Cambridge University Press, 2010).

Watal, Jayashree, *Intellectual Property Rights in the WTO and Developing Countries* (The Hague: Kluwer Law International, 2001).

Wesley, Michael, 'Who Calls the Tune? Asia Has to Dance to Duelling Trade Agendas', *The Conversation*, 19 October 2014.

White House, 'Presidential Memorandum regarding Withdrawal of the United States from the Trans-Pacific Partnership Negotiations and Agreement'; available at www.whitehouse.gov/the-press-office/2017/01/23/presidential-memorandum-regarding-withdrawal-united-states-trans-pacific [accessed on 21 April 2017].

World Intellectual Property Organization, 'Who Filed the Most Madrid Trademark Applications in 2016?' 15 March 2017; available at www.wipo.int/export/sites/www/ipstats/en/docs/infographic_madrid_2016.pdf [accessed on 21 April 2017].

'Who Filed the Most PCT Patent Applications in 2016?' 15 March 2017; available at www.wipo.int/export/sites/www/ipstats/en/docs/infographic_pct_2016.pdf [accessed on 21 April 2017].

World Trade Organization, 'China – Measures Affecting Trading Rights and Distribution Services for Certain Publications and Audiovisual Entertainment Products', WT/DS363/R, 12 August 2009, Panel Report.

'China – Measures Affecting Trading Rights and Distribution Services for Certain Publications and Audiovisual Entertainment Products', WT/DS363/AB/R, 21 December 2009, Appellate Body Report.

Yu, Peter K., 'Access to Medicines, BRICS Alliances, and Collective Action' (2008) 34 *American Journal of Law and Medicine* 345–94.

'The ACTA/TPP Country Clubs', in Dana Beldiman (ed.), *Access to Information and Knowledge: 21st Century Challenges in Intellectual Property and Knowledge Governance* (Cheltenham: Edward Elgar, 2014).

'Are Developing Countries Playing a Better TRIPS Game?' (2011) 16 *UCLA Journal of International Law and Foreign Affairs* 311–43.

'Currents and Crosscurrents in the International Intellectual Property Regime' (2004) 38 *Loyola of Los Angeles Law Review* 323–443.

'The International Enclosure Movement' (2007) 82 *Indiana Law Journal* 827–907.

'The Middle Intellectual Property Powers', in Randall Peerenboom and Tom Ginsburg (eds.), *Law and Development in Middle-Income Countries: Avoiding the Middle-Income Trap* (New York: Cambridge University Press, 2014).

'The Middle Kingdom and the Intellectual Property World' (2011) 13 *Oregon Review of International Law* 209–62.

'The RCEP and Trans-Pacific Intellectual Property Norms' (2017) 50 *Vanderbilt Journal of Transnational Law* 673–740.

'Sinic Trade Agreements' (2011) 44 *U.C. Davis Law Review* 953–1028.

'Six Secret (and Now Open) Fears of ACTA' (2011) 64 *SMU Law Review* 975–1094.

'A Tale of Two Development Agendas' (2009) 35 *Ohio Northern University Law Review* 465–93.

'Thinking about the Trans-Pacific Partnership (and a Mega-Regional Agreement on Life Support)' (2017) 21 *SMU Science and Technology Law Review* [forthcoming].

'TPP and Trans-Pacific Perplexities' (2014) 37 *Fordham International Law Journal* 1129–81.

'TRIPS and Its Discontents' (2006) 10 *Marquette Intellectual Property Law Review* 369–410.

'Virotech Patents, Viropiracy, and Viral Sovereignty' (2014) 45 *Arizona State Law Journal* 1563–662.

Yu, Peter K. et al., 'Speeches: U.S. Industries, Trade Associations, and Intellectual Property Lawmaking' (2002) 10 *Cardozo Journal of International and Comparative Law* 5–35.

Yusuf, Abdulqawi A., 'TRIPS: Background, Principles and General Provisions', in Carlos M. Correa and Abdulqawi A. Yusuf (eds.), *Intellectual Property and International Trade: The TRIPS Agreement*, 2nd edn (Alphen aan den Rijn: Kluwer Law International, 2008).

8

BRICS in the Emerging Energy Trade Debate

JENYA GRIGOROVA AND JULIA MOTTE BAUMVOL

I. Introduction

It is a truth universally acknowledged that a single state must be in want of cooperation. This cannot be any more universal, or any more true, when applied to the energy sector. No state can strive to be an energy island, and cooperation between energy producers (exporters), and energy consumers (importers) is inevitable. This is even more the case for the BRICS countries, not only because of their central (and rising) role in the international scene but also because energy was, and still is, one of the cornerstones of their cooperation.

In this chapter, we are less concerned with the role of energy as a brick of the BRICS, however, and more with its catalyzing role in the relationships between the BRICS and third countries. Our focus is on the role that BRICS countries play in the context of the (re)emerging energy–trade debate. We aim to identify points of convergence in the activities in the sector, and to determine whether these points of convergence are the result of streamlined cooperation when it comes to trade in energy, or mere coincidences.

Defining energy is central for this chapter. However, this task is quite burdensome, since energy is one of those concepts that were born outside the legal world and for which lawyers can only borrow definitions coined in other scientific fields. For the purposes of our study, we prefer a definition that is as broad as possible and that will allow us to grasp the intricacies of the complex relationships between the BRICS and the outside world. In this vein, we define energy as 'the action (product and process) through which energy rich natural resources are consumed and transformed to respond to a series of societal and individual human requirements for heat and power'.[1]

---

[1] Gabrielle Marceau, 'The WTO in the emerging energy governance debate' (2010) 5(3) *Global Trade and Customs Journal* 83–93 at 83.

II.   Setting the Stage: BRICS, Energy and the WTO

A.   The BRICS Countries and Energy

At a first glance, there are more differences than similarities between the BRICS countries in the energy field. If each of these countries faces very different issues in realizing their growth potential, this is particularly true in the energy sector, where the differences involve at least three main points.

First, the BRICS countries play very different roles in the international energy scene, because of their very different profiles. Brazil is a signifi-cant energy producer. Increasing domestic oil production has been a long-term goal of the government, and discoveries of large offshore oil deposits have transformed Brazil into a strong fossil fuel exporter. Limited eco-nomic growth and corruption scandals implicating Petrobras, however, have dampened short-term prospects in the sector. Almost 45 percent of primary energy demand in Brazil is met by renewable energy, making its energy sector one of the least carbon-intensive in the world.[2]

The Chinese, Indian and South African economies are substantially dependent on coal. China is, by far, the world's largest consumer and producer of coal,[3] but it also deploys substantial renewable power gen-eration capacity. India is entering a sustained period of rapid growth in energy consumption. Its energy mix is also extremely reliant on coal, mak-ing it an important coal consumer.[4] Demand for oil is also increasing in India. While China and India are net oil importers, and China is one of the biggest gas importers, Russia remains the world's largest exporter of natural gas and the second largest producer and exporter of crude oil.[5]

Secondly, there are important differences between the BRICS countries in terms of energy policy choices. Not only are their energy-related legis-lations very dissimilar, but there are also important divergences in terms of priorities. Some of these concern the abovementioned differences in profile. Others are harder to explain. For instance, while Brazil has always been a pioneer in the renewable energy field, in particular when it comes to bioethanol, Russia is heavily industrializing its fossil fuel production. In its

---

[2] International Energy Agency, country profile; available at www.iea.org/countries/non-membercountries/brazil/ [accessed on 1 November 2016].
[3] International Energy Agency, 'Key World Energy Statistics 2015'.
[4] International Energy Agency, 'World Energy Outlook 2015', *Executive Summary*.
[5] International Energy Agency, 'Key World Energy Statistics 2015'.

quest for long-lasting self-sufficiency in terms of energy supply, China has recently been going through a drastic transition to a less energy-intensive model for growth. It is expected to introduce an emissions trading scheme in 2017, covering the power sector and heavy industry.[6]

Despite these differences, a more detailed analysis of the energy policies within the BRICS countries proves that there are some, and probably even many, common elements. These serve as the nexus for discovering the extent to which one can talk about an enantiosis of the BRICS in the energy sector.[7] For example, in spite of important liberalization initiatives, large-scale privatization has not affected major state-owned companies in the oil and gas subsectors. Brazil's Petrobras,[8] Russia's Gazprom,[9] India's Oil and Natural Gas Corporation,[10] and China's National Petroleum Corporation[11] remain state-trading enterprises and are duly notified as such to the WTO.[12] Their status seems to be related less to cooperation between the countries, and more to a convergence in terms of the governance of the central economic sectors.

The main line of convergence, where cooperation is central, concerns the attention paid to the relationship between energy issues and sustainable development. As stated in several BRICS declarations, 'the implementation of the concept of sustainable development, comprising, inter alia, the Rio Declaration, Agenda for the 21st Century and multilateral environmental agreements, should be a major vector in the change of

---

[6] For further analysis, see Jeff Swartz, 'China's National Emissions Trading System' (2016) 6 *ICTSD Global Platform on Climate Change, Trade and Sustainable Energy* 1–34.

[7] See Chapter 1 of this book for a definition of this term.

[8] For further developments, see Adilson de Oliveria, 'Brazil's Petrobas: Strategy and Performance', in David Victor, David Hults and Mark Thurber (eds.), *Oil and Governance: State-Owned Enterprises and the World Energy Supply* (Cambridge: Cambridge University Press, 2011), pp. 515–557.

[9] See Nadejda Victor and Inna Sayfer, 'Gazprom: the Struggle for Power', in David Victor, David Hults and Mark Thurber (eds.), *Oil and Governance: State-owned Enterprises and the World Energy Supply* (Cambridge: Cambridge University Press, 2011), pp. 655–701.

[10] See Varun Rai, 'Fading Star: Explaining the Evolution of India's ONGC', in David Victor, David Hults and Mark Thurber (eds.), *Oil and Governance: State-Owned Enterprises and the World Energy Supply* (Cambridge: Cambridge University Press, 2011), pp. 753–809.

[11] See Binbin Jiang, 'China National Petroleum Corporation (CNPC): A Balancing Act between Enterprise and Government', in David Victor, David Hults and Mark Thurber (eds.), *Oil and Governance: State-Owned Enterprises and the World Energy Supply*(Cambridge: Cambridge University Press, 2011), pp. 379–418.

[12] Eighty percent of South Africa's Engen is currently owned by Malaysia's Petronas, and South Africa declares, before the competent WTO bodies, that it does not maintain any state trading enterprises.

paradigm of economic development',[13] and the BRICS countries, convinced of 'the important role of renewable energy as a means to address climate change'[14] and of 'the importance of cooperation and information exchange in the field of development of renewable energy resources',[15] support the development and use of renewable energy resources.

This concern about renewable energy sources is at the heart of a series of national energy policy choices. Examples include the promotion of biofuels or the implementation of national ETS schemes. It cannot be ignored that China's decision to launch a national ETS system in 2017 goes hand in hand with India's 'Perform, Achieve and Trade' initiative, and its developing renewable energy credit market,[16] with some initiatives at a state (not federal) level in Brazil, and current discussions on this issue in Russia. Whether this cooperation appears ex ante or ex post, after a leadership position has been assumed by one of the BRICS countries, is of little importance for the outside world. What matters is mainly that such an alignment in policies is gradually becoming a common rationale.

Thirdly, the differences among the BRICS countries put them in very different positions in terms of their participation in the international energy debate. This debate, in all of its complexities and specificities, is not the topic of this chapter. Suffice it to say, however, that it can be roughly narrowed down to two groups of forums: those putting together net exporters (OPEC and the Gas Exporting Countries Forum) or net importers (IEA), on the one hand, and those connecting exporters to importers, on the other hand. The latter have remained largely regionalized (OLADE, Energy Charter) or underinstitutionalized, and their mandate has always been somewhat limited (for instance, the World Energy Council, or IRENA). Most of these forums were established during the Cold war, before the emergence of the BRICS countries as power actors on the international stage. It is therefore not surprising that they have small roles to play. This is not the case for the Gas Exporting Countries Forum where Russia is one of the lead actors, for IRENA, or for the WTO, which is the focus of this chapter.

---

[13] First BRIC Summit, *Joint Statement of the BRIC Countries Leaders*, 16 June 2009, Yekaterinburg, Russia, § 7.

[14] Third BRICS Summit, Sanya Declaration of the BRICS Leaders Meeting, 14 April 2011, Sanya, Hainan, China, at 18.

[15] *Ibid.*, § 18.

[16] See Jeff Swartz, 'China's National Emissions Trading System', 1–34.

B. The BRICS Countries in the WTO

If the main reason for seeing the BRICS countries as a group is rooted in their discontent with the current international order, the WTO is the exception that proves the rule. Apart from South Africa, the BRICS countries have been extremely active on the WTO front. This was not the case, however, in the beginning of the multilateral trading system, when Brazil and India were the only actors at this stage, and they remained somewhat discreet. The accessions of China (2001) and Russia (2012) to the WTO have, in this sense, marked the end of an era.

As Brendan Vickers put it, acting alone or in concert, the BRICS countries have clearly emerged as major players in the WTO system.[17] They have assumed 'twin roles as system supporters and change agents in multilateral trade'.[18] They have thus become the anti-agent of the developed countries, and their economic rise has made compromises ever more difficult, because 'neither of those groups is powerful enough to overwhelm the others and this has led to an inevitable stalemate and bottleneck'.[19]

The role of the BRICS countries in the WTO has been subject to extensive scholarship, mainly from the international relations perspective, with special interest in the shifting of powers in the multilateral trading system. This chapter is, however, strictly concerned with their role in the emerging energy debate at the WTO, and does not aim to generalize its conclusions. With the accessions of China and Russia to the WTO, the energy–trade debate became streamlined within the multilateral trading system. The accession process provided the perfect opportunity to put energy issues on the negotiations table: trade in energy (gas, lurking in the background of China's accession, was largely discussed in the working party for Russia's accession).

C. Energy and the WTO

The WTO is not the only forum, not even the first one that comes to mind, when discussing energy. The energy debate has not always been the center

---

[17] Brendan Vickers, 'The Role of the BRICs in the WTO: System-Supporters or Change Agents in Multilateral Trade?' in Amrita Narlikar, Martin Daunton, and Robert M. Stern (eds.), *The Oxford Handbook on the World Trade Organization* (Oxford: Oxford University Press, 2012), pp. 254–273 at 269.

[18] *Ibid.*, at 283.

[19] Mitsuo Matsushita, 'A View on Future Roles of The WTO: Should There Be More Soft Law in the WTO?' (2015) 17(3) *Journal of International Economic Law* 701–715 at 701.

of attention at the WTO. On the contrary, for a long time energy remained at the periphery of trade negotiations for various reasons. These are, however, not the issues that we wish to discuss here. What matters is that the energy debate is making its way (back) to the WTO. More and more cases are brought before the WTO's Dispute Settlement Body (DSB) that are closely related to trade in the energy sector. After twenty years of testing, the dispute settlement system of the WTO has proven a stable enough forum for these sorts of cases, and some of the BRICS countries are actively starting to push the energy agenda through the DSB.

III. The BRICS Countries and Energy-Related Disputes within the WTO

A. General Observations

Until recently, few energy-related cases had been brought to the attention of the DSB. This phenomenon can easily be related to international relations and policy studies, in particular to empirical literature on dispute initiation in the WTO.[20] The pattern is, however, rapidly changing, and more and more energy-related cases are, or will be, adjudicated by the panels and the Appellate Body.

This recent wave of cases is clearly not a coincidence. What is happening, in fact, is a paradigm shift in the energy debate, which is gradually being brought to the WTO forum. The first signs were seen at the time of China's accession. Energy-wise, China is, however, on a quest for self-sufficiency, although its high dependence on coal has been subject to regular criticism in terms of environmental protection and the reduction of gas emissions. Russia's accession is what added fuel to the debate. Indeed, Russia is rapidly becoming the main player in the field. The most obvious explanation for its interest in the WTO dispute settlement mechanism is the fact that its main market has been slowly slipping away. Deteriorating relations between the EU and Russia in the energy field are, also, directly relevant for improving China-Russia relations. It remains to be seen whether this is related to geopolitical conjuncture or to a mid- to long-term cooperation strategy.

---

[20] See Horn Henrik, Petros Mavroidis and Nordstrom Hakan, 'Is the Use of the WTO Dispute Settlement System Biased?' (1999) *CEPR Discussion Paper No. 2340*, and for a detailed bibliographical note, Henok Asmelash, 'Energy Subsidies and WTO Dispute Settlement: Why Only Renewable Energy Subsidies Are Challenged?' (2015) 18 (2) *Journal of International Economic Law* 261–285 at 262.

B. Energy and the GATT

Most energy-related cases brought before the DSB concern government involvement in the sector, in particular subsidies for renewable energy production.

The first report issued by the Appellate Body in this line concerned the feed-in tariff program in the Canadian province of Ontario.[21] Brazil, China and India were third parties in the proceedings. Their arguments mainly concerned the interpretation of the government procurement derogation of Article III:8, the 'hottest' issue at the appellate stage.[22] Brazil's pleadings, by far more elaborate than those of India and China, summarized rather clearly what the BRICS position could have been on this issue, namely that 'the purpose of any governmental action can only be assessed on a case-by-case basis, and should be informed by the functions performed by a given government in each sector of its economy'.[23] This issue was again discussed more recently, in direct relation to India's energy initiative, the National Solar Mission.[24] Following the Appellate Body's approach in *Canada – Renewables*, the panel found that the electricity purchased by the government was not in a competitive relationship with solar cells and modules. This ruling was later upheld by the Appellate Body.[25]

These recent cases have also given rise to some very innovative arguments brought by the BRICS countries in relation to the exceptions provided in GATT Article XX. For instance, *India – Solar cells* was one of those very rare occasions where the defendant relied on GATT Article XX (j), *in casu* – arguing that its lack of domestic manufacturing capacity in solar cells and modules makes them 'products in general or local

---

[21] Report of the Appellate Body, Canada – Certain Measures Affecting the Renewable Energy Generation Sector, WT/DS412/AB/R, 6 May 2003. For comments, see, among others, Luca Rubini, 'Ain't Wastin' Time No More: Subsidies for Renewable Energy, the SCM Agreement, Policy Space, and Law Reform' (2012) 15 (2) *Journal of International Economic Law* 525–579; or Rika Koch, 'International Trade Law Challenges by Subsidies for Renewable Energy' (2015) 49 (5) *Journal of World Trade* 757–780.

[22] On this point, see for instance Arwell Davies, 'The GATT Article III: 8 (a) Procurement Derogation and Canada – Renewable Energy' (2015) 18 (3) *Journal of International Economic Law* 543–554.

[23] Report of the Appellate Body, Canada – Certain Measures Affecting the Renewable Energy Generation Sector, WT/DS412/AB/R, 6 May 2013, at 2.199.

[24] Report of the Panel, India – Certain Measures Relating to Solar Cells and Solar Modules, WT/DS456/R, 24 February 2016.

[25] Report of the Appellate body, India – Certain Measures Relating to Solar Cells and Solar Modules, WT/DS456/AB/R, 16 September 2016.

short supply'. Furthermore, in *Canada – Renewables*, Brazil argued that GATT Article XX provides useful guidance for assessing whether a government procurement program pursues a governmental purpose, in particular with relation to examining the contribution of a measure to its objective. Brazil's legal reasoning was not followed by the Appellate Body. In its report, the Appellate Body called for a holistic interpretation of Article III:8 (a), requiring consideration of the linkages between the different terms used in the provision and the contextual connections with other parts of Article III, as well as with other provisions of the GATT 1994.[26] However, it adopted a textual interpretation of the term 'purpose', comparing the French, English and Spanish versions of the word. It also asserted that GATT Article XVII:2 provided a relevant context for interpretation of the words 'governmental purposes' in Article III:8(a), because it refers to 'imports of products for immediate or ultimate consumption in governmental use'.[27]

C.   Energy and the General Agreement on Trade in Services (GATS)

One of the main reasons why the issue of energy services has been the subject of discussion is because the W/120 classification, commonly followed by WTO members, lacks a specific category for energy services.[28] Although this may have had some impact on commitments in the area, it has not hindered the possibility of bringing cases related to energy services. On the contrary, a recent case brought by Russia may prove that the debate is less about interpreting the specific commitments in the field and more about the way GATS disciplines will be interpreted so as to reflect the specificities of the energy sector.

As mentioned, Russia is the biggest gas exporter in the world, and the gas market remains, in its biggest part, a regional one, highly dependent on the uninterrupted functioning of pipelines. The main consumers of Russian gas are China and the EU. While cooperation with China has been growing, relations between Russia and the EU are much more difficult.

---

[26] *Ibid.*, at 5.57.   [27] *Ibid.*, at 5.66–5.68.

[28] See Mireille Cossy, 'The Liberalization of Energy Services: Are PTAs More Energetic than the GATS?' in Juan Marchetti and Martin Roy (eds.), *Opening Markets for International Trade in Services* (Cambridge: Cambridge University Press, 2009), pp. 405–434; Mireille Cossy, 'Energy Services under the General Agreement on Trade in Services' in Yulia Selivanova (ed.), *Regulation of Energy in International Trade Law* (The Hague: Kluwer, 2011), pp. 149–180; or Francesco Meggiolaro, 'Energy Services in the Current Round of WTO Negotiations' (2005) 11 (3) *International Trade and Regulation* 97–108.

The WTO has recently become a new front in the ongoing energy battle (rather resembling a love-hate scenario where none of the parties can exist without the other, but both insist on being right).

Having lurked in the background for some time, Russia's discontent with the EU energy legislation, the Third Energy Package, has recently culminated in a request for the establishment of a panel.[29] The complexities of the case, mainly focused on access to pipeline services by Russian providers in the Hungarian, Lithuanian and Croatian markets, mirror the complexities of the energy relations between Russia and the EU. A panel was established, and the outcome of its decision will be of utmost interest for legal scholarship, both in the fields of WTO law and international energy relations. What can be said for now is that this the second energy case brought before the DSB, following the *Canada – Renewables* case, serves as proof that the energy debate is slowly making its way back to the DSB. The WTO is on the way to becoming the forum for future energy battles between exporters and importers. This case may also be the marker of an expected, but still surprising in terms of timing, cooperation, as Brazil, India and China have reserved their third-party rights.

D.   Energy and the Subsidies and Countervailing Measures (SCM) Agreement

As previously mentioned, the bulk of energy-related cases brought before the DSB concern state involvement in the energy makets, mainly in the form of subsidies. Over the past few years, renewable energy subsidies have become an important source of trade disputes.[30] China has been at both ends of the complaints on these issues. For instance, in 2012, it launched a case against the EU's legislation on renewable energy generation.[31] This dispute, which is still in its consultation phase and closely resembles *Canada –Renewables*, arose as a challenge to the domestic content requirement attached to the Greek and Italian tariff programs. A case was also brought by the United States against China's program for grants, funds and awards to enterprises manufacturing wind power

---

[29] Request for the establishment of a panel by the Russian Federation, European Union and its Member States – Certain Measures Relating to the Energy Sector, WT/DS476/2, 28 May 2015.

[30] See Asmelash, 'Energy Subsidies and WTO Dispute Settlement' at 261.

[31] Request for consultations by China, European Union and certain Member States – Certain Measures Affecting the Renewable Energy Generation Sector, WT/DS452/1, 7 November 2011.

equipment,[32] challenging the measures under Articles 3 and 25 of the SCM Agreement. The dispute was resolved at the consultation stage, following China's agreement to terminate the program as of February 2011.[33]

IV. The BRICS Countries and Energy Trade Negotiations within and outside the WTO

The WTO is not all about dispute resolution. It is also the multilateral forum for discussing all issues related to trade liberalization. The Doha Program concerned only indirectly the energy sector,[34] but as both the accession of China and Russia and the recent reemergence of the debate within the dispute settlement system show, energy has made its way (back) to the negotiating table. It seems that at this particular negotiating table, however, the BRICS countries are playing such different roles that it is impossible to see any convergence, let alone cooperation. Outside the WTO forum, they have conducted trade-related energy negotiations since the beginning of their cooperation, recognizing that 'energy is an essential resource for improving the standard of living of our people and that access to energy is of paramount importance to economic growth with equity and social inclusion.'[35] In this regard, BRICS countries declare their support for the diversification of energy supply, for the development of renewable energy production, for securing energy transit routes and creating new energy investments and infrastructure.[36] The BRICS strategy to achieve these goals as a coherent group has mostly been unsuccessful. This lack of coordination stems mainly from the fact that each country addresses different energy issues.[37] The current trade negotiations regarding the energy sector are conducted individually (or regionally) and can be summarized in two ongoing debates: trade facilitation and environmental goods and services.

---

[32] Request for consultations by the United States, China – Measures concerning wind power equipment, WT/DS419/1, 6 January 2011.

[33] See Asmelash, 'Energy Subsidies and WTO Dispute Settlement' at 277.

[34] See Simonetta Zarrilli, 'Doha Work Programme: Possible Impact on Energy Trade' (2003) 19 (4) *Journal of Energy and Natural Resources Law* 399–413.

[35] Second BRIC Summit, *BRIC Summit Joint Statement*, 14 April 2010, Brasília, Brazil, at 9.

[36] First BRIC Summit, *Joint Statement of the BRIC Countries Leaders*, 16 June 2009, Yekaterinburg, Russia, at 8 and 9.

[37] Sajal Mathur and Meghna Dasgupta (eds.), *BRICS Trade Policies, Institutions and Areas for Deepening Cooperation* (Centre for WTO Studies, 2013), p. 330; available at wtocentre.iift .ac.in [accessed on 1 November 2016].

A. Trade Facilitation

At the Ninth WTO Ministerial Conference, held in Bali in December 2013, WTO members concluded negotiations on a Trade Facilitation Agreement (TFA), as part of a wider 'Bali Package'.[38] The purpose of the TFA is to expedite the movement, release and clearance of goods, including goods in transit. It also sets out measures for effective cooperation between customs and other appropriate authorities on trade facilitation and customs compliance issues.

The main point of contact between the TFA and the energy debate is on issues related to transit. As James Nedumpara puts it, 'Trade facilitation assumes significance in light of the need for providing security for transit energy infrastructure'.[39] The insufficiencies and inadequacies of GATT Article V to tackle issues related to transit in the energy sector have been largely discussed in legal scholarship.[40] The final version of the TFA addresses some of these issues[41] and provides long-awaited clarifications of Article V, in particular supporting the argument that transit *via* pipelines is a mode of transit covered by WTO law.[42]

Issues of energy transport via pipelines and electricity grids were discussed during the TFA negotiations. For instance, in 2012, Egypt and

---

[38] World Trade Organization, Ministerial Conference, Ninth Session, *The Bali Ministerial Declaration*, WT/MIN(13)/DEC, adopted on 7 December 2013.

[39] James Nedumpara, 'Energy Security and the WTO Agreements', in Sajal Mathur (ed.), *Trade, the WTO and Energy Security: Mapping The Linkages for India* (Springer, 2014), pp. 15–73 at 58.

[40] See, among others, Danae Azaria, 'Energy Transit under the Energy Charter Treaty and the General Agreement on Tariffs' (2009) 27(4) *Journal of Energy and Natural Resources Law* 559–596; Mireille Cossy, 'Energy Transit and Transport in the WTO', in Joost Pauwelyn (ed.), *Global Challenges at the Intersection of Trade, Energy and the Environment* (Graduate Institute of Geneva, 2010), pp. 113–121; Lothar Ehring and Yulia Selivanova, 'Energy Transit', in Yulia Selivanova (ed.), *Regulation of Energy and International Trade Law* (Kluwer, 2011), pp. 49–104; or Vitaliy Pogoretskyy, 'Freedom of Transit and the Principles of Effective Right and Economic Cooperation: Can Systemic Interpretation of GATT Article V Promote Energy Security and the Development of an International Gas Market?' (2013) 16(2) *Journal of International Economic Law* 313–352.

[41] See, among others, Danae Azaria, 'Energy Transit under the Energy Charter Treaty and the General Agreement on Tariffs' 559–596; Cossy, 'Energy Transit and Transport in the WTO', pp. 113–121; Lothar Ehring and Yulia Selivanova, 'Energy Transit', pp. 49–104; or Vitaliy Pogoretskyy, 'Freedom of Transit and the Principles of Effective Right and Economic Cooperation', 313–352.

[42] See Mikella Hurley, 'Energy Transit in the Tangled Web of RTAs: The Relationship between GATT Articles V and XXIV in the Context of Energy Goods', in Freya Baetens and José Caiado (eds.), *Frontiers of International Economic Law: Legal Tools to Confront Interdisciplinary Challenges* (Brill Nijhoff, 2014), pp. 205–235 at 216.

Turkey sent a communiqué opposing the idea of GATT Article V disciplines being interpreted so as to govern the transit of energy products via fixed infrastructure and proposing a separate provision on the issue.[43] Despite several other initiatives on this issue, the adopted document does not expressly include energy transit infrastructure.[44] The BRICS countries did send proposals to the Negotiating Group on Trade Facilitation. However, they did not send them as a coherent group, and more importantly, they were not active in the debates surrounding energy issues. Indeed, they did not tackle a single proposal on the matter, probably because issues related to energy transit are of minor importance to China, India and Brazil, while Russia only entered the debate at a later –almost the final– stage of negotiations, when it acceded to the WTO. All BRICS countries but South Africa have ratified the TFA.[45] The agreement was supposed to enter into force when two-thirds of the WTO members notify their acceptance, according to Article X:3 of the Marrakesh Agreement. This happened on 22 February 2017.

Along with these individual positions on trade facilitation negotiations within the WTO forum, BRICS countries undertook collective negotiations in other forums.[46] The BRICS Contact Group for Economic and Trade Issues (CGETI), established in 2013, adopted a Trade and Investment Cooperation Framework with a specific disposition concerning trade facilitation.[47] Its substantial content is very similar to that of the TFA. The main purpose of the framework is to enhance information exchange on trade and investment policies and to improve the transparency of trade in line with the respective laws and regulations of BRICS countries. It also seeks to enhance communication and cooperation in the areas of standardization, certification, inspection and quarantine. Similarly, the BRICS Trade and Investment Facilitation Action Plan, adopted at the Fourth

---

[43] WTO Negotiating Group on Trade Facilitation, Communication from Egypt and Turkey, *Discussion Paper on the Inclusion of the Goods Moved via Fixed Infrastructure into the Definition of Traffic in Transit*, TN/TF/W/179, 4 June 2012.

[44] For the draft, see WTO Negotiating Group on Trade Facilitation, *Draft Consolidated Negotiating Text*, TN/TF/W/165/Rev.14., 27 March 2013. For the final document, see WTO, Preparatory Committee on Trade Facilitation, *Agreement on Trade Facilitation*, WT/L/931, adopted on 15 July 2014.

[45] China ratified the Agreement on 4 September 2015, Brazil on 26 March 2016, and the Russian Federation and India on 22 April 2016.

[46] Fourth BRICS Summit, *Delhi Declaration*, 29 March 2012, New Delhi, India, at 34.

[47] BRICS Contact Group for Economic and Trade Issues, *BRICS Trade and Investment Cooperation Framework*, adopted in Durban on 26 March 2013.

BRICS Summit, highlighted five main trade-facilitation principles and suggested immediate actions, such as the simplification and harmonization of national policies.[48]

The Trade and Investment Cooperation Framework and the BRICS Trade and Investment Facilitation Action Plan are not TFA-plus commitments. They distance themselves from the TFA not only by their broad wording, but also by their little guidance on how to achieve these general commitments. These BRICS documents recall the key principles of the TFA without mentioning energy-related issues. The BRICS countries also went beyond this substantial linkage with the TFA and adopted a declaration to promote the effectiveness of their TFA commitments. In the declaration and action plan, adopted at the BRICS Sixth Summit, states reaffirmed their support for an open, inclusive, nondiscriminatory, transparent and rule-based multilateral trading system. For this purpose, they were set to 'look forward to the implementation of the Agreement on Trade Facilitation' and 'call(ed) upon international partners to provide support to the poorest, most vulnerable WTO members to enable them to implement this Agreement, which should support their development objectives'.[49] The BRICS Business Council is currently working on this subject in order to propose operational tools to implement the TFA among the BRICS countries. Its second annual report recommend organizing a roundtable among BRICS customs authorities to discuss measures that could be adopted by the governments to facilitate trade and to advance cooperation initiatives, including the provision of technical assistance for all countries on the implementation of their commitments related to the TFA.[50] These trade facilitation negotiations were mainly promoted by the Russian BRICS presidency. There is little information about their current status or results. The BRICS summit, organized by India in October 2016, lead to minor improvements in the matter. The final communiqué mainly focused on a desired orientation of international cooperation in the field towards the issue of access to clean energy technology and finance, and related this to the achievement of Sustainable Development Goals.

---

[48] *Ibid.*

[49] Sixth BRICS Summit, *Fortaleza Declaration and Action Plan*, 15 July 2014, Fortaleza, Brazil, at 21.

[50] See BRICS Business Council Second Annual Report, *Facing Challenges, Building Confidence*, 2015, p. 8; available at http://infobrics.org [accessed on 1 November 2016].

B. Environmental Goods and Services

The BRICS countries have adopted highly dissonant strategies on Environmental Goods and Services (EGS) negotiations. The issue had always been on the 'trade-liberalization' agenda, but it was specifically singled out in the Doha Ministerial Declaration:

> 31. With a view to enhancing the mutual supportiveness of trade and environment, we agree to negotiations, without prejudging their outcome, on: (iii) the reduction or, as appropriate, elimination of tariff and non-tariff barriers to environmental goods and services.[51]

Increasing access to, and use of, EGS can bring benefits, highly valued by the BRICS, including reducing air and water pollution, improving energy and resource efficiency and facilitating solid-waste disposal, to name a few.[52] In short, well-managed trade liberalization in EGS can facilitate the BRICS countries' achievement of sustainable development goals laid out in global mandates such as the Johannesburg Plan of Implementation, the UN Millennium Development Goals and various multilateral environmental agreements (MEAs).[53]

The lack of a universally accepted definition of EGS meant that trade delegates have struggled over the scope of goods and services that would be taken up for liberalization,[54] mainly whether only goods intended solely for environmental protection purposes should be included, as opposed to goods that may have both environmental and nonenvironmental uses.[55] Under this matter, Brazil suggested that ongoing negotiations had privileged a definition of environmental goods with the

---

[51] WTO, Ministerial Conference, *Doha Ministerial Declaration*, WT/MIN(01)/DEC/1, 20 November 2001.

[52] See in this vein, Veena Jha, 'Environmental Priorities and Trade Policy for Environmental Goods: A Reality Check', ICTSD Trade and Environment Series Issue Paper No. 7, 2008.

[53] Edmundo Claro, Lucas, N., Mahesh Sugathan, Mario Marconini and Enrique Lendo, 'Trade in Environmental Goods and Services and Sustainable Development: Domestic Considerations and Strategies for WTO Negotiations', ICTSD Environmental Goods and Services Series, Policy Discussion Paper, International Centre for Trade and Sustainable Development, Geneva, Switzerland, 2007, p. xii.

[54] For general observations, see Alexey Vikhlyaev, 'Environmental Goods and Services: Defining Negotiations or Negotiating Definitions' (2004) 38 (1) *Journal of World Trade* 93–122; or Thomas Cottier and Donah Baracol-Pinhao, 'Environmental Goods and Services: The Environmental Area Initiative Approach and Climate Change', in Thomas Cottier (ed.), *International Trade Regulation and The Mitigation of Climate Change* (Cambridge: Cambridge University Press, 2009), pp. 395–419.

[55] See Veena Jha, 'Trade Flows, Barriers and Market Drivers in Renewable Energy Supply Goods', ICTSD Trade and Environment Issue Paper 1, 2009.

various 'lists' that focused on high-technology products of little interest to developing countries. It suggested that the definition of environmental goods should cover products such as renewable energy, including ethanol and biodiesel. It also pointed out that improved market access for products derived from incorporating cleaner technologies, such as 'flexi fuel' engines and vehicles, could also encourage the use of environmentally efficient products and be supportive of the developmental concerns of developing countries, as these vehicles would use fuels obtained from the processing of natural resources in developing countries.[56] China, in contrast, has put forward a proposal calling for a 'common list' including environmental goods of export interest to both developed and developing countries. It further suggested a 'development list' that would be derived from the common list and comprise goods eligible for special and differential treatment in the form of lower levels of reduction commitments for developing countries.[57]

China is also the only BRICS state to participate in the ongoing Environmental Goods Agreement (EGA) negotiation.[58] The EGA aims to lower trade barriers on a number of important environmental goods. The participants are considering products in several significant areas of environmental protection and climate change mitigation, including those that contribute to generating clean and renewable energy, improving energy efficiency, controlling air pollution, managing waste and treating waste water.[59] The participating members account for the majority of global trade in environmental goods and have declared that the entire WTO membership would benefit from the tariff reductions that would arise from the agreement. In the scope of these negotiations, China's main proposal is to grant members three years to remove tariffs for certain products, while developing countries would have different staging options.

The EGA negotiation goes beyond the scope of the WTO. The EGA was built on efforts made by the APEC, an international organization that

---

[56] WTO, Committee on Trade and Environment, Submission by Brazil, *Environmental Goods for Development, Paragraph 31 (iii)*, TN/TE/W/59, 8 July 2005.

[57] WTO, Committee on Trade and Environment, Submission by China, *Statement by China on Environmental Goods at the Committee on Trade and Environment Special Session Meeting, Paragraph 31 (iii)*, TN/TE/W/42, 6 July 2004.

[58] Joint Statement Regarding the Launch of the Environmental Goods Agreement Negotiations, Geneva, Switzerland, 8 July 2014; available at http://trade.ec.europa.eu/ [accessed on 1 November 2016].

[59] The European Commission's website hosts all the available information concerning the EGA negotiations: http://trade.ec.europa.eu/doclib/press/index.cfm?id=1116 [accessed on 1 November 2016].

includes Russia and China as members.[60] APEC members have been promoting strong negotiations in the EGS domain. The 2012 Vladivostok
Declaration lists, in its Appendix C, fifty-four environmental goods for
which APEC members commit to reduce tariffs to 5 percent or less by
the end of 2015. Amongst these fifty-four goods are solar panels, solar
water heaters, wind turbines and gas turbines used for electrical power
generation.[61] To date, little effort has been made by China and Russia to
transpose these regional tariffs reductions to the multilateral WTO forum.

From a collective point of view, the BRICS countries have been adopting general commitments regarding renewable energy. The BRICS Business Council established an 'Energy and green economy Working Group'
in 2013, with a mandate to discuss current issues on electricity, renewable energy, solar power, natural gas, oil and hydropower and to avoid
plurilateral initiatives that go against the fundamental principles of transparency, inclusiveness and multilateralism.[62] It contributed to the adoption of a 'Memorandum of Mutual Understanding in Energy Saving and
Energy Efficiency' on 20 November 2015. According to the memorandum, to promote access to energy-efficient technologies, the parties will
identify a list of energy-efficient and clean technologies in which they are
interested, and they will create a record (database) of relevant data on
energy -efficient technologies in BRICS countries. The parties will also
activate cooperation between the public sector, private companies and
international financial institutions to encourage investments in energy-
efficient projects and technologies, and will foster the institutionalizing of
energy cooperation within BRICS. The first steps of this institutionalization have recently emerged. The BRICS New Development Bank (NDB)
has approved its first package of loans, worth some USD 811 million. The
four projects in Brazil, China, South Africa and India are all in the renewal
energy development sphere.[63]

V. Conclusion

The energy debate is making its (re)emergence in the multilateral trading system, and it appears that the BRICS countries are playing a central

---

[60] Kyong Su Lim and Hyeri Park, 'APEC's Liberalization Efforts on Environmental Goods',
KIEP Research Paper, (2015) 5(4) *World Economy Update*.

[61] APEC 2012 Leaders' Declaration, Vladivostok, Russia, 8 September 2012, Annex C, 'APEC
List of Environmental Goods'.

[62] Fourth BRICS Summit, *Delhi Declaration*, 29 March 2012, New Delhi, India, at 16.

[63] For further information concerning these loans, see http://ndb.int/ [accessed on 1 November 2016].

role in this process. Today, we see a growing proliferation of energy-related cases brought before the DSB. Their contribution to enriching the case law on the interpretation of WTO law and the extent to which they relate to sector-specific concerns, or general tendencies, are yet to be discussed in legal scholarship. For now, and in relation to the focus of this chapter, we have highlighted the participation of some, if not all, of the BRICS countries and the leading role that China and Russia are attempting to play in this emerging debate. From a legal point of view, this debate is, for now, mainly focused on GATT Articles III:8 and XX of the GATT 1994, the SCM Agreement and the interpretation of GATS disciplines in light of the specificities of the energy sector.

Energy issues are, indeed, an essential pillar in cooperation between the BRICS countries. But they are also key elements in the relations between the BRICS countries and the rest of the world. Russia and China are the main actors when it comes to trade negotiations, in particular those concerning trade barriers. Brazil and India keep a low profile on energy cooperation issues, while at the same time deploying large-scale renewable energy projects. The rationale behind this discrepancy lies in the divergence of the interests of BRICS countries in the field: while Russia and China are dependent on energy cooperation, Brazil and India are aiming for self-sufficiency. South Africa remains the odd one out, both within and outside the WTO forum. This combination of convergences and discrepancies is what defines the enantiosis of BRICS in the emerging energy trade debate.

VI. References

Asmelash, Henok, 'Energy Subsidies and WTO Dispute Settlement: Why Only Renewable Energy Subsidies Are Challenged?' (2015) 18 (2) *Journal of International Economic Law* 261–285.

Azaria, Danae, 'Energy Transit under the Energy Charter Treaty and the General Agreement on Tariffs' (2009) 27(4) *Journal of Energy and Natural Resources Law* 559–596.

BRICS Business Council Second Annual Report, *Facing Challenges, Building Confidence* (2015); available at http://infobrics.org [accessed on 1 November 2016].

Claro, Edmundo, Lucas, N., Sugathan, Mahesh, Marconini, Mario and Lendo, Enrique, 'Trade in Environmental Goods and Services and Sustainable Development: Domestic Considerations and Strategies for WTO Negotiations', *ICTSD Environmental Goods and Services Series, Policy Discussion Paper* (International Centre for Trade and Sustainable Development, Geneva, 2007).

Cossy, Mireille, 'Energy Services under the General Agreement on Trade in Services', in Yulia Selivanova (ed.), *Regulation of Energy in International Trade Law* (Kluwer, 2011), pp. 149–180.

'Energy Transit and Transport in the WTO', in Joost Pauwelyn (ed.), *Global Challenges at the Intersection of Trade, Energy and the Environment* (Graduate Institute of Geneva, 2010), pp. 113–121.

'The Liberalization of Energy Services: Are PTAs More Energetic Than the GATS?' in Juan Marchetti and Martin Roy, (eds.), *Opening Markets for International Trade in Services* (Cambridge University Press, Cambridge, 2009), pp. 405–434.

Cottier, Thomas and Baracol-Pinhao, Donah, 'Environmental Goods and Services: The Environmental Area Initiative Approach and Climate Change', in Thomas Cottier (ed.), *International Trade Regulation and The Mitigation of Climate Change* (Cambridge: Cambridge University Press, 2009), pp. 395–419.

Davies, Arwell, 'The GATT Article III:8 (a) Procurement Derogation and Canada – Renewable Energy' (2015) 18 (3) *Journal of International Economic Law* 543–554.

Ehring, Lothar and Selivanova, Yulia, 'Energy Transit', in Yulia Selivanova (ed.), *Regulation Of Energy and International Trade Law* (The Hague: Kluwer, 2011), pp. 49–104.

Eliason, Antonia, 'The Trade Facilitation Agreement: A New Hope for the World Trade Organization' (2015) 14 (4) *World Trade Review* 643–670.

Horn, Henrik, Mavroidis Petros and Hakan Nordstrom, 'Is The Use of the WTO Dispute Settlement System Biased?' (1999) *CEPR Discussion Paper* No. 2340.

Hurley, Mikella, 'Energy Transit in the Tangled Web of RTAs: The Relationship between GATT Articles V and XXIV in the Context of Energy Goods', in Freya Baetens and José Caiado (eds.), *Frontiers of International Economic Law: Legal Tools to Confront Interdisciplinary Challenges* (Leiden: Brill Nijhoff, 2014), pp. 205–235.

International Energy Agency, 'Key World Energy Statistics 2015'. Paris: International Energy Agency.

'World Energy Outlook 2015: Executive Summary'. Paris: International Energy Agency.

Jha, Veena, 'Environmental Priorities and Trade Policy for Environmental Goods: A Reality Check', ICTSD Trade and Environment Series Issue Paper No.7, 2008.

Jiang, Binbin, 'China National Petroleum Corporation (CNPC): A Balancing Act between Enterprise and Government', in David Victor, David Hults and Mark Thurber (eds.), *Oil and Governance: State-Owned Enterprises and The World Energy Supply* (Cambridge: Cambridge University Press, 2011), pp. 379–418.

Koch, Rika, 'International Trade Law Challenges by Subsidies for Renewable Energy' (2015) 49 (5) *Journal of World Trade* 757–780.

Lim, Kyong Su and Park, Hyeri, 'APEC's Liberalization Efforts on Environmental Goods', KIEP Research Paper, (2015) 5(4) *World Economy Update*.

Mathur, Sajal and Dasgupta, Meghna (ed.), *BRICS Trade Policies, Institutions and Areas for Deepening Cooperation* (Centre for WTO Studies, 2013); available at http://wtocentre.iift.ac.in [accessed on 1 November 2016].

Matsushita, Mitsuo, 'A View on Future Roles of The WTO: Should There Be More Soft Law in the WTO?' (2015) 17(3) *Journal of International Economic Law* 701–715.

Meggiolaro, Francesco, 'Energy Services in the Current Round of WTO Negotiations' (2005) 11 (3) *International Trade and Regulation* 97–108

Nedumpara, James, 'Energy Security and the WTO Agreements', in Sajal Mathur (ed.), *Trade, the WTO and Energy Security: Mapping The Linkages for India* (Springer, 2014), pp. 15–73.

Oliveira, Adilson de, 'Brazil's Petrobas: Strategy and Performance', in David Victor, David Hults and Mark Thurber (eds.), *Oil and Governance: State-Owned Enterprises and The World Energy Supply* (Cambridge: Cambridge University Press, 2011), pp. 515–557.

Pogoretskyy, Vitaliy, 'Freedom of Transit and the Principles of Effective Right and Economic Cooperation: Can Systemic Interpretation of GATT Article V Promote Energy Security and the Development of an International Gas Market?' (2013) 16(2) *Journal of International Economic Law*, 313–352.

Rai, Varun, 'Fading Star: Explaining the Evolution of India's ONGC', in David Victor, David Hults and Mark Thurber (eds.), *Oil and Governance: State-Owned Enterprises and The World Energy Supply* (Cambridge: Cambridge University Press, 2011), pp.753–809

Rubini, Luca, 'Ain't Wastin' Time No More: Subsidies for Renewable Energy, the SCM Agreement, Policy Space, and Law Reform' (2012) 15 (2) *Journal of International Economic Law* 525–579.

Swartz, Jeff, 'China's National Emissions Trading System' (2016) 6 *ICTSD Global Platform on Climate Change, Trade and Sustainable Energy* 1–34.

Vickers, Brendan, 'The Role of the BRICs in the WTO: System-Supporters or Change Agents in Multilateral Trade?' in Amrita Narlikar, Martin Daunton, and Robert M. Stern (eds.), *The Oxford Handbook on the World Trade Organization* (Oxford: Oxford University Press, 2012), pp. 254–273.

Victor, Nadejda and Sayfer, Inna, 'Gazprom: The Struggle for Power', in David Victor, David Hults and Mark Thurber (eds.), *Oil and Governance: State-Owned Enterprises and The World Energy Supply* (Cambridge: Cambridge University Press, 2011), pp. 655–701.

Vikhlyaev, Alexey, 'Environmental Goods and Services: Defining Negotiations or Negotiating Definitions' (2004) 38 (1) *Journal of World Trade* 93–122.

WTO Committee on Trade and Environment, Submission by Brazil, *Environmental Goods for Development, Paragraph 31 (iii)*, TN/TE/W/59, 8 July 2005.

Submission by China, *Statement by China on Environmental Goods at the Committee on Trade and Environment Special Session Meeting, Paragraph 31 (iii)*, TN/TE/W/42, 6 July 2004.

WTO, Negotiating Group on Trade Facilitation, Communication from Egypt and Turkey, *Discussion Paper on the Inclusion of the Goods Moved via Fixed Infrastructure into the Definition of Traffic in Transit*, TN/TF/W/179, 4 June 2012.

Draft Consolidated Negotiating Text, TN/TF/W/165/Rev.14., 27 March 2013.

Zarrilli, Simonetta, 'Doha Work Programme: Possible Impact on Energy Trade' (2003) 19 (4) *Journal of Energy and Natural Resources Law* 399–413.

9

The BRICS Bank

On the Edge of International Economic Law and the New Challenges of Twenty-First-Century Capitalism

CHRISTIANE ITABAIANA MARTINS, LIER PIRES FERREIRA
AND RICARDO BASÍLIO WEBER

I. Introduction

Contemporary world politics has been through numberless changes, following the fall of the Berlin Wall in 1989 and the end of USSR in 1991, both of which formally marked the end of the bipolar world politics of Cold War in the 1900s. Almost three decades later, it seems that a new world order is about to come forth, bringing down the traditional hegemonic vertical relationships among Western-civilized northern countries and developing countries in general.

One of the dimensions of this new international world order is the blossoming of new power centers since the 1990s, configuring a multipolar international scenario that is reformulating the relationships between developed and developing countries. The emergence of BRICS is a fundamental event in this new era. The acronym 'BRIC' was created by Goldman Sachs economist Jim O'Neill, who wrote a report titled *Building Better Global Economic BRIC*,[1] which considered only four countries: Brazil, Russia, India and China. In 2011, at the coalition meeting held in China (Sanya), talks accomplished the incorporation of South Africa as a new member of the group, inaugurating the BRICS format.[2]

---

[1] Andrew Hurrell, 'Narratives of Emergence: Rising Powers and the End of the Third World?' (2013) 33(2) *Revista Economia Política*; available at www.scielo.br/scielo.php?script=sci_arttext&pid=S0101-31572013000200001&lng=pt&nrm=iso [accessed on 8 July 2016].

[2] Jim O'Neill, 'Building Better Global Economic BRICs', 2001; available at www.goldmansachs.com/our-thinking/archive/archive-pdfs/build-better-brics.pdf [accessed on 3 October 2016].

The first phase of the negotiation process that culminated in the creation of the group began in 2006, leading to the first official meeting of the BRIC countries in 2009 in Russia (Yekaterimburg).[3] Since then, many formal and informal meetings, conferences and talks have taken place, with different levels of representation, involving entrepreneurs, ministers and a host of authorities from member countries, but always focused on the establishment of agreements between the members regarding a series of themes on the international agenda.

Despite the commitment of BRICS countries to the main objectives and principles embodied by the coalition, however, they have not yet been able to attain a high level of cohesion, nor have they achieved a sound political platform enabling them to strategically take advantage of their power and influence over the international relations arena. Notwithstanding, BRICS countries play a strategic role in the emerging multipolar world order on many grounds, from their large territory and population to their high economic growth levels, even those still to be achieved. Despite many inconsistencies and contradictions, due to the huge diversity of political interests contemplated by its membership, the BRICS coalition remains fundamental to any strategic thinking focused on the reconfiguration of the world economy, in the sense that this concept was used by Braudel[4] and Wallerstein.[5]

This chapter aims to shed some light on one of the main initiatives of the group, the creation of the New Development Bank (NDB) in 2014, as a result of talks in its sixth meeting, which was held in Brazil (Fortaleza). The new bank was established to provide financial support to infrastructural and pro-development projects in developing countries. The New Development Bank (NDB) was funded with USD 100 billion in reserves; its most fundamental impact, however, will be on the economic juridical logic that has governed relations between Bretton Woods institutions and developing countries since the 1944 Bretton Woods Conference and the organization of the International Monetary Fund (IMF) and the Bank for International Reconstruction and Development (BIRD), which have always acted on behalf of Western developed countries.

---

[3] Diego Santos Vieira de Jesus, 'De Nova York a Durban: o processo de institucionalização do BRICS' [From New York to Durban: The institutionalization proccess of BRICS] (2013) 12(1) *Revista Oikos* 32–62.

[4] Fernand Braudel, 'Os jogos das trocas' [The Games of Exchange], n *Civilização material, economia e capitalismo*, séculos XV–XVIII (São Paulo: Martins Fontes, 1996), vol. III.

[5] Immanuel Wallerstein, *The Capitalist World-Economy* (Cambridge: Cambridge University Press, 1979).

II. International Economic Law and the Contemporary World Economy

The current international monetary and financial systems were established in July 1944, three years after the first two drafts of the legal agreements were individually submitted by Harry Dexter White (US) and John Maynard Keynes (England),[6] at the Conference of Bretton Woods, New Hampshire (US). The norms, rules and principles to be the basis for the operation of both international systems were embodied in two main international institutions: the IMF and the World Bank or BIRD.[7]

Both institutions were conceived under the aegis of Keynesianism and were a legacy of the outstanding success achieved by its policies in fighting the economic consequences of the 1929 financial crisis. Those policies were first implemented by the US president Frank Delano Roosevelt. Politically, the World Bank and IMF reflected the American perception of the role of international institutions as providing political stability for the new international order, under American hegemony. In general, this system was based on the juridical economic management of global exchange relations, configuring a new international economic law as a body of rules, principles and norms that regulated international economic relations and the exchange of capital, merchandise and services, as well as the integration of political processes and international policies for the promotion of development.

International economic law has always been ideologically oriented, with a sound liberal basis, driven by the promotion of free trade and the free movement of capital. Closely related to the international political economy, it has always been supported by the strong intervention of the state in the economy, especially when economic crises broke out, emphasizing the strategic role of states and governments in the world economy.

Juridical rules and economic theory were thus closely associated, giving rise to the specific design, content and format of those economic and financial institutions, which may have been responsible for keeping the international economy from facing another economic depression after the Second World War. In addition, the high levels of free trade and the free movement of capital worldwide, when combined, made it possible for

---

[6] See Fobe, Nicole Julie, 'Uma proposta esquecida – o bancor' [The Forgotten Proposal – the Bancor] (2014) 10(2) *Revista Direito GV* 441–450.

[7] See Carlos Márcio B. Cozendey, *Instituições de Bretton Woods: desenvolvimento e implicações para o Brasil* [Bretton Woods Institutions: Development and Implications to Brazil] (Brasília: FUNAG, 2013).

the IMF and the World Bank to hold the resources to provide financial aid and rescue packages to help countries facing economic crisis. Those institutions were also able to formulate development projects and strategies in numerous countries and were responsible for one of the longest periods of economic growth in history: the so-called Golden Age of Capitalism.

Those years of steady economic growth in Europe and North America, from the 1940s to the 1970s, had positive effects worldwide; in Latin America, Brazil, Mexico and Argentina were able to succeed in their strategies of development based on state-led industrialization policies, resulting in high levels of industrialization and economic growth.

Nowadays, however, although the IMF and the World Bank have played the same role as previously, they have not been able to achieve the same results. What happened?

There are many differences between the world economy in the second half of the twentieth century and the second decade of the twenty-first century, not only in economic but also in political matters. Economically, globalization has led to a high level of internationalization of the productive process, maximizing the financialization of capital and reorganizing, at the same time, the institutional channels of creation and distribution of wealth. Those changes have empowered great multinational corporations[8] and contributed to the emergence of a new principle, such as the rise in asymmetric relations between peoples and domestic groups worldwide.[9]

In the political sphere, the bipolarity of the Cold War era has been altered, and a new multipolar world order has come into being, under the leadership of the United States, now in alliance with local forces that are more or less able to project their power internationally.

According to the world system theory, the world economy comprises a continuum of production chains, connected across borders and involving members of the countries of the center, members of the countries of the periphery and members of the countries of the semi-periphery, depending on the levels of industrialization or the extent to which technology has been incorporated in the production process in each country. Overall, what makes hegemony hard to overcome is precisely the structural

---

[8] Lier Pires Ferreira Júnior, *Estado, Globalização e Integração Regional: Políticas exteriores de desenvolvimento e inserção internacional da América Latina no final do século XX* [State, Globalization and Regional Integration: Development Foreign Policies and International Relations of Latin America at the End of Twentieth Century] (Rio de Janeiro: América Jurídica, 2003).

[9] Zygmunt Bauman, *A riqueza de poucos beneficia todos nós?* [The Wealth of Some Helps Us all?] (Rio de Janeiro: Zahar, 2015).

constraints that associate the development of the center with the development of the other strata, mainly in the circles of growth or expansion of the world economy. In periods of crisis, however, the structural relationships among different regions and countries that are built into the production process through global production chains become loosened, and the ties that were once responsible for the close association of countries in a socially productive process weaken, making room for change in those relationships.

After each crisis that erupted following the end of the Bretton Woods system in the 1970s, more and more of the ties that usually had bound together those economies, through their relations of production in the world economy, were dismantled. This explains why the world economy is currently in a period of great transformation or transition. One clear response is the establishment of the BRICS New Development Bank, which was created to provide resources to finance development projects without subordinating debtor countries to the harsh policies of the conditions traditionally imposed by Bretton Woods institutions.[10]

The world economy is currently reconfiguring the traditional ties and structural positions between countries[11] in the international social division of labor. The result is that developing countries will not have to implement the macroeconomic policies that developed countries usually had constrained or forced them to accept, even though they themselves had never adopted them. Those policies had the effect of deepening the structural subordination of the periphery[12] and the semi-periphery to the center,[13] as implemented by the Bretton Woods institutions in the negotiating process with each debtor country.

These changes also pose a challenge to the traditional structures of international economic law, generating discontent and criticism of its main institutions. In this new multipolar world order, in which the world economy is assuming new characteristics,[14] neither new institutions such

---

[10] Ha-Joon Chang, *Chutando a escada: Estratégia do desenvolvimento em perspectiva histórica* [Kicking away the Ladder: Development Strategies in Historical Perspective] (São Paulo: Unesp, 2004).

[11] Robert Keohane and Joseph Nye, 'Power and Interdependence in the Information Age' (1998) 77(5) *Foreign Affairs* 158–165.

[12] Braudel, Braudel, 'Os jogos das trocas'.

[13] Thomas Piketty, *A economia da desigualdade* [The Inequality Economy] (Rio de Janeiro: Intrínseca, 2015).

[14] Julio Aguirre and Rúben Lo Vuolo, '*Variedades de capitalismo*. Una aproximación al estudio comparado del capitalismo y sus aplicaciones para América Latina' [Varieties of Capitalism: One Approach to the Study of Comparative Analisys of Capitalism and its Practice

as the WTO, which emerged from the old GATT, nor the traditional United Nations system or different sorts of regional integration agreements (among which the European Union is an outstanding example, albeit now highly contested since the approval of Brexit) are able to lead given the complexity and multiplicity of forces, new actors and interests emerging in those stormy seas of contemporary international politics. The BRICS NDB has its roots in this transition era, and its goal is to make it possible for new and old actors to negotiate on a new basis in the complex game of international relations.

III.   The BRICS Bank and Its Political Meaning

The BRICS coalition represents a new initiative of cooperation in international relations. Two years after the first report was issued by Jim O'Neill, two analysts from Goldman Sachs, Dominic Wilson and Roopa Purushothaman, carried away by the potential of this new group of countries, wrote a document analyzing the group, '*Dreaming with BRIC: the path to 2050*'.[15]

Both studies worked as a self-fulfilling prophecy, yielding the basis for the collective action of the group at the margins of the sixty-first General Assembly of the United Nations in 2006, when the first meeting of the foreign ministers of the BRIC countries took place.[16] The main goals of its members were the reform of the international governance apparatus and the creation of new institutions that would express the new configuration of forces in the international scenery, reflecting the new economic status of the emerging markets. The group had a sound basis of legitimacy as it covered 25.91 percent of the earth's surface, included 43.03 percent of the planet's population and 18 percent of the world GDP (25 percent of the GDP per capita) within its borders; it also had 15 percent of world trade and, more impressively, represented 46.3 percent of global economic growth, from 2000 to 2008.[17]

---

in Latin America] *Documento de Trabalho CIEPP* n. 85 (Buenos Aires: Centro Interdisciplinario para el estudio de politicas publicas, 2013).

[15] 'Dreaming with BRICs: the path to 2050', 2003; available at www.goldmansachs.com/our-thinking/archive/brics-dream.html [accessed on 6 November 2016].

[16] BRICS Policy Center, *Policy Brief: A Coodenação dos BRICs nos Fóruns Multilaterais, Núcleo de Política Internacional e Agenda Multilateral*, BRICS Policy Center and Centro de Estudos e Pesquisas BRICS, August 2012.

[17] George Bronzeado Andrade, 'Banco dos BRICS: a institucionalização de um novo organismo internacional para o desenvolvimento sustentável das nações emergentes.

206   CHRISTIANE ITABAIANA MARTINS *ET AL.*

These geopolitical assets made it possible for the group to coordinate their positions in some multilateral negotiations; they also enabled an agenda of regular meetings between its members, as well as resulted in influence over a series of themes and negotiations on the international agenda (the G-20, the reform of quotas and representation in the IMF, and participation in a rescue package to fight the financial crisis of 2008). In all those opportunities, the group worked in collaboration with the multilateral institutions; this collaboration was a theme of all its declarations and documents.

The group also seemed to represent a force for reform of the international world order, and this reformist character has been reflected in its initiatives; for example, the creation of the NDB and the proposition for a new international currency that would substitute for the US dollar in international trade. On these occasions the group showed itself eager to lead movements of reform or change in the traditional mechanisms of international governance.

The perception that the coalition has some inconsistencies led some analysts to understand it as a coalition of variable geometry,[18] which can be seen as a limitation of new coalitions of developing countries that remain unable to attain a solid basis of cohesion in more than one theme of the international agenda. On the contrary, the BRICS platform was only able to achieve an ad-hoc power equilibrium regarding each theme of the international agenda. This meant that it was never able to generate an authentic anti-hegemonic movement.[19] As a legacy of the process through which the group came into being, the basis for the selection of BRICS members was their levels of economic growth, not the identification of common interests. This resulted in a group with a large

Uma esfinge a ser decifrada' [BRICS Bank: Institutionalization of a New International Organization for the Sustainable Development of Emerging Nations: One Sphinx to be Deciphered] 2° Seminário De Relações Internacionais da Associação Brasileira De Relações Internacionais (Abri): Graduação E Pós-Graduação, 28 e 29 de agosto de 2014; available at www.seminario2014.abri.org.br/resources/anais/21/1407030812_ARQUIVO_ArtigoparaABRI2014-GeorgeBronzeadodeAndrade.pdf [accessed on 6 November 2016].

[18] Hermes Moreira Junior, 'Os BRICS e a Recomposição da Ordem Global: Estratégias de Inserção Internacional das Potências Emergentes' [BRICS and the reorganization of Global Order: Strategies of International Relations of Emerging Markets] (December 2011–March 2012) 3 (9–10) *Revista Conjuntura Austral* 71–89

[19] Cristina S. Pecequilo, 'Os EUA e o ciclo neoconservador: avaliações preliminares sobre a presidência George W. Bush' [The USA and the Neoconservative Circle: Preliminary Observations on George W.Bush´s Presidency] in Fundação Alexandre de Gusmão (ed.), *O Brasil No Mundo Que Vem Aí- II Conferência Nacional de Política Externa* (Brasília: FUNAG, 2008), vol. 1.

asymmetry of interests among its members, yet whose aspirations for influence over international order has helped them share the lead in some agenda itesm, for which there was some common ground over some issues and for some time.

Those challenges to the establishment of BRICS leadership paved the way for other strategies to achieve consensus on strategic themes considered fundamental by members of the coalition. This was the case at the Fifth BRICS Summit in Durban in 2013, which focused on the development of a long-term coordination mechanism to address key questions of global economy and politics, as well as economic growth and international security. A further advance in the institutionalization of the group, however, came through the creation of new ventures, such as the BRICS Business Council and the Multilateral Agreement over Cooperation and Co-Finance for Sustainable Development, and scheduled series of meetings and consultation processes regarding new areas of cooperation to be created.[20]

The ever-growing dialogue among BRICS countries and the creation of the BRICS Business Council resulted in a close relationship between the public and private interests represented in the group, which led to the creation of the BRICS Development Bank from inside the Business Council. This connection of the interests of the business sector to those of the government representatives of the member countries would bear fruit, because the strategy for creating the new bank was always conceived in association with the local development banks. At the first meeting of the Business Council, in August 2013, the final document noted the public-private partnerships among entrepreneurs and the governments of countries, at the same time encouraging the public authorities to speed up realization of the project of the new bank.[21] It was in this context that the Agreement for Co-Financing of Infrastructure for Africa was signed, providing incentives and guidance for agreements between the development banks of the country members, with the goal of enabling them to finance the projects of interest of more than one African state and enabling the investment of entrepreneurs and firms from each member country.[22]

---

[20] Ethekwini Declaration, Durban, South Africa, 27 March 2011; available at www.brics5.co.za/fifth-brics-summit-declaration-and-action-plan/ [accessed on 22 February 2015].

[21] BRICS Joint Statement; available at www.brics5.co.za/joint-statement-of-the-brics-business-forum-2013/ [accessed on 27 February 2015].

[22] Carlos Tautz and João Roberto Lopes Pinto, 'Quem são os proprietários dos BRICS' [Who Are the BRICS Owners?} available at www.corecon-rj.org.br/pesquisa_2014/brics.pdf [accessed on 23 February 2015].

Since Durban 2013, a new institutional logic, based on the norms of international economic law, is guiding the international initiatives of the BRICS. This logic is the basis on which the NDB will work, as connected to and moved forward by the Business Council.

The NDB was formally created in Brazil (Fortaleza) in 2014 at the Sixth BRICS Summit, where the talks reaffirmed that the new bank was an alternative to capitalist banks, which served only the interests of great corporations. In contrast, the new bank was seen as working for the sustainable economy and against the hegemonic power relations preserved through the financial relations operated by traditional banks. NDB was created following the same pattern as IMF and BIRD, however. Its reserves in 2015 were USD 100 billion, which were to come from the country members over seven years, in growing installments, as agreed in the 2014 Treaty for the Establishment of a BRICS Contingent Reserve Agreement (CRA).[23] According to the BRICS members, this treaty 'shall contribute to strengthening the global social safety net and complement existing international monetary and financial agreements'.[24] In this sense, countries other than BRICS members could take loans and become members of the bank, as long as the original members remained in control of 55 percent of the total assets.

The NDB was thus created to provide resources with which to invest in infrastructure in peripheral and semi-peripheral countries, including the BRICS member countries. Originally, the NDB was to be an alternative to the Bretton Woods institutions, financing projects that were strategic for BRICS members, making them stronger economicall,y and investing in building infrastructure for development. In the original agreement, Brazil had the right to appoint the president of the Management Council, Russia was to appoint the Governor's Council and India was entitled to appoint the first president of the NDB. China retained the right to be the country where the bank was placed. The African regional center of the bank was placed in South Africa. According to the original agreement, the presidency of the bank would be shared in turn among the BRICS members, with five- year terms. After India, Brazil would appoint the president of the bank, followed by Russia, South Africa and China.

---

[23] Treaty for the Establishment of a BRICS Contingent Reserve Arrangement, Fortaleza, 15 July 2014; available at http://brics.itamaraty.gov.br/media2/press-releases/220-treaty-for-the-establishment-of-a-brics-contingent-reserve-arrangement-fortaleza-july-15 [accessed on 4 December 2016].

[24] *Ibid.*

IV.   BRICS New Development Bank: Challenges Ahead

Widely understood as an alternative to Bretton Woods institutions, the NDB could jeopardize the traditional control that central countries possess over the resources and loans given to peripheral and semi-peripheral countries. It is the first international financial institution free from 'Euro-American' hegemony. Traditionally, international economic law and the Bretton Woods institutions worked as powerful political channels through which central countries were able to project their influence over the world economy, mainly in their vertical relationships with developing countries. Bretton Woods institutions were used by central countries to control and restrain economic and political free action in order to enforce their own interests against the aims of the peripheral countries. The IMF, the World Bank and the WTO worked as instruments to make sure that the macroeconomic policies of developing countries would be framed according to the interests of the central countries.

Nevertheless, it is possible to understand the creation of the NDB as a strenuous effort to improve BRICS influence over Bretton Woods financial institutions. The performance of BRICS countries in the G-20 – fighting for changes in IMF quotas, for example – offers evidence that they are eager to have a good relationship and to take part in the multilateral institutions of the old order, helping them adjust to the new power configuration of the twenty-first century.

According to Baumann,[25] there are many possibilities for building a peaceful and even a harmonious relationship between Bretton Woods institutions and the NDB; however, there are some challenges for the NDB. The first challenge is to gain the confidence of the central countries and reassure them that the NDB is not a threat to Bretton Woods institutions, but instead is another way to establish multilateral cooperation in the international environment.

The BRICS history shows that its members are accustomed to making all sorts of efforts to build a basis on which to improve the potential for collective action inside the group.[26] Cooperation for development appears to be the main goal through which those efforts can be combined towards a long-term common agenda.

[25] Renato Baumann, 'Os Novos Bancos de Desenvolvimento: Independência Conflitiva ou Parcerias estratégicas?' [The New Development Banks: Conflicting Independence or Strategic Partnership?] (2016) 43 *Radar* 37–46.

[26] Adriana Erthal Abdenur and Mayara Folly, 'O Novo Banco de Desenvolvimento e a Institucionalização dos BRICS '[**The New** Development Bank and the BRICS Institutionalization], in *BRICS: Estudos e Documentos* (BRASÍLIA: FUNAG, 2015).

A second challenge involves making the bank a real success on its own terms, which means that it must be able to effectively finance development in developing countries, on an alternative basis to the traditional modus operandi characteristic of the Bretton Woods institutions. Meeting this challenge would bring concrete results in terms of a new international economic governance that would be more fair, more inclusive and more democratic.[27] If this challenge were met there would be a substantial gain in legitimacy for the group, which explains why NDB assumes preeminence in the agenda of the coalition. In fact, many analysts believe that the BRICS countries cannot translate their economic emergent market status into political influence, because the coalition has not yet been able to overcome the internal diversity of interests, which results in inconsistencies when the group has to take part in more ambitious negotiations or political projects. In contrast, China and Russia make it clear how fundamental the capacity to pursue an autonomous foreign policy is to projecting power in the international scenario.

A third challenge lies in the economic, social, cultural and political diversity that characterizes the BRICS member countries. Brazil, South Africa and India are democracies, but Russia is a kind of semi-democracy, and China may be considered an autocracy. The coalition also works with low levels of institutionalization, what means that there are no institutional devices or mechanisms aiming to harmonize interests or economic policies, as is the case in the European Union, for example. The consequence is that each BRICS member country pursues independent or autonomous foreign policies in relation to the other members of the coalition. These countries thus, individually, compete among themselves in business areas, such as ore production (South Africa, Brazil and Russia). China is well known for signing bilateral commercial agreements with Russia, Brazil and South Africa. Another fundamental difference can be seen when one considers judicial rules: Each country has its own laws and juridical regime. These rules directly affect deals and cooperation efforts that can have an impact on the liability of the ambitious settlement deals inside the group. A significant question is how much the NDB projects will be affected by any divergent interests between the country-members.[28]

The fourth challenge is closely related to the previous one. The diversity of interests among its members and its low levels of institutionalization

---

[27] *Ibid.*

[28] Andrade, 'Banco dos BRICS: a institucionalização de um novo organismo internacional para o desenvolvimento sustentável das nações emergentes'.

encourage other countries to offer agreements to some BRICS members, which go against the objectives of the group and threaten cohesion. We can assume that central countries and Bretton Woods institutions will not be restrained in trying to stop the NDB project from going further. Central countries are not used to acting submissively and will always try to co-opt countries against the NDB. The Transpacific Partnership Agreement – a US initiative – is a clear example. The TPA threatens the priority given to BRICS agreements and to the NDB, on which Brazilian foreign policy is expending a great deal of effort.[29]

The fifth challenge is the impact of the international financial crisis on the economic growth of some BRICS members, especially Brazil and Russia. The effects of the crisis can override O'Neill's presumptions. In this scenario, BRICS could be converted into TICKS (meaning the exclusion of Russia and Brazil and the inclusion of Taiwan and South Korea).[30]

The sixth and last challenge to the NDB is the clear understanding that BRICS members have to share about the fundamental importance of their internal and external relationships and alliances. In other words, they must preserve the basis of the group's collective action such as it is, bearing the mark of being created to address the lack of influence over International Order from the new emergent countries. In this sense, its members have to cultivate, among themselves, as with other developing countries, a new basis of relationships, which must be as fair, democratic, horizontal an open as possible. The reason this is so strategic from a BRICS perspective is that the members need to be conscious that the legitimacy of the group comes from its political project, which represents a challenge to the traditional way that Bretton Woods institutions used to operate.

From this perspective, the main risk to the NDB lies in the threat to this kind of relationship posed by China's great political and economic power. In particular, the NDB must find ways to make sure that the projects that it will finance will really promote the development of the countries who receive the loans and that the way the bank will manage its governance and its relationships to creditor countries will stand in sharp contrast to the way Bretton Woods institutions always operated.

---

[29] Isabel Versiani, "Brasil não descarta aderir ao Tratado Transpacífico' diz ministro' [Brazil Does Not Give Up to Take Part in Transpacific Partnership, Says Minister], Folha de São Paulo, 14 October 2015; available at www1.folha.uol.com.br/mercado/2015/10/1693809-brasil-podera-aderir-ao-tratado-transpacifico-diz-ministro.shtml [accessed on 6 November 2016].

[30] Marcos Troyjo, 'Sobre a Morte dos BRICS e a Ascensão dos Ticks' [On the Death of BRICS and the Rising of TICKS], Folha de São Paulo, 10 Feburary 2016.

V. Conclusion

Despite the political discourse that emphasizes the anti-hegemonic character of the new bank, all the documents issued by the group note that the NDB was set up as a political initiative through the entrepreneurial representation of the BRICS countries, gathered in the new Business Council. As such, it was conceived as a new institution to finance development projects in association with the governments of those countries. This initiative is a threat to Bretton Woods institutions and to the norms and rules of international economic law; however, this threat is often neutralized by the group, which insists that the NDB should work as part of the multilateral system and was never intended to replace those institutions. On the contrary, NDB is envisioned to increase the number of resources and credit lines at the disposal of developing countries to finance their development, while at the same time projecting the influence of BRICS countries into the international economic scene. In other words, the political character of the bank is undeniable, notwithstanding the possibilities of its operation in harmony with Bretton Woods institutions.

The new bank may also assume other political meanings, depending on the interests and foreign policy objectives of each member of the BRICS. For Brazil, the new bank may represent a valuable economic and political asset that may increase its international projection of power and influence, mostly in Latin America; it may also offer an opportunity to succeed in bargains with its traditional Western allies, among which the United States is the best example. In addition, through its deeper integration into BRICS, Brazil has been able to come closer to Asian markets than ever before. Another Brazilian objective that is achieved by its participation in the NDB is to establish a good relationship with some of the largest and more powerful emerging countries, such as India and China. In the same vein, Brazil's cultivation of those partnerships may provide access to Chinese capital and investments and increase its commercial relationships with other members of the NDB. Chinese investments in Brazilian infrastructure are being negotiated right now, and the consequences they may have on domestic politics remain to be seen.

Russian interests in NDB are highly specific, which reflects its past and history as a hegemon of the Cold War era. This history continues to influence its international status; as a country widely known for its outstanding military industry, Russia shows great potential in the development of high technology in nuclear weapons and other kinds of war devices. It also shows a remarkable scientific performance and high levels in its social development performance.[31] The country's economic development figures, however, do not show the same dynamism as shown by its political ambitions in the international arena. In this sense, the NDB is a strategic objective of Russian foreign policy as its participation in the bank may provide investments that would contribute to accelerating its levels of economic activity. This role is even more significant when international prices of oil and gas are extremely low. The current political tensions between Moscow and Western countries (Ukraine and Syria) may turn the NDB into a viable alternative to attracting capital away from the Bretton Woods institutions and their harsh policies of conditionality.

In India, the NDB may offer great support for its astonishing economic development. India may become a superpower in the twenty-first century, as the country has completed twenty-three years of its highest levels of economic growth.[32] Its scientific and technological development has made it the fourth leading country in the nuclear/war industry.[33] In addition to its outstanding performance in information technology, software and services,[34] the country was able to develop a space program to the highest of standards, which launched its first spaceship to Mars in 2013.[35] In the social sphere, India shows outstanding performance in strengthening its democracy, increasing the efficiency of its public sector, and implementing education reform and policies designed to fight poverty.[36] The

---

[31] Victoria V. Panova, 'Rússia nos BRICS: visão e interpretação prática. Semelhanças e diferenças. Coordenação dos BRICS dentro das estruturas de instituições multilaterais' [Russia in BRICS: Vision and Practical Interpretation: Differences and Similarities. BRICS Coordination inside the Structure of Multilateral Institutions] (2015) 47(1) *Contexto Internacional* 47–80; available at www.scielo.br/scielo.php?script=sci_arttext&pid=S0102–85292015000100047&lng=pt&nrm=iso [accessed on 8 July 2016].

[32] Arindan Banik and Fernando Padovani, 'Índia em transformação: o novo crescimento econômico e as perspectivas pós-crises' [Changes in India: The New Economic Development and the Post-Crisis Perspectives] (2014) 22(50) *Revista de Sociologia e Política* 67–93; available at www.scielo.br/scielo.php?script=sci_arttext&pid=S0104–44782014000200006&lng=pt&nrm=iso [accessed on 8 August 2016].

[33] Global Firepower, 'The Complete Global Firepower List Puts the Military Powers of the World into Full Perspective'; available at www.globalfirepower.com/countries-listing.asp [accessed on 8 April 2016].

[34] Bank and Padovani, 'Índia em transformação'.

[35] Pedro Carvalho de Mello, O B de BRICS: Potencial de consumo, recursos naturais e economia brasileira [The B of BRICS: Potential of Comsumption, Natural Resources and Brazilian Economy] (São Paulo: Saint Paul Editora, 2012).

[36] João Feres Jr. and Verônica Toste Daflon, 'Ação afirmativa na Índia e no Brasil: um estudo sobre a retórica acadêmic' [Affirmative Policies in India and in Brazil: A Study on Academic Rhetoric] (2015) 17(40) *Sociologias* 92–123; available at www.scielo.br/scielo.php?script=sci_arttext&pid=S1517–45222015000300092&lng=pt&nrm=iso [accessed on

country has also passed legislation to fight prejudice through affirmative policies.

This high level of economic growth has made India eager to find new financing sources that would allow it to take the greatest advantage of these developments. The NDB would be the perfect financial source for India, in clear contrast to Bretton Woods institutions, which have been unable to provide the capital to finance the needs of development in Africa, Asia and Latin America. In this sense, the new bank might provide access to Chinese capital without the threat of a direct and asymmetric relationship between India and the Chinese dragon.

China is the largest economic power in BRICS and has strategic interests in NDB that are deeply associated with its status in international relations.[37] The country underwent a period of radical economic reforms that resulted in a combination of two systems.[38] Politically, there is no democracy or social rights, and economically, the country takes advantage of market forces and, at the same time, resorts to an efficient economic planning model to stimulate or induce the behavior of private agents and to correct market failures.[39] The Chinese economic model is heterodox, combining trade liberalization with state control and the presence of special regimes for strategic sectors of the economy.[40] This economic model is based on an association between the increase in exports and the rise in the amount of foreign reserves in dollars,[41] as well as high levels of external direct investment,[42] which has been provided by Asian industries from

8 August 2016].[Affirmative Policies in India and in Brazil: a Study on Academic Rhetoric]

[37] Paulo G. Fagundes Visentini, 'Novíssima China e o sistema internacional' [The Very New China and the International System] (2011) 19(1) *Revista Sociologia e Política* 131–141.

[38] Julio Aguirre and Rúben Lo Vuolo, '*Variedades de capitalismo. Una aproximación al estudio comparado del capitalismo y sus aplicaciones para América Latina*' [Varieties of Capitalism. One Approach to the Study of Comparative Analisys of Capitalism and its Practice in Latin America], *Documento de Trabalho CIEPP* n. 85 (Buenos Aires: Centro Interdisciplinario para el estudio de politicas publicas, 2013).

[39] Ha-Joon Chang, *The East Asian Development Experience: The Miracle, the Crisis and the Future* (Penang: Third World Network, 2006).

[40] Nicholas R. Lardy, *Integrating China into the Global Economy* (Washington DC: Brookings, 2004).

[41] André Moreira Cunha, 'A ascensão da China à condição de potência econômica: há algo de novo no modelo asiático? Trabalho apresentado no XIII' [The Rise of China to theSstatus of Economic Power: Is There Something New in the Asian Model?], Encontro Nacional de Economia Política, realizado em João Pessoa, de 20 a 23 de maio, 2008; available at www .anpec.org.br/encontro2008/artigos/200807091508220-.pdf [accessed on 8 May 2016].

[42] Lardy, *Integrating China into the Global Economy.*

Hong Kong, Taiwan and South Korea. The characteristics of the development model has given China[43] great autonomy in the management of its economic policy,[44] leading to a capacity to align its economy policy with its own interpretation of its national interest.[45]

However, the Chinese political economy,[46] which combines strong political autonomy with the absence of limits or restraints on the government's role[47] in the economy or society,[48] stands in opposition to one of the mandatory objectives of the NDB: the economic sustainability of the projects to be financed. China has always been concerned with maintaining a great deal of autonomy and preserving free political space for the behavior of its government because of its ambitious foreign policy objectives. It is prepared to lead a new configuration of forces at the forefront of a new world economic order, helping Asia and the Global South to free themselves from economic and financial conditions of dependence and the restraint imposed by the Western countries through their control over the Bretton Woods institutions.[49]

For China to take part in BRICS means to keep push one of the more relevant mechanisms of expression of its ever-growing global power, however, it also means that it must put the brakes on some of its foreign policy ambitions. It would never have a status similar to the one it would have

---

[43] Martin Jacques, *When China Rules the World: The End of the Western World and The Birth of a New Global Order* (London: Penguin, 2009).

[44] Gary Gereffi and Fernandez-Stark Karina, 'Global Value Chain Analysis: A Primer', Center on Globalization, Governance & Competitiveness (CGGC) Duke University Durham, North Carolina, USA, 31 May 2011; available at www.cggc.duke.edu/pdfs/2011–05–31_ GVC_analysis_a_primer.pdf [accessed on 8 May 2016].

[45] André Moreira Cunha and Luciana Acioly, 'China: ascensão à condição de potência global– características e implicações') [China: The Rise to the Status of Global Power: Characteristics and Implications], in J. Cardoso Jr., L. Acioly and M. Matijascic (eds.), *Trajetórias Recentes de Desenvolvimento: estudos de experiências internacionais selecionadas* (Brasília: Instituto de Pesquisa Econômica Aplicada, 2009).

[46] Alexandre Queiroz Guimarães, 'A economia política do modelo econômico chinês: o estado, o mercado e os principais desafios' [The Political Economy of Chinese Economic Model: Sate, Market and the Main Challenges] (2012) 20(4) *Revista Sociologia e Política*; available at http://www.scielo.br/scielo.php?script=sci_arttext&pid=S0104– 44782012000400009&lng=pt&nrm=iso#7a [accessed on 8 May 2016].

[47] Minxin Pei, *China's Trapped Transition: The Limits of Developmental Autocracy* (Harvard University Press, 2009).

[48] James Kynge, *A China Sacode O Mundo* [China Shakes the World] (Brazil: Globo Livros, 2007).

[49] Ho-Fung Hung, 'O braço direito dos Estados Unidos? O dilema da República Popular da China na crise global' [The Right Arm of United States? The Popular Chinese Republic Dillema in the Global Crisis] (2011) (89) *Novos Estudos – CEBRAP* 17–37.

if it acted alone in the formal structures of international economic law or in the Bretton Woods institutions. The NDB is one among many international agreements in which China is taking part, as some other investment banks for financing infrastructure in Asia, such as the Asian Infrastructure Investment Bank (AIIB), as well as any other multilateral agreements.[50] The NDB represents for China one mechanisms among others that could be used to project its great power and influence in the international order, being of relative importance for its foreign policy objectives; however, Chinese ambition would never be restrained by its ties to the bank. It seems that China is expanding its reach to regions with low strategic costs and projecting influence to make itself ready for the moment when it will face the United States on an equal one-to-one basis, for a frank and open dialogue.

South Africa was the last country to join BRICS and has a history associated with apartheid, the ethnic racial policy of segregation that came to an end only in the 1990s, as a result of the mobilization of a great deal of national and international pressure. As the country with the most modest levels of economic growth in BRICS, it is the one that has the most to gain from the NDB. The strategic presence of South Africa in BRICS was conceived to provide a pathway to obtaining projects for the coalition on the African continent. Its presence in the NDB may not only consolidate its status as a regional power in the African continent but may also allow the country to gain access to credit lines, other markets and partnerships with larger economies.

South Africa is the only member of BRICS that is not among the ten largest economies in the world; however, it has seen steady growth over recent years, being an example of a country that has been able to consolidate its democracy. Its presence in BRICS is strategic, as the other members compete for its natural resources and for access to its markets: The growing competition among developing countries, BRICS members included, is becoming more and more clear, and investment levels on the African continent are rising. China and India have a strong presence in South Africa and there are already harsh disputes between them.[51]

[50] Marcos Antônio Macedo Cintra and Eduardo Costa Pinto, 'China em transformação: transição e estratégias de desenvolvimento' [China in Transition: Changes and Development Strategies], Instituto de Economia, UFRJ, Texto para Discussão 006/2015; available at www.ie.ufrj.br/images/pesquisa/publicacoes/discussao/2015/TD_IE_006_2015_CINTRA_PINTO.pdf [accessed on 8 May 2016].

[51] 'BRICS competem para ganhar terreno na África: Recursos naturais e mercados africanos estão na mira dos investidores' [BRICS Dispute Influence in Africa: Natural Resources

No definitive conclusions can be drawn about the NDB, as its effective work still is very recent. However, many possible inferences can be made, based on the diversity of perspectives on international relations entertained by the countries that take part in it. In the quest for another kind of policy and another perspective on development outside the established patterns imposed by the countries of the global economic center, the BRICS countries all compromised and took risks to pursue alternative political roads to free themselves from the harsh conditionality policies of Bretton Woods institutions. The NDB does not have enough funds to supply the needs of peripheral countries, however, not even those of its members. So it is not about to replace Bretton Woods institutions, but it will work in collaboration with them in some measure to increase the resources to finance development projects, through less rigid and more flexible criteria. Over the long term, however, a growing political influence of BRICS countries in the international order will follow.

In the future, the growing influence of the NDB could even contribute to a reform of the policies and governance of Bretton Woods institutions, opening new political and economic spaces for BRICS in the new international order that is under construction.

VI. References

Abdenur, Adriana Erthal and Folly, Mayara, 'O Novo Banco de Desenvolvimento e a Institucionalização dos BRICS', in *BRICS: Estudos e Documentos* (Brasília: FUNAG, 2015).

Aguirre, Julio and Vuolo, Rúben Lo, 'Variedades de capitalismo. Una aproximación al estudio comparado del capitalismo y sus aplicaciones para América Latina', *Documento de Trabalho CIEPP n. 85* (Buenos Aires: Centro Interdisciplinario para el estudio de políticas publicas, 2013).

Andrade, George Bronzeado, 'Banco dos BRICS: a institucionalização de um novo organismo internacional para o desenvolvimento sustentável das nações emergentes. Uma esfinge a ser decifrada', 2º Seminário De Relações Internacionais da Associação Brasileira De Relações Internacionais (Abri): Graduação E Pós-Graduação, 28 e 29 de agosto de 2014; available at www.seminario2014.abri.org.br/resources/anais/21/1407030812_ARQUIVO_ArtigoparaABRI2014-GeorgeBronzeadodeAndrade.pdf [accessed on 6 November 2016].

and African Markets on the Target of Investors]; available at http://noticias.r7.com/internacional/brics-competem-para-ganhar-terreno-na-africa-26032013 [accessed on 15 August 2016].

Banik, Arindan and Padovani, Fernando, 'Índia em transformação: o novo cresci-mento econômico e as perspectivas pós-crises' (2014) 22(50) *Revista de Sociologia e Política* 67–93; available at www.scielo.br/scielo.php?script=sci_arttext&pid=S0104-44782014000200006&lng=pt&nrm=iso [accessed on 8 August 2016].

Bauman, Zygmunt, *A riqueza de poucos beneficia todos nós?* (Rio de Janeiro: Zahar, 2015).

Baumann, Renato, 'Os Novos Bancos de Desenvolvimento: Independência Confli-tiva ou Parcerias estratégicas?' (2016) 43 *Radar* 37–46.

Braudel, Fernand, 'Os jogos das trocas', in *Civilização material, economia e capital-ismo*, séculos XV–XVIII (São Paulo: Martins Fontes, 1996), vol. III.

BRICS Policy Center, *Policy Brief: A Coodenação dos BRICs nos Fóruns Multilaterais*, Núcleo de Política Internacional e Agenda Multilateral, BRICS Policy Center and Centro de Estudos e Pesquisas BRICS, Agosto de 2012.

Chang, Ha-Joon, *Chutando a escada: Estratégia do desenvolvimento em perspectiva histórica* (São Paulo: Unesp, 2004).

The East Asian Development Experience: The Miracle, the Crisis and the Future (Penang: Third World Network, 2006).

Cintra, Marcos Antônio Macedo and Pinto, Eduardo Costa, 'China em transfor-mação: transição e estratégias de desenvolvimento', Instituto de Economia, UFRJ, Texto para Discussão 006/2015; available at www.ie.ufrj.br/images/pesquisa/publicacoes/discussao/2015/TD_IE_006_2015_CINTRA_PINTO .pdf [accessed on 8 May 2016].

Cozendey, Carlos Márcio B., *Instituições de Bretton Woods: desenvolvimento e impli-cações para o Brasil* (Brasília: FUNAG, 2013).

Cunha, André Moreira, 'A ascensão da China à condição de potência econômica: há algo de novo no modelo asiático? Trabalho apresentado no XIII', Encon-tro Nacional de Economia Política, realizado em João Pessoa, de 20 a 23 de maio, 2008; available at www.anpec.org.br/encontro2008/artigos/200807091508220-.pdf [accessed on 8 May 2016].

Cunha, André Moreira and Acioly, Luciana, 'China: ascensão à condição de potên-cia global–características e implicações', in J. Cardoso Jr, L. Acioly and M. Matijascic (eds.), *Trajetórias Recentes de Desenvolvimento: estudos de exper-iências internacionais selecionadas* (Brasília: Instituto de Pesquisa Econômica Aplicada, 2009).

Feres Jr, João and Daflon, Verônica Toste, 'Ação afirmativa na Índia e no Brasil: um estudo sobre a retórica acadêmic' (2015) 17(40) *Sociologias* 92–123; available at www.scielo.br/scielo.php?script=sci_arttext&pid=S1517-45222015000300092&lng=pt&nrm=iso [accessed on 8 August 2016].

Fobe, Nicole Julie, 'Uma proposta esquecida – o bancor' (2014) 10(2) *Revista Direito GV* 441–450.

Gereffi, Gary and Fernandez-Stark, Karina, 'Global Value Chain Analysis: A Primer', Center on Globalization, Governance & Competitiveness (CGGC) Duke University Durham, North Carolina, USA, 31 May 2011; available at www.cggc.duke.edu/pdfs/2011-05-31_GVC_analysis_a_primer.pdf [accessed on 8 May 2016].

Guimarães, Alexandre Queiroz, 'A economia política do modelo econômico chinês: o estado, o mercado e os principais desafios' (2012) 20(4) *Revista Sociologia e Política*; available at www.scielo.br/scielo.php?script=sci_arttext&pid=S0104-44782012000400009&lng=pt&nrm=iso#7a [accessed on 8 May 2016].

Hung, Ho-Fung, 'O braço direito dos Estados Unidos? O dilema da República Popular da China na crise global' (2011) (89) *Novos Estudos – CEBRAP* 17–37.

Hurrell, Andrew, 'Narratives of Emergence: Rising Powers and The End of Third Word?' (2013) 33(2) *Revista Economia Política*; available at www.scielo.br/scielo.php?script=sci_arttext&pid=S0101-31572013000200001&lng=pt&nrm=iso [accessed on 8 July 2016].

Jacques, Martin, *When China Rules the World: The End of the Western World and The Birth of a New Global Order* (London: Penguin, 2009).

Jesus, Diego Santos Vieira de, 'De Nova York a Durban: o processo de institucionalização do BRICS' (2013) 12(1) *Revista Oikos* 32–62.

Júnior, Lier Pires Ferreira, *Estado, Globalização e Integração Regional: Políticas exteriores de desenvolvimento e inserção internacional da América Latina no final do século XX* (Rio de Janeiro: América Jurídica, 2003).

Keohane, Robert and Nye, Joseph, 'Power and Interdependence in yhe Information Age' (1998) 77(5) *Foreign Affairs*.

Kynge, James, *A China Sacode O Mundo* (Brazil: Globo Livros, 2007).

Lardy, Nicholas R., *Integrating China into the Global Economy* (Washington, DC: Brookings Institution Press, 2004).

Mello, Pedro Carvalho de, *O B de BRICS: Potencial de consumo, recursos naturais e economia brasileira* (São Paulo: Saint Paul Editora, 2012).

Moreira Jr, Hermes, 'Os BRICS e a Recomposição da Ordem Global: Estratégias de Inserção Internacional das Potências Emergentes' (Dec 2011–Mar 2012) 3 (9–10) *Revista Conjuntura Austral* 71–89.

O'Neill, Jim, 'Building Better Global Economic BRICs', 2001; available at www.goldmansachs.com/our-thinking/archive/archive-pdfs/build-better-brics.pdf [accessed on 3 October 2016].

Panova, Victoria V., 'Rússia nos BRICS: visão e interpretação prática. Semelhanças e diferenças. Coordenação dos BRICS dentro das estruturas de instituições multilaterais' (2015) 47(1) *Contexto Internacional* 47–80; available at www.scielo.br/scielo.php?script=sci_arttext&pid=S0102-85292015000100047&lng=pt&nrm=iso [accessed on 8 July 2016].

Pecequilo, Cristina S., 'Os EUA e o ciclo neoconservador: avaliações preliminares sobre a presidência George W. Bush', in Alexandre de Gusmão Fundação (ed.), *O Brasil No Mundo Que Vem Aí- II Conferência Nacional de Política Externa* (Brasília: FUNAG, 2008), vol. 1.

Pei, Minxin, *China's Trapped Transition: The Limits of Developmental Autocracy* (Cambridge, MA: Harvard University Press, 2009).

Piketty, Thomas, *A economia da desigualdade* (Rio de Janeiro: Intrínseca, 2015).

Tautz, Carlos and Pinto, João Roberto Lopes, 'Quem são os proprietários dos BRICS'; available at www.corecon-rj.org.br/pesquisa_2014/brics.pdf [accessed on 23 February 2015].

Troyjo, Marcos, 'Sobre a Morte dos BRICS e a Ascensão dos Ticks', Folha de São Paulo, 10 Feburary 2016.

Versiani, Isabel, "Brasil não descarta aderir ao Tratado Transpacífico'. diz ministro', Folha de São Paulo, 14 October 2015; available at www1.folha.uol.com. br/mercado/2015/10/1693809-brasil-podera-aderir-ao-tratado-transpacifico-diz-ministro.shtml [accessed on 6 November 2016].

Visentini, Paulo G. Fagundes, 'Novíssima China e o sistema internacional' (2011) 19(1) *Revista Sociologia e Política* 131–141.

Wallerstein, Immanuel, *The Capitalist World-Economy* (Cambridge: Cambridge University Press, 1979).

10

The Political Economy Challenges of Financial Regulation in BRICS Economies

A Case Study of Capital Markets Regulation in India

DEBANSHU MUKHERJEE

I. An Overview of Capital Markets Regulation in BRICS Economies

BRICS economies (Brazil, Russia, India, China and South Africa) represent the four largest emerging markets. This chapter examines the political economy challenges that arise in the regulation of capital markets operating in such economies. It uses the Indian experience of capital market regulation and the functioning of the capital market regulator, the Securities and Exchange Board of India (SEBI), as a test case to pinpoint specific issues that arise in this regard. Before the case of the Indian capital market regulation and its associated issues is discussed in detail, a cursory reference to the regulatory regimes of other BRICS nations is apposite.

The Brazilian capital market is a highly regulated sector.[1] The entities responsible for capital market regulation include the Comissão de Valores Mobiliários (CVM), the Central Bank (BCB) and the Conselho Monetário Nacional (CMN).[2] CMN is responsible for setting national policy, and BCB is a 'licensing body and prudential regulator'.[3] CVM is the Brazilian securities regulator and is responsible for market development, the efficient functioning of the market, protection of investors, access to

---

[1] Law Business Research, *International Capital Market Review: Brazil*, p. 23; available at www.pinheironeto.com.br/Documents/Artigos/The-International-Capital-Markets-Review-Brazil.jpg.pdf [accessed on 2 November 2016].

[2] IOSCO, 'Financial Sector Assessment Program: Brazil- IOSCO Objectives and Principles of Securities Regulation Detailed Assessment of Implementation (2013)', p. 29; available at www.imf.org/external/np/fsap/fsap.aspx [accessed on 2 November 2016].

[3] *Ibid.*

appropriate information, and market supervision and sanctions.[4] In terms of the legislative framework, federal laws lay down the general rules for the regulation of capital markets, including rules applicable to different agents functioning in the market and rules establishing market regulators and their respective limits and powers. The subordinate legislation regulating the market includes CVM instructions, Central Bank circulars and CMN resolutions.[5]

The Russian capital market is regulated by Federal Law No. 39-FZ [On the Securities Market] of 22 April 1996, which provides a legal framework for the conduct of primary and secondary capital market transactions.[6] There has been much change in the institutional framework over the years in terms of the institution regulating the capital markets and a transition from the Federal Commission for the Securities Market (FCSM), which was abolished in 2004, to the Federal Service for the Financial Markets (FSFM) whose regulatory functions were assimilated into the Bank of Russia through a legislative amendment in 2013.[7]

The Chinese Securities Regulatory Commission (CSRC) is responsible for the regulation of equity markets in China. The functions of CSRC include, inter alia, 'enactment of [binding] quasi-legislation, including regulations and guidelines; supervision of listed entities on the Chinese Securities market; reactive enforcement and imposition of fines etc. on delinquent market participants'.[8]

The South African capital market system is regulated through the Financial Services Board (FSB), Department of Trade and Industries (DTI), South African Reserve Bank (SARB) and Johannesburg Stock Exchange (JSE); the JSE serves as a self-regulatory institution.[9] The FSB is

---

[4] Securities and Exchange Commission of Brazil, 'Legal Mandates of CVM'; available at www.cvm.gov.br/subportal_ingles/menu/about/mandates.html [accessed on 2 November 2016].

[5] Law Business Research, *International Capital Market Review: Brazil*, p. 23; available at www.pinheironeto.com.br/Documents/Artigos/The-International-Capital-Markets-Review-Brazil.jpg.pdf [accessed on 2 November 2016].

[6] International Monetary Fund, *Russian Federation: Detailed Assessment of Observance of IOSCO Objectives and Principles of Securities Regulation*, IMF Report 12/53; available at www.imf.org/external/pubs/ft/scr/2012/cr1253.pdf [accessed on 2 November 2016].

[7] Lidings, 'Abolition of the FCSM and establishment of financial markets 'mega-regulator' on the basis of Bank of Russia', 2013; available at www.lidings.com/eng/legalupdates2?id=95 [accessed on 2 November 2016].

[8] Tianshu Zhou, 'Is The CSRC Protecting a 'Level Playing Field' in China's Capital Markets: Public Enforcement, Fragmented Authoritarianism and Corporatism' (2015) 15(2) *Journal of Corporate Law Studies* 377–406 at 378.

[9] International Monetary Fund, *South Africa: Detailed Assessment of Implementation on IOSCO Principles – Securities Markets*, p. 8; available at www.imf.org/external/pubs/ft/scr/2010/cr10355.pdf [accessed on 2 November 2016].

regulated by the Financial Services Board Act 1980, and is appointed by the Ministry of Finance. The FSB has wide powers over 'financial advisors and intermediaries, collective investment scheme operators (CIS), pension funds and insurance companies'.[10] It also has investigative and supervisory powers. The DTI has regulatory powers over the 'listing of public companies, the offering process for primary offerings of securities or for the regulation of ongoing periodic disclosure requirement for these companies'.[11] The DTI and the JSE collectively promulgate and regulate the supervisory standards in this regard. The SARB regulates issues pertaining to cross-border listings and foreign securities offerings.[12]

From the perspective of policy formulation, emerging markets represent a unique challenge. These markets are characterized by volatility[13] and transitional characteristics,[14] which render policy making an act of creating a balance between policy flexibility to account for uncertainties and policy certainty to retain investor confidence in the market.[15] Despite the recognition of such general identifiers of emerging markets, a nuanced definition of the term is yet to emerge.[16]

A number of approaches have been taken to define such markets. Some scholars have adopted a quantitative approach, using quantifiable factors such as GDP, industrial production, consumer prices, trade balance and foreign reserves to distinguishemerging markets from their developed counterparts.[17] Arnold and Quelch take such an approach, identifying the following factors as the characteristics of emerging markets:

> First is the absolute level of economic development, usually indicated by the average GDP per capita, or the relative balance of agrarian and industrial/commercial activity... Second is the relative pace of economic

---

[10] *Ibid.*   [11] *Ibid.*   [12] *Ibid.*

[13] Emerging markets may be volatile due to domestic policy instability, natural disasters and external price shocks. See Ashoka Mody, 'What Is an Emerging Market?' IMF Working Paper WP/04/177, p. 5; available at www.imf.org/external/pubs/ft/wp/2004/wp04177.pdf [accessed on 2 November 2016]. See also Ana Maria Santacreu, 'The Economic Fundamentals of Emerging Market Volatility', Economic Synopses 2015, No. 2; available at https://research.stlouisfed.org/publications/economic-synopses/2015/01/30/the-economic-fundamentals-of-emerging-market-volatility/ [accessed on 2 November 2016].

[14] See Mody, 'What Is an Emerging Market?'   [15] *Ibid.*

[16] Olga E. Annushkina, et al., 'How Do Emerging Markets Differ from Developing Markets? A Conceptual and Empirical Analysis', in Hemant Merchant (ed.), *Handbook of Contemporary Research on Emerging Markets* (Boston: Edwin Elgar, 2016), p. 3.

[17] See David J. Arnold and John A. Quelch, 'New Strategies in Emerging Markets'; available at http://sloanreview.mit.edu/article/new-strategies-in-emerging-markets/ [accessed on 2 November 2016]. See also S. T. Cavusgil, 'Measuring the Potential of Emerging Markets: An Indexing Approach' (1997) 40(1) *Business Horizons* 87–91.

development, usually indicated by the GDP growth rate. Third is the system of market governance and, in particular, the extent and stability of a free-market system; if the country is in the process of economic liberalization from a command economy, it is sometimes defined as a "transitional economy".[18]

Others have taken a more qualitative approach to the issue and have proceeded by examining institutional impediments peculiar to such markets in an effort to distinguish them from developed economies.[19] Miller for example, provides the following benchmarks for identifying emerging markets:

> 1. Physical characteristics, in terms of an inadequate commercial infrastructure as well as inadequacy of all other aspects of physical infrastructure (communication, transport, power generation); 2. Socio-political characteristics which include, political instability, inadequate legal framework, weak social discipline, and reduced technological levels, besides (unique) cultural characteristics; 3. Economic characteristics in terms of limited personal income, centrally controlled currencies with an influential role of government in economic life, expressed, beside other, in managing the process of transition to market economy.[20]

The BRICS economies demonstrate most of these characteristics and limitations.

A number of studies have also investigated the role of the government in such markets and have used the incidence of government control and the quality of governance as defining characteristics of such markets. Scholars such as Liu, Li and Xue note the prevalence of government ownership in emerging markets.[21] In some countries, the poor quality of governance also serves as an impediment to market development in such markets. As Marquis and Raynard indicate in this regard,

> Emerging markets are characterized by greater informality and less developed government and regulatory infrastructures, suggesting that market regulation, corporate governance, transparency, accounting standards, and

---

[18] Arnold and Quelch, 'New Strategies in Emerging Markets'.

[19] See Aziz Sunje and Emin Civi, 'Emerging Markets: A Review of Conceptual Frameworks', 203–216 at 208; available at www.opf.slu.cz/vvr/akce/turecko/pdf/Sunje.pdf [accessed on 2 November 2016].

[20] Russell R. Miller, *Selling to Newly Emerging Markets* (Westport CT: Quorum Books, 1998), p. 17, as cited in Sunje and Civi, 'Emerging Markets: A Review of Conceptual Frameworks'.

[21] See, for example, Yi Liu, Yuan Li and Jiaqi Xue, 'Ownership, Strategic Orientation and Internationalization in Emerging Markets' (2011) 46(3) *Journal of World Business* 381–393 at 381.

intellectual property protection may not be as reliable or mature as those in more advanced economies. To further complicate matters, emerging market governments have been shown to be particularly susceptible to external conflicts, coups, and internal tensions, which increases the risk of unstable resource exchanges and information flows.[22]

Some of these statements also hold true for BRICS economies.

In the context of capital markets, Rojas-Suarez identifies four pillars for promoting market development: 'macroeconomic stability, sound banking systems, high institutional quality and an adequate regulatory and supervisory framework.'[23] Because of the characteristic volatility and transience of emerging nations, the capital markets in such nations are often underdeveloped and illiquid, with high transaction costs.[24] Additionally, the weakness of regulatory, legal and monitoring mechanisms in such markets also creates information asymmetries that in turn provide an avenue for opportunism and misuse by unscrupulous market players.[25] Furthermore, the weakness of enforcement mechanisms (due to inadequate legal system) affects the enforceability of the legal contracts operative in such markets, further contributing to the transactions cost associated with operating in the market.[26] To develop robust capital markets in the BRICS economies, the regulatory processes (for both rule making and enforcement) therefore need to be carefully considered.

II. Capital Markets Regulation in India

SEBI was established as a nonstatutory advisory body in 1988 under the Ministry of Finance.[27] The grant of statutory legitimacy to SEBI, and its emergence as an independent capital market regulator are attributable to a number of political and economic factors.

---

[22] Chris Marquis and Mira Reynard, 'Institutional Strategies in Emerging Markets' (2015) 9(1) *The Academy of Management Annals* 291–335 at 300; available at http://dx.doi.org/10.1080/19416520.2015.1014661 [accessed on 2 November 2016].

[23] Liliana Rojas-Suarez, 'Towards Strong and Stable Capital Markets in Emerging Market Economies', CGD Policy Paper 042, 2014, p. 1; available at www.cgdev.org/sites/default/files/towards-stable-markets-emerging-market-economies.pdf [accessed on 2 November 2016].

[24] *Ibid.*

[25] Marquis and Reynard, 'Institutional Strategies in Emerging Markets' at 300.   [26] *Ibid.*

[27] SEBI (Securities and Exchange Board of India), *Annual Report 2014–15*, p. 179; available at www.sebi.gov.in/cms/sebi_data/attachdocs/1450427865050.pdf [accessed on 2 November 2016].

The promulgation of the Securities and Exchange Board of India Ordinance in 1992, which can be regarded as the first step towards the present regulatory structure, was undertaken at a time when India was moving towards an economic outlook that viewed market liberalization as a desirable policy for improving the overall viability of its economic system.[28] This paradigm shift was the result of a balance of payment crisis in 1991, which had had a crippling effect on the Indian economy and had compelled the ruling government to introduce radical economic reforms.[29] These included, inter alia, 'a swift transition to a market-determined exchange rate regime, dismantling of trade restrictions, a move towards current account convertibility and a gradual opening-up of the capital account'.[30] There was also a shift in favor of non-debt creating inflows of external finance coupled with the liberalization of industrial and foreign investment policies.[31]

In terms of capital market reforms during this period, the existing regulatory regime under the Capital Issues (Control) Act, 1947 (CIC Act) was dismantled.[32] The CIC Act had imposed prohibitions on the raising of capital by nongovernmental incorporated entities without the prior consent of the central government.[33] The act was administered by the Controller of Capital Issues (Controller), which not only had the power to deny consent to capital issues but also had the mandate to determine the pricing of issues, particularly the level of premium that could be charged in a public issue.[34] This led to a largely inefficient situation, making a foray into the Indian capital market a cumbersome prospect. Apart from the inefficient

[28] ASSOCHAM (Associated Chambers of Commerce of India), 'The Indian Capital Market: Growth with Governance', p. 7; available at www.pwc.in/assets/pdfs/publications-2010/india-captial-market.pdf [accessed on 2 November 2016].

[29] *Ibid.*

[30] Rakesh Mohan, 'Capital Flows to India', in *Financial Globalization and Emerging Market Capital Flows*, Bank for International Settlements Paper No. 44, p. 236; available at www.bis .org/publ/bppdf/bispap44m.pdf [accessed on 2 November 2016]. See also Rakesh Mohan, 'Capital Account Liberalisation and Conduct of Monetary Policy: The Indian Experience' (2009) 2(2) *Macroeconomics & Finance in Emerging Market Economies* 215–238; available at www.bis.org/review/r070619c.pdf [accessed on 2 November 2016].

[31] SEBI (Securities and Exchange Board of India), *Annual Report 1992-1993*, p. 2; available at www.sebi.gov.in/cms/sebi_data/attachdocs/1321419421330.pdf [accessed on 2 November 2016].

[32] B. A. Prakash, *The Indian Economy Since 1991* (New Delhi: Dorling Kindersley India, 2009), p. 535.

[33] S. 3, Capital Issues (Control) Act 1947.

[34] S. Guruswami, *Indian Financial System*, 2nd edn (New Delhi: Tata McGraw-Hill, 2009), pp. 555–56.

processing of applications leading to delays, interference by the Controller led to the underpricing of issues and consequently their oversubscription, thereby diminishing the profit potential of such issues.[35] The introduction of economic reforms in 1991 led to the repeal and reformulation of a number of laws regulating markets, and the CIC Act was amongst the first legislation to be subjected to such a process.[36] The Securities and Exchange Board of India Ordinance, dated January 30, 1992 (later replaced by the Securities and Exchange Board of India Act, 1992 (SEBI Act)) established SEBI as a statutory body. The CIC Act was repealed first by an ordinance (the Capital Issues (Control) Repeal Ordinance, 1992) and later by legislation (the Capital Issues (Control) Repeal Act, 1992).[37] These developments entrusted the task of capital market regulation to SEBI. A number of simultaneous developments also increased the importance of SEBI in the capital market landscape. These included the establishment of a new stock market (National Stock Exchange in 1992) and other institutions for trade facilitation (such as the National Securities Clearing Corporation Ltd. in 1995); introduction of technological reforms to reform stocks trading; and the opening of the Indian capital market to foreign investors.[38]

It must be noted that despite its statutory legitimization in 1992, the regulatory impact of SEBI in its early years of functioning was limited; it was not vested with adequate powers to effectively carry out its functions.[39] SEBI's mandate was to ensure the development of a fair and efficient capital market in the country and to provide a mechanism for investor protection against unfair and fraudulent market practices'[40] however, despite such a far-reaching mandate, SEBI's autonomy and independence were curtailed by its dependence on the central government in the exercising

[35] Ibid.

[36] N. K. Sengupta, Government and Business, 6th edn (New Delhi: Vikas Publishing House, 2007), p. 165.

[37] SEBI (Securities and Exchange Board of India), Annual Report 1994–95, p. 1; available at http://www.sebi.gov.in/cms/sebi_data/attachdocs/1321419837830.pdf [accessed on 2 November 2016].

[38] John Armour and Priya Lele, 'Law, Finance and Politics: The Case of India' (2009) 43(3) Law & Society Review 491–526 at 503.

[39] C. R. L. Narasimhan, 'SEBI: When Personalities Matter', The Hindu, 25 February 2002; available at http://www.thehindu.com/2002/02/25/stories/2002022500141700.htm [accessed on 2 November 2016].

[40] See Securities and Exchange Board of India Act, 1992 [The preamble to the Act provides as follows: 'An Act to provide for the establishment of a Board to protect the interests of investors in securities and to promote the development of, and to regulate, the securities market and for matters connected therewith or incidental thereto. Furthermore, s. 11(1)

of its essential regulatory functions.[41] Additionally, a number of legislative flaws such as lack of jurisdiction over issuers of securities, nondelegation of powers under the Securities Contracts Regulation Act, 1956, and a lack of adequate adjudicatory machinery to address investor complaints rendered SEBI a largely toothless regulator.[42]

The repeal of the CIC Act, the abolition of the office of Controller of Capital Issues in 1992, and the simultaneous (and arguably hasty) enactment of the SEBI Act culminated in a regulatory vacuum, which enabled the perpetuation of unfair market and pricing practices[43], which led to a number of large-scale stock market scams between 1991 and 2001.[44] These scams resulted in huge losses and a reduction in investor confidence in the capital markets.[45] After two significant parliamentary deliberations,[46] a comprehensive legislative reform process was initiated, which enhanced SEBI's regulatory potential.[47] The said reforms also granted a higher degree of autonomy and independence to SEBI, thereby severing, to a

provides that 'it shall be the duty of the Board to protect the interests of investors in securities and to promote the development of, and to regulate the securities market, by such measures as it thinks fit.'].

[41] M. S. Sahoo, 'Historical Perspective of Indian Securities Laws'; available at www.icsi .edu/webmodules/programmes/31nc/historicalperspectiveofsecuritieslaws-mssahoo.doc [accessed on 2 November 2016].

[42] *Ibid.*

[43] Shaji Vikraman, 'Explained: How India's New Securities Market Regulator Found its Feet'; available at http://indianexpress.com/article/explained/explained-how-indias-new-securities-market-regulator-found-its-feet/ [accessed on 2 November 2016].

[44] Sucheta Dalal, '10 Years of Financial Scams'; available at http://suchetadalal.com/?id= baebd5a4–0b2c-eda7–492e8a70763c&base=sub_sections_content&f&t=10+years+of+ financial+scams [accessed on 2 November 2016].

[45] Arindam Ghosh, 'Reforms in Capital Market in India and the Role of SEBI' (2011) 16 *Vidyasagar University Journal of Commerce* 35–45 at 36; available at http://14.139.211.206: 8080/jspui/bitstream/123456789/503/1/p3.pdf [accessed on 2 November 2016].

[46] See Lok Sabha Secretariat, *Report of the Joint Parliamentary Committee on Stock Market Scam and Matters Relating Thereto – Volume I*, 2002; available at www.watchoutinvestors .com/JPC_REPORT.PDF [accessed on 2 November 2016]; Ministry of Finance, *Action Taken Report on the Report of the Joint Parliamentary Committee on Stock Market Scam and Matters Relating Thereto*, 2003; available at http://finmin.nic.in/the_ministry/dept_eco_ affairs/UTI&JPC/ATRMay2003.pdf [accessed on 2 November 2016]; Supreena Narayan, 'Financial Market Regulation-Security Scams in India with historical evidence and the role of corporate governance', MPRA Paper, 2004; available at https://mpra.ub.uni-muenchen .de/id/eprint/4438 [accessed on 2 November 2016].

[47] See Securities Law (Amendment) Act 1995, Securities Law (Amendment) Act 1999; Securities Laws (Second Amendment) Act 1999; SEBI (Amendment) Act 2002; Securities Law (Amendment) Act 2004; Securities Law (Amendment) Act 2014. See also, P. K. Jalan, *Encyclopaedia of Economic Development: Volume 3* (New Delhi: Sarup and Sons, 2005).

large extent, its dependence on the central government for approval of its actions.[48] Today, SEBI has a unique presence in the Indian regulatory context. Subsequent amendments to the SEBI Act and associated legislation have ensured the delegation of greater powers to the regulator.[49] Most recently, the Securities Law (Amendment) Act 2014[50] has granted SEBI increased authority for search and seizure and the power to order the disgorgement of unfair gains, including the authority to order the attachment of property and arrest of delinquent persons, and has authorized the establishment of special courts to ensure speedy remedy in securities law disputes.[51] With its enhanced powers, SEBI has focused on 'establishing a framework of regulation to ensure transparency of trading practices, speedy settlement procedures, enforcement of prudential norms and full disclosure for investor protection'.[52] Over the years the exercise of SEBI's mandate has spawned regulations for 'merchant (investment) banks, disclosure requirements, substantive corporate governance rules (the so-called Clause 49 of the Listing Agreement), a takeover law and the prohibition of insider trading'.[53]

---

[48] A factor that remains unresolved in terms of the independence of SEBI pertains to the tenure of its board members, who may be removed at the pleasure of the government. See International Monetary Fund, *India: Financial Sector Assessment Program – Detailed Assessments Report on IOSCO Objectives and Principles of Securities Regulation*, p. 15; available at https://www.imf.org/external/pubs/ft/scr/2013/cr13266.pdf [accessed on 2 November 2016].

[49] The legislative intent to increase SEBI's powers can be gauged from the statement of objects and reasons of such enactments. For instance, the Securities Law (Amendment) Act 2014 provides as follows: '2. The nature of the securities market and the environment in which it operates is dynamic and the laws governing it have to be responsive to market needs. The governance of the securities market through the Board has withstood the test of time, including judicial scrutiny. However, based on the experience gained over the years, it has become necessary to further strengthen the regulatory provisions to ensure effective enforcement of the securities market related laws while ensuring its orderly development'.

[50] Securities Laws (Amendment) Act 2014.

[51] For a detailed discussion See PRS Legislative Research, *Legislative Brief: The Securities Law Amendment Bill 2013*; available at www.prsindia.org/uploads/media/Securities %20(A)/Brief-%20Securities%20Laws%20(A)%20Bill,%202013.pdf [accessed on 2 November 2016]; PRS Legislative Research, *Addendum to PRS Legislative Brief on the Securities Laws (Amendment) Bill 2013*; www.prsindia.org/uploads/media/Securities %20(A)/Addendum_to_Legislative_Brief_on_Securities_Laws_(A)_Bill.pdf [accessed on 2 November 2016].

[52] Montek S. Ahluwalia, 'India's Economic Reforms'; available at http://planningcommission .nic.in/aboutus/speech/spemsa/msa012.pdf [accessed on 2 November 2016].

[53] John Armour and Priya Lele, 'Law, Finance and Politics: The Case of India' (2009) 43(3) *Law & Society Review* 491–526 at 503.

III. SEBI's Regulatory Mandate

In terms of the legislative mandate under the SEBI Act, the primary function of SEBI is to protect the interests of investors and promote the development of the securities market.[54] While the expression 'securities market' is not statutorily defined, SEBI understands the import of this term
to include the 'market for long-term debt and equity shares'.[55] The regulatory jurisdiction of SEBI extends to both primary and secondary capital markets.[56] In the former it regulates the conduct of public issues of
securities by incorporated entities. In the latter, it supervises auction and
dealer markets and regulates the conduct of stock exchanges and over-
the-counter arrangements.[57] SEBI also performs regulatory oversight of
the mutual funds market in India and administers the Securities and
Exchange Board of India (Mutual Funds) Regulations, 1996.[58] SEBI also
regulates both the primary and secondary corporate debt market and the
market for foreign portfolio investment. SEBI's jurisdiction extends over
issuers of securities, intermediaries and any persons directly or indirectly
associated with the securities market.[59]

The SEBI Act prescribes a range of functions to be undertaken by the
regulator.[60] These can be largely classified into (a) registration and regulation of the working of entities functioning in the securities market, including include issuers, intermediates, depositories, participants, custodians
of securities, foreign institutional investors, credit rating agencies, venture
capital funds and collective investment schemes including mutual funds;
(b) prohibiting fraudulent and unfair trade practices relating to securities
markets including insider trading and forward dealing; (c) regulation of
matters relating to issue of capital, transfer of securities by public companies including substantial acquisition of shares and takeover of companies;
and (d) the promotion of investor education and training of intermediaries and of securities markets, and of research for the development of the
securities market.[61]

To effectively discharge these functions, SEBI is empowered to exercise a number of investigative and adjudicatory powers.[62] As discussed

---

[54] See s. 11, Securities and Exchange Board of India Act 1992.
[55] SEBI (Securities and Exchange Board of India), 'FAQs on Secondary Market'; available at
www.sebi.gov.in/faq/smdfaq.html [accessed on 2 November 2016].
[56] *Ibid.* SEBI (Securities and Exchange Board of India), *Annual Report 2014–15*, p. 36, 42;
available at www.sebi.gov.in/cms/sebi_data/attachdocs/1450427865050.pdf [accessed on
2 November 2016].
[57] *Ibid.*   [58] *Ibid.*, p. 64.   [59] Ibid., pp. 70, 74.
[60] See s. 11, 11A, Securities and Exchange Board of India Act 1992.   [61] *Ibid.*
[62] See s. 11(3), 11(4), 11B, 11C, 11D, Securities and Exchange Board of India Act 1992.

earlier, such powers have been considerably expanded over the years and have been deemed indispensable in facilitating regulation of the securities market.[63]

SEBI also has certain legislative powers,[64] which manifest largely in the power to make regulations consistent with the legislative framework.[65] Such regulations have to be promulgated and notified in the prescribed manner and placed before Parliament for validation.[66] Initially, the prior sanction of the central government was necessary for formulating regulations under the act;[67] however, this requirement was removed by an amendment in 1994, thereby granting greater autonomy to the regulator in terms of initiating the regulation-making process.[68] Except for these provisions, however, the SEBI Act provides no guidance as to the manner in which the regulation- making process is to be carried out in practice.[69] SEBI regularly uses expert committees to suggest reforms to the existing framework; they consist of representatives from a wide range of interest groups.[70] A wider public consultation process is also conducted, although evidence suggests that such consultations are not uniformly conducted in all cases.[71] Regulations framed by SEBI are part of subordinate legislation and are binding on the entities to which they apply.[72] Violation of such regulations may attract penalties under the SEBI Act.[73]

IV. Political Economy Challenges in the Indian Capital Markets

Contemporary literature suggests the relevance of politico-economic factors in financial regulation and the need to account for such factors during policy formulation and implementation.[74] Pagno and

---

[63] *Ibid.*
[64] s. 30, 11(i), Securities and Exchange Board of India Act 1992.
[65] SEBI also routinely issues circulars (under s. 11(i), Securities and Exchange Board of India Act 1992), directives, guidelines and FAQs.
[66] S. 30, 31, Securities and Exchange Board of India Act 1992.
[67] See s. 30, (unamended) Securities and Exchange Board of India Act 1992.
[68] S. 17, Securities Law (Amendment) Act 1995, pp. 36 and 47; available at http://lawmin.nic .in/legislative/textofcentralacts/1995.pdf [accessed on 2 November 2016].
[69] Arpita Pattanaik and Anjali Sharma, 'Regulatory Governance Problems in the Legislative Function at RBI and SEBI', 2015; available at https://ajayshahblog.blogspot.com/2015/09/ regulatory-governance-problems-in.html [accessed on 2 November 2016].
[70] See Table 10.1.   [71] *Ibid.*
[72] See generally, Sukhdev Singh v. Bhagat Ram, AIR 1975 SC 1331.
[73] Chapter VI, Securities and Exchange Board of India Act 1992.
[74] See for e.g., Randall Kroszner, 'On the Political Economy of Banking and Financial Reform in Emerging Markets', CRSP Working Paper No. 472; available at http://ssrn .com/abstract=143555 [accessed on 2 November 2016] or http://dx.doi.org/10.2139/ssrn

Molpin[75] offer the following reasons to explain this causal relationship. Firstly, politico-economic factors may determine the effectiveness of the regulatory process and may impede the efficient implementation of a particular regulatory measure.[76] An understanding of the impact of such factors can thus provide an insight into regulatory failure and serve as a useful guide for better policy formulation and implementation.[77] Secondly, an analysis of such factors can provide insight into the interest groups that influence policy towards a particular regulatory outcome.[78] Several scholars have emphasized the importance of the role played by interest groups in determining the shape of regulatory reform.[79] As one author notes,

> Capital market reforms must . . . be understood as the outcome of political negotiations and interest group activity: as the result of a political process that produces new institutions and is driven by the interplay of national regulation, transnational economic actors, intergovernmental regulatory cooperation and global capital markets.[80]

A due regard to such factors may enable insight into 'the constituencies [that] are sustaining a certain regulatory outcome, why they are currently dictating the rules, and how and why the balance of power can shift against them'.[81] Such an analysis may not only be useful in predicting the direction of policy change but may also be influential in determining a feasible mechanism for guiding the policy in a desired direction.[82]

.143555/ [accessed on 2 November 2016]; Peter Mooslechner et al. (eds.), *The Political Economy of Financial Market Regulation: The Dynamics of Inclusion and Exclusion* (Boston: Edward Elgar, 2006); Stephan Haggard, Chung Lee and Sylvia Maxfield (eds.), *The Political Economy of Finance in Developing Countries* (Ithaca, NY: Cornell University Press, 1993); R. D. Geoffrey Underhill and Xiaoke Zhang, 'Setting the Rules: Private Power, Political Underpinnings, and Legitimacy in Global Monetary and Financial Governance' (2008) 84(3) *International Affairs* 535–554; available at http://dare.uva.nl/document/2/63616 [accessed on 2 November 2016].

[75] Marco Pagano and Paolo Volpin, 'The Political Economy of Finance', Center for Economic Policy Research Discussion Paper No. 3231, 2002; available at www.researchgate.net/profile/Marco_Pagano/publication/5216148_The_Political_Economy_of_Finance/links/02bfe5141e1ee16c2b000000.pdf [accessed on 2 November 2016].

[76] *Ibid.*, pp. 17–20, at 3.   [77] *Ibid.*   [78] *Ibid.*

[79] See generally, Mooslechner et al. (eds.), *The Political Economy of Financial Market Regulation.*

[80] Sebastian Heilmann, 'Research Group on Equity Market Regulation: Capital Market Reforms as an Economic and Political Process', p. 1; available at www.cs.unsyiah.ac.id/~frdaus/PenelusuranInformasi/File-Pdf/regem_no1eng.pdf [accessed on 2 November 2016].

[81] Pagano and Volpin, 'The Political Economy of Finance' at 3.   [82] *Ibid.*

In the context of the capital markets, such an analysis must have both a domestic and international dimension. This is largely due to the transnational interconnectedness of capital markets and the specific relevance of international actors and politico-economic events in influencing domestic capital market policies.[83] The existence and influence of the politico-economic dimension in the policy-making process may proceed through an examination of the involvement of particular actors in the process and the influence of such actors in shaping the content of the policy. In the Indian context, a significant corpus of capital market reform is dictated through the regulations made by the SEBI. A prominent, yet relatively underanalyzed element in this context is the role played by private entities in shaping such regulations. This section also examines the impact of international actors on the Indian capital markets regulator, particularly in the context of domestic policy reforms initiated at the behest of such actors.

Domestic Factors

This section examines the role of private influence in public policy formulation. The presence and dominance of private control of the regulatory process have been exhaustively examined in the literature.[84] The phenomenon of 'regulatory capture'[85] is often used to refer to such control and is defined as a systematic attempt by private sector groups to shape the direction of a particular regulatory policy in a way that is favorable to the interests of such groups.[86] A number of explanations have been offered for this phenomenon. One set refers to the characteristics and strengths of such private sector actors, which place them in a superior position to influence policy. Such a position may be through the virtue of (a)

---

[83] See Beth A. Simmons, 'The International Politics of Harmonization: The Case of Capital Market Regulation' (2001) 55(3) *International Organization* 589–620; available at https://dash.harvard.edu/handle/1/3382976 [accessed on 2 November 2016].

[84] See George Stigler, 'The Theory of Economic Regulation' (1971) 2(2) *Bell Journal of Economics & Management Science* 3–21; available at www.ppge.ufrgs.br/giacomo/arquivos/regulacao2/stigler-1971.pdf [accessed on 2 November 2016]. See e.g. Doris Fuchs, *Business Power in Global Governance* (Boulder: Lynne Reiner, 2007); Underhill and eZhang, 'Setting The Rules: Private Power, Political Underpinnings, and Legitimacy in Global Monetary and Financial Governance'.

[85] See generally, Stigler, 'The Theory of Economic Regulation'.

[86] *Ibid.* See generally, Eleni Tsingou, 'Transnational Private Governance and the Basel Process: Banking Regulation, Private Interests and Basel II', in Andreas Nolke and Jean-Christophe Graz (eds.), *Transnational Private Governance and Its Limits* (London: Routledge, 2008).

superior financial resources, which allows such actors to attain better access to the regulators;[87] or the (b) superior technical and expertise[88] possessed by such actors, which may compel the regulators to involve such entities in the policy formulation process.

Another set of explanations focuses on the structural power of private institutions and the influence that this power has on the industry regulators.[89] This power is based on the phenomenon of corporate flight and the constrained regulatory environment created by fear of such flight.[90] The global financial system is characterized by the free mobility of capital across nations.[91] The relative ease with which financial assets can be moved across countries ensures that governments and policy makers are often wary of promulgating policies that may adversely effect prominent private industry groups.[92] This structural aspect of private influence may compel regulators to grant such groups a greater say, thereby influencing the policy formulation process.[93] Some scholars have attempted to highlight the unfairness of the policy-making process on the basis that the process fails to provide democratic representation for all stakeholders affected by a prospective policy decision, leading to a closed-door policy framing process in which only the opinions of select 'epistemic communities' are considered during policy formulation.[94]

The next section attempts to examine the role played by private actors in the policy formulation process undertaken by SEBI. Private entities can be involved in such a process in two different ways.

---

[87] Stefano Pagliari and Kevin L. Young, 'Leveraged Interests: Financial Industry Power and the Role of Private Sector Coalitions' (2014) 21(21) *Review of International Political Economy* 575–610.

[88] Tsingou, 'Transnational Private Governance and the Basel Process'.

[89] See Fuchs, *Business Power in Global Governance*, p. 103.

[90] See Geoffrey Garrett, 'Global Markets and National Politics', p. 795; available at www.people .fas.harvard.edu/~iversen/PDFfiles/Garrett1998.pdf [accessed on 2 November 2016]; Terutomo Ozawa, 'The Dynamics of Multinational Corporation Impacted Comparative Advantage: Relevancy to Ricardo's View on Cross-Border Investment and Samuelson's Skepticism about Globalization', 2013; available at http://academiccommons.columbia .edu/catalog/ac%3A159661 [accessed on 2 November 2016].

[91] *Ibid.*

[92] Pagliari and Young, 'Leveraged Interests: Financial Industry Power and the Role of Private Sector Coalitions'.

[93] *Ibid.*

[94] *Ibid.* See also, Leonard Seabrook and Eleni Tsingou, 'Revolving Doors and Linked Ecologies in the World Economy: Policy Locations and the Practice of International Financial Reform', CSGR Working Paper 260/09; available at http://wrap.warwick.ac.uk/1849/ 1/WRAP_Seabrooke_26009.pdf [accessed on 2 November 2016].

Firstly, private actors may be a part of the committees created by the regulator to shape the regulatory policy for a particular issue. Such committees are usually created through board resolutions passed by SEBI on an ad hoc basis to provide policy advice to the regulator on specific regulatory issues. The advice of such committees is not binding, and the final content of a particular regulation is required to be validated in the manner discussed earlier, as per the procedure laid down in the SEBI Act.[95] In practice, however, most recommendations are translated into regulations. Tables 10.1 and 10.2 profile the participants of the committees created by SEBI between 2007–2015.[96]

The following findings emerge from this analysis: (a) The committees were comprised of a wide range of participants from the public and the private sector. The public sector members included representatives of SEBI and the Ministry of Finance, officials of the Reserve Bank of India, judicial officers (including retired judges and presiding officers of tribunals) and the management personnel of government-owned companies and banks. There was a significant representation from the private sector; approximately 32 percent were personnel of private companies, banks and financial service providers. The committees were also very strongly constituted of professionals practicing in law firms and consultancy firms, as well as representatives of professional associations and stock exchanges. A small percentage of the members were eminent scholars in educational institutions of high repute. Some were independent professionals. In two committees there were also representatives from the media. (b) Of the eighteen committees surveyed, representatives from private corporations and banks were involved in fourteen. (c) SEBI seems to have adopted an expertise-oriented approach when selecting members of different committees, taking into account the nature of expertise required for the adequate handling of issues by a particular committee. This is particularly evident through an examination of the constitution of the Alternative Investment Policy Advisory Committee (2015)[97] and Committee on Infrastructure Funds.[98] As a consequence of the adoption of this approach, not all

---

[95] See the discussion accompanying footnotes 65 and 66.
[96] The details of the constitution of these committees have been taken from the SEBI website. See SEBI, 'Committees'; available at www.sebi.gov.in/sebiweb/committees/CommitteesAction.do?doList=yes [accessed on 2 November 2016].
[97] SEBI, Alternative Investment Policy Advisory Committee 2015; available at www.sebi.gov.in/cms/sebi_data/committees/1458547585621.pdf [accessed on 2 November 2016].
[98] SEBI Press Release PR No.108/2007; available at www.sebi.gov.in/sebiweb/committees/CommitteesAction.do?doList=yes [accessed on 2 November 2016].

Table 10.1 *Representation of Different Actors on Committees Constituted by SEBI between 2007–2015*

Committee	Total Members (Including Chairman and Member Secretary)	Govt. Officers	Judicial Officers (including retired judges, officers of tribunals)	Govt.-Controlled Enterprises (including government companies and canks)	Private Companies, Banks etc.	Law Firms/ Consultancy Firms/ Lawyers	Professional Associations (including stock exchanges)	Educational Institutions	Others
					Representation				
Committee on Infrastructure Funds (2007)	4	1			3				
Takeover Regulation Advisory Committee (2009)	12	3	1		4	2	1	1	
Committee for Review of Structure of Market Infrastructure Institutions (2010)	6	3			2			1	
High Powered Advisory Committee on Consent Orders and Compounding of Offences (2011)	4	2	1			1			
Primary Market Advisory Committee (2011)	18	5		1	4	3	3	1	1
Depository System Review Committee (2012)	5	2						2	1
Corporate Bonds & Securitization Advisory Committee	28	9		5	8	3	3		

	Committee									Total
19	High Level Committee for Reviewing the SEBI (Prohibition of Insider Trading) Regulations, 1992	3	2		2	5	3	2		2
4	Technical Advisory Committee (2013)						1		3	
16	SEBI Advisory Committee on Mutual Funds (2013)	1			2	8	3	2		2
10	Risk Management Review Committee (2013)	1				7			2	
6	Committee on Clearing Corporations (2013)	2				1			3	
8	Advisory Committee for SEBI Investor Protection and Education Fund (2014)	3				1			1	3
7	Qualified Audit Report Review Committee (2015)	2						5		
18	Secondary Market Advisory Committee (2015)	4				6		5	2	1
22	Alternative Investment Policy Advisory Committee (2015)	5				13	1	2	1	
5	SEBI Takeover Panel (2015)		2	1	1		1	1		
17	Committee on Disclosures and Accounting Standards (2015)	5		1	1	6	1	3	1	
	TOTAL	51	6	10	68	19	27	18	10	209

Table 10.2 *Representation of Different Actors on Different Committees Constituted by SEBI between 2007–2015 (Percentages)*

Govt. Officers	Judicial Officers (including retired judges, officers of Tribunals)	Govt. Controlled Enterprises (including Government Companies and Banks)	Private Companies, Banks, etc.	Law Firms/ Consultancy Firms/ Lawyers	Professional Associations (including stock exchanges)	Educational Institutions	Others
24.4	2.8	4.7	32.5	9	12.9	8.6	4.7

committees have representatives from all categories. (d) At least 20 percent of the members of most committees are representatives from government agencies. A number of committees also have retired government officers as their members.

A second means by which private entities may participate in the regulation formulation process is through the public consultation process conducted by SEBI before implementing the proposed regulations. However, scholars have expressed concern about the efficacy of such a process, in particular the lack of uniformity and transparency with which the consultation process is conducted.[99] Pattnaik and Sharma point out four distinct problems with the public consultation process undertaken by SEBI, which render it of suspicious efficacy.[100] Firstly, they note that public comments are not invited for a substantial corpus of regulations, which are then issued without going through this process.[101] Secondly, most consultation documents issued by the regulator lack a cost-benefit analysis of the prospective regulations on different stakeholders or multiple proposals/solutions to identified issues.[102] Thirdly, not only is an inadequate amount of time provided for submitting public comments but also 'the time lag between the public consultation and the issue of final regulation is high'.[103] This often renders such comments nugatory or irrelevant. Fourthly, there is no provision for the publication of responses to the comments received by the regulator.[104] This poses a significant question regarding adequate consideration being provided by SEBI to concerns raised by the public in general. It also makes it difficult to estimate the

---

[99] Pattanaik and Sharma, 'Regulatory Governance Problems in the Legislative Function at RBI and SEBI'.

[100] *Ibid.*   [101] *Ibid.*   [102] *Ibid.*   [103] *Ibid.*   [104] *Ibid.*

extent to which such entities influence policy formulation and shape regulatory reform.

International Factors

The transnational regulatory landscape relating to global capital market regulation is a deeply interconnected system.[105] The need for transnational cooperation for capital market regulation has increased since the liberalization of capital markets across the globe and is a product of the peculiar dynamics of this market.[106] As one author notes,

> Global capital markets pose dilemmas for national financial regulators. On the one hand, financial liberalization ... has increased competition in banking, which in turn has encouraged some firms to take on more risk. Innovative financial instruments and strategies and accounting and reporting standards that are difficult to compare across jurisdictions have compromised transparency ... On the other hand, national regulatory authorities are finding it increasingly difficult to achieve their purposes unilaterally. The speed with which international transactions take place, the complex structure of many financial contracts, and the multi-country network of branches and affiliates through which these transactions pass often impede efforts of national authorities to properly supervise and regulate financial markets. Competitive concerns are also important. As in other areas of economic activity, national regulators typically prefer to avoid rules that raise costs for national firms or that encourage capital or financial activity to migrate to under-regulated jurisdictions.[107]

The primary standard-setting authority in this landscape is the International Organization of Securities Commissions (IOSCO).[108] The IOSCO is 'the standard setting body for the world's securities markets and promotes international co-operation for sharing of information and providing mutual assistance'.[109] It comprises not only national securities markets regulators across the globe but also 'self regulatory associations, securities exchanges or trade associations with self-regulatory responsibilities located across the globe'.[110] As with several other international associations on technical matters, it is largely driven by the experiences of the developed economies. SEBI's association with the IOSCO

---

[105] See Simmons, 'The International Politics of Harmonization'.

[106] See Philip G. Cerny, 'The Deregulation and Re-Regulation of Financial Markets in a More Open World', in Philip G. Cerny (eds.), *Finance and World Politics: Markets, Regimes, and States in the Post-hegemonic Era* (Cheltenham: Edward Elgar, 1993), p. 51.

[107] Simmons, 'The International Politics of Harmonization' at 590.

[108] SEBI, *Annual Report 2014–15*, p. 170.   [109] *Ibid.*   [110] *Ibid.*

has involved participation in the 'various meetings and committees of IOSCO [and] cooperation in investigations/ enforcement/supervisory matters with other overseas regulators under the framework of mutual collaboration provided under the IOSCO multilateral memorandum of understanding'. Other international institutions with which SEBI has been closely associated are the Financial Stability Board, a body 'mandated by the G-20 to promote implementation of financial sector regulatory reforms in the world'[111] and the Joint Forum, which is 'a co-operative cross-sector group established in 1996 to deal with issues common to the banking, securities and insurance sectors, including the regulation of financial conglomerates'.[112] SEBI's engagement with these entities has involved cooperation on several fronts, including participation in 'plenary meetings and [contributions] to various work streams through responses to surveys, questionnaires and reviews' carried out by the entity.[113] With all these institutions SEBI submits itself to periodic reviews through their mandated procedure and participates in similar exercises with regard to the regulators of other countries. The result of SEBI's interactions with such associations has largely been a move towards regulatory harmonization and a challenge to keep Indian securities law in sync with globally accepted standards. In its annual report, SEBI acknowledged this phenomenon in the following manner:

> On numerous occasions the vast and varying international experience gathered by SEBI through its international engagements with global bodies has been carefully applied to its domestic policy formulation. The deliberations and valuable knowledge sharing efforts at the international level translate to the formulation and adoption of global standards. Such standards are, time and again, adopted by SEBI in its domestic rule-making. While on the one hand, this demonstrates SEBI's commitment towards the international community, on the other hand it enhances and lends the necessary breadth and depth to SEBI's own policy formation.[114]

V. Conclusion

Voters typically have little interest in financial regulation, and the lawmaking function in this area is invariably delegated to financial regulators,

---

[111] *Ibid.*   [112] *Ibid.*

[113] SEBI, 'Financial Stability Board'; available at www.sebi.gov.in/cms/sebi_data/internationalAffr/IA_FSB.html [accessed on 2 November 2016].

[114] SEBI *Annual Report 2014–15*, p. 173.

who are not directly accountable to the voters. While such delegation provides regulators with much-needed flexibility to respond to the dynamics of financial markets, it also makes them susceptible to 'capture'. The rule-making processes of India's capital markets regulator suggest that several local and international political economic considerations may be affecting the content of regulations. As far as local factors are concerned, an examination of the regulation-making committees set up by SEBI in the past indicates that privately regulated actors (either directly or through their advisors) seem to have a high degree of involvement in the regulation-making process. While such actors may bring technical expertise to the process, they also make the system more susceptible to capture by private interests. In the absence of a robust public consultation process, a limited set of wealthy market participants may be in a position to have disproportionate influence on the content of regulation in comparison with the public in general. Given that inequality among market participants and the resource constraints of the regulators are also common to other BRICS economies, such capture may be possible (and may even be taking place) in those markets as well. In relation to international factors, while IOSCO may help with the international harmonization of capital markets regulations, it is possible that its philosophy largely reflects the realities and experiences of the developed markets (which are in turn influenced by their local political economy considerations).

The Indian experience suggests that the financial market regulators of the BRICS economies may be vulnerable to regulatory capture. The governments of the BRICS nations should consider carrying out a detailed study of the regulation-making processes of their financial market regulators to understand the influence of political economy factors on the content of their regulations. Further, given the common challenges faced by the BRICS economies in the regulation of financial markets, greater coordination in responding to such challenges may be useful for developing robust markets in these economies. The financial market regulators of the BRICS economies should set up a common platform under the aegis of BRICS for knowledge creation and training of personnel for developing appropriate internal expertise to respond to the challenges posed by the political economy factors discussed in this chapter. Such a forum will also enable better representation of their ideas and requirements at forums such as IOSCO, such that their common interests are better protected both internally within BRICS and externally at such international forums.

VI. References

Ahluwalia, Montek S., 'India's Economic Reforms'; available at http://planningcommission.nic.in/aboutus/speech/spemsa/msa012.pdf [accessed on 2 November 2016].

Annushkina, Olga E. et.al., 'How Do Emerging Markets Differ from Developing Markets? A Conceptual and Empirical Analysis', in Hemant Merchant (ed.), *Handbook of Contemporary Research on Emerging Markets* (Cheltenham: Edward Elgar, 2016).

Armour, John and Lele, Priya, 'Law, Finance and Politics: The Case of India' (2009) 43(3) *Law & Society Review* 491–526.

Arnold, David J. and Quelch, John A., 'New Strategies in Emerging Markets' (1998) 40(1) *Mit Sloan Management Review* 7–20; available at http://sloanreview.mit.edu/article/new-strategies-in-emerging-markets/ [accessed on 2 November 2016].

ASSOCHAM (Associated Chambers of Commerce of India), 'The Indian Capital Market: Growth with Governance'; available at www.pwc.in/assets/pdfs/publications-2010/india-captial-market.pdf [accessed on 2 November 2016].

Cavusgil, S. T., 'Measuring the Potential of Emerging Markets: An Indexing Approach' (1997) 40(1) *Business Horizons* 87–91.

Cerny, Philip G., 'The Deregulation and Re-regulation of Financial Markets in a More Open World', in Philip G. Cerny (eds.), *Finance and World Politics: Markets, Regimes, and States in the Post-hegemonic Era* (Cheltenham: Edward Elgar, 1993).

Dalal, Sucheta, '10 Years of Financial Scams'; available at http://suchetadalal.com/?id=baebd5a4–0b2c-eda7–492e8a70763c&base=sub_sections_content&f&t=10+years+of+financial+scams [accessed on 2 November 2016].

Fuchs, Doris, *Business Power in Global Governance* (Boulder: Lynne Reiner, 2007).

Ghosh, Arindam, 'Reforms in Capital Market in India and the Role of SEBI' (2011) 16 *Vidyasagar University Journal of Commerce* 35–45; available at http://14.139.211.206:8080/jspui/bitstream/123456789/503/1/p3.pdf [accessed on 2 November 2016].

Guruswami, S., *Indian Financial System*, 2nd edn (New Delhi: Tata McGraw-Hill, 2009).

Haggard, Stephan, Lee, Chung and Maxfield, Sylvia (eds.), *The Political Economy of Finance in Developing Countries* (Ithaca, NY: Cornell University Press, 1993).

Heilmann, Sebastian, 'Research Group on Equity Market Regulation: Capital Market Reforms as an Economic and Political Process'; available at www.cs.unsyiah.ac.id/~frdaus/PenelusuranInformasi/FilePdf/regem_no1eng.pdf [accessed on 2 November 2016].

International Monetary Fund, *India: Financial Sector Assessment Program – Detailed Assessments Report on IOSCO Objectives and Principles of*

Securities Regulation; available at www.imf.org/external/pubs/ft/scr/2013/cr13266.pdf [accessed on 2 November 2016].

Russian Federation: Detailed Assessment of Observance of IOSCO Objectives and Principles of Securities Regulation, IMF Report 12/53; available at www.imf.org/external/pubs/ft/scr/2012/cr1253.pdf [accessed on 2 November 2016].

South Africa: Detailed Assessment of Implementation on IOSCO Principles – Securities Markets; available at www.imf.org/external/pubs/ft/scr/2010/cr10355.pdf [accessed on 2 November 2016].

IOSCO, '*Financial Sector Assessment Program: Brazil – IOSCO Objectives and Principles of Securities Regulation Detailed Assessment of Implementation* (2013)'; available at www.imf.org/external/np/fsap/fsap.aspx [accessed on 2 November 2016].

Jalan, P. K., *Encyclopaedia of Economic Development: Volume 3* (New Delhi: Sarup and Sons, 2005).

Kroszner, Randall, '*On the Political Economy of Banking and Financial Reform in Emerging Markets*', CRSP Working Paper No. 472; available at SSRN: http://ssrn.com/abstract=143555 or http://dx.doi.org/10.2139/ssrn.143555/ [accessed on 2 November 2016].

Law Business Research, 'International Capital Market Review: Brazil'; available at www.pinheironeto.com.br/Documents/Artigos/The-International-Capital-Markets-Review-Brazil.jpg.pdf [accessed on 2 November 2016].

Lidings, 'Abolition of the FCSM and Establishment of Financial Markets 'Mega-Regulator' on the Basis of Bank of Russia', 2013; available at www.lidings.com/eng/legalupdates2?id=95 [accessed on 2 November 2016].

Liu, Yi, Li, Yuan and Xue, Jiaqi, 'Ownership, Strategic Orientation and Internationalization in Emerging Markets' (2011) 46(3) *Journal of World Business* 381–393.

Lok Sabha Secretariat, Report of the Joint Parliamentary Committee on Stock Market Scam and Matters Relating Thereto – Volume *I*, 2002; available at www.watchoutinvestors.com/JPC_REPORT.PDF [accessed on 2 November 2016].

Marquis, Chris and Reynard, Mira, 'Institutional Strategies in Emerging Markets' (2015) 9(1) *Academy of Management Annals* 291–335; available at http://dx.doi.org/10.1080/19416520.2015.1014661 [accessed on 2 November 2016].

Miller, Russell R., *Selling to Newly Emerging Markets* (Westport CT: Quorum Books, 1998).

Ministry of Finance, 'Action Taken Report on the Report of the Joint Parliamentary Committee on Stock Market Scam and Matters Relating Thereto', 2003; available at http://finmin.nic.in/the_ministry/dept_eco_affairs/UTI&JPC/ATRMay2003.pdf [accessed on 2 November 2016].

Mody, Ashoka, 'What Is an Emerging Market?' IMF Working Paper WP/04/177; available at www.imf.org/external/pubs/ft/wp/2004/wp04177.pdf [accessed on 2 November 2016].

Mohan, Rakesh, 'Capital Account Liberalisation and Conduct of Monetary Policy: The Indian Experience' (2009) 2(2) *Macroeconomics & Finance in Emerging Market Economies* 215–238; available at www.bis.org/review/r070619c.pdf [accessed on 2 November 2016].

Mohan, Rakesh, 'Capital Flows to India', in *Financial Globalization and Emerging Market Capital Flows*, Bank for International Settlements Paper No. 44; available at www.bis.org/publ/bppdf/bispap44m.pdf [accessed on 2 November 2016].

Mooslechner, Peter, Schuberth, Helene and Weber, Beat (eds.), *The Political Economy of Financial Market Regulation: The Dynamics of Inclusion and Exclusion* (Cheltenham: Edward Elgar, 2006).

Narasimhan, C. R. L., 'SEBI: When Personalities Matter', *The Hindu*, 25 February 2002; available at www.thehindu.com/2002/02/25/stories/2002022500141700.htm [accessed on 2 November 2016].

Narayan, Supreena, 'Financial Market Regulation-Security Scams in India with Historical Evidence and the Role of Corporate Governance', MPRA Paper, 2004; available at https://mpra.ub.uni-muenchen.de/id/eprint/4438 [accessed on 2 November 2016].

Ozawa, Terutomo, 'The Dynamics of Multinational Corporation Impacted Comparative Advantage: Relevancy to Ricardo's View on Cross-border Investment and Samuelson's Skepticism about Globalization', 2013; available at http://academiccommons.columbia.edu/catalog/ac%3A159661 [accessed on 2 November 2016].

Pagano, Marco and Volpin, Paolo, 'The Political Economy of Finance', Center for Economic Policy Research Discussion Paper No. 3231, 2002; available at www.researchgate.net/profile/Marco_Pagano/publication/5216148_The_Political_Economy_of_Finance/links/02bfe5141e1ee16c2b000000.pdf [accessed on 2 November 2016].

Pagliari, Stefano and Young, Kevin L., 'Leveraged Interests: Financial Industry Power and The Role of Private Sector Coalitions' (2014) 21(21) *Review of International Political Economy* 575–610.

Pattanaik, Arpita and Sharma, Anjali, 'Regulatory Governance Problems in The Legislative Function at RBI and SEBI', 2015; available at https://ajayshahblog.blogspot.com/2015/09/regulatory-governance-problems-in.html [accessed on 2 November 2016].

Prakash, B. A., *The Indian Economy since 1991* (New Delhi: Dorling Kindersley India, 2009).

PRS Legislative Research, 'Addendum to PRS Legislative Brief on the Securities Laws (Amendment) Bill 2013'; www.prsindia.org/uploads/media/Securities%20(A)/Addendum_to_Legislative_Brief_on_Securities_Laws_(A)_Bill.pdf [accessed on 2 November 2016].

'Legislative Brief: The Securities Law Amendment Bill' 2013; available at www.prsindia.org/uploads/media/Securities%20(A)/Brief-%20Securities %20Laws%20(A)%20Bill,%202013.pdf [accessed on 2 November 2016].

Rojas-Suarez, Liliana, 'Towards Strong and Stable Capital Markets in Emerging Market Economies', CGD Policy Paper 042, 2014; available www.cgdev.org/ sites/default/files/towards-stable-markets-emerging-market-economies.pdf [accessed on 2 November 2016].

Sahoo, M. S., 'Historical Perspective of Indian Securities Laws'; available at www.icsi .edu/webmodules/programmes/31nc/historicalperspectiveofsecuritieslaws-mssahoo.doc [accessed on 2 November 2016].

Santacreu, Ana Maria, 'The Economic Fundamentals of Emerging Market Volatility', Economic Synopses 2015, No. 2; available at https://research .stlouisfed.org/publications/economic-synopses/2015/01/30/the-economic-fundamentals-of-emerging-market-volatility/ [accessed on 2 November 2016].

Seabrook, Leonard and Tsingou, Eleni, 'Revolving Doors and Linked Ecologies in the World Economy: Policy Locations and the Practice of International Financial Reform', CSGR Working Paper 260/09; available at http:// wrap.warwick.ac.uk/1849/1/WRAP_Seabrooke_26009.pdf [accessed on 2 November 2016].

Securities and Exchange Commission of Brazil, 'Legal Mandates of CVM'; available at www.cvm.gov.br/subportal_ingles/menu/about/mandates.html [accessed on 2 November 2016].

Securities and Exchange Board of India) (SEBI), 'FAQs on Secondary Market'; available at www.sebi.gov.in/faq/smdfaq.html [accessed on 2 November 2016].

'Annual Report 1992–1993'; available at www.sebi.gov.in/cms/sebi_data/ attachdocs/1321419421330.pdf [accessed on 2 November 2016].

'Annual Report 1994–95'; available at www.sebi.gov.in/cms/sebi_data/ attachdocs/1321419837830.pdf [accessed on 2 November 2016].

'Annual Report 2014–15'; available at www.sebi.gov.in/cms/sebi_data/ attachdocs/1450427865050.pdf [accessed on 2 November 2016].

'Alternative Investment Policy Advisory Committee 2015'; available at www .sebi.gov.in/cms/sebi_data/committees/1458547585621.pdf [accessed on 2 November 2016].

'Committees'; available at www.sebi.gov.in/sebiweb/committees/ CommitteesAction.do?doList=yes [accessed on 2 November 2016].

'Financial Stability Board'; available at www.sebi.gov.in/cms/sebi_data/ internationalAffr/IA_FSB.html [accessed on 2 November 2016].

'Press Release PR No.108/2007'; available at www.sebi.gov.in/sebiweb/ committees/CommitteesAction.do?doList=yes [accessed on 2 November 2016].

Sengupta, N. K., *Government and Business*, 6th edn (New Delhi: Vikas Publishing House, 2007).

Simmons, Beth A., 'The International Politics of Harmonization: The Case of Capital Market Regulation' (2001) 55(3) *International Organization* 589–620; available at https://dash.harvard.edu/handle/1/3382976 [accessed on 2 November 2016].

Stigler, George, 'The Theory of Economic Regulation' (1971) 2(2) *Bell Journal of Economics & Management Science* 3–21; available at www.ppge.ufrgs .br/giacomo/arquivos/regulacao2/stigler-1971.pdf [accessed on 2 November 2016].

Sunje, Aziz and Civi, Emin, 'Emerging Markets: A Review of Conceptual Frameworks' 203–216; available at www.opf.slu.cz/vvr/akce/turecko/pdf/Sunje.pdf [accessed on 2 November 2016].

Tsingou, Eleni, 'Transnational Private Governance and the Basel Process: Banking Regulation, Private Interests and Basel II', in Andreas Nolke and Jean-Christophe Graz (eds.), *Transnational Private Governance and Its Limits* (London: Routledge, 2008).

Underhill, R. D. Geoffrey and Zhang, Xiaoke, 'Setting The Rules: Private Power, Political Underpinnings, and Legitimacy in Global Monetary and Financial Governance' (2008) 84(3) *International Affairs* 535–554; available at http:// dare.uva.nl/document/2/63616 [accessed on 2 November 2016].

Vikraman, Shaji, 'Explained: How India's New Securities Market Regulator Found Its Feet'; available at http://indianexpress.com/article/explained/ explained-how-indias-new-securities-market-regulator-found-its-feet/ [accessed on 2 November 2016].

Zhou, Tianshu, 'Is The CSRC Protecting a 'Level Playing Field' in China's Capital Markets: Public Enforcement, Fragmented Authoritarianism and Corporatism' (2015) 15(2) *Journal of Corporate Law Studies* 377–406.

11

Contract Law in the BRICS Countries

A Comparative Approach

SALVATORE MANCUSO

I. Introduction

Created as a platform for dialogue and cooperation between countries that represent 43 percent of the world's population, the BRICS (not only from the economic and financial point of view) is particularly impressive today.

The BRICS countries, perhaps deliberately, do not dwell on the nature of their legal status, making it difficult to classify and determine accurately what the BRICS is. What is possible is rather to show what it is not: It is neither simply a regular summit nor a simple international organization. It would thus be better to try to understand the legal implications of the BRICS by thinking differently and considering how it is developing: It is then evident that the BRICS is a bearer of relatively stable 'legal flows' in different domains that are the expression of globalization, which brings with it the need for comparison and relationships between systems that are profoundly different.[1]

The decision-making processes used by the BRICS in dealing with the different issues to be tackled unfold following two main lines that are often converging and strictly interconnected. The first relates to the ambit of the 'coordination' between heads of state and governments within the summits and all the preparatory activity behind it. The second refers to the inter-ministerial level. Following the traditional institutional and diplomatic path, the results of the summits are disclosed through official statements that include more prospective issues of common interest, with the aim of fostering work in progress that closely follows the strong economic and social challenges affecting the five countries.

---

[1] Lucia Scaffardi, 'Pensare l'im-possibile: BRICS, tra miraggio e realtà', in Lucia Scaffardi (ed.), *BRICS: Paesi emergenti nel prisma del diritto comparato* (Turin: Giappichelli, 2012), p. 162.

Decisions on the issues facing BRICS are not the result of extemporaneous actions, but instead are supported by preparatory analysis carried out by joint working groups; sometimes these analyses are based on the results of previous meetings held by representatives of the various departments or key people involved in the matters leading to the creation of shared strategies. Today, thanks to the preparatory work carried out by these working groups, the heads of state and governments of the BRICS countries can share a common position on particular themes that can determine collective action.

One of the areas of discussion concerns legal aspects of the BRICS activities, particularly in the domain of commercial law and arbitration other than international law. On 12 December 2014, after a meeting held in Brasília, Brazil, the BRICS Legal Forum was created. Its goal is to promote integration among the BRICS countries to achieve infrastructure investments, thereby enabling integrated legal–economic development. It is a forum for discussion of the way to promote the realization of BRICS countries' objectives through the use of proper legal principles, because those countries are already engaged in internal decision-making procedures, dispute resolution mechanisms, relationships with and participation in different international organizations and the creation of common institutions.

Another objective of the Legal Forum is to enhance mutual understanding about the legal systems of the member countries, promote legal cooperation and coordination and protect the diversity of the legal culture in each member country. It does so by enabling an exchange of respective experiences on common legal issues. The economic cooperation among the BRICS countries will result in regional trade, investments and financial transactions. These activities need a common legal platform on which they can be performed efficiently, together with a simple, quick and reliable system of dispute resolution, and the BRICS Legal Forum could represent the place to elaborate on such common legal instruments. It is designed to serve as the think tank instrument on BRICS legal issues and to be the long-term instrument of legal cooperation for the BRICS countries.

Contract law is a pivotal element in commercial transactions. The importance of pursuing BRICS legal research in the area of contract law can be deduced from the 2015 Strategy for BRICS Economic Partnership document signed at the 2015 BRICS Summit held in Ufa (Russia): It stated that improving the transparency of the trade and investment climate in the framework of international obligations and national legislation and creating favorable conditions for the development of mutual trade and foreign direct investment in the BRICS countries are among the goals to be pursued to expand trade and investment cooperation. The same document notes that one of the main areas of BRICS countries' educational cooperation is the establishment of networks of researchers and the development of joint projects in areas of mutual interest.[2]

II. Methodologies in Comparative (Contract) Law

A. Comparative Law

Comparative law is the main tool for endeavors aiming to achieve legal approximation. It is 'a broad church embracing a variety of beliefs and approaches, even if the members of the church sometimes seem more interested in pursuing that which divides them than that which binds them together'.[3]

Discourses on comparative law have always revolved around the grouping of the world's legal systems into legal systems or – more recently – legal traditions. It is certainly true that present research on comparative law rests on the general idea that legal systems are converging (or convergent) rather than diverging (or divergent) and that such convergence should be promoted further through comparative work.

Micro-comparison focuses on specific legal institutions and problems in investigating the rules used and principles applied to solve specific problems or issues.[4] In macro-comparison the object of the comparative analysis is related to the methods by which different legal materials are analyzed, the way in which comparisons are made and disputes are settled, and the methods used by the jurists.[5]

---

[2] The 2015 Strategy for BRICS Economic Partnership document signed at the 2015 BRICS Summit held in Ufa (Russia); available at http://infobrics.org/blog/documents/4868/ [accessed on 26 October 2016].

[3] Hector L. MacQueen, 'The Common Frame of Reference in Europe' (2010) 25(1) *Tulane European & Civil Law Forum* 1–19, at 17.

[4] On the difference between macro- and micro-comparison, see Jaakko Husa, 'Legal families', in Jan Smits (ed.), *Elgar Encyclopedia of Comparative Law*, 2nd edn (Cheltenham: Edward Elgar, 2012), p. 491; Esin Örücü, *The Enigma of Comparative Law* (Leiden: Martinus Nijhoff, 2004).

[5] Konrad Zweigert and Hein Kotz, *Introduction to Comparative Law*, 3rd edn (Oxford: Clarendon Press, 1998), p. 4.

B. Comparative Law in the BRICS Context and the Importance of a Mixed Jurisdiction

Comparative law research today is based on the concept of legal tradition,[6] and the idea of a Western legal tradition is often placed at the center of the legal universe.[7] Such a Western legal tradition contains common principles and values, such as concepts of rule of law, democracy, the monopoly of the state and its bodies in the law-making process, the role of the state in the economy, the relationship between the state and the citizens, the protection of fundamental rights by the state and the separation of powers.[8]

The five BRICS countries do not share all the principles of the Western legal tradition as just described briefly. Two examples serve as a reference. The approach and interpretation of the concept of 'rule of law' in the BRICS countries, such as the Chinese concept of 'rule by law' and the quest for the way forward to the application of that concept in China, are quite different from those of the Western countries (especially European and United States). The strong role of the state in the economy of these five countries is another difference: The 'state capitalism' in Brazil, Russia and South Africa and the Chinese 'socialist market economy' are definitely divergent from the Western trend to limit the role of the state in the economy and strongly promote privatization.

If the question of legal research in the ambit of the BRICS is considered using the traditional approach that classifies legal systems into legal families, then the BRICS has a different legal framework. Indeed, of the five BRICS countries, three are generally considered as belonging to the civil law family (Brazil, Russia and China), one is a common law country (India), and one is a mixed jurisdiction (South Africa).

Yet, that classification is obviously debatable. Russian company law has been highly influenced by US company law. India has great legal diversity

---

[6] Glenn H. Patrick, 'A concept of legal tradition' (2008–9) 34 *Queen's Law Journal* 427; Glenn H. Patrick, *Legal Traditions of the World* (Oxford: Oxford University Press, 2014), pp. 1–30.

[7] Against this central role of the Western legal tradition, see P. G. Monateri, 'Black Gaius: a quest for the multicultural origins of the "Western legal tradition"' (2000) 51(3) *Hastings Law Journal* 1–72 at 3.

[8] On the concept of the Western legal tradition, see Harold J. Berman, *Law and Revolution: The Formation of the Western Legal Tradition Law* (Cambridge, MA: Harvard University Press, 1983); Harold J. Berman, 'The Western legal tradition in a millennial perspective: past and future' (2000) 60 *Louisiana Law Review* 739–63; Alan Watson, 'Legal culture v legal tradition', in Mark Van Hoecke (ed.), *Epistemology and Methodology of Comparative Law* (Oxford: Hart, 2004); David B. Goldman, *Globalization and the Western Legal Tradition* (Cambridge: Cambridge University Press, 2007).

and legal pluralism with various indigenous, Hindu or Islamic laws being applied more or less officially. Modern Chinese law is commonly associated with the civil law legal family due to the civil law legal tradition's great influence exercised on it[9] and to its 'codification' through detailed statutory law and its development following the Romano-Germanic path. However, the strong presence of the socialist pattern and the common law influences deriving from the adoption of Hong Kong institutions[10] could lead to Chinese law being considered as a hybrid mixed system.[11]

There are many advantages of having a mixed jurisdiction in the group. With its mixture of Roman–Dutch and common law, South Africa shares both civil law and common law experiences. Its legal background can serve as a bridge and element of dialogue between the two main legal traditions of the world (following Glenn's taxonomy[12]) and facilitate the methodological approach to highlighting similarities among the five BRICS countries, also taking into account the other commonalities described earlier.

C.   Comparative Contract Law

Comparative contract law is already a subject of legal study with its own independent legitimacy and solid traditions. Universities around the world offer courses on comparative contract law, and many scholars are engaged in research efforts on the comparative analysis of contractual systems in different jurisdictions or dedicating their research to a microcomparison of specific aspects of contract law. Therefore, there is no need to justify or explain the need for the analysis and comparison of the regulations that different countries provide for contracts.

---

[9] On the influence exercised by German law on the development of Chinese law, using Japan and Taiwan as access doors, see Albert H. Y. Chen, *An Introduction to the Legal System of the PRC*, 4th edn (Hong Kong: Lexis Nexis, 2011).

[10] Jianfu Chen, 'Modernisation, Westernisation, and globalisation: legal transplant in China', in Jorge Costa Oliveira and Paulo Cardinal (eds.), *One Country, Two Systems, Three Legal Orders – Perspectives of Evolution: Essays on Macau's Autonomy after the Resumption of Sovereignty by China* (Berlin: Springer, 2009).

[11] Ignazio Castellucci, 'Chinese law: a new hybrid', in Eleanor Cashin Ritaine, Seán Patrick Donlan and Martin Sychold (eds.), *Comparative Law and Hybrid Legal Traditions* (Zurich: Schulthess, 2010).

[12] Glenn H. Patrick, *Legal Traditions of the World*, pp. 1–30; see also John W. Head, *Great Legal Traditions* (Durham: Carolina Academic Press, 2011), bringing Chinese law to the same level as civil and common law.

Any international contract involves comparative considerations. A contract with foreign elements potentially deals with the laws of a variety of countries – the laws of the countries where each of the parties has its place of business, the laws of the countries where the performance of the contractual obligations will take place and the laws of the other jurisdictions with which the transaction might have connections. The choice of the law that will govern the contract is a matter to be dealt by using the private international law principles.

Thus, an international contract is – in theory – subject to the national law of a single country. In principle, therefore, it should be sufficient to obtain proper knowledge about such law to deal properly with the rights and obligations arising from that contract. It might also be very useful to pay equal attention to those laws that could also – at least theoretically – be applicable to the same contract. Having such additional knowledge could be extremely useful in making the best choice on the law governing the contract. It could also be important in assessing the possible interference by other laws caused by some specific conditions or overriding mandatory rules attached to the contract. It is even more important to understand how the other party could interpret the contract and the implied meaning of a certain legal term, clause or formulation; this is because most contracts are written in the English language and adopt English legal terms, the construction and meaning of which can be different and unfamiliar to anyone not versed in the common law tradition, regardless of which law has been chosen as the governing law of the contract. Knowledge of foreign legal systems and foreign legal concepts is obtained using the comparative methodology.

The setting of contract law in international trade has an obvious and inevitable economic dimension that could lead the comparative analysis to consideration of comparative law and economics. Globalization – in the sense of a process of Americanization of the worldwide legal culture –is among the factors attesting to the existence of an intellectual environment that is favorable to the reception of law and economics around the world. Comparative law and economics combines the instruments and methodologies of both these disciplines (comparative law and economic analysis of law) to enable the better understand of the reasons for the existing legal rules and institutions and their evolution; it is a dynamic approach to law focusing on the study of phenomena of legal divergence and convergence.[13]

---

[13] Ugo Mattei, Luisa Antoniolli and Andrea Rossato, 'Comparative law and economics', *Encyclopedia of Law and Economics* (Cheltenham: Edward Elgar, 2000), vol. I, pp. 505–38.

This chapter does not deal with contract law and economics or – more generally – with comparative law and economics. The reason is simple: It aims to offer the first hints of the common principles of BRICS contract law and of the way forward to develop a methodological approach for comparative legal studies in the ambit of the BRICS. Its focus is pure comparative contract law, then, or, perhaps better, comparative law applied to contract law.

III.   Terms of Comparison: The Contract Law System in the BRICS Countries

To provide the terms of comparison from which fully fledged research will start, this chapter first describes briefly how the contract law system is structured in the five BRICS countries, leaving all the different aspects of the regulation of contractual obligations to more exhaustive and specific works referring to each country.

A.   Brazil

Brazil is a civil law country, and its law has been codified in the past. Brazilian contract law was first influenced by research undertaken by the Brazilian doctrine of the nineteenth century and then highly influenced by Roman law, Portuguese law, the German Pandectist School and the French codification. These influences led Brazil to adopt a liberal approach to contract law in the old 1916 Civil Code, an approach rooted in the principles of freedom of contract and of no interference from statutory law, except for those cases in which the contract has been entered into irregularly.[14]

In the twentieth and twenty-first centuries, the Brazilian doctrine turned its attention to Portuguese, Italian and US law. From Portuguese and Italian law Brazil adopted the approach based on deeper intervention by the state to introduce mandatory rules that cannot be excluded or modified by the parties; this approach's ultimate aim was to protect the weaker party of the contractual relationship to restore a proper balance in the parties' contractual relations. US law influenced the regulation of several types of contracts. The result of the combination of these two approaches was the switch from the liberal to a more socially oriented approach to contract law, expressed in the new 2002 Civil Code.[15]

---

[14] Luciano Benetti Timm, 'Contract law', in Fabiano Deffenti and Welber Barral (eds.), *Introduction to Brazilian Law* (The Hague: Kluwer, 2011), p. 85.
[15] Ibid., p. 86.

Brazilian contract law makes a distinction between the existence, the validity and the effectiveness of contracts and is based on two fundamental pillars: freedom of contract and solidarity. The freedom of contract entails the sufficiency of the consent to enter into a valid contract, the principle of sanctity of contract, that of privity of contract and the possibility for the parties to create a contract that is not included in the statutory law. The solidarity pillar limits the freedom of contract, giving the social interest a larger role than the private interest of the contractual parties. The consequence is the application of the principle of strict good faith in contractual relations, the predominance of the social function of the contract and the principle of contractual fairness, which should be maintained during the contractual life.[16]

B. Russia

Russia is a civil law country, and the Russian legal system is codified with the main branches of law each having its own thematic code. Russian contract law has deeper connections with the German side of the civil law family, although it has some specific features that distinguish it from German contract law; its Roman origins are evident, and the vocabulary clearly derives from the two major systems in the civil law family.[17]

The primary source of Russian contract law is statutory law. As in the other continental systems, contract law mainly finds its place in the civil code, even though there are other statutes (always at the federal level) pertaining to specific contracts and the protection of consumer rights.[18] The Russian Civil Code was adopted in four different parts, the last in 2008. The code appears to be partially Soviet and partially Western: modern but without a full break from the past.[19] It generally intends to establish the legal background for a market economy as conceived in the West (according to the principles on the freedom of economic activity, freedom of contract and a great variety of types of contracts), but it maintains several rules that are not in line with a full market economy (such as excessive formality and detail in the regulation of contract relations, the possibility for the state agencies of interfering in the validity

---

[16] Ibid., pp. 90ff.

[17] Christopher Osakwe, 'Modern Russian law of contract: a functional analysis', (2002) 24 *Loyola of Los Angeles International and Comparative Law Review* 112–264 at 119.

[18] Ibid., p. 123.

[19] Christopher Osakwe, *Russian Civil Code Annotated* (Moscow: Moscow State University Press, 2000), p. 27.

of a contract and retaining state enterprises and similar forms of Soviet-inherited institutions).[20]

In the same year, 2008, a step towards the improvement of the Civil Code was taken with these aims: aligning it with the new stage of development of market relations, incorporating the experiences of the application and the interpretation of the code by the courts, putting the code in line with the European law using related experiences in legal development, and ensuring the stability of the law.[21] The result was a set of new rules that has subsequently been divided into parts, three of which have already been approved; two of these three approved parts concern contractual matters that are mainly in line with the jurisprudential application of the code with reference to some practical issues.[22]

The code is a federal law, and the norms of the civil legislation contained in the other laws must be in line with it.[23] In Russia there is no duality between civil and commercial law. All matters are included in the Civil Code, even though there is duality in the code itself: Some rules are applicable to commercial relations only, while others are reserved for non-commercial relations. In contract law, an example of this duality is the liability for breach of contractual obligations: Fault is requested in non-commercial relations but not in commercial relations. Another example is the possibility of using some of the contracts provided for in the code only for commercial relations.[24]

Regulation of contracts in the Russian Civil Code has two parts: The first one contains the general principles of obligations and contract law, while the second deals with the law of specific contracts.[25] The code introduces the freedom of contract as one of the pillars of Russian civil legislation,[26] breaking with the past, when contractual relations were admitted only within the limits fixed by the code. The freedom of contract is not as expansive as in the common law jurisdictions due to a large number of mandatory rules, of which the lack of applications determines the invalidity of the clause or the contract itself. Moreover, judges tend to

---

[20] Maria Yeremova, Svetlana Yakovleva and Jane Henderson, *Contract Law in Russia* (Oxford: Hart, 2014), p. 14.

[21] Decree of the President of the Russian Federation of 18 July 2008 n. 1108 on the Perfection of Civil Legislation, para. 1.

[22] See in detail Yeremova, Yakovleva and Henderson, *Contract Law in Russia*, p. 15.

[23] Art. 3(2), Russian Civil Code.

[24] Yeremova, Yakovleva and Henderson, *Contract Law in Russia*, p. 42.

[25] Osakwe, 'Modern Russian law of contract', at 122.

[26] Art. 1(1), Art. 421, Russian Civil Code.

bring atypical contracts back to the types set forth in the code, therefore submitting them to the compulsory rules indicated by the code for the chosen contract.

The second pillar in Russian contract law is that of the exact performance placed by the Russian Civil Code in the chapter related to the liability for the nonperformance of obligation, which provides that the payment of a penalty and the compensation of the losses in the case of improper performance of the obligation will not enable the debtor to evade the performance of the obligations in kind, unless otherwise stipulated by the law or by the contract.[27] Then the debtor must perform the contractual obligation as agreed in the contract, and the code gives the creditor several instruments (like pledge and punitive damages) to secure his or her right to receive the correct performance of the contractual obligation.[28]

In Russian contract law, a contract concluded out of commercial activities can be concluded validly without consideration (*rectius*, without a correspondent performance from the other party), even though the code establishes a presumption that contracts have a valuable consideration unless arising differently from the law or the content of the agreement.[29] The 2012 modification introduced the principle of good faith into the Russian Civil Code as the obligation to act in good faith while entering into, performing and enforcing civil obligations;[30] the violation of this duty entitles the other party to claim the damages suffered.[31] The introduction of these principles entails the incorporation into the Civil Code of a previous interpretation of the general principles on contractual obligations by the Russian courts, which did not hesitate previously to ignore or change contractual terms considered to be adopted in bad faith by one party to eliminate the adverse consequences that their application would have generated.[32]

Case law and commercial practices are also important in Russian contract law. The Supreme Court of Arbitration of the Russian Federation renders advisory opinions (not in the context of the decision of a case) that are binding on future cases. The Supreme Court formulates such opinions if there is a lack of uniformity among the lower courts on a specific question of law; it does not create new legal rules, but merely interprets

---

[27] Art. 396(1), Russian Civil Code.
[28] Yeremova et al., *Contract Law in Russia*, p. 44.
[29] Art. 423(3), Russian Civil Code.   [30] Art. 1(3), Russian Civil Code.
[31] Art. 10(4), Russian Civil Code.   [32] Yeremova et al., *Contract Law in Russia*, p. 48.

and clarifies existing rules.[33] Business practices include any general rule of conduct that is widely accepted in business activities and that does not contravene legislation or contractual terms and conditions.[34]

C. India

India is a common law jurisdiction. The law relating to contracts is found in the Indian Contract Act of 1872. The act is not intended to cover the whole contract law applicable by the Indian courts[35]: Any situation not contemplated there shall be governed by the principles of justice, equity and good conscience – that is, these principles are applied as done in English law – unless the Indian conditions are different,[36] and, to determine the Indian conditions and circumstances, a court will consider local customs and trade usages.[37]

Any agreement enforceable by law is considered a contract under Indian law. Under the Indian Contract Act an agreement is a promise or a set of promises, and a promise is an accepted proposal. To be enforceable by law an agreement must be the result of the free consent of the parties to the contract on a lawful object and for a lawful consideration, and must not be declared as void by the law. When required, the contract must be entered into by adopting the formal legal requirements. A contract can be modified or terminated in the same way it was entered into.[38] The intention to create a legally binding relation is not expressly indicated in the Indian Contract Act as a requirement for a valid contract; however, this intention is considered to be included in the requirement of a valid proposal that becomes a promise[39] if accepted. Therefore a proposal ends up into a contract if it is made with the intention to be legally bound by the subsequent eventual acceptance. The creation of a valid contract becomes the source of legally binding obligations for the parties to the contract. The right to the performance of the contractual obligations is considered a

---

[33] Osakwe, 'Modern Russian law of contract', 124.   [34] Ibid., 126.

[35] The Indian Contract Act's preamble explains that it has been enacted 'to define and amend certain parts of the law relating to contracts'. See also Ministry of Law, *Thirteenth Report (Contract Act 1872)* (Government of India, 1958), p. 2; *Irrawaddy Flotilla Co. v. Bugwandass* (1891) 18 I.A. 121, 129.

[36] I. C. Saxena, 'India', in Joseph Minattur (ed.), *Contractual Remedies in Asian Countries* (New York: Oceana, 1975).

[37] S. 1, Indian Contract Act, 1872.

[38] Nilima Bhadbhade, *Contract Law in India*, 3rd edn (The Hague: Kluwer, 2016), p. 39.

[39] The Indian Contract Act (see Section 37) uses the word 'promise' to identify the binding obligation arising from a valid contract.

personal right to the creditor, and the doctrine of privity of contract prevents its enforcement against any other person different from the debtor.[40]

D. China

In modern Chinese law, the term 'contract' started to be used frequently in the late 1970s, when foreign legal literature on contracts was introduced into the country. The Chinese contract law is to be found in the 1986 General Principles of Civil Law and in the 1999 Contract Law. A contract in Chinese law is an agreement by which natural persons, legal persons or other entities, as equal parties, create, modify or terminate relationships of civil rights and duties.[41] To have a valid contract under Chinese law, it is necessary to have the consensus of the parties and for the object of the contract to be legal; Chinese law also attaches great importance to the equal status of the parties to a contract, since such equality is considered to be an essential pillar in the transition process from a planned to a market economy[42]; therefore, a contract into which the government enters to exercise its public authority is not governed by the Contract Law.[43] The Contract Law does not apply to any matter concerning personal status, such as marriage or guardianship.[44] In Chinese law a contract is considered to be a civil juristic act and is one of the possible sources of legal obligations.[45]

E. South Africa

As mentioned earlier, South Africa is the only recognized mixed jurisdiction among the five BRICS jurisdictions: It has a combination of Roman–Dutch and common law. South African contract law is not codified, meaning that, with its dependence on judicial precedent, there are inevitably gaps and uncertainties in the law that can only partially be filled by the legal literature.

In today's South African Roman–Dutch law, a contract is an agreement that is, or is meant to be, enforceable at law. Common law is less relevant to South African contract law, since its influence has not changed the Roman–Dutch structure of South African contract law, although it has

---

[40] Bhadbhade, *Contract Law in India*, pp. 40ff.   [41] Art. 2 (1), 1999 Chinese Contract Law.
[42] Mo Zhang, *Chinese Contract Law* (Leiden: Martinus Nijhoff, 2006), p. 36.
[43] Bing Ling, *Contract Law in China* (Hong Kong: Sweet & Maxwell, 2002), p. 4.
[44] Art. 2(2), Chinese Contract Law of 1999.   [45] Ling, *Contract Law in China*, p. 6.

been quite important.[46] The attempt to replace Roman–Dutch law with English law was unsuccessful,[47] and therefore the application of Roman–Dutch law was maintained. Thus, after a number of fluctuating case decisions, the English doctrine of consideration was kept out of South African contract law,[48] while the doctrine of quasi-mutual assent was instead transplanted without too much difficulty.[49] Conversely, the idea of developing the concept of good faith in South African law was rejected by jurisprudence, and the violation of good faith was not accepted as an independent ground to set aside or not enforce contractual obligations.[50]

Roman–Dutch contract law represents a considerable evolution of Roman law. In it every agreement stipulated seriously and with proper intention is considered as a valid contract, and the distinction between *stipulatio* and *pactum* existing in Roman law no longer exists.

IV. Terms of Comparison: Other Useful Experiences in Contract Law Approximation

A. UNIDROIT Principles

The UNIDROIT Principles of International Commercial Contracts turned twenty in 2014. They represent a private codification or 'restatement' of the general part of international contract law.[51] They were prepared by a group of independent experts from all the major legal systems around the world, and they are not intended to be ratified by states to be incorporated into their respective domestic laws.[52]

---

[46] R. H. Christie, *The Law of Contract in South Africa*, 5th edn (Durban: Lexis Nexis, 2006).

[47] See the recommendation from the Colebrooke Bigge Law Commission of 1826 from George McCall Theal, 'The report of Commissioners Bigge and Colebrooke' (6 September 1826) *Records of the Cape Colony from February 1793 to April 1831*, vols. XVII–XVIII; see also Vernon Valentine Palmer, *Mixed Jurisdictions Worldwide: The Third Legal Family*, 2nd edn (Cambridge: Cambridge University Press, 2014), p. 32.

[48] Christie, *The Law of Contract*, p. 10. The author underlines that the lack of introduction does not necessarily mean that the doctrine of consideration can be entirely forgotten in South Africa.

[49] R. H. Christie, 'The doctrine of quasi-mutual assent' (1976) *Acta Juridica* 149.

[50] Christie, *The Law of Contract*, p. 16, where the author indicates a number of cases in which the attempt to introduce such a concept was rejected.

[51] Michael Joachim Bonell, *An International Restatement of Contract Law: The UNIDROIT Principles*, 3rd edn (Leiden: Brill, 2009).

[52] In Bruno Zeller, 'The UNIDROIT Principles of Contract Law: is there room for their inclusion into domestic contracts?' (2006–07) 26 *Journal of Law and Commerce* 155, the author advances the argument 'that the theoretical or soft law stage has passed and the Principles have entered into the phase of 'case-hardened' law'.

The UNIDROIT Principles cover international commercial contracts in general, providing a comprehensive set of rules dealing with all the most important topics of general contract law. The drafting style of the UNIDROIT Principles follows the pattern of civil codes rather than that of common law statutes; the drafters tried to use as concise and straightforward a language as possible to facilitate their understanding by nonlawyers and deliberately avoided the use of any terminology peculiar to any given legal system, with the aim of creating a sort of legal *lingua franca* referring to contract law that could be used and generally understood throughout the world.[53]

The UNIDROIT Principles represent a mixture of the different legal traditions of the world. In the drafting process, the preference was given to solutions that are generally accepted at the international level (the 'common core' approach). However, when it was necessary to make a choice between conflicting rules, the preference was given not to the rule that was adopted by the majority of countries but rather to that among the rules under consideration that seemed to be particularly well suited to cross-border transactions (the 'better rule' approach). At the very end, 'the Principles contain much that is recognisable in many legal systems of the world even when it does not fully accord in its detail with the law of any particular country.'[54]

B.   Draft Common Frame of Reference of European Private Law and the Principles of European Contract Law

The unveiling of the Draft Common Frame of Reference for European Private Law (DCFR) was the event in the field of European private law that drew the most attention in the past decade. It is a text bringing forward a set of annotated rules to which the European and national legislators as well as the European and national courts and arbitral tribunals can refer when seeking a commonly acceptable solution to a given problem at the European level. The DCFR was also drafted as an instrument that the parties to a contract (regardless of whether they are cross-border or

---

[53] Michael Joachim Bonell, 'The UNIDROIT Principles 2010: an international restatement of contract law'; available at www.law.georgetown.edu/cle/materials/unidroit/2011.pdf [accessed on 26 October 2016].

[54] Paul Finn, 'Symposium paper: the UNIDROIT Principles: an Australian perspective' (2010) 17 *Australian International Law Journal* 193 at 194.

domestic) can incorporate into their agreement.[55] It is not intended to be transformed into applicable law, and it will therefore remain a set of standard terms developed at the academic level by request of the European Commission.[56] The drafters of the DCFR drafters have been very clear on the academic nature of ttheir activity and that they do not want to enter into the political debate regarding the opportunity of their adoption.[57]

According to the EU Commission 2004 communication, 'The Way Forward',[58] the DCFR should contain 'principles, definitions and model rules'.[59] The DCFR was initially conceived as a set of principles, concepts and terminology that would be understood commonly across the European Union and that would be used consistently in future legislation as well as in revising and improving the existing texts.[60] The model rules would consequently form part of a wider instrument than general contract law, since the working group dealt with different aspects of private law, on the assumption that contract law could not be considered without reference to other parts of private law.[61]

As stated, the DCFR does not consider exclusively contract law; it includes matters pertaining traditionally to the area of the law of obligations or connecting the law of obligations to property law, according to the civil law systems.[62] The DCFR extends to ten books. Book I covers general provisions: the field of application of the rules, the interpretation and development of the text, the essential definitions and the computation of time. Book II deals with contracts and other juridical acts. Book III is

---

[55] Christian von Bar, 'A common frame of reference for European private law – academic efforts and political realities' (May 2008) 12(1) *Electronic Journal of Comparative Law* 1–10; available at www.ejcl.org/121/art121-27.pdf [accessed on 26 October 2016].

[56] On the DCFR see Christian von Bar and Eric Clive (eds.), *Principles, Definitions and Model Rules of European Private Law: Draft Common Frame of Reference (DCFR)* (Munich: Sellier, 2009), 6 volumes.

[57] Luisa Antoniolli and Francesca Fiorentini, 'Introduction', in Luisa Antoniolli and Francesca Fiorentini (eds.), *A Factual Assessment of the Common Frame of Reference* (Munich: Sellier, 2011).

[58] Communication from the Commission to the European Parliament and the Council – European Contract Law and the Revision of the Acquis: The Way Forward, COM(2004)651fin., of 11 October 2004.

[59] For an analysis of the meaning of such words, see Antoniolli and Fiorentini, 'Introduction', p. 12.

[60] Martijn W. Hesselink, 'The Common Frame of Reference as a source of European private law' (2009) 83(4) *Tulane Law Review* 919–971.

[61] Hector L. MacQueen, 'The Common Frame of Reference in Europe', at 3.

[62] Reiner Schulze, 'The academic draft of the CFR and the EC Contract Law', in Reiner Schulze (ed.), *The Common Frame of Reference and the Existing EC Contract Law* (Munich: Sellier, 2008).

dedicated to obligations (contractual and noncontractual) and the rights and obligations arising from them; it is divided into seven chapters dealing, respectively, with general provision, performance, remedies for nonperformance, plurality of creditors and debtors, change of parties, set-off and mergers, and prescriptions. Book IV deals with specific contracts and the rights and obligations arising from them; it is divided into eight parts, each referring to a specific contract (sale, lease of goods, services, mandates, commercial representation in its different forms, loans, personal security and donations). Book V refers to the benevolent intervention in another's affair. Book VI regulates noncontractual liability arising from damage caused to another. Book VII covers unjustified enrichment. Book VIII deals with the acquisition and loss of ownership of goods. Book IX is on proprietary security in movable assets. Book X refers to trusts.

The DCFR was preceded by the product of the Lando Commission on European Contract Law,[63] namely the Principles of European Contract Law (PECL), which were a mix of civil law and common law elements that to a considerable degree matched the position of the mixed system of Scots contract law and – more importantly for our purposes – the position in South Africa.[64] They incorporated the set of principles underlying European contract law resulting from a comparative analysis of the principles of contract law of the members of the EU at the time when the research was conducted; this is the reason why the PECL themselves were considered as a mixed system.[65]

The primary objective of the PECL was to serve as a basis for a European code of contracts; however, the principles were also intended to serve other purposes dealing with international contracts.[66] The PECL were produced in the form of a series of articles; a commentary on how each article related to each other, on the principles as a whole and on the

---

[63] On the differences between the PECL and the DCFR, see Hugh Beale, 'The development of European private law and the European Commission's action plan on contract law' (2005) X *Juridica International* 4–16 at 13 and ff.

[64] Hector L. MacQueen, 'Scots law and the road to the new ius commune', *Ius Commune Lectures on European Private Law No. 1*, Universities of Maastricht, Utrecht, Leuven and Amsterdam in Co-operation with the Free University of Amsterdam and the University of Liege (Maastricht, 2000).

[65] MacQueen, 'The Common Frame of Reference in Europe', at 4; with more emphasis on the entire system of European private law, see Jan Smits, *The Making of European Private Law: Toward a Ius Commune Europaeum as a Mixed Legal System* (Antwerp: Intersentia, 2002).

[66] Ole Lando, 'Principles of European contract law: an alternative to or a precursor of European legislation?' (1992) 40(3) *American Journal of Comparative Law* 573–585.

different national laws was attached to each article.[67] The PECL are the set of principles that underlie European contract law resulting from a comparative analysis of the principles of contract law of the country members of the EU at the time the research was conducted. After some revision, the PECL were incorporated into the DCFR.

The importance of the work that produced the PECL lies in the evidence that, if a functional approach that takes into consideration the application of the legal principles to concrete cases instead of concepts or rules as declaimed in books is used, there are very few major differences of substance in the field of contract law and the solution given to most real cases will be broadly similar. Therefore, the main differences lie in the language and the concepts used by the various contract laws (across Europe).[68]

The PECL/DCFR approach is thus an academic attempt toward convergence using comparative rule making by representative groups. It is an endeavor to formulate common rules capable of working on a systematic basis. This research is a clear example of the principle put forward earlier: mixed legal systems can be considered as potential sources of inspiration for legal approximation, not only of contract law, since the mixed systems represent models of how law might develop in a context (in this case, Europe) that is drawing closer together in the framework of an ever-closer union of countries and jurisdictions.

C. Principles of Asian Contract Law

The initiative for the creation of Principles of Asian Contract Law (PACL) came from a proposal made by the following scholars: Shiyuan Han (China), Wang Zejian (Taiwan), Young Jun Lee (South Korea), Naoki Kanayama and Naoko Kano (Japan). The aim of the PACL, which are focused on East Asia, is to create a set of rules and principles that are appropriate for Asian countries. By giving common rules to an economically growing environment, the PACL are intended to be applied as general rules of contract law in the Asian countries.

This project has not been supported or authorized by any government; it is a purely scholarly initiative. The three current chairmen are Shiyuan Han (China), Naoki Kanayama (Japan) and Young Jun Lee (South Korea).

---

[67] For the PECL see generally Ole Lando and Hugh Beale (eds.), *Principles of European Contract Law Parts I and II* (The Hague: Kluwer, 2000); Ole Lando, Eric Clive, André Prüm and Reinhard Zimmermann (eds.), *Principles of European Contract Law Part III* (The Hague: Kluwer, 2003).

[68] Beale, 'The development of European private law', at 7.

The jurisdictional teams include Cambodia, China, Hong Kong, Taiwan, Indonesia, Japan, Myanmar, Nepal, Singapore, South Korea, Thailand and Vietnam. Although this initiative is presently still a scholarly exercise, it is worth mentioning since China is involved in it and it seems potentially to be open to the involvement of other Asian countries, including India.

Several meetings have been held regarding the PACL, dealing with different aspects of contract law. The teams are organized by jurisdiction and led by a 'jurisdictional reporter' to take into account the status of Hong Kong, Taiwan and Macau. These reporters are specialists in contract and comparative law; proficient in English, the language used to carry out such a project; and in charge of drafting the articles, comments and notes. All the 'jurisdictional reporters' are members of the PACL drafting group. Together with the 'jurisdictional reporters,' 'nominated reporters' review the different drafts, working closely with the original drafters and taking into account the work of the jurisdictional reporters as well as generally considering the coherence and the level of detail across the different chapters of the PACL. Up to now five chapters of the PACL have been drafted.[69]

V. Object of the Comparison

There is not much to say about the object of comparison, since the research will be conducted following the comparative approach that has been tested the most. Therefore, the purpose of the questionnaire will be not only to gain knowledge on the law that is written in the books but also – and more importantly – to understand how the rules work and are applied in practice. The goal is indeed to understand the real differences and how to identify real similarities. The comparative analysis has already demonstrated how similar (or even identical) rules can lead to different operational results and, vice versa, how different rules can lead to the same operational result, due to the action of different legal formants.[70] The

---

[69] On the PACL project, see Shiyuan Han, 'Principles of Asian contract law: an endeavor of regional harmonization of contract law in East Asia' (2013) 58 *Villanova Law Review* 589–599; Jung-joon Ka, 'Introduction to PACL', in Tony Angelo, Luca Castellani and Yves-Louis Sage (eds.), The New Zealand Association for Comparative Law, Hors Série, Vol XVII, 2014 – Contributions to the Study of International Trade Law and Alternative Dispute Resolution in the South Pacific (Wellington, NZ: Association de Législation Comparée du Pacifique & New Zealand Association for Comparative Law, 2014), pp. 55–66.

[70] One fundamental approach followed by the project is the dynamic comparative law methodology principally developed by Rodolfo Sacco during the last thirty years. Sacco's theory is based on the assumption that a list, albeit exhaustive, of all the reasons given for

analysis of the contract law in the five BRICS countries will therefore take into account what these legal formants are and how they operate in each country to determine the operational rules in the area of contract law.

The importance of concepts and technicalities will not be underestimated, leading us to deal with the issues of legal traditions and languages. The word 'contract' can be misleading if not accompanied by a definition of what it is intended to address. Indeed, the concept underlying this word differs between the civil law and the common law legal tradition. Using the tools provided by the questionnaire, the endeavor to identify the common principles of BRICS contract law will clearly identify the ambit of the research not only by determining what is included and what is excluded but also by explaining on what exactly the researchers are requested to conduct their research.

VI.   'Principles of the BRICS Contract Law' Project

If, therefore, the process that we are witnessing in the BRICS continues according to the conditions summarized in this chapter, the law will have to confront in a bivector manner the legal globalization of the Anglo-Saxon or the Western matrix and another, different, Asian matrix. Neither of these lines of geo-legal globalization can manage without the contribution of comparative legal studies. The development of legal research in the BRICS in the ambit of its Legal Forum has been already directed towards key areas identified as crucial to support trade and investments within the member countries.

The research project, The Principles of BRICS Contract Law (PBCL)[71], was launched by the Centre for Comparative Law in Africa at the University of Cape Town in line with these general objectives. The PBCL project tries to find and restate the common core of existing BRICS contract law, considering that the common principles of BRICS contract law (or, better, the PBCL) can become a modern BRICS *lex mercatoria* or *ius commune* when developed.

---

the decisions made by the courts is not the entire law; neither are the statutes or the definitions of legal doctrines given by scholars the entire law. Therefore, it is necessary to analyze the full, complex relationship among what he calls the 'legal formants' of a system – that is, all those elements that make up any given rule of law among statutes, general propositions, particular definitions, reasons, holdings and so on – to know what the law is. The theory is summarized in Rodolfo Sacco, 'Legal formants: a dynamic approach to comparative law' (1991) 39 *American Journal of Comparative Law* 1–34 (Part I), 343–401 (Part II).

[71] The full title of the project is 'The Principles of BRICS Contract Law – A Comparative Study of General Principles Governing International Commercial Contracts in the BRICS Countries'.

The project will begin with the drafting of national reports, which have two functions. The first is to establish the position in a particular jurisdiction, and the second is to provide the material for a comparative analysis, which in turn could form the basis of a draft of general principles governing international commercial contracts in the BRICS countries. A questionnaire has been drafted by the national reporters using the UNIDROIT Principles of International Commercial Contracts as a reference; it will provide a more exact indication of the specific issues or research topics to be addressed in the national reports; thereby guiding their preparation.

When the national reports are completed, a comparative analysis will follow, drafted by he comparatists among the national reporters based on all the national reports; this analysis will then be circulated among the national reporters for comment. The methodology adopted for the 'Common Core of European Private Law' research project (the Common Core Project) could be helpful in preparing this comparative analysis.[72]

The same procedure could be followed for the drafting of the soft law rules. After the comparative analysis has been finalized and the common principles of contract law of the BRICS countries identified, the national reporters will meet to discuss and validate them. Having a single guiding mind behind the comparative analysis and draft soft law rules would ensure uniformity of style from the outset.

It is very unlikely that the PBCL will become the applied law of the BRICS countries. However, the result of this research could be useful for the BRICS countries when amending their national contract laws. Additionally, the PBCL may play a role in arbitration and dispute resolution.

VII.   References

Antoniolli, Luisa and Fiorentini, Francesca, 'Introduction', in Luisa Antoniolli and Francesca Fiorentini (eds.), *A Factual Assessment of the Common Frame of Reference* (Munich: Sellier, 2011).

---

[72] The bibliography on the Common Core Project is now extremely vast. On the project itself, see Mauro Bussani and Ugo Mattei, 'The common core approach to European private law' (1997–1998) 3 *Columbia Journal of European Law* 339–356; Mauro Bussani and Ugo Mattei (eds.), *The Common Core of European Private Law* (The Hague: Kluwer, 2003). On contract law in particular, see Rudolf B. Schlesinger (ed.), *Formation of Contracts: A Study of the Common Core of Legal Systems* (Dobbs Ferry, New York: Oceana Publications, Inc. and London: Stevens & Sons, 1968), work that was a source of inspiration for the Common Core Project.

Bar, Christian von, 'A common frame of reference for European private law – academic efforts and political realities' (May 2008) 12(1) *Electronic Journal of Comparative Law* 1–10; available at www.ejcl.org/121/art121-27.pdf [accessed on 26 October 2016].

Bar, Christian von and Clive, Eric (eds.), *Principles, Definitions and Model Rules of European Private Law: Draft Common Frame of Reference (DCFR)* (Munich: Sellier, 2009), 6 volumes.

Beale, Hugh, 'The development of European private law and the European Commission's action plan on contract law' (2005) X *Juridica International* 4–16.

Berman, Harold J., *Law and Revolution: The Formation of the Western Legal Tradition Law* (Cambridge, MA: Harvard University Press, 1983).

'The Western legal tradition in a millennial perspective: past and future' (2000) 60 *Louisiana Law Review* 739–63.

Bhadbhade, Nilima, *Contract Law in India*, 3rd edn (The Hague: Kluwer, 2016).

Bonell, Michael Joachim, 'The UNIDROIT Principles 2010: an international restatement of contract law'; available at www.law.georgetown.edu/cle/materials/unidroit/2011.pdf [accessed on 26 October 2016].

Bonell, Michael Joachim, *An International Restatement of Contract Law: The UNIDROIT Principles*, 3rd edn (Leiden: Brill, 2009).

Bussani, Mauro and Mattei, Ugo, 'The common core approach to European private law' (1997–1998) 3 *Columbia Journal of European Law* 339–356.

(eds.), *The Common Core of European Private Law* (The Hague: Kluwer, 2003).

Castellucci, Ignazio, 'Chinese law: a new hybrid', in Eleanor Cashin Ritaine, Seán Patrick Donlan and Martin Sychold (eds.), *Comparative Law and Hybrid Legal Traditions* (Zurich: Schulthess, 2010).

Chen, Albert H. Y., *An Introduction to the Legal System of the PRC*, 4th edn (Hong Kong: Lexis Nexis, 2011).

Chen, Jianfu, 'Modernisation, Westernisation, and globalisation: legal transplant in China', in Jorge Costa Oliveira and Paulo Cardinal (eds.), *One Country, Two Systems, Three Legal Orders – Perspectives of Evolution: Essays on Macau's Autonomy after the Resumption of Sovereignty by China* (Berlin: Springer, 2009).

Christie, R. H., 'The doctrine of quasi-mutual assent' (1976) *Acta Juridica* 149–156.

The Law of Contract in South Africa, 5th edn (Durban: Lexis Nexis, 2006).

Finn, Paul, 'Symposium Paper: the UNIDROIT Principles: an Australian perspective' (2010) 17 *Australian International Law Journal* 193–196.

Glenn, H. Patrick, 'A concept of legal tradition' (2008-9) 34 *Queen's Law Journal* 427–446.

Legal Traditions of the World (Oxford: Oxford University Press, 2014).

Goldman, David B., *Globalization and the Western Legal Tradition* (Cambridge: Cambridge University Press, 2007).

Han, Shiyuan, 'Principles of Asian contract law: an endeavor of regional harmonization of contract law in East Asia' (2013) 58 *Villanova Law Review* 589–599.

Head, John W., *Great Legal Traditions* (Durham: Carolina Academic Press, 2011).

Hesselink, Martijn W., 'The Common Frame of Reference as a source of European private law' (2009) 83(4) *Tulane Law Review* 919–971.

Husa, Jaakko, 'Legal families', in Jan Smits (ed.), *Elgar Encyclopedia of Comparative Law*, 2nd edn (Cheltenham: Edward Elgar, 2012).

Ka, Jung-joon, 'Introduction to PACL', in Tony Angelo, Luca Castellani and Yves-Louis Sage (eds.), *The New Zealand Association for Comparative Law, Hors Série*, Vol *XVII, 2014 – Contributions to the Study of International Trade Law and Alternative Dispute Resolution in the South Pacific* (Wellington, NZ: Association de Législation Comparée du Pacifique & New Zealand Association for Comparative Law, 2014).

Lando, Ole, 'Principles of European contract law: an alternative to or a precursor of European legislation?' (Summer 1992) 40(3) *American Journal of Comparative Law* 573–585.

Lando, Ole and Beale, Hugh (eds.), *Principles of European Contract Law Parts I and II* (The Hague: Kluwer, 2000).

Lando, Ole, Clive, Eric, Prüm, André and Zimmermann, Reinhard (eds.), *Principles of European Contract Law Part III* (The Hague: Kluwer, 2003).

Ling, Bing, *Contract Law in China* (Hong Kong: Sweet & Maxwell, 2002).

MacQueen, Hector L., 'The Common Frame of Reference in Europe' (2010) 25(1) *Tulane European & Civil Law Forum* 1–19.

'Scots law and the road to the new ius commune', *Ius Commune Lectures on European Private Law No. 1*, Universities of Maastricht, Utrecht, Leuven and Amsterdam in co-operation with the Free University of Amsterdam and the University of Liege (Maastricht, 2000).

Mattei, Ugo, Antoniolli, Luisa and Rossato, Andrea, 'Comparative law and economics', *Encyclopedia of Law and Economics* (Cheltenham: Edward Elgar, 2000), vol. I.

Ministry of Law, *Law Commission of India, Thirteenth Report (Contract Act 1872)* (Government of India, 1958): available at http://lawcommissionofindia.nic.in/1-50/report13.pdf [accessed 4 December 2016].

Monateri, P. G., 'Black Gaius: a quest for the multicultural origins of the 'Western legal tradition'' (2000) 51(3) *Hastings Law Journal* 1–72.

Örücü, Esin, *The Enigma of Comparative Law* (Leiden: Martinus Nijhoff, 2004).

Osakwe, Christopher, 'Modern Russian law of contract: a functional analysis' (2002) 24 *Loyola of Los Angeles International and Comparative Law Review* 112–264.

Russian Civil Code Annotated (Moscow: Moscow State University Press, 2000).

Palmer, Vernon Valentine, *Mixed Jurisdictions Worldwide: The Third Legal Family*, 2nd edn (Cambridge: Cambridge University Press, 2014).

Sacco, Rodolfo, 'Legal formants: a dynamic approach to comparative law' (1991) 39 *American Journal of Comparative Law* 1–34 (Part I), 343–401 (Part II).

Saxena, I. C., 'India', in Joseph Minattur (ed.), *Contractual Remedies in Asian Countries* (New York: Oceana, 1975).

Scaffardi, Lucia, 'Pensare l'im-possibile: BRICS, tra miraggio e realtà', in Lucia Scaffardi (ed.), *BRICS: Paesi emergenti nel prisma del diritto comparato* (Turin: Giappichelli, 2012).

Schlesinger, Rudolf B. (ed.), *Formation of Contracts: A Study of the Common Core of Legal Systems* (Dobbs Ferry, NY: Oceana Publications and London: Stevens & Sons, 1968).

Schulze, Reiner, 'The academic draft of the CFR and the EC Contract Law', in Reiner Schulze (ed.), *The Common Frame of Reference and the Existing EC Contract Law* (Munich: Sellier, 2008).

Smits, Jan, *The Making of European Private Law: Toward a Ius Commune Europaeum as a Mixed Legal System* (Antwerp: Intersentia, 2002).

Theal, George McCall, 'The report of Commissioners Bigge and Colebrooke' (6 September 1826) *Records of the Cape Colony from February 1793 to April 1831*, vols. XVII–XVIII.

Timm, Luciano Benetti, 'Contract law', in Fabiano Deffenti and Welber Barral (eds.), *Introduction to Brazilian Law* (The Hague: Kluwer, 2011).

Watson, Alan, 'Legal culture v legal tradition', in Mark Van Hoecke (ed.), *Epistemology and Methodology of Comparative Law* (Oxford: Hart, 2004).

Yeremova, Maria, Yakovleva, Svetlana and Henderson, Jane, *Contract Law in Russia* (Oxford: Hart, 2014).

Zeller, Bruno, 'The UNIDROIT Principles of Contract Law: is there room for their inclusion into domestic contracts?' (2006–07) 26 *Journal of Law and Commerce* 115–127.

Zhang, Mo, *Chinese Contract Law* (Leiden: Martinus Nijhoff, 2006).

Zweigert, Konrad and Kotz, Hein, *Introduction to Comparative Law*, 3rd edn (Oxford: Clarendon Press, 1998).

12

Consumer Protection Law in the BRICS Countries and Their Future Cooperation

JIA YAO

I. Introduction

As an emerging power among the developing countries, the BRICS countries have become an important pillar of the steady growth of the world economy and play a more and more important role in international affairs. As the representatives of countries with emerging markets, they have an economic basis for cooperation, complementarity of resource endowments and comparative advantages in the export trade; their complementary relationship remains the dominant position. They also have common interests, are in similar development stages, and want to gain a greater say in the international financial and trade systems. Because the BRICS countries are quite different in terms of economic development, competitive advantages, cultures, customs, and religious practices, they have quite different legal systems.

The international community generally believes that the BRICS countries are the engine with which to deal with the international financial crisis and to stimulate global economic growth by trying to redraw the world map of creating wealth. The population of the BRICS countries – Brazil, Russia, India, China and South Africa – accounts for 43 percent of the world's population; their total economic output accounts for 23 percent of the world economy; their middle class group has reached 600 million, which is the sum of that of the United States and the European Union; and they are the world's largest market. According to the International Monetary Fund, the growth rate of BRICS countries will remain higher than that of developed countries and other emerging markets until 2030.[1]

---

[1] 'What Brics Summit achieved'; available at www.iol.co.za/business/opinion/what-brics-summit-achieved-1888295 [accessed on 4 December 2016].

The BRICS countries have moved to a consumption-led economic growth mode in recent years that relies on boosting domestic demand to promote economic development, especially in China and India. In the process of developing a consumer economy, consumers themselves are undoubtedly the most important subjects to protect, but to date they have not been protected as well as expected in BRICS countries. The BRICS countries should attempt not only to make full use of their advantages in capital, resources, market, technology, human resources and cooperation in economics and trade but also to promote communication and cooperation in the consumption-driven economy and improve cooperation in enforcement of consumer protection laws.

II.   A Short History

Eight BRICS summits have been held since 2009: Yekaterinburg 2009, Brasília 2010, Sanya 2011, New Delhi 2012, Durban 2013, Fortaleza 2014, Ufa 2015 and Goa 2016. The summit on the subject of 'consumption' was the sixth BRICS summit in 2014, where the theme was 'Inclusive Growth: Sustainable Solutions'. The concept of inclusive growth was first proposed by the Asian Development Bank in 2007 and then widely adopted by the international community. Inclusive growth is the growth of equality of opportunity, and its most fundamental aim is to share economic growth fairly and reasonably. It seeks coordinated social and economic development and sustainable development to bring about equality and equity, rather than the simple pursuit of economic growth. Inclusive growth requires sharing the benefits of globalization, protecting vulnerable groups, strengthening small and medium enterprises, opposing investment and trade protectionism, and emphasizing the maintenance of social stability.

A.   Consumption Economy in BRICS

The BRICS countries have been given distinctive labels based on their dominant economies, such as 'World granary' Brazil, 'World oil station' Russia, 'World office' India, 'World factory' China and 'World mineral' South Africa. These labels reflect not only characteristics of their development but also their potential advantages of development.

The actual consumption expenditure of residents and the public expenditure of governments were highest in Brazil, followed by South Africa, China, Russia and India. In terms of their individual expenditure and gross fixed capital formation, the situation is totally different: The price of housing, medical care and education is generally lower than while the price level of machinery and equipment, and this is a common characteristic of the BRICS countries.[2]

Investigation of the actual expenditure of residents in the BRICS countries from 2000 to 2011 shows that their actual consumption accounts for a high proportion of GDP in Russia, Brazil and South Africa, so the ratio of the per capita actual expenditure equivalent to the world average level of GDP is higher than their per capita GDP.[3] The actual expenditure of residents accounts for a low proportion of GDP in China, so per capita actual expenditure equivalent to the world average level of GDP is far lower than its per capita GDP, which further widens the gap between China and Russia, Brazil, and South Africa in the level of actual consumption of residents.[4]

B.   Requirements of UN Guidelines for Consumer Protection

On 9 April 1985, the United Nations General Assembly passed Resolution 39/248, adopting the 'United Nations Guidelines for Consumer Protection'. It mainly set out the 'legislative goals' and the 'general principles' of consumer protection standards. At its thirteenth session, held in Doha from 21 to 26 April 2012, the United Nations Conference on Trade and Development was entrusted to conduct analysis and research and help all member states, in particular developing countries and countries with economies in transition, to formulate and implement competition and consumer protection policies, promote the sharing of best practices and carry out peer reviews with regard to their implementation.

The UN discussed issues of consumer protection through General Assembly resolutions on 22 December 2015. It recognized that member states should further strengthen the protection of consumers over the long term, and therefore the General Assembly should be committed to respond to the impacts of market and technology developments on consumers; for example, to give consumers cross-border redress when they are harmed by fraudulent and deceptive commercial practices; to promote

---

[2] Fangdong Yu, 'A Comparative Study of Price Level and Economic Power of BRICS Countries: Analysis of the Results of the World Bank 2011 International Comparison Project' (2015) (7) *World of Survey and Research* 3–8 at 7.

[3] Ibid.

[4] Yiming Cai and Yuyu Zhong, 'Basic Consumption and Economic Strength of BRICS: 2000–2010' (2014) (6) *Journal of Strategy and Decision-Making* 62–69 at 67.

and protect consumer privacy and the free flow of information worldwide; to respond to the influences of electronic commerce to consumers; to protect consumer interests in financial services, which the recent financial crisis has placed a renewed focus on; and to continue to fight against falsely labeled and counterfeit products.

C. Consumer Protection in BRICS

Brazilian president Collor de Mello signed Law No. 8078 on 11 September 1990 creating the Consumer Defense Code. This code was the first of its kind in Brazil, establishing guidelines for consumer protection in keeping with the 1988 Federal Constitution.[5] This code is mainly used to adjust the relationship between consumers and the industrial, trade, service and other enterprises, such as importers. It sets all procedural norms, from the pre-production stage through the whole process of a product entering the market, and it also regulates advertising campaigns. The Consumer Rights Protection Association, a nongovernmental and nonprofit organization, mainly provides guidance in implementation of the consumer protection laws.

In Brazil, there is no doubt that the most effective way to address infringement of consumer rights is group litigation, especially consumer group litigation. Brazil has created a unique mechanism based on the US group dispute settlement mechanism.

The Russian parliament approved the federal law, Consumer Rights and Interests Protection Law, in 1992. This law is intended to protect consumers and promote a market economy and the development of private enterprises. Some lawyers realized that a revival of private enterprise would require the protection of intellectual property, fair trading rules, restrictive practices legislation, consumer protection and product liability. The other CIS countries later developed similar laws and regulations in accordance with this Russian law.

This consumer law has subsequently been revised many times. In December 2007, new rules were added about the return of complex technical commodities, such as cars, refrigerators, computers, washing machines and other goods. The law also first stipulated the rules of online shopping: the rules governing remote sales are now the same as the rules of traditional sales. This law was also made applicable to any kind of service, and

---

[5] Emilio J. Cárdenas and Pinheiro Neto, 'Legal Memoranda' (1990) 24 *University of Miami Inter-American Law Review*, 143–159 at 158.

the current law has virtually no loopholes that could be used by unscrupulous manufacturers and traders.

In some cases, however, Russian consumers have complained that the courts took too much time to handle cases of consumer rights and interests; the process, from submitting a complaint to the court ruling, could sometimes take several months. It is worth noting that consumers often use other methods to protect their rights and interests and only start legal proceedings when they no longer have any options. This is despite the fact that, when consumers think their rights have been infringed, they can seek legal protection under any conditions, they have no burden of cost, and they are exempt from taxes in such legal proceedings.[6]

The Indian Consumer Protection Act was established in 1986. It relates to the laws of contract, tort, railways, telegraphs, telephones, post, air travel, insurance, electricity, water, housing, medicine, banking, finance, engineering, motor vehicles, hotel industry, entertainment, cooperative societies, tourism agencies, sales tax and transport.

The Consumer Protection Act provides for the establishment of the Consumer Protection Commission, whose mandate is to prevent business practices from having an adverse effect on competition, to promote and sustain competition in markets, to protect the interests of consumers and to ensure the freedom of trade for other participants in the markets. Its legislative intent was to clear all hurdles in promoting competition among business units, whether of domestic or foreign origin, provide better protection of the interests of the consumers against various types of exploitation and unfair dealings, and enable the establishment of Consumer Protection Councils and other authorities for the settlement of consumer disputes. It is indeed a very progressive piece of social welfare legislation. Unlike other laws, which are basically punitive or preventive in nature, the provisions are compensatory. Since 1986, the law has been amended three times to address deficiencies and shortcomings, and there is still scope for further improvements.

China enacted the Law of the PRC on the Protection of Consumer Rights and Interests in 1993 in response to pressure exerted by international consumer movements to reduce the volume of Chinese counterfeit and shoddy products. Although this legislation was primarily related to protecting consumer rights and interests, it has yet to directly address

---

[6] 'Law on Consumer Protection of Russia'; available at www.russia-online.cn/Overview/ detail_12_558.shtml [accessed on 3 November 2016].

the issue of consumer protection.[7] However, because there was no mature market in China at that time, the consumers preferred relying on regulatory law and policies rather than consumer law, particularly given that the nature of the consumer law was unclear in jurisprudence.[8] For two decades, the law was not implemented to any degree.

China revised the consumer law in 2013, and the new law came into effect in 2014, introducing a number of important reforms to the Chinese retail environment. Regarding allegations of counterfeiting, the onus of proof is now on the retailer to prove innocence for the first six months after the sale, rather than on the consumer to prove wrongdoing, as previously; penalties for fraud and false advertising have been increased; class-action lawsuits against retailer malfeasance have been made easier to file (although limited to state consumer associations and their local branches); for online and other types of delivery purchases, consumers are not required to provide a reason for returns within seven days of purchase; and greater restrictions now apply to retailers' collection and use of consumer data. In addition, the law added new rules to protect the security of consumers' personal information, which is very good progress.

South Africa, as is well known, is one of the best examples worldwide of a mixed system of law. Roman law, Roman-Dutch law, English law, indigenous (African) law and modern legislation (particularly a highly modern and progressive constitution) have all contributed to a system that is as diverse and mixed as one can imagine.[9] Since the establishment of the new government, South Africa has enacted a series of laws to protect the rights of consumers. The Consumer Protection Act of 2008, the first legislation in South Africa that specifically regulated franchising, came into force on 31 March 2011. The long-awaited final regulations, setting out the detail of how the act should be applied, were released in April.[10] This act is the core of South Africa's consumer protection legal system.

To establish a fair, orderly and healthy market, the Consumer Protection Act constrains irrational market behaviors, sets up a dispute settlement

---

[7] Mary Ip, 'Chinese Consumer Law: Recent Development and Implication' (2001) 6(2) *International Journal of Business* 111–134 at 113.

[8] Junke Xu, 'Who Will Protect Chinese Consumers? The Past, Present and Future of Consumer Protection Legislation in China' (2011) 24 *Loyola Consumer Law Review* 22–64 at 53.

[9] Jannie Otto, 'The History of Consumer Credit Legislation in South Africa' (2010) 16 *Fundamina* 257–258.

[10] Eugene Honey, 'South Africa-Consumer Protection Act Regulations at Last' (2011) 9(3) *International Journal of Franchising Law* 35–38.

mechanism and defines consumer, consumer rights and supplier obligations. It sets up a strict liability system, in which suppliers now have the obligation to make fair deals and follow safety rules, such as their responsibilities for promoting environmental protection.

Consumer organizations are responsible for enforcement of the consumer act and the supervision of the market. They include the National Consumer Commission, National Credit Regulator, provincial consumer protection organizations and nongovernmental organizations. The main dispute settlement mechanism is use of nonlitigation settlement. Litigation as a final remedy, however, can provide judicial protection for consumers, which is the key factor determining the efficiency of the law.

III.   BRICS Cooperation: Past, Present and Future

In the international economy, the BRICS countries' cooperation is demonstrated in two ways. On the one hand, BRICS countries jointly take part in global economic governance, accelerate the growth of new markets and inclusion of the voice and representation of developing countries in the international finance system, speed up the reform pace of the international monetary fund share and governance structure, maintain the multilateral trade system and promote the Doha round negotiations at the same time. On the other hand, they push forward global development, advocate partnership in global development, and protect the new markets and common interests of developing countries in decreasing poverty and promoting sustainable development, climate change, and energy safety, thereby contributing actively to global development.

The issue of consumer protection is related to the domestic law of each country, and consumer rights are directly related to the realization of human rights, economic development, consumption development and the founding of the New Development Bank. The five BRICS countries, however, have not called for special conferences on the promotion of consumption development and cooperation or carried out any influential activities to promote communication in this respect. For example, the theme of the Sixth BRICS Summit in July 2014 was 'Sustainable Solutions to Realize Inclusive Growth'. The concept of inclusive growth, which was first presented by the Asian Development Bank and then adopted internationally, means advocating the growth of equal opportunities so that economic growth is shared in an equal and just way. Meanwhile, B. B. L. Madhukar, Secretary General of the BRICS Chamber of Commerce and Industry in Delhi, said that, through the BRICS New Development Bank and a Contingency Reserve Fund, BRICS countries can cooperate in the fields of expertise and technology transfer, energy, tourism, IT development, education, health care, food security, production distribution and food pricing management.[11]

In addition, the BRICS International Competition Conference – as well as earlier conferences hosted by the Federal Anti-Monopoly Service of Russia in 2009, the State Administration for Industry and Commerce of the People's Republic of China in 2011 and the Competition Commission of India in 2013 – created a solid platform on which BRICS member states can deepen their relations in the field of competition regulation. The theme for the fourth BRICS International Competition Conference was 'Competition and Inclusive Growth' (2015). The conference explored, among other things, the intersection between competition policy and economic development. This is an important issue for BRICS member states, as they are uniquely placed to promote and expand an appreciation of competition regulation that recognizes the specific needs and demands of the developing world.[12]

On the international and regional levels, nongovernmental consumer organizations in the BRICS countries have more closely communicated and cooperated with each other in recent years. For example, Asian consumer organizations took part in the Asian Conference on Millennium Development Goals and the Consumer Movement, which was jointly organized by Consumers International Asia Pacific Office and the United Nations Conference on Trade and Development on 23 August 2005 in Kuala Lumpur. At the Fifth United Nations Conference to Review all Aspects of the Set of Multilaterally Agreed Equitable Principles and Rules for the Control of Restrictive Business Practices, which was held in Antalya, Turkey, from 14–18 November 2005, they issued a Declaration of Consumer Leaders 'Pro-Poor, Pro-Rural, Pro-Women'. In this declaration, they reviewed the scope and nature of the activities of the consumer movement in Asia and came to many common understandings.[13] In

---

[11] 'BRICS Development Bank to Benefit Developing Countries: Indian Businessman'; available at http://news.xinhuanet.com/english/business/2014-07/13/c_133480654.htm [accessed on 3 November 2016].

[12] 'Competition Commission Hosts 4th BRICS International Competition Conference'; available at www.durban.gov.za/Resource_Centre/new2/Pages/Competition-Commission-hosts-4th-BRICS-International-Competition-Conference.aspx [accessed on 3 November 2016].

[13] Consumers International (NGO), 'Declaration of Consumer Leaders 'Pro-Poor, Pro-Rural, Pro-Women"; available at http://unctad.org/Sections/wcmu/docs/tdrbpconf6p012_en.pdf [accessed on 3 November 2016].

addition, the 'Report on Consumer Rights Protection of Industrial and Commercial System in China in 2015' issued in March 2016 is the first officially published report, symbolizing a new step toward the transparency of consumer rights protection.

China has cooperated with the other BRICS countries on consumer protection. In 2016 the State Administration for Industry and Commerce of the PRC and Federal Anti-Monopoly Service of Russia signed a Memorandum of Understanding, pledging to continue to cooperate in the fields of competition law and advertisement supervision. They strengthened a cooperative project of personal information protection together with emerging countries. The State Administration for Industry and Commerce of the PRC, together with the German Federal Ministry of Justice and Consumer Protection and the Ministry of Justice of Brazil, have had joint seminars about protecting consumer information and held trainings on international laws and practices of protecting consumer information. At these seminars, they shared the current workplace situation regarding personal information protection and explored the problems that will confront the protection of consumer personal information in the future.[14] Finally, to meet the needs of Russian consumers who buy online, China will build a new logistics center in Suifenhe, a border city of China.

IV.   Incentive Mechanisms of Cooperation in BRICS

Cooperation among BRICS countries mainly focuses on two elements: cooperation in the global economic governing platform and economic cooperation in trade, investment, finance, energy and infrastructure construction. Even though there are disagreements and differences in the social systems, ideologies, cultural traditions and the like of the five countries, their common interests greatly outweigh their disagreements and differences. Closer and well-coordinated cooperation between the BRICS is the cornerstone of a successful reform of the international legal order. In more concrete terms, this means finding novel ways to first formulate policies and subsequently implement them based on creative laws.[15]

In recent decades, there has been great growth in consumption in the BRICS countries. From 2000–2009, consumption increased threefold, from USD 1.4 trillion to USD 4.2 trillion. BRICS countries could become

---

[14] State Administration for Industry and Commerce, *Report on Consumer Rights Protection of Industrial and Commercial System in China in 2015*, 16 March 2016; available at http://www.cicn.com.cn/zggsb/2016-03/16/cms83461article.shtml [accessed on 3 November 2016].

[15] See Chapter 1 by Rostam J. Neuwirth.

the main global driving force in the auto, luxury and tourism markets and will have strong consumer markets in the future. According to data published by the World Tourism Organization in 2012, for the first time, the total number of tourists throughout the world was more than one billion, a greater than 4 percent increase from the year before. International tourism consumption has increased eight times since 2000.

In recent years, bilateral trade between India and China has increased ten times, and China has become the biggest trade partner of India. Even though the Chinese economy has reached a massive size, its development still partially relies on the recovery of the economies of advanced countries to ensure a successful transition towards a consumption economy development mode. China, as the major representative of emerging countries, will certainly play a more important role in the future G-20 agenda. Meanwhile, experience from the economic transition of China will provide a very good 'testing field' for BRICS countries searching for an alternative development mode.

After the world financial crisis in 2008, the economic development of every country faced huge challenges; economic growth slowed down, and inflation increased. There were also challenges in pushing economic growth through consumption. According to the data released by a Brazilian economic research institution, the Fundação Getúlio Vargas (FGV), the economy in Brazil dropped 6.7 percent in January 2015, and the consumer confidence of Brazil dropped 4.9 percent in February 2015 to its lowest level since September 2005. Brazil's consumer confidence dropped 34 percent from the peak in April 2012, and has been 26 percent lower than the average over last five years (Figure 12.1).[16]

As well as in Brazil, consumer confidence has decreased greatly in China[17] and Russia[18]. Consumer confidence in South Africa increased to -9 in the first quarter of 2016 from -14 in the fourth quarter of 2015,[19] but it is in an era of stagflation, and consumer confidence probably will remain low for a long time. Compared with consumer confidence in Brazil,

[16] 'Brazil Became the First Depressed Country among BRICS Countries'; available at http://view.inews.qq.com/a/FIN2015120204104802 [accessed on 3 November 2016].

[17] Gordon Orr, 'China in 2016: Fewer Jobs, Lower Consumer Confidence'; available at www.linkedin.com/pulse/china-2016-fewer-jobs-lower-consumer-confidence-gordon-orr [accessed on 3 November 2016].

[18] Armine Sahakyan, 'Consumer Confidence Tanking in Russia and Other CIS Countries, Surveys Indicate; available at www.huffingtonpost.com/armine-sahakyan/consumer-confidence-tanki_b_9845066.html [accessed on 3 November 2016].

[19] 'South Africa Consumer Confidence 1982–2016'; available at www.tradingeconomics.com/south-africa/consumer-confidence [accessed on 3 November 2016].

Depressed Consumer Confidence
(2005 = 100; s.a.)

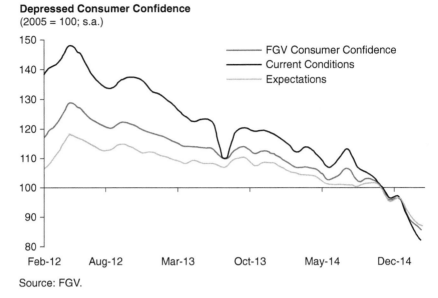

Source: FGV.

Figure 12.1 Depressed consumer confidence in Brazil.
Source: Brazil Became the First Depressed Country among BRICS Countries; available
at http://view.inews.qq.com/a/FIN2015120204104802.

Russia, China and South Africa, the consumer confidence of India was
at the top of the world rankings in 2015 (Figure 12.2).[20]

Since the financial crisis increasing sustainable consumption is necessary for the economic development of all the BRICS countries. India is
relatively optimistic, but the other four countries of BRICS have low consumer confidence. In other words, the countries of BRICS are all facing
the same or similar challenges of economic development and the same or
similar legal problems.

Countries that do not have a mature market economy usually have
problems implementing consumer protection law, because it covers not
only consumers' legal rights and interests but also contract law, tort
law and competition law, product quality law, advertisement law, the
relevant laws of consumer administrative organizations and consumer
associations, criminal law and procedural law. Even some of the clauses

[20] 'Nielsen: India tops global confidence ranking in Q1'; available at www
.thehindubusinessline.com/news/nielsen-india-tops-global-confidence-rankings-in-q1/
article8611493.ece?textsize=large&test=1 [accessed on 3 November 2016].

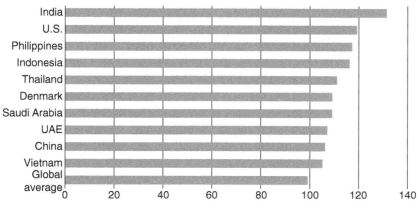

Most Confident Consumers
India tops the list of 61 countries

Source: Nielsen. CCI 3Q 2015

*based on respondents with online access. India's July-September rating was unchanged from the previous quarter, U.S. posted the biggest increase of 18 points and China dropped 1 point

Bloomberg

Figure 12.2   Indian consumer confidence tops the list of 61 countries.
Source: 'Indian Consumer Confidence Tops No.1 in the World'; available at http://wallstreetcn.com/node/225694.

in a single consumer law have encountered obstacles to their implementation, such as the unconditional return of goods purchased online and consumer public welfare lawsuit systems. When consumption economy development encounters bottlenecks, countries around the world need more perfect laws and law enforcement mechanisms to safeguard the realization of the rights and interests of consumers and thereby improve consumer confidence.

The development of tourism and the cross-border goods flow that is part of cross-border e-commerce also requires countries to strengthen their cooperation in the consumer protection arena. As mentioned earlier, the tourism industries of the BRICS countries have developed rapidly. How to protect consumer rights in tourism has become an important question for countries around the world and members of BRICS.

In BRICS, measures for the protection of consumers are not perfect yet, and many problems need to be resolved by the fuller implementation of each country's own consumer protection law. From a global viewpoint, however, there are common understandings of and foundations for consumer protection, as manifested in the United Nations Guidelines for Consumer Protection; these guidelines are the operative requirements of consumer protection movements in all countries. They advocate the adoption of an international standard for consumer protection, as done with other widely accepted international standards in terms of food and water. In terms of medicine, an appropriate standard and regulation or a control system should also be maintained.[21] International law at the UN level is an important basis of law on which countries can reinforce consumer protection.

V.   Future Legal Cooperation in BRICS

BRICS cooperation has a large and grand strategy: to adhere to the 'big market, big circulation, unicom, communication' strategic positioning. To be specific, the BRICS platform takes economic cooperation as the starting point and quickly expands it to the areas of finance, trade, science and technology, health, agriculture, the humanities and others areas to closely connect the five countries in the market and provide each member with more opportunities and better prospects for development. At the same time, along with enhanced cohesion and international influence, the BRICS countries are working together to develop the field of international economy, politics and security. To strengthen the BRICS platform as a coordinating mechanism that aims to solve major issues in the international economic and political fields has become a consensus goal of the five countries.

However, innovation in cooperation in the legal field has many challenges. On the one hand, this kind of innovation needs a driving force; on the other hand, the cooperation must have some basis in legal principles and regulations. This section suggests how to enhance cooperation in the consumer protection field through concrete efforts.

The common features of BRICS in the consumer protection field are rapid economic development, consumer protection laws established around the same time but unsatisfactorily enforced and not congruent with the fast-developing economy, and the recognition that the development of a consumer economy inherently requires a guarantee of consumer human rights and a realization of 'consumer sovereignty'. The Sustainable Development Goals and the requirements in the United Nations Guidelines for Consumer Protection are the basis, foundation and bond

---

[21] Articles 79–86.

for these countries to promote their cooperation in consumer protection field. The means to cooperation mainly involve the official cooperation and communications provided by the UN, as well as cooperation and communications among official bodies and the NGOs of BRICS countries.

On 22 December 2015, the UN's General Assembly agreed to construct a powerful consumer law and supervision structure. This includes an effective dispute resolution and compensation mechanism that gives consumer associations across countries the ability to cooperate. Whenever possible, they should help recover losses for consumers who were cheated during cross-border business. This structure will promote economic vitality and consumer welfare and confirm that there is a common interest for member countries in protecting consumer privacy and the free exchange of information.

For cooperation among the BRICS countries to be enhanced, they must make full use of the cooperation resources and platform of the UN. To actualize the Sustainable Development Goals and United Nations Guidelines for Consumer Protection, the UN General Assembly, each continent, and each region need to engage in communication and cooperation on the issue of consumer protection.

Second, it is necessary to strengthen the cooperation and communication among BRICS official institutions. As noted earlier, the summits of the BRICS countries, although they are not directly related to consumer protection cooperation, still lay the foundation for promoting consumption economic development and consumer protection. In the meantime, the BRICS countries are also undertaking continuous exchanges and cooperation on issues of protecting consumers and their personal information in the era of e-commerce. In addition to the intergovernmental cooperation, many countries have set up consumer associations, semi-official organizations with responsibilities for monitoring and protecting the legitimate rights and interests of consumers. Such communication and cooperation among the governing bodies of countries, such as authorities governing and regulating the market or associations protecting consumers, may be more effective than summits in protecting consumers.

Third, it is necessary to enhance cooperation and exchange between national science and research institutes, intelligences, universities and nongovernmental organizations of the BRICS countries, which are relatively flexible. They include agencies involved in product quality improvement, consumer rights protection and consumer public interest litigation, which can cooperate to perfect the legal texts and enforce existing laws.

Existing consumer protection laws should be amended to focus on the development of the economy and to protect the consumers in new areas, such as online shopping. At the same time the BRICS countries should focus on enhancing the implementation of consumer law, coordinating its relationship with other domestic administrative law. Some scholars have also put forward the question whether consumer protection is possible in a global economy. It is difficult to enforce consumer law internationally, as domestic 'common law' remedies will continue to affect the local suppliers of goods and services who supply them in a physical form.[22] It is thus important for the BRICS to discuss the implementation of consumer law.

The economies of members of BRICS have developed rapidly in recent years, with fast-growing e-commerce and retail entities, but there are still issues of counterfeit and shoddy commodities and the infringement of intellectual property rights. Such problems are commonly faced by developing countries. For example, a booming economy with high taxation and an urban and relatively young population eager to have access to consumer goods – from unsophisticated ones to luxury goods –could naturally be seen as an ideal market for pirated goods and counterfeits.[23] Russia joined the WTO very late; it is one of the few more industrialized countries that was not a member of the WTO before 2012, and IP rights have been an important issue of contention. The international community had provided a great deal of aid to India, but it has not yet adopted TRIPS.[24]

VI. Conclusion

Brazil, Russia, India, China and South Africa differ in many ways, but they can learn from each other and achieve coordinated development. Since 2009, there have been eight BRICS summits, which have improved communication and cooperation. In recent years, they have tried to make the transition from economies of the 'investment-driven type' to a 'consumption-driven type'. Because increasing consumption has become the new economic focal point of these countries, it is important to highlight the protection of consumer rights. How should cooperation on

---

[22] John Goldring, 'Consumer Protection, Globalization and Democracy' (1998) 6 *Cardozo Journal of International and Comparative Law* 5–6.

[23] Cristina Guerra and Ricardo Pinho, 'Combating Intellectual Property Infringement at the Border: A Look at the Systems in Brazil, Argentina, and Uruguay' (2013) 5 *Landslide* 29–33.

[24] J. Benjamin Bai, Keith D. Lindenbaum, Yi Qian and Cynthia Ho, 'From Infringement to Innovation: Counterfeiting and Enforcement in the BRICs' (2007) 5 *Northwestern Journal of Technology and Intellectual Property* 523–543 at 532.

consumer protection among BRICS countries be realized and enhanced? This is a very challenging problem, because it is not only an economic problem but also a problem of human rights protection, which will mostly depend on the completion, perfection and development of the law systems of each country.

At present, the similar problems encountered in the development of BRICS countries can be solved through cooperation in the legal arena and improved communication, and the countries should find a balance between cooperative creativity and institutional practicability. Legal cooperation in the field of consumer protection is a new opportunity of this century, and it should be deepened, paying attention to institutional practicability and effects, which will bring about a more significant coalition of BRICS countries and fundamentally promote their development.

VII.   References

Bai, J. Benjamin, Lindenbaum, Keith D., Qian, Yi and Ho, Cynthia, 'From Infringement to Innovation: Counterfeiting and Enforcement in the BRICs' (2007) 5 *Northwestern Journal of Technology and Intellectual Property* 523–543.

'Brazil Became the First Depressed Country among BRICS Countries'; available at http://view.inews.qq.com/a/FIN2015120204104802 [accessed on 3 November 2016].

'BRICS Development Bank to Benefit Developing Countries: Indian Businessman'; available at http://news.xinhuanet.com/english/business/2014-07/13/c_133480654.htm [accessed on 3 November 2016].

Cai, Yiming and Zhong, Yuyu, 'Basic Consumption and Economic Strength of BRICS: 2000–2010' (2014) (6) *Journal of Strategy and Decision-Making* 62–69.

Cárdenas, Emilio J. and Neto, Pinheiro, 'Legal Memoranda' (1990) 22 *The University of Miami Inter-American Law Review*, 143–159.

'Competition Commission Hosts 4th BRICS International Competition Conference'; available at www.durban.gov.za/Resource_Centre/new2/Pages/Competition-Commission-hosts-4th-BRICS-International-Competition-Conference.aspx [accessed on 3 November 2016].

Consumers International (NGO), 'Declaration of Consumer Leaders 'Pro-Poor, Pro-Rural, Pro-Women''; available at http://unctad.org/Sections/wcmu/docs/tdrbpconf6p012_en.pdf [accessed on 3 November 2016].

Crabb, Kelly, 'Providing Legal Services in Foreign Countries: Making Room for the American Attorney' (1983) 83 *Columbia Law Review* 1767–1823.

Goldring, John, 'Consumer Protection, Globalization and Democracy' (1998) 6 *Cardozo Journal of International and Comparative Law* 5–6.

Guerra, Cristina and Pinho, Ricardo, 'Combating Intellectual Property Infringement at the Border: A Look at the Systems in Brazil, Argentina, and Uruguay' (2013) 5 *Landslide* 29–33.

Honey, Eugene, 'South Africa-Consumer Protection Act Regulations at last' (2011) 9(3) *International Journal of Franchising Law* 35–38.

Ip, Mary, 'Chinese Consumer Law: Recent Development and Implication' (2001) 6(2) *International Journal of Business* 111–134.

'Law on Consumer Protection of Russia'; available at www.russia-online.cn/Overview/detail_12_558.shtml [accessed on 3 November 2016].

'Nielsen: India Tops Global Confidence Ranking in Q1'; available at www.thehindubusinessline.com/news/nielsen-india-tops-global-confidence-rankings-in-q1/article8611493.ece?textsize=large&test=1 [accessed on 3 November 2016].

Orr, Gordon, 'China in 2016: Fewer Jobs, Lower Consumer Confidence'; available at www.linkedin.com/pulse/china-2016-fewer-jobs-lower-consumer-confidence-gordon-orr [accessed on 3 November 2016].

Otto, Jannie, 'The History of Consumer Credit Legislation in South Africa' (2010) 16 *Fundamina* 257–258.

Sahakyan, Armine, 'Consumer Confidence Tanking in Russia and Other CIS Countries, Surveys Indicate; available at www.huffingtonpost.com/armine-sahakyan/consumer-confidence-tanki_b_9845066.html [accessed on 3 November 2016].

'South Africa Consumer Confidence 1982–2016'; available at http://www.tradingeconomics.com/south-africa/consumer-confidence [accessed on 3 November 2016].

State Administration for Industry and Commerce, *Report on Consumer Rights Protection of Industrial and Commercial System in China in 2015*, March 16 2016; available at www.cicn.com.cn/zggsb/2016-03/16/cms83461article.shtml [accessed on 3 November 2016].

Verbiscus, Lauren, 'Economic Globalization and the Need for Legal Innovation' (2013) 21 *Michigan State University College Law Review* 779–820.

Warf, Barney, 'Global Dimensions of U.S. Legal Services' (2001) 53 *Professional Geographer* 398–406.

Xu, Junke, 'Who Will Protect Chinese Consumers? The Past, Present and Future of Consumer Protection Legislation in China' (2011) 24 *Loyola Consumer Law Review* 22–64.

Yu, Fangdong, 'A Comparative Study of Price Level and Economic Power of BRICS Countries: Analysis on the Results of World Bank 2011 International Comparison Project' (2015) (7) *World of Survey and Research* 3–8.

13

A Dispute Resolution Centre for the BRICS?

FERNANDO DIAS SIMÕES

I. International Arbitration and Economic Globalization

In a world subject to increasing globalization, there is a clear tendency to settle business disagreements by means of arbitration. Twining defines globalization as 'those processes which tend to create and consolidate a unified world economy, a single ecological system and a complex network of communications that covers the whole globe, even if it does not penetrate to every part of it.'[1] Globalization is an economic phenomenon as well as a political and legal one. It has served as a catalyst for internationally agreed rules of behavior in trade, finance, taxation and many other areas.[2] Economic globalization cannot be understood apart from global business regulation and the legal construction of the markets on which it increasingly depends.[3] International arbitration has become the foremost technique for resolving disputes between states, individuals and corporations in almost every aspect of international trade, commerce and investment.[4] It is now considered the 'normal' method to resolve international business disputes, and practically all international agreements contain arbitration clauses.[5] This trend can be explained by the increased globalization of business and expansion of international trade, which have led to a change in the way in which international business disputes are solved.[6]

---

[1] William Twining, *Globalisation and Legal Theory* (Cambridge: Cambridge University Press, 2000), p. 4.

[2] See Jeffrey Sachs, 'International economics: unlocking the mysteries of globalization' (1998) 110 *Foreign Policy* 97–111.

[3] Terence C. Halliday and Pavel Osinsky, 'Globalization of law' (2006) 32 *Annual Review of Sociology* 447.

[4] Nigel Blackaby, Constantine Partasides, Alan Redfern and Martin Hunter, *Redfern and Hunter on International Arbitration*, 5th edn (Oxford: Oxford University Press, 2009), p. 1.

[5] Klaus P. Berger, *International Economic Arbitration* (Deventer, Boston: Kluwer Law and Taxation Publishers, 1993), p. 8, n. 62.

[6] David J. McLean, 'Toward a new international dispute resolution paradigm: assessing the congruent evolution of globalization and international arbitration' (2009) 30 *University of Pennsylvania Journal of International Law* 1087–1097.

International arbitration has been transformed and institutionalized as the foremost mechanism for the resolution of transnational disputes. In fact, it has become a key institution for the developing international market.[7] As a central mechanism of cross-border dispute settlement, an analysis of international arbitration helps provide an understanding of the impact of globalization on the international practice of law.[8] Indeed, globalization requires and inspires a large number of business actors, many of which are not located in well-established centres of international trade, to take part in cross-border transactions.[9]

II.   The Proliferation and Specialization of Arbitral Institutions

The globalization process has raised the level of conflict and competition within the market of international arbitration. The system is confronted with growing demand from the business community, compelling the international arbitration community (arbitrators, arbitration centres and lawyers) to listen to the needs of the market and offer a fitting answer to the challenges of globalization and technology in transnational trade. Trying to cater to the needs of local and international business communities, national and international legal systems around the world have taken a firm pro-arbitration stance, enacting modern legal frameworks to support arbitration proceedings. The astonishing expansion of the market for international commercial arbitration is also evidenced by the multiplication of arbitral institutions and organizations.[10] The market is global and requires wide-ranging legal support and, accordingly, there are now arbitration service providers on a worldwide scale. International arbitration has become a market.[11]

---

[7] Yves Dezalay and Bryant G. Garth, 'Merchants of law as moral entrepreneurs: constructing international justice from the competition for transnational business disputes' (1995) 29 *Law and Society Review* 27–64.

[8] Shahla F. Ali, 'Approaching the global arbitration table: comparing the advantages of arbitration as seen by practitioners in East Asia and the West' (2009) 28 *Review of Litigation* 735–789.

[9] S. I. Strong, 'Navigating the borders between international commercial arbitration and U.S. federal courts: a jurisprudential GPS' (2012) *Journal of Dispute Resolution* 119–216.

[10] Katherine L. Lynch, *The Forces of Economic Globalization: Challenges to the Regime of International Commercial Arbitration* (The Hague: Kluwer Law International, 2003), pp. 111–112.

[11] Aleksandar Goldstajn, 'Choice of international arbitrators, arbitral tribunals and centres: legal and sociological aspects', in Petar Sarcevic (ed.), *Essays on International Commercial Arbitration* (London: Graham & Trotman, 1989), p. 29; Jacques Werner, 'International

Institutional arbitration is different from ad hoc arbitration. The former is managed by a professional provider of arbitration services and is generally organized pursuant to the procedural rules approved by that institution. In contrast, ad hoc arbitration is carried out without an administering authority and generally without the support of institutional procedural rules. Certainly, both institutional and ad hoc arbitration have advantages and disadvantages.[12] Still, many experienced international practitioners prefer institutional arbitration to ad hoc arbitration because of the enhanced predictability, stability and international expertise provided by the former. The benefits arising from the integration of institutional arbitration rules are substantial. Particularly at the outset of arbitration between inexperienced parties from different legal cultures, an institution's role in moving proceedings along can be highly constructive and efficient.[13] The agreement to submit the case to an arbitral institution introduces an element of certainty and predictability into the dispute resolution proceedings. The parties have the chance to familiarize themselves with the rules under which the arbitration will proceed.[14] Furthermore, the administrative support provided by the arbitral institution allows the arbitrators to devote their full attention to deciding the dispute, avoiding the waste of time and resources that could result from a process that had to be created from scratch.[15] Finally, institutional supervision and guidance considerably reduce the probability that the arbitrators will make avoidable procedural errors or that one party will not be given a fair chance to present its case. As a consequence, it is more likely that the parties will accept the arbitral award voluntarily, or that not being the case, that national courts will enforce it.[16] Because of its purported advantages, institutional arbitration, rather than ad hoc arbitration, is becoming the prevalent type of arbitration on which parties depend for the settlement of their disputes.

---

commercial arbitrators: from merchant to academic to skilled professional' (1998) 4(3) *Dispute Resolution Magazine* 22–24.

[12] See Anne V. Schlaepfer and Angelina M. Petti, 'Institutional versus ad hoc arbitration', in Elliott Geisinger and Nathalie Voser (eds.), *International Arbitration in Switzerland: A Handbook for Practitioners*, 2nd edn (Alphen aan den Rijn: Kluwer Law International, 2013), pp. 13–24.

[13] Gary B. Born, *International Arbitration and Forum Selection Agreements: Drafting and Enforcing*, 4th edn (Alphen aan den Rijn: Kluwer Law International, 2013), pp. 44, 59.

[14] Arden C. McClelland, 'International arbitration: a practical guide to the system for the litigation of transnational commercial disputes' (1977) 17 *Virginia Journal of International Law* 729–754, at 736–737.

[15] Ibid., p. 737.   [16] Ibid.

The expansion of international trade and the propagation of international arbitration have led to a dramatic multiplication in the number of arbitral institutions. Virtually every major trading city in the world has at least one – if not several – institutions that deliver arbitration services. Most of these institutions are affiliated with local chambers of commerce. This makes sense, as arbitration hubs are normally located in economic focal points. Most if not all existing arbitration hubs serve as commercial or financial centres as well. Some popular locations for international arbitration proceedings also reflect historically established trading routes. London, Geneva, Paris, Singapore and New York have historically been some of the global hubs of international arbitration. Highly regarded institutions, such as the International Court of Arbitration of the International Chamber of Commerce, the London Court of International Arbitration or the American Arbitration Association, have traditionally taken the biggest share of the market. For many years the choice of a place of arbitration was rather easy – only a few centres handled considerable international arbitration cases.

As international arbitration is becoming a global business, the market of international arbitration is expanding, and many cities and jurisdictions are now positioning themselves to collect a share of that market. Plans for the creation of new arbitral institutions are announced almost daily.[17] As more venues refresh and harmonize their legal systems to achieve an international benchmark, parties may feel persuaded to select them as the seat of their arbitration proceedings, looking beyond the 'traditional' options.

---

[17] In 2016 alone, plans for the creation of the following arbitral institutions were announced: in India, in Gujarat (available at http://timesofindia.indiatimes.com/city/vadodara/Gujarat-to-get-first-arbitration-centre/articleshow/50495527.cms [accessed on 25 October 2016]) and Mumbai (available at www.mumbaimirror.com/mumbai/others/International-arbitration-centre-to-open-in-August-at-Nariman-Point/articleshow/51759979.cms [accessed on 25 October 2016]); in China, in Pingtan (available at http://english.cri.cn/12394/2015/12/30/4082s910637.htm [accessed on 25 October 2016]) and Chongqing (available at www.china.org.cn/china/2016-04/28/content_38349463.htm [accessed on 25 October 2016]); in the United Arab Emirates (available at www.seatrade-maritime.com/news/middle-east-africa/emirates-maritime-arbitration-centre-starts-operations-in-the-uae.html [accessed on 25 October 2016]); in Cambodia (available at www.khmertimeskh.com/news/24705/another-commercial-arbitration-center-planned [accessed on 25 October 2016]); in Barbados (available at www.loopnewsbarbados.com/content/barbados-will-benefit-arbitration-centre [accessed on 25 October 2016]); in Sri Lanka (available at www.news.lk/news/politics/item/7461-pm-to-open-an-international-arbitration-centre-in-colombo [accessed on 25 October 2016]); and in the Bahamas (available at www.jamaicaobserver.com/news/Bahamas-seeking-to-become-international-arbitration-centre_55792 [accessed on 25 October 2016]).

One important recent trend concerns specialization. Arbitral institutions can be divided into generalist and specialist institutions. The former administer the resolution of any form of dispute, while the latter specialize in arbitrations arising from specific types of activities or trade. Specialized arbitral institutions have been created, for instance, to settle disputes regarding maritime transportation, construction, commodities, foodstuffs (e.g. coffee, grain, sugar), architects, chartered surveyors and the stock exchange. Normally these institutions operate under the control of national or international professional organizations.

Another noticeable trend in the arbitration market in the last few years is regionalization. Markets are increasingly being integrated through economic regional organizations. As a result, arbitral institutions try to cater to such regional needs. This phenomenon has led to the creation of arbitral institutions that aim to serve as arbitral hubs for such regional markets. Even though these institutions may develop to achieve a global status, they focus on regional disputes. This is what happens, for instance, with Singapore and Hong Kong for Asia; with Dubai for the Middle East; with Istanbul for Eurasia; and with Mexico City for Latin America. Regional markets are united by economic links and, in some cases, by a common language. Regional arbitral institutions are designed to address better the cultural, linguistic and economic specificities of such commercial relations.

China has been particularly keen on creating arbitral institutions specifically devoted to a particular geographical scope. The Chinese European Arbitration Centre (CEAC), based in Hamburg, was launched in 2008, focusing on China-related disputes, namely international contracts with Chinese parties, joint venture agreements with Chinese or Chinese-controlled parties and contracts with subsidiaries of Chinese companies in other countries.[18] The China–Africa Joint Arbitration Centre (CAJAC), with branches in both Shanghai and Johannesburg, was created in August 2015, focusing on disputes involving African and Chinese businesses. In December 2015 an arbitral institution was created in Fujian Province, Southeastern China, to deal mainly with civil and commercial contract and property rights disputes involving parties from the Chinese mainland and Taiwan.[19] The members of the Forum for Economic and Trade

---

[18] See www.ceac-arbitration.com/index.php?id=2 [accessed on 25 October 2016]. See also Eckart Brodermann and Thomas Weimann, 'CEAC', in Gerhard Wegen and Stephan Wilske (eds.), *Getting the Deal through Arbitration 2012* (London: Law Business Research Ltd, 2012), pp. 15–19.

[19] See http://english.cri.cn/12394/2015/12/30/4082s910637.htm [accessed on 25 October 2016].

Cooperation between China and Portuguese-Speaking Countries (Macau Forum) have also called for the promotion of Macau as a centre for arbitration of commercial disputes between enterprises from the mainland and Portuguese-speaking countries.[20]

III. A Dispute Resolution Centre for the BRICS

India assumed the chairmanship of the BRICS for the year 2016 and hosted the Eighth BRICS Summit on 15 and 16 October 2016 in Goa.[21] In the run-up to the BRICS Summit, India initiated a number of events to foster new cooperation mechanisms for the member states, one of which was the 'Conference on International Arbitration in BRICS: Challenges, Opportunities and Road Ahead,' which took place in New Delhi on 27 August 2016. The conference was jointly organized by the Department of Economic Affairs of India's Ministry of Finance, the Federation of Indian Chambers of Commerce & Industry and the Indian Council of Arbitration.[22] The event brought together national and international experts from the BRICS countries in the field of international arbitration. The goal was to discuss the need to develop and establish an efficient and effective international arbitration mechanism for members of the BRICS. According to India's Department of Economic Affairs, the conference was envisioned as an important step towards a better understanding of the legal framework governing international arbitration involving the BRICS member states.[23] The Indian finance minister, Arun Jaitley, said in a statement, 'It appears obvious that an efficient and effective measure for the resolution of any commercial or investment dispute by investors or

---

[20] See Fernando Dias Simões, *Commercial Arbitration between China and the Portuguese-Speaking World* (Alphen aan den Rijn: Kluwer Law International, 2014).

[21] See BRICS India 2016, 'Eighth BRICS Summit'; available at http://brics2016.gov.in/content/innerpage/8th-summit.php [accessed on 25 October 2016].

[22] ZeeBiz WebTeam, 'Arun Jaitley wants a "world class" BRICS arbitration mechanism', *Zeebiz*, 28 August 2016; available at www.zeebiz.com/india/news-arun-jaitley-wants-a-world-class-brics-arbitration-mechanism-5464 [accessed on 25 October 2016].

[23] Press Trust of India, 'Finance Minister to inaugurate BRICS meet on arbitration', *Business Standard*, 24 August 2016; available at www.business-standard.com/article/international/finance-minister-to-inaugurate-brics-meet-on-arbitration-116082400587_1.html [accessed on 25 October 2016]; KNN – Knowledge & News Network, 'Jaitley to inaugurate conference on "Intl Arbitration in BRICS: Challenges, Opportunities & Road Ahead" on Aug 27', KNN – Knowledge & News Network, 24 August 2016; available at http://knnindia.co.in/news/newsdetails/global/jaitley-to-inaugurate-conference-on-intl-arbitration-in-brics-challenges-opportunities-road-ahead-on-aug-27 [accessed on 25 October 2016].

trading entities between the BRICS nations is imperative to encourage further economic activity and cooperation'.[24] Jaitley called for the setting up of a task force of experts and officers to build world-class arbitration centres and to achieve higher growth in the globally challenging environment. He believed there is a need both for a credible international dispute resolution mechanism among the BRICS countries to resolve all the trade-related issues among them and for an effective system to implement the arbitration awards quickly. Jaitley added that once this mechanism was set up, it could be extended to non-BRICS nations.[25] The idea of a BRICS arbitration centre was also discussed in three technical sessions with representatives of the five countries.[26] The government of India pledged its full support for the development and establishment of an international arbitration mechanism for the resolution of commercial and investment disputes among the BRICS nations.[27]

The idea of setting up a specialized arbitration centre devoted to intra-BRICS disputes stemmed from several criticisms directed at the existing framework for commercial and investment-related dispute resolution. The first concerned the institutional setting in which dispute resolution currently takes place. The Indian finance minister, Arun Jaitley, argued that some institutions, particularly in the developed world, have monopolized the international arbitration process and created arbitrators who are familiar with processes all over the world.[28] In his opinion 'Those jurisdictions dominated the pie as far as international arbitration was

---

[24] Press Trust of India, 'Finance Minister'.

[25] ZeeBiz WebTeam, 'Arun Jaitley wants'. See also SME Times News Bureau, 'BRICS nations need to engage on own arbitration centres: FM', *SME Times*, 29 August 2016; available at www.smetimes.in/smetimes/news/top-stories/2016/Aug/29/brics-nations-need-to-engage-on-own-arbitration-centres1633507.html [accessed on 25 October 2016]; *The Hindu*, 'Own arbitration tool must for BRICS', *The Hindu*, 27 August 2016; available at www.thehindu.com/business/Economy/own-arbitration-tool-must-for-brics/article9040735.ece [accessed on 25 October 2016].

[26] Shreeja Sen, 'Arun Jaitley proposes task force for arbitral centres for Brics countries', *Live Mint*, 27 August 2016; available at www.livemint.com/Politics/y9OTm8JZKnNrhSOSnFqkDL/Arun-Jaitley-pitches-for-Brics-arbitration-platform.html [accessed on 25 October 2016].

[27] Jackwell Feris and Jonathan Ripley-Evans, 'Challenges, opportunities and road ahead for international arbitration in BRICS', *Bizcommunity*, 1 September 2016; available at www.bizcommunity.com/Article/196/547/150226.html [accessed on 25 October 2016].

[28] Press Trust of India, 'Arun Jaitley pitches for BRICS arbitration platform to cut dependence on developed nations', *Economic Times*, 28 August 2016; available at http://economictimes.indiatimes.com/news/economy/policy/arun-jaitley-pitches-for-brics-arbitration-platform-to-cut-dependence-on-developed-nations/articleshow/53890040.cms [accessed on 25 October 2016].

concerned'.[29] Jaitley added that developing countries often have expressed apprehension about arbitral awards from those well-established arbitral institutions, which they frequently perceive as being biased against them.[30] He argued that India, like other developing economies, has been a victim of the inherent structural bias that prevails in the traditional frameworks of international arbitration.[31] The solution to this problem would be the creation of arbitral centres as far as the BRICS nations are concerned.[32] The idea is that the BRICS countries would create a mechanism for disputes among them, developing arbitration capabilities, capacity building and their own arbitration centres.[33]

The second criticism was targeted at arbitration tribunals. During the conference the Indian economic affairs secretary, Shaktikanta Das, criticized the lack of adequate representation of the developing nations in the arbitration process.[34] The law minister, Ravi Prasad, lamented the scarcity of international arbitrators from the BRICS nations, asking, 'Why do we see very few arbitrators from BRICS countries in the world dispute redressal mechanism? Why should there be a presumption that fast alternative arbitration can come and come only from arbitrators who are from the western world?'[35] Jaitley argued that the BRICS member countries should have a pool of international-level arbitrators and arbitration lawyers, among others.[36]

The third critique regarded the protection of the interests of emerging economies. Ravi Prasad stressed in his speech that dispute resolution mechanisms should keep in mind the concerns of 'locals'. He said that the Indian experience with bilateral investment treaties was that their interpretation has often been ambiguous,[37] emphasizing that

---

[29] SME Times News Bureau, 'BRICS nations'.

[30] Ibid.; The Hindu, 'Own arbitration tool'; Press Trust of India, 'Arun Jaitley pitches'.

[31] Abhishek Dwivedi, 'India pursues a new investment arbitration regime to protect itself', *Swarajya*, 18 September 2016; available at http://swarajyamag.com/world/india-pursues-a-new-investment-arbitration-regime-to-protect-itself [accessed on 25 October 2016].

[32] Sen, 'Arun Jaitley proposes task force'.

[33] SME Times News Bureau, 'BRICS nations'; Press Trust of India, 'Arun Jaitley pitches'.

[34] The Hindu, 'Own arbitration tool'.

[35] Murali Krishnan, 'Why do BRICS countries produce so few global arbitrators, asks Law MinRavi Shankar Prasad', *Bar & Bench*, 28 August 2016; available at http://barandbench.com/brics-countries-produce-global-arbitrators-asks-law-min-ravi-shankar-prasad [accessed on 25 October 2016].

[36] ZeeBiz WebTeam, 'Arun Jaitley wants'; SME Times News Bureau, 'BRICS nations'; The Hindu, 'Own arbitration tool'.

[37] Krishnan, 'Why do BRICS countries'.

the country's sovereign right to regulate investments needs consideration.[38] Shaktikanta Das added that there is a need for balancing the interests of private investors and the overwhelming public needs of the country while deciding disputes.[39] 'Pursuit of global business order should be balanced with public policy for overwhelming public good', he added.[40] In his opinion developing countries, including India, should build capacity instead of playing the victim, because the structure of international arbitration was heavily biased towards the developed countries: 'The key is to develop local capabilities in the BRICS countries, so we can deal with these issues.'[41]

IV.   Prospects and Challenges

The BRICS aims to promote economic cooperation and trade exchange between parties from its member states. The BRICS brings together five major emerging economies, comprising 43 percent of the world population, 30 percent of the world GDP and a 17 percent share of the world trade.[42] Disputes are an inevitable occurrence in many international transactions and are further intensified by increased globalization and market liberalization. Different commercial and legal expectations, cultural traditions, political implications and geographic locations are all causes of disagreement and disputes between parties.[43] When these disputes cannot be determined through negotiation, they need to be resolved pursuant to a legal process that merits the trust of the parties. Investors need a fair, flexible and reliable dispute resolution process to ensure that their international disputes are resolved effectively.

The development of the market of international arbitration is directly dependent on the quality of the services provided by arbitral institutions. If it is true that the arbitration is only as good as the arbitrators, that same relationship holds when we consider the institutions that deliver

---

[38] Sen, 'Arun Jaitley proposes'.   [39] Ibid.
[40] Siliconindia, 'International arbitration structure skewed in favour of developed nations', *Siliconindia*, 28 August 2016; available at www.siliconindia.com/news/general/International-Arbitration-Structure-Skewed-In-Favour-Of-Developed-Nations-nid-197971-cid-1.html [accessed on 25 October 2016].
[41] Ibid.
[42] BRICS India 2016, 'About BRICS'; available at http://brics2016.gov.in/content/innerpage/about-usphp.php [accessed on 25 October 2016].
[43] Loukas A. Mistelis, 'International arbitration – corporate attitudes and practices'. 12 perceptions tested: myths, data and analysis research report' (2004) 15 *American Revue of International Arbitration* 525–591.

arbitration services.[44] The increasing integration of the different world-wide economies into the global market has led to escalating competition between arbitration systems. In principle competition between arbitral institutions and between venues for arbitration proceedings will benefit users of international arbitration. Parties and their counsel will be faced with a strategic choice of venue, with different cities and countries trying to present themselves as the best option.[45]

At the Conference on International Arbitration in BRICS, members of the Indian government argued that the existing arbitral institutions are not suited to settling intra-BRICS disputes, because they are biased towards developed economies, rely mainly on arbitrators from Western nations and often fail to take into account the specific public interests pursued by developing countries. Members of the BRICS have identified, inter alia, the need to set up a neutral institution for the resolution of intra-BRICS commercial and investment disputes; to develop the expertise and skills of legal professionals in international arbitration among BRICS nations to support and ensure the success of the BRICS international arbitration mechanism; to ensure adequate representation of arbitrators from emerging economies to avoid structural bias and partiality or the perception thereof by arbitrators originating from the developed world; and to reform the existing investor state arbitration mechanism under the International Centre for the Settlement of Investment Disputes (ICSID) and under bilateral investment treaties to account for the unique circumstances and challenges of emerging economies.[46]

The New Delhi conference signaled significant discontent from the members of the BRICS with the current market for international arbitration. The solution to the problem, in the opinion of the Indian government, was to create a specific institution for intra-BRICS dispute settlement. However, this proposal is not entirely new. In October 2015 the Shanghai International Economic and Trade Arbitration Commission (Shanghai International Arbitration Centre) launched the BRICS Dispute Resolution Centre Shanghai.[47] Created with the support of the China Law Society and other members of the BRICS legal community, the centre provides alternative dispute resolution services for commercial disputes between parties from the BRICS countries. The BRICS Dispute

---

[44] René David, *Arbitration in International Trade* (Kluwer Law, 1985), p. 39.
[45] For a general overview, see Michael Ostrove, Claudia Salomon and Bette Shifman (eds.), *Choice of Venue in International Arbitration* (Oxford University Press, 2014).
[46] Feris and Ripley-Evans, 'Challenges, opportunities and road ahead'.
[47] See www.shiac.org/BRICS/index_E.aspx [accessed on 25 October 2016].

Resolution Centre, as advocated by the Indian government, would apparently have broader jurisdiction, having the competence to settle not only commercial but also investor–state disputes.

This proposal was made to realize part of India's mission for its tenure as chairing the BRICS: 'Building Responsive, Inclusive and Collective Solutions'. One of the objectives that India pledged to pursue during its chairmanship was 'institution building to further deepen, sustain and institutionalise BRICS cooperation'. The creation of a BRICS-centred arbitral institution is in line with the purpose of fostering new cooperation mechanisms for the BRICS nations. A similar idea has also been mulled over in other fields. After setting up the New Development Bank to rival the International Monetary Fund and the World Bank, the BRICS countries are considering the creation of a credit rating agency, with the aim of ending the dominance of existing credit rating agencies.[48]

The proposal to create its own arbitral centre is another example of the BRICS nations' dissatisfaction with the current international institutional landscape. According to Feris and Ripley-Evans, 'The BRICS nations regard themselves as the de facto vanguard of emerging economies, duty-bound to ensure that an international arbitration mechanism is developed which has regard to factors relevant to emerging economies in the resolution of disputes'.[49] Currently all the members of the BRICS have their own system and structure for international law and domestic dispute resolution. The idea is to create a whole new forum for these countries, with jurisdiction over intra-BRICS investor–state or commercial disputes, instead of referring them to the traditional arbitral centres, mainly based in developed countries. However, is the creation of yet another arbitral institution truly necessary, and will this centre create value-added options for disputing parties?

Some commentators reply affirmatively to this question. The attorney general of India, Mukul Rohatgi, said at the conference, 'The BRICS countries collectively constitute more than half of the population and economy of the world. In such a scenario, these nations should come together and form a common law and ease into common dispute resolution. This systematic synchronisation of law will be a helpful setup'.[50] The minister

---

[48] Prasanta Sahu, 'After bank, BRICS nations now mull rating agency', *Financial Express*, 11 September 2016; available at www.financialexpress.com/economy/after-bank-brics-nations-now-mull-rating-agency/373278 [accessed on 25 October 2016].

[49] Feris and Ripley-Evans, 'Challenges, opportunities and road ahead'.

[50] Avni Shrivastav, 'Third BRICS Legal Forum begins in Delhi', *Live Law*, 11 September 2016; available at www.livelaw.in/third-brics-legal-forum-begins-delhi [accessed on 25 October 2016].

of law, Ravi Shankar Prasad, added, 'Dispute resolution system has a slant of the old in the world which is going forward. However, now we are quite keen to have a robust arbitration system. An alternative and efficacious dispute redressal system is the need of the hour today'.[51] In a similar vein, Feris argued that an efficient and effective measure for the resolution of commercial or investment disputes between the BRICS nations is imperative to encourage further economic activity and cooperation.[52] In his opinion, the economic opportunities and benefits for cooperation appear to far outweigh the challenges of establishing an arbitration centre.[53]

From a different perspective, some authors have argued that the creation of a new dispute resolution centre is not necessarily the most efficient way to address the deficiencies of the existing arbitration system. Kaszubska identified several problems. First, there is a lack of cohesion, as some BRICS countries do not recognize each other's arbitral awards.[54] Second, many countries take a long time to enact enforcement proceedings, leading to judicial delays.[55] While acknowledging that greater coordination among the BRICS countries might help to bridge some of the cultural, regulatory and judicial disparities, thus fueling investment and trade in these countries, Kaszubska considered that the creation of a new arbitral forum would not be a golden solution.[56] After setting up an arbitral centre, it would be necessary to ensure its sustainability. Arbitral institutions prosper only if the number of proceedings that they administer increases. Thus, they actively market and promote arbitration in the hope of attracting more cases and increasing their revenues. Institutional specialization may be beneficial for disputing parties, as it gives them the possibility of choosing the institutions with which they feel greater affinity. Disputing parties from the BRICS may also benefit from the existence of an arbitral institution specifically devoted to disputes that emerge within this economic bloc. Potential arbitration users should, however, take a close look at whether the new centre offers a useful alternative. The BRICS Dispute

---

[51] Ibid.

[52] Jackwell Feris, 'An international arbitration system for BRICS – is it an imperative for further economic cooperation', Lexology, 18 August 2016; available at www.lexology.com/library/detail.aspx?g=6541959b-3054-4821-a55a-672e00c4776c [accessed on 25 October 2016].

[53] Feris and Ripley-Evans, 'Challenges, opportunities and road ahead'.

[54] Katarzyna Kaszubska, 'A BRICS-only arbitration forum will not be the panacea imagined', The Wire, 9 September 2016; available at http://thewire.in/64641/a-brics-only-arbitration-forum-will-not-be-the-panacea-they-are-hoping-for [accessed on 25 October 2016].

[55] Ibid.   [56] Ibid.

Resolution Centre Shanghai, for instance, has not received a single arbitration application since its inception.[57] Kaszubska considered it preferable to advocate structural reforms of the existing arbitral institutions to ensure that developing countries are adequately represented on arbitration panels.[58]

There are several questions that need to be addressed by the BRICS nations in future meetings.

First, while there was a consensus in the New Delhi conference regarding the need for an arbitral mechanism, it was less clear whether this mechanism would be developed as an independent arbitral body or whether the arbitral bodies already established in the regions concerned should be utilized for this purpose.[59]

Second, it is necessary to discuss and implement measures to ensure the neutrality of the new arbitral centre or reinforce the neutrality of the pre-existing centres. Neutrality is regarded as one of the most important features of international arbitration. Dozens of different arbitral centres exist around the world, and they all aim to be perceived as neutral and impartial. However, none of them can avoid being associated with a specific legal and cultural background, expressed in a certain institutional culture. The institutional culture of each arbitral centre is molded by a combination of different factors,[60] with location perhaps the most important. Other factors that influence the institutional culture are the centre's membership, leadership and administrative structure; diversity of staff, background of arbitrators; and official or most frequently used languages. The success of an institution specializing in arbitration matters within the BRICS countries is naturally dependent on a strong image of neutrality. Such an arbitral institution could not hope to be recognized as credible if it did not appear neutral to all parties and stakeholders.

Third, it is vital to ensure that arbitral centres (whether newly created or preexisting) are endowed with lists of qualified arbitrators with diverse backgrounds. One of the major advantages of arbitration is that it allows parties to select who will settle their dispute. As arbitrators play the decisive role in determining how the arbitration proceedings are carried out, the choice of the right arbitrator is one of the most important issues that the parties need to consider. This decision typically takes into account

---

[57] Ibid.   [58] Ibid.
[59] Feris and Ripley-Evans, 'Challenges, opportunities and road ahead'.
[60] See Fernando Dias Simões, 'Institutional culture in international arbitration' (2016) 27(3) *Australasian Dispute Resolution Journal* 188–197.

factors such as the prospective arbitrators' experience in international proceedings, experience in the place where the arbitration is to be held, language skills, availability and academic background. When designating a party-appointed arbitrator, the parties ponder all of these aspects to ensure that the selected person has credibility with the other arbitrators.[61]

A BRICS-centred arbitral institution should provide the parties with a roster of qualified professionals who can be called on to serve as arbitrators. It is imperative that the parties are able to make informed, thoughtful selections of arbitrators from lists made up only of competent professionals. These individuals should have a minimal level of proven competence, hearing management skills and analytical ability. They should have the necessary skills to create confidence in parties and thus enhance the reputation of the center. One of the most important tests for any institution is its ability to appoint suitable arbitrators. 'Suitability' is an amorphous concept. However, it is increasingly being recognized that an arbitrator must be not only technically competent but also culturally sensitive and demonstrate an appreciation for the concerns of all the parties.[62]

Cultural awareness is particularly important in this regard, as parties come from countries with different social and legal backgrounds. The plural composition of the list of arbitrators is a key condition for the success of an arbitral institution with jurisdiction over intra-BRICS disputes. The list of arbitrators should naturally include arbitrators from the different member states to provide the parties with vast freedom of choice. Even though neutrality is not directly or necessarily dependent on nationality, if all or most of the arbitrators come from one of the members states of the BRICS, that may inculcate a perception of favoritism, thus affecting the centre's image of neutrality and impartiality. On the other hand, if most arbitrators come from developed countries, the criticism about their lack of regard for the interests of developing nations may resurface.

Fourth, the BRICS member states need to consider the adoption and implementation of suitable arbitration rules. All arbitration proceedings are subject to some legal and regulatory systems. The BRICS Dispute Resolution Centre should draft and enact its own arbitration rules. The aim

---

[61]　Tom Ginsburg and Richard M. Mosk, 'Becoming an international arbitrator: qualifications, disclosures, conduct, and removal', in Daniel M. Kolkey, Richard Chernick and Barbara Reeves Neal (eds.), *The Practitioner's Handbook of International Arbitration and Mediation* (New York: Juris Net, 2012), pp. 339 and 343.

[62]　Michael J. Moser and Peter Yuen, 'Arbitration outside China', in Michael J. Moser (ed.), *Managing Business Disputes in Today's China: Duelling with Dragons* (Alphen aan den Rijn: Kluwer Law International, 2007), pp. 87 and 112.

should be the adoption of rules that are highly flexible, provide the disputants with the maximum autonomy, take into account the different legal cultures and backgrounds present and limit the amount of judicial intervention – in a word, rules that suit the interests of disputing parties from the BRICS. Each arbitral institution has its own distinct characteristics and predilections.[63] The centre should cater to the needs of investors and businessmen from the BRICS and understand the nature of their transactions, the likely nature of future disputes and their problems and expectations.

It is essential to set up a group of experts to work on further developing these ideas. This task force should undertake an exhaustive review of international arbitration systems. It should analyze international treaties, consider the arbitration laws of other countries and examine the arbitration rules of other institutions. In developing the centre, it is important to ensure that all the stakeholders, specifically the relevant governments and their judiciaries, are actively involved.[64] Opening the discussion to practitioners, commercial entrepreneurs, professional associations and other interested parties is vital. Networking is useful if new members, new ideas and new cultures are to be included. An open mind toward modernization, by adopting rules to suit the needs of the parties – that is, the end users and the market – should be recognized as essential.[65]

Fifth, it is necessary not to duplicate efforts.[66] The BRICS Dispute Resolution Centre Shanghai already focuses on intra-BRICS commercial disputes. Member states should make sure that the jurisdiction of the two centres does not overlap to avoid waste of human and material resources.

Sixth, BRICS member states also need to consider whether the International Centre for the Settlement of Investment Disputes (ICSID) still serves their interests as emerging economies. If the answer is negative, they need to decide whether there is a need to establish an investment dispute settlement institution that takes into account specific factors relevant to emerging economies when resolving investment disputes.[67] Currently, of the five member states, only China is a member of the Convention on the Settlement of Investment Disputes between States and Nationals of other States of 1965 (ICSID Convention), which established the ICSID under

---

[63] Born, *International Arbitration*, p. 57.
[64] Feris and Ripley-Evans, 'Challenges, opportunities and road ahead'.
[65] Ignacio Gomez-Palacio, 'International commercial arbitration: two cultures in a state of courtship and potential marriage of convenience' (2009) 20 *American Review of International Arbitration* 235–256 at 238.
[66] Feris and Ripley-Evans, 'Challenges, opportunities and road ahead'.
[67] Feris, 'An international arbitration system'.

the auspices of the World Bank. The BRICS member states should discuss whether the creation of an arbitral institution should include an investment dispute resolution mechanism and not merely be an institution for the settlement of commercial disputes. The creation of such an institution must reflect the close relations between the BRICS countries while providing a further instrument for increasing economic cooperation.[68]

Finally, the BRICS member states need to decide whether, in addition to creating a new arbitral institution or remodeling the existing ones, they are going to draft new trade and investment treaties providing for the use of such arbitral institutions in the case of disputes.[69] If this is the case, the member states need to discuss how such international investment agreements would differ from the existing investment treaties, which already provide protection to investors between certain BRICS member states.[70]

V. Conclusion

In the global market of international arbitration, success is measured by how effective arbitral institutions are in transforming their jurisdiction into a hub for arbitration that parties are willing to travel to in the case that any dispute arises. Setting up an arbitral institution requires long-term strategic planning, patience and constant monitoring. The first stage is the creation of the centre, with a proper structure (management board, administrative staff, list of arbitrators and physical infrastructure) and legal framework (namely institutional rules). After the inception of the centre, it is necessary to 'put it on the market': to let potential 'clients' know that a new institution has been created with a view to satisfying their potential needs for dispute resolution services. This entails marketing the idea and convincing traders of its potential and advantages. Any BRICS-centred institutions, whether created from scratch or based on preexisting institutions, should publicize their work adequately. Otherwise, many parties will not know about the arbitration opportunities that they offer. However, this is not enough. The usefulness of a centre will only be assessed when parties actually refer real disputes to it. Naturally, this may take several years.

Once a centre has been created and put on the market, it has to establish a good reputation to persuade parties to choose it as a provider of arbitration services. However, this creates a sort of chicken-and-egg problem, as a centre is unlikely to be able to establish a good track record for ten to fifteen years. Two problems spring from this: a lack of interest and

[68] Ibid.   [69] Ibid.   [70] Ibid.

a lack of funds.[71] The popularity of international arbitration is dependent on market forces and whether the demands of customers are satisfied. For a centre to prove its quality, it needs to be used. Only in this third stage will the centre enter into action. During the two first phases, the centre is in a standby position. Nevertheless, such an initial stage should not mean inactivity. Quite to the contrary, during this period the centre ought to promote its services actively, making itself noticed. Because of its novelty and inexperience, the centre needs to engage in a continuous effort that may be under the radar, but is essential for achieving noticeable results in the future. The development of a fully active caseload is a gradual process. It will be a decade or longer before a sufficiently large number of companies will have used the BRICS Dispute Resolution Centre.

The expansion of international trade and the propagation of international arbitration have led to the emergence of multiple arbitral institutions throughout the world. These institutions compete fiercely to attract arbitration proceedings. International arbitration is now a global business, the market of international arbitration is expanding and many cities and jurisdictions are positioning themselves to collect a share of that market. The emergence of new arbitral centres is enlarging the pool of available institutions, giving parties the possibility to choose institutions with closer cultural affinity and greater geographic or linguistic convenience. However, the unfolding of the globalization process also puts pressure on legal cultures: National legal cultures that were more or less autonomous are now subject to a multiplicity of external pressures because of the increasing number of transnational interactions.[72] Culturally diversified participants are entering the global competition. This cultural multiplicity results in the modification of the market, which is increasingly populated and influenced by non-European and non-Western countries, companies and individuals. Such cultural diversity requires arbitration practitioners to be cognizant of different approaches to arbitration taken in various countries.[73]

Similarly, every arbitral institution has a distinct culture, a particular way of acting that distinguishes it from other institutions. Institutions are social communities as well. They often function in a world of their own,

---

[71] Robert Clow and Patrick Stewart, 'International arbitration: storming the citadels' (1990) 9 *International Financial Law Review* 10–13.

[72] Tom Ginsburg, 'The culture of arbitration' (2003) 36 *Vanderbilt Journal of Transnational Law* 1335–1345 at 1337.

[73] Sharon Thomas, 'International arbitration: a historical perspective and practice guide connecting four emerging world cultures: China, Mexico, Nigeria, and Saudi Arabia' (2006) 17 *American Review of International Arbitration* 183–238 at 183–184.

performing similarly to a city or country and having a particular culture that expresses itself through the behaviors, values and assumptions of the diverse groups and individuals that make up the institution. In the field of arbitration, the most important factors determining institutional culture appear to be communication, expectation and understanding. Regardless of how developed and convergent the systems and processes might be, each arbitral institution necessarily has its own distinctive culture that makes it attractive to some and unattractive to others.[74]

International arbitration is deeply dependent on the neutrality of arbitral institutions and arbitral tribunals. To be perceived as culturally unbiased and neutral, arbitral institutions should pay close attention to the differences among the national cultures and different legal traditions of the parties. Their institutional architecture should be transparent and flexible to accommodate a diversity of cultural and legal backgrounds and expectations. The goal is to ensure that each party feels that it is taking part in the arbitration proceedings in a fair and equitable manner, with no preconceived ideas or hidden bias. Achieving this objective often requires inherent tensions to be addressed and compromises reached. A shared debate among actors from the different cultures to determine the most adequate form and principles of the arbitration mechanism is demanded. Opening the discussion to government officials, practitioners, commercial entrepreneurs, professional associations and other interested parties is of the essence. This requires an open mind towards new members, new ideas and new cultures. Arbitral institutions will only succeed in a globalized world if they are willing to commit constantly to modernization, not only by adopting rules to suit the ever-changing needs of the market but also by understanding and addressing the different cultural and legal backgrounds and expectations of their end users. These are some of the factors that the BRICS member states should bear in mind when establishing their own arbitral institution.

VI. References

Ali, Shahla F., 'Approaching the global arbitration table: comparing the advantages of arbitration as seen by practitioners in East Asia and the West' (2009) 28 *Review of Litigation* 735–789.

Berger, Klaus P., *International Economic Arbitration* (Deventer: Kluwer Law and Taxation Publishers, 1993).

---

[74] Won Kidane, *China–Africa Dispute Settlement: The Law, Economics and Culture of Arbitration* (Wolters Kluwer International, 2012), p. 288.

Blackaby, Nigel, Partasides, Constantine, Redfern, Alan and Hunter, Martin, *Redfern and Hunter on International Arbitration*, 5th edn (Oxford: Oxford University Press, 2009).

Born, Gary B., *International Arbitration and Forum Selection Agreements: Drafting and Enforcing*, 4th edn (Alphen aan den Rijn: Kluwer Law International, 2013).

BRICS India 2016, 'About BRICS'; available at http://brics2016.gov.in/content/innerpage/about-usphp.php [accessed on 25 October 2016].

Brodermann, Eckart and Weimann, Thomas, 'CEAC', in Gerhard Wegen and Stephan Wilske (eds.), *Getting the Deal through: Arbitration 2012* (London: Law Business Research Ltd, 2012).

Clow, Robert and Stewart, Patrick, 'International arbitration: storming the citadels' (1990) 9 *International Financial Law Review* 10–13.

David, René, *Arbitration in International Trade* (Deventer: Kluwer Law, 1985).

Dezalay, Yves and Garth, Bryant G., 'Merchants of law as moral entrepreneurs: constructing international justice from the competition for transnational business disputes' (1995) 29 *Law and Society Review* 27–64.

Dwivedi, Abhishek, 'India pursues a new investment arbitration regime to protect itself', *Swarajya*, 18 September 2016; available at http://swarajyamag.com/world/india-pursues-a-new-investment-arbitration-regime-to-protect-itself [accessed on 25 October 2016].

Feris, Jackwell, 'An international arbitration system for BRICS – is it an imperative for further economic cooperation', *Lexology*, 18 August 2016; available at www.lexology.com/library/detail.aspx?g=6541959b-3054-4821-a55a-672e00c4776c [accessed on 25 October 2016].

Feris, Jackwell and Ripley-Evans, Jonathan, 'Challenges, opportunities and road ahead for international arbitration in BRICS', *Bizcommunity*, 1 September 2016; available at www.lexology.com/library/detail.aspx?g=a5432c38-44ca-4283-ac7d-3f92d46f2766 [accessed on 25 October 2016].

Ginsburg, Tom, 'The culture of arbitration' (2003) 36 *Vanderbilt Journal of Transnational Law* 1335–1345.

Ginsburg, Tom and Mosk, Richard M., 'Becoming an international arbitrator: qualifications, disclosures, conduct, and removal', in Daniel M. Kolkey, Richard Chernick and Barbara Reeves Neal (eds.), *The Practitioner's Handbook of International Arbitration and Mediation* (New York: Juris Net, 2012).

Goldstajn, Aleksandar, 'Choice of international arbitrators, arbitral tribunals and centres: legal and sociological aspects', in Petar Sarcevic (ed.), *Essays on International Commercial Arbitration* (London: Graham & Trotman, 1989).

Gomez-Palacio, Ignacio, 'International commercial arbitration: two cultures in a state of courtship and potential marriage of convenience' (2009) 20 *American Review of International Arbitration* 235–256.

Halliday, Terence C. and Osinsky, Pavel, 'Globalization of law' (2006) 32 *Annual Review of Sociology* 447–470.

Kaszubska, Katarzyna, 'A BRICS-only arbitration forum will not be the panacea imagined', *The Wire*, 9 September 2016; available at http://thewire.in/64641/a-brics-only-arbitration-forum-will-not-be-the-panacea-they-are-hoping-for [accessed on 25 October 2016].

Kidane, Won, *China–Africa Dispute Settlement: The Law, Economics and Culture of Arbitration* (Alphen aan den Rijn: Wolters Kluwer International, 2012).

KNN – Knowledge & News Network, 'Jaitley to inaugurate conference on 'Intl Arbitration in BRICS: Challenges, Opportunities & Road Ahead' on Aug 27', *KNN – Knowledge & News Network*, 24 August 2016; available at http://knnindia.co.in/news/newsdetails/global/jaitley-to-inaugurate-conference-on-intl-arbitration-in-brics-challenges-opportunities-road-ahead-on-aug-27 [accessed on 25 October 2016].

Krishnan, Murali, 'Why do BRICS countries produce so few global arbitrators, asks Law MinRavi Shankar Prasad', *Bar & Bench*, 28 August 2016; available at http://barandbench.com/brics-countries-produce-global-arbitrators-asks-law-min-ravi-shankar-prasad [accessed on 25 October 2016].

Lynch, Katherine L., *The Forces of Economic Globalization: Challenges to the Regime of International Commercial Arbitration* (The Hague: Kluwer Law International, 2003).

McClelland, Arden C., 'International arbitration: a practical guide to the system for the litigation of transnational commercial disputes' (1977) 17 *Virginia Journal of International Law* 729–754.

McLean, David J., 'Toward a new international dispute resolution paradigm: assessing the congruent evolution of globalization and international arbitration' (2009) 30 *University of Pennsylvania Journal of International Law* 1087–1097.

Mistelis, Loukas A., 'International arbitration – corporate attitudes and practices. 12 perceptions tested: myths, data and analysis research report' (2004) 15 *American Revue of International Arbitration* 525–591.

Moser, Michael J. and Yuen, Peter, 'Arbitration outside China', in Michael J. Moser (ed.), *Managing Business Disputes in Today's China: Duelling with Dragons* (Alphen aan den Rijn: Kluwer Law International, 2007).

Ostrove, Michael, Salomon, Claudia and Shifman, Bette (eds.), *Choice of Venue in International Arbitration* (Oxford: Oxford University Press, 2014).

Press Trust of India, 'Arun Jaitley pitches for BRICS arbitration platform to cut dependence on developed nations', *Economic Times*, 28 August 2016; available at http://economictimes.indiatimes.com/news/economy/policy/arun-jaitley-pitches-for-brics-arbitration-platform-to-cut-dependence-on-developed-nations/articleshow/53890040.cms [accessed on 25 October 2016].

'Finance Minister to inaugurate BRICS meet on arbitration', *Business Standard*, 24 August 2016; available at www.business-standard.com/article/ international/finance-minister-to-inaugurate-brics-meet-on-arbitration-116082400587_1.html [accessed on 25 October 2016].

Sachs, Jeffrey, 'International economics: unlocking the mysteries of globalization' (1998) 110 *Foreign Policy* 97–111.

Sahu, Prasanta, 'After bank, BRICS nations now mull rating agency', *Financial Express*, 11 September 2016; available at www.financialexpress.com/ economy/after-bank-brics-nations-now-mull-rating-agency/373278 [accessed on 25 October 2016].

Schlaepfer, Anne V. and Petti, Angelina M., 'Institutional versus ad hoc arbitration', in Elliott Geisinger and Nathalie Voser (eds.), *International Arbitration in Switzerland. A Handbook for Practitioners*, 2nd edn (Alphen aan den Rijn: Kluwer Law International, 2013), pp. 13–24.

Sen, Shreeja, 'Arun Jaitley proposes task force for arbitral centres for Brics countries', *Live Mint*, 27 August 2016; available at www.livemint .com/Politics/y9OTm8JZKnNrhSOSnFqkDL/Arun-Jaitley-pitches-for-Brics-arbitration-platform.html [accessed on 25 October 2016].

Shrivastav, Avni, 'Third BRICS Legal Forum begins in Delhi', *Live Law*, 11 September 2016; available at www.livelaw.in/third-brics-legal-forum-begins-delhi [accessed on 25 October 2016].

Siliconindia, 'International arbitration structure skewed in favour of developed nations', *Siliconindia*, 28 August 2016; available at www .siliconindia.com/news/general/International-Arbitration-Structure-Skewed-In-Favour-Of-Developed-Nations-nid-197971-cid-1.html [accessed on 25 October 2016].

Simões, Fernando Dias, *Commercial Arbitration between China and the Portuguese-Speaking World* (Alphen aan den Rijn: Kluwer Law International, 2014).

'Institutional culture in international arbitration' (2016) 27(3) *Australasian Dispute Resolution Journal* 188–197.

SME Times News Bureau, 'BRICS nations need to engage on own arbitration centres: FM', *SME Times*, 29 August 2016; available at www.smetimes .in/smetimes/news/top-stories/2016/Aug/29/brics-nations-need-to-engage-on-own-arbitration-centres1633507.html [accessed on 25 October 2016].

Strong, S. I., 'Navigating the borders between international commercial arbitration and U.S. federal courts: a jurisprudential GPS' (2012) *Journal of Dispute Resolution* 119–216.

The Hindu, 'Own arbitration tool must for BRICS', *The Hindu*, 27 August 2016; available at www.thehindu.com/business/Economy/own-arbitration-tool-must-for-brics/article9040735.ece [accessed on 25 October 2016].

Thomas, Sharon, 'International arbitration: a historical perspective and practice guide connecting four emerging world cultures: China, Mexico, Nigeria, and

Saudi Arabia' (2006) 17 *American Review of International Arbitration* 183–238.

Twining, William, *Globalisation and Legal Theory* (Cambridge: Cambridge University Press, 2000).

Werner, Jacques, 'International commercial arbitrators: from merchant to academic to skilled professional' (1998) 4(3) *Dispute Resolution Magazine* 22–24.

ZeeBiz WebTeam, 'Arun Jaitley wants a "world class" BRICS arbitration mechanism', *Zeebiz*, 28 August 2016; available at www.zeebiz.com/india/news-arun-jaitley-wants-a-world-class-brics-arbitration-mechanism-5464 [accessed on 25 October 2016].

14

Legal and Policy Aspects of Space Cooperation in the BRICS Region

Inventory, Challenges and Opportunities

YUN ZHAO

I. Introduction

Since the launch of the first artificial satellite in 1957,[1] international society has emphasized the importance of cooperation in space. The United Nations has advocated the principle of international space cooperation on various occasions, to be demonstrated by the adoption of a series of documents elaborating on this principle. The most recent achievement is the adoption by the UN General Assembly (UNGA) in 1996 of the Declaration on International Cooperation in the Exploration and Use of Outer Space for the Benefit and in the Interest of All States, Taking into Particular Account the Needs of Developing Countries.[2] This document illustrates the means (formal requirements) and factors (substantive requirements) to be considered in applying the principle of international space cooperation. It is to be noted that it elaborates this principle in the broadest sense, encouraging space cooperation to be carried out in various manners and approaches and at all levels.[3]

While emphasizing the importance of space cooperation at the international level, one cannot disregard the special role that bilateral or regional cooperation can play in promoting the development of space activities and

---

[1] On 4 October 1957, the Union of Soviet Socialist Republics (USSR) launched 'Sputnik-1', the first artificial satellite. See further: Steve Garber, 'Sputnik and the Dawn of the Space Age', 10 October 2007; available at http://history.nasa.gov/sputnik/ [accessed on 26 May 2016].

[2] UNGA resolution 51/122, 13 December 1996.

[3] Ibid., Articles 2, 4. The modes of cooperation as listed include governmental and non-governmental cooperation; cooperation in commercial and noncommercial matters; and global, multilateral, regional or bilateral cooperation. International cooperation can also be conducted among countries at all levels of development, including between space-faring

ensuring the realization of space security.[4] With more and more countries joining the space club, international space cooperation will face many
challenges and difficulties in view of the diversified state interests in this
strategic field,[5] and bilateral and regional cooperation has proven to be a
feasible and relatively easy way for countries with similar history and culture to work together in the space field, ultimately leading to space cooperation at the international level.[6]

The BRICS countries – Brazil, Russia, India, China and South Africa –
all being developing countries, grouped together and formed a flexible
political and economic bloc in 2009. This provides a platform for these five
countries on which to coordinate and cooperate on various issues. While
space activities are not specifically mentioned in the area of cooperation,

and non–space-faring nations, and cooperation between developing and developed countries. While taking an open attitude towards the formal elements of cooperation, the resolution emphasizes the importance of several substantive requirements for long-term cooperation. The principle of party autonomy should be respected in the first place in international
space cooperation. The countries themselves are in a position to decide on the appropriateness and effectiveness of certain modes of cooperation; however, it is necessary to set minimum standards for such cooperation in order to protect the rights and legitimate interests
of countries.

[4] Frank A. Rose, 'Promoting the Long-Term Sustainability and Security of the Space Environment'; available at www.state.gov/t/avc/rls/2015/250140.htm [accessed on 26 May 2016].

[5] Challenges include the traditional legal issue of the delimitation between airspace and outer
space; with more emerging space-faring countries and different national interests, it is
becoming more difficult for these countries to cooperate with each other to reach a consensus on this issue. See further: Michael Listner, 'Could Commercial Space Help Define
and Delimitate the Boundaries of Outer Space?' 29 October 2012, *Space Review*; available
at www.thespacereview.com/article/2180/1 [accessed on 26 May 2016]. Moreover, with the
prevalence of space militarization and potential space weaponization, due to the different
interests of various countries, it is not realistic for these space-faring countries to cooperate in a smooth way to reach a consensus on a particular initiative in a short period of
time. As example is the Prevention of the Placement of Weapons in Outer Space and of
the Threat or Use of Force against Outer Space Objects drafted by Russia and China, as its
potential for becoming an internationally binding treaty is pessimistic due to conflicts of
interests between various states. See further: Michael Listner and Rajeswari P. Rajagopalan,
'The 2014 PPWT: A New Draft but with the Same and Different Problems', 11 August 2014,
Space Review; available at www.thespacereview.com/article/2575/1 [accessed on 26 May
2016].

[6] For example, China reached bilateral agreements with Brazil in developing the Chinese-
Brazilian Earth Resources Satellites (CBERS). This bilateral cooperative framework has
proven to be the most successful South–South space cooperation model and has led to
fruitful results. For the development of bilateral agreements, see further: Jose Monserrat
Filho, 'Brazilian-Chinese Space Cooperation: An Analysis', (1997) 13 *Space Policy* 153–170.
For more background information on the CBERS program, see further: www.cbers.inpe.br/
ingles/satellites/history.php [accessed on 26 May 2016].

the open and flexible nature of this platform does allow for intra-BRICS space cooperation. With the economic paradigm created by the BRICS, space exploration and cooperation among the BRICS members are both a necessity and a reality.[7]

This chapter examines the ongoing intra-BRICS space cooperation, of which bilateral cooperation is the main feature. This chapter then analyzes the reasons for the current situation and identifies the difficulties and barriers in carrying out multilateral cooperation among the BRICS members. It concludes that the widely accepted principle of space cooperation also applies to the BRICS members and that more efforts are needed to realize the wider scope of space cooperation among the members.

II. A Short History

The BRICS members share common views regarding cooperation and coordination on a wide variety of issues. It is argued that they are 'free-riding on a liberal system that provides them with great competitive advantages without taking on major responsibilities'.[8] The first BRIC summit was held in 2009, and the BRICS members hold summits annually, as well as specific meetings, if necessary, to coordinate policies in international affairs, including the reform of international institutions and financial systems.[9] BRICS, working as a whole, also has cooperated with other economic blocs, such as the European Union (EU).[10]

Space cooperation stands out as a major area for cooperation in the original framework, and the BRICS members, all being space-faring nations, have already cooperated in some form, and their efforts have become increasingly interwoven in this strategic field. As observed by Firsing, 'the friendly relationship between the BRICS countries can blast off into space'.[11] It is noted, however, that there is no program of space

---

[7] Marsha Freeman, 'BRICS Nations Aim for the Moon and Mars'; available at www .larouchepub.com/other/2014/4148brics_moon_mars.html [accessed on 26 May 2016].

[8] Miguel Otero-lglesias, 'China, the Euro and the Reform of the International Monetary System'; available at www.academia.edu/2446804/China_the_Euro_and_the_Reform_of_ the_International_Monetary_System [accessed on 7 December 2016].

[9] Alex Tuai, 'Introduction to BRICS'; available at http://ampglobalyouth.org/students/ introduction-to-brics/ [accessed on 26 May 2016].

[10] Irina Z. Yarygina, 'BRICS-EU-CIS Cooperation: Problems and Challenges'; available at www.leap2020.net/euro-brics/2014/10/22/brics-eu-cis-cooperation-problems-and-challenges/?lang=en [accessed on 26 May 2016].

[11] Scott Firsing, 'Space, BRICS' Next Frontier', *Daily Maverick*, 10 October 2011; available at www.dailymaverick.co.za/opinionista/2011-10-10-space-brics-next-frontier/# .VwtMo-_ovcs [accessed on 26 May 2016].

cooperation among the BRICS countries; the ongoing cooperation is largely limited to bilateral levels.[12]

A. China

The successful launch of the Dong Fang Hong-1 satellite signified the start of the space age in China.[13] Since then, space technologies have developed rapidly; so far China has launched more than one hundred satellites for scientific, military and commercial purposes.[14] The first decade of the twenty-first century witnessed the launch of six Chinese astronauts into space on three occasions.[15]

China has acceded to four space treaties (1967 Outer Space Treaty,[16] 1968 Rescue Agreement,[17] 1972 Liability Convention[18] and 1975 Registration Convention[19]). It is a member of many international space organizations.[20] To facilitate regional cooperation, China, working

---

[12] Two typical examples of bilateral cooperation among BRICS countries are as follows: first, in June 2014, Russia and China signed a memorandum of understanding on cooperation between Russia and China to synchronize their satellite navigation system, the GLONASS navigation system and China's Beidou; secondly, on 6 July 1988, the governments of Brazil and China signed a partnership agreement involving INPE (National Institute for Space Research) and CAST (Chinese Academy of Space Technology) to develop a program to build and operate two advanced remote-sensing satellites, called the CBERS Program (China-Brazil Earth Resources Satellite).

[13] See further: 'China's First Man-made Satellite'; available at www.chinaculture.org/gb/en_aboutchina/2003-09/24/content_26079.htm [accessed on 26 May 2016].

[14] These satellites are mainly used for communication, observation and navigation; for more history and the latest information about China's satellites, see the website of the Chinese official satellite launching center; available at www.cgwic.com/ [accessed on 26 May 2016].

[15] For more information about Chinese astronauts: 'List of Chinese astronauts'; available at https://en.wikipedia.org/wiki/List_of_Chinese_astronauts [accessed on 26 May 2016].

[16] Treaty on Principles Governing the Activities of States in the Exploration and Use of Outer Space, Including the Moon and Other Celestial Bodies, 610 UNTS 205.

[17] Agreement on the Rescue of Astronauts, the Return of Astronauts and the Return of Objects Launched into Outer Space, 672 UNTS 119.

[18] Convention on the International Liability for Damage Caused by Space Objects, 961 UNTS 187.

[19] Convention on Registration of Objects Launched into Outer Space, UNGA resolution 3235 (XXIX).

[20] China participates in activities organized by the International Committee on Global Navigation Satellite Systems, International Space Exploration Coordination Group, Inter-Agency Space Debris Coordination Committee, Group on Earth Observations, World Meteorological Organization and other inter-governmental international organizations. See further: Information Office of the State Council of the People's Republic of China, 'China's Space Activities in 2011 (Part V. International Exchange and Cooperation)', 29

together with several other countries in the region, set up the Asia-Pacific Space Cooperation Organization (APSCO) in 2005.[21]

To elaborate on its space policy, the Chinese government has so far released White Papers on Space Activities in 2000, 2006 and 2011, all placing the principle of international cooperation in a high position when conducting space activities.[22] So far, Russia, Brazil and South Africa have undertaken cooperative activities.[23] As identified in the 2011 White Paper, key cooperation areas include 'scientific research areas, remote sensing applications, communications satellites applications, satellite navigation systems applications, human spaceflight (space lab/space station), space TT&C cooperation and support, commercial satellite projects, personnel exchanges and training'.[24]

B. Russia

The former Soviet Union launched the first artificial satellite in 1957, marking the start of the space age for human beings.[25] During the Cold War period, Russia and the United States were the two superpowers competing with each other in the space field. After the Cold War, Russia has remained a highly developed country in the field of space technologies.[26] Since the retirement of the space shuttle program, Russia's Soyuz spacecraft has been the sole transport vehicle for astronauts traveling to and from the International Space Station (ISS).[27]

The president of the Russian Federation is in charge of the general management of space activities. The Russian government, in particular the

December 2011; available at www.china.org.cn/government/whitepaper/node_7145648 .htm [accessed on 26 May 2016].

[21] See further: 'History of APSCO'; available at www.apsco.int/AboutApscosS .asp?LinkNameW1=History_of_APSCO&LinkNameW2=Signing_of_APSCO_ Convention&LinkCodeN3=11172&LinkCodeN=17 [accessed on 26 May 2016].

[22] Yun Zhao, *National Space Law in China: An Overview of the Current Situation and Outlook for the Future* (Leiden: Brill Nijhoff, 2015), p. 11.

[23] See note 20, 'Bilateral Cooperation' in 'China's Space Activities in 2011 (Part V. International Exchange and Cooperation)'.

[24] See note 20, 'Key Cooperation Areas' in 'China's Space Activities in 2011 (Part V. International Exchange and Cooperation)'.

[25] Stephan Hobe, 'Historical Background', in Stephan Hobe et al. (eds.), *Cologne Commentary on Space Law: Outer Space Treaty* (Luxemburg: Carl Heymanns Verlag, 2009), vol. 1, p. 4.

[26] Francis Lyall and Paul B. Larsen, *Space Law: A Treatise* (Ashgate Publishing, 2009), p. 1.

[27] Anthony Wood, 'American Independence in Space: Ending Reliance on the Soyuz Spacecraft by 2017', 12 January 2015; available at www.gizmag.com/nasa-boeing-spacex-iss-soyuz-dragon-cst100-roscosmos/35543/ [accessed on 26 May 2016].

Ministry of Defense, coordinates matters of international space cooperation and supervises international space projects on behalf of the Russian Federation.[28] The Federal Space Agency (Roscosmos), as an independent authority in charge of civil space activities, undertakes international space cooperation with foreign space entities and international organizations.[29] It can be party to international agreements for the purpose of space cooperation.

At the moment, Russia is a member of the four space treaties (Outer Space Treaty, Rescue Agreement, Liability Convention and Registration Convention). It has intergovernmental agreements with around twenty countries, including China, Brazil, India and South Africa. Russia is also a partner state to the 1998 Intergovernmental Agreement on the ISS.[30]

C. India

India is a major space-faring nation in the Asia-Pacific region, and it is seen by the international community as an emerging space power capable of achieving its goals using a cost-effective and time-efficient approach. The principle of international cooperation is a major part of India's space policy.[31] India has currently reached cooperation agreements with more than thirty countries in the areas of the peaceful use of outer space,[32] such as for remote sensing of Earth, satellite communication, launch services, telemetry and tracking support, space exploration, space law and capacity building.[33]

---

[28] See further: 'Section II. Organization of Space Activity' of 'Law of the Russian Federation 'About Space Activity'', Decree No. 5663-1 of the Russian House of Soviets.

[29] Elizabeth Howell, 'Roscosmos: Russia's Space Agency', 17 May 2016; available at www.space .com/22724-roscosmos.html [accessed on 26 May 2016].

[30] Agreement among the Government of Canada, Governments of the Member States of the European Space Agency, the Government of Japan, the Government of the Russian Federation, and the Government of the United States of America Concerning Cooperation on the Civil International Space Station, 1998.

[31] See further: 'India's Space Policy'; available at www.isro.gov.in/indias-space-policy [accessed on 26 May 2016].

[32] The countries that cooperate with India in the field of outer space include the major space-faring nations, Russia, the United Kingdom, the United States and Japan; in addition to these major space countries, Syria, Spain, Sweden, Thailand, Norway, Peru, The Netherlands, Ukraine, Argentina, Australia, Brazil, Brunei Darussalam, Bulgaria, Canada, Chile Egypt, France, Germany, Hungary, Indonesia, Israel, Italy, Kazakhstan, Mauritius, Mongolia, Myanmar, Republic of Korea and Saudi Arabia and Venezuela are also involved.

[33] Staff writer, 'India Has Space Cooperation with 33 Nations', 30 July 2014; available at www .ndtv.com/india-news/india-has-space-cooperation-with-33-nations-599448 [accessed on 26 May 2016].

The Indian Space Research Organization (ISRO), as a national space bureau, undertakes the responsibility to manage civil space programs, which includes maintaining existing cooperation at an optimum level.[34] Over recent years, as ISRO has become increasingly mature in experience and technological capabilities, the scope for cooperation has become multifaceted and advanced.[35] In addition to this cooperation in traditional space areas, ISRO is also pursuing cooperation in advanced areas of space science and technology, including deep-space navigation and communication support for space exploration missions, the joint realization of Earth observation satellites with advanced scientific instruments, capacity building and disaster management support.[36]

In response to the UNGA Resolution (45/72 of 11 December 1990), the Centre for Space Science and Technology Education in Asia and the Pacific (CSSTEAP) has been set up in India.[37] The main objective of this regional institution is to enhance member countries' knowledge, understanding and practical experience in those aspects of space science and technology that have the potential for a greater impact on their economic and social development, including the preservation of the environment.[38] This center is affiliated with the UN, and its space-related education programs are providing rich resources for space industry development in the Asia-Pacific region. CSSTEAP could also be seen as an international cooperation platform for the BRICS countries. As well as India's existing space cooperation with Russia and Brazil,[39] negotiations and

---

[34] See more information about ISRO at www.isro.gov.in/about-isro/genesis [accessed on 26 May 2016].

[35] ISRO has had the benefit of international cooperation since its inception. The establishment of the Thumba Equatorial Rocket Launching Station (TERLS); the conduct of the Satellite Instructional Television Experiment (SITE) and Satellite Telecommunication Experiment Project (STEP); the launches of Aryabhata, Bhaskara, Ariane Passenger Payload Experiment (APPLE), IRS-IA, IRS-IB satellites, INSAT series of satellites, Mission to Moon, Human Space Flight Programme Initiatives, etc., have components of international cooperation; available at www.isro.gov.in/international-cooperation#sthash .fKpalCHq.dpuf [accessed on 26 May 2016].

[36] Staff writer, 'India Has Space Cooperation with 33 Nations'.

[37] The Center for Space Science and Technology Education in Asia and the Pacific (CSSTEAP) was established in India on 1 November 1995 under an agreement signed initially by ten member countries of the region. It is hosted by the government of India with the Department of Space (DOS) as the nodal agency. For more information about CSSTEAP, see: www.cssteap.org/, [accessed on 26 May 2016].

[38] See more about the background of the CSSTEAP; available at www.cssteap.org/ background; [accessed on 26 May 2016].

[39] More information about 'International Cooperation'; See further: www.isro.gov.in/ international-cooperation [accessed on 26 May 2016].

discussions are well on the way for cooperation between India and other BRICS members.[40]

D. *Brazil*

Brazil has had a space program since the 1960s, and the national governmental organization related to the Brazilian space industry is the Brazilian Space Agency (abbreviated in Brazilian Portuguese as AEB).[41] The AEB is a civilian authority under the aegis of the Executive Office of the President of Brazil, established by law on 10 February 1994. The AEB is responsible for formulating and coordinating Brazilian space policy, and it plays a role in facilitating Brazilian governmental autonomy over the space sector.[42]

Brazil's strategy for space is outlined in its 2005 National Program of Space Activities (PNAE) nine-year plan.[43] In the past decade, the Brazilian space program has largely focused on 'utilitarian satellite designs used for communications and observation,'[44] and thus, at the current stage, Brazil is focused on the development of space-based applications addressing the needs of citizens.[45]

The AEB pays special attention to the promotion of international cooperation and has sought to promote the technological capacity of the Brazilian space industry to meet the needs of the country.[46] Intergovernmental framework agreements were signed with nine countries and one international organization regarding cooperation for the peaceful uses

[40] K. S. Jayaraman, 'India and China Sign Space Cooperation Pact', 22 September 2014; available at http://spacenews.com/41942india-and-china-sign-space-cooperation-pact/ [accessed on 26 May 2016].
[41] See more information about Global Space Programs; available at www.spacefoundation .org/programs/public-policy-and-government-affairs/introduction-space/global-space-programs [accessed on 26 May 2016].
[42] See the official website of the AEB; available at www.aeb.gov.br/institucional/sobre-a-aeb/ [accessed on 26 May 2016].
[43] Brazil National Program of Space Activities (2005–2014); available at www.aeb.gov.br/ wp-content/uploads/2013/03/PNAE_INGLES.pdf [accessed on 26 May 2016].
[44] Matthew Bodner, 'Russia to Propose BRICS Space Station', 27 January 2015; available at www.themoscowtimes.com/business/article/russia-to-propose-brics-space-station/ 514972.html [accessed on 26 May 2016]; São José Dos Campos, 'Brazil's Space Programme', 8 August 2015; available at www.economist.com/news/americas/21660572-rocket-science-hard-rocket-diplomacy-harder-ten-nine-ten [accessed on 26 May 2016].
[45] 'The Space Sector in Brazil – An Overview'; available at www.globalsecurity.org/space/ library/report/2003/brazilspace.pdf [accessed on 26 May 2016].
[46] See the official website of the AEB; available at www.aeb.gov.br/institucional/sobre-a-aeb/ [accessed on 26 May 2016].

of outer space.[47] These agreements are generators of new international instruments and initiatives that have led to the development of bilateral space programs.

E.   South Africa

The South African National Space Agency (SANSA) was established in 2010 to promote the use of space and cooperation with other space-faring countries, with the intent of optimizing and maximizing the advantages of space-related services and applications to society.[48]

The start of South Africa's relationship with outer space dates back to the 1950s, and since then it has been an active participant in the international space field with an indispensable space infrastructure. Until now, however, South Africa has had no independent launching capability.[49] It identifies one of the aims of space activities in its National Space Agency Act as to 'foster international cooperation in space-related activities'[50] by encouraging research in space science, promoting scientific engineering through human capital and creating an environment where its space technologies could be utilized within the national industrial framework.[51] Some achievements have been realized by the SANSA, such as the signing of the JRC/SANSA collaboration agreement.[52]

III.   BRICS Cooperation: Past, Present and Future

A.   China-Russia Space Cooperation

The cooperation between China and Russia is mainly driven by the political and economic needs of both countries at the international

---

[47] See the official website of the AEB; available at www.aeb.gov.br/institucional/sobre-a-aeb/ [accessed on 26 May 2016].

[48] See more information at the official website of the SANSA: available at www.sansa.org.za/ overview/history [accessed on 26 May 2016].

[49] Keith Campbell, 'South Africa to Relook at Space Launch Capability to Strengthen Space Skills', 5 March 2010; available at www.engineeringnews.co.za/article/sa-to-look-again-at-space-launch-capability-and-strengthen-space-skills-2010-03-05 [accessed on 26 May 2016].

[50] South Africa National Space Agency Act, 36 of 2008, section 4 (e).

[51] See more information at the official website of the SANSA: available at www.sansa.org.za/ overview/history [accessed on 26 May 2016].

[52] 'Scientific cooperation agreement with South Africa's Space Agency'; available at https://ec. europa.eu/jrc/en/news/scientific-cooperation-agreement-south-africa-s-space-agency-7004 [accessed on 26 May 2016].

level.[53] China started its cooperation with the Former Soviet Union in the 1950s in the sales of missiles.[54] In May 1990, both countries signed an agreement to cooperate on ten projects in the fields of satellite navigation, space surveillance, propulsion, satellite communications, materials, intelligence sharing and space system testing.[55]

To date China has cooperated closey with Russia in a wide range of space activities, including satellite navigation, joint deep-space research, moon exploration and manned space missions.[56] A joint subcommittee on space cooperation was established in 2000 to provide a forum for regular meetings between the prime ministers of the two countries.[57] In 2002, both countries agreed to cooperate in thirteen areas, including remote sensing, telecommunications and navigation.[58] The work of this subcommittee led to the conclusion of two multiannual cooperation agreements for projects such as moon and Mars missions.[59] Most recently, the China National Space Administration signed a cooperation agreement with Russia's space agency Roscosmos, concerning navigation technologies and the use of the Russian satellite navigation system GLONASS.[60] This agreement provides the basis for deeper and broader cooperation between the two countries.[61]

---

[53] See more: 'Russia and China: From Cooperation to Synergy', 12 October 2011; available at www.rt.com/politics/official-word/russia-china-economy-putin-637/ [accessed on 26 May 2016].

[54] Brian Harvey, *China's Space Program – From Conception to Manned Spaceflight* (Chichester: Springer-Praxis, 2004), p. 24.

[55] Mark A. Stokes, 'China's Strategic Modernization: Implications for the United States', September 1999, at 184; available at https://fas.org/nuke/guide/china/doctrine/chinamod.pdf [accessed on 26 May 2016].

[56] Matthew Bodner, 'Russia, China Sign Space Exploration Agreement', *Moscow Times*, 19 May 2014; available at www.themoscowtimes.com/business/article/russia-china-sign-space-exploration-agreement/500463.html [accessed on 26 May 2016].

[57] See further: 'Chinese, Russian PMs Sign Joint Communique', 3 November 2000; available at http://en.people.cn/english/200011/03/eng20001103_54286.html [accessed on 26 May 2016].

[58] Pravda. Ru, 'Russia, China Specify Areas of Bilateral Space Cooperation', 12 August 2002; available at www.pravdareport.com/news/world/12-08-2002/15694-0/#sthash.U2ruipnu.dpuf [accessed on 26 May 2016].

[59] Charlotte Mathieu, European Space Policy Institute, 'Assessing Russia's Space Cooperation with China and India: Opportunities and Challenges for Europe', Report 12, June 2008, at 21.

[60] See: 'Russia, China Sign Range of Space Industry Agreements'; available at http://sputniknews.com/world/20151217/1031906991/russia-china-space-industry.html [accessed on 26 May 2016].

[61] Staff Writers, 'Russia, China Sign Range of Space Industry Agreements', *Space Daily*, 21 December 2015; available at www.spacedaily.com/reports/Russia_China_Sign_Range_of_Space_Industry_Agreements_999.html [accessed on 26 May 2016].

China and Russia also cooperate in international forums on important legal issues. For example, in the field of nonweaponization in outer space, both countries co-sponsored the draft Treaty on the Prevention of the Placement of Weapons in Outer Space and of the Threat or Use of Force against Outer Space Objects (PPWT) at the Conference on Disarmament in Geneva in February 2008, and resubmitted a new version of the PPWT on 10 June 2014.[62]

B. China-Brazil Space Cooperation

China and Brazil started cooperating on space ventures in 1984 when the two governments reached a complementary agreement on space cooperation, in the framework agreement on cooperation in science and technology.[63] Four years later, both countries, represented by theBrazilian National Institute for Space Research (INPE) and Chinese Academy of Space Technology (CAST), signed an agreement on a cooperative program to develop, build and operate two remote sensing satellites named the China-Brazil Earth Resources Satellite (CBERS).[64] The cooperative agreement between China and Brazil is the first successful example of space cooperation between developing countries.[65]

The CBERS project, benefiting both countries, represents the first successful South-South cooperation in the field of space technology around the world. China, having initiated its economic reform in the late 1970s, needs an international strategic partner to cooperate in developing advanced space technologies. This coincided with Brazil's urgent needs to establish new international partnerships after the fall of its military regime, in particular in developing medium-size satellites.[66] After successful launches of the first two remote sensing satellites (CBERS-1 and CBERS-2) in 1999 and 2003, respectively, China and Brazil extended

---

[62] Michael Listner and Rajeswari Pillai Rajagopalan, 'The 2014 PPWT: A New Draft but with the Same and Different Problems', *Space Review*, 11 August 2014; available at www.thespacereview.com/article/2575/1 [accessed on 26 May 2016].

[63] See further: 'China–Brazil Earth Resources Satellite Program'; available at https://en.wikipedia.org/wiki/China%E2%80%93Brazil_Earth_Resources_Satellite_program [accessed on 26 May 2016].

[64] See more information on the background of cooperation at the CBERS Official website; available at www.cbers.inpe.br/ingles/satellites/history.php [accessed on 26 May 2016].

[65] V. Leister, 'South to South Cooperation in Outer Space: The Brazil-China Agreement', *Proceedings of the 32nd IISL Colloquium on the Law of Outer Space*, October 1989, Torremolinos-Malaga (Washington: AIAA, 1990), at 15.

[66] Filho Josémonserrat, 'Brazilian-Chinese Space Cooperation: An Analysis', (1997) 13 *Space Policy* 153–170.

their cooperation by launching new satellites, with Brazil assuming more responsibility (50 percent for each party, instead of 30 percent for Brazil and 70 percent for China in the first two satellite launches).[67]

The cooperation benefits not only the two countries but also other developing countries, as the 'CBERS Program' was initiated for the free distribution of remote sensing images to all African countries, thereby featuring an open access data policy.[68] Through this cooperative project, both countries 'transformed themselves from data users to exporters.'[69] The China-Brazil cooperation provides a vivid example of cooperation between two major developing countries in the high-technology field, regardless of the difference in their stages of space development.[70]

C. Russia-Brazil Space Cooperation

Russia and Brazil have undertaken much cooperation in the space field. As a highly advanced nation, Russia was able to provide opportunities for Brazil to participate in relevant space activities and help Brazil to improve its space capabilities. Russia assisted Brazil in updating the Brazilian Satellite Launch Vehicle (VLS-1) after a deadly accident on 23 August 2003.[71] The more spectacular achievement resulting from the bilateral cooperation was the boarding of the first Brazilian astronaut, Marcos Pontes, on the Russian Soyuz TMA-8 in 2006.[72] In 2012, Brazil became the first state outside Russia to host a station of the Russian Global Navigation Satellite System (GLONASS), which marked a new stage in the cooperation between these two countries.[73]

---

[67] Brian Harvey, *China's Space Program – From Conception to Manned Spaceflight*, p. 155.

[68] See more about the CBERS data policy; available at www.obt.inpe.br/cbers/documentos/appl_07_2004.pdf [accessed on 26 May 2016].

[69] H. Altemani de Oliveira, 'China-Brasil: Perspectivas de Cooperacion Sur-Sur', (2006) 23 *Nueva Sociedad* 138–147.

[70] Huayu Liu, 'Space Cooperation between China and Brazil', (2014) 3 *Aerospace China* 12–14.

[71] See further: 'Brazilian Rocket Explodes on Pad: Many Dead'; available at www.spacedaily.com/news/rocketscience-03zu.html [accessed on 26 May 2016].

[72] Editors of Encyclopædia Britannica, 'Marcos Pontes'; available at http://global.britannica.com/biography/Marcos-Pontes [accessed on 26 May 2016].

[73] Jürgen Treutler, 'Brazil and Russia Boost Space Cooperation with New Glonass Station', *Moscow Times*, 16 September 2015; available at www.themoscowtimes.com/business/article/brazil-and-russia-boost-space-cooperation-with-new-glonass-station/531086.html [accessed on 26 May 2016].

D. South Africa

Brazil, Russia and South Africa, as members of the Missile Technology Control Regime (MTCR), cooperate closely on the issue of export control over missile technologies and products.[74]

Mark Shuttleworth, a South African citizen, became the second space tourist on the International Space Station (ISS), with Russian assistance.[75] Russia further assisted South Africa in launching its first earth orbiting satellite, Sumbandila, in September 2009.[76] The countries signed the RadioAstron-VLBI agreement in 2013, allowing South Africa to participate in the VLBI project led by the Astro Space Centre of Lebedev Physical Institute in Moscow.[77] The South Africa-Brazil project on the A-to-A missile (20-km range) is yet another example of bilateral cooperation within the BRICS.[78]

E. India

China and India are seen to be in an Asian space race, and there is already some progress in the field of space cooperation with the recent decision of the two countries to work together on a joint system of satellites; this will allow the two BRICS members to be more independent in space activities[79] and thus moving beyond the former framework agreement on sharing remote-sensing data.[80]

---

[74] See further: 'The Missile Technology Control Regime at a Glance', November 2015; available at www.armscontrol.org/factsheets/mtcr [accessed on 26 May 2016].

[75] See more about Mark Shuttleworth; available at www.southafrica.net/za/en/articles/entry/article-southafrica.net-mark-shuttleworth [accessed on 26 May 2016].

[76] Scott Firsing, 'BRICS Are Conquering the Developing World and Space Is Next', International Policy Digest, 3 October 2011; available at http://intpolicydigest.org/2011/10/03/brics-are-conquering-the-developing-world-and-space-is-next/ [accessed on 26 May 2016].

[77] See more: 'RadioAstron: Space VLBI Mission'; available at www.asc.rssi.ru/radioastron/ [accessed on 26 May 2016].

[78] Defense Industry Daily staff, 'South Africa, Brazil's A-Darter SRAAM Hits Target', 3 November 2015; available at www.defenseindustrydaily.com/south-africa-brazil-to-develop-adarter-sraam-03286/ [accessed on 26 May 2016].

[79] 'United in Space: China, India Pave the Way to BRICS Cooperation in Space', 13 April 2016; available at http://sputniknews.com/science/20160413/1037917928/china-india-brics-space-satellite.html [accessed on 26 May 2016].

[80] K. S. Jayaraman, 'India and China Sign Space Cooperation Pact', 22 September 2014; available at http://spacenews.com/41942india-and-china-sign-space-cooperaton-pact [accessed on 26 May 2016].

Indo-Brazil cooperation in space technology is an ongoing process. Under the Indo-Brazil Committee, the two countries signed the Agenda on S&T Cooperation in January 1996, underlining bilateral cooperation in strategic areas, including space technology.[81] The Indian Space Research Organization (ISRO) and the Brazilian Space Agency (AEB) signed a Memorandum of Understanding (MOU) at Bangalore on 1 March 2002 for Cooperation in Space.[82]

Cooperation between India and Russia started in the 1960s when the Former Soviet Union assisted India in setting up the Thumba Equatorial Rocket Launching Station (TERLS).[83] The two countries have reached agreements to cooperate in a number of fields, including the development of launchers, satellite navigation, moon exploration and manned spaceflight.[84]

IV.   The Main Incentives for BRICS Cooperation

A.   Features of BRICS Space Cooperation

BRICS is a bloc aiming for cooperation, instead of competing with other international organizations, and it exercises the principles of openness, transparency and inclusiveness.[85] Space cooperation exists in a wide range of activities among the BRICS members, from space research, space technology to space exploratory projects.[86] Such cooperation varies in degree,

---

[81] Boekholt Patries, Nagle Monique, Rannala Ruta and Vullings Wieneke, 'International S&T Collaboration: Background', Report 3: Country Analysis non-EU, 1 April 2009; available at http://ec.europe.eu/research/iscp/pdf/drivers_sti_annex_3.pdf [accessed on 26 May 2016].

[82] The MOU mentions cooperation between India and Brazil in the following broad areas: cooperative programs in satellites and use of sounding rockets; studies related to satellite communications, space-based remote sensing and meteorology applications; operation of satellite ground stations and satellite mission management; organization of training programs; and the exchange of technical and scientific personnel to participate in the studies and joint working groups to examine specific issues. See more; available at www.isro.gov .in/hi/node/1025#sthash.gCvRTXOt.dpuf [accessed on 26 May 2016].

[83] Wisconsin Project on Nuclear Arms Control, 'India Missile Milestones: 1947–2005', *The Risk Report 11.6* (2005).

[84] Charlotte Mathieu, 'Assessing Russia's Space Cooperation with China and India: Opportunities and Challenges for Europe', at 24.

[85] Zhang Yan, 'BRICS Works for Shared Prosperity', *The Hindu*, 13 April 2011; available at www.hindu.com [accessed on 26 May 2016].

[86] Hartosh Singh Bal, 'BRICS in Space'; available at http://latitude.blogs.nytimes.com/2012/ 08/30/india-and-china-race-to-send-a-mission-to-mars/?_r=2 [accessed on 26 May 2016].

but the trend is clear, in that all the members are exploring ways to further the cooperation to a deeper level.[87]

BRICS, as a distinct entity, while seeking independence in economic and social development, emphasizes the importance of interdependence among its members.[88] The combination of independence and interdependence vividly shows the strategy of BRICS members in seeking a distinct role in international society.

It is clear from the discussions above that the current space cooperation among the BRICS members is primarily of bilateral nature. The bilateral cooperation is mutually beneficial to each two countries, irrespective of their developmental stage. Taking the China-Brazil cooperation as an example, both countries, making the most of their best political and technical talents, 'accomplished an excellent job at saving, resuming and enlarging' their 'historical joint project on space cooperation.'[89]

The BRICS members are mainly developing countries. As observed by Wood and Weigel, 'governments in developing countries that start satellite programs often seek support from foreign sources for technological capacity building'.[90] The China-Brazil cooperation provides the exact example for the above statement, with Brazil achieving indigenous launching capability in the end.

B.   Difficulties in Space Cooperation

Building on common interests, the BRICS members form an economic bloc, aiming to speak with a common voice and take joint actions in international economic and financial affairs.[91] Such cooperation is limited, however, for historical and cultural reasons. Compared to many other international organizations, the BRICS members are situated in four

---

[87] Marsha Freeman, 'BRICS Nations Aim for the Moon and Mars', *Executive Intelligence Review*, 5 December 2014; available at www.larouchepub.com/other/2014/4148brics_moon_mars.html [accessed on 26 May 2016].

[88] Saira Syed, 'Bric Nations Become Increasingly Interdependent', 14 April 2011; available at www.bbc.com/news/business-13046521 [accessed on 26 May 2016].

[89] Jose Monserrat Filho, 'Brazilian – Chinese Space Cooperation: An Analysis', (1997) 13(2) *Space Policy* 153–170 at 169.

[90] Danielle Wood and Annalisa Weigel, 'Building Technological Capability within Satellite Programs in Developing Countries', (2011) 69 *Acta Astronautica* 1110–1122, at 1120.

[91] More information about 'Information about BRICS'; available at http://brics.itamaraty.gov.br/about-brics/information-about-brics [accessed on 26 May 2016].

different continents, geographically distant from each other. They differ drastically in culture, religion, population and political systems.[92]

The concept of a strategic triangle including China, Russia and India, as put forward by the former Russian prime minister, has never taken shape, with the main challenge coming from the mistrust between India and China.[93] A real alliance is not on the agenda of these three countries.

China and Russia are major space-faring nations, belonging to the first tier of countries in the space club. There are abundant opportunities and areas for these two countries to cooperate on the one hand; but on the other, China and Russia are in competition with each other in the self-contained space market. For example, both countries, as major launching services providers, are competing for space launch contracts in the international market.[94] Both are 'attempting to capture the space market there and to reap the geographical benefits'.[95] Russia also still needs to keep its technological lead ahead of China.

The relationship between China and India has proved to be a more daunting issue, preventing cooperation at a deeper level. The historical relationship, territorial struggles and the position regarding Tibet have all contributed to mistrust between the two sides.[96] This has seriously affected bilateral cooperation, which will in turn add difficulty to achieving multilateral cooperation among the BRICS members. It will take time for the two countries to rebuild mutual trust and thus multilateral cooperation seems unlikely in the near future.[97] More importantly, there is no sign of the need for both sides to have multilateral cooperation with the BRICS regime in the space field, as both countries already had clear goals

---

[92] Nouriel Roubini, 'The BRICS: An Analysis', 18 June 2009; available at www.forbes.com/2009/06/17/bric-brazil-russia-india-china-renminbi-yekaterinberg-opinions-columnists-roubini.html [accessed on 26 May 2016].

[93] Charlotte Mathieu, 'Assessing Russia's Space Cooperation with China and India – Opportunities and Challenges for Europe', (2010) 66 Acta Astronautics 355–361, at 359.

[94] Baikonur Kazakhstan, 'Russians Fear Chinese Competition in Space', 16 October 2003; available at www.spacedaily.com/2003/031016073258.88ekcvxk.html [accessed on 26 May 2016].

[95] Ajey Lele and Ciro Arevalo Yepes, 'Prospects and Opportunities for Space Collaboration with Latin America: What can India Contribute and Gain?' (2013) 29 Space Policy 190–196, at 193.

[96] Colonel Stuart Kenny, 'China and India: A 'New Great Game' Founded on Historic Mistrust and Current Competition'; available at www.defence.gov.au/ADC/Publications/IndoPac/Kenny_IPS_Paper.pdf [accessed on 26 May 2016].

[97] Amardeep Athwal, China-India Relations: Contemporary Dynamics (New York: Routledge, 2008), p. 109.

and plans to develop their own space programs on their own or with other countries.[98]

V. Law and Aspects of the Future BRICS Agenda

The BRICS members have rich human and natural resources, as well as economic and political weight in the international forum. They share the understanding of a more balanced and fair international order, instead of a polarized world. This naturally extends to cooperation on a wide range of international issues, including in high technology.[99] Space cooperation can be carried out in a wide range of areas at different levels. At the lowest level, countries can work together on information-sharing or application of remote sensing data;[100] at a higher level, members can work in the fields of satellite navigation, joint deep space exploration, moon exploration and manned space missions, etc.[101] The wide scope of areas and broad range of space activities provide flexibility for the states to negotiate on possible means and models of cooperation. There is no doubt that the BRICS members will continue to seek approaches to widen the areas for cooperation.[102]

It would be thus very important for the members to plan carefully for possible cooperation. The interests and constraints of all the members must be considered, by mapping a complete picture that accounts for country-by-country variances. It is believed that 'the decision to cooperate in space can be understood as part of a broad alignment process that crosses the domestic and international policy lines'.[103]

---

[98] Lindsay Hughes, 'Off and Rocketing: The Brewing India-China Space Race', 10 April 2013; available at www.futuredirections.org.au/publication/off-and-rocketing-the-brewing-india-china-space-race/ [accessed on 26 May 2016].

[99] See further: 'Main Areas and Topics of Dialogue between the BRICS'; available at http://brics. itamaraty.gov.br/about-brics/main-areas-and-topics-of-dialogue-between-the-brics [accessed on 26 May 2016].

[100] Such as the successful practice in natural disaster response by sharing the satellite remote sensing data, which could be regarded as good model on which to conduct international space cooperation in general disaster management. See more: Atsuyo Ito, *Legal Aspects of Satellite Remote Sensing* (Leiden: Martinus Nijhoff, 2011), p. 188.

[101] One of the manned space missions may be a proposed BRICS space station, see more: Matthew Bodner, 'Russia to Propose BRICS Space Station'; available at www.themoscowtimes.com/business/article/russia-to-propose-brics-space-station/514972.html [accessed on 26 May 2016].

[102] Marsha Freeman, 'BRICS Nations Aim for the Moon and Mars'.

[103] Laura M. Delgado-Lopez, 'Sino- Latin American Space Cooperation: A Smart Move' (2012) 28 *Space Policy* 7–14, at 13.

Based on the current achievements in cooperation between the BRICS members in the traditional earth-based areas, the five member states should form a long-term vision for space cooperation: setting the purpose, aims and principles for space cooperation within the bloc; a medium-term action plan outlining specific goals to be achieved with regard to the development of space technology and space activities. The BRICS members should also have a short-term plan identifying possible space projects and exploratory activities for cooperation. A systemic roadmap would help the BRICS members to have a common ground on which to continue and expand their space cooperation.

In the process of achieving a roadmap of space cooperation for BRICS members, a legal mechanism is crucial for the sustainable development of the collaboration mechanism, and well-established dispute resolution is especially important for addressing cross-border disputes and deepening ties in the space-related finance, trade and investment. Most recently, the BRICS Dispute Resolution Shanghai Centre was established in Shanghai, and considering the previous situation where was no alternative dispute resolution channels among BRICS members, this new center in Shanghai is a significant event in legal cooperation within the bloc.[104]

While multilateral cooperation seems difficult at the current stage, we cannot exclude the possibility of improvements in political and social relationships among the BRICS members in future. The BRICS Summit mechanism provides opportunities for the BRICS members, in particular China and India, to exchange views.[105] Since entering the 21st century, China and India have developed rapidly in their economies; the two countries are both strategic competitors and cooperating partners.[106] These cooperative areas expand quickly, moving beyond the traditional economic field, and these developments help the two countries to build trust. As major members of BRICS, China, India and Russia have formed good triangle of working relationships, which may also help to soften the bitter relationship between China and India.[107]

---

[104] Lijun Du, 'China, Brazil, India, South Africa and Russia Forge Legal Framework', *Shanghai Daily*, 11 April 2016; available at www.shanghaidaily.com/business/Benchmark/China-Brazil-India-South-Africa-and-Russia-forge-legal-framework/shdaily.shtml [accessed on 26 May 2016].

[105] Wuzhou Li, 'Significance of the BRICS Mechanism', *China Today*, July 2014; available at http://m.183read.com/magazine/article/article_id/250316 [accessed on 26 May 2016].

[106] Amardeep Athwal, *China-India Relations: Contemporary Dynamics*, p. 109.

[107] Nivedita Das Kundu, 'Russia-India-China: Prospects for Trilateral Cooperation', at 5–6; available at www.helsinki.fi/aleksanteri/english/publications/contents/ap_3-2004.pdf [accessed on 26 May 2016].

VI.   Conclusion

BRICS are major players in space activities and are developing rapidly into the major space powers of the new millennium. While the BRICS members are in different stages of space development, they should 'use each other's scientific and technological potential at maximum'.[108] With China, India and Russia leading the way, the other BRICS nations, as members of this economic bloc, should be able to participate and benefit from these projects. At the BRICS Summit in July 2015 in Ufa, Russia, the BRICS members agreed to 'actively engage in the joint application of space technologies, satellite navigation, including GLONASS and BeiDou, as well as the latest achievements in space science'.[109]

It may be that each of the BRICS members have already had extensive cooperation programs with non-BRICS countries; within the bloc, a wide range of bilateral cooperation has been in place and it is expected that such bilateral cooperation will continue to play an increasingly important role to elevate the space capability of the members. Multilateral space cooperation is not common at the moment within the bloc; and while multilateral cooperation would be a welcomed process, it is necessary to be realistic in view of the historical and cultural differences among the members and the strategic implications of space technologies and space activities.

VII.   References

'Brazilian Rocket Explodes on Pad: Many Dead'; available at www.spacedaily.com/news/rocketscience-03zu.html [accessed on 26 May 2016].

'China – Brazil Earth Resources Satellite program'; available at https://en.wikipedia.org/wiki/China%E2%80%93Brazil_Earth_Resources_Satellite_program [accessed on 26 May 2016].

'China's First Man-Made Satellite'; available at www.chinaculture.org/gb/en_aboutchina/2003-09/24/content_26079.htm [accessed on 26 May 2016].

'Chinese, Russian PMs Sign Joint Communique', 3 November 2000; available at http://en.people.cn/english/200011/03/eng20001103_54286.html [accessed on 26 May 2016].

---

[108] Ajey Lele and Ciro Arevalo Yepes, 'Prospects and Opportunities for Space Collaboration with Latin America: What can India Contribute and Gain?'

[109] Viktor Kuzmin, 'Will BRICS Join Forces in Space?' 4 August 2015; available at http://in.rbth.com/world/2015/08/04/will_brics_join_forces_in_space_44569 [accessed on 26 May 2016].

'Global Space Programs'; available at www.spacefoundation.org/programs/public-
policy-and-government-affairs/introduction-space/global-space-programs
[accessed on 26 May 2016].

'History of APSCO'; available at www.apsco.int/AboutApscosS.asp?LinkNameW1=
History_of_APSCO&LinkNameW2=Signing_of_APSCO_Convention&
LinkCodeN3=11172&LinkCodeN=17 [accessed on 26 May 2016].

'India's Space Policy'; available at www.isro.gov.in/indias-space-policy [accessed on
26 May 2016].

'Information about BRICS'; available at http://brics.itamaraty.gov.br/about-brics/
information-about-brics [accessed on 26 May 2016].

'List of Chinese Astronauts'; available at https://en.wikipedia.org/wiki/List_of_
Chinese_astronauts [accessed on 26 May 2016].

'Main Areas and Topics of Dialogue between the BRICS'; available at http://brics.
itamaraty.gov.br/about-brics/main-areas-and-topics-of-
dialogue-between-the-brics [accessed on 26 May 2016].

'Mark Shuttleworth'; available at www.southafrica.net/za/en/articles/entry/article-
southafrica.net-mark-shuttleworth [accessed on 26 May 2016].

The Missile Technology Control Regime at a Glance', November 2015, www
.armscontrol.org/factsheets/mtcr [accessed on 26 May 2016].

'RadioAstron: Space VLBI Mission', www.asc.rssi.ru/radioastron/, [accessed on 26
May 2016].

'Russia and China: From Cooperation to Synergy', 12 October 2011, www.rt
.com/politics/official-word/russia-china-economy-putin-637/ [accessed on
26 May 2016].

'Russia, China Sign Range of Space Industry Agreements', http://sputniknews.com/
world/20151217/1031906991/russia-china-space-industry.html   [accessed
on 26 May 2016].

'Scientific Cooperation Agreement with South Africa's Space Agency', see: https://
ec.europa.eu/jrc/en/news/scientific-cooperation-agreement-south-africa-s-
space-agency-7004 [accessed on 26 May 2016].

'The Space Sector in Brazil – An Overview', http://www.globalsecurity.org/space/
library/report/2003/brazilspace.pdf [accessed on 26 May 2016].

'United in Space: China, India Pave the Way to BRICS Cooperation in Space', 13
April 2016, http://sputniknews.com/science/20160413/1037917928/china-
india-brics-space-satellite.html [accessed on 26 May 2016].

Athwal, Amardeep, *China-India Relations: Contemporary Dynamics* (New York:
Routledge, 2008).

'Background of Cooperation', CBERS official website: www.cbers.inpe.br/ingles/
satellites/history.php, [accessed on 26 May 2016].

Bal, Hartosh Singh, 'BRICS in Space'; available at http://latitude.blogs.nytimes
.com/2012/08/30/india-and-china-race-to-send-a-mission-to-mars/?_r=2
[accessed on 26 May 2016].

Bodner, Matthew, 'Russia, China Sign Space Exploration Agreement', *Moscow Times*, 19 May 2014; available at www.themoscowtimes.com/business/article/russia-china-sign-space-exploration-agreement/500463.html [accessed on 26 May 2016].

'Russia to Propose BRICS Space Station', *Moscow Times*, 27 January 2015; available at www.themoscowtimes.com/business/article/russia-to-propose-brics-space-station/514972.html [accessed on 26 May 2016].

Boekholt, Patries, Nagle Monique, Rannala Ruta and Vullings Wieneke, 'International S&T Collaboration: Background', Report 3: Country Analysis non-EU, 1 April 2009; available at http://ec.europe.eu/research/iscp/pdf/drivers_sti_annex_3.pdf [accessed on 26 May 2016].

'Brazil National Program of Space Activities (2005–2014)'; available at www.aeb.gov.br/wp-content/uploads/2013/03/PNAE_INGLES.pdf [accessed on 26 May 2016].

Campbell, Keith, 'South Africa to Relook at Space Launch Capability to Strengthen Space Skills', 5 March 2010; available at www.engineeringnews.co.za/article/sa-to-look-again-at-space-launch-capability-and-strengthen-space-skills-2010-03-05 [accessed on 26 May 2016].

Campos, São José Dos, 'Brazil's Space Programme', 8 August 2015; available at www.economist.com/news/americas/21660572-rocket-science-hard-rocket-diplomacy-harder-ten-nine-ten [accessed on 26 May 2016].

Das Kundu, Nivedita, 'Russia-India-China: Prospects for Trilateral Cooperation', at 5–6, www.helsinki.fi/aleksanteri/english/publications/contents/ap_3-2004.pdf, [accessed on 26 May 2016].

Defense Industry Daily Staff, 'South Africa, Brazil's A-Darter SRAAM Hits Target', 3 November 2015; available at www.defenseindustrydaily.com/south-africa-brazil-to-develop-adarter-sraam-03286/ [accessed on 26 May 2016].

Delgado-Lopez, Laura M., 'Sino- Latin American Space Cooperation: A Smart Move', (2012) 28 *Space Policy* 7–14.

Du, Lijun, 'China, Brazil, India, South Africa and Russia Forge Legal Framework', *Shanghai Daily*, 11 April 2016; available at www.shanghaidaily.com/business/Benchmark/China-Brazil-India-South-Africa-and-Russia-forge-legal-framework/shdaily.shtml [accessed on 26 May 2016].

Filho, Jose Monserrat, 'Brazilian-Chinese Space Cooperation: An Analysis', (1997) 13 *Space Policy* 153–170.

Firsing, Scott, 'BRICS Are Conquering the Developing World and Space Is Next', 3 October 2011, *International Policy Digest*, http://intpolicydigest.org/2011/10/03/brics-are-conquering-the-developing-world-and-space-is-next/ [accessed on 26 May 2016].

Firsing, Scott, 'Space, BRICS' Next Frontier', *Daily Maverick*, 10 October 2011, www.dailymaverick.co.za/opinionista/2011-10-10-space-brics-next-frontier/#.VwtMo-_ovcs [accessed on 26 May 2016].

Freeman, Marsha, 'BRICS Nations Aim for the Moon and Mars', *Executive Intelligence Review*, 5 December 2014; available at www.larouchepub.com/other/2014/4148brics_moon_mars.html [accessed on 26 May 2016].

Garber, Steve, 'Sputnik and The Dawn of the Space Age', 10 October 2007, http://history.nasa.gov/sputnik/ [accessed on 26 May 2016].

Harvey, Brian, *China's Space Program – From Conception to Manned Spaceflight* (Chichester: Springer-Praxis, 2004).

Hobe, Stephan et al. (eds.), *Cologne Commentary on Space Law: Outer Space Treaty* (Luxemburg: Carl Heymanns Verlag 2009), vol. 1.

Howell, Elizabeth, 'Roscosmos: Russia's Space Agency', 17 May 2016; available at www.space.com/22724-roscosmos.html [accessed on 26 May 2016].

Hughes, Lindsay, 'Off and Rocketing: The Brewing India-China Space Race', 10 April 2013; available at www.futuredirections.org.au/publication/off-and-rocketing-the-brewing-india-china-space-race/ [accessed on 26 May 2016].

India Has Space Cooperation with 33 Nations', 30 July 2014, www.ndtv.com/india-news/india-has-space-cooperation-with-33-nations-599448 [accessed on 26 May 2016].

Information Office of the State Council of the People's Republic of China, 'China's Space Activities in 2011', 29 December 2011; available at www.china.org.cn/government/whitepaper/node_7145648.htm [accessed on 26 May 2016].

Ito, Atsuyo, *Legal Aspects of Satellite Remote Sensing* (Leiden: Martinus Nijhoff, 2011).

Jayaraman, K. S., 'India and China Sign Space Cooperation Pact', 22 September 2014; available at http://spacenews.com/41942india-and-china-sign-space-cooperation-pact/ [accessed on 26 May 2016].

Kazakhstan, Baikonur, 'Russians Fear Chinese Competition in Space', 16 October 2003; available at www.spacedaily.com/2003/031016073258.88ekcvxk.html [accessed on 26 May 2016].

Kenny, Colonel Stuart, 'China and India: A 'New Great Game' Founded on Historic Mistrust and Current Competition'; available at www.defence.gov.au/ADC/Publications/IndoPac/Kenny_IPS_Paper.pdf [accessed on 26 May 2016].

Kuzmin, Viktor, 'Will BRICS Join Forces in Space?' 4 August 2015, http://in.rbth.com/world/2015/08/04/will_brics_join_forces_in_space_44569 [accessed on 26 May 2016].

Leister, V., 'South to South Cooperation in Outer Space: The Brazil-China Agreement', *Proceedings of the 32nd IISL Colloquium on the Law of Outer Space*, October 1989, Torremolinos-Malaga (Washington, DC: AIAA, 1990).

Lele, Ajey, and Ciro, Arevalo Yepes, 'Prospects and Opportunities for Space Collaboration with Latin America: What Can India Contribute and Gain?' (2013) 29 *Space Policy* 190–196.

Li, Wuzhou, 'Significance of the BRICS Mechanism', *China Today*, July 2014; available at http://m.183read.com/magazine/article/article_id/250316 [accessed on 26 May 2016].

Listner, Michael and Rajagopalan, Rajeswari P., 'The 2014 PPWT: A New Draft but with the Same and Different Problems', 11 August 2014, *Space Review*, www.thespacereview.com/article/2575/1, [accessed on 26 May 2016].

'Could Commercial Space Help Define and Delimitate the Boundaries of Outer Space?' 29 October 2012, *Space Review*, www.thespacereview.com/article/2180/1, [accessed on 26 May 2016].

Liu, Huayu, 'Space Cooperation between China and Brazil', (2014) 3 *Aerospace China* 12–14.

Lyall, Francis and Larsen, Paul B., *Space Law: A Treatise* (New York: Ashgate Publishing 2009).

Mathieu, Charlotte, 'Assessing Russia's Space Cooperation with China and India – Opportunities and Challenges for Europe', (2010) 66 *Acta Astronautics* 355–361.

Oliveira, H. Altemani de, 'China-Brasil: Perspectivas de Cooperacion Sur-Sur', (2006) 23 *Nueva Sociedad* 138–147.

Otero-lglesias, M., 'China, the Euro and the Reform of the International Monetary System', www.academia.edu/2446804/China_the_Euro_and_the_Reform_of_the_International_Monetary_System [accessed on 7 December 2016].

Pravda.Ru, 'Russia, China Specify Areas of Bilateral Space Cooperation', 12 August 2002, www.pravdareport.com/news/world/12-08-2002/15694-0/#sthash.U2ruipnu.dpuf, [accessed on 26 May 2016].

Rose, Frank A., 'Promoting the Long-Term Sustainability and Security of the Space Environment'; available at www.state.gov/t/avc/rls/2015/250140.htm [accessed on 26 May 2016].

Roubini, Nouriel, 'The BRICs: An Analysis', 18 June 2009, www.forbes.com/2009/06/17/bric-brazil-russia-india-china-renminbi-yekaterinberg-opinions-columnists-roubini.html, [accessed on 26 May 2016].

Russia, China Sign Range of Space Industry Agreements', 21 December 2015, *Space Daily*, www.spacedaily.com/reports/Russia_China_Sign_Range_of_Space_Industry_Agreements_999.html [accessed on 26 May 2016].

Saira, Syed, 'Bric Nations Become Increasingly Interdependent', 14 April 2011, www.bbc.com/news/business-13046521 [accessed on 26 May 2016].

Stokes, Mark A., 'China's Strategic Modernization: Implications for the United States', September 1999; available at https://fas.org/nuke/guide/china/doctrine/chinamod.pdf [accessed on 26 May 2016].

Treutler, Jürgen, 'Brazil and Russia Boost Space Cooperation with New Glonass Station', *Moscow Times*, 16 September 2015; available at www.themoscowtimes.com/business/article/brazil-and-russia-boost-space-cooperation-with-new-glonass-station/531086.html [accessed on 26 May 2016].

Tuai, Alex, 'Introduction to BRICS'; available at http://ampglobalyouth.org/students/introduction-to-brics/ [accessed on 26 May 2016].

Wisconsin Project on Nuclear Arms Control, 'India Missile Milestones: 1947–2005', *Risk Report* 11.6 (2005).

Wood, Anthony, 'American Independence in Space: Ending Reliance on the Soyuz Spacecraft by 2017', 12 January 2015; available at www.gizmag.com/nasa-boeing-spacex-iss-soyuz-dragon-cst100-roscosmos/35543/ [accessed on 26 May 2016].

Wood, Danielle, and Weigel, Annalisa, 'Building Technological Capability within Satellite Programs in Developing Countries', (2011) 69 *Acta Astronautica* 1110–1122.

Yarygina, I. Z., 'BRICS-EU-CIS Cooperation: Problems and Challenges'; available at www.leap2020.net/euro-brics/2014/10/22/brics-eu-cis-cooperation-problems-and-challenges/?lang=en [accessed on 26 May 2016].

Zhang, Yan, 'BRICS Works for Shared Prosperity', 13 April 2011 *The Hindu*, www.hindu.com [accessed on 26 May 2016].

Zhao, Yun, *National Space Law in China: An Overview of the Current Situation and Outlook for the Future* (Leiden: Brill Nijhoff, 2015).

15

For a BRICS Agenda on Culture and the Creative Economy

LILIAN RICHIERI HANANIA AND ANTONIOS VLASSIS

I. Introduction

This chapter highlights how culture and creative industries may support the BRICS's contribution to global governance and help it to make a difference in tackling domestic and global problems. As emerging economies with contrasting features, the BRICS countries should embrace opportunities created both by their aincreased collaboration and by the so-called creative economy, which is characterized by business convergence and interdependence resulting from technological innovation and creativity.[1] By so doing they would benefit not only from economic growth but also from fundamental conditions conducive to more human and sustainable development in increasingly multicultural societies. The respect and promotion of cultural diversity are a prerequisite for that, with implications regarding democracy and pluralism – which unfortunately remain a challenge in some of those countries.[2]

'Cultural diversity' is understood here according to the 2005 United Nations Educational, Scientific and Cultural Organization (UNESCO) Convention on the Protection and Promotion of the Diversity of Cultural

---

[1] Rostam J. Neuwirth, 'Global Market Integration and the Creative Economy: The Paradox of Industry Convergence and Regulatory Divergence' (2015) 18(1) *Journal of International Economic Law* 21–50.

[2] For instance, see Jonathan McClory, 'Creative Russia: lessons from Berlin', *The Guardian*, 2013; available at www.theguardian.com/culture-professionals-network/culture-professionals-blog/2013/sep/25/russia-culture-st-petersburg-berlin [accessed on 8 March 2016], who states, 'The future development of Russia's creative industries is surely stymied by the country's current political climate and its opposition to political and cultural diversity'.

Expressions (CDCE).[3] It 'refers to the manifold ways in which the cultures of groups and societies find expression . . . , whatever the means and technologies used' (article 4.1 CDCE).

Since '[c]ultural diversity can be protected and promoted only if human rights and fundamental freedoms, such as freedom of expression, information and communication, as well as the ability of individuals to choose cultural expressions, are guaranteed' (article 2.1 CDCE), it implies the 'recognition of equal dignity of and respect for all cultures, including the cultures of persons belonging to minorities and indigenous peoples' (article 2.3 CDCE) as well as of vulnerable groups in general. Moreover, cultural diversity is 'one of the roots of development, understood not simply in terms of economic growth, but also as a mean to achieve a more satisfactory intellectual, emotional, moral and spiritual existence' (article 3 of the Universal Declaration on Cultural Diversity – UDCD).[4] The contribution of cultural diversity to sustainable development is confirmed in the CDCE (Preamble, articles 2.6 and 13 CDCE).

The CDCE focuses on cultural goods, services and industries, adopting as such an economic and material perspective. It offers a comprehensive framework for cultural policies and international cultural cooperation with the aim of attaining more balanced international exchanges of cultural goods and services and therefore better global governance of the cultural sector. It responds pertinently to the creative economy and should be used as 'a coordination framework to promote regulatory coherence' in such a context.[5] Since its negotiations the CDCE has generated the inclusion of cultural considerations in international discussions and in the last several years has become fundamental in efforts to achieve

---

[3] UNESCO, Convention on the Protection and Promotion of the Diversity of Cultural Expressions, adopted on 20 October 2005 and in effect since March 2007; available at http://en.unesco.org/creativity/convention/about/2005-convention-text [accessed on 25 March 2016]. On this convention, its purpose and its object, see Lilian Richieri Hanania, *Diversité culturelle et droit international du commerce* (Paris: La Documentation française, 2009), as well as Lilian Richieri Hanania (ed.), *Cultural Diversity in International Law: The Effectiveness of the UNESCO Convention on the Protection and Promotion of the Diversity of Cultural Expressions* (London: Routledge, 2014); and Antonios Vlassis, *Gouvernance mondiale et culture: de l'exception à la diversité* (Liège: Presses universitaires de Liège, 2015).

[4] UNESCO, Universal Declaration on Cultural Diversity, 2001, available at http://unesdoc.unesco.org/images/0012/001271/127162e.pdf [accessed on 22 March 2016].

[5] On this subject see Lilian Richieri Hanania, 'The UNESCO Convention on the Diversity of Cultural Expressions as a coordination framework to promote regulatory coherence in the creative economy' (2015) *International Journal of Cultural Policy* 1–20.

better and socially mindful global governance. Among other things, it has contributed to the recognition of the role of culture in the United Nations (UN) Sustainable Development Goals (SDGs) in 2015.[6]

Despite the different positions defended by the BRICS countries during the CDCE negotiations, notably regarding its relationship with other international treaties, particularly with trade agreements,[7] we propose that the CDCE should be at the heart of a future BRICS agenda on the creative economy. Four members of the BRICS are already parties to the CDCE: India since 15 December 2006, South Africa since 21 December 2006, Brazil since 16 January 2007 and China since 30 January 2007. The first step in such an agenda would be the CDCE ratification by the Russian Federation.

The BRICS's rapprochement regarding the explicit integration of culture in the UN SDGs offers interesting perspectives for the cultural field. A landmark in the 2012–2015 international mobilization in favor of the inclusion of culture in the post-2015 development agenda, 'Culture: Key to Sustainable Development', an international congress, was held in China in May 2013. Organized by the Hangzhou local authorities and UNESCO, which had developed strong links since the inscription of the West Lake Cultural Landscape of Hangzhou within the UNESCO World Heritage List in 2011,[8] this international meeting was attended by 500 participants from eighty-two countries, including representatives of national authorities, civil society and academics from the BRICS countries.[9] The BRICS

---

[6] United Nations, Transforming our World: The 2030 Agenda for Sustainable Development, Resolution adopted by the General Assembly on 25 September 2015, Seventieth session, A/RES/70/1, 21 October 2015; available at www.un.org/ga/search/view_doc.asp?symbol=A/RES/70/1&Lang=E [accessed on 16 March 2016].

[7] China and South Africa favored nonsubordination of the CDCE to trade agreements, while India objected to a binding convention that could counterbalance the international trade regime. The Chinese delegation noted that 'the Convention should become a reference for the World Trade Organization and other international bodies. In this regard, all the international regimes would function as a whole' (free translation) See UNESCO, Avant-projet de Convention sur la protection de la diversité des contenus culturels et des expressions artistiques: Partie II: commentaires spécifiques des Etats-membres (2004), p. 87.

[8] Antonios Vlassis, 'Culture in the post-2015 development agenda: the anatomy of an international mobilization' (2015) 36(9) Third World Quarterly 1649–62.

[9] Forty-six participants from China; seven participants from India, notably experts in the field of cultural heritage and the craft industry; and two each from Russia, Brazil and South Africa. See UNESCO, List of Attendees to the Congress; available at www.unesco.org/new/fileadmin/MULTIMEDIA/HQ/CLT/pdf/Book15.pdf [accessed on 13 April 2016]. One of the main outcomes of the congress was the 'Hangzhou Declaration', which included nine actions to place culture at the core of policies for sustainable development.

countries seemed to be divided on the link between culture and sustainable development, however. In September 2013, the Group of Friends on Culture and Development was launched within the UN General Assembly with nearly thirty countries, including South Africa and Brazil, but China, India and Russia decided not to join. In addition, UNESCO organized two special thematic debates on 'Culture and Development' at the UN General Assembly in 2013 and 2014. Although many high representatives from economically developing countries participated in the debates, the only representative from a BRICS country was the minister of culture from South Africa.

Nevertheless, in the 2015 BRICS Agreement on Cooperation in the Field of Culture,[10] the BRICS explicitly recognized 'the contribution of cultural heritage to the sustainable development agenda' (article 4) and creative industries 'as a pillar of sustainable development' (article 12). The 2016 Goa Declaration adopted at the eighth BRICS Summit recognized 'the important role of culture in sustainable development and in fostering mutual understanding and closer cooperation' as well.[11] The adoption of the 2030 Agenda for Sustainable Development, with cultural concerns notably being included in paragraphs 8 and 36 of the SDGs Declaration,[12] as well as Targets 4.5, 4.7, 8.9, 11.4 and 12.b,[13] should also ultimately help

See UNESCO, 'The Hangzhou Declaration: heralding the next era of human development'; available at www.unesco.org/new/en/culture/themes/dynamic-content-single-view/news/the_hangzhou_declaration_heralding_the_next_era_of_human_development/#.Vw5mtKSLShc [accessed on 13 April 2016].

[10] BRICS, Agreement between the Governments of the BRICS States on Cooperation in the Field of Culture, Ufa, Russia, 9 July 2015; available at www.brics.utoronto.ca/docs/150709-culture-agreement-en.html [accessed on 5 April 2016].

[11] *The Indian Express*, '8th BRICS Summit Goa Declaration: Here is the full text adopted by the member nations', 16 October 2016; available at http://indianexpress.com/article/india/india-news-india/8th-brics-summit-goa-declaration-here-is-the-full-text-adopted-by-the-member-nations/ [accessed on 1 December 2016].

[12] Paragraph 8 reads, 'We envisage a world of universal respect for human rights and human dignity, the rule of law, justice, equality and non-discrimination; of respect for race, ethnicity and cultural diversity'; and paragraph 36: 'We pledge to foster intercultural understanding, tolerance, mutual respect and an ethic of global citizenship and shared responsibility. We acknowledge the natural and cultural diversity of the world and recognize that all cultures and civilizations can contribute to, and are crucial enablers of, sustainable development' (United Nations, Transforming our World, pp. 4, 10).

[13] These targets refer to Goals 4 ('Ensure inclusive and equitable quality education and promote lifelong learning opportunities for all'), 8 ('Promote sustained, inclusive and sustainable economic growth, full and productive employment and decent work for all'), 11 ('Make cities and human settlements inclusive, safe, resilient and sustainable') and 12 ('Ensure sustainable consumption and production patterns'). (United Nations, Transforming our World, pp. 17, 20, 22, 23).

diminish differences and encourage engagement among the BRICS countries on this matter.

Attempts to attain the SDGs and promote economic growth through the strengthening of creative industries require actions at the local, national and international levels. The CDCE offers a suitable legal framework for national policies and international cooperation to create a favorable environment for creativity and cultural diversity.[14] A BRICS agenda on the creative economy should address these two aspects: the adoption and implementation of appropriate national cultural policies and measures (Section I) and the enhancement of international cultural cooperation (Section II).

II. National Cultural Policies and Measures

The CDCE recognizes the legitimacy of policies and measures 'related to the protection and promotion of the diversity of cultural expressions' (article 3 CDCE) and reaffirms the parties' sovereign right to act in favor of the diversity of cultural expressions within their territory (articles 2.2 and 5 CDCE). Its call for the parties to integrate culture into development policies, as well as its flexibility regarding cultural policies, allows countries to implement the CDCE in different fields. Policies legitimated under the CDCE may, for instance, focus on cultural heritage, if needed to protect and promote the diversity of cultural expressions (notably for countries that are not parties to the 2003 Convention for the Safeguarding of the Intangible Cultural Heritage, but are parties to the CDCE, e.g. South Africa),[15] or may even be adopted outside traditional cultural sectors (e.g.

---

[14] The 2003 UNESCO Convention for the Safeguarding of the Intangible Cultural Heritage (CSICH), adopted on 17 October 2003 and in effect since 20 April 2006; available at www .unesco.org/culture/ich/en/convention [accessed on 4 April 2016], might also have a complementary role to play for some of the BRICS countries. In fact, China, India and Brazil are among the main players regarding the CSICH implementation and as of June 2017, they have inscribed fifty-nine elements on the List of Intangible Cultural Heritage – 39, 12 and 8, respectively. These countries see traditional cultural resources and contemporary cultural expressions as a continuum and tend to include under the term of 'creative economy' many cultural pursuits that might be identified as intangible cultural heritage. See UNESCO-UNDP, *Creative Economy Report 2013 Special Edition: Widening Local Development Pathways* (Paris: UNESCO-UNDP, 2013), p. 69. By contrast, South Africa is not a party to the CSICH, whereas Russia has inscribed only two elements on the above-mentioned list.

[15] See, on the link between the two conventions, Lilian Richieri Hanania, 'Protection mechanisms for cultural expressions under threat' (2014) 2 *Transnational Dispute Management – Art and Heritage Disputes* 2–6; available at www.transnational-dispute-management.com/ article.asp?key=2095 [accessed on 4 April 2016].

varied sectors involved with information and communications technology (ICT) in the digital age).[16] In the context of the creative economy, those policies and measures require a high level of creativity and openness to the future from lawyers and policy makers.[17]

To take full advantage of their creative potential, the BRICS nations should map their creative sectors to identify their weaknesses and strengths, thereby enabling appropriate policies to be adopted and implemented to create the right environment for cultural and creative industries. Such an environment should encourage 'individuals and social groups: (a) to create, produce, disseminate, distribute and have access to their own cultural expressions' (article 7(a) CDCE). It should also foster 'access to diverse cultural expressions from within their territory as well as from other countries of the world' (article 7(b) CDCE). Policies might focus on specific communities and sectors or be transversal,[18] targeting mainstream effects, such as investments in infrastructure, innovation, new technologies, education and capacity building as well as an effective respect for fundamental freedoms.

The following subsections provide a brief overview of the state of the BRICS countries' cultural industries and their existing cultural policies, testifying once more to significant discrepancies among them.

A.   The BRICS Countries' Cultural Industries

According to a recent study, global 'cultural exports have doubled over the past 10 years, reaching a total of USD 212.8 billion in

---

[16] Lilian Richieri Hanania, 'Le débat commerce-culture à l'ère numérique: quelle application pour la Convention de l'UNESCO sur la diversité des expressions culturelles?' (2015), 3–10; available at http://papers.ssrn.com/sol3/papers.cfm?abstract_id=2600647 [accessed on 4 April 2016], as well as Lilian Richieri Hanania, 'The UNESCO Convention on the Diversity of Cultural Expressions as a coordination framework', 6–10' and Lilian Richieri Hanania, L'extension de l'exception culturelle aux secteurs issus des nouvelles technologies, RIJDEC, Le renouvellement de l'exception culturelle à l'ère du numérique (2015); available at www.coalitionfrancaise.org/wp-content/uploads/2015/10/RIJDEC-Le-renouvellement-de-lexception-culturelle-%C3%A0-l%C3%A8re-du-num%C3%A9rique-22-10-15.pdf [accessed on 4 April 2016].

[17] Rostam J. Neuwirth, 'The UNESCO Convention and future technologies: a journey to the center of cultural law and policymaking', in Lilian Richieri Hanania and Anne-Thida Norodom (eds.), Diversity of cultural expressions in the digital era (Buenos Aires: Teseo, 2016), available at www.teseopress.com/diversityofculturalexpressionsinthedigitalera/ [accessed on 4 April 2016].

[18] CISAC, The Creative Industries and the BRICS – A Review of the State of the Creative Economy in Brazil, Russia, India, China and South Africa (CISAC, 2014); available at www.cisac.org/Media/Studies-and-Reports/Publications-PDF-files/CISAC-BRICS-STUDY-20146 [accessed on 4 April 2016], p. 5.

2013'.[19] Regarding trade in cultural services, the available statistics show that exports increased globally on average by 10 percent annually between 2003 and 2012, accounting for USD 150 billion in 2013.[20] Despite the growing importance of the creative sectors in the BRICS economies, 'the BRICS . . . have not yet unlocked the full economic potential and benefits of the creative economy. The economic contribution of the creative industries to the GDP of BRICS countries is between 1–6% only', while in the United States, for instance, such industries account for 11 percent of the GDP.[21] In addition, the economic benefits deriving from cultural diversity and creativity[22] may result not only from the activity of cultural and creative industries per se but also and more generally from the creativity and innovation that cultural diversity brings to the economy.[23]

The BRICS countries have, nevertheless, expanded their participation in the cultural sector, with China, Brazil and Russia controlling 436, 310 and 219 affiliates abroad in the sectors of publishing, printing and recorded media in 2012, respectively.[24] Moreover, since 2010 China has been the leading exporter of cultural goods in the world, and India has emerged as the fifth-largest exporter of those goods.[25] In the global market in 2013, visual arts and crafts accounted for 71 percent of exports of cultural goods, showing an increase of 185 percent between 2004 and 2013 mostly due to trade in jewelry (gold).[26] The value of South Africa's exports of cultural and natural heritage goods also doubled from 2004 to

---

[19] UNESCO and UIS, *Cultural Trade Flows Infographic* (2016); available at www.uis.unesco .org/culture/Documents/cult-trade-infographic-final-EN.pdf [accessed 22 March 2016].

[20] UNESCO and UIS, *The Globalisation of Cultural Trade: A Shift in Consumption – International Flows of Cultural Goods and Services 2004–2013* (2016), p. 69; available at www .uis.unesco.org/culture/Documents/international-flows-cultural-goods-report-en.pdf [accessed on 22 March 2016]. According to the 2009 UNESCO Framework for Cultural Statistics, cultural domains comprise cultural and natural heritage; performance and celebration; visual arts and crafts; books and press; audiovisual and interactive media; and design and creative services, including architecture, design and advertising services. Ibid., pp. 13–14.

[21] CISAC, *The Creative Industries and the BRICS*, pp. 4, 10. Growth in exports of creative goods 'significantly outpace[s] global economic growth' (ibid., p. 4).

[22] See, for instance, UNCTAD, *World Creative Economy Report 2010 – Creative Economy: A Feasible Development Option* (Geneva: UNCTAD, 2010); available at http://unctad.org/en/ Docs/ditctab20103_en.pdf [accessed on 25 March 2016].

[23] See, for instance, articles 1 and 9 UDCD and Lilian Richieri Hanania, 'Bringing cultural diversity to discussions on social and labor issues', pp. 121–135. Regarding the effects of this link on international trade agreements, see Lilian Richieri Hanania, 'The UNESCO Convention on the Diversity of Cultural Expressions as a coordination framework', 1–20 and 'Le débat commerce-culture à l'ère numérique', 3–10.

[24] UNESCO and UIS, *The Globalisation of Cultural Trade*, p. 79.

[25] Ibid., pp. 11 and 33.   [26] Ibid., pp. 39 and 45.

Table 15.1 *Film Production/National Market Share (%)*

	2011	2012	2013	2014
China	588/53.6	745/48.5	638/58.7	618/54.5
India	1255/89	1602/91.5	1724/–	1966/–
Russia	64/15.8	75/16.1	73/18.4	123/18.7
Brazil	100/12.4	83/10.3	129/18.6	114/12.3
South Africa	25/17	19/–	25/11.2	23/6.3

Source: European Audiovisual Observatory, *Focus: World Film Market Trends (2005–2015).*

2013.[27] The future of creative industries has also been considered promising for Russia,[28] despite the lack of governmental incentives, a few reasons being the absence of clear policies for the creative sector, excessive bureaucracy and corruption, as well as the fact that 'most cultural organizations are still state-owned and their participation in commercial activities is somewhat restricted in the law'.[29]

The global cinema market offers useful insights into the expansion of the film industry in the BRICS. Although the five countries actively participate in the global film market, the disparities are significant between India and China, on the one hand, and Russia, Brazil and South Africa, on the other, in terms of cinema production and the national market share (Table 15.1). China remains the most important cinema market in terms of gross box office receipts, followed by India and Russia (Table 15.2). South Africa is one of the few African countries with a structured film industry based on networks of production studios, distribution and exhibition chains and one of the continent's largest theatrical markets. Moreover, China shows the highest and steadiest growth potential, whereas the

[27] Ibid., p. 42.

[28] Ibid., p. 10. Moscow has recently hosted the First World Summit for Creative Industries. See Rossiyskaya Gazeta, 'Moscow will host the World Summit for Creative Industries', *Russia beyond the Headlines,* 2014; available at http://rbth.com/business_calendar/2014/03/04/ moscow_will_host_the_world_summit_for_creative_industries_34761.html [accessed on 8 March 2016].

[29] Katja Ruutu, Aleksander Panfilo, and Päivi Karhunen, *Cultural Industries in Russia – Northern Dimension Partnership on Culture* (2009), pp. 9–10; available at www .northerndimension.info/images/Cultural_Industries_in_Russia.pdf [accessed on 4 April 2016].

Table 15.2 *Gross Box Office (in USD Billion)/Average Admissions per Capita*

	2011	2012	2013	2014
China	2.03/0.3	2.74/0.3	3.54/0.4	4.82/0.6
India	1.47/2.2	1.60/2.5	1.60/2.2	1.50/2.0
Russia	1.17/1.2	1.20/1.1	1.34/1.2	1.15/1.2
Brazil	0.86/0.7	0.84/0.8	0.74/0.7	0.82/0.8
South Africa	0.05/0.4	0.09/0.5	0.09/0.7	0.07/–

Source: European Audiovisual Observatory, *Focus: World Film Market Trends* (2005–2015).

film market growth of India, Russia, Brazil and South Africa fluctuates (Table 15.2).

B. *Existing Action for Creative Industries*

Taking the illustration of the film industry, China has developed strict and centralized cinema policies supporting the national film industry via tariffs, quotas, subsidies and tax credits (and, unfortunately, censorship),[30] whereas India remains characterized by very low state intervention in the film industry, a commercially dynamic private entertainment industry, a strongly decentralized film system and prolific cinema production, shot in more than twenty local languages.[31] South Africa's film policy aims to attract foreign film productions. For their part, Russia and Brazil have developed film policies marked by screen quotas: in 2012 Russia introduced a 20 percent quota for Russian films in cinemas, while in Brazil since 1932 a minimum number of days a year must be devoted to local productions.[32] In addition, both countries have various co-production treaties. Russia joined the European co-production fund *Eurimages* in 2011 and has film agreements with major European countries such as Italy, France, Spain and Germany. Brazil has several co-production agreements with Latin American and European countries and is a main pillar

---

[30] Antonios Vlassis, 'Soft power, global governance and rising powers: the case of China' (2016) 22(4) *International Journal of Cultural Policy* 481–96.

[31] Antonios Vlassis, 'Les puissances émergentes dans la bataille mondiale de l'attraction: Bollywood, vecteur du soft power de l'Inde' (2016) 55 *Interventions Économiques* 1–21; available at https://interventionseconomiques.revues.org/2867 [accessed on 4 April 2016].

[32] See Lilian Richieri Hanania, *Diversité culturelle et droit international du commerce*, p. 71.

of the multilateral co-production program IBERMEDIA, which includes Spain, Portugal and several countries in Latin America. With regard to national support, the Russian Cinema Fund, a public funding system established in 2010 with a budget of USD 110 million, has provoked criticism, since a big portion of its funding is distributed to seven leading production companies.[33]

More broadly, South Africa provides an interesting example of a dynamic partnership between civil society and national authorities in the cultural sector. The Cultural and Creative Industries Federation, created in 2014, aims to prevent the fragmentation of the sector and to foster its economic potential. It is built on a strong partnership among several South African stakeholders, such as the Ministry of Arts and Culture, the Department of Trade and Industry, the Department of Communications and many players in the cultural and creative industries.

According to the quadrennial reports from the CDCE parties,[34] between 2005 and 2010, China opened up a range of cultural industry sectors to nonpublic capital and supported private performing groups via funding, government procurement, performance venues and equipment, simplified approval processes, talent cultivation and commendation as well as rewards.

The Brazilian Ministry of Culture has organized a series of workshops on cultural policies for artists and cultural professionals and entrepreneurs in all the states of the Federation. The Brazilian international audiovisual cooperation policy, aimed at international co-productions and the promotion of Brazilian films in the international audiovisual market (through the allocation of USD 35.7 million), is also an important innovative initiative. Moreover, the 'Creative Brazil Plan' is part of the strategy to promote the creative economy[35] but faces several challenges,[36] including

---

[33] In 2010, the Federal Antimonopoly Service called for more transparency in the Russia Cinema Fund's decision-making procedures. See European Audiovisual Observatory, *Focus: World Film Market Trends* (Strasbourg: European Audiovisual Observatory, 2005–2016).

[34] Brazil submitted its report in 2012, China in 2013 and India in 2015. South Africa has still not provided its report. See UNESCO, *Periodic Reports – Innovative Examples*; available at http://en.unesco.org/creativity/monitoring-and-reporting/periodic-reports/innovative-examples [accessed on 13 April 2016].

[35] For more information on Brazilian policies for the diversity of cultural expression, see Brazil, *Relatório periódico quadrienal sobre as medidas para proteger e promover a diversidade das expressões culturais* (2012); available at http://en.unesco.org/creativity/sites/creativity/files/periodic_reports/old/brazil_report_ownformat_pt_2012.pdf [accessed on 4 April 2016].

[36] Claudio Accioli, Kalinka Iaquinto, Solange Monteiro and Thais Thimoteo, 'Can Brazil become a creative economy?' (2011) *Brazilian Economy* 20–8.

instability and a lack of continuity in policies, as illustrated by the rapid dissolution of the Creative Economy Secretariat within the Brazilian Ministry of Culture. Finally, Brazilian local and grassroots cultural initiatives have been fostered through the creation of 'Culture Points' all over the country within the 'Living Culture' program.[37] Part of a national cultural system that brings together Brazilian states and municipalities, the 'Living Culture' program considers culture to be a key factor in the development of and access to citizenship.

Such a local perspective, close to citizens, seems to be a fundamental factor in the effectiveness of national policies and measures that intend to promote creativity, cultural diversity and the flourishing of creative industries. Indeed, '[i]t is first and foremost at [the] local level that culture and creativity are lived and practised on a daily basis'.[38] The promotion and multiplication of 'creative cities' in the BRICS countries may be a step in that direction. Except for South Africa, 'creative cities' have been acknowledged in the BRICS countries by UNESCO and incorporated into the UNESCO Creative Cities Network (UCCN) created in 2004.[39] Each of these cities is recognized as having placed creativity and cultural industries at the heart of sustainable urban development, local development plans, and cooperation at the international level. Indeed, to foster access by their citizens to diversified cultural offerings, international cultural cooperation must be reinforced as well.

III. International Cultural Cooperation

Following previous summit declarations, the BRICS Agreement on Cooperation in the Field of Culture was adopted in 2015.[40] Still subject to

---

[37] See Giuliana Kauark and Lilian Richieri Hanania, 'Social and cultural development through cultural diversity – the Living Culture Programme', in *Mapping Cultural Diversity – Good Practices from around the Globe* (Asia-Europe Foundation, German Commission for UNESCO and U40 Group, 2010), pp. 17–21; available at www.unesco.de/fileadmin/medien/Dokumente/Kultur/U40/Mapping_Cultural_Diversity_FINAL.pdf [accessed on 4 April 2016].

[38] UNESCO, UNESCO Creative Cities Network, 'Why creativity? Why cities?' 2016; available at http://en.unesco.org/creative-cities/content/why-creativity-why-cities [accessed on 30 March 2016].

[39] UNESCO, *UNESCO Creative Cities Network* (2016); available at http://en.unesco.org/creative-cities/home [accessed on 30 March 2016]. The UCCN is currently composed of 116 cities, including 5 cities in Brazil (Florianópolis, Curitiba, Santos, Belém and Salvador), 1 in the Russian Federation (Ulyanovsk), 2 in India (Varanasi and Jaipur) and 8 in China (Beijing, Chengdu, Hangzhou, Shanghai, Shunde, Suzhou, Shenzhen and Jingdezhen).

[40] BRICS, Agreement between the Governments of the BRICS States on Cooperation in the Field of Culture.

ratification, and despite being very vaguely worded and weakly binding, it represents the first step in the strengthening of cooperation by the BRICS countries regarding different cultural sectors.

In its preamble, it recalls the commitment of those countries to 'openness, inclusiveness, equality, respect for cultural diversity, and mutual respect and learning'. While referring to the 'laws and policies of their states,' the agreement reflects the obligation by the parties to 'develop and promote cooperation and exchanges' in several cultural sectors. The areas of cooperation include 'music and dancing, choreography, theatre, circus, archives, publishing and libraries, museums, cultural heritage, fine, decorative and applied arts, audio-visual works, and . . . other creative activities provided for by [the] Agreement' (article 1) as well as intangible cultural heritage (article 4) and traditional knowledge and cultural expressions (article 7).

Cooperation should cover the following: training; skills upgrading; exchanges of researchers, experts and students; joint programs and exchange of information (article 2); prevention of illicit importing, exporting and transferring of cultural property (article 3); 'protection, preservation, restoration, return and utilisation of cultural heritage objects'; support and assistance in managing cultural heritage sites and in inscribing those sites in the World Heritage List (article 4); organization of festivals, exhibitions and performances of traditional expressions (article 6); consultations on matters of common interest (article 7); exchanges involving young teams and performers (article 8); 'exchange of copies of documents and materials related to the culture, history, social and political development' of each BRICS country (article 9); cooperation among libraries and museums (article 10); book translation and exchanges in the printing and publishing sector (article 11); cooperation among agencies in the field of creative industries (article 12); and selection, co-production and exchanges of audiovisual works and 'participation of audio-visual professionals in international activities as per the rules and regulations of the Parties' states' (article 5). In fact, audiovisual co-production efforts among the BRICS countries have so far been quite limited. In 2014, India signed audiovisual co-production treaties with China and Brazil, whereas co-production agreements between China and Brazil, China and Russia, and India and Russia are currently under discussion.

The 2015 agreement is without prejudice to other multilateral exchanges and bilateral cooperation among the BRICS countries. It could particularly stimulate international cooperation among the BRICS countries that are parties to the CDCE. Most importantly, it could ultimately contribute to welding together the BRICS countries around cultural issues, building common positions and creating momentum for action – and perhaps leading to ratification of the CDCE by Russia and more active participation in its implementation by India and South Africa, which seem to have kept a low profile regarding the convention.

Using the CDCE as a framework for cooperation with regard to cultural and creative industries, collaboration among the BRICS countries should imply, inter alia, addressing together situations of vulnerability of cultural expressions; promoting dialogue on cultural policy; encouraging professional cultural exchanges and sharing best practices to improve cultural public sector institutions; strengthening partnerships with and among civil society, NGOs and the private sector; sharing information, data, knowledge and expertise; promoting the use of new technologies; and encouraging co-production and co-distribution agreements (articles 12 and 19 CDCE). Joint and collaborative projects should be set up in all those fields. Coordination among the BRICS countries that are parties to the CDCE pursuant to article 21 should likewise be promoted in different international fora. The significant differences in circumstances existing in those countries may undoubtedly have a positive impact in motivating the countries to develop new and innovative solutions and proposals for global challenges.

Furthermore, the BRICS countries should contribute to the International Fund for Cultural Diversity (IFCD, article 18 CDCE),[41] investing in projects in developing and least developed countries selected according to the principles of the CDCE and with no 'political, economic or other conditions that are incompatible with [its] objectives' (article 18.6 CDCE). Since the IFCD may benefit projects both in the BRICS and in lower-income countries, it could be the first tool to address the CDCE principle of 'international solidarity and cooperation' aiming at 'enabling countries . . . to create and strengthen their means of cultural expression, including their cultural industries' (article 2.4 CDCE).

As of June 2017, China's contribution to the IFCD amounts to USD 470,000, far more than the contribution of very developed countries in terms of cultural industries and the main actors in international development aid; for example, Denmark, Sweden, Italy, Australia and the United Kingdom. India's contributions to the IFCD have been irregular,

---

[41] See Antonios Vlassis, 'Culture development and technical and financial assistance on the basis of the Convention', in Richieri-Hanania (ed.), *Cultural Diversity in International Law*, pp. 167–80.

reaching USD 45,000. However, no Chinese or Indian project has received IFCD funds so far. Both an important donor and a receiver, Brazil has contributed USD 300,000 to the IFCD, and two Brazilian projects have received resources from it: a project providing training to indigenous film-makers with a focus on programming for children (USD 97,580) and a project for empowering indigenous creators from different communities in Brazil by promoting their participation in the digital publishing sector (USD 90,950). South Africa contributed USD 11,000 once to the IFCD in 2009, but remains one of the most dynamic countries in terms of receiving IFCD resources, revealing an effective partnership between civil society and national authorities in the cultural sector.[42] Five projects have been funded (USD 410,000 in total) dealing with capacity and creative industry development.

Finally, cooperation among the BRICS countries in favor of lower-income countries could provide the latter with best practices and lessons learned. The significant differences existing among the BRICS countries would be an advantage in that respect, allowing for easier replicability and adaptability of policies and measures according to national circumstances. The CDCE may also provide guidance in this respect. Its article 14 ('Cooperation for Development') highlights the specific needs of developing countries and the objective of fostering 'the emergence of a dynamic cultural sector'. Among the means to be used, it includes the strengthening of cultural industries, 'capacity-building through the exchange of information, experience and expertise, as well as the training of human resources', transfer of technology and know-how and financial support. The latter could be sought inter alia through the BRICS' New Development Bank (NDB BRICS).[43]

Innovative collaborative partnerships should equally be sought and 'shall, according to the practical needs of developing countries, emphasize

---

[42] It is noteworthy that national coalitions for cultural diversity were established in South Africa and in Brazil before the adoption of the CDCE. The first national coalition was created in Canada in 1998 to mobilize the country's cultural organizations. At the present date, there are forty-three national coalitions, gathering more than 600 professional organizations in the cultural field that are main players in the CDCE implementation. On the contrary, there are no coalitions for cultural diversity in China, Russia and India.

[43] The NDB BRICS 'shall mobilize resources for infrastructure and sustainable development projects in BRICS and other emerging economies and developing countries' and 'shall support public or private projects through loans, guarantees, equity participation and other financial instruments'. See article 1, BRICS, Agreement on the New Development Bank (2014), Fortaleza, Brazil, 15 July 2014; available at http://ndbbrics.org/agreement.html [accessed on 11 April 2016].

the further development of infrastructure, human resources and policies, as well as the exchange of cultural activities, goods and services' (article 15 CDCE). Furthermore, the BRICS countries, guided by the CDCE, could 'facilitate cultural exchanges with developing countries by granting, through the appropriate institutional and legal frameworks, preferential treatment to artists and other cultural professionals and practitioners, as well as cultural goods and services from developing countries' (article 16 CDCE). In fact, despite the difficulty in characterizing the BRICS as 'developed countries' under the CDCE, the operational guidelines on article 16 of the CDCE have surpassed 'pure operationalization' by adding this statement: 'developing countries are encouraged to offer a preferential treatment to other developing countries, in the framework of South–South cooperation.'[44]

IV. Conclusion

The BRICS should embrace opportunities generated by the creative economy through the elaboration of a strategic agenda on culture and the creative economy, having the CDCE at its heart. At the national and international levels, they should pursue the SDGs and economic growth through the strengthening of creative industries. To capitalize on their creative assets, the BRICS agenda on culture and the creative economy should notably comprise the following elements:

1. Collaboration to identify weaknesses and strengths in the BRICS countries' creative sectors for appropriate policies to be implemented, allowing the creation of a favorable environment for cultural and creative industries;
2. Innovative partnerships at the local level among the civil society and the public and private sectors as well as the promotion of creative cities;
3. Dialogue on cultural policies and exchange of best practices, the significant differences existing among these countries' creative sectors being an indication that they might learn considerably from each other in varied cultural fields;
4. Based on the 2015 BRICS Agreement on Cooperation in the Field of Culture, collaboration to promote exchanges of cultural goods and

---

[44] For a discussion on this matter, see RIJDEC, 'Les directives opérationnelles et autres techniques de mise en œuvre de la convention sur la diversité des expressions culturelles dans un contexte numérique' (2015), p. 18, presented at UNESCO in June 2015.

services among the BRICS countries and to develop their cultural and creative industries;

5. Welding the BRICS around issues regarding global cultural governance, with the aim of leading to ratification of the CDCE by Russia, promoting the CDCE as a framework for cooperation with regard to cultural and creative industries, and building common positions in different international fora; and

6. Cooperation in favor of least-developed countries in terms of cultural and creative industries, the IFCD and the NDB BRICS being possible sources of financial support.

Setting a strategic agenda in the field of culture and the creative economy requires leadership from a national government or an alliance of BRICS governments with the political will to take the initiative and to provide the substantial human and financial resources needed to implement such an agenda. It also requires the building of a strong BRICS partnership and support for a more decisive role for organizations of cultural professionals, both in the BRICS space and worldwide. In fact, strong synergies among civil society organizations in the cultural field in the BRICS countries are a condition for the effective implementation of this agenda and for improving their influence on external cultural affairs.

V.   References

Accioli, Claudio, Iaquinto, Kalinka, Monteiro, Solange and Thimoteo, Thais, 'Can Brazil become a creative economy?' (2011) *The Brazilian Economy* 20–28.

BRICS, 'Agreement between the Governments of the BRICS States on Cooperation in the Field of Culture' (Ufa, Russia, 2015); available at www.brics.utoronto .ca/docs/150709-culture-agreement-en.html, [accessed on 5 April 2016].

CISAC, *The Creative Industries and the BRICS – A Review of the State of the Creative Economy in Brazil, Russia, India, China and South Africa* (CISAC, 2014); available at www.cisac.org/Media/Studies-and-Reports/Publications-PDF-files/CISAC-BRICS-STUDY-20146 [accessed on 4 April 2016].

European Audiovisual Observatory, *Focus: World Film Market Trends* (Strasbourg: European Audiovisual Observatory, 2005–2016).

Indian Express, '8th BRICS Summit Goa Declaration', 16 October 2016; available at http://indianexpress.com/article/india/india-news-india/8th-brics-summit-goa-declaration-here-is-the-full-text-adopted-by-the-member-nations/ [accessed on 1 December 2016].

Kauark, Giuliana and Richieri Hanania, Lilian, 'Social and Cultural Development through Cultural Diversity – The Living Culture Programme', in *Mapping Cultural Diversity – Good Practices from around the Globe* (Asia-Europe

Foundation, German Commission for UNESCO and U40 Group, 2010), pp. 17–21; available at www.unesco.de/fileadmin/medien/Dokumente/ Kultur/U40/Mapping_Cultural_Diversity_FINAL.pdf [accessed on 4 April 2016].

McClory, Jonathan, 'Creative Russia: Lessons from Berlin', *The Guardian*, 2013; available at www.theguardian.com/culture-professionals-network/ culture-professionals-blog/2013/sep/25/russia-culture-st-petersburg-berlin [accessed on 8 March 2016].

Neuwirth, Rostam J., 'Global Market Integration and the Creative Economy: The Paradox of Industry Convergence and Regulatory Divergence' (2015) 18(1) *Journal of International Economic Law* 21–50.

'The UNESCO Convention and Future Technologies: A Journey to the Center of Cultural Law and Policymaking', in Lilian Richieri Hanania and Anne-Thida Norodom (eds.), *Diversity of Cultural Expressions in the Digital Era* (Buenos Aires: Teseo, 2016); available at www.teseopress.com/ diversityofculturalexpressionsinthedigitalera/ [accessed on 4 April 2016].

Relatório periódico quadrienal sobre as medidas para proteger e promover a diversidade das expressões culturais (2012); available at http://en.unesco .org/creativity/sites/creativity/files/periodic_reports/old/brazil_report_ ownformat_pt_2012.pdf [accessed on 5 April 2016].

Richieri Hanania, Lilian, 'Bringing Cultural Diversity to Discussions on Social and Labor Issues', in Lilian Richieri Hanania (ed.), *Cultural Diversity in International Law: The Effectiveness of the UNESCO Convention on the Protection and Promotion of the Diversity of Cultural Expressions* (London/New York: Routledge, 2014), pp. 121–135.

(ed.), *Cultural Diversity in International Law: The Effectiveness of the UNESCO Convention on the Protection and Promotion of the Diversity of Cultural Expressions* (London: Routledge, 2014).

Diversité culturelle et droit international du commerce (Paris: La Documentation française, 2009).

'Le débat commerce-culture à l'ère numérique: quelle application pour la Convention de l'UNESCO sur la diversité des expressions culturelles?' (2015); available at http://papers.ssrn.com/sol3/papers.cfm?abstract_id=2600647 [accessed on 4 April 2016].

'L'extension de l'exception culturelle aux secteurs issus des nouvelles technologies', in RIJDEC – Réseau international des juristes pour la diversité des expressions culturelles, *Le renouvellement de l'exception culturelle à l'ère du numérique*, 25 October 2015; available at www.coalitionfrancaise.org/wp-content/uploads/2015/10/RIJDEC-Le-renouvellement-de-lexception-culturelle-%C3%A0-l%C3%A8re-du-num%C3%A9rique-22-10-15.pdf [accessed on 4 April 2016].

'Protection Mechanisms for Cultural Expressions under Threat' (2014) 2 *Transnational Dispute Management – Art and Heritage Disputes* 2–6;

available at www.transnational-dispute-management.com/article.asp?key=2095 [accessed on 4 April 2016].

'The UNESCO Convention on the Diversity of Cultural Expressions as a Coordination Framework to Promote Regulatory Coherence in the Creative Economy' (2015) *International Journal of Cultural Policy* 1–20.

RIJDEC, 'Les directives opérationnelles et autres techniques de mise en œuvre de la convention sur la diversité des expressions culturelles dans un contexte numérique' (2015), presented at UNESCO June 2015.

Rossiyskaya, Gazeta, 'Moscow will Host the World Summit for Creative Industries', *Russia beyond the Headlines*, 20 March 2014; available at http://rbth.com/business_calendar/2014/03/04/moscow_will_host_the_world_summit_for_creative_industries_34761.html [accessed on 8 March 2016].

Ruutu, Katja, Panfilo, Aleksander, and Karhunen, Päivi, *Cultural Industries in Russia – Northern Dimension Partnership on Culture* (2009), pp. 9–10; available at www.northerndimension.info/images/Cultural_Industries_in_Russia.pdf [accessed on 4 April 2016].

UNCTAD, United Nations Conference on Trade and Development, *World Creative Economy Report 2010 – Creative Economy: A Feasible Development Option* (Geneva: UNCTAD, 2010); available at http://unctad.org/en/Docs/ditctab20103_en.pdf [accessed on 25 March 2016].

UNESCO, *Avant-projet de Convention sur la protection de la diversité des contenus culturels et des expressions artistiques: Partie II: commentaires spécifiques des Etats-membres* (Paris, 2004).

Convention on the Protection and Promotion of the Diversity of Cultural Expressions (Paris, 2005); available at http://en.unesco.org/creativity/convention/about/2005-convention-text [accessed on 25 March 2016].

'The Hangzhou Declaration: Heralding the Next Era of Human Development'; available at www.unesco.org/new/en/culture/themes/dynamic-content-single-view/news/the_hangzhou_declaration_heralding_the_next_era_of_human_development/#.Vw5mtKSLShc [accessed on 13 April 2016].

'List of Attendees to the Hangzhou Congress'; available at www.unesco.org/new/fileadmin/MULTIMEDIA/HQ/CLT/pdf/Book15.pdf [accessed on 13 April 2016]

'Periodic Reports – Innovative Examples'; available at http://en.unesco.org/creativity/monitoring-and-reporting/periodic-reports/innovative-examples [accessed on 13 April 2016].

'Universal Declaration on Cultural Diversity' (Paris, 2001); available at http://unesdoc.unesco.org/images/0012/001271/127162e.pdf [accessed on 22 March 2016].

UNESCO Creative Cities Network, 'Why creativity? Why cities?' 2016; available at http://en.unesco.org/creative-cities/content/why-creativity-why-cities [accessed on 30 March 2016].

UNESCO and UNESCO Institute for Statistics (UIS), 'Cultural Trade Flows Infographic' (2016); available at www.uis.unesco.org/culture/Documents/cult-trade-infographic-final-EN.pdf [accessed on 22 March 2016].

'The Globalisation of Cultural Trade: A Shift in Consumption – International Flows of Cultural Goods and Services 2004–2013' (2016); available at www.uis.unesco.org/culture/Documents/international-flows-cultural-goods-report-en.pdf [accessed on 22 March 2016].

UNESCO-UNDP, *Creative Economy Report 2013 Special Edition: Widening Local Development Pathways* (Paris: UNESCO-UNDP, 2013).

United Nations, 'Transforming our World: The 2030 Agenda for Sustainable Development', Resolution adopted by the General Assembly on 25 September 2015, Seventieth session, A/RES/70/1, 21 October 2015; available at www.un.org/ga/search/view_doc.asp?symbol=A/RES/70/1&Lang=E [accessed on 16 March 2016].

Vlassis, Antonios, 'Culture development and technical and financial assistance on the basis of the Convention', in Lilian Richieri Hanania (ed.), *Cultural Diversity in International Law: The Effectiveness of the UNESCO Convention on the Protection and Promotion of the Diversity of Cultural Expressions* (London: Routledge, 2014), pp. 167–80.

'Culture in the Post-2015 Development Agenda: The Anatomy of an International Mobilization' (2015) 36(9) *Third World Quarterly* 1649–62.

Gouvernance mondiale et culture: de l'exception à la diversité (Liège: Presses universitaires de Liège, 2015).

'Les puissances émergentes dans la bataille mondiale de l'attraction: Bollywood, vecteur du soft power de l'Inde' (2016) 55 *Interventions Économiques* 1–21; available at https://interventionseconomiques.revues.org/2867 [accessed on 4 April 2016].

'Soft Power, Global Governance and Rising Powers: The Case of China' (2016) 22(4) *International Journal of Cultural Policy* 481–96.

16

Making Lawyers in BRICS

Histories, Challenges and Strategies for Legal Education Reform

FABIO DE SA E SILVA

I. Introduction

Attempts to study and imagine BRICS as a new 'pole' in the global order normally end up in a paradox. On the one hand, many investments have sought to help the BRICS countries achieve better economic cooperation and greater political synergy. On the other hand, there are many obstacles to such cooperation and synergy. Geographic distance, language and cultural barriers, and remarkable differences in institutional histories and trajectories of development are but a few of the most commonly noted obstacles.

Law and lawyers are an inevitable part of this scenario. There is a broad consensus that new, innovative legal tools will be necessary to cement the desired cooperation and synergy among BRICS. Accordingly, there are both needs and opportunities for at least some degree of 'legal integration' in this would-be 'bloc', which could – or even should – start at the level of law school. There is also wide recognition that there are severe limitations

Many of the informal exchanges with sociolegal scholars, on which this chapter is based, took place at the annual meetings of the Law and Society Association and the Brazilian Network for Empirical Legal Studies, in addition to the activities of the GLEE (Globalization and Lawyering in Emerging Economies) project at Harvard Law School. GLEE's international, interdisciplinary, and interinstitutional team has produced insightful examinations of issues related to the corporate law sector in Brazil, India and China. For the enriching exchanges I have had in these venues, I am particularly thankful to David B. Wilkins, David M. Trubek, Marc Galanter, Bryant Garth, Mihaela Papa, Louise G. Trubek, Scott L. Cummings, Jay Krishnan, Vic Khanna, Nick Robinson, Arpita Gupta, Sida Liu, Xueyao Li and Jin Dong, in addition to the fantastic Brazilian sociolegal community that these venues involved. Any failures in this and other attempts I have made to make sense of such a vast amount of information are clearly my sole responsibility.

to such integration. In a recent note for the recently launched *BRICS Law Journal*, for example, Maleshin states that 'despite a considerable desire, both on political and academic levels, to establish closer connections in the field of legal education in the BRICS, there are some problems which complicate it'.[1] He specifically lists language, geographical remoteness and variation in educational models and legal systems.

This chapter addresses the paradox, with the aim of illuminating the next steps in the legal domain of the BRICS conversation. To do so, the chapter comparatively examines the histories, challenges and strategies of legal education reform in Brazil, Russia, India, China and South Africa. While the core of the analysis relies on secondary data and accounts, the chapter also benefits from informal exchanges with – and learning from – sociolegal scholars from, or strongly connected with, legal developments in these countries.

The chapter contains two sections, after this introduction. Section II presents the main substantive findings from our inquiry. Section III discusses the implications of such findings for theories on lawyers, governance and globalization, as well as for the BRICS project.

II.   A Comparative History of Legal Education in BRICS: Different Trajectories, Converging Challenges

While the histories of law school education in the BRICS countries are considerably different, they follow converging patterns of development and faced similar challenges at the turn of the twenty-first century. These similarities can be found in three roughly conceived stages. The first stage ends in the late twentieth century. Amid the political, economic and institutional instabilities that marked this period in world history, law schools survived and became a core feature of higher education systems in the BRICS countries. The quality of the education they provided and the relative prestige of their graduates in society, however, were somewhat low.

These developments led legal education in the BRICS countries to the 'critical' situation that would characterize the second stage. At this stage, each and all of the BRICS countries realized that, despite producing many *law graduates*, their law schools were not able to nurture *lawyers* with the ability to meet the needs of their increasingly complex societies.

---

[1] Dmitry Maleshin, 'Chief Editor's Note on Legal Education in BRICS Countries' (2015) 2(1) *BRICS Law Journal* 4–6 at 5.

This resulted in the 'reforms' that characterized the third stage. At this stage, the BRICS countries enacted new standards for the accreditation and operation of their law schools, hoping this would encourage pedagogic innovation and improve the quality of legal training. However, the advent of these reforms coincided with the BRICS countries' emergence and integration into a globalized economy, which have created opportunities, but have also posed challenges, as we will see.

A.   Stage 1: Pathways and Dysfunctions of BRICS Legal Education in the 'Age of Extremes'

What we now call BRICS are indeed countries with strikingly different historical paths. While China and Russia have long had widespread powerful influence, Brazil, India and South Africa took shape essentially as modern colonies. In the twentieth century, each of these countries experienced in a particular way what Hobsbawm called the 'Age of Extremes': Russia was at the center of the Soviet Union; China saw the violent, radical 'Cultural Revolution'; India was involved in Gandhi's legendary independence movement; Brazil underwent a military coup and a four-decade authoritarian regime; and South Africa endured the apartheid regime – to name just some of the major social and political processes in these countries.[2]

These historical situations and incidents had obvious effects on the formation of legal education systems in these countries. In Brazil, for example, law schools were introduced because local elites were searching for alternative ways to train their members, who were about to take control of a newly independent state. As such, law schools were an arena for elite socialization in public affairs and the training of statesmen, much of which occurred informally, through a 'hidden curriculum'.[3] In imperial Russia, law schools were initially responsible for training members for high-level positions in the state and the church, but this changed radically with the 1917 revolution and the formation of the Soviet Union. Law schools were then subject to strong control by the state, and most of the legal work that

---

[2] Eric J. Hobsbawm, *The Age of Extremes: The Short Twentieth Century, 1914–1991* (London: Michael Joseph, 1994).

[3] See Sérgio Adorno, *Os aprendizes do poder. O bacharelismo liberal na política brasileira* (São Paulo: Paz e Terra, 1988); A. Venâncio Filho, 'Análise histórica do Ensino Jurídico no Brasil', in *Encontros da UnB: ensino jurídico* (Brasília: UnB, 1979); Raimundo Faoro, *Os donos do Poder – Formação do patronato político brasileiro*, 3rd edn (São Paulo: Globo, 2001).

absorbed the graduates of these schools was conducted within the public sector or state-owned enterprises.[4]

In India, law schools are an old part of the higher education system, but were deeply distrusted by the local elite, who would send their youth to earn law degrees at the prestigious Oxford and Cambridge universities. In China, law schools were also introduced during imperial times, but were greatly reconfigured after the Cultural Revolution to become centers of 'political education'.[5] In South Africa, law schools were subjected to similar recasting: to reflect apartheid laws, a 'dual' law school system was established, with higher-quality institutions being almost exclusively for white students, and lower-quality institutions for black students.

In the twentieth century, however, these pathways took converging directions, and similarities grew amid the vast sea of differences. Unfortunately, what united law schools in the BRICS countries were not achievements, but structural dysfunctions. On the one hand, legal education both resisted and expanded into a sizeable law school infrastructure everywhere in the BRICS countries. On the other hand, both the average quality of the programs provided by such law schools and the relative prestige of their graduates in society were generally very low.

India offers a good example. As local elites rejected their legal education system from its very inception, law schools had no incentives to pursue higher-quality training. By default, Indian law degree programs were part-time, with most schools offering night classes for students who had other jobs during the day – just as did their young, inexperienced faculty. This 'lassitude in Indian legal education further was fed by the typical two–year degree program, a course of study that simply was too short to develop the critical thinking and practical skills necessary to effectively practice law'.[6]

In Brazil, things evolved in a similar direction. Once the first republic was consolidated in the mid-1930s, lawyers were gradually replaced with bureaucrats at the higher end of state power. As a result, law schools

---

[4] Kathryn Hendley, Peter Murrell and Randi Ryterman, 'Agents of Change or Unchanging Agents? The Role of Lawyers within Russian Industrial Enterprises' (2001) 26 *Law & Social Inquiry* 685–715.

[5] 'In a sense, there was no formal legal education in China between 1957 and 1977, in particular during the Great Cultural Revolution, which is generally considered to have ended in 1976.' See John Mo and Weidong Li, 'Legal Education in the PRC' (2002) 4 *Journal of the History of International Law* 189–190.

[6] Lovely Dasgupta, 'Reforming Indian Legal Education: Linking Research and Teaching' (2010) 59(3) *Journal of Legal Education* 432–449 at 433.

became mere providers of general (liberal arts) higher education, which the children of working classes aspired to attend. Accordingly, by the late 1980s – after decades of expansion in the system to accommodate this new demand – Brazil had accredited hundreds of law schools, which produced thousands of law graduates every year, but most of these graduates would not search for jobs in the legal market. In fact, the vast majority would do work of mid-level complexity in the state bureaucracy or in the market of other services, such as real estate.[7]

In the 'dual system' that existed in South Africa, the historical black universities (HBUs), which provided training for the majority of would-be lawyers in the country, were extremely underresourced. For example, research in 1994 established that 'the student/staff ratio is generally much higher at the HBUs', 'library resources at HBUs do not compare at all with those at HWUs', 'academic support programs either do not exist at HBUs or are totally inadequate, compared to support programs at HWUs', and 'administrative support at HBUs does not compare well with that at HWUs'.[8]

Even within the 'white' hemisphere of this racially divided legal education system, however, serious pedagogical shortcomings existed. The apartheid regime required law schools to undertake a depoliticized approach to legal pedagogy so as not to threaten the status quo with substantive discussions about freedom, equality and justice. Accordingly, legal education – even at elite institutions – was a highly formalistic enterprise, closed to critical thinking and skills development. As summarized by Greenbaum, 'It was inevitable that the effects of a positivist approach to law, which enabled the enactment of racist legislation while claiming adherence to the rule of law, albeit in its most impoverished and formalist

---

[7] It should be noted that there is a cadre of elite professionals – or grand jurists – that enjoys high levels of economic success and political power in Brazil, but these are not the products of outstanding law school education, nor is their success due to their professional excellence. Their secret is a combination of family capital, attendance at particular elite schools, and ties with the state. See Yves Dezalay and Bryant Garth, *The Internationalization of Palace Wars: Lawyers, Economists and the Contest to Transform Latin American States* (Chicago: University of Chicago Press, 2002); Fabiano Engelmann, 'O espaço da arbitragem no Brasil: notáveis e experts em busca de reconhecimento' (2012) 20(44) *Revista de Sociologia e Política* 155–176; Joaquim Falcão 'Lawyers in Brazil', in Richard L. Abel & Philip S.C. Lewis (eds.), *Lawyers in Society* (Berkeley: University of California Press, 1988–1989). This story is not exclusive to Brazil, as parallels exist in other BRICS countries. In the Indian case, for example, see Marc Galanter and Nick Robinson, 'India's Grand Advocates: A Legal Elite Flourishing in the Era of Globalization' (2013) 20(3) *International Journal of the Legal Profession*.

[8] John B. Kaburise, 'The Structure of Legal Education in South Africa' (2001) 51 *Journal of Legal Education* 363–371 at 365.

interpretation, would percolate down through the teaching of 'black letter' law at universities'.[9]

In China and Russia, the development of law school infrastructure took place relatively later and in a much more time-compressed manner, but its general direction was similar to that of Brazil, India and South Africa. In China, for example, law school education was restored in 1978. By 1996 – less than twenty years later – law degree programs were being offered in more than 300 law schools to more than 60,000 students. This growth was boosted by the 'urgent need for rebuilding China's formal legal system' and the lack of available professionals to take jobs in different sectors of the Chinese state and economy.[10] This spillover made legal jobs and law school credentials extremely popular among prospective students in China, but this momentum was confined to the 1990s, with law soon becoming a 'much less appealing major that only attracted those who have no background or connection in the government'.[11]

As in China, law school education in Russia was restored only in the mid-1980s, after decades of constraint by the political regime.[12] When the Soviet Union collapsed in the 1990s, 'the number of educational institutions training lawyers grew dramatically'.[13] As time went by, however, Russians saw the surfacing of dysfunctions similar to those of the other BRICS countries. Russian legal education came to be defined – even if stereotypically – as having a 'surplus' of law schools with low-quality training programs, insufficient orientation towards practice, and a lack of attention to professional ethics.[14] As a local newspaper reported recently,

---

[9] Lesley A. Greenbaum, 'Re-Visioning Legal Education in South Africa: Harmonising the Aspirations of Transformative Constitutionalism with the Challenges of Our Educational Legacy', 2014, at 4; available at http://ssrn.com/abstract=2575289 [accessed on 2 November 2016].

[10] Zhizhou Wang, Sida Liu and Xueyao Li, 'Internationalizing Chinese Legal Education in the Early 21st Century' (2017) 16(2) *Journal of Legal Education*; Xianyi Zeng, 'Legal Education in China' (2001) 43 *South Texas Law Review* 707–716 at 707; John Mo and Weidong Li, 'Legal Education in the PRC' (2002) 4 *Journal of the History of International Law* 189–190.

[11] Wang et al., 'Internationalizing Chinese Legal Education in the Early 21st Century'.

[12] Valentina Smorgunova, 'Legal Education in Modern Russian Universities', 2015; available at www.ialsnet.org/wordpress/wp-content/uploads/2015/08/Smorgunova.pdf [accessed on 8 July 2016].

[13] Ibid. From this author's perspective, the 'boom was caused not only by the demand, but also by the need to overcome those constraints which were artificially imposed during the Soviet period'. This seemingly refers to what she calls a 'technocratic approach and underestimation of the relevance of social and humanities knowledge', which in her view were hallmarks of the Soviet Union. She adds, 'in the USSR there were 4 times more graduates in the field of engineering than un the USA, and about 1.5 more times than in Germany'.

[14] Olga Shepeleva and Asmik Novikova, 'The Quality of Legal Education in Russia: The Stereotypes and the Real Problems' (2014) 2(1) *Russian Law Journal* 106–120.

The last decade has seen rapid growth in the number of law schools, especially in the number of private law schools and law faculties at non-core
estate universities. This trend has provoked sharp criticism from the Prime
Minister Dmitry Medvedev, who promised to reduce the number of such
institutions. 'The number of people with a degree in law is extremely high
and very often they cannot find a job,' he said. If they do find a job, it is
often even more dangerous.[15]

In the late twentieth century the BRICS states and economies were deeply
reconfigured, and these dysfunctions in their legal education systems – a
sizeable law school infrastructure that was unable to provide good-quality
education and nurture professionals with enough prestige – would be
increasingly seen as 'critical'. In consequence, an era of legal education
reforms would be inaugurated in all the BRICS countries. These reforms
characterize what we see as a 'second stage' in the modern history of
BRICS law school education, which we address next.

B.   Stage 2: Late Twentieth Century – State Reconfiguration, 'Crises' and Reforms in BRICS Legal Education

By the late twentieth century, the BRICS countries had gone through
major transformations. Brazil had moved past an authoritarian regime,
enacted a new constitution, and elected its first civil president in about
forty years. Russia had returned to being an autonomous state after the
fall of the Berlin Wall and the dissolution of the Soviet Union. India was
charting the new terrain of postcolonialism. China had ceased its 'Cultural
Revolution', enacted a new constitution, and moved towards a 'socialist
market economy'. South Africa had ended the apartheid regime, enacted
its 'transformative' constitution and elected its first black president.

   This context put legal education under renewed pressure. Arguably,
skillful and sophisticated lawyers were necessary to mediate the more
complex business transactions, as well as the social and political conflicts
characteristic of the urban, modern, industrial, economies that BRICS
countries were rapidly turning into; however, law schools in BRICS were
largely unable to meet the needs for this new cadre of professionals. This
contradiction took the form of a general critique of law schools and

---

[15] *St. Petersburg Times*, 26 February 2014; available at www.sptimes.ru [accessed on 23
December 2016]. But see Shepeleva and Novikova, 'The Quality of Legal Education in
Russia', who argue the alleged surplus and lack of quality in Russian legal education are
partly due to market incentives, such as nepotism in recruiting processes, especially for
government law jobs.

growing feelings of a 'crisis' in legal education. A series of debates and initiatives to reform legal education resulted.

Regardless of the diversity that marks the BRICS domain, these reforms resulted from similar processes and included similar features. First, they involved multiple stakeholders, such as the bar, government authorities, law school faculty and administrators, and – sometimes, at least – interest groups in the market economy and civil society. Second, these reforms emphasized new standards for law school accreditation and operation, including changes in the curriculum and definitions of degree requirements.

South Africa, Brazil and India provide insightful examples of how these reforms proceeded. In South Africa, the process was driven by changes in state politics that ended the apartheid regime. Law schools were faced with two primary challenges: they needed to overcome the 'dual system' that had prevailed under apartheid laws, which created separation and inequality between white and black lawyers,[16] and they needed to meet the demands of the new legal system, committed to the 'transformative' ideals that underlay the 1994 South African Constitution.[17]

The process began immediately after the 1994 elections, with the Minister of Justice convening several meetings with law school deans. As a result, the three-year postgraduate degree was changed to a (cheaper and more accessible) four-year undergraduate degree.[18] Curricular recommendations were formulated to reflect changes in the country's political system. They included an 'integrated approach to legal education, rather than the traditional approach that separated the theory of law from practice' and an acceptance that 'it is not enough to provide students with knowledge about the law, without developing their skills to apply such

---

[16] 'The late Chief Justice, Pius Langa, in his submission to the Truth and Reconciliation Commission (TRC), described the many indignities suffered by black lawyers, in being prevented from obtaining chambers near to the courts and being excluded from advocates' robing rooms'. See Greenbaum, 'Re-Visioning Legal Education in South Africa' at 4.

[17] See Karl Klare, 'Legal Culture and Transformative Constitutionalism' (1998) 14 *South African Journal on Human Rights* 150; David McQuoid-Mason, 'Developing the Law Curriculum to Meet the Needs of the 21st Century Legal Practitioner: A South African Perspective' (2004) 24 *Obiter* 101–108; David McQuoid-Mason, 'Transforming Legal Education for a Transforming Society: The Case of South Africa', Paper delivered at the International Conference on the Future of Legal Education, Georgia State University, 2008; available at www.learningace.com/doc/917667/f889c321c67076e82a625b60852dd949/mcquoid-mason220208 [accessed on 2 November 2016].

[18] See Qualification of Legal Practitioners Amendment Act 1997.

knowledge or inculcating them with the necessary values concerning the practice of the law'.[19]

In Brazil, a similar process took place. As in South Africa, Brazilians had been highly critical of the dominant law school system, its formalistic approach to law and its disengagement from debates about social, political and economic development.[20] In 1992 and 1993, expert commissions were established at the bar and the Ministry of Education with the goal of making assessments and recommendations about legal education in the country. These commissions convened meetings and seminars, whose results were adopted by the ministry in 1994 as 'new curricular guidelines' for law school operation in Brazil. These 'guidelines' did not affect the basic structure of the law degree (a five-year undergraduate program), but they brought considerable innovation in curricular matters: the program became more interdisciplinary, included a 'practical' component, and was supposed to integrate lectures, research and community service.[21]

The story of law school reform in India had a different character and timeline, and perhaps a more successful outcome than in South Africa and Brazil. Conversations about the 'crisis' of legal education in India began immediately after independence in 1948, when a national commission to improve higher education made several recommendations with regard to law schools. An additional push to this process came in 1961, when the Advocates Act created the 'Bar Council of India' with authority to make legal reforms and set standards for legal education.

---

[19] See Greenbaum, 'Re-Visioning Legal Education in South Africa', 6–7; McQuoid-Mason, 'Transforming Legal Education for a Transforming'.

[20] José Eduardo Faria, *A reforma do ensino jurídico* (Porto Alegre: Sergio Antonio Fabris, 1987); Luis Alberto Warat, 'Confissões Pedagógicas diante da Crise do Ensino Jurídico', in *OAB Ensino Jurídico: diagnósticos, perspectivas e propostas* (Brasília: OAB, 2002); Joaquim Falcão, *Os advogados: ensino jurídico e mercado de trabalho* (Recife: Fundação Joaquim Nabuco, Massangana, 1984); Roberto Lyra Filho, *O Direito que se Ensina Errado* (Brasília: Centro Acadêmico de Direito da UnB, 1980); José Geraldo de Sousa Jr, 'Movimentos Sociais e Práticas Instituintes de Direito: perspectivas para a pesquisa sociojurídica no Brasil', in *OAB Ensino Jurídico: 170 anos de cursos jurídicos no Brasil* (Brasília: OAB, 1997).

[21] Inês da Fonseca Pôrto, *Ensino jurídico, diálogos com a imaginação – Construção do Projeto Didático no Ensino Jurídico* (Porto Alegre: Sérgio Antônio Fabris, 2000); Fabio Sa e Silva, *Ensino Jurídico: A Descoberta de Novos Saberes para a Democratização do Direito e da Sociedade* (Porto Alegre: Sergio Antonio Fabris, 2007); Loussia P. M. Felix, 'Da Reinvenção do Ensino Jurídico- Considerações sobre a Primeira Década', in OAB – Conselho Federal e Comissão de Ensino Jurídico do Conselho Federal da OAB (Ed.), *OAB Recomenda – Um Retrato dos Cursos Jurídicos* (Brasília: OAB, 2001); André Macedo de Oliveira, *Ensino Jurídico, diálogo entre teoria e prática* (Porto Alegre: Sergio Antonio Fabris, 2004).

Although the Council played an important role, for example, in the extension of the LL.B. program from three to five years,[22] it was never able to exercise the leadership the act expected. Instead, law school reform in India owed much to individual leadership. Indian law school reformers had long wished to see a 'model national law school' established to serve as an example of new standards of excellence in legal education,[23] but this was only accomplished in 1986, when the National Law School of India University (NLSIU) was established in Bangalore. Central in this move was the 'dynamic' Delhi University Law Professor N. R. Madhav Menon. During his deanship at NLSIU, not only did Menon implement the five-year LL.B. program but he also changed the curriculum to emphasize ana-lytical skills and practical experience through clinics and internships. His changes were successful, and eighteen other National Law Schools were created in accordance with the NLSIU model.[24]

In Russia and China, these processes of reform became part of the very efforts to rebuild local infrastructure for legal education. As such, the primary objective of the reforms was to rationalize the systems as

---

[22] This extension was a contentious issue in Indian law school reform. Successful implementation of this new model would only take place in 1986 (see the later discussion).

[23] Lovely Dasgupta, 'Reforming Indian Legal Education: Linking Research and Teaching'. This aspiration was reinforced by a prior Ford Foundation initiative for legal education reform, which attempted to establish a three-year program, similar to the J.D. degree in the United States, at 'model law schools' in India; see Jay Krishnan, 'Professor Kingsfield Goes to Delhi: American Academics, the Ford Foundation, and the Development of Legal Education in India' (2004) 46 (4) *American Journal of Legal History* 447–499. US–driven initiatives for law school reforms have been constant in BRICS countries. Regarding Brazil, for example, see David M. Trubek, 'Reforming Legal Education in Brazil: From the Ceped Experiment to the Law Schools at the Getulio Vargas Foundation', Univ. of Wisconsin Legal Studies Research Paper No. 1180 (2011); available at http://ssrn.com/abstract=1970244 [accessed on 2 November 2016]. Regarding Russia, see William Burnham et al., *Assessments of the Current State of Russian Legal Education: Opportunities for Targeted Funding with Maximum Impact, Report for USAID–Russia*, 2003; available at http://pdf.usaid.gov/pdf_docs/PBAAE047.pdf [accessed on 10 July 2016].

[24] Madhav Menon, *The Transformation of Indian Legal Education: A Blue Paper* (Cambridge, MA: Harvard Law School Center on the Legal Profession, 2012); Madhav Menon, *Turning Point: The Story of a Law Teacher – Memoirs of Padmashree Prof. N. R. Madhava Menon* (New Delhi: Universal Law Publishing, 2009); Deepa Badrinarayana, 'India's State of Legal Education: The Road from NLSIU to Jindal' (2013) 63 *Journal of Legal Education* 521–523; Krishnan, 'Professor Kingsfield Goes to Delhi', 447–499; Jonathan Gingerich and Nick Robinson, 'Responding to the Market: The Impact of the Rise of Corporate Law Firms on Elite Legal Education in India', in David B. Wilkins, Vikramaditya Khanna and David M. Trubek (eds.), *The Indian Legal Profession in an Age of Globalization* (Cambridge University Press, forthcoming); Sushma Gupta, *History of Legal Education* (New Delhi: Deep and Deep Publications Pvt Ltd, 2006).

they took shape. For example, a recent account from Russia emphasizes, 'Till 1995 the higher legal education was not strictly standardized, and universities were allowed to experiment both in terms of the content of legal training, and in terms of its forms and duration'.[25] The Ministry of Education then introduced 'first-generation state educational standards' to regulate the 'specialist in law' degree, a five-year program that follows standards for higher education in Russia that date back to the Soviet Union. In 2000, 'second-generation standards' were introduced to regulate the master's degree.[26]

Reports from China point to a similar path. In 1995, the Juris Master's (J.M.) degree was created. In 1997, the Ministry of Education instituted the Guidance Committee for Legal Education in Higher Education Institutions, which worked to 'standardize undergraduate law programs by establishing a general law major with 14 uniform "core courses" ... along with a number of electives'.[27]

As these experiences of legal education reforms were becoming mature – sometimes producing their first results, sometimes showing their limitations and calling for additional 'generations' of reforms – the BRICS countries were hit by new winds of transformation. Needless to say, this would affect the debates about and prospects for their law schools.

C.   Stage 3: Early Twenty-First Century – Globalization, BRICS Emergence and Current Challenges

In the early twenty-first century, accelerated changes added yet another layer of complexity to the debates about legal education reforms in the BRICS countries. Their economies became more developed and more integrated with the global marketplace. BRICS societies became structurally reconfigured, with large groups experiencing upward mobility and social fabrics as a whole growing more diversified. BRICS itself emerged as a would-be 'bloc', arguably challenging the hegemons of the existing world order.

In addition to habitual issues of access and quality, BRICS law schools were now confronted with more strategic questions. How could they train lawyers able to meet the challenges (new and old) of their fast-changing contexts? How sufficient were the existing repertoires of law school reform

---

[25] Smorgunova, 'Legal Education in Modern Russian Universities', p. 4.

[26] Ibid.; Peter B. Maggs, Olga Schwartz and William Burnham, *Law and Legal System of the Russian Federation*, 6th edn (New York: Juris Publishing, 2015).

[27] Wang et al., 'Internationalizing Chinese Legal Education in the Early 21st Century'; Mo and Li, 'Legal Education in the PRC' 189–190.

in enabling the 'right' standards to be achieved? What new opportunities had globalization and the emergence of the BRICS countries themselves presented? How could the BRICS countries take the most advantage of these new opportunities?

There have now been few initiatives to place studies about legal education and law school reforms in BRICS in this particular context, but the available accounts reveal at least three critical (and in many ways overlapping) tensions, which should encourage further investigation and reflection.

The first tension is between local and global forces. All major initiatives of legal education reform in the BRICS countries these days have an international component. In China, for example, law schools have made consistent, significant investments in recruiting faculty with foreign credentials and engaging with the foreign audience of scholars and practitioners. As Wang, Liu and Li have documented, more than 70 percent of the faculty recruited at Shanghai Jiao Tong and Tsinghua law schools in the past five years have foreign law degrees.[28] Similarly, 40.3 percent and 50 percent of the faculty in these two law schools, respectively, have at least one foreign-language publication.[29] Authors also reveal that various joint initiatives have emerged between China, the United States and European institutions – from student exchanges to joint and dual degrees.

In Russia, the process has been influenced by regional contingencies. Having adhered to the Bologna process in 2003, Russia agreed to move past the five-year specialization model and to embrace the European model, with its four-year 'bachelor's' degree followed by a two-year 'master's' degree. Compliance with the Bologna model may bring relative advantages to Russian students and faculty, when it comes, for example, to mobility across the borders of the EU. To be sure, this has encouraged Russians to rethink other aspects of their curriculum and confront the more structural problems of their legal education system, like its lack of practical and ethical preparation.[30]

This greater internationalization of law school reforms raises many issues. Hierarchies in local legal fields can be subverted,[31] questions of authorship and cognitive justice can emerge,[32] and ties with imperial

[28] Wang et al., 'Internationalizing Chinese Legal Education in the Early 21st Century', 13.
[29] Ibid., 12.
[30] Shepeleva and Novikova, 'The Quality of Legal Education in Russia'.
[31] Yves Dezalay and Bryant Garth, *The Internationalization of Palace Wars: Lawyers, Economists and the Contest to Transform Latin American States* (Chicago: University of Chicago Press, 2002).
[32] Fabio Sa e Silva, 'Hegemonia e contra-hegemonia na globalização do direito: a 'advocacia de interesse público' nos Estados Unidos e na América Latina, (2015) 6(10) *Direito e Praxis*

powers (old and new) can be reconstructed.[33] Scholars need to pay close attention to the way these dynamics play out in the near future.

A second visible tension lies between public and private. In Brazil and India, for example, public law schools have been both at the top of the professional hierarchies and at the forefront of innovation, but these hegemonies have been challenged by private institutions like Jindal Global Law School, near Delhi, in India,[34] and by FGV Law Schools in São Paulo and Rio de Janeiro, in Brazil.[35] These institutions have invested in new pedagogic approaches to law, built strong international connections and embraced the mission of training lawyers to operate in a 'global' context. There are still other ways in which the private sector may be a driver of changes in legal education and the legal field. For example, studies have shown that while Brazilian schools have been relatively slow to respond to current market needs for high-quality corporate lawyers, a whole industry of continuing legal education, study abroad programs and in-house training in law firms and General Counsels' offices has grown.[36] Many of these programs receive support, direct or not, from the private sector.

Of course, this is not to say that the state has lost significance. For example, when Brazil sought to become a big player in international trade, the government and the private sector worked together to create a new cadre of lawyers who could advocate before the WTO.[37] Accordingly, it

---

310–376; Fabio Sa e Silva, 'Lawyers, Governance, and Globalization: The Diverging Paths of 'Public Interest Law' across the Americas' (2015) 5(5) *Oñati Socio-legal Series* 1329–1350; Boaventura de Sousa Santos (ed.). *Cognitive Justice in a Global World: Prudent Knowledge for a Decent Life* (Lanham: Lexington, 2007); Boaventura de Sousa Santos, *Epistemologies of the South. Justice against Epistemicide* (Boulder: Paradigm Publishers, 2014); Scott L. Cummings and Louise G. Trubek, 'Globalizing Public Interest Law' (2009) 13 *UCLA Journal of International Law & Foreign Affairs* 1–53.

[33] Dezalay and Garth, *The Internationalization of Palace Wars.*

[34] Deepa Badrinarayana, 'India's State of Legal Education: The Road from NLSIU to Jindal'; Jonathan Gingerich and Nick Robinson, 'Responding to the Market: The Impact of the Rise of Corporate Law Firms on Elite Legal Education in India', in David B. Wilkins, Vikramaditya Khanna and David M. Trubek (eds.), *The Indian Legal Profession in an Age of Globalization* (Cambridge University Press, forthcoming).

[35] Luciana G. Cunha and José G. Ghirardi, 'Legal Education in Brazil: The Challenges and Opportunities of a Changing Context', in Luciana G. Cunha, Daniela M. Gabbay, José G. Ghirardi, David M. Trubek and David B. Wilkins (eds.), *The Brazilian Legal Profession in the Age of Globalization* (Cambridge University Press, forthcoming).

[36] Ibid.

[37] Gregory C. Shaffer, Michelle Ratton Sanchez Badin and Barbara Rosenberg, 'Trials of Winning at the WTO: What Lies behind Brazil's Success' (2008) 41 *Cornell International Law Journal* 383–501; Alvaro Santos, 'Carving out Policy Autonomy for Developing Countries in the World Trade Organization: The Experience of Brazil & Mexico' (2012) 52 *Journal of International Law* 551–995; Badin Sanchez and Ratton Michelle,

is of extreme importance that scholars critically examine how law school reforms will take shape amid competition and cooperation between the state and the market – both of which are also being reconstructed as we speak.

The third tension lies between the economy and the polity. While globalization and the emergence of BRICS create pressure for institutional transformations at many levels, including law schools, there seems to be a tendency for concerns about economic integration and growth to dominate the debates and formulations in this area[38].

A careful examination of the literature reveals that there are competing concerns among BRICS scholars and practitioners, such as about social development and the rule of law; however, except for recurring references to clinical legal education[39] and pro bono[40] work (additional expressions of the international character of the current processes of legal education reform), there have been only modest efforts to integrate these issues into the conversation. Doing so seems to be another challenge not only for scholars but also for policy makers, social activists and whoever else in and around BRICS is willing to take the law seriously.

III. Conclusion

This chapter comparatively examined the histories, challenges and strategies of legal education reforms in the BRICS countries. It sought to address a fundamental paradox that exists in current debates about the BRICS,

---

'Developmental Responses to the International Trade Legal Game: Cases of Intellectual Property and Export Credit Law Reforms in Brazil', in David Trubek et al. (ed.), *Law and the New Developmental State: The Brazilian Experience in Latin American Context* (Cambridge: Cambridge University Press, 2013).

[38] For instance, Laurence Boulle, 'Isolationism, Democratisation and Globalisation: Legal Education in a Developing Country', in William Van Caenegem and Mary Hiscock (eds.), *The Internationalisation of Legal Education: The Future Practice of Law* (Cheltenham: Edward Elgar, 2014), pp. 48–69, at 66, notes that, in South Africa's prestigious University of Witwatersrand Law School, the Mandela Institute 'was rebranded as having and 'international economic law' focus'.

[39] See, for example, the essays in Frank S. Bloch (ed.), *The Global Clinical Movement: Educating Lawyers for Social Justice* (New York: Oxford University Press, 2011).

[40] See, for example, Arpita Gupta, 'Pro Bono and Corporate Legal Sector in India', HLS Program on the Legal Profession Research Paper No. 2013–4, 2013; available at http://ssrn.com/abstract=2344257 [accessed on 11 July 2016]; J. Dong, 'Do Institutional Variations Impact Chinese Lawyers' Attitudes on Pro Bono?' Paper presented at 'The Chinese Legal Profession in the Age of Globalization' Conference, Harvard Center Shanghai, 7–8 August 2015; Fabio Sa e Silva, 'Doing Well and Doing Good in an Emerging Economy: The Social Construction of Pro Bono among Corporate Lawyers and Law Firms in Sao Paulo', in Luciana G. Cunha et al. (eds.), *The Brazilian Legal Profession in the Age of Globalization*.

wherein aspirations about integration and synergy coexist with persisting findings that there are many obstacles to such integration and synergy.

Using this approach, I found legal education systems in the BRICS to be 'similar in their differences'. Although there is a great variation in the trajectories, characteristics and the 'making of' these systems, they all face similar challenges in the early twenty-first century. They have to meet the needs of their changing societies at a time when such changes have been accelerated. They have undergone a 'first generation' of law school reforms, which sought to set basic standards to deal with issues of access and quality. These reforms provide them with some, but not all, the resources they need to deal with what lies ahead.

The literature about this new period is still very scarce, but what is available shows that, as the BRICS countries navigate new waters, they are treading amid contradictory forces locally and globally, within the public and the private sectors, within the economy and the polity. Arguably, this is a context of good opportunities for cooperation and learning among BRICS themselves. More dialogue between BRICS authorities in education, science and technology has already resulted in joint forums, such as the BRICS Think Tanks Council[41] and the BRICS Global University League,[42] but these can be just the beginning of a new arena, and potentially a new pole, of global law and policy. For example, the BRICS New Development Bank can easily become a source of innovation in investment practices,[43] thus requiring new forms of expertise and inviting new experiments in legal training.

---

[41] 'BRICS Think Tanks Council Set Up'; available at www.bricsforum.com/2013/03/15/brics-think-tanks-council-set-up/ [accessed on 11 July 2016].

[42] 'BRICS Global University Summit in Moscow'; available at http://en.brics2015.ru/allnews/20151028/618957.html [accessed on 11 July 2016].

[43] About the bank, see: http://ndbbrics.org/index.html [accessed on 11 July 2016]. About the construction of innovative investment practices, at least in bilateral investment treaties between Brazil and Angola, see Fabio Morosini and Michelle R. Sanchez-Badin, 'Macunaima Looking for a Place in the African Savanas', paper presented at the NYU Law & Development Colloquium, New York: NYU, 2015; Fabio Morosini and Michelle R. Sanchez-Badin, 'The New Brazilian Agreements on Cooperation and Facilitation of Investments (ACFIs): Navigating between Resistance and Conformity with the Global Investment Regime', paper presented at the 'Grappling with Investor-State Dispute Settlement in and beyond the Trans-Pacific Partnership and Transatlantic Trade and Investment Partnership Symposium', Stockton: University of the Pacific, 2016. About the need for lawyers with new skills in light of alternative development models, see Fabio Sa e Silva and David M. Trubek, ' Legal Professionals and Development Strategies: Corporate Lawyers and the Construction of the Telecoms Sector in Brazil (1980s–2010s)', *Law & Social Inquiry* (forthcoming).

In any event, such imaginative initiatives should not be constrained to business issues. The legitimacy – if not the success – of future conversations about legal reforms in the BRICS will require that they also include issues of social justice and civil liberties.

IV. References

Adorno, Sérgio, *The Apprentices of Power: Liberal Lawyership in Brazilian Politics* (São Paulo: Paz e Terra, 1988).

Badrinarayana, Deepa, 'India's State of Legal Education: The Road from NLSIU to Jindal' (2013) 63 *Journal of Legal Education* 521–523.

Bloch, Frank. S. (ed.), *The Global Clinical Movement: Educating Lawyers for Social Justice* (New York: Oxford University Press, 2011).

Boulle, Laurence, 'Isolationism, Democratisation and Globalisation: Legal Education in a Developing Country', in William Van Caenegem and Mary Hiscock (eds.), *The Internationalisation of Legal Education: The Future Practice of Law* (Cheltenham: Edward Elgar. 2014).

Burnham, William, Maggs, Peter B., Luzin, Vladimir and Shokina, Elena, *Assessments of the Current State of Russian Legal Education: Opportunities for Targeted Funding with Maximum Impact, Report for USAID–Russia*, 2003; available at http://pdf.usaid.gov/pdf_docs/PBAAE047.pdf [accessed 10 Jul 2016].

Cummings, Scott L. and Trubek, Louise G., 'Globalizing Public Interest Law' (2009) 13 *UCLA Journal of International Law & Foreign Affairs* 1–53.

Cunha, Luciana G. and Ghirardi, José G., 'Legal Education in Brazil: The Challenges and Opportunities of a Changing Context', in Luciana G. Cunha, Daniela M. Gabbay, José G. Ghirardi, David M. Trubek and David B. Wilkins (eds.), *The Brazilian Legal Profession in the Age of Globalization* (Cambridge University Press, forthcoming).

Dasgupta, Lovely, 'Reforming Indian Legal Education: Linking Research and Teaching' (2010) 59(3) *Journal of Legal Education* 432–449.

De Sa e Silva, Fabio, 'Doing Well and Doing Good in an Emerging Economy: The Social Construction of Pro Bono among Corporate Lawyers and Law Firms in Sao Paulo', in Luciana G. Cunha, Daniela M. Gabbay, José G. Ghirardi, David M. Trubek and David B. Wilkins (eds.), *The Brazilian Legal Profession in the Age of Globalization* (Cambridge University Press, forthcoming).

De Sa e Silva, Fabio, *Ensino Jurídico: A Descoberta de Novos Saberes para a Democratização do Direito e da Sociedade* (Porto Alegre: Sergio Antonio Fabris, 2007).

'Hegemonia e contra-hegemonia na globalização do direito: a 'advocacia de interesse público' nos Estados Unidos e na América Latina' (2015) 6(10) *Direito e Praxis* 310–376.

'Lawyers, Governance, and Globalization: The Diverging Paths of 'Public Interest Law' across the Americas' (2015) 5(5) *Oñati Socio-legal Series* 1329–1350.

De Sa e Silva, Fabio and Trubek, David M., 'Legal Professionals and Development Strategies: Corporate Lawyers and the Construction of the Telecoms Sector in Brazil (1980s–2010s)', *Law & Social Inquiry* (forthcoming).

Dezalay, Yves and Garth, Bryant, *The Internationalization of Palace Wars: Lawyers, Economists and the Contest to Transform Latin American States* (Chicago: University of Chicago Press, 2002).

Dong, Jin, 'Do Institutional Variations Impact Chinese Lawyers' Attitudes on pro bono?' Paper presented at 'The Chinese Legal Profession in the Age of Globalization' Conference, Harvard Center Shanghai, 7–8 August 2015.

Engelmann, Fabiano, 'Arbitration in Brazil: Notables and Experts in Search of Recognition' (2012) 20(44) *Revista de Sociologia e Política* 155–176.

Falcão, Joaquim, 'Lawyers in Brazil', in Richard L. Abel and Philip S. C. Lewis (eds.), *Lawyers in Society* (Berkeley: University of California Press, 1988–1989).

Lawyers: Legal Education and the Market for Legal Services (Recife: Fundação Joaquim Nabuco, Massangana, 1984).

Faoro, Raimundo, *The Power Owners: The Formation of the Brazilian Patronage*, 3rd edn (São Paulo: Globo, 2001).

Faria, José Eduardo, *The Reform of Legal Education* (Porto Alegre: Sergio Antonio Fabris, 1987).

Felix, Loussia P. M., On the Reinvention of Legal Education – Considerations on the First Decade', in OAB – Conselho Federal e Comissão de Ensino Jurídico do Conselho Federal da OAB (ed.), *OAB Recomenda – Um Retrato dos Cursos Jurídicos* (Brasília: OAB, 2001).

Filho, A. Venâncio, 'A Historical Analysis of Legal Education in Brazil', in *Encontros da UnB: ensino jurídico* (Brasília: UnB, 1979).

Filho, R. Lyra, *The Law that Is Taught Wrongly* (Brasília: Centro Acadêmico de Direito da UnB, 1980).

Galanter, Marc and Robinson, Nick, 'India's Grand Advocates: A Legal Elite Flourishing in the Era of Globalization' (2013) 20(3) *International Journal of the Legal Profession* 241–265.

Gingerich, Jonathan and Robinson, Nick, 'Responding to the Market: The Impact of the Rise of Corporate Law Firms on Elite Legal Education in India', in David B. Wilkins, Vikramaditya Khanna and David M. Trubek (eds.), *The Indian Legal Profession in an Age of Globalization* (Cambridge University Press, forthcoming).

Greenbaum, Lesley A., 'Re-Visioning Legal Education in South Africa: Harmonising the Aspirations of Transformative Constitutionalism with the Challenges of Our Educational Legacy', 2014; available at http://ssrn.com/abstract=2575289[accessed on 2 November 2016].

Gupta, Arpita, 'Pro Bono and Corporate Legal Sector in India', HLS Program on the Legal Profession Research Paper No. 2013-4, 2013; available at http://ssrn.com/abstract=2344257 [accessed on 11 July 2016].

Gupta, Sushma, *History of Legal Education* (New Delhi: Deep and Deep Publications, 2006).

Hendley, Kathryn, Murrell, Peter and Ryterman, Randi, 'Agents of Change or Unchanging Agents? The Role of Lawyers within Russian Industrial Enterprises' (2001) 26 *Law & Social Inquiry* 685–715.

Hobsbawm, Eric J., *The Age of Extremes: The Short Twentieth Century, 1914–1991* (London: Michael Joseph, 1994).

Kaburise, John B., 'The Structure of Legal Education in South Africa' (2001) 51 *Journal of Legal Education* 363–371.

Klare, Karl, 'Legal Culture and Transformative Constitutionalism' (1998) 14 *South African Journal on Human Rights* 146–188.

Krishnan, Jayanth, 'Professor Kingsfield Goes to Delhi: American Academics, the Ford Foundation, and the Development of Legal Education in India' (2004) 46 (4) *American Journal of Legal History* 447–499.

Maggs, Peter B., Schwartz, Olga and Burnham, William, *Law and Legal System of the Russian Federation*, 6th edn (New York: Juris Publishing, 2015).

Maleshin, Dmitry, 'Chief Editor's Note on Legal Education in BRICS Countries' (2015) 2(1) *BRICS Law Journal* 4–6.

McQuoid-Mason, David, 'Developing the Law Curriculum to Meet the Needs of the 21st Century Legal Practitioner: A South African Perspective' (2004) 24 *Obiter* 101–108.

'Transforming Legal Education for a Transforming Society: The Case of South Africa'. Paper delivered at the International Conference on the Future of Legal Education, Georgia State University, 2008; available at www.learningace.com/doc/917667/f889c321c67076e82a625b60852dd949/mcquoid-mason220208 [accessed on 2 November 2016].

Menon, Madhava, *The Transformation of Indian Legal Education: A Blue Paper* (Cambridge, MA: Harvard Law School Center on the Legal Profession, 2012).

Turning Point: The Story of a Law Teacher – Memoirs of Padmashree Prof. N. R. Madhava Menon (New Delhi: Universal Law Publishing, 2009).

Mo, John and Li, Weidong, 'Legal Education in the PRC' (2002) 4 *Journal of the History of International Law* 189–190.

Morosini, Fabio and Sanchez-Badin, Michelle R., 'Macunaima Looking for a Place in the African Savannas'. Paper presented at the NYU Law & Development Colloquium, New York: NYU, 2015.

Morosini, Fabio and Sanchez-Badin, Michelle R., 'The New Brazilian Agreements on Cooperation and Facilitation of Investments (ACFIs): Navigating between Resistance and Conformity with the Global Investment Regime'. Paper presented at the 'Grappling With Investor-State Dispute Settlement In and Beyond the Trans-Pacific Partnership and Transatlantic Trade and Investment Partnership Symposium', Stockton: University of the Pacific, 2016.

Oliveira, André Macedo de, *Legal Education, a Dialogue between Theory and Practice* (Porto Alegre: Sergio Antonio Fabris, 2004).

Pôrto, Inês da Fonseca, *Legal Education: Dialogues with the Imagination – Construção do Projeto Didático no Ensino Jurídico* (Porto Alegre: Sérgio Antônio Fabris, 2000).

Sanchez-Badin, Michelle, 'Developmental Responses to the International Trade Legal Game: Cases of Intellectual Property and Export Credit Law Reforms in Brazil', in David M. Trubek, Helena Alviar Garcia, Diogo R. Coutinho, and Alvaro Santos (eds.), *Law and the New Developmental State: the Brazilian experience in Latin American context* (Cambridge: Cambridge University Press, 2013).

Santos, Alvaro, 'Carving out Policy Autonomy for Developing Countries in the World Trade Organization: The Experience of Brazil & Mexico' (2012) 52 *Journal of International Law* 551–995.

Santos, Boaventura de Sousa (ed.), *Cognitive Justice in a Global World: Prudent Knowledge for a Decent Life* (Lanham, MD: Lexington, 2007).

Epistemologies of the South: Justice against Epistemicide (Boulder: Paradigm Publishers, 2014).

Shaffer, Gregory, Sanchez, Michelle R. and Rosenberg, Barbara, 'Trials of Winning at the WTO: What Lies behind Brazil's Success' (2008) 41 *Cornell International Law Journal* 383–501.

Shepeleva, Olga and Novikova, Asmik, 'The Quality of Legal Education in Russia: The Stereotypes and the Real Problems' (2014) 2(1) *Russian Law Journal* 106–120.

Smorgunova, Valentina, 'Legal Education in Modern Russian Universities', 2015; available at www.ialsnet.org/wordpress/wp-content/uploads/2015/08/Smorgunova.pdf [accessed on 8 July 2016].

Sousa Jr., José Geraldo de, 'Social Movements and Practices that Institute Law: Perspectives for Sociolegal Research in Brazil', in *OAB Ensino Jurídico: 170 anos de cursos jurídicos no Brasil* (Brasília: OAB, 1997).

Trubek, David M., 'Reforming Legal Education in Brazil: From the Ceped Experiment to the Law Schools at the Getulio Vargas Foundation'. University of Wisconsin Legal Studies Research Paper No. 1180 (2011); available at http://ssrn.com/abstract=1970244[accessed on 2 November 2016].

Wang, Zhizhou, Liu, Sida and Li, Xueyao, 'Internationalizing Chinese Legal Education in the Early 21st Century' (2017) 16(2) *Journal of Legal Education*.

Warat, Luis Alberto, 'Pedagogical Confessions Facing the Crisis of Legal Education', in *OAB Ensino Jurídico: diagnósticos, perspectivas e propostas* (Brasília: OAB, 2002).

Zeng, Xianyi, 'Legal Education in China' (2001) 43 *South Texas Law Review* 707–716.

~

Conclusion

BRICS Lawyers as Bricklayers

ROSTAM J. NEUWIRTH, ALEXANDR SVETLICINII AND
DENIS DE CASTRO HALIS

*We can't create foundations, but we can build a superstructure... Those who
believe that life consists in change because change implies movement, should
remember that there must be an underlying thread of unity or the change, being
unmeaning, will cause conflict and clash.*[1]

In an age of the proliferation of international organizations and international agreements and an increase in the number of international actors,
each time a new element is added, it is crucial to examine what, if any-
thing, it is effectively bringing to the current global governance debate.
This is the principal question we raised in the beginning of this book in
critically inquiring about the future role of the BRICS countries in the
concert of global governance. More concretely, this book translated this
fundamental question about BRICS, as a young and recent addition to the
international community, into four sets of questions. First and foremost,
why should the BRICS countries cooperate at all? As a second question, it
is necessary to assess where or in what areas they should focus their cooperation. Related to this, it is important to consider, as a third question,
the precise means for their cooperation or how to cooperate in the areas
chosen for cooperation. Fourth and last, what should be the objective of
their cooperation and what purposes will it serve? Together, these four
sets of questions should serve as the benchmarks for a critical assessment
of what the BRICS countries' role in the establishment of a future global
governance system will be.

Regarding the first question, it is hard to believe that in the global information society of the twenty-first century, there are still countries where
the knowledge of other countries' history, culture, traditions or people is

[1] Rabindranath Tagore, 'Talks in China: section II', in Rabindranath Tagore, *The English Writ-
ings of Rabindranath Tagore: Essays* (New Delhi: Atlantic, 2007), vol. IV, p. 777.

meager and insufficient. Such lack of knowledge creates an obstacle to trade and investment, as well as cooperation in other fields. Unfortunately, it still exists, as proven by the recent initiation of closer relations between the BRICS countries, some of which are even geographic neighbors. This fact can already be taken as a principal answer to the question about the possible and expected benefits of closer cooperation between the BRICS countries. Their cooperation – currently organized as a strategic partnership based on a 'dialogue and cooperation platform' – is certainly warranted and beneficial, not only for each of these countries individually and for all of them collectively in their plurilateral relations but also, most importantly, for the wider global community. Clearly, regardless of the recent skepticism or disappointment being voiced by various commentators abouthe BRICS, their cooperation must continue and continue to deepen and improve, if only because those countries represent almost half of the world's population.

There are, however, additional reasons for cooperation, as identified throughout the various chapters of this book. One important reason is the BRICS countries' diversity in terms of their politics, economics, culture, history and law. As discussed in Chapter 1, when BRICS is understood as an enantiosis, like a *discordia concors* or 'discord in harmony', its brief history of organized cooperation proves that ideas or concepts, yoked together by an act of free will, can 'mutually, set off and enhance each other'.[2] In short, the countries' diverse or apparently contradictory nature is not an obstacle, but instead the main reason for their comparison and closer consideration through cooperation. This conceptual or linguistic finding is best illustrated and confirmed by the core of their initial basis of cooperation, that is, international trade. It is well established, and is confirmed in Chapter 2, that the diversity in resources, factor endowments or technological capabilities, as well as other factors, is hailed as the 'fundamental rationale behind trade'. These differences, which are prevalent between the BRICS countries, have also been specifically confirmed in the areas of company law (Chapter 4), energy trade (Chapter 8), the exploration of outer space (Chapter 14), culture and the cultural industries (Chapter 15) and legal education (Chapter 16). Similarly, not only do their resources or various endowments diverge, but so may their interests. This was also confirmed by the BRICS countries' participation in various international organizations, such as the WTO, the IMF or the World Bank (Chapters 3 and 9), the creation of an alternative dispute settlement

---

[2] T. Gibbons, *Rhetoric; or, a View of its Principal Tropes and Figures* (London: J. and W. Oliver, 1767), p. 248.

system through international arbitration (Chapter 13), as well as various regulatory areas including competition law, investment and development cooperation (Chapters 4–6), consumer protection (Chapter 12) and the creative economy (Chapter 15). *Mutatis mutandis*, the same findings may also be applied to other areas where no BRICS cooperation has yet materialized. Yet, even divergent interests may still give rise to the 'BRICS factor' or, in other words, commitments to cooperation by some or all of the BRICS countries (Chapter 7).

The diversity displayed in these areas and manifested in corresponding interests, in turn, provides the basic rationale for their cooperation, as was proven in concrete terms by the establishment of the BRICS as a 'dialogue and cooperation platform' in the first place. This earned them various qualifications as a 'multi-centre legal network'[3] or a 'coalition of variable geometry' (Chapter 9). Meanwhile, the initial rationale has been confirmed by explicit achievements, such as an improved cooperation through the WTO Dispute Settlement Mechanism (Chapter 3) and the subsequent establishment of the so-called 'BRICS Bank' or the New Development Bank (NDB; Chapter 9). There may be more implicit achievements resulting from the initial years of the BRICS-coordinated cooperation. These may be, at first, achievements that are more theoretical or seemingly abstract due to their conceptual nature, which – paradoxically and eventually – will create major differences. An example could be the changing status of Africa in the world economy through the transformation of development policies by the BRICS (Chapter 5). It may be too early for other achievements or impacts to materialize, such as the conclusion of the Regional Comprehensive Economic Partnership (RCEP) Agreement (Chapter 7) or other international norm-setting activities. Perhaps indirectly, the change in the terminology of the World Bank's 2016 Development Indicators Report, which abandoned the dichotomy of 'developing and developed countries',[4] is another such achievement and possible example of the BRICS countries' emerging soft power.[5]

As one achievement is already better than none, their cooperation – as any form of cooperation between different countries – is unquestionable

---

[3] See Lucia Scaffardi, 'BRICS, a Multi-Centre "Legal Network"?' (2014) 5 *Beijing Law Review* 140–148.

[4] See also Rostam J. Neuwirth, 'Global law and sustainable development: change and the "developing–developed country" terminology', (2016) *European Journal of Development Research* 1–15, doi:10.1057/s41287-016-0067-y; available at http://link.springer.com/article/10.1057/s41287-016-0067-y [accessed on 22 December 2016].

[5] See also Oliver Stuenkel, 'Do the BRICS Possess Soft Power?' (2016) 9(3) *Journal of Political Power* 353–367.

and must continue. This means that the second question, namely the areas on which they should focus their cooperation, gains greater significance. In this regard, the numerous and equally diverse areas highlighted in the chapters of this book show that there is no limitation in terms of areas for cooperation. Here, the spectrum may range from broader macroeconomic or global trade, investment or development policies to concrete, microeconomic or very specific issues, such as the regulatory framework for foreign direct investment based on company law (Chapter 4), the regulation of financial markets (Chapter 10), intellectual property rights (Chapter 7), or support for the cultural industries (Chapter 15), as well as law school curricula (Chapter 16).

On a general note, it seems to be a general characteristic of the present time that, in a state of growing complexity, opposites tend not to be mutually exclusive, but rather to converge to reveal their potential complementarity. This is why numerous dichotomous distinctions between apparent opposites, such as the local and the global, the close and the remote, and the public and the private, can no longer be relied upon. For example, it is possible to argue that the BRICS countries' global cooperation in outer space, for instance, by joint projects in satellite or navigation technologies, creates benefits for individuals locally. Therefore, put briefly, there can and should be no prima facie limitations in terms of possible areas for their cooperation. This also means that the BRICS countries must remain open to new areas of cooperation whenever the necessity arises. It is the same complexity, which is creating connections between all areas or phenomena in this world of increasing interdependence and interconnectedness, that requires a critical assessment of the intrinsic links connecting them, as well as the dynamics governing them. In this regard, the conclusion drawn from the illustrations provided throughout this book is that a dynamic movement in concentric circles from the core economic or trade areas via trade-related to nontrade concerns seems to be the direction of current and future BRICS cooperation.

Ultimately, the dynamics governing the existing and possible new areas of joint BRICS activities are inextricably linked to the third question about the precise means for their cooperation. In this regard, it is the self-designated nature of a 'dialogue and cooperation platform' that forms the starting point. This means that, to date, BRICS cooperation relies primarily on regular visits and meetings at different levels of governance or varying representations of civil society. Except for the NDB, the BRICS mode of cooperation has little permanent and comprehensive institutional backing. The status quo therefore invites the question of the future setup and, specifically, whether the BRICS should ponder the establishment of an institutionalized structure and organization. In this regard, another principal characteristic of our time poses a serious challenge to institutions worldwide, that is, the noticeable acceleration of the pace of change. The acceleration of change puts pressure on institutions in terms of providing stability, certainty and predictability against the backdrop of drastic societal or technological changes. While institutions may provide stability in changing conditions, they may also resist internal change through reforms, thereby hampering the realization of desirable change in order to provide stability in a sustainable manner.

At this stage, for the BRICS countries, the chosen institutional nature of a 'dialogue and cooperation platform' seems adequate and better suited to the present global context. Building on their diversity and backed by a sincere solidarity, the BRICS countries can first enhance their cooperation by coordinating their policies within the existing international organizations, as exemplified by their activities within the WTO or UNESCO, rather than by creating new ones (Chapters 3 and 15). This approach will help to foster their strength as a 'coalition of variable geometry' (Chapter 9), and whenever needed, it can be supported by the ad hoc establishment of new individual institutions such as the NDB or, for instance, one or more BRICS dispute resolution centers. The same applies to the ad hoc creation of 'BRICS alliances' as outlined by Peter K. Yu for the realm of international trade and intellectual property rights negotiations (Chapter 7). When necessary, BRICS cooperation can also be complemented by individual international agreements, following the examples of the 2014 Treaty for the Establishment of a BRICS Contingent Reserve Arrangement (CRA) or the 2015 BRICS Agreement on Cooperation in the Field of Culture (Chapter 15).

In following a kind of looser setup with an open method of coordination, the BRICS governments will be more flexible in reacting to sudden changes, rather than going through lengthy and paralyzing institutional procedures, as for example, the EU has been experiencing with the failed EU Constitutional Treaty and the recent Brexit movement, or those of the United Nations, with its continuous failure to reform itself and 'deliver as one'.[6] Such an open method of coordination also helps to keep it

---

[6] See also United Nations High Level Panel on Coherence, *Delivering as one: Report of the High-level Panel on United Nations System-wide Coherence in the Areas of Development, Humanitarian Assistance and the Environment*, G.A. A/61/583 (20 November 2006); available at https://daccess-ods.un.org/TMP/746690.034866333.html [accessed on 22 December 2016].

receptive to other countries or regional organizations when their participation or cooperation is useful, such various BRICS alliances like the one with the Bay of Bengal Initiative for Multi-Sectoral Technical and Economic Cooperation (BIMSTEC) member countries, which participated in the 2016 Goa BRICS Summit.

Yet to take full advantage of their diversity, as well as their flexibility in cooperation, the BRICS countries will need to strengthen their unity, as the quote from the Indian poet Rabindranath Tagore's talks in China in 1924 warns. The reason is that diversity and change, without an underlying thread of unity, is likely to cause conflict and clashes, or at least unnecessary friction stemming from a lack of coherence. Thus, to secure coherence in all the endeavours envisaged by the BRICS, both past, present and future, they must first have recourse to new ideas and novel concepts, which will be extracted and elaborated from a fruitful dialogue. However, to guarantee that the dialogue will be fruitful, a reliable source of information must be provided. In this regard, regular and frequent summit meetings are certainly helpful, but are not adequate in the long run, especially as the volume of data or related policies increases with each of them.

Therefore, it will be necessary to strengthen the encouraging calls for the BRICS to function as a 'multi-centre legal network'. In other words, it will be necessary to use existing and to create novel legal tools and instruments based on a novel conception of law. The reason is that as unity is the thread against clashes and conflicts vis-a-vis change, it is the law that provides the mortar holding the bricks of different layers of life, particularly politics and economics, together, especially in turbulent times characterized by rapid and drastic change. Thus, for the time being, the designation as a dialogue and cooperation platform suffices to meet the BRICS needs, but only if it is supported by a legal network built on the comparison and recognition of the diversity of law and laws. To this end, a joint e-governance initiative aimed at establishing a BRICS-Law database, which will be fed on a constant basis with each BRICS country's data pertinent to legislation or legislative reform, should be established. This database can then gradually evolve with the widening and deepening scope of the fields of cooperation chosen. Ideally, it should be accompanied by the creation of a joint committee (made up of related functional units in the foreign ministries of all BRICS countries) that oversees the management of the database and the overall coherence in the pursuit and implementation of the actions laid down in the BRICS countries' declarations.

With their strategic partnership using a 'dialogue and cooperation platform' of variable geometry supported by a multicenter and multipurpose network and open to cooperation in the form of so-called BRICS alliances, the fourth and, for the time being, final question about the purpose and objectives of BRICS cooperation will be easier to address. In fact, the BRICS Heads of States outlined and reiterated the principal objectives in the Goa Declaration formulated during the Eighth BRICS Summit held in Goa (India) on October 15–16, 2016, which reads:

> Recalling all our previous declarations, we emphasise the importance of further strengthening BRICS solidarity and cooperation based on our common interests and key priorities to further strengthen our strategic partnership in the spirit of openness, solidarity, equality, mutual understanding, inclusiveness and mutually beneficial cooperation. We agree that emerging challenges to global peace and security and to sustainable development require further enhancing of our collective efforts.[7]

Thus, based on the main reasons given, their purpose can be defined as truly making a difference in the existing global and local governance structures. More concretely, their purpose and main reason to exist were said to reside in making a noticeable and tangible difference in all areas in which people around the world feel that important matters have not been addressed adequately or at all. This point has also been outlined by stating that 'BRICS countries represent an influential voice on the global stage through our tangible cooperation, which delivers direct benefits to our people'.[8]

These and other commitments mean that BRICS will try to tackle most of the global objectives laid down in the sustainable development goals (SDGs) and to meet individual expectations in the BRICS countries and beyond. These and additional objectives, it is submitted, will automatically result from dialogue and cooperation between the BRICS countries in a vast array of different fields by means of including and connecting governments and individuals, as well as other stakeholders from these and other countries. Supported by the individual opportunities in person-to-person

---

[7] See Paragraph 2 of the Goa Declaration at Eighth BRICS Summit, 16 October 2016, Government of India, Ministry of Foreign Affairs; available at www.mea.gov.in/bilateral-documents.htm?dtl/27491/Goa+Declaration+at+8th+BRICS+Summit [accessed on 22 December 2016].

[8] See Paragraph 3 of the Goa Declaration at Eighth BRICS Summit, 16 October 2016, Government of India, Ministry of Foreign Affairs; available at www.mea.gov.in/bilateral-documents.htm?dtl/27491/Goa+Declaration+at+8th+BRICS+Summit [accessed on 22 December 2016].

contacts at all levels, a unifying thread of cooperation by means of the law will not only eventually strengthen the BRICS cooperation but also help to lay the true foundations of the global community and its future governance structure: hence the notion of BRICS-Lawyers functioning as BRICS-Layers.

INDEX

CPSIA information can be obtained
at www.ICGtesting.com
Printed in the USA
LVHW052225070119
603029LV00021B/265